ENCYCLOPEDIA OF
COMMUNICATION and INFORMATION

ENCYCLOPEDIA OF
COMMUNICATION
and INFORMATION

Volume 2

Edited by Jorge Reina Schement

MACMILLAN REFERENCE USA

GALE GROUP
————*————
™
THOMSON LEARNING

New York • Detroit • San Diego • San Francisco
Boston • New Haven, Conn. • Waterville, Maine
London • Munich

Encyclopedia of Communication and Information

Copyright © 2002 by Macmillan Reference USA, an imprint of Gale Group

Macmillan Library Reference USA   Macmillan Library Reference USA
300 Park Avenue South   27500 Drake Road
New York, NY 10010   Farmington Hills, MI 48331–3535

Library of Congress Cataloging-in-Publication Data

Encyclopedia of communication and information/edited by Jorge Reina Schement.
        p. cm.
    Includes bibliographical references and index.
    ISBN 0-02-865386-6 (set : hardcover : alk. paper)-ISBN 0-02-865383-1 (v. 1 :
    hardcover : alk. paper)-ISBN 0-02-865384-X (v. 2 : hardcover : alk. paper)-
    ISBN 0-02-865385-8 (v. 3 :hardcover : alk. paper)
        1. Communication-Encyclopedias. I. Schement, Jorge Reina.
    P87.5.E53 2001
    302.2"03-dc21   2001031220

Printed in United States of America

10 9 8 7 6 5 4 3 2 1

G

▣ GAYS AND LESBIANS IN THE MEDIA

In 1997, when Ellen DeGeneres announced on the cover of *Time* magazine that she was a lesbian, and her television character "came out" on the situation comedy *Ellen*, media attention was unprecedented. Partly due to a changing social climate that tolerated gays and lesbians more than in the past and partly due to the fact that television and film depictions of homosexuals were becoming more visible and accurate, a historic moment in media occurred. For one of the few times in television history, the lead character in a major program was homosexual and not shown as a lonely, evil, or homicidal character.

The history of the depiction of gays and lesbians in the mainstream media is a tale of negative and oppressive images. For some time their stories have been limited to suicide, murder, and evil. Vito Russo in *The Celluloid Closet* (1987) lists more than forty examples of the ways gay or lesbian characters in films have died. The rest of his book details the effeminate and sissy stereotypes of gay men in movies, the butch and aggressive women identified as lesbian, and the general images of most homosexuals as victims and villains.

Given the historical invisibility of accurate images of gays and lesbians in mainstream movies and print publications, many gays and lesbians resorted to creating their own media, as Edward Alwood discusses in *Straight News: Gays, Lesbians, and the News Media*(1996). Some of the earliest publications were a 1924 Chicago-area gay newsletter called *Friendship and Freedom*, a 1934 publication titled *The Chanticleer*, and a 1947 Los Angeles-area lesbian newsletter called *Vice Versa*. Beginning with the modern gay movement in the early 1950s in Los Angeles, *ONE* became the first widely circulated homosexual magazine, selling two thousand copies a month. Along with *The Ladder*, published by the Daughters of Bilitis from 1956 to 1970, and the *Mattachine Review*, published from 1955 to 1964, these important gay and lesbian media contributed to a growing sense of community and identity. The tradition continues with such widely circulated national magazines as *The Advocate* (first published in 1967, making it the longest continuously published gay magazine), *Lesbian News*, *Out*, and many other less-commercialized local newspapers, underground "zines," independent films, cable television shows, and World Wide Web sites that are produced by and for gay and lesbian audiences.

It should be remembered that these community-based media emerged as a reaction to mainstream films, newspapers, radio programs, and television shows that were slow in recognizing gay and lesbian lives. From the 1930s to the late 1960s, the Motion Picture Production Code was used to self-regulate Hollywood movies, and it set out a list of forbidden topics, including "any inference of sexual perversion," (i.e., homosexuality). Before 1930, many pre-code films had explicit references to homosexuals and numerous depictions of cross-dressing, but it was not until 1961 that the subject of homosexuality became more overtly depicted. The humorous, innocent sissy characters that were typical of the 1930s and 1940s gave way in the 1960s and 1970s to homosexual characters who

Shirley MacLaine (left) and Audrey Hepburn play the leads in the 1961 film version of The Children's Hour, *in which MacLaine's character is in love with Hepburn's character. (Bettmann/Corbis)*

were almost always lonely, predatory, and pathological. Consider, for example, William Wyler's two film versions of Lillian Hellman's play *The Children's Hour*. According to Vito Russo (1987), censors prohibited the 1936 movie (called *These Three*) from depicting a lesbian character; she was changed to a heterosexual woman in love with her colleague's boyfriend. The 1961 version (using the original title of *The Children's Hour*), on the other hand, showed a lesbian character in love with her female colleague, even though the lesbian committed suicide in the end.

As television became more popular, stereotypical images of the effeminate, lonely gay man and the masculine, tough lesbian were dispersed more widely. With an increasingly active gay movement, pressure against the media emerged in 1973 when the Gay Activist Alliance (GAA) in New York confronted executives at the American Broadcasting Company (ABC) about unfavorable treatment of homosexuality. That same year, ABC became the first U.S. television network to air a made-for-television movie about a gay topic, *That Certain Summer*. Within a few years, most major situation comedies, drama shows, and talk shows incorporated gay issues, typically as a special episode, but rarely in terms of a continuing character or plot. By the mid-1980s, however, any attention given to gay issues was, as Larry Gross (1994) points out, almost always framed in terms of AIDS, where gays were once again portrayed as victims or villains.

Following the activism of the Gay & Lesbian Alliance Against Defamation (GLAAD) during the 1990s, there has been a trend toward more accurate and fair images of gays and lesbians in the media. According to Peter Nardi (1997), some of this is due to an increase in the production of media by gays and lesbians themselves. However, the mainstream media are also increasingly devoting more attention to gay images, especially in light of major social, legal, and political issues that have focused on gays and lesbians. Such controversial topics as "gays-in-the-military" and "gay marriage" generated many magazine cover stories, radio and television news features, and central attention on television talk shows. The talk show coverage usually did not contain the disparaging and distorted language that once would have been the norm, yet sometimes there was a sensational and exploitative tone, as Joshua Gamson describes in his analysis of tabloid talk shows in *Freaks Talk Back* (1998).

Television sitcoms, dramas, and news shows have increasingly included continuing characters who are gay or lesbian and stories with gay or lesbian themes. No longer are these forbidden topics or ones used to generate a laugh at the expense of the gay character. During the 1999–2000 television season, around thirty lesbian and gay characters (mostly created after *Ellen* broke new ground) appeared in prime-time shows, including *Will and Grace*, a comedy with two openly gay characters in lead roles; the adult cartoon shows, *Mission Hill* and *The Simpsons*; and dramas such as *NYPD Blue* and *Dawson's Creek*. However, Marguerite Moritz (1994) and Darlene Hantzis and Valerie Lehr (1994) argue that the price paid for the increase in depictions of gays and lesbians in the media is that these new characters look no different from everyone else in television. They are mostly white, middle class, typically desexualized, generally existing outside of any gay or lesbian social context and friendship circles, not threatening to heterosexuals, and usually free from oppression. This minimizes the real-life political, sexual, and social differences that often arise from having to live in a society where people continue to discriminate against and commit violence against gays and lesbians.

A more fair and balanced portrayal of gays and lesbians is also due in part to an increasingly tolerant climate in the media workplace. This new climate allows gay and lesbian employees to have domestic partner benefits, to work with less fear of job discrimination, and, thus, to be visibly present, organized, and open with their comments and creative skills.

The combination of changing societal attitudes toward gays and lesbians, advocacy by gay media watchdog groups, and openness to diversity in the workplace has contributed to a visibility of more accurate images of gays and lesbians in the media.

See also: FILM INDUSTRY, HISTORY OF; SEX AND THE MEDIA; TALK SHOWS ON TELEVISION; TELEVISION BROADCASTING, PROGRAMMING AND.

Bibliography

Alwood, Edward. (1996). *Straight News: Gays, Lesbians, and the News Media.* New York: Columbia University Press.

Gamson, Joshua. (1998). *Freaks Talk Back: Tabloid Talk Shows and Sexual Nonconformity.* Chicago: University of Chicago Press.

Gross, Larry. (1994). "What Is Wrong with This Picture? Lesbian Women and Gay Men on Television." In *Queer Words, Queer Images,* ed. R. Jeffrey Ringer. New York: New York University Press.

Hantzis, Darlene, and Lehr, Valerie. (1994). "Whose Desire? Lesbian (Non)sexuality and Television's Perpetuation of Hetero/sexism." In *Queer Words, Queer Images,* ed. R. Jeffrey Ringer. New York: New York University Press.

Moritz, Marguerite. (1994). "Old Strategies for New Texts: How American Television Is Creating and Treating Lesbian Characters." In *Queer Words, Queer Images,* ed. R. Jeffrey Ringer. New York: New York University Press.

Nardi, Peter M. (1997). "Changing Gay & Lesbian Images in the Media." In *Overcoming Heterosexism and Homophobia: Strategies That Work,* eds. James Sears and Walter Williams. New York: Columbia University Press.

Russo, Vito. (1987). *The Celluloid Closet: Homosexuality in the Movies,* revised edition. New York: Harper & Row.

PETER M. NARDI

■ GENDER AND THE MEDIA

The importance of gender in Western culture is illustrated throughout almost all forms of popular communication. From nursery rhymes that provide children with lessons on what boys and girls are made of, to bestsellers that claim that men and women are from different planets, media images are thought to reflect and, in some instances, perpetuate or exaggerate differences between the sexes. The important role that the media play in representing and affecting attitudes and beliefs about gender has been documented in a long history of research that has explored not only the ways in which gender is portrayed, but also the ways in which viewers respond to and are influenced by images of males and females.

Gender Portrayals in Media

Although portrayals of gender have shown considerable changes over the years, media content continues to feature disparities in the ways in which males and females are represented. This characterization applies to both sheer numbers, or "head counts," and to the manner in which males and females are characterized.

Frequency of Male Versus Female Portrayals

Although the underrepresentation of females in television programming is a phenomenon that researchers have long noted, recent analyses suggest that the proportion of female characters has increased over the years. For example, the content analysis by Nancy Signorielli and Aaron Bacue (1999) of prime-time programming reported trends toward greater representation of female characters between 1967 and 1998, though females continue to represent only 40 percent of the characters in programs aired during the 1990s (up from previous figures of approximately 34 percent).

Of course, the representation of gender varies widely as a function of the genre in question. For example, daytime soap operas, prime-time situation comedies, and prime-time dramas tend to feature more equitable gender representations. However, these genres appear to be the exception rather than the norm. For example, many researchers have noted that programming for children is particularly likely to feature an overabundance of male versus female characters. The analysis by Teresa Thompson and Eugenia Zerbinos (1995) of television cartoons found that among major characters, males outnumbered females more than three to one, and that among minor characters, males outnumbered females almost five to one. Similarly, Signorielli and Bacue (1999) reported that in prime-time programming, action adventure programs feature only 30 percent females (up from 20 percent during the 1960s).

Nonfiction programming also continues to underplay the appearance of females. For example, the content analysis by Dhyana Ziegler and Alisa White (1990) of network newscasts found that only 12 percent of the news correspondents were female. Similarly, television and newspaper reports of sporting events continue to vastly ignore participation by females. Susan Tyler Eastman and Andrew Billings (2000) content analyzed sports reporting on two television programs (ESPN's *SportsCenter* and CNN's *Sports Tonight*) and two newspapers (*The New York Times* and *USA Today*) over a five-month period in 1998.

Coverage of women's sports accounted for only 17 percent of sports coverage in *USA Today,* 9 percent in *The New York Times,* 6 percent on *SportsCenter,* and 4 percent on *Sports Tonight.*

The Nature of Gender Portrayals

In addition to the frequency of representation, numerous studies have pointed out that the manner in which males and females are portrayed is often very stereotypical. For example, the Thompson and Zerbinos (1995) analysis of children's cartoons showed that male characters were more likely than female characters to show ingenuity, to use aggression, to show leadership, to express opinions, to issue threats, and to show anger. In contrast, female characters were more likely than male characters to show affection, to ask for advice or protection, and to engage in routine services.

These behavioral differences found in children's programming parallel other studies concerning portrayals of marital status and occupational roles. Signorielli and Bacue (1999) reported that although a majority of both male and female prime-time characters were portrayed as working outside of the home, working status was evident for a larger percentage of male (76%) than female (60%) characters. Similarly, content analyses of marital and parental roles suggest that the family lives of female characters are portrayed as more important than those of male characters. For example, the content analysis by Donald Davis (1990) of prime-time programs found that among male characters, 60 percent had an unknown marital status and 71 percent had an unknown parental status. For women, these figures were only 31 percent and 48 percent for marital and parental status, respectively.

In addition to noting behavioral and occupational characteristics of media characters, media portrayals of females tend to focus on appearance and sexuality much more than do portrayals of males. This differential attention to appearance can be seen across a number of different types of characteristics. In general, female television characters are younger than male characters, are more likely to be shown displaying sexual behaviors, more likely to be portrayed as thin or physically fit, and are more likely to be shown in revealing or "skimpy" clothing. Similarly, Amy Malkin, Kimberlie Wornian, and Joan Chrisler (1999) found that media that are targeted specifically toward women, such as women's magazines, are much more likely to feature stories concerning dieting, appearance, and fitness than are media targeted toward men.

Uses of Media

Do these differential portrayals of gender translate into different patterns of media consumption for males and females? In some respects, the answer to this question is "no." According to Nielsen Media Research (1998), although females tend to watch slightly more television than do males, these differences vary substantially by the time of day in question and by the age of the viewer. However, the most striking gender differences in media use pertain not to overall consumption, but to differential liking of and reaction to specific types of programming or media portrayals.

Many of the gender differences in media preferences documented in the literature are consistent with stereotypical notions of what males and females should be expected to enjoy. In general, males express greater enjoyment than females for sporting events and sports-related news, for action-adventure programming, and for sexually explicit adult entertainment. In contrast, females tend to report greater enjoyment of entertainment best characterized as drama or romance, including sad films and soap operas. In addition, Tracy Collins-Standley, Su-lin Gan, Hsin-Ju Jessy Yu, and Dolf Zillmann (1996) found that these types of gender differences that are typical among adult media consumers are also evident among children as early as nursery school, though they do appear to increase as children age.

Possible explanations for why these gender differences exist are numerous and complex. Some research has focused on different aspects of media content that may help to explain the differential preferences of males and females. For example, some researchers have explored the idea that viewers respond more favorably to programming that features same-sex characters. Consistent with this idea, entertainment generally enjoyed more by females than males, such as soap operas and "tear-jerkers," tends to focus more on female characters, while typical male-oriented fare such as sports and action adventures tends to focus more on male than female characters. In addition to the gender of the characters, other researchers have

pointed out that many differences in the media preferences of males and females may reflect differential responses to images of violence. In general, males have a greater affinity than do females for portrayals of aggression featured in a wide range of entertainment including sports, cartoons, horror films, and war films.

In addition to focusing on media content, other researchers have focused on aspects of gender role socialization that may help explain the media preferences of males and females. For example, given that boys are taught from a very early age that displays of sadness are inappropriate for males, whereas girls are taught that displays of anger and aggression are inappropriate for females, viewers may be less likely to enjoy entertainment that elicits emotional responses that are deemed "inappropriate" for one's gender. Furthermore, from this perspective, viewers who do not strongly internalize societal standards of gender-role expectations should be less likely than more-traditional viewers to show typical patterns of gender differences in media preferences. Support for this position has been reported in several studies showing that, in some instances, gender-role self-perceptions (i.e., masculinity and femininity) predict media preferences beyond that explained by biological sex alone.

Effects of Gender Portrayals on Viewers

In addition to examining the differential viewing preferences of males and females, a sizable amount of research has also examined the ways in which images of gender influence the attitudes, beliefs, and behaviors of viewers. Many of these studies have explored the idea that television viewing may lead to greater gender stereotyping, particularly among younger viewers. Although some researchers such as Kevin Durkin (1985) have argued that other social influences, such as parents and peers, overwhelm the influence that the media play in gender-role development, many studies employing a variety of methodologies have reported small to moderate relationships between television viewing and endorsement of traditional gender-role attitudes.

Some researchers have also voiced concerns that unrealistic media images of women focusing on appearance and body size may serve to set a standard of female beauty that is unnaturally thin. From this perspective, media consumption may lead to very harmful behavioral consequences, such as bulimia and anorexia nervosa. Consistent with these concerns, Kristin Harrison and Joanne Cantor (1997) reported that among women in their sample, media use (and particularly magazine reading) predicted an increased drive for thinness and a greater level of body dissatisfaction.

Finally, some research on media and gender has focused attention specifically on male viewers and the ways in which media images of gender influence their attitudes and beliefs about women. In particular, numerous studies have suggested that some portrayals of females (particularly sexual portrayals) may lead to increased acceptance of sexual aggression or sexual callousness. Although most of the research in this area has focused on the effects of pornography, a sizable amount of research has explored more mainstream entertainment fare, such as R-rated movies. For example, Daniel Linz, Edward Donnerstein, and Steven Penrod (1987) have conducted a series of studies showing that long-term exposure to R-rated horror films, such as *Texas Chainsaw Massacre,* quickly desensitize viewers to sexual aggression, leading to lower levels of concern about actual instances of victimization.

Given the evidence suggesting that media images of gender may lead to harmful or negative effects, some research has explored the possibility that media content may be used to affect the attitudes of viewers in prosocial or beneficial ways. In this regard, research suggests that in some cases, media portrayals may be successful in reducing sex-role stereotyping. For example, Robert Liebert and Joyce Sprafkin (1988) reported that nine- to twelve-year-old children expressed greater acceptance of nontraditional gender-role behaviors (e.g., careers for girls, nurturant behavior for boys) after viewing *Freestyle,* a thirteen-part television series featuring nontraditional gender portrayals. Also, Joyce Jennings, Florence Geis, and Virginia Brown (1980) showed that exposure to commercials featuring women in nontraditional roles increased the self-confidence of women.

Despite this success, other studies have suggested that gender-role attitudes and beliefs may be so firmly entrenched for some viewers that attempts at counter-stereotyping may meet with considerable challenges. For example, Ronald Drabman and his colleagues (1981) showed children a video that featured a female physician (Dr.

Mary Nancy) and a male nurse (Dr. David Gregory). When asked to recall the video, more than 95 percent of the first- and second-graders in the sample incorrectly identified the physician as male and the nurse as female. Similarly, Suzanne Pingree (1978) found that eighth-grade boys in her sample reported more gender stereotyping after viewing commercials featuring nontraditional portrayals of women than after viewing traditional portrayals. These results should not be interpreted as suggesting that positive media images of gender are inconsequential. Rather, they point to the importance of considering how the existing attitudes and beliefs of viewers about gender play a role in their interpretation of nontraditional portrayals.

Conclusion

The portrayal of gender has shown considerable changes over the years, with female characters now receiving greater and more-favorable representation. However, traditional portrayals of gender are still prevalent, with these differences reflected both in terms of the preferences of viewers and in the ways in which viewers are affected by media content. As media images of men and women continue to progress and as researchers devote more attention to the ways in which media content can be used for prosocial ends, popular images of males and females may move away from reflecting or perpetuating gender stereotypes, and move toward celebrating differences and enhancing equality.

See also: BODY IMAGE, MEDIA EFFECT ON; PORNOGRAPHY; SOAP OPERAS; TELEVISION BROADCASTING, PROGRAMMING AND; VIOLENCE IN THE MEDIA, ATTRACTION TO; VIOLENCE IN THE MEDIA, HISTORY OF RESEARCH ON.

Bibliography

Collins-Standley, Tracy; Gan, Su-lin; Yu, Hsin-Ju Jessy; and Zillmann, Dolf. (1996). "Choice of Romantic, Violent, and Scary Fairy-Tale Books by Preschool Girls and Boys." *Child Study Journal* 26:279–302.

Davis, Donald M. (1990). "Portrayals of Women in Prime-Time Network Television: Some Demographic Characteristics." *Sex Roles* 23:325–333.

Drabman, Ronald S.; Robertson, Stephen J.; Patterson, Jana N.; Jarvie, Gregory J.; Hammer, David; and Cordua, Glenn. (1981). "Children's Perception of Media-Portrayed Sex Roles." *Sex Roles* 7:379–389.

Durkin, Kevin. (1985). "Television and Sex-Role Acquisition: 2. Effects." *British Journal of Social Psychology* 24:191–210.

Eastman, Susan Tyler, and Billings, Andrew C. (2000). "Sportscasting and Sports Reporting: The Power of Gender Bias." *Journal of Sports & Social Issues* 24:192–213.

Harrison, Kristen, and Cantor, Joanne. (1997). "The Relationship Between Media Consumption and Eating Disorders." *Journal of Communication* 47:40–67.

Jennings, Joyce (Walstedt); Geis, Florence L.; and Brown, Virginia. (1980). "Influence of Television Commercials on Women's Self-Confidence and Independence of Judgment." *Journal of Personality and Social Psychology* 38:203–210.

Liebert, Robert M., and Sprafkin, Joyce. (1988). *The Early Window: Effects of Television on Children and Youth,* 3rd edition. New York: Pergamon Press.

Linz, Daniel; Donnerstein, Edward; and Penrod, Steven. (1987). "Sexual Violence in the Mass Media: Social Psychological Implications." In *Review of Personality and Social Psychology, Vol. 7: Sex and Gender,* eds. Phillip Shaver and Clyde Hendrick. Beverly Hills, CA: Sage Publications.

Malkin, Amy R.; Wornian, Kimberlie; and Chrisler, Joan C. (1999). "Women and Weight: Gendered Messages on Magazine Covers." *Sex Roles* 40:647–655.

Nielsen Media Research. (1998). *1998 Report On Television.* New York: Nielsen Media Research.

Pingree, Suzanne. (1978). "The Effects of Nonsexist Television Commercials and Perceptions of Reality on Children's Attitudes about Women." *Psychology of Women Quarterly* 2:262–277.

Signorielli, Nancy, and Bacue, Aaron. (1999). "Recognition and Respect: A Content Analysis of Prime-Time Television Characters Across Three Decades." *Sex Roles* 40:527–544.

Thompson, Teresa L., and Zerbinos, Eugenia. (1995). "Gender Roles in Animated Cartoons: Has the Picture Changed in 20 Years?" *Sex Roles* 32:651–673.

Ziegler, Dhyana, and White, Alisa. (1990). "Women and Minorities on Network Television News: An Examination of Correspondents and Newsmakers." *Journal of Broadcasting & Electronic Media* 34:215–223.

MARY BETH OLIVER
CHAD MAHOOD

GEOGRAPHIC INFORMATION SYSTEMS

Information systems may be broadly divided into nonspatial and spatial categories. Most information systems, including management information systems, do not refer their data to a spatial coordinate system. For example, payroll records are usually linked to a person rather than a specific location. Spatial information systems refer data to some coordinate system. For example, architectural software records the spatial relationship of beams to the foundation of a building but not necessarily to the location of the beams or the building on Earth's surface. Geographic information systems (GISs) are a subset of spatial information systems that do refer information to location.

Locations in a GIS are usually referred either directly or indirectly to coordinates denoted by latitude, longitude, and elevation or depth—or some projection of these onto a flat surface. The sciences of geodesy (concerned with the size and shape of Earth and the determination of exact positions on its surface) and cartography (concerned with the creation of maps) are therefore integral parts of geographic information science in general and of geographic information systems in particular. The combination of science and technology required for a GIS is reflected in the range of available GIS software. Some GIS software has been developed from specialized architectural drawing packages, some from computerized mapping systems, some from geographic extensions of relational databases, and others from mathematical graphing and visualization software. GISs vary in sophistication from systems that simply show the location of items ("what–where systems") or that allow the user to search for information with a location-based query ("where–what systems") to relational databases that are searchable by feature, attribute, relative location, and absolute location.

Conceptual Elements

Conceptually, a GIS consists of a data input subsystem, a data storage and retrieval subsystem, a data manipulation and analysis subsystem, and a reporting subsystem. The data input subsystem may include arrays of values (raster data or imagery), points, lines or areas constrained by coordinates (vector data), or tables of attribute data. Common data input methods include raster scans of existing maps or images, satellite and aircraft imaging systems, digitizing the vertices of map points, lines, or areas to generate vector files (electronic line drawings), uploads of coordinate data from global positioning system (GPS) receivers, or uploads of flat files of attribute data.

The data storage and retrieval subsystem is usually a relational database similar to those used in other branches of information science with extensions for manipulating location-based or georeferenced metadata and data. Georeferenced data are usually stored in one of three forms: raster, vector, or flat files. Noncoordinate-based locations, such as street addresses, may be referred to coordinate-based locations through a process known as geocoding, which assigns coordinates to each feature.

The data manipulation and analysis subsystem translates the data into a common format or formats, transforms the data into a common map projection and datum for compilation, performs calculations, and facilitates analysis of the data with regard to shape, contiguity, orientation, size, scale, neighborhood, pattern, and distribution with location-based queries. Therefore, this manipulation and analysis component of a GIS enables geographic knowledge management. Such systems are used to estimate landslide current risk, calculate property values and tax assessments, and manage wildlife habitat.

Some sophisticated GISs also allow the user to take geographic knowledge management to the next level by incorporating a modeling capability. The modeling capability allows the user to adjust variables and mathematical relationships between variables (algorithms) in the situation represented by the GIS to help determine the probable cause of the situation and to simulate what might occur if the situation were to change. Some GISs automate this last capability via built-in or modular computer programs such that the GIS becomes a geographic decision support system (GDSS). GDSSs are used to model the effect of various land-use policies on urban growth, the effect of timber cutting patterns on soil erosion, and the effect of toxic waste dumps on groundwater quality. The accuracy of a GDSS is commonly evaluated with time-series historical and real-time data.

The reporting subsystem of the GIS displays the processed information in tabular, graphic (e.g., histograms, pie charts, and surfaces), or map form, depending on the information need of the user and the capability of the GIS. The first two types of report are similar to those of most other information reporting systems. The map form links GIS to the sciences of geodesy and cartography as well as computer mapping, image processing, and visualization technologies.

Physical Elements

Physically, a GIS usually consists of input hardware and software, magnetic or optical storage, a central processing unit with GIS software, and output hardware and software. The advent of networks and the Internet has resulted in a phenomenal increase in the variety and amount of input hardware for GISs. Traditional sources of geographic information (input) include scanners, digitizing tables, keyboards, pointers, and mice. Software for GIS input includes raster-to-vector conversion programs, image processing and classification programs, geocoding packages, and various digitizing packages for translating analog maps and drawings into a vector-based GIS.

The heart of a GIS is computer hardware and software. Growth in the number and capability of computers was essential to the development and widespread use of GISs. Rapid increases in the performance/price ratio of computer hardware and decreases in overall cost for entry-level computer systems between 1985 and 2000 facilitated the rapid growth of GISs. Input hardware such as color scanners and GPS receivers decreased by a factor of ten during that period. A usable workstation including a central processing unit, disk storage, CD-ROM drive, monitor, random-access memory (RAM), keyboard, and mouse decreased in cost from several thousand dollars in 1985 to less than $1,000 in 2000.

Affordable input and processing hardware expanded the market for GIS software from tens of thousands of users to hundreds of thousands of users between 1985 and 2000. This resulted in the evolution of easy-to-use commercial GIS software with graphic user interfaces from the previous, difficult-to-use UNIX-based command-line systems of the mid-1980s. Similarly, the cost of sophisticated graphic user interface (GUI) GIS software decreased to less than $3,000 and simple systems to less than $100. The core technology necessary for GIS is now well developed, and the price of GIS technology is no longer a barrier to its widespread use.

The Information

While technology and its cost were key factors in the explosive growth of geographic information science after 1985, the primary fuel for the adoption of GIS and the development of geographic information science was the availability of low-cost, entry-level geographic information from federal, state, provincial, and tribal governments. Efforts by the U.S. Geological Survey, the Bureau of the Census, the National Oceanic and Atmospheric Administration (NOAA), the Environmental Protection Agency (EPA), the military, and academia led to the development of a limited number of data formats and metadata exchange standards based on those of the Library of Congress and the Federal Geographic Data Committee. These agencies made their data and standards available to the public and the value-added industry at little or no cost. These early efforts led to increased governmental and public awareness of the utility of GIS and, at least, the beginnings of interoperability with regard to GIS software, data, and metadata.

The Future

The growth rate of GISs seems likely to increase. The advent of the Internet has resulted in new possibilities for geographic information capture, exchange, storage, analysis, and dissemination. Internet map and geographic information servers, distributed storage, federated electronic clearinghouses, online data access, enhanced visualization tools viewable through simple and GPS-aware Internet browsers and other thin-clients decrease the cost barriers for the GIS and flatten its learning curve still further. The economies of scale and tremendous value added by networking geographic information systems allow users to share expensive information resources such as satellite data for collaborative education, research, and planning purposes, all of which used to be prohibitively expensive.

Low-cost, high-accuracy GPS receivers in combination with wireless telecommunications are rapidly increasing the amount of georeferenced information. GISs are now used to help manage the construction and maintenance of both the wired and wireless parts of the Internet as well as to synchronize its servers. As bandwidth expands and compression techniques improve, large amounts of real-time, raster-based information, including satellite imagery and three-dimensional visualizations, will be added to Internet-based GISs. Wireless networks, bandwidth, GPS, satellite imagery, and improved visualization make geographic information more plentiful and easier

for users to interpret. This will drive the demand for ancillary georeferenced information. For example, if users know where they are via GPS, they may wish to query an Internet-based GIS to find the nearest restaurant. Eventually, georeferenced information will increase to the point where the terms "information system" and "geographic information system" are synonymous in the minds of most users and information scientists.

See also: DATABASES, ELECTRONIC; DIGITAL COMMUNICATION; INTERNET AND THE WORLD WIDE WEB; KNOWLEDGE MANAGEMENT; SATELLITES, TECHNOLOGY OF; TELECOMMUNICATIONS, WIRELESS; VISUALIZATION OF INFORMATION.

Bibliography

Clarke, Keith C. (1995). *Analytical and Computer Cartography.* New York: Prentice-Hall.

Clarke, Keith C. (1999). *Getting Started with Geographic Information Systems.* New York: Prentice-Hall.

Daskin, Mark S. (1995). *Network and Discrete Location: Models, Algorithms, and Applications.* New York: Wiley.

DeMers, Michael N. (1997). *Fundamentals of Geographic Information Systems.* New York: Wiley.

Korfhage, Robert R. (1997). *Information Storage and Retrieval.* New York: Wiley.

Laudon, Kenneth C., and Laudon, Jane P. (2000). *Management Information Systems.* New York: Prentice-Hall.

Star, Jeffery E., and Estes, John E. (1990). *Geographic Information Systems: An Introduction.* Upper Saddle River, NJ: Prentice-Hall.

RICHARD BECK

■ GLOBALIZATION OF CULTURE THROUGH THE MEDIA

The received view about the globalization of culture is one where the entire world has been molded in the image of Western, mainly American, culture. In popular and professional discourses alike, the popularity of Big Macs, *Baywatch,* and MTV are touted as unmistakable signs of the fulfillment of Marshall McLuhan's prophecy of the Global Village. The globalization of culture is often chiefly imputed to international mass media. After all, contemporary media technologies such as satellite television and the Internet have created a steady flow of transnational images that connect audiences worldwide. Without global media, according to the conventional wisdom, how would teenagers in India, Turkey, and Argentina embrace a Western lifestyle of Nike shoes, Coca-Cola, and rock music? Hence, the putatively strong influence of the mass media on the globalization of culture.

The role of the mass media in the globalization of culture is a contested issue in international communication theory and research. Early theories of media influence, commonly referred to as "magic bullet" or "hypodermic needle" theories, believed that the mass media had powerful effects over audiences. Since then, the debate about media influence has undergone an ebb and flow that has prevented any resolution or agreement among researchers as to the level, scope, and implications of media influence. Nevertheless, key theoretical formulations in international communication clung to a belief in powerful media effects on cultures and communities. At the same time, a body of literature questioning the scope and level of influence of transnational media has emerged. Whereas some scholars within that tradition questioned cultural imperialism without providing conceptual alternatives, others have drawn on an interdisciplinary literature from across the social sciences and humanities to develop theoretical alternatives to cultural imperialism.

Cultural Imperialism and the Global Media Debate

In international communication theory and research, cultural imperialism theory argued that audiences across the globe are heavily affected by media messages emanating from the Western industrialized countries. Although there are minor differences between "media imperialism" and "cultural imperialism," most of the literature in international communication treats the former as a category of the latter. Grounded in an understanding of media as cultural industries, cultural imperialism is firmly rooted in a political-economy perspective on international communication. As a school of thought, political economy focuses on material issues such as capital, infrastructure, and political control as key determinants of international communication processes and effects.

In the early stage of cultural imperialism, researchers focused their efforts mostly on nation-states as primary actors in international relations.

They imputed rich, industrialized, and Western nation-states with intentions and actions by which they export their cultural products and impose their sociocultural values on poorer and weaker nations in the developing world. This argument was supported by a number of studies demonstrating that the flow of news and entertainment was biased in favor of industrialized countries. This bias was clear both in terms of quantity, because most media flows were exported by Western countries and imported by developing nations, and in terms of quality, because developing nations received scant and prejudicial coverage in Western media.

These concerns led to the rise of the New World Information Order (NWIO) debate, later known as the New World Information and Communication Order (NWICO) debate. Although the debate at first was concerned with news flows between the north and the south, it soon evolved to include all international media flows. This was due to the fact that inequality existed in news and entertainment programs alike, and to the advent of then-new media technologies such as communication satellites, which made the international media landscape more complex and therefore widened the scope of the debate about international flows.

The global media debate was launched during the 1973 General Conference of the United Nations Educational, Scientific, and Cultural Organization (UNESCO) in Nairobi, Kenya. As a specialized agency of the United Nations, the mission of UNESCO includes issues of communication and culture. During the conference, strong differences arose between Western industrialized nations and developing countries. Led by the United States, the first group insisted on the "free flow of information" doctrine, advocating "free trade" in information and media programs without any restrictions. The second group, concerned by the lack of balance in international media flows, accused Western countries of invoking the free flow of information ideology to justify their economic and cultural domination. They argued instead for a "free and balanced flow" of information. The chasm between the two groups was too wide to be reconciled. This eventually was one of the major reasons given for withdrawal from UNESCO by the United States and the United Kingdom—which resulted in the *de facto* fall of the global media debate.

A second stage of research identified with cultural imperialism has been associated with calls to revive the New World Information and Communication Order debate. What differentiates this line of research from earlier cultural imperialism formulations is its emphasis on the commercialization of the sphere of culture. Research into this area had been a hallmark of cultural imperialism research, but now there is a deliberate focus on transnational corporations as actors, as opposed to nation-states, and on transnational capital flows, as opposed to image flows. Obviously, it is hard to separate the power of transnational corporations from that of nation-states, and it is difficult to distinguish clearly between capital flows and media flows. Therefore, the evolution of the debate is mainly a redirection of emphasis rather than a paradigm shift.

It has become fashionable in some international communication circles to dismiss cultural imperialism as a monolithic theory that is lacking subtlety and increasingly questioned by empirical research. Cultural imperialism does have some weaknesses, but it also continues to be useful. Perhaps the most important contribution of cultural imperialism is the argument that international communication flows, processes, and effects are permeated by power. Nevertheless, it seems that the concept of globalization has in some ways replaced cultural imperialism as the main conceptual umbrella under which much research and theorizing in international communication have been conducted.

Media, Globalization, and Hybridization

Several reasons explain the analytical shift from cultural imperialism to globalization. First, the end of the Cold War as a global framework for ideological, geopolitical, and economic competition calls for a rethinking of the analytical categories and paradigms of thought. By giving rise to the United States as sole superpower and at the same time making the world more fragmented, the end of the Cold War ushered in an era of complexity between global forces of cohesion and local reactions of dispersal. In this complex era, the nation-state is no longer the sole or dominant player, since transnational transactions occur on subnational, national, and supranational levels. Conceptually, globalization appears to capture this complexity better than cultural imperialism. Second, according to John Tomlinson (1991), global-

ization replaced cultural imperialism because it conveys a process with less coherence and direction, which will weaken the cultural unity of all nation-states, not only those in the developing world. Finally, globalization has emerged as a key perspective across the humanities and social sciences, a current undoubtedly affecting the discipline of communication.

In fact, the globalization of culture has become a conceptual magnet attracting research and theorizing efforts from a variety of disciplines and interdisciplinary formations such as anthropology, comparative literature, cultural studies, communication and media studies, geography, and sociology. International communication has been an active interlocutor in this debate because media and information technologies play an important role in the process of globalization. Although the media are undeniably one of the engines of cultural globalization, the size and intensity of the effect of the media on the globalization of culture is a contested issue revolving around the following question: Did the mass media trigger and create the globalization of culture? Or is the globalization of culture an old phenomenon that has only been intensified and made more obvious with the advent of transnational media technologies? Like the age-old question about whether the egg came before the chicken or *vice versa*, the question about the relationship between media and the globalization of culture is difficult to answer.

One perspective on the globalization of culture, somewhat reminiscent of cultural imperialism in terms of the nature of the effect of media on culture, but somewhat different in its conceptualization of the issue, is the view that the media contribute to the homogenization of cultural differences across the planet. This view dominates conventional wisdom perspectives on cultural globalization conjuring up images of Planet Hollywood and the MTV generation. One of the most visible proponents of this perspective is political scientist Benjamin Barber, who formulated his theory about the globalization of culture in the book *Jihad vs. McWorld* (1996). The subtitle, "How Globalism and Tribalism Are Reshaping the World," betrays Barber's reliance on a binary opposition between the forces of modernity and liberal democracy with tradition and autocracy.

Although Barber rightly points to transnational capitalism as the driving engine that brings Jihad

A McDonalds advertisement from the 2000 Beijing Chaoyang International Business Festival illustrates how global that particular aspect of Western culture has become. During its first ten years in China (1990 to 2000), the food chain expanded to include 270 stores in 50 Chinese cities. (Reuters NewMedia Inc./Corbis)

and McWorld in contact and motivates their action, his model has two limitations. First, it is based on a binary opposition between Jihad, what he refers to as ethnic and religious tribalism, and McWorld, the capital-driven West. Barber (1996, p. 157) seemingly attempts to go beyond this binary opposition in a chapter titled "Jihad Via McWorld," in which he argues that Jihad stands in "less of a stark opposition than a subtle counterpoint." However, the evidence offered in most of the book supports an oppositional rather than a contrapuntal perspective on the globalization of culture. The second limitation of Barber's book is that he privileges the global over the local, because, according to him, globalization rules via transnational capitalism. "[T]o think that globalization and indigenization are entirely coequal forces that put Jihad and McWorld on an equal footing is to vastly underestimate the force of the new planetary markets. . . . It's no contest" (p. 12). Although it would be naïve to argue that the local defeats the global, Barber's argument does not take into account the dynamic and resilient nature of cultures and their ability to negotiate foreign imports.

Another perspective on globalization is cultural hybridity or hybridization. This view privileges an understanding of the interface of globalization and localization as a dynamic process and hybrid product of mixed traditions and cultural forms. As such, this perspective does not give prominence to globalization as a homogenizing force, nor does it believe in localization as a resistive process opposed to globalization. Rather, hybridization advocates an emphasis on processes of mediation that it views as central to cultural globalization. The concept of hybridization is the product of interdisciplinary work mostly based in intellectual projects such as postcolonialism, cultural studies, and performance studies. Hybridization has been used in communication and media studies and appears to be a productive theoretical orientation as researchers in international media studies attempt to grasp the complex subtleties of the globalization of culture.

One of the most influential voices in the debate about cultural hybridity is Argentinean–Mexican cultural critic Nestor García-Canclini. In his book *Hybrid Cultures* (1995), García-Canclini advocates a theoretical understanding of Latin American nations as hybrid cultures. His analysis is both broad and incisive, covering a variety of cultural processes and institutions such as museums, television, film, universities, political cartoons, graffiti, and visual arts. According to García-Canclini, there are three main features of cultural hybridity. The first feature consists of mixing previously separate cultural systems, such as mixing the elite art of opera with popular music. The second feature of hybridity is the deterritorialization of cultural processes from their original physical environment to new and foreign contexts. Third, cultural hybridity entails impure cultural genres that are formed out of the mixture of several cultural domains. An example of these impure genres is when artisans in rural Mexico weave tapestries of masterpieces of European painters such as Joan Miró and Henri Matisse, mixing high art and folk artisanship into an impure genre.

In media and communication research, the main question is "Have transnational media made cultures across the globe hybrid by bringing into their midst foreign cultural elements, or have cultures always been to some extent hybrid, meaning that transnational mass media only strengthened an already-existing condition?" There is no obvious or final answer to that question, because there is not enough empirical research about media and hybridity and because of the theoretical complexity of the issue. What does exist in terms of theoretical understanding and research results points to a middle ground. This position acknowledges that cultures have been in contact for a long time through warfare, trade, migration, and slavery. Therefore, a degree of hybridization in all cultures can be assumed. At the same time. this middle ground also recognizes that global media and information technologies have substantially increased contacts between cultures, both in terms of intensity and of the speed with which these contacts occur. Therefore, it is reasonable to assume that transnational mass media intensify the hybridity that is already in existence in cultures across the globe. Consequently, the globalization of culture through the media is not a process of complete homogenization, but rather one where cohesion and fragmentation coexist.

See also: CULTURAL STUDIES; CULTURE AND COMMUNICATION; CULTURE INDUSTRIES, MEDIA AS; CUMULATIVE MEDIA EFFECTS; MCLUHAN, HERBERT MARSHALL; POLITICAL ECONOMY; SOCIAL CHANGE AND THE MEDIA; SOCIAL GOALS AND THE MEDIA; SOCIETY AND THE MEDIA.

Bibliography

Appadurai, Arjun. (1996). *Modernity at Large.* Minneapolis: University of Minnesota Press.

Barber, Benjamin. (1996). *Jihad vs. McWorld.* New York: Ballantine Books.

Bhabba, Homi. (1994). *The Location of Culture.* London: Routledge.

Featherstone, Mike. (1990). *Global Culture.* London: Sage Publications.

García-Canclini, Nestor. (1995). *Hybrid Cultures.* Minneapolis: University of Minnesota Press.

Gerbner, George; Mowlana, Hamid; and Nordenstreng, Kaarle. (1994). *The Global Media Debate.* Norwood, NJ: Ablex.

Golding, Peter, and Harris, Phil. (1997). *Beyond Cultural Imperialism.* London: Sage Publications.

Kraidy, Marwan M. (1999). "The Global, the Local, and the Hybrid: A Native Ethnography of Glocalization." *Critical Studies in Mass Communication* 16(4):456–476.

Mattelart, Armand. (1983). *Transnationals and the Third World.* London: Bergin and Harvey

Robertson, Roland. (1992). *Globalization.* London: Sage Publications.

Schiller, Herbert. (1991). "Not Yet the Post-Imperialist Era." *Critical Studies in Mass Communication* 8(1):13–28.

Schiller, Herbert. (1992). *The Ideology of International Communication.* New York: Institute for Media Analysis.

Straubhaar, Joseph D. (1991). "Beyond Media Imperialism: Assymetrical Interdependence and Cultural Proximity." *Critical Studies in Mass Communication* 8(1):39–59.

Tomlinson, John. (1991). *Cultural Imperialism.* Baltimore, MD: Johns Hopkins University Press.

Tomlinson, John. (1999). *Globalization and Culture.* Chicago: University of Chicago Press.

Tufte, Thomas. (1995). "How Do Telenovelas Serve to Articulate Hybrid Cultures in Contemporary Brazil?" *Nordicom Review* 2:29–35.

Varis, Tapio. (1984). "The International Flow of Television Programs." *Journal of Communication* 34(Winter):143–152.

MARWAN M. KRAIDY

■ GLOBALIZATION OF MEDIA INDUSTRIES

In the 1960s, Canadian professor Marshall McLuhan predicted that television media would create a "global village" where "time ceases, space vanishes." McLuhan's prophecies have come true, but even he could not have predicted the degree of globalization and convergence of technology that now exists throughout media communications. Since the 1960s, the rise of global media and multinational media companies has greatly influenced—if not transformed—the ways in which people think and interact, as well as how they gain access to and communicate information. With globalization, constraints of geography are reduced, but social and cultural interconnectivity across time and space is increased. Media are obviously important to globalization; they provide an extensive transnational transmission of cultural products, and they contribute to the formation of communication networks and social structures.

The manner in which media have expanded globally, yet converged technologically since the mid-1970s, is quite remarkable in its scope and integration. Millions of people now listen to "local" radio from a computer anywhere in the world. Modern television has changed the way that world affairs are conducted. Online users can access video graphics on any one of millions of websites. U.S. films are "greenlighted" (i.e., given the go-ahead for production) based on their

On May 31, 2000, Cable News Network (CNN) founder Ted Turner spoke to the CNN World Report Conference in Atlanta, Georgia. From an initial 200 employees in 1980, CNN had grown to include 4,000 people in 37 bureaus worldwide by 2000. (AFP/Corbis)

potential to attract a global audience. Advances from satellite technology to digitally based, increasingly interactive media have made such a global media environment possible.

The Rise of Global Media

When the first communications satellite, *Telstar I*, was launched in 1962, few people predicted the major effect that satellite technology would have on global media. Although satellites helped to deliver such transforming events as the first moon walk and coverage of the Olympics in the 1960s, modern global media industries can be traced to 1975—the year when Home Box Office (HBO), a service owned by Time, Inc., decided to use satellite technology to show a championship boxing match to subscribers in two U.S. cable television systems. The experiment proved so successful—even enlightening—that HBO soon began to use satellites to distribute more programming, not only to its own systems but to cable system operations throughout the United States.

HBO's entry marked the beginning of the explosive growth of cable television in the United States—from only 12 percent of U.S. homes in 1975 to nearly 70 percent in 2000—and opened the floodgates for other media companies that quickly saw the value of using satellites to expand their business.

The greater significance of HBO's "experiment" was that television industries no longer viewed themselves as "earthbound"—tied strictly to telephone lines or broadcast station signals—and bounded by their geographic borders. Worldwide transmission and distribution of media communication—information, entertainment, persuasion—was viewed as an attractive opportunity for media companies and individuals and entrepreneurs with the vision to take their media products to the global market.

The most globally minded media visionary was Ted Turner, who first used satellite technology to turn his "local" independent television station into "Superstation" WTBS. This led to the formation of the Cable News Network (CNN) in 1980. Many people thought that Turner was "crazy" for establishing a cable news network that would always be on the air, but CNN soon grew to have enormous influence on viewers around the globe.

CNN is considered by many people to be the "flagship" for media globalization. Turner transformed his Atlanta-based company into a credible international news service. The company's aggressive strategy of covering news whenever and wherever it happens, of breaking the news first, and of going live from the scene is important to the globalization of media industries. Former U.S. President George H. W. Bush once even quipped, "I learn more from CNN than I do from the CIA."

By the mid-1980s, various countries began to subscribe to CNN's satellite feeds. In less than twenty years from its creation, CNN (or CNN International) had viewers in more than 150 nations around the world. One of CNN's most intriguing concepts is "CNN World Report," a truly international newscast that presents stories from almost every point of the globe.

The emergence of CNN also sparked the development or expansion of other international news services, including BBC World, a television service started in 1995 that has grown to reach some 167 million weekly viewers in nearly 200 countries.

A second significant satellite channel began within a year of CNN's debut. On August 1, 1981, Warner Amex Satellite Entertainment Company launched Music Television (MTV), the first full-time music video channel. Rock-'n'-roll, radio, television, and youth culture around the globe would never be the same. MTV asked viewers to "think globally, act locally." The music and entertainment channel affected nearly every aspect of world popular culture—music, fashion, art, advertising, and movies. MTV has grown to the point where it is delivered to nearly 70 million households in the United States and to more than 100 million households in Europe, Asia, South America, and Russia. Together, CNN and MTV illustrate the emerging importance of communication—not only to reduce time and space but to convey both news and entertainment values to a global audience.

Globalization and the Internet

As satellite-delivered cable television continued to expand throughout the 1980s, the development and growing use of personal computers and the Internet added new dimensions and opportunities in worldwide media. In the early 1990s, the large increase of desktop computers and connections over the public telephone networks allowed for the exchange of messages (e-mail), computer bulletin-board postings, information files, and computer programs with tens of thousands of other computers in the same network.

The Internet came of age as a communications medium with the creation of the World Wide Web (i.e., the Internet's graphical interface) by British engineer Tim Berners-Lee in 1991 and the invention of the first graphical browser (i.e., Mosaic) in 1993 by Marc Andressen at the National Center for Supercomputing Applications (NCSA) at the University of Illinois.

In 1989, America Online (AOL) launched a text-only service for Macintosh and Apple II computers; they added a Windows version in 1993. AOL, led by cofounder Steve Case, soon focused on building a "global community" of subscribers and entered into international partnerships with media companies in Latin American and in specific key countries such as Germany and Japan. In 1993, AOL acquired Global Network Navigator as a platform for direct Internet service. A joint venture with German conglomerate Bertelsmann AB created European online services in 1993. By the end of 1993, AOL had more than half a million members. After launches in the United Kingdom, Canada, and France in 1996 and in Japan in 1997, AOL passed the point where they had one million members outside of the United States.

In the late 1990s, when other online services focused on games, shopping, and business, AOL aggressively sought to "brand" its name throughout the world. Through these attempts to have its name considered to be synonymous with the Internet, AOL secured and interconnected subscribers in fourteen countries—including Australia, Brazil, Canada, France, Germany, Hong Kong, Japan, Latin America, and the United Kingdom—and seven languages. By 2000, AOL had 21 million customers in the world—3.2 million of which live outside the United States. AOL-owned CompuServe has 2.5 million subscribers.

AOL is the largest of thousands of companies that use the "information superhighway" to transmit media content, sell or advertise products, or send information. The Internet carries enormous amounts of information—combining voice, video, graphics, data, and computer services—around the globe. The Internet and other media technologies are empowering members of virtual communities throughout the world. New digital-age printing costs little to operate and reaches audiences of millions in an almost instantaneous fashion. In sum, the Internet speeds the delivery of information and communication throughout the world, but it also eases the individual user's access to that information and communication.

Globalization of Media Ownership

The growth of any media industry is predicated on the economic potential for growth and expansion. Part of the reason for globalization is not only the development of technology, but also the growth of multinational companies that seek to expand economic opportunities throughout the world. Through consolidation, global media companies are becoming increasingly larger in size but fewer in number. New technologies of digitization and multimedia and network integration have allowed for rapid structural globalization of communication. Rupert Murdoch owns media properties in the United States, Europe, Asia, and his native Australia. Japanese companies, such as Matsushita and Sony, own U.S. movie studios. These "conglomerates" seek to "vertically integrate" to control all aspects of production, distribution, and exhibition of content.

Successful channels such as Murdoch's Star TV are conglomerates of national and regional channels designed to meet the different political and cultural needs of their respective audiences in China, India, and other countries. Other multinational consortiums also own satellites and cable/DBS (direct broadcast satellite) systems in Europe, and Japan has several DBS systems. Companies such as Sony and Matsushita equip many of their new television sets and videocassette recorders with built-in DBS receivers.

AOL purchased CompuServe in 1998 and Netscape in 1999 and works with "strategic world-class partners" such as Bertelsmann AB (Europe, Australia), Cisneros Group of Companies (Latin America), Royal Bank (Canada), Mitsui & Co., Ltd., and Nihon Keizai Shimbun (Nikkei) in Japan. Mitsui owns 40 percent of AOL Japan, while Nikkei owns 10 percent. AOL also developed a partnership with China.com, a Chinese- and Eng-lish-language service that began in Hong Kong in 1999. The $181 billion merger between AOL and Time Warner in 2001 further expanded the boundaries of global media conglomerations. AOL is the world's largest Internet service provider (ISP) and instant messaging (IM) service, while Time Warner is an entertainment empire that owns and operates popular video programming networks, multiple sports franchises, magazines, music recording labels, a broadcast television network, and the second largest cable system operator in the United States, as well as companies that produce and distribute films and television programming. AOL Time Warner's combined resources and infrastructure suggest almost unlimited possibilities for the production, distribution, and exhibition of media content on a global scale. This trend for companies to consolidate and to develop multinational partnerships is expected to continue.

Continuing Convergence and the Transition to a Digital World

As the companies that own the media industries become larger, the lines that once separated the various media also will become smaller. Convergence refers to the melding of the computer, the television, the telephone, and satellites into a unified system of information acquisition, delivery, and control. These are held together by a global network of satellite dishes, copper, coaxial, fiber-optic wires, and the accelerating flow of digital bits and bytes.

Communication theorists, computer specialists, media moguls, telecommunications leaders, and Wall Street investors have found common ground in the belief that the Internet is evolving into the premier medium of the twenty-first century. Already, by the year 2000, nearly one billion people were using the Internet on a regular basis. Because of its ability to convey both sequential and nonsequential writing, e-mail, audio and visual images, animation, audio conferencing, and multimedia presentations, the Internet has become the embodiment of the global information superhighway. Philips Electronics, a U.S. company, has already introduced "WebTV." In 1999, AOL signed pacts with DirecTV, Hughes Network System, Philips, and Network Computer to help bring interactivity to the television experience.

Convergence of technology increases the power of large multinational companies, but it also empowers individuals with the ability to choose their channels and to dispatch their own descriptions of what is happening to a rapidly expanding online audience. For example, first-hand information and eyewitness accounts of the Serbian conflict of the 1990s came from the professional corps of print and broadcast reporters, but it also came from amateurs who had computers, modems, cellular telephones, digital cameras, and access to e-mail. The riveting and insightful e-mail dialogue between two high school students, one in Kosovo and the other in Berkeley, California, was recycled in newspapers and read throughout the world. Using websites and chat groups on the Internet, monks, farmers, housewives, paramilitary leaders, and propagandists in Serbia, Kosovo, Albania, Macedonia, and Montenegro told, with varying degrees of accuracy and trustworthiness, about their beleaguered cities, towns, and refugee camps.

Emerging technologies are rapidly transforming the global media landscape. The Internet and the World Wide Web, wireless communications, and digital video technology are creating a new global communication environment in which the roles of media consumer and content creator often blur. Increasingly, media consumers from throughout the world have unprecedented choice and control over the media experience, selecting not just what they watch, read, or hear, but when and where they do so.

By the late 1990s, much voice, sound, and image communication was being converted to digital coding, a system that grew out of computer and data applications. Advances in transmission systems have also greatly facilitated the capabilities of modern telecommunications, making it possible to send messages, whether voice, data, or image, across different communication routes and computer systems. Digitalization will bring crystal clear, "high-definition" pictures and hundreds of additional channels, but it will also make television sets interactive, similar to personal computers.

Ramifications of Media Globalization

The digital age has the potential to provide an unprecedented richness of new sources of information, diversity of views, and a variety of perspectives that will not be bound by geographic or even political barriers. However, the free flow of information across any boundary is not without detractors. For "information rich" countries such as the United States and many Western European countries, the global flow of information across national boundaries is a positive consequence of globalization. However, the flow of media content is not equal between developed and developing countries. The globalization of media content means cultural values are far more likely to be transmitted from the United States to other countries than to the United States from other countries. Some would go so far as to say that "globalization" of the media industries is Westernization.

Certainly, all forms of information and entertainment contribute to social learning, the process by which people come to know their society and its rules and absorb its values, beliefs, and attitudes. U.S. movies, television, music, and magazines compete with and sometimes replace native versions in many countries. Advocates of the "global village" can aim at spreading Western culture and lifestyle through the mass media or strive for a real global culture of democratically integrated markets, ideas, and potentials. This new media, which will not divide along the traditional lines of delivery that were established by print, broadcast, and cable, will provide shared media experiences that will be created at least in part by those same people who receive it.

See also: CABLE TELEVISION, HISTORY OF; COMMUNITY NETWORKS; DIGITAL COMMUNICATION; DIGITAL MEDIA SYSTEMS; GLOBALIZATION OF CULTURE THROUGH THE MEDIA; INTERNET AND THE WORLD WIDE WEB; McLUHAN, HERBERT MARSHALL; SATELLITES, HISTORY OF; TELECOMMUNICATIONS, WIRELESS.

Bibliography

Flournoy, Don M.; Carter, Jimmy; and Stewart, Robert K. (1999). *CNN: Making News in the Global Market.* Luton, Eng.: University of Luton Press.

Gershon, Richard. (1996). *The Transnational Media Corporation: Global Messages and Free Market Competition.* Mahwah, NJ: Lawrence Erlbaum.

Greco, Albert N., ed. (2000). *The Media and Entertainment Industries.* Boston: Allyn & Bacon.

Gross, Lynne Schafer, ed. (1995). *The International World of Electronic Media.* New York: McGraw-Hill.

Kai, Hafez. (1999). "International News Coverage and the Problems of Media Globalization: In Search of a 'New Global-Local Nexus.'" *Innovation* 12(1):47–62.

McGrath, Tom. (1996). *MTV: The Making of a Revolution.* Philadelphia, PA: Running Press.

McLuhan, Marshall. (1967). *The Medium Is the Message.* New York: Penguin Books.

Winston, Brian. (1998). *Media Technology and Society: A History from the Telegraph to the Internet.* London: Routledge.

ROGER COOPER

■ GREELEY, HORACE (1811–1872)

Two features of Horace Greeley's life make him notable in the fields of communication and journalism. The first is his rise to publisher of one of the most powerful newspapers in the nineteenth century, the *New York Tribune.* The second is his career as a writer of editorials and lectures for the popular "lyceums"(i.e., lecture series that provided education to the public on a variety of topics).

In his autobiography, *Recollections of a Busy Life* (published four years before his death), Greeley recalled the misery of his family's chronic, debt-ridden existence when he was a child: "Hunger, cold, rags, hard work, contempt, suspicion, unjust reproach, are disagreeable; but debt is infinitely worse than them all" (Greeley, 1868, p. 96). This statement characterizes the drive that turned a child from an impoverished farm family into one of the most influential newspaper editors of the nineteenth century.

Greeley took his first job on the path to journalism in East Poultney, Vermont, as a printer's apprentice, at the age of fifteen. In 1831, he went to work in Pennsylvania for the *Erie Gazette,* and later, he worked as a printer in New York City for the *Spirit of the Times,* the *Morning Post,* and the *Commercial Advertiser.* In 1834, two events that would shape Greeley's influence on the world of newspapers and on his own career as a politically minded publisher occurred: (1) he founded his *New Yorker,* a literary magazine, and (2) he joined the Whig party of New York. Joining forces with Thurlow Weed, an editor of the *Albany Evening Journal,* and William H. Seward, the Whig candidate for governor of New York in 1837, Greeley founded the *Jeffersonian,* a Whig paper. In 1840, Greeley also initiated the *Log Cabin,* a Whig paper designed to support the presidential candidacy of William Henry Harrison. Once Harrison was

elected, and after Harrison's untimely death soon after he became president, Greeley published the first issue of his own newspaper, the *New York Tribune,* on April 10, 1841. Described as "A New Morning Journal of Politics, Literature and General Intelligence," the newspaper promised "to advance the interests of the people, and to promote their Moral, Political and Social well-being."

Thus began Greeley's tenure as an editor who crusaded against slavery, capital punishment, class injustice, and marital infidelity and who wrote editorials in favor of labor rights, protective tariffs, westward expansion, and women's rights (not suffrage). Greeley was a strong shaper of public opinion whose own views were loyal to Whig party causes, such as protection of industry, but who desired his newspaper to be politically neutral. Believing that newspapers should provide a forum for debate, Greeley's newspaper featured writings by such luminaries of the nineteenth century as Margaret Fuller and Karl Marx. The *New York Tribune* was known for its quality reporting of local, national, and international events, for its inclusion of various genres of writing, such as poetry and criticism, and for its embodiment of the virtues of a free press. It became one of the first great American newspapers, reaching a circulation of almost 300,000 by 1860. One of Greeley's most famous editorials, "The Prayer of Twenty Millions," was a plea to President Abraham Lincoln to authorize military commanders to free slaves during 1862. Lincoln's famous reply, that his concern was saving the Union, regardless of slavery, shows how Greeley's clout led many leaders of the day to engage with him editorially.

Throughout his lifetime, Greeley championed a variety of causes, some of them seemingly contradictory. He advocated protective tariffs but supported the presidential candidacy of the Republican party, which favored tariff reduction. He was apparently an inelegant speaker with a squeaky voice and a literary style, both of which combined with his eccentric and ill-fitting dress to give an impression of a well-schooled but painfully awkward orator. Nonetheless, Greeley gave extensive lectures on labor, education, and farming techniques throughout the country at agricultural fairs and lyceums. He was known as an articulate and opinionated speaker.

Greeley wrote twelve books in his lifetime, and four of them encapsulate his career as a journalist and statesman. The first, *Hints Toward Reforms* (1853), is a 400-page collection of his lectures at lyceums and agricultural fairs. Characterized as "editorials on legs," these lectures range widely in topic from labor to religion to slavery, thereby showing Greeley's own range of interests. The second, *A History of the Struggle for Slavery Extension or Restriction in the United States,* is an excessively detailed account of slavery in the United States, overlaid with Greeley's political commentary on the ordinances and bills that fueled the institution of slavery from the eighteenth century onward. This book, published in 1856, has been praised for its journalistic detail and research. The third, *An Overland Journey, from New York to San Francisco, in the Summer of 1859,* is a travelogue of Greeley's ventures west to California, complete with details of modes of transport and the variety of natural phenomena he witnessed. It is this work that may have contributed to Greeley's fame for the phrase "Go west, young man," which was actually coined by John Soule, an Indiana editor, in 1851. Finally, Greeley's 1868 autobiography, *Recollections of a Busy Life,* traces his life from the Puritan New England roots through his newspaper days. Included in this book are accounts of the U.S. Civil War and a discussion of the deaths of his children (he lost five out of seven). Comprehensive and evocative, it is considered to be on par with Benjamin Franklin's famous autobiography.

Greeley was the Republican candidate for president in 1872, but he was soundly defeated by the incumbent, Ulysses S. Grant, in an election that coincided with tragedy in Greeley's personal life, as he faced his wife's death and his own failing health.

See also: NEWSPAPER INDUSTRY, HISTORY OF.

Bibliography

Greeley, Horace. (1850). *Hints Toward Reforms.* New York: Harper & Brothers.

Greeley, Horace. (1856). *A History of the Struggle for Slavery Extension or Restriction in the United States, from the Declaration of Independence to the Present Day.* New York: Dix, Edwards.

Greeley, Horace. (1859). *An Overland Journey from New York to San Francisco in the Summer of 1859.* New York: C. M. Saxton, Barker.

Greeley, Horace. (1868). *Recollections of a Busy Life.* New York: J. B. Ford.

Hale, William Harlan. (1950). *Horace Greeley: Voice of the People.* New York: Harper & Brothers.

The campaign materials for Horace Greeley's 1872 run for the presidency included sheet music for "Horace Greeley's Grand March." (Bettmann/Corbis)

Lunde, Erik S. (1981). *Horace Greeley.* Boston: G. K. Hall

Maihafer, Harry J. (1998). *The General and the Journalists: Ulysses S. Grant, Horace Greeley, and Charles Dana.* Washington, DC: Brasseys.

Parton, James. (1882). *The Life of Horace Greeley, Editor of the New York Tribune.* Boston: Houghton, Mifflin.

Schulze, Suzanne. (1992). *Horace Greeley: A Bio-Bibliography.* Westport, CT: Greenwood.

Stoddard, Henry Luther. (1946). *Horace Greeley: Printer, Editor, Crusader.* New York: G. P. Putnam.

Van Deusen, Glyndon G. (1953). *Horace Greeley: Nineteenth-Century Crusader.* New York: Hill and Wang.

SUSAN ROSS

GRIFFITH, D. W. (1875–1948)

David Wark "D. W." Griffith advanced the motion picture from a cheap amusement to an art form. Ironically, this theater-trained dramatist and would-be playwright developed many of the cinematic techniques that lifted the motion picture out of the shadow of the stage and gave it its own language and style.

Griffith began acting in films in 1907 at a salary of five dollars per day working under early director Edwin Porter. Griffith was hesitant to act in films, fearing this could hurt his stage career, but he needed the money. His playwriting background also helped draw him to the movies because he could earn extra money by writing story ideas for films. His story ideas soon landed him a job with the Biograph Company. Between 1908 and 1910, he directed 206 short one-reel films, averaging about two films per week. Each reel of film lasted approximately ten minutes. From 1910 to 1912, Griffith directed 104 two-reel films. Initially, there was resistance in the industry to extending a film beyond one reel. Biograph even released some two-reelers as separate films, such as *His Trust, Part I* and *His Trust, Part II* (also referred to as *His Trust* and *His Trust Fulfilled*). However, demand from customers to see both parts of a two-reel film together eventually led to the success of the longer films.

Across these hundreds of films can be seen the incremental steps of creating an art form. While early filmmakers such as Porter and the Lumière brothers (Louis and Auguste) used moving cameras, close-up shots, excellent photographic composition, and editing techniques, it was Griffith who understood the use of these techniques to create meaning. Griffith discovered what it meant to use close-up shots juxtaposed with long-range shots or medium shots. Griffith gradually developed his techniques of editing film so that the changes in camera angles, distance from the subject, pace of edits, and sequence of edits all carried meaning for the viewer. Griffith learned to direct the viewer's attention to specific detail in a scene, ensuring that the viewer would be led to specific conclusions related to the plot of the film script. In short, Griffith showed how the filmmaker could gain control over the emotional response that the audience had to a film.

Many of these advances were the result of changing the basic unit around which a film was built—from the individual scene to the individual shot. Early filmmakers relied on the scene as the basic unit of action. Thus, the camera would often capture an entire scene of action in one take. Griffith began using several takes from multiple camera angles to create one scene using each shot to

specific advantage. This was, perhaps, his most important contribution to the art.

In 1913, Griffith stretched the running time of a movie to four reels with *Judith of Bethulia*. He went on to create the first American feature-length film two years later with *The Birth of a Nation*, which was twelve reels in length. With this film, Griffith brought together for the first time in one film most of the basic cinematic techniques that are still used in modern filmmaking. Still considered to be one of the most remarkable cinematic successes in the history of motion pictures, *The Birth of a Nation* was as controversial as it was successful (financially and artistically).

The film (based on the 1905 novel *The Clansmen* by Thomas Dixon) reflected the racial bias of Griffith's upbringing as the son of a Confederate Army officer. As with many of his films, the story line of *The Birth of a Nation* was built around the ravages of the American Civil War. Griffith emphasized the villainy of a mixed-race character and showed his abhorrence for the romantic intentions that a former slave showed toward the daughter of a white family. In general, he portrayed African Americans as being innately inferior to Caucasians. The "heroes" in the section of the film set in the post-Civil War era were the members of the Ku Klux Klan, a group that grew in power, influence, and infamy in the wake of the film. Due to the inflammatory content of *The Birth of a Nation*, protests and attempts to censor it were common. However, these only served to further the fame of the film and draw the audience to the theaters. By some estimates, the film, which had an original budget of between $110,000 and $125,000, grossed as much as $50 million during it run at the box office.

Griffith was surprised to be accused of being anti-Negro. He had failed to understand the need for equality among the races, believing it was enough that the film's white characters had treated the African Americans kindly. Still, he seems to have realized the error of his prejudice in the making of his next film, *Intolerance* (1916), although that film was as big a financial failure as *The Birth of a Nation* had been a success. *Intolerance,* which departed from the successful narrative style that Griffith had refined, relied instead on a new technique of montage that wound four stories around each other in order to emphasize the movie's idea or theme of intolerance—at the expense of focusing on telling a specific story. The American audience of 1916 could

D. W. Griffith directs one of his early silent movies. (Bettmann/Corbis)

not cope with the demands of viewing this advanced style, and it has taken decades for film audiences and many filmmakers to become sophisticated enough to begin to appreciate the montage method. Soviet filmmakers did appreciate his innovation, however, and began to use montage techniques to bolster the focus on ideas and emotions in the propaganda films that followed the Russian Revolution.

Griffith participated in the formation of United Artists in 1919, along with Mary Pickford, Charlie Chaplin, and Douglas Fairbanks. However, his last successful film, *Way Down East*, was made only two years later in 1921. After that, critics became more hostile as he lost touch with public taste. Griffith finally left United Artists in 1924, due to his own mounting debt and the dismal box office performance of his films. After a monumental failure with *The Struggle* in 1931, Griffith gave up directing.

While Griffith established many of the modern film techniques, some even way ahead of their time, his subject matter failed to keep up with the changing world of the 1920s and 1930s. He fought losing battles against the star system (which gave prominence and power to the actors), as well as other shifts in the culture of the film industry. He lived his last seventeen years on a remnant of his once vast fortune.

See also: CHAPLIN, CHARLIE; FILM INDUSTRY, HISTORY OF; FILM INDUSTRY, PRODUCTION PROCESS OF; LUMIÈRE, AUGUSTE/LUMIÈRE, LOUIS.

Bibliography

Ellis, Jack C. (1979). *A History of Film*. Englewood Cliffs, NJ: Prentice-Hall.

MacIntyre, Diane. (1997–1998). "The D. W. Griffith Canon." <http://www.mdle.com/ClassicFilms/BTC/direct5.htm>.

O'Dell, Paul. (1970). *Griffith and the Rise of Hollywood*. New York: A. S. Barnes.

Parshall, Gerald. (1998). "The First Prince of Babylon." *U.S. News & World Report* 124(21):58.

Schickel, Richard. (1984). *D. W. Griffith: An American Life*. New York: Simon & Schuster.

Williams, Martin. (1980). *Griffith: First Artist of the Movies*. New York: Oxford University Press.

STEPHEN D. PERRY

GROUP COMMUNICATION

Families, friendship circles, work teams, committees, and sports teams are all examples of groups. Individuals belong to many types of groups. The quality of people's everyday lives depends in important ways on the groups to which they belong. Much of the work and many of the decisions that shape the world depend on the actions that groups take. Groups are important because they influence the way in which people experience and understand the world. The study of group communication helps further the understanding of how groups function in influencing individuals and society. Additionally, the study of groups can lead to innovations in such things as technology, government, and organizational policy.

Defining a Group

To understand groups, there must be some way of determining what makes a collection of people a group. The number of members can be used to distinguish groups from other forms of social behavior, such as crowds, organizations, and interpersonal relationships. Groups, which are obviously bigger in size than interpersonal relationships but smaller than crowds or organizations, typically have around five members (but can be as large as twenty members). This supports the theory that the ideal decision-making group consists of five members (plus or minus two). While it is useful, the number of members does not capture exactly what makes a collection a group.

A group is not a crowd or a mob. As with crowds (such as those that gather for sporting events or around the scene of an accident), groups focus their attention on particular matters of interest. Unlike crowds, groups are more than just a collection of individuals. People come together in groups to accomplish a set of goals and to work together to accomplish those goals. Crowds disperse once the event that draws their attention is over, but a group remains intact.

A group is not an organization. As with organizations (such as business firms or school districts), a group has rules and expectations that help members accomplish shared goals. Unlike organizations, groups do not develop a bureaucracy to organize members and do not hire managers to enforce the rules. Instead, members of small groups typically know each other, develop informal rules and norms, and monitor each other's behavior.

A group is not an interpersonal pairing of two individuals. As with interpersonal relationships (such as those between friends, parents and children, or coworkers), group members interact with each other and influence each other at a personal level. Groups, however, include at least three people who have a common relationship and develop a sense of mutual belonging that differs from any interpersonal relationship that might exist between any two given members of the group.

Because the number of members is just a useful starting point for understanding groups, it is important to understand that a collection becomes a group only when the members (1) share a goal, (2) hold expectations over each other about participating in and belonging to the group, (3) create identities for the group and its members, and (4) influence each other and develop strategies and tactics to control each other and maintain the group.

Function of Group Communication

The term "group communication" refers to the messages that are exchanged by group members. These messages, whether verbal or nonverbal, are important to groups because it is through the exchange of messages that group members participate, maintain the group identity, determine goals, motivate participation, and do the many things that keep the group intact. For example, a soccer team can be considered to be a group, but one would not expect a soccer team to exist or compete with other soccer teams without exchanging messages. How would team members share information about the game plan? How would they make collective decisions in executing the game plan? How would members build the relationships that help each member understand who to trust in the critical moments of a game? How would members create the team spirit that motivates each member to play their best game possible?

Examining group communication is fundamental to understanding groups. The messages that are exchanged by group members provide evidence of the nature of the group. The messages that are exchanged identify whether the group is a social group or a task group. The messages also reveal what roles specific members play in a group. Imagine a family trying to decide what to do during the two weeks in the summer when all the family members are free to do something as a family. Should they go on vacation, stay home and relax, paint the house, or have some parties with extended family and friends? The types of messages that are exchanged and the manner in which the messages are exchanged can be used to describe such group characteristics as the structure of the family, who is in control, and the group's collective identity. However, messages are more than just a signal about what the group is.

Group communication is important because it is through messages that groups make decisions, manage conflict, and build the rapport that is necessary to keep the group going in difficult circumstances. The exchange of messages shapes what the group will be and what the group can accomplish. The way in which, for example, a family exchanges messages about pending choices shapes important features, such as how members understand each other, whether they will respect each other, and whether they will be motivated to make the decision happen.

The Importance of Studying Group Communication

The study of group communication often challenges folk wisdom. It is a common belief, for example, that more communication is better. Research suggests, however, that group discussion leads to the polarization of opinions; that is, group decisions tend to be either more cautious or more risky after group discussion of a choice. This occurs because group members want to appear correct, which leads them to exaggerate their positions in the direction that the group favors. Shifts toward more risky or cautious decisions also occur because group members tend to present more arguments that support the direction that the group favors. More communication, then, is not in principle better than less communication. The point of studying group communication is to provide insight into the sometimes hidden aspects of groups.

Studying group communication can reveal why particular decisions are made while other decisions are not. One might believe, for example, that people are individuals who make their own choices based on personal beliefs and values. However, studies on such diverse things as how

people choose candidates for elected office or how people select which technology to adopt show that individuals are quite susceptible to the influence of the opinion leaders in the most important small groups to which they belong. Indeed, the ways in which individuals express their personal identity are often intimately tied to what their peer groups deem fashionable at the time.

Studying group communication refines, and often changes, the everyday beliefs about how groups work. It is an important field of study because it allows for a better understanding of how groups cooperate, make decisions, influence their members, accomplish their goals.

Specific Subjects of Study

Group communication touches many aspects of group life. The study of group communication tends to focus on group processes and how group communication can be improved. The topics that have been most important in the study of group communication all relate to the exchange of messages. Researchers study how group factors influence the exchange of messages; they also study the reverse, which is how the exchange of messages influences the group. The latter area has become increasingly important in the field of group communication.

"Group dynamics" is a general term created early in the history of the study of groups. Kurt Lewin coined the term to refer to what happens in group situations. The point was to draw attention to the fact that what happens in groups is active and vibrant and is not simply determined by larger social and historical forces. Many of the other key topical areas emerged from this term.

"Leadership" is one of the first, and longest lasting, areas in the study of groups. The goal in this area is to understand what makes leaders effective. If researchers can identify these factors, then it may be possible to develop methods and training from which all groups could benefit.

"Decision making" is another dominant area in group communication research. The goal in this area is to understand the factors that influence groups to make good decisions and bad decisions. The hope is that decision-making practice can be improved by figuring out these factors.

"Social influence" refers to how the messages produced by group members affect the conformity (and deviance) of group members. This includes the study of power, conformity, deviance, and leadership.

"Group process" refers to the functions that communication plays in groups and to the way in which communication in groups becomes patterned and sequenced over time. There is a great deal of interest in how group process affects group outcomes such as decisions and leadership. These interests include, for example, how computer-mediated communication influences group communication.

"Conflict" refers to how group members manage their individual differences within groups and how group members manage their differences with other groups.

Evolution of the Study of Group Communication

The rhetorical, the social-psychological, and the pragmatic traditions heavily influence the study of group communication. These traditions share a focus on how people persuade and influence each other but each has a unique approach.

Researchers in the rhetorical tradition identify the practices that speakers use to persuade audiences, and they are especially concerned with judging the performance of persuasive acts. Rhetorical studies develop standards for good persuasion (i.e., persuasion that is both effective and ethical). Group researchers following rhetorical approaches have contributed by developing discussion protocols and standards for assessing the quality of group discussion. Researchers and teachers of group communication have drawn from rhetoric and argumentation in their development of discussion agendas and rules for critical thinking. There was a great deal of interest in the early twentieth century that small groups could be formed among citizens to discuss important matters of the day, thus leading to better judgment by citizens on important public matters. It did not take long, however, to realize that simply gathering people together in the same place to talk does not cause good discussion. Those in the speech-communication field took on the task of cultivating good discussion habits in their students. They trained students in principles of discussion as well as public speaking. Their work was motivated to improve the quality of public discourse. They developed ideas such as the "standard agenda," which was a tool a group could use to improve the quality of the decision-making discussion.

Researchers in the social-psychological tradition identify how the beliefs and attitudes of group members are changed by a variety of social factors. Social-psychological studies compile the effects of such social factors as power, roles, and identity. The antecedents of group communication in this tradition are found in early investigations of whether groups could be more successful at accomplishing tasks than an individual could be. These results showed that groups were in fact likely to be more productive. Individuals were less productive in the groups than when they worked on their own. This apparent paradox motivated researchers to discover how groups influence individuals. The study of group influence on the beliefs and attitudes of members drew increasing attention with the events and social circumstances surrounding Adolf Hitler's rise and fall, the Holocaust, and the mobilization of allied support for the war effort. There was a great deal of interest in studying conformity—in particular, the formation of the "group mind" and how groups influence individual beliefs and attitudes. The study of conformity preceded much of later social-psychological research. From the early experimental research, a whole new area of study in facilitating group communication emerged. Researchers who engaged in this area of study developed many techniques that help small groups communicate and make better judgments. In addition, many innovations in using groups to aid individual therapy and to help manage organizations emerged from this initial movement to help citizens.

Researchers in the pragmatic tradition identify the sequences of communication among group members and how those sequences become patterned (i.e., conventional ways group members communicate). Pragmatic researchers assess how communication patterns influence what groups can and cannot accomplish due to their patterns of communication. This area of research has many different starting points. The researchers in this tradition recognize that messages have multiple functions. These researchers focused on the content and relational aspects of a message. Every message has content, or information value, and every message makes a "meta-comment" on the relationship between the speaker and the hearer. The same message content can be used to signal a request or an order. These researchers were very interested in how group members negotiated the variety of meanings that messages have. To study this, they looked at the interaction between messages.

Contemporary group communication finds its roots in the above three basic areas. While some research remains clearly rhetorical, social-psychological, or pragmatic, some blending of the three has taken place. The study of group communication has always focused on how discussion among group members can be used to help groups cooperate to achieve larger goals. The advent of computer and telecommunication networks has not altered this quest, but it has brought about opportunities for group interaction that were impossible and even inconceivable in the past. Communication technologies such as e-mail, cellular telephones, and group support systems make it possible for groups to meet without being in the same place at the same time. Even more interesting than the possibility of compressing time and space, these tools make it possible to alter or provide new forums for interaction. New channels can be made available to group members, and decision and discussion aids can be designed to aid group interaction via the technology. The use of new technology raises questions about whether groups can emerge and function without meeting face-to-face or whether technology can aid group effectiveness. Many of the issues that motivated the original research on groups apply to technologically supported groups.

The goal of developing better forms of discussion occurred in four unique but related eras in the evolution of group communication research. In each era, a new use of discussion emerged and is marked by a different set of assumptions about groups and the strategies for improving group communication. The first period, 1900 to 1920, is marked by an interest in improving democracy and the responsiveness of government. Group discussion and training in effective discussion were seen as ways to facilitate widespread participation in democratic governance. The second period, 1930 to 1950, is marked by an interest in using groups to help individuals learn about themselves. Group discussion and training in effective discussion were seen as ways to help people help themselves. It was during this time that movements such as T-groups (therapy groups) and Alcoholics Anonymous emerged. The third period, 1960 to 1980, is marked by an interest in improving the effectiveness of organizations. Group discussion and training in effective discussion were seen as ways to foster employee involvement in organizational goals and to shape the commitment of members to the organizational mission. This is the era when the concept of teams and teamwork became very popular. The fourth period, 1980 to the present, is marked by an interest in knowledge. Group discussion and training in effective discussion include the use of new communication technology that enhances the mobility, memory, and efficiency of group members.

Examples of Scholars Working in Group Communication

Some of the scholars who have worked in the area of group communication are Kurt Lewin, Solomon Asch, B. Aubrey Fisher, and M. Scott Poole. In addition to forming the area of group dynamics, Lewin's efforts contributed to the development of methods and techniques for improving group discussion. Asch was a leader in the study of compliance and developed novel methods to show how groups influence individual conformity to the group. Fisher developed an interactional view of group communication and a phase model of group decision processes and leadership emergence. Poole, one of the contemporary leaders in the study of groups, has developed structuration theory, an innovative view of group communication. He has also pioneered communication research on the use of technology to support group decision making.

See also: GROUP COMMUNICATION, CONFLICT AND; GROUP COMMUNICATION, DECISION MAKING AND; GROUP COMMUNICATION, DYNAMICS OF; GROUP COMMUNICATION, ROLES AND RESPONSIBILITIES IN; INTERPERSONAL COMMUNICATION; ORGANIZATIONAL COMMUNICATION; PUBLIC SPEAKING; RHETORIC.

Bibliography

Asch, Solomon. (1955). "Opinions and Social Pressures." *Scientific American* 193(5):31–55.

Brilhart, John K.; Galanes, Gloria J.; and Adams, Katherine L. (2001). *Effective Group Discussion: Theory and Practice,* 10th edition. New York: McGraw-Hill.

Cathcart, Robert, and Samovar, Larry. (1992). *Small Group Communication: A Reader,* 6th edition. Dubuque, IA: Wm. C. Brown.

Cathcart, Robert; Samovar, Larry; and Henman, Linda. (1996). *Small Group Communication: Theory and Practice,* 7th edition. Dubuque, IA: Brown & Benchmark.

Fisher, B. Aubrey. (1970). "Decision Emergence: Phases in Group Decision Making." *Speech Monographs* 37:53–66.

Lewin, Kurt. (1951). *Field Theory in Social Science.* New York: Harper.

Poole, M. Scott; Seibold, David; and McPhee, Robert. (1985). "Group Decision-Making as a Structural Process." *Quarterly Journal of Speech* 71:74–102.

MARK AAKHUS

GROUP COMMUNICATION, CONFLICT AND

What is conflict? Is it the clash of personalities? Is it a difference of opinion? Is it a misunderstanding? Is it the attempt to right a wrong? Is it a contest for scarce resources? Group members engage in conflict for all these reasons. It seems that everyone knows conflict when they see it. Yet, when individuals experience conflict, they find it difficult, at best, to understand it and deal with it. The same is true for those who study it.

How and Why Groups Engage in Conflict

Group communication researchers pay special attention to how conflict is expressed, created, and managed through communication. While they recognize numerous causes for conflict, they focus on the variety of ways in which group members use messages to express conflict. Researchers' special interest lies in how people use messages to manage the "causes" of conflict, such as the scarcity of resources, differences between personalities, differences between ideas, and even differences about how to handle differences.

Group communication researchers are keen to learn the ways in which communication itself contributes to conflict. Consider how group members' beliefs about conflict can differ depending on their habits for handling conflict. One group member may handle conflict through avoidance. Such a person will change topics, become quiet, or avoid contact when he or she anticipates that conflict will occur. That person probably believes that talk, instead of solving conflict, will only makes it worse. Thus, from this perspective, talking about conflict only draws attention to the things that cannot be changed (e.g., personalities, scarce resources, habits). Another group member may handle conflict through confrontation and persuasion. Such a person will raise questions, challenge what others say, and will generally speak up when conflicts emerge. That person probably understands that personalities differ and resources are usually unequally distributed. However, this group member sees talk as a way to remove misunderstanding between group members and to influence group members to act differently. Group communication researchers investigate how communicating about conflict changes the conflict circumstances and whether talk ends or continues a conflict.

How messages are used to resolve conflicts is a central concern in the study of group communication. This focus has consequences. What group communication researchers know about conflict concentrates on the conflict between group members, the conflict styles of individual group members, and the conflict management techniques that serve as a vehicle for resolving conflict. The result is a preference for studying conflict styles of group members and how to make conflict productive by turning it into cooperative decision making. The assumption is that conflict is an inherently bad thing that should be eliminated. How conflict happens in groups and how groups influence the conflict behavior of their members are two things that are not as well understood. Such a shift in focus draws attention to conflict as a source of growth, innovation, and quality decision making.

Conflict can be useful if it brings about needed change, test ideas, challenges illegitimate authority, or leads to increased cohesiveness. Group development researchers generally agree that groups go through a conflict phase. B. Aubrey Fisher (1970), in particular, suggests that groups can cycle through many conflict phases during decision making. During the conflict phase, group members are testing their ideas and opinions against each other, but they are doing even more. It is during the conflict phase that opinion leaders emerge. The conflict phase helps group members learn what their roles will be, how decisions will be made, and what the group will value. These are important issues that the group must continuously negotiate.

How individuals prefer to handle their own conflicts shapes the understanding of how conflicts happen. Avoiders, for example, tend not to see talk as a useful way to solve conflict, while competers see talk as a useful way to resolve conflict but not necessarily as a way to cooperate. Thus, group communication can help people understand their own habits and views of conflict. This can help individuals and groups learn how better to handle the conflicts that they face.

Conflict Styles and Tactics

The term "conflict style" refers to a person's inclination to act in a particular way when faced with conflict. Styles differ in terms of how much concern a person shows for self (competitiveness) and how much concern a person shows for the other (cooperativeness). According to the classic description of conflict styles set forth by Robert Blake and Jane Mouton (1964), five styles can be distinguished in this way: forcing, smoothing, withdrawing, compromise, and collaboration. Forcing involves high competition and low cooperation on the part of an individual. Smoothing is the opposite because it involves low competition and high cooperation. Withdrawing involves low competition and low cooperation. Compromise involves moderate competition and moderate cooperation. Collaboration, which is often taken to be the ideal style, involves high competition and high cooperation. These five styles are popular in training literature on conflict management because the distinctions help people understand and adapt to how others engage in conflict. It is generally believed that no one style is best but that each style has advantages and disadvantages. For example, collaboration seems best but is very time consuming. A competitive style seems bad because it escalates the conflict, but escalation is sometimes needed to move the conflict forward.

There is controversy over whether styles are the most accurate way to describe how people engage in conflict. First, critics point out that styles refer to what people believe they do in conflict rather than what people actually do. Second, critics point out that styles refer to individuals rather than the groups and contexts, which ignores the fact that people can behave quite differently depending on the group norms or context.

The term "tactics" refers to specific conflict behaviors and provides a useful alternative to the term "styles." When people deny a situation or make noncommittal and irreverant remarks, they are avoiding conflict; that is, they are staying away from issues or concerns that are important to the group members. Alan Sillars (1980) distinguishes avoidance tactics, like those just described, from competitive and collaborative tactics. Competitive tactics include personal criticism, rejection, hostile jokes, and denial of responsibility. Competitive tactics engage people in overt conflict and often contribute to conflict escalation. Collaborative tactics include descriptive statements, concessions, supportive remarks, and soliciting statements. Collaborative tactics engage people in overt conflict but enable participants to cooperate in resolving the conflict.

The identification of tactics makes it possible to understand how a conflict unfolds when people in conflict communicate. Studying tactics draws attention closer to the messages that group members use to engage in conflict. Tactics help researchers see how conflicts escalate and de-escalate due to the types of messages that are exchanged. In addition, tactics can be used to understand how messages can be used to change the escalation of conflict into cooperation. For example, if one group member uses personal criticism, hostile jokes, and other competitive tactics, another group member may use descriptive statements, concessions, and other collaborative tactics to make the discussion more productive.

How People Should Engage in Conflict

Imagine a leading member of a social club proposing that member dues be raised. When the person makes this proposal, another leading member disagrees and points out problems with the proposal. The person who proposed the measure defends the position against what feels like an attack. The person who is opposed to the measure continues to disagree by picking on very fine details of the proposal. The disagreement escalates until the group and the meeting stand in a stalemate. What should be done? What often happens in a discussion about positions, as in this example, is that people begin to feel that they are being attacked personally, rather than that their ideas are being attacked. A discussion can turn into a hostile exchange of barbs or into a steely silence quite quickly.

Group communication researchers have addressed the question about how people should engage in conflict. The central idea has two parts. Group members should minimize relational conflict and encourage conflict about ideas. Such advice suggests that it is better to "separate the person from the problem" and "to be tough on ideas and easy on people." This advice could be applied to the situation of the social club.

The messages exchanged by the two leaders in the example escalated the relational conflict and made their ideas secondary concerns. Their discussion became focused on creating the impression of winning or at least avoiding looking like a loser to the other group members. The attack on the proposal led to defensiveness on the part of the proposer, who in turn made the proposal look good in the face of criticism. This only gave the other leader more ground on which to attack. A cycle of defense-attack followed. Most communication research advice suggests that situations like this one should be avoided for the sake of group relations and the group's ability to accomplish its goals. These situations can be avoided by fostering cooperation in the face of an escalating conflict.

The solution, according to most communication research, would involve separating the people from the problem. Thus, another group member should intervene and say, "Let's have the whole group examine this proposal along with some other proposals members may have." This gives the discussion back to the group and draws attention away from the two combatants. The next part of the solution is to be tough on ideas and easy on people. Thus, another group member should intervene and say, "Okay, now that we have more proposals, let's identify the pros and cons for each one." This gives everyone permission to be hard on the issues but soft on the people.

Numerous techniques have been developed over the years to foster "productive" conflict (i.e., conflict that is neither too hot nor too cold and that is neither too hard on the people nor too soft on the issues). These techniques that are designed to help groups cooperate include graduated and reciprocal initiatives in tension reduction (GRIT), reflective thinking, problem-purpose-expansion technique, and facilitation/mediation.

GRIT was proposed by Charles Osgood (1962). It is a method intended to foster cooperation during conflict. The method involves at least one party making cooperative, even conciliatory, moves, without letting down his or her guard. The strategy helps counter the hostile and aggressive moves of the other party. In using GRIT, one person competes for a period of time and then begins to cooperate. When the person begins to cooperate, it must be announced to the other party. This communicates that one could compete but chooses to cooperate, thus suggesting that the other party should follow this approach as well.

Reflective thinking was first proposed by John Dewey (1910). It was later developed by group researchers such as Dennis Gouran (1982) to serve as a way to improve problem solving. Reflective thinking is a five-step procedure that helps groups thoroughly analyze a situation and develop a solution: (1) define the problem, (2) analyze the problem, (3) suggest possible solutions, (4) select a solution, and (5) plan implementation. This procedure helps participants focus their interaction and cooperate on rational problem solving.

The problem-purpose-expansion technique was proposed by Roger Volkema (1983). The technique is designed to help conflicted parties avoid an overly narrow discussion that misses opportunities for resolution. It is easy for conflicted groups to become obsessed with a particular description of the problem. Volkema's technique encourages parties to be creative in developing different ways to understand a problem. They then brainstorm solutions for each different way of understanding the problem. This generates creativity and opportunities for cooperation.

Groups can also use experts, such as mediators and facilitators, to help manage conflict. Mediators and facilitators know a variety of techniques, understand different models for analyzing group communication, and possess experience in helping groups. Facilitators generally specialize in helping groups communicate better when faced with a complex problem to solve. They are especially useful because they help groups avoid destructive conflict that can emerge in decision making. Mediators specialize in helping groups once conflict has been expressed and begins to debilitate the group. Mediators help groups resolve conflicts and restore the ability to work together.

See also: GROUP COMMUNICATION; GROUP COMMUNICATION, DECISION MAKING AND; GROUP COMMUNICATION, DYNAMICS OF; GROUP COMMUNICATION, ROLES AND RESPONSIBILITIES IN; ORGANIZATIONAL COMMUNICATION.

Bibliography

Blake, Robert R., and Moutin, Jane S. (1964). *The Managerial Grid*. Houston: Gulf Publishing.

Dewey, John. (1910). *How We Think*. Boston: Heath

Fisher, B. Aubrey. (1970). "Decision Emergence: Phases in Group Decision Making." *Speech Monographs* 37:53–66.

Folger, Joseph P.; Poole, M. Scott; and Stutman, Randall K. (1997). *Working Through Conflict: Strategies for Relationships, Groups, and Organizations*, 3rd edition. New York: Longman.

Gouran, Dennis. (1982). *Making Decisions in Groups*. Glenview, IL: Scott, Foresman.

Hocker, Janice, and Wilmot, William. (1991). *Interpersonal Conflict*, 3rd edition. Dubuque, IA: Wm. C. Brown.

Osgood, Charles. (1962). *An Alternative to War and Surrender*. Urbana: University of Illinois Press.

Sillars, Alan. (1980). "Attributions and Communication in Roommate Conflicts." *Communication Monographs* 47:180–200.

Volkema, Roger. (1983). "Problem Formulation in Planning and Design." *Management Science* 29(6):639–652.

MARK AAKHUS

■ GROUP COMMUNICATION, DECISION MAKING AND

A decision is a choice among two or more alternatives. For example, a hiring committee makes a decision when it chooses one of the five candidates under consideration for a new job opening. A jury makes a decision when it chooses whether the defendant is guilty or not guilty. Decisions are sometimes hard to identify, as when a soccer team moves down the field to score a goal and their choices are made on the fly in the face of ever-changing conditions. Many of the decisions made by work groups are similar, especially when the work group is managing a crisis when a deadline is pending. The term "decision making" refers to the process that groups go through to identify alternative choices and the logical or appropriate way to select an alternative to implement.

Role of Communication in Group Decision Making

Communication plays a central role in group decision making. Group decisions primarily result from the opinions that group members have about an issue or course of action. Individual opinions can and do change as a result of group communication. Communication affects group decision making in at least two important ways.

First, group members influence each other through the messages they exchange. When one member opposes the idea of another member, for example, then the group must reconcile the difference in some way. If a low-status person in the group raises a good idea, it is likely to be rejected publicly by the group members. It is interesting to note, however, that the opinion of low-status members will slowly influence each member's private beliefs. The consequence, in the long run, is that the low-status group member's willingness to express a contradictory opinion can have a real effect on the decisions of a group. The low-status member, however, is less likely to get credit for the good idea than the more high-status members of the group.

Second, group communication is typically patterned, and these patterns influence the course of decision making. For example, some groups develop communication patterns that are extremely polite and formal. These habits can make it difficult to raise a difference of opinion and the speaker often has to "water down" his or her disagreement to the degree that the opposition seems pointless. Other groups embrace open conflict. In these groups, the simple act of agreeing or supporting another person's comments can easily be taken by that person as a challenge. Thus, group communication has a variety of effects on decision making, in particular in the role communication plays in the formation of decisions and in decision-making outcomes.

Approaches to Understanding Decision-Making Communication

Consideration of the functional and decision-emergence approaches to the study of communication in group decision making helps show how communication influences group decisions.

Functional Approach

Since the 1920s, communication teachers have taught students that particular functions are necessary for good group decision making. For example, students are often taught a "standard agenda" that they can apply to all group decisions. A standard agenda prescribes functions that every group should perform: (1) define the problem, (2) identify criteria for a good solution, (3) generate alternative solutions, (4) assess alternatives, and (4) choose a solution. These functions define what groups should do.

Functional approaches specify the functions groups should perform to make good decisions. Randy Hirokawa (1985) has developed a functional approach that both challenges and advances the idea behind using a standard agenda for group decision making. Hirokawa and his colleagues have found "critical functions" that groups must perform to make good decisions; these functions are similar to the standard agenda. They also found that groups that make "bad decisions" begin their discussions by generating and evaluating alternatives. Groups that make "good decisions" begin by analyzing the problem and generating alternatives, and then they evaluate alternatives.

Thus, the way group members communicate affects the quality of the decisions that are made by a group. Communication also influences what members talk about. How this happens has been addressed in particular by researchers who explain decision emergence.

Decision-Emergence Approach

Early research on group decision making suggests that all group decisions go through a particular set of phases: groups (1) orient themselves to the task, (2) engage in conflict with each other, (3) develop some standards about making a choice, and (4) create solutions. This differs from the functional approach because these phases describe how decisions emerge (rather than prescribing the phases a group should go through). Communication researchers have challenged the phase model proposed in early research on groups.

Thomas Scheidel and Laura Crowell (1964) studied how people exchanged messages during decision making and found that decisions emerge in a spiral fashion. For example, a member will put a proposal forward and it will be accepted. The group will continue the discussion only to find that the proposal is inadequate. Then they will spiral back to modify or reject the proposal that was once accepted. Thus, it is better to characterize this form of group decision making in terms of two steps forward, followed by one step back, and then two steps forward.

B. Aubrey Fisher (1970) discovered that both the phase and spiral models of decision making explain how decisions emerge. He found that some group decisions emerge in a pattern that looks very much like a standard agenda. Other group decisions, however, seem never to move toward concrete solutions and instead remain stuck in the debate over alternatives. Fisher explains that discussion about choices involves more than the task before the group. Indeed, it also involves the relationships among the group members. The spiraling in decision-making discussion is a reflection of how the group members manage their relationships and work through interpersonal conflict.

M. Scott Poole (1983) and his colleagues have developed an even more advanced explanation than Fisher's explanation of decision emergence. Poole argues against a phase model. Instead of phases, research by Poole and his colleagues shows how groups are actually managing multiple tracks of activity that correspond to what other researchers have called phases. These multiple tracks include the task, the member relationships, and the discussion focus. Thus, similar to phase models, Poole argues that groups must manage many developmental demands. Poole's point, however, is that decision-making group members are constantly managing these demands. Thus, decision-making communication may appear chaotic. This is the case because the communication among group members serves multiple purposes. The group is solving the decision, but it is also working out the relationship among the members and maintaining a common focus in the discussion.

Common Difficulties in Group Communication

There are numerous barriers to effective decision making that involve communication. Three of the most common difficulties are groupthink, polarization, and inferential errors.

Groupthink

Groupthink occurs when group members value consensus above all else. The result is that group members feel extraordinary pressure to agree and have little if any means to disagree or oppose the will of the group. Irving Janis (1972) developed this concept. There are five conditions that contribute to groupthink: an authoritarian style leader, isolation from other groups and people, lack of explicit decision procedures, group members sharing similar viewpoints, and group members being under high pressure to make a decision. A project team facing a deadline may not adequately consider new information that runs contrary to a selected position because the members fear that including the new information means missing the deadline.

Polarization

When groups make decisions, the group decision tends to be either riskier or more cautious than the decision that individual group members would make outside of the group. When groups begin their discussion by leaning toward guaranteed outcomes, they tend to experience a cautious shift; that is, the group makes a decision that is more cautious than an individual would have made on his or own. When a group begins the discussion by leaning toward taking a change, it tends to experience risky shift. A group of friends, for example, may go to a much scarier or risqué movie than any one of them would ever see when alone.

Inferential Errors

Individuals and groups are prone to errors when their judgments are based on data. These are called inferential errors. The way a problem is framed, for example, can influence how group members judge the evidence. Two groups can make very different judgments of the same evidence, depending on past success or failure in decision making. Past failure can induce risky behavior by groups, while past success can make groups more conservative. The previous decision outcomes frame judgment of the evidence in a current choice. When groups make successful choices, it tends to stick to what works and is less willing to see evidence in new ways. When groups make unsuccessful choices, they are willing to try something new. The football team that is losing because of bad plays and miscues will be likely (in order to win) to abandon the original plan and even try plays that have not been well practiced.

Overcoming Problems

Groups can overcome a problem by designating or hiring a person to be a facilitator. The facilitator is a type of group leader who helps improve the group's procedures so the group is more effective in accomplishing its goals. A facilitator helps a group identify problems in the decision-making processes and shows the group how to correct those problems. Facilitators can also diffuse unproductive conflict by helping groups regulate the expression of frustrations while helping the group find a path toward a solution.

Vigilance, according to Dennis Gouran (1990), is sensitivity to careful examination of the information on which a choice rests. Vigilance can be cultivated in a group by developing an attitude toward critical thinking, by an appreciation for listening, and by a willingness to explore alternatives. Vigilance depends on the leadership in a group. Gouran explains that leaders help groups move toward a goal through "counteractive influence." Group leaders must be aware of anything that influences a group to deviate from accomplishing its goals. Group leaders must provide the necessary behavior to counteract those influences. For example, leaders can become skeptics when groupthink emerges or sensitive when hostilities escalate.

Robert's Rules of Parliamentary Procedure (or Robert's Rules of Order, as they are commonly known) were created to provide a common set of procedures for decision-making groups. The rules make clear how a proposal should be handled, thus helping to reduce or eliminate conflict over procedures and to contribute to group productivity. For example, these rules specify how a member can put a motion, or proposal, up for consideration by the group. This encourages members to have a thoughtful proposal and gives the group members a fair way to prevent discussion on every thought of every group member. The rules help balance power and influence among the members of a group.

Nominal group technique is a procedure to help groups discover the best ideas and promote consensus building among members. The essence of the technique involves having the members of the group write their ideas on cards. The cards are then collected and the ideas are posted. The group then discusses and evaluates those ideas. The benefit of this technique is twofold. First, individuals tend to be more productive when working individually in the presence of others. Second, the cards enable members to bring up unpopular ideas while remaining anonymous.

Group decision-support systems (GDSSs) combine computers and specialized software to help groups make better decisions. A GDSS provides group discussion and decision-making tools such as brainstorming and voting. When groups use a GDSS, they work in a room where they can interact with each other by talking or by using the GDSS. The GDSS makes it possible for group members to input all of their ideas at the same time, maintains a record of their contributions, and provides groups with the opportunity to interact anonymously. The features of a GDSS, in many ways, combine the insights of facilitation, vigilance, Robert's Rules of Order, and nominal group technique.

See also: GROUP COMMUNICATION; GROUP COMMUNICATION, CONFLICT AND; GROUP COMMUNICATION, DYNAMICS OF; GROUP COMMUNICATION, ROLES AND RESPONSIBILITIES IN.

Bibliography

Fisher, B. Aubrey. (1970). "Decision Emergence: Phases in Group Decision Making." *Speech Monographs* 37:53–66.

Fisher, B. Aubrey, and Ellis, Don. (1990). *Small Group Decision Making: Communication and the Group Process,* 3rd edition. New York: McGraw-Hill.

Gouran, Dennis. (1990). *Making Decisions in Groups: Choices and Consequences.* Prospect Heights, IL: Waveland Press.

Hirokawa, Randy. (1985). "Discussion Procedures and Decision-Making Performance." *Human Communication Research* 12:203–224.

Janis, Irving. (1972). *Victims of Groupthink.* Boston: Houghton-Mifflin.

Pavitt, Charles, and Curtis, Ellen. (1994). *Small Group Discussion: A Theoretical Approach,* 2nd edition. Scottsdale, AZ: Gorsuch Scarisbrick.

Poole, M. Scott. (1983). "Decision Development in Small Groups III: A Multiple Sequence Model of Group Decision Development." *Communication Monographs* 50:321–341.

Scheidel, Thomas, and Crowell, Laura. (1964). "Idea Development in Small Group Discussion Groups." *Quarterly Journal of Speech* 50:140–145.

MARK AAKHUS

■ GROUP COMMUNICATION, DYNAMICS OF

The study of group dynamics is a search for the social influences that affect the way people behave in groups. "Dynamics" is a term used to refer to the factors that often lie just outside one's awareness but that have an effect on how people behave. Social influence in small groups includes factors such as power, developmental phases, conformity, deviance, networks, and norms.

Importance of Understanding Dynamics

In one of the earliest known social science experiments, a researcher named M. Ringlemann tested whether individuals were more productive in groups. He had people pull a rope and measured the force each person exerted while pulling compared with how much the whole group pulled. He discovered that the group exerted more total force with each person added to the group. Yet, even though the group exerted more total force as members were added, each individual actually exerted less force while pulling. The Ringlemann effect, as it is known, still highlights the central issues in group dynamics research. It shows the advantages and disadvantages of groups, but it also suggests that people have a social influence on each other that may go unnoticed by the group members.

Muzafer Sherif's experiments in the 1930s dramatically demonstrated that individuals in groups can be significantly influenced by forces that are beyond the awareness of the individuals within the groups. He created a novel experiment using a stationary pinpoint of light in a completely darkened room. In such conditions, the light appears to move even though it does not. Sherif recorded individual's estimates of how much the stationary light in the darkened room moved. He then recorded the estimates that groups of people made about the movement of light. Sherif found that individual estimates varied a great deal. When in groups, however, individual estimates slowly converged toward a group consensus. For example, one subject individually estimated that the light moved as much as seven inches while two other subjects individually estimated that there was one to two inches of movement. When these subjects viewed the light as a group, they ultimately judged the light movement to be a little more than two inches. The group members mutually influenced each other as they all tried to develop a better estimate of the light movement. The experiment demonstrated that groups develop norms that influence the behavior and judgment of the individual members.

One goal of group dynamics research is to identify social influences and then design techniques or procedures to counteract the negative aspects of social influence and optimize the positive aspects. The Ringlemann effect, for example, suggests that to improve overall group performance, it may be helpful to let groups know both their group performance and their individual performance on a task. This would allow the individual to see what happens to his or her individual performance relative to the group performance. Sherif's light experiment suggests that groups need to develop "anchors" for their judgments. Group members can use decision criteria, for example, to counteract the pressure to conform in groups.

Power

Power is an ambiguous concept. It refers to resources and force possessed by an individual to influence other people. One person may be able to take and give rewards from others and thus make others act as he or she wishes. Thus, power is a characteristic of an individual. On the other hand, power refers to the mutual influence people hold over each other. The ability to give and take rewards is only powerful to the extent that others value those rewards. Thus, power is a feature of the relationship between people.

The earliest discussion of power focused on individual characteristics. John French and Bertram Raven, in 1959, proposed five bases of power: (1) reward, (2) coercive, (3) legitimate, (4) referent, and (5) expert. Reward power is the capacity of one person to control access to things that others value. Friends influence each other by giving out or holding back compliments, time together, and access to other people. Coercive power is the capacity of an individual to threaten and punish another. A friend can coerce another to do something by threatening to gossip and divulge personal information, in which case, the friendship itself comes into question. Legitimate power is the capacity of one individual to demand something from another on a rightful basis. A parent can impose a curfew, and a boss can demand that an employee show up for work on time. Referent power is the capacity of one person to get others to do things due to respect, attractiveness, and admiration. A child obeys a curfew not simply because a parent can impose curfews but because the child respects his or her parents. An employee puts out an extra effort not because the boss has the right to ask but because the employee likes and admires his or her boss as a person. Expert power results from a person's superior skills and abilities. Players may obey their coach because he or she played the game in the past and was an excellent and successful athlete.

It is clear in these definitions that power is possessed by individuals but that power depends on the relationship between the "powerful" and the "powerless." As French and Raven put it, power is the difference between the maximum force that one person can bring to bear and the maximum resistance that another person can bring to bear. Thus, someone may be incredibly charming and successful but unable to make referent power work on someone who is resistant to charm.

The power concept draws attention to the "nonrational" ways in which people influence each other. Group members do not always take action based on evidence and information; instead, they act because of the influence of reward, coercive, legitimate, referent, and expert power. Power has both positive and negative consequences for decision making. For example, a group can act on the referent power of a group member who has significant and relevant accomplishments and experience with a certain issue rather than treating that member's opinion as being no more informed than those of the other members. This contributes to decision-making efficiency for the whole group. If, however, that member's referent power on a particular issue is extended to other issues where the member's opinion is in fact no more informed than those of the rest of the group, it may result in quicker decision making but the decision quality would likely be lower.

Group Development Phases

All groups go through phases where their member's interaction is dominated by certain topics and issues. The research of Robert Bales (1953) suggests that groups tack back and forth over task and relational issues. For example, a group may exert such an enormous effort to solve a task that frustration builds up between various members. The group may then almost abandon the task and concentrated instead on repairing the relationships among the group members. This means that what a group is supposed to do and talk about may be significantly influenced by the phase of development that the group is going through. A coach may want a team to focus on preparation for a tournament but team members may be in a phase where they are trying to repair their relationships with each other after conflicts from a previous game. Thus, it may be difficult for the team to focus on the task when relational issues dominate their concerns.

Bruce Tuckman (1965) proposed that development phases actually occur in a typical order or pattern. He developed a scheme to describe the issues and topics that dominate groups in particular stages of development: (1) forming, (2) storming, (3) norming, (4) performing, and (4) adjourning. Forming is the initial formation of a group. In this phase, group members are exchanging information, orienting themselves toward each other, and creating attraction to the group. It is likely that talk is overly polite and tentative. Storming is the struggle to come together as a group. In this phase, participants are testing each other, vying for various roles in the group, expressing dissatisfaction, and arguing about procedures. It is likely that overt disagreement and criticism mark talk in the group. Members may actively avoid group meetings. Norming is the coming together of group members. In this phase, groups become more cohesive, members better understand their roles and status in the group, and shared goals and values emerge. It is likely that talk is more harmonious and supportive and marked by phrases of inclusion such as "we" and "us." Performing is a phase of high productivity of group members. The group members are cooperating to achieve tasks and abide by the norms and standards of behavior that they have agreed on. It is likely that the talk is focused on decision making and problem solving and not on conflict and relationships. Adjourning is when the group completes its tasks. In this phase, the group members reduce their dependence on each other and renegotiate their obligations. Emotion and regret mark the talk in this phase.

Conformity

Conformity means that a person accepts a course of action because the majority has agreed on it or because it is socially acceptable. There are two types of conformity: compliance and private acceptance. Compliance occurs when someone goes along with the group without accepting the group's norms or point of view. A person might change his or her style of dress to impress people in the majority (or to avoid criticism) but not to become like those people. Private acceptance, on the other hand, refers to the personal adoption of the majority opinion. Thus, compliance occurs when a person publicly agrees with the majority but privately disagrees. Private acceptance occurs when a person publicly and privately agrees with the majority.

Solomon Asch (1955) demonstrated conformity through an experiment. He was interested in the conditions that led an individual to conform to the majority's judgment. In his experiment, participants viewed two cards. One line was printed on the first card, while three lines of different length were printed on the second card. The participants were asked to report which line on the second card matched the line on the first card. The subject of the experiment was always the last person in the group to report. All of the other participants were secretly given directions to report wrong answers. This was repeated several times. Because the task was so simple, the subject most likely knew that the participants were reporting wrong answers. Yet, three-fourths of the subjects reported at least one conforming answer during the experiment. About one-third of all the responses by all the subjects were conforming. These results created a great deal of interest because the experiment demonstrated that people will conform to a majority. It was less clear, however, why people conformed.

The number of group members who express the majority opinion can influence conformity. It seems that when more group members are in agreement with each other, it is more likely that conformity will occur among the other members. While the number of people in a majority influences conformity, an individual is more likely to be influenced to conform by how the majority came to hold an opinion. There is more pressure to conform when an individual believes that each person in the majority has individually developed an opinion that is consistent with the majority. There is less pressure to conform when an individual thinks that the members of the majority are simply complying themselves.

The number of potential allies influences conformity. When another person disagrees with the majority, the amount of a subject's conformity

GROUP COMMUNICATION, DYNAMICS OF • 385

decreases. This is especially true when the potential ally consistently rejected the majority or converted from the majority to the minority. If a potential ally began by disagreeing with the majority and then shifted to the majority, it did not help the subject resist conformity.

Deviance

There are many forms of deviance. It is typical to understand deviance as something bad, such as when someone drops out of a group, rebels against a group, or sabotages a group. While such forms of deviance are not always bad, other forms of deviance, such as innovation, are very likely to be good; that is, innovative deviance can help a group solve problems or adapt to new situations. A "devil's advocate" in a group can prevent a group from making an unwise, ill thought-out decision. Deviance is a way that group members show their independence or anticonformity.

Deviant behavior and the deviants themselves are likely to be negatively judged by group members. Deviants, however, can be judged positively. Groups tolerate deviants who have group-centered motives. Members who deviate only after careful conformity to group norms during the early formation of the group are judged positively. Group members who have high status also have more latitude to deviate.

While groups do not always like deviants, expression of a minority opinion can weaken the influence of a majority. In particular, when a minority consistently expresses a dissenting opinion, it can have a long-term effect. Research by Serge Moscovici (1985) and others has shown that majority influence leads to compliance while minority influence leads to private acceptance. Thus, someone might be persuaded by a minority opinion and yet still comply in public with the majority view. The influence of a minority opinion may not be seen in an immediate decision, but it may be seen in a later decision.

Networks

The concept of a network refers to the patterns of message exchange among group members. The patterns of message exchange suggest different roles for group members. When one group member tends to be the recipient and sender of most of the messages in the group, that person is considered central to the group network. The pattern of message exchange might resemble a wheel—in which case, the other group members may exchange nearly all of their messages through one person (the hub) while exchanging few if any messages with each other (the spokes). An example of the wheel might be evident in a family where the children have grown up and moved out of the house. If the children primarily speak to their mother to find out what is going on in the family, while speaking little to each other, then they would have formed a wheel pattern of communication. It is important to notice that where one is in the network helps define the role one plays in the group.

There are numerous network patterns that can emerge in groups. Five patterns have received a great deal of attention: (1) wheel, (2) chain, (3) Y, (4) circle, and (5) comcon. The wheel pattern was described above, in the example where siblings speak primarily to their mother and not to each other. Groups with wheel patterns tend to make decisions quicker than groups that have other patterns. Groups with wheel patterns also gain clarity because one member handles all the messages, leaving less room for misinterpretation.

The chain pattern means that each group member primarily speaks to only two other people in the group. For example, Bill, Jill, Stan, and Jan work on the "complaint project team" in a company's service department. Their job is to investigate complaints. Bill's job is to take complaints from customers and get an accurate description. He informs Jill of the complaint. Jill organizes the complaints and transmits them to Stan. Stan investigates the complaints and creates alternative ways to handle the complaints. Stan hands off the alternatives to Jan. Jan decides on a course of action to take on each complaint and implements it. In the chain, Jill exchanges messages with Bill and Stan but not Jan. Jill is connected to Jan through Stan. Likewise, Bill is connected to Stan through Jill, and so on. The chain pattern in small groups tends to be a slower way to make decisions than the other patterns. The people in the middle of the chain tend to be seen as leaders because they have the most control of message flow in the network.

The Y pattern is a combination of the wheel and the chain. The preceding example of the "complaint project team" can be used to show a Y. The team could be organized so that both Bill and

Jill take complaints and then hand the complaints to Stan, who then sends recommendations to Jan. In this Y pattern, Stan would be the most central position in the network. The Y pattern is not quite as efficient as the wheel.

The circle pattern is like an "unbroken" chain. There is no one central person in a circle pattern, although each person still only exchanges messages with two other people. The hypothetical project team could be organized in a circle: Bill takes complaints, Jill compiles and categorizes complaints, Stan investigates and recommends courses of action, Jan decides which course of action, and then Jan directs Bill on how to handle the customer. Circle patterns are similar to chains in terms of efficiency.

The comcon (completely connected) pattern or all-channel pattern exists when all group members exchange messages with all of the other members. To reflect the comcon pattern, the complaint team could be organized as follows: Bill specializes in taking complaints, Jill specializes in compiling and categorizing complaints, Stan specializes in investigating complaints, and Jan specializes in choosing and implementing a course of action. The group might generally follow a chain pattern, but the members meet regularly to discuss how to improve the complaint handling process. They actively share insights and frustrations with each other. The comcon pattern is likely to have a higher degree of satisfaction because no member is isolated from the rest.

Norms

Norms define what is appropriate and inappropriate. Norms are standards that group members use to judge actions and positively or negatively sanction behavior. Norms are generally understood by group members (but often only on an implicit basis). Group members tend to learn norms indirectly, as in Sherif's experiment with the stationary light described earlier. Norms are involved in conformity and deviance, are what groups create as they develop, and are represented in the patterns of communication of group members.

See also: GROUP COMMUNICATION; GROUP COMMUNICATION, CONFLICT AND; GROUP COMMUNICATION, DECISION MAKING AND; GROUP COMMUNICATION, ROLES AND RESPONSIBILITIES IN.

Bibliography

Asch, Solomon. (1955). "Opinions and Social Pressures." *Scientific American* 193(5):31–55.

Bales, Robert F. (1953). *Interaction Process Analysis: A Method for the Study of Small Groups.* Cambridge, MA: Addison-Wesley.

Forsyth, Donelson. (1983). *An Introduction to Group Dynamics.* Monterey, CA: Brooks/Cole.

French, John R. P., Jr., and Raven, Bertram. (1959). "The Bases for Social Power." In *Studies in Social Power*, ed. Dawn Cartwright. Ann Arbor, MI: Institute for Social Research.

Moscovici, Serge. (1985). "Social Influence and Conformity." In *The Handbook of Social Psychology*, 3rd edition, ed. Gardner Lindzey and Elliot Aronson. New York: Random House.

Pavitt, Charles, and Curtis, Ellen. (1994). *Small Group Discussion: A Theoretical Approach,* 2nd edition. Scottsdale, AZ: Gorsuch Scarisbrick.

Sherif, Muzafer. (1935). "A Study of Some Social Factors in Perception." *Archives of Psychology* 27(187):1–60.

Tuckman, Bruce. (1965). "Developmental Sequence in Small Groups." *Psychological Bulletin* 63:382–399.

MARK AAKHUS

▮ GROUP COMMUNICATION, ROLES AND RESPONSIBILITIES IN

A group is a collectivity of individuals who are united by a common goal. Groups may vary substantially from one another in any number of ways, including their purpose, the way in which they emerge and evolve, their structure, their longevity, and their size. Groups may be formed for task completion, economic gain, social support, personal development and change, spiritual growth, or any of a number of other reasons. They may emerge and evolve quite naturally, or they may be developed and maintained through planning and conscious effort. Groups may have a very transitory existence, or they may be stable over time. Their structure and operations can be causal, or they can be formal. Whatever the specific nature or structure of a group, communication is critical to its emergence and ongoing dynamics.

There is no single view as to the minimum or maximum number of members needed to constitute a group. However, size is an important factor that affects the communication and other dynamics with any group. As compared to a two-person relationship, the presence of additional members provides extra resources to assist with the activities of the group and to provide input into planning, decision making, and problem resolution. However, a larger group requires a greater leadership effort in order to set and maintain direction, develop consensus on plans and goals, keep all parties informed and engaged, and identify and integrate the range of member expectations and perspectives.

Task and Social Dimensions

Groups are created to serve any number of goals. Often, the stated objective is to undertake and complete a specific task. Examples of group tasks include organizing a social event, painting a house, and carrying out a community-service project. Groups may also be formed and maintained primarily to create positive morale and to help members achieve a sense of personal or social well-being. Social clubs, discussion groups, and support groups are examples. Often, they are formed to help individuals who are lonely or are seeking support for overcoming personal difficulties.

To a greater or lesser extent, most groups serve a combination of task goals and social goals. Even in highly task-oriented groups, such as a construction crew or emergency room team—where successful task performance is the overriding goal—good morale and supportive work relationships are important. This is especially the case if members of a task group will be working together for a period of time. In these cases, good morale and a positive social climate often contribute to task effectiveness. Conversely, poor morale can undermine productivity and effectiveness.

Communication in Groups

In a two-person relationship, there is the possibility of only one reciprocal communication link. That is, person A can talk to person B. In a group of three persons, there are six possible message-processing relationships: person A with person B, person A with person C, person B with person C, persons A and B with person C, persons A and C with person B, and persons B and C with person A. In a group of four members, this increases to twenty-five potential relationships. In other words, increasing the size of the group by just one more person (from three people to four people) creates the possibility of nineteen addi-

tional communication relationships (Kephart, 1950). Thus, as the size of a group increases, the number and complexity of the communication relationships that are involved increases exponentially—creating many new opportunities, as well as many new challenges.

Group Development

Typically, groups go through four predictable stages as they develop: forming, storming, norming, and performing (Tuckman, 1965; Fisher, 1974).

Forming consists of getting acquainted, discussing how the group might begin its work, exploring where and when the members will meet, identifying the purposes of the group, and sharing other initial concerns. Storming refers to the dynamics that occur as individuals in the group begin to express differing perspectives, preferences, and opinions that must be entertained and addressed in some manner as the group begins its work. This stage may be either quite brief or fairly extensive—depending on the individuals, the range of views expressed, and the purpose of the group. Norming is the stage in group development at which goals, directions, and methods of operating are clarified and agreed upon. Once the norming stage is completed, the group can move forward more rapidly and effectively to the performing stage, where the goals of the group are accomplished.

While it is typical for newly formed groups to move through this sequence, the process of group development is not usually as logical as this description might suggest. Even in groups that have been performing at a high level for some time, it is not uncommon for the earlier three stages to reoccur periodically as a group pursues its work.

Decision Making

A variety of approaches are available for making decisions in a group. Among these approaches are consensus, compromise, majority vote, decision by leader, and arbitration (Wilson and Hanna, 1986).

Consensus requires all members of a group to arrive at a decision with which everyone genuinely agrees. Compromise involves decisions that result from negotiation and a give-and-take in order to arrive at a decision that is acceptable to all members of a group. Under majority vote, the final decision is the one that is supported by the majority of the group. In the decision by leader approach, the leader imposes his or her decision on the entire group. Formal negotiation and arbitration often involve facilitation by an impartial "third party" who helps to reconcile opposing positions.

Roles and Responsibilities

In most groups, particular roles (i.e., patterns of behavior) emerge. In a classic article on this subject, Kenneth Benne and Paul Sheats (1948) identified three broad categories of roles that typically occur during group interactions: task completion roles, group building and support roles, and individualistic roles.

Task completion roles are those roles that are related to the completion of a given job or activity. Examples of task completion roles include information seeker, opinion seeker, information giver, recorder, coordinator, and evaluator–critic.

Group building and support roles are those roles that are related to encouraging the social development of the group. Examples of these roles include encourager, harmonizer, compromiser, gatekeeper/expediter, observer, and follower.

Individualistic roles are generally the less desireable roles. These roles contribute negatively to the group both in terms of progress toward completion of a task and group development and climate. Examples of individualistic roles include aggressor, blocker, recognition seeker, dominator, and special-interest pleader.

Leadership

A particularly critical role in any group is that of leader. Essentially, the role consists of guiding the group. A great deal has been written about leadership, and there are many different points of view on the topic. Summarizing this literature in a simple way, Michael Useem (1998) explains that leadership requires a vision of what needs to be done and why, as well as a commitment to action (i.e., to implementation of the vision).

At a more microscopic level, the leadership role involves two sets of responsibilities: group maintenance functions and group achievement functions (Baird and Weinberg, 1981). Group maintenance activities include promoting participation, managing interaction, promoting cooperation, assuring that the needs and concerns of the members are addressed, arbitrating conflict, protecting the rights of individuals, modeling exemplary behavior, promoting group development, and assuming responsibilities for group dynamics. Group achievement functions include informing, planning, orienting, integrating, representing, coordinating, clarifying, evaluating, and motivating.

There are various theories about what constitutes effective leadership and how one acquires the necessary attributes to become a leader. One classical approach—the "great man" theory—holds that "leaders are born not made." Popular in the 1800s and early 1900s, this view held that some individuals inherit natural abilities that are necessary for effective leadership, while others do not.

"Trait" approaches, which were particularly popular in the first half of the twentieth century, contend that certain traits, such as being self-confident or outgoing, are essential if one is to be an effective leader. If one has these traits, they are likely to be successful in leadership roles.

Beginning in the 1950s, theories of leadership began to emphasize the importance of learned behaviors in effective leadership. Early behavioral theories often suggested that there was one best way to lead all groups in all situations, but subsequent theories have suggested the importance of situational leadership—adapting one's approach and behaviors to the particular group and circumstances that are involved in a given situation. More recent approaches see leadership as a set of social and communicative competencies and values that can and should be learned.

Conclusion

An understanding of roles and responsibilities is important for comprehending the dynamics of groups. An appreciation of the concepts is also very helpful for functioning effectively within groups and for contributing to group productivity and cohesiveness.

See also: GROUP COMMUNICATION; GROUP COMMUNICATION, CONFLICT AND; GROUP COMMUNICATION, DECISION MAKING AND; GROUP COMMUNICATION, DYNAMICS OF; INTERPERSONAL COMMUNICATION.

Bibliography

Baird, John E., Jr., and Weinberg, Sanford B. (1981). *Group Communication*, 2nd edition. Dubuque, IA: Brown.

Benne, Kenneth, and Sheats, Paul. (1948). "Functional Roles of Group Members." *Journal of Social Issues* 4:41–49.

Covey, Stephen. (1992). *Principle-Centered Leadership.* New York: Simon & Schuster.

Fisher, B. Aubrey. (1970). "Decision Emergence: Phases in Group Decision-Making." *Speech Monographs* 37:53–66.

Goleman, Daniel. (1994). *Emotional Intelligence.* New York: Bantam Books.

Kephart, William M. (1950). "A Quantitative Analysis of Intra-Group Relationships." *American Journal of Sociology* 55:544–549.

Komives, Susan R.; Lucas, Nancee; and McMahon, Timothy R. (1998). *Exploring Leadership.* San Francisco: Jossey-Bass.

Ruben, Brent D., and Stewart, Lea. (1998). *Communication and Human Behavior,* 4th edition. Boston: Allyn & Bacon.

Tichy, Noel M. (1997). *The Leadership Engine.* New York: Harper.

Tuckman, Bruce W. (1965). "Developmental Sequence in Small Groups." *Psychological Bulletin* 63:384–399.

Useem, Michael. (1998). *The Leadership Moment.* New York: Random House.

Wheatley, Margaret J. (1992). *Leadership and the New Science.* San Francisco: Berrett-Koehler.

Wilson, Gerald L., and Hanna, Michael S. (1986). *Groups in Context.* New York: Random House.

BRENT D. RUBEN

GUTENBERG, JOHANNES
(ca. 1400–1468)

Although no piece of printing in existence bears the name of Johannes Gutenberg, documentary evidence, as well as a large body of testimony from contemporary writers, identifies him as the inventor of printing by movable type in the Western world.

Gutenberg was born in Mainz, Germany, to a well-to-do father who was probably involved in the cloth trade (as well as dealing with precious metals) and a mother who was the daughter of a shopkeeper. The different social backgrounds of his parents made it impossible for Gutenberg to be part of the patrician class, so, out of necessity, he became a self-reliant entrepreneur. Probably through the affiliation of his father's family with the society of the mint, Gutenberg learned metallurgy and casting techniques. He left Mainz around 1429 due to civic conflicts and during the next five years honed his metalworking skills—skills that would play a major role in his invention.

Gutenberg was active in Strasbourg between 1434 and 1444, and, based on a document concerning a lawsuit brought against him in 1439, scholars have inferred that Gutenberg was already experimenting with some kind of printing technique at that time. Gutenberg's next major documented appearance is in Mainz in 1448, when a relative obtained a loan for him. What is known about the next seven years comes from a document, dated November 6, 1455, that summarizes a lawsuit brought against Gutenberg by Johann Fust, a money broker and Gutenberg's business partner. Fust sought repayment of two loans: the first loan may have been made around 1450 for the purpose of setting up a new printing establishment, secured by equipment; and the second two years later, in 1452, as an investment in "the work of the books." It is likely that Gutenberg lost the action Fust brought against him. At the close of the legal proceedings, two print shops, it is speculated, were operating in Mainz. As a result of the lawsuit, Gutenberg forfeited one of these shops, and Fust, with the help of Peter Schöffer (a scribe who would later become his son-in-law), operated that shop. Scholars have surmised that Gutenberg continued to operate the unforfeited print shop through the late 1450s and perhaps into the 1460s. Gutenberg received a pension from the Archbishop of Mainz in January 1465 and died sometime before February 26, 1468.

There is much continued speculation about whether or not Gutenberg, working in Europe, was aware of printing techniques that were already being used in Asia by that time. The invention of movable type made from clay is recorded in China between 1041 and 1049. Later, these ceramic letters were replaced by wooden ones. In 1234, metal characters were used in the production of a fifty-volume Korean etiquette book. Certainly, the Western alphabet is more conducive to building new words and texts by simply reshuffling letters than is the Asian system of ideographs, and it is this attribute on which Gutenberg's invention is based. Although whether Gutenberg is the actual inventor of movable printing is a matter of serious debate, the evidence does indicate that he assembled a number of technologies that were already in existence and adopted them for the purposes of printing. For example, presses used in the produc-

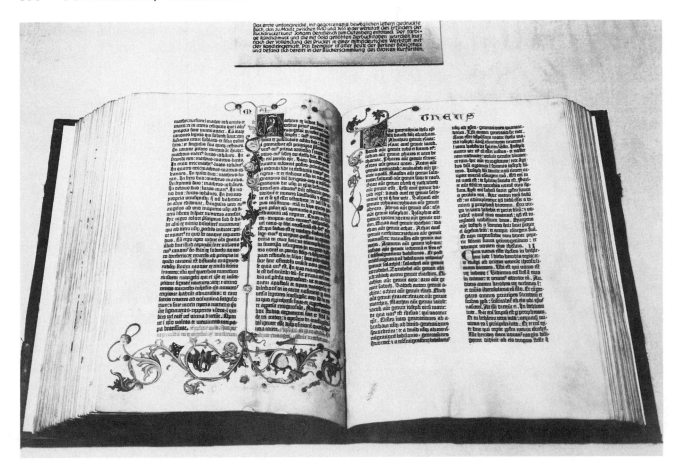

The Gutenberg Bible features richly illuminated copy. (Bettmann/Corbis)

tion of wine were adapted to serve the needs of printing, and ink that already existed was reformulated for the printing press. The one clearly new invention—and the key to the advancement of printing—was the adjustable type mold.

Gutenberg realized that the assembly of numerous interchangeable characters into text pages so that an impression could be transferred onto a surface, such as parchment or paper, required each metal letter to be exactly rectangular and in reverse relief. The process to create such a letter began with the cutting of a piece of steel or other hard metal, called a "punch," that resulted in an engraved relief image of a letter in reverse. The punch was then driven, with one blow, into a rectangular bar of copper, producing a matrix that differed in width depending on the width of the letter; for example, the letter "m" was wider than the letter "i." The matrix was then positioned into the adjustable type mold that allowed for this variation in letter width. The type mold consisted of several parts, held together by iron screws in such a way that each time an individual letter was cast,

the mold could be separated quickly into two halves and then quickly reassembled after the cast letter had been released from the mold. The metal used to cast the type consisted of lead, tin, and antimony. The result of this invention, and the assemblage of relevant technologies, was the ability to produce uniform and accurate impressions over long press runs, a method ideally suited to the production of multiple copies, thus satisfying the growing demand for reading material.

The major work to originate from Gutenberg's workshop was the forty-two-line Bible, often referred to as the Gutenberg Bible. The book is a reflection of the daring, skill, and artistic and intellectual aptitude of its creator. Gutenberg proved that his printing technique could produce a book of high quality without compromise. Even today, this level of mastery is rarely matched and never surpassed in quality.

Although various methods of printing had been in use earlier in Asia and methods of printing with movable type may have been developed in Europe before Gutenberg, his genius lay in the assembly of processes and the perfecting of them into one unified craft. This craft, capable of standardization and establishment in other places, permitted the rapid duplication of texts, thus changing the structure of communication forever. Books and knowledge became available to a wider sector of society and promoted economic progress through the diffusion of practical skills and scientific discovery. In essence, through the power of the printed book, no field of human endeavor was left untouched.

See also: ALPHABETS AND WRITING; PRINTING, HISTORY AND METHODS OF.

Bibliography

Ing, Janet. (1988). *Johann Gutenberg and His Bible: A Historical Study.* New York: The Typophiles.

Kapr, Albert. (1996). *Johann Gutenberg: The Man and His Invention,* trans. Douglas Martin. Brookfield, VT: Ashgate Publishing.

MARCELLA GENZ

HAINES, HELEN E. (1872–1961)

While many people may not be familiar with who Helen Haines was, she made numerous contributions during her lifetime to the American Library Association, the library press, library education, and the American intellectual freedom movement.

The eldest of five daughters born in Brooklyn, New York, to Benjamin Reeve, a wool broker, and Mary Hodges Haines, a woman who was both strong willed and well read, Helen Haines did not receive a formal education. Instead, she was homeschooled by her mother. Haines read voraciously and by the age of nineteen had written her first work, *History of New Mexico from the Spanish Conquest to the Present Time, 1530–1890, with Portraits and Bibliographical Sketches of Its Prominent People.* This book marked the beginning of a lengthy writing career that included more than one hundred articles for publications such as *Library Journal, Publishers' Weekly, Dial,* and the *Pasadena Star-News* and three books for Columbia University Press—*Living with Books* (1935, 1950) and *What's in a Novel* (1942). The former works were and still remain the best-selling books within the library science series of Columbia University Press.

The career of Helen Haines started by necessity and chance. In 1892, Haines had to take a job to help support her family. It so happened that her neighbor, Mary Wright Plummer, was the director of the Library School of Pratt Institute, an active member in the American Library Association (ALA), and a good friend of Richard Rogers Bowker, publisher of *Publishers' Weekly* and *Library Journal.* Plummer arranged an introduction for Haines, and shortly thereafter Haines began working as Bowker's assistant. By 1896, Haines had assumed a new role as managing editor of *Library Journal,* a position that required her to attend all ALA conferences. Not only did Haines attend, she functioned as the recorder of the ALA, and made many notable contributions. She argued on behalf of collecting fiction in public libraries and championed the cause of reading widely on all subjects regardless of their controversial nature. By taking such stances, she gained a powerful position within the ALA; by 1907, she was elected vice-president. Her work for both the ALA and for Bowker also impressed the Carnegie Corporation and directors of library schools. Although tuberculosis forced Haines to relocate from Brooklyn to Pasadena, California, in 1908, thus ending her full-time association with the ALA and *Library Journal,* Haines remained active in the library world.

In 1921, Charles C. Williamson, a consultant for the Carnegie Corporation (and later the director of the Library School of Columbia University), had written a report about the state of library training programs in the United States. Before its general release, he asked Haines to critique it. Her comments, along with her work for library training programs at the Los Angeles Public Library, University of California at Berkeley, and University of Southern California, helped shape the future of library education. Like Williamson, Haines stressed the need for librarians to possess a liberal arts education before embarking on a library training program. She called for the scholarization of library schools and their placement in universities that had, at their center, research libraries. She also spoke on the importance of librarians as professionals. No longer should librarianship be regarded as busy work for women; instead, librarians should function as both teachers and scholars. When the first edition of *Living with Books* appeared in 1935, it was one of the first true textbooks aimed at training librarians in the art of book selection. But *Living with Books* functioned more than just as a textbook; it helped to shape the burgeoning intellectual freedom movement.

Haines covered a variety of topics in *Living with Books*. Some would even be considered controversial for the time, including birth control, race relations, and censorship. On the latter subject, she wrote (1935, pp. 174–175), "Thus, the practice of official censorship (the restriction or suppression of literature deemed subversive or harmful) has continued in varying manifestations to our own day. . . . [C]ensorship and copyright lie at the roots of publishing history." Haines's words would be prophetic. Sixteen years later, the *Freeman*, a conservative political magazine, denounced her as a communist sympathizer.

In 1938, Forrest Spaulding, director of the Des Moines Public Library, developed a Bill of Rights for his library stating, among other matters, that "book selection should not be influenced by the writer's race, religion, politics, or nationality." With Haines's help, the ALA revised and adopted that Bill of Rights in June 1939 and, one year later, formed a Committee on Intellectual Freedom. Also in 1940, Haines became chair of the newly formed California Library Association Committee on Intellectual Freedom (CLA–CIF), the first state organization of its kind. During her tenure, the CLA–CIF challenged the Los Angeles County loyalty oaths and worked closely with the ALA to challenge similar issues.

Haines also became more outspoken about censorship, discrimination, and the Soviet Union. Her 1950 revision of *Living With Books* (p. 371) urged its readers to get a balanced view of the Soviet Union by reading widely about it: "Thus in a locked battle between capitalism and communism that now divides the two great world powers, materials of both defense and attack must be freely available for public information and study." However, for the January 1952 issue of *Freeman*, Oliver Carlson, a freelance journalist who often

contributed to the publication, wrote a scathing review of the revision of *Living with Books*. Entitled "A Slanted Guide to Library Selection," the Carlson review took quotes from the book out of context to make a case that Haines was a communist sympathizer. In "Red Hunting" circles, the accusation carried weight—it allowed right-wing conservatives to say that communists were disguising themselves as little old ladies who loved and recommended books. Because the ALA had an active Office of Intellectual Freedom in place, Haines's reputation remained untarnished. However, the accusation—made when Haines was in very poor health—was hurtful and cruel.

By 1951, Haines had become both America's expert on book selection and a key figure in the intellectual freedom movement. Because she also enjoyed great credibility, using *Living with Books* as the forum to spread her message that access to literature about the Soviet Union prompted better relations between it and the United States, Haines would not only be heard, but also believed. To honor her writings and her efforts, the ALA awarded Haines its Lippincott award in 1951.

Although Haines died in 1961, her legacy continues to be felt. Through the 1970s, *Living with Books* remained the standard text on book selection, and it is still referenced on many collection development course syllabi. Training for librarianship takes place on the graduate level, typically on campuses with a large research library. The ALA, through its Intellectual Freedom office, routinely battles challenges to intellectual freedom, the most recent and notable being the Communications Decency Act of 1996. And, for those without a formal education, Haines remains the role model; through unfettered access to books, anyone can influence the world.

See also: COMMUNICATIONS DECENCY ACT OF 1996; LIBRARIANS; LIBRARIES, FUNCTIONS AND TYPES OF.

Bibliography

Crawford, Holly. (1997). "Freedom Through Books: Helen Haines and Her Role in the Library Press, Library Education, and the Intellectual Freedom Movement." Unpublished dissertation, Graduate School of Library and Information Science, University of Illinois, Urbana-Champaign.

Haines, Helen E. (1925). "The Teaching of Book Selection." *Library Journal* 50:693–697.

Haines, Helen E. (1935, 1950). *Living With Books.* New York: Columbia University Press.

Haines, Helen E. (1939). "Values in Fiction." *Booklist* 36:99–102.

Haines, Helen E. (1942). *What's in a Novel.* New York: Columbia University Press.

Haines, Helen E. (1946). "Ethics of Librarianship." *Library Journal* 71:848–851.

Haines, Helen E. (1948). "Balancing the Books, Reason Enthroned." *Library Journal* 73:149–154.

Williamson, Charles C. (1921). *Training for Library Service: A Report Prepared for the Carnegie Corporation of New York.* New York: The Carnegie Corporation.

HOLLY CRAWFORD

HEALTH COMMUNICATION

Health communication is a rich, exciting, and relevant area of study that investigates and elucidates the many ways that human and mediated communication dramatically influences the outcomes of health-care and health-promotion efforts. While health communication is a relatively young area of communication inquiry and education, research and writing on this topic has grown tremendously since the early 1980s, generating increasing numbers of important research findings and publications. A major reason for the tremendous growth and development of inquiry related to health communication is the importance of this research area for addressing complex and challenging health-care demands in society and guiding the promotion of public health.

Communication is at the very center of health-care and health-promotion efforts. To gather relevant diagnostic information from health-care consumers, doctors, nurses, and other health-care providers depend on their ability to communicate effectively by asking pertinent questions, interpreting responses, and probing for more detailed information. Consumers depend on their own ability to communicate with health-care providers when seeking help, identifying health problems, interpreting health-care recommendations and treatment strategies, and negotiating their way through the often complex modern health-care systems. At the broader system-wide level, communication is the primary mechanism that professionals have for engendering cooperation and coordination. In a large hospital, for example, the efforts of physicians, nurses, pharmacists, laboratory technicians, therapists, and administrative personnel must be carefully coordinated in order to accomplish treatment goals.

Similarly, communication is an important element of health-promotion efforts (i.e., campaigns designed to influence public health knowledge, attitudes, and behaviors in order to help reduce health risks and encourage the adoption of healthy behaviors and lifestyles). The campaigners must be able to communicate successfully with their intended audiences if the important messages about relevant health risks and appropriate health-preserving behaviors are going to be heeded. In health-promotion efforts, care must be taken to craft messages that are appropriate and compelling for the target audiences and to guarantee that the messages are delivered to these audiences through the most effective communication channels possible. The effectiveness of communication in virtually all health-care and health-promotion activities is directly related to the potency of the health outcomes achieved, and in many cases these outcomes can mean life or death for health-care consumers.

Health Communication as an Important Area of Study

A large and developing body of scholarly research in the area of health communication powerfully illustrates the centrality of communication processes in achieving important health-care and health-promotion goals. For example, Gary Kreps and Dan O'Hair (1995) have reported a series of studies showing the influences of communication strategies and programs (introduced at individual, dyadic, group, organizational, and societal levels) on health knowledge, behaviors, and outcomes. Similarly, a study by Sheldon Greenfield, Sherrie Kaplan, and John Ware (1985) has clearly demonstrated the positive influences of increased patient–provider communicative involvement in directing health-care treatment in achieving desired health outcomes. In addition, James Dearing and his colleagues (1996) have illustrated the positive influences of social marketing and diffusion-based communication campaign strategies in encouraging at-risk populations to adopt important health-risk-prevention behaviors. Large-scale longitudinal (multi-year) communication intervention programs, such as the Stanford Five City Heart Health Program and the Minnesota Heart

Health Communication Program also demonstrate the positive influences of these campaigns on promoting adoption of lifestyle changes to prevent cardiovascular disease and reducing gaps in public health knowledge. There is great potential for the use of strategic programs in the area of health communication to provide health-care consumers and providers with needed health information and to help address important public health needs.

In response to the growing body of health communication research and intervention work, there is increasing recognition within the academic world and throughout the health-care delivery system that health communication is a most important and relevant area of inquiry for addressing salient health-care and health-promotion issues. This recognition is also occurring in many of the major centers for public health policy (such as the Centers for Disease Control and Prevention, the National Institutes of Health, other agencies of the U.S. Department of Health and Human Services, and the World Health Organization). In fact, the National Cancer Institute (1999), the largest institute in the National Institutes of Health, identified health communication as one of the institute's major areas of research support and investment for reducing the national cancer burden and fighting the war against cancer.

Health communication issues are increasingly a primary topic of large-scale funded research programs sponsored by numerous major foundations, health-care corporations, and government agencies. It is especially common for these organizations to fund the development and implementation of important campaigns for promoting public health and preventing the spread of serious health threats. Increased funding for research has spurred tremendous growth in inquiry, education, and publication in the area of health communication. Similarly, scholarly divisions and interest groups related to health communication have been established in many social scientific professional societies. For example, almost all of the communication discipline's professional associations, such as the International Communication Association, the National Communication Association, the American Public Health Association, and several regional communication societies, have interest groups or divisions devoted to health communication. In addition, there is strong interest in health communication by medical, nursing, pharmacy, and other allied health professions. Health communication is closely aligned with other areas of social inquiry such as health administration, health psychology, medical sociology, and health anthropology. Well-attended scholarly conferences presenting state-of-the-art research and intervention programs for health communication are held on a regular basis, both in the United States and internationally. Indeed, increasing numbers of theses and dissertations written by graduate students concern health communication, and courses in health communication have become standard fare in many undergraduate and graduate communication and public health educational programs across the United States and around the world.

There is no doubt that education and research in the area of health communication is achieving a higher level of disciplinary maturation than ever before—generating stronger scholarly interest, support, and productivity. However, the powerful, complex, and widespread influences of communication on health care and health promotion demand careful examination, leading to the systematic study of health communication. There is still much to be learned about health communication, and there are many areas where knowledge of health communication can be applied to enhancing the quality of public health. As scholarly inquiry in this area grows, new and exciting areas of examination have developed.

Need for Relevant Health Information

Health information is the primary commodity of health communication. Consumers of health care depend on the quality of the health information that they can access to make important health-care choices. There are many different sources of health information available today. In addition to gathering health information directly from their health-care providers, consumers can consult their public libraries (or, if available, a local university or medical library) that have access to reference books, journals, and computerized sources, such as the National Library of Medicine's Medline database. There is a large and growing list of health information services available to consumers via the Internet, which has rapidly become an extremely powerful source of health information for both consumers and health-care providers. However, the sheer number of information sources and the incredible volume of health information that is available today can sometimes overload and confuse consumers.

Consumers can obtain information about specific health-care issues from advocacy groups (e.g., the Alzheimer's Association, the American Cancer Society, and the American Heart Association), health-care delivery centers (e.g., hospitals, clinics, and health maintenance organizations), and research organizations (e.g., the World Health Organization, the Centers for Disease Control and Prevention, and the National Institutes of Health). Government health agencies typically provide excellent, up-to-date information on most serious diseases. For example the National Cancer Institute operates a toll-free telephone information system, the Cancer Information Service, which can be accessed from anywhere in the United States at 1–800–4–CANCER. The hotline operators try to answer any questions about cancer, and they provide referral and treatment information when it is needed. The operators can also have searches conducted on the Physician Data Query database in order to access the latest information about cancer treatment and clinical research that is being conducted.

Health Communication and Health Informatics

One area of tremendous growth in the study of health communication is the way in which computer-based technologies can be used to process and disseminate relevant health information. The dawn of the information-oriented society has spawned a communication revolution in modern health care that has changed the way health care is delivered. Quality health care is closely tied to the widespread availability of health information. Unprecedented levels of health information are now available to both consumers and health-care providers via a broad range of new and more traditional communication channels (e.g., the Internet, interactive CD-ROM programs, television, and different print media).

The use of new communication technologies to process and disseminate health information has spawned an exciting new area of inquiry, health informatics. Health informatics involves the study of computer-based dissemination of information. As information technologies advance, there are a variety of new computer-based tools and media for disseminating and accessing health information.

There are also new mechanisms (based on advances in areas such as artificial intelligence and decision sciences) for manipulating, interpreting, and applying health information. Health informatics scholars are interested in studying the ways computer-based information systems can be used to

1. disseminate relevant information to key audiences,
2. increase public knowledge about important health-care treatment and risk prevention issues,
3. promote the adoption of healthy behaviors and lifestyles by the public,
4. facilitate adoption of the best treatment modalities and technologies by health-care providers,
5. encourage collaboration and multidisciplinary consultation in health-care treatment,
6. facilitate, when relevant, patient entry into appropriate clinical trials (controlled scientific studies of new and promising treatment modalities, usually conducted at major medical centers),
7. enhance social support and psychosocial adaptation for health-care consumers and their caregivers.

The widespread availability of relevant and accurate health information offers the great promise of demystifying many of the complexities and uncertainties of health care and the health-care system for consumers, shedding light on health-care processes and treatment strategies that were once only the domain of health-care professionals. Access to relevant and timely health information can help consumers participate fully in health-care decision-making and encourage greater cooperation and collaboration between health-care providers and consumers than ever before. This health information revolution can also help health-care professionals access state-of-the-art prevention, diagnostic, and treatment information and, through easy contact with other providers, engage in multidisciplinary consultation with other health professionals in coordinating health-care services. New communication technologies have also helped promote increasing use of telemedicine (i.e., health-care services delivered via interactive communication channels such as computer, video, and teleconferencing technologies) to assist consumers in remote and isolated geographic locations. However, on the negative side, this information revolution has also led to a general overload of available health information that is of limited quality and that inevitably serves to confuse and misdirect health care consumers and providers, thereby decreasing the quality of health-care choices that are made. Scholars of health communication have an opportunity to help promote public health by focusing on the role of information in the modern health-care system. Research on health communication can help to sort out the ways in which communication can most profitably inform consumers and providers about relevant health issues, identify the best ways to develop and present high-quality health information to key audiences, and encourage effective collaborative decision-making in modern health-care efforts.

Major Levels and Areas of Inquiry

There are many important areas of health communication education and inquiry that range from the intrapersonal study of health beliefs and attitudes to the mass-mediated dissemination of health information within and across societies. A good framework for describing the primary levels of the analysis of health communication differentiates between intrapersonal, interpersonal, group, organizational, and societal levels of inquiry. The ability of scholars to examine the influences of communication on health outcomes at multiple levels of interaction occurring within a broad range of social settings clearly illustrates the power and pertinence of inquiry into health communication, yet it also illustrates the complexity of this area of inquiry.

Intrapersonal health communication inquiry examines the internal mental and psychological processes that influence health care, such as the health beliefs, attitudes, and values that predispose health-care behaviors and decisions. Scholars focusing on these intrapersonal issues in health communication often benefit from adopting a psychological frame of reference to their inquiry, examining the ways in which health communicators process information, create meanings, and craft messages. There has been excellent progress in integrating health communication and health psychology scholarship, and there should be further opportunities for collaboration between these interrelated areas of inquiry. Some of the issues

scholars might examine from an intrapersonal perspective include the development of unique health beliefs within different cultural groups that influence the health behaviors of individual members of these cultures, the ways in which certain health-related attitudes and values might predispose certain target audiences toward accepting or rejecting advice provided in campaigns for health promotion, and the emotional effects of specific health threats (e.g., breast cancer) and treatment strategies (e.g., radical mastectomy) on health-care consumers. The intrapersonal perspective on health communication provides unique insights into the personal orientations, expectations, and predispositions held by the different participants in the health-care system and enables health communicators to adjust their messages to these particular psychological variables.

Interpersonal health communication inquiry examines relational influences on health outcomes, focusing on the study of provider–consumer relationships, dyadic (face-to-face) provision of health education, therapeutic interaction, and the exchange of relevant information in health-care interviews. This provocative area of inquiry focuses on the development of cooperative relationships between mutually dependent participants in the modern health-care system, such as the study of provider–patient relations, interprofessional relations among health-care providers, and multicultural relations within the health-care system. Relationship development is a complex social process that develops incrementally as relational partners exchange messages and get to know one another. The stronger the interpersonal relationships that health-care participants can develop with one another, the more likely they are to develop trust in one another, share relevant health information, and work cooperatively during challenging, complex, and sometimes even tense situations.

Relationship development is very important to health-care delivery, from the point of view of both the provider and the consumer. Health-care providers need to encourage their patients to trust them, provide them with full information about symptoms and past health behaviors, listen carefully to instructions and to provide informed consent explanations (in which health-care providers are legally required to explain the costs and benefits of alternative treatments and identify the relative implications of the treatment strategies that are recommended), and to follow carefully the treatment protocols that are prescribed for them. Health-care consumers depend on relationship development to gain the trust and concern of their providers, to gather full information from providers about treatment options, and to encourage providers to allow them to participate actively in making important treatment decisions.

The interpersonal perspective has been a dominant area of health communication inquiry over the years, focusing directly on important health-care delivery issues. It is a complex area of study, with many different personal, psychological, cultural, linguistic, and nonverbal variables at play. Care must be taken when studying interpersonal aspects of health communication to address fairly the important cultural, political, and power issues that underlie interpersonal relations in the delivery of health care.

Group health communication inquiry examines the role communication performs in the interdependent coordination of members of collectives (e.g., health-care teams, support groups, ethics committees, and families) as the group members share relevant health information in making important health-care decisions. Health-care teams are comprised of specialists from different professional backgrounds (e.g., medicine, pharmacy, nursing, therapy) who work together to help plan and implement complex treatment strategies for the same patient. As specialization of services and technologies continues to increase, there is a growing dependence on health-care teams in the delivery of modern health care, as well as growing interdependence among the different members of these health-care teams. However, due to differences in professional knowledge, specialization, and orientation toward the consumer's health care, it is common for differences of opinion to emerge between members of health-care teams. These differences of opinion, while sometimes uncomfortable for team members to deal with, can be very useful, because they highlight different aspects of health care that all members of a team may not have been aware of. By sharing such information, the team can make more informed choices about treatment strategies. It is important, though, for team members to be willing to accept points of view that are different from their own and to use group communication

effectively to work through conflict and make good health-care decisions.

There are many difficult ethical issues concerning quality of care, access to care, consumer dignity, and end-of-life issues that have led to the widespread use of ethics committees in health-care systems to ensure that fair and moral choices are made in health care. (These committees also help guard health-care systems from legal problems and litigation claims.) Ethics committees are often comprised of different health-care professionals, religious leaders, bio-ethicists, health-care administrators, lawyers, and concerned lay individuals (often representing the consumer or a consumer advocacy group). These individuals meet to communicate about complex ethical choices that often have to made in health-care systems, such as who among many applicants should get access to specialized, yet limited, treatment equipment and resources (e.g., organ transplants). Group communication among the members of these ethics committees is the primary process by which ethical decisions are reached.

The growing complexities of modern health-care delivery, with new diagnostic tools and sophisticated treatment technologies and strategies, demand greater input from groups of individuals to make difficult and challenging health-care decisions. Interdependent health-care providers, administrators, and consumers must learn how to share relevant information and coordinate efforts in group settings. Because communication performs such important functions in group coordination and information exchange, a communication perspective is particularly appropriate for the study of health-care teams, ethics committees, and other decision-making groups.

Organizational health communication inquiry examines the use of communication to coordinate interdependent groups, mobilize different specialists, and share relevant health information within complex health-care delivery systems to enable effective multidisciplinary provision of health care and prevention of relevant health risks. With the rise of managed care, the delivery of health-care services has become increasingly controlled by financial and bureaucratic concerns. There is growing frustration among many consumers about the quality of care they receive and their ability to participate actively in making important health-care decisions. There are many important opportunities for scholars in the area of health communication to examine ways to promote greater receptivity, flexibility, and sensitivity toward consumers within the increasingly complex and highly regulated modern health-care system.

Communication between different interdependent departments in health-care systems is crucial for coordinating health-care efforts. For example, in-patients receiving treatment in hospitals are housed within specific hospital wards, yet they are often sent to different departments (e.g., radiology, surgery, therapy) for treatment. It is important for these departments to share information about the consumers they serve, to keep track of the consumers' needs and activities as they move through the hospital, and to coordinate the care of these patients. Organizational communication tracks the ways these departments share information, coordinate activities, and adapt to each other as they share the accomplishment of organizational goals.

Societal health communication inquiry examines cultural influences on health care and the generation, dissemination, and utilization of health information communicated via diverse media to the broad range of professional and lay audiences in society that influence health education, promotion, and health-care practices. Social marketing has been widely adopted by communication scholars as an important strategic framework for designing sophisticated campaigns of health promotion. In the past, research focusing on societal inquiry was conducted primarily by communication scholars who specialized in media studies and examined the ways that various media can deliver messages on health promotion and risk prevention to targeted audiences. However, as efforts at health promotion have become more and more sophisticated, using multiple message strategies and delivery systems, there are increasing opportunities for greater participation by communication scholars (and others) with expertise in analyzing the intrapersonal, interpersonal, group, and organizational levels of health communication.

Health Communication Channels

Inquiry into health communication also involves examination of many communication channels. Face-to-face communication between providers and consumers, members of health-care teams, and support group members are the focus of many studies. A broad range of both personal communication media (e.g., telephone, mail, fax, e-mail) and mass communication media (e.g., radio, television, film, billboards) are also the focus of much research. More and more, the new communication technologies that have developed have been examined as important media for health communication. These new media, especially the interactive computer technologies and the Internet, have become increasingly important sources for relevant health information and support for many consumers and health-care providers. For this reason, they will be a most promising topic for future research.

Settings for Health Communication

The settings for the study of health communication are quite diverse and include the wide range of settings where health information is generated and exchanged, such as homes, offices, schools, clinics, and hospitals. Scholars of health communication must be aware of the widespread nature of health communication so they can design and conduct studies in many diverse field settings. Research has examined such diverse issues as the role of interpersonal communication in developing cooperative provider–consumer relationships, the role of comforting communication in providing social support to those who are troubled, the effects of various media and presentation strategies on the dissemination of health information to those who need such information, the use of communication to coordinate the activities of interdependent health-care providers, and the use of communication for administering complex health-care systems. Since the study of health communication encompasses such a broad range of media, channels, levels, and settings, it is a convergent research area that benefits from the work of scholars representing multiple research traditions, disciplines, methodologies, and theoretical perspectives. Indeed, health communication is a "transdisciplinary" area of inquiry, attracting researchers who represent multiple related social scientific, humanist, and technical disciplines and conduct research that focuses on a diverse set of health issues in a broad range of health-care settings.

Conclusion

Health communication is an exciting multifaceted area of applied communication inquiry that examines the role of messages, message exchange, and information about health care and health outcomes. Evidence suggests that communication plays extremely important functions in health care and health promotion. Future study of health communication will help identify the primary communication mechanisms that are at work in modern health care and health promotion, thereby guiding effective and strategic use of communication by health-care consumers and providers. Knowledge about the role of communication in health care, coupled with the skills to access and share relevant health information effectively, will help both consumers and providers get the most out of the modern health-care system.

See also: GROUP COMMUNICATION; HEALTH COMMUNICATION, CAREERS IN; INTERPERSONAL COMMUNICATION; ORGANIZATIONAL COMMUNICATION; PROVIDER–PATIENT RELATIONSHIPS; PUBLIC HEALTH CAMPAIGNS.

Bibliography

Dearing, James W.; Rogers, Everett M.; Meyer, Gary; Casey, Mary K.; Rao, Nagesh; Campo, Shelly; and Henderson, Geoffrey M. (1996). "Social Marketing and Diffusion-Based Strategies for Communicating with Unique Populations: HIV Prevention in San Francisco." *Journal of Health Communication: International Perspectives* 1(4):342–364.

Flora, June A.; Maccoby, Nathan; and Farquhar, John W. (1989). "Communication Campaigns to Prevent Cardiovascular Disease: The Stanford Community Studies." In *Public Communication Campaigns*, 2nd ed., eds. Ronald E. Rice and Charles K. Atkins. Newbury Park, CA: Sage Publications.

Greenfield, Sheldon; Kaplan, Sherrie; and Ware, John, Jr. (1985). "Expanding Patient Involvement in Care: Effects on Patient Outcomes." *Annals of Internal Medicine* 102:520–528.

Kreps, Gary L. (1988). "The Pervasive Role of Information in Health and Health Care: Implications for Health Communication Policy." In *Communication Yearbook*, Vol. 11, ed. James A. Anderson. Newbury Park, CA: Sage Publications.

Kreps, Gary L.; Bonaguro, Ellen W.; and Query, James L. (1998). "The History and Development of the Field of Health Communication." In *Health Communication Research: A Guide to Developments and Direction,* eds. Lorraine D. Jackson and Bernard K. Duffy. Westport, CT: Greenwood Press.

Kreps, Gary L., and O'Hair, Dan, eds. (1995). *Communication and Health Outcomes.* Cresskill, NJ: Hampton Press.

Kreps, Gary L., and Thornton, Barbara C. (1992). *Health Communication: Theory and Practice,* 2nd ed. Prospect Heights, IL: Waveland Press.

National Cancer Institute. (1999). *The Nation's Investment in Cancer Research: A Budget Proposal for Fiscal Year 2001.* NIH Publication No. 99-4373. Bethesda, MD: National Institutes of Health.

Pavlik, John V.; Finnegan, John R.; Strickland, Daniel; Salman, Charles T.; Viswanath, K.; and Wackman, Daniel B. (1993). "Increasing Public Understanding of Heart Disease: An Analysis of the Minnesota Heart Health Program." *Health Communication* 5(1):1–20.

Rogers, Everett M (1994). "The Field of Health Communication Today." *American Behavioral Scientist* 38(2):208–214.

GARY L. KREPS

■ HEALTH COMMUNICATION, CAREERS IN

Study in the area of health communication can serve as good preparation for individuals who want to work in a number of very important arenas related to the modern health-care delivery and health promotion. In fact, communication knowledge and skills are in high demand in the modern health-care system because there are many important health-care functions that are related to communication. The combination of well-developed oral, written, and media communication skills, along with an understanding of the way the health-care system operates is very powerful and of great utility in health-care industries. Students of health communication can perform very important roles in health care and health promotion, helping to improve quality of care and to enhance efforts at health promotion.

Education and Training

Education is one of the growing areas of opportunity for scholars who have graduate degrees in health communication. These scholars are increasingly in demand at universities and colleges to serve as faculty in communication programs, as well as in educational programs related to the health professions. Many health-care professions (e.g., medicine, nursing, pharmacology, physical therapy, psychology) require practicing health-care providers to seek continuing-education credits to maintain their professional licensing, and many hospitals and medical centers have well-developed continuing-education programs for their professional staff. Training in health communication is an important and high-demand area of study. Topics such as provider–consumer relations, interviewing skills, multicultural relations, ethical decision-making, interprofessional relations, and health-care team development are very attractive to practicing health-care providers. Scholars in these areas can provide a great educational service to health-care professionals, health-care delivery systems, and consumers by helping providers develop and refine their skills in health communication.

Health-Care Advocacy and Support

With the growing emphasis on public advocacy, consumerism, and empowerment in research, both undergraduate and graduate students of health communication are well prepared for important information intermediary and advocacy careers within the health-care delivery system. New career opportunities with job titles such as "patient advocate," "health information specialist," and "patient relations officer" are helping to enhance the modern health-care system by providing relevant health information to both providers and consumers. These new information and advocacy professionals help to identify and fulfill the specific information needs of consumers and providers. They relieve a great deal of strain on the modern health-care system by disseminating relevant health information that can encourage and empower consumers to practice disease prevention and self-care and to become active partners with health-care providers in the health-care enterprise.

Ideally, these specialists help identify appropriate sources of relevant health information that are available to consumers, gather data from consumers about the kinds of challenges and constraints they face within the modern health-care system, and develop and field test information dissemination methods meant to enhance consumers' medical literacy. Such efforts help consumers negotiate their ways through health-care bureaucracies and develop communication strategies for working effectively with health-care providers. These professionals also act as information intermediaries for health-care providers and administrators by gathering relevant information

and feedback from consumers about the nature of the health-care problems these consumers are coping with, their needs within the health-care system, and their reactions to the services they have received within the health-care system. The consumer information that the information intermediaries can provide enables health-care providers and administrators to understand and meet the needs of their clients.

Health Education and Dissemination

There are growing opportunities for specialists in health communication to work as health educators, health science writers, and as health reporters. There is a tremendous need for individuals in the health-care, pharmaceutical, and health-care technology industries who can translate complex technical health treatment and research information for lay audiences. This applies to information provided both orally (in health education and counseling efforts) and in writing (for newspapers, websites, magazines, pamphlets, and advertising). Students of health communication are typically well trained to present technical information to different audiences and have developed strong oral and written communication skills that prepare them for these career opportunities. Similar opportunities within the broad health-care industries are available to students who are skilled as audio, video, film, and new media producers and can effectively present relevant health information to different audiences via these powerful media channels.

Health Promotion

With the growth of efforts at health promotion in the modern health-care system, there are growing opportunities for people to develop and administer campaigns related to health communication. Communication professionals are well suited to collect audience analysis data for guiding message development and communication strategies for campaigns. They develop and field test messages strategies for health promotion, gather formative evaluation data for refining these messages, and identify appropriate communication channels for delivering these messages. Health campaigns are typically mounted by local, state, regional, and national public health agencies, by health-care and consumer-advocacy organizations, and by health-care delivery systems—all of

A traveling health educator visits a class in South Carolina to teach children about health-related topics ranging from dental care to anatomy. (Annie Griffiths Belt/Corbis)

which are good potential employers for experts in health communication.

Research and Evaluation

The are many research and evaluation opportunities available for scholars in health communication because advocacy groups, health-care delivery systems, and government public health agencies have made significant investments in developing public health education communication programs. These communication programs include print materials (e.g., brochures, booklets, and posters), television and radio programs (e.g., public service announcements), interactive media (e.g., CD-ROMs), and websites for providing health information to key audiences via the Internet. Scholars in health communication are in great demand to help these organizations and government agencies evaluate the effectiveness of their current health information delivery programs, to help them tailor their message strategies for specific targeted audiences, and to help

them develop new and improved health information dissemination strategies and technologies. Such evaluation research can also help consumers decide which of the many available sources of health information are the most credible, accurate, and up-to-date sources.

Health Sales and Account Management

The area of health sales is an exciting area of employment opportunity for students of health communication. Companies that sell pharmaceuticals, medical equipment, and health supplies all need sales personnel who can communicate effectively within the health-care system. They need people who can understand the complexities of health-care delivery yet explain those complexities in laymen's terms to diverse audiences. The companies also want sales personnel who can establish good working relationships with health-care customers, who can manage standing accounts, and who can develop new accounts.

See also: HEALTH COMMUNICATION;
PROVIDER–PATIENT RELATIONSHIPS; PUBLIC
HEALTH CAMPAIGNS.

Bibliography

Du Prè, Athena. (1999).*Communicating about Health:
Current Issues and Perspectives.* Mountain View, CA:
Mayfield Publishing.

Jackson, Lorraine D., and Duffy, Bernard K., eds.
(1998). *Health Communication Research: A Guide to
Developments and Direction.* Westport, CT: Greenwood Press.

Kreps, Gary L., and Thornton, Barbara C. (1992).
Health Communication: Theory and Practice, 2nd ed.
Prospect Heights, IL: Waveland Press.

Sharf, Barbara F. (1997). "The Present and Future of
Health Communication Scholarship: Overlooked
Opportunities." *Health Communication* 11(2):
195–199.

GARY L. KREPS

HEARST, WILLIAM RANDOLPH (1863–1951)

William Randolph Hearst defined twentieth-century media for better and for worse. His style of journalism emphasized a focus on the audience, and that approach has resulted in the look and content of today's mass media.

Born in San Francisco on April 29, 1863, to George Hearst and Phoebe Apperson Hearst, William was raised with all the strength and inspiration that a self-made multimillionaire and a well-educated woman could impart in one of the most exceptional environments of the century. San Francisco bred larger-than-life figures of success and failure. Although his parents demanded a high standard, they provided excellent examples of the rewards that would accrue from such efforts.

Around the time that Hearst, studying at Harvard, was discovering an interest in media, his father acquired a small newspaper, *The San Francisco Examiner,* as compensation for a debt owed to him. Hearst sent a letter to his father requesting that he be given control of the newspaper. "I am convinced that I could run a newspaper successfully," he wrote. "With enough money to carry out my schemes—I'll tell you what I would do!" In 1887, at the age of twenty-three, Hearst named himself "Proprietor" of *The Examiner* and devoted

both his energy and his intellect to disparaging those who felt that his fortune and his position were unwarranted. Through a combination of long hours, hard work, and nearly unlimited resources, Hearst developed a set of principals of journalism that were devoted to providing an advocate for the average person as much as to providing useful information. He spared no expense to hire the best reporters of the day and encouraged them to use a style of prose designed to entertain as much as to inform. "The Monarch of the Dailies"—as Hearst referred to his newspaper—began a crusade for the people. Corruption and muckraking exposed civic decay. Exposés were standard fare. Hearst established his publishing "dynasty" with the 1895 purchase of a second newspaper, *The New York Journal.* Now firmly established on both coasts of the United States, his creation of *The Chicago American* in 1900 established him as a force throughout the country. By the 1920s, "The Chief"—a nickname given to Hearst—was the owner of a chain of more than twenty-four newspapers that had been carefully chosen to reach as many people as possible.

Hearst emphasized the importance of talent (as much as content) in writing to convey information to the public. With this in mind, he hired writers such as Stephen Crane, Mark Twain, and Jack London to work for his newspapers. Sensationalist stories, the hallmark of "Yellow Journalism" (which emphasized flamboyant interpretation over objective presentation and was a style first associated with Joseph Pulitzer and his *New York World*), drew in a large audience—at one point, one in four people in America read a Hearst newspaper.

The coverage of the events leading to the Spanish-American War provided a significant incident in the rivalry between Hearst and Pulitzer. Reporting on the Cuban rebellion against Spanish rule, correspondents from both papers filed a string of lurid accounts. Starving women and children, abuse toward prisoners, and valiant rebels fighting to be free were regular features in both newspaper chains. Stories that featured women were particularly inflammatory as well as circulation building. The drawing "Spanish Dons Search American Women" by Frederic Remington is an example of this sensationalism. However, in 1897, Remington cabled Hearst that everything was quiet in Havana. Remington wanted to return to the United States. Hearst replied, "Please remain. You furnish the pictures, I'll furnish the war." The sensational stories continued. By the time the *Maine* was sunk in Havana Harbor on February 15, 1898, Hearst and Pulitzer had managed to build U.S. public opinion to a point where intervention on the part of President William McKinley and the United States was demanded. "Remember the *Maine!*" became an international cry for justice. As a result of the involvement of Hearst and Pulitzer, the Spanish-American War has since become known as the first media war. In later years, however, Hearst recognized the need for balance. A 1933 memo to his editors emphasized that fair and impartial reporting was essential to the people's interest. "Give unbiased news of all creeds and parties," it read.

Hearst, not wanting to limit his influence to the newspaper world, launched his first magazine, *Motor*, in 1903, shortly after his marriage to Millicent Willson (with whom he would have five sons). He expanded his dominance of print media with the purchase or start of many other magazines, including *Cosmopolitan*, *Chicago Examiner*, *Boston American*, *Daily Mirror*, and *Harper's Bazaar*. Hearst also eventually moved into radio broadcasting and the film industry (where he produced several movies starring Marion Davies, who was his mistress from 1917 until his death). His political interests resulted in Hearst being elected to the U.S. House of Representatives (1903–1907), but his separate bids to become mayor of New York City, governor of New York State, and president of the United States all proved unsuccessful.

It is undeniable that Hearst's style of news reporting, whether through Yellow Journalism excess or reader-friendly emphasis, reached audiences in ways that journalists still strive to imitate. His legacy is more physically apparent at San Simeon—also known as Hearst Castle—in California. This lavish estate created by Hearst during the later period of his life is now a state historical monument and houses an extensive collection of Hearst memorabilia.

See also: JOURNALISM, HISTORY OF; NEWSPAPER INDUSTRY, HISTORY OF; PULITZER, JOSEPH.

Bibliography

Loe, Nancy. (1988). *William Randolph Hearst: An Illustrated Biography*. Santa Barbara, CA: Sequoia Communications.

This *"Hearst for Mayor"* poster was part of William Randolph Hearst's campaign to become the mayor of New York City. (Corbis)

Swanberg, W. A. (1961). *Citizen Hearst: A Biography of William Randolph Hearst*. New York: Scribner.
Tebbel, John. (1952). *The Life and Good Times of William Randolph Hearst*. New York: Dutton.

MARK REID ARNOLD

■ HOME AS INFORMATION ENVIRONMENT

In the information age—the frenetic era of the networked computer, the Internet-surfing consumer, and the digital commodity—there have been rapid advancements in information technology (IT). These advancements have increasingly affected the way people interact in their daily living spaces, including the workplace, public areas such as libraries and shopping centers, and the private dwelling known as the home.

While specific definitions depend on the area of research or interest level, IT can loosely be described as any device or service that has an electronic origin and is used by people to process data. This data can be the music from a home stereo system, the picture from a television, the bit stream of a personal computer, a voice from a telephone, or virtually any other thing found in the home. A synonym often used for IT based in the home is "media."

While media has a substantial presence in all three living spaces, IT is most obvious and arguably most dynamic within the home. This statement may seem counterintuitive at first glance; anecdotes about enormous corporate budgets providing employees with limitless access to new and innovative technologies abound. However, on further reflection, viewing the home as the dominant space for the presence and diversity of information technology is understandable since the home serves multiple functions in the lives of most Americans.

The home is capable of serving in any capacity that is desired by its dwellers, thanks to an ever-present environment of sophisticated information technology. The following are some of the more popular functions of the home:

- entertainment (perform leisure activities),
- marketplace (purchase goods and services),
- neighborhood (engage fellow community members),
- office (accomplish business tasks),
- refuge (minimize societal exposure), and
- school (educate oneself).

Most Americans spend the majority of their time in their homes, usually with other people. More often than not, people at home are engaged with some IT appliance. Technology that is devoted to the mundane tasks of cooking, cleaning, opening garage doors, and waking people up blends effortlessly with more stimulating entertainment-based devices. Channeling music from radio stations to home theater systems, sending international e-mail messages from the living room, or viewing real-time stock quotes from a television or cellular telephone are mundane, nearly automatic tasks of many daily household routines. This attention to media is significant. Americans consume on average slightly more than

nine hours of IT entertainment media every day of the year—a figure that has remained remarkably constant since the mid-1990s and will likely continue with moderate annual increases into the early 2000s. This saturation of the home with IT has a price. Americans have maintained a significant media spending level—at least $500 per person per year since the mid-1990s, an amount that is likely to double by the mid-2000s.

With this complex portrait of the home as an information technology center being so dominant, it is useful to review the history of IT. Doing so will show that while the modern home is without doubt more sophisticated than its historical counterparts, it is nevertheless still the progeny of a late-nineteenth-century phenomenon—the rise of modern mass media. So while the modern home is a target for aggressively priced personal computers, sophisticated digital home theater systems, and the compelling promises of a global Internet, its function as a primary center of IT-based mass media activity has remained relatively unchanged since the late 1800s.

Origins of Home-Based Information Technology

Few information technologies that affect home users were created solely for the purpose of serving the needs of home consumers without the notion of profit. Purely charitable reasons for inventing, producing, and distributing IT devices and services were and are nonexistent in the history of American IT in regard to the home. In fact, most IT devices slated for the home were designed as lures for corporate business—specifically, to gain their advertising dollars. One advantage of most IT media in the home, with the exception of non-icon components of the Internet, is that user literacy is not required either to buy or to use the information technology. This allows even people who do not have reading or writing skills to have the opportunity to experience a nearly constant stream of entertainment, communication, and information.

The telephone, available to homes in the 1870s, was touted as a tool for commerce and was accepted more rapidly by businesses than home consumers. Today, telephones are still more common in business offices than in individual residences: 99 percent of businesses have at least one telephone versus 95 percent for households.

A decade after news of the *Titanic* disaster reached American ears via telegraph in 1912 and only two years after Pennsylvania's KDKA in 1920 became the first operating radio station licensed by the federal government, radio broadcasters were selling airtime to advertisers. As the novelty and immediacy of radio entered and grew within the daily routines of home listeners, so too did the presence of advertisers.

Television was designed less for the enjoyment of home consumers and more as an advertising vehicle for corporate customers of the television networks. Cable television initially extended that idea and later added other channels on a subscription or pay-per-view basis. Commercial advertising rates have grown exponentially as a result of the popularity of television. Corporations have become willing to pay millions of dollars for single commercials during major sporting events such as the Super Bowl.

Overview of Information Technology in the Home

The home has never been completely isolated from new technology, nor has it ever been a completely safe haven from the pressures of work or the offerings of the entertainment industry. What has changed most markedly about IT in the home is not its basic functions—creating entertainment, promoting communication, and organizing information—but rather the type of information technology. The telephone allowed voice conversations, and the Internet allowed instant text communication via e-mail and instant-chat software. Broadcast television gave viewers several video channels to view. Cable television later provided dozens of such channels, and satellite television promises similar channels in bundles numbering in the hundreds.

As early as 1880, IT in the home was touted as revolutionary. In reference to the telephone, *Scientific American* saw the new device as ". . . nothing less than a new organization of society—a state of things in which every individual, however secluded, will have at call every other individual in the community" (Marvin, 1988). Similar proclamations have been made about every new technology since that time, even those that no longer exist, such as the videotext and videodisc, or those that have yet to enter mainstream use, such as high-definition television (HDTV) and Internet-based telephony. However, it was the telephone with its straightforward design and simple instructions that first put IT into the homes of the American public.

Patented by Alexander Graham Bell in 1876, the telephone made its way into the first home a year later, and it has captivated users ever since. Its resilient design, still basically the same as when it was first invented, has allowed people in disparate areas to communicate in ways that were unimaginable prior to its invention.

Yet, even though the telephone generated attention and had at its inception a unique ability to "cheat time," it did not diffuse rapidly into American homes. It took eighty years from the time of its invention to penetrate 75 percent of homes, and it was not until 1970 that it reached a penetration level of 93 percent.

Minority household penetration rates consistently rank 8 to 10 percentage points lower than their white counterparts. According to Alexander Belinfante (1998), the telephone gap between white and minority households in 1984 was approximately 13 percent. In 1999, white households had a national average telephone penetration rate of 95 percent, approximately 8 percent higher than the black and Hispanic rates of 86.9 percent and 86.7 percent, respectively. Such differences persist with respect to other IT devices as well.

Radio, the next technology to diffuse within the home, would show the vast potential for Americans to consume IT in their homes. It is still the benchmark by which all subsequent devices and services are compared; its low one-time price, immediate value to the consumer, and astonishingly fast acceptance by home consumers created the first ubiquitous home IT device.

Even the Great Depression, with its effect of diminishing personal expenditures on information goods and service by 25 percent, failed to slow the growth of radio receivers in the home. In 1929, less than a decade after commercial radio programming was introduced and only five years after national broadcasting began, the household penetration of radio was above 30 percent. In 1931, that percentage had jumped to more than 50 percent. By the end of the 1930s, close to 80 percent of all U.S. households had at least one radio. In 1950, that percentage was at 95 percent, and by 1970, radio penetration was at 99 percent, where it has remained constant. Approximately 12,000 FM (frequency modulation) and AM (amplitude modulation) radio stations transmit their signals to home users in the United States.

Television, while more expensive initially than radio, diffused even more rapidly into American households. In 1950, barely a decade after its public display at the 1939 World's Fair, television was in 9 percent of households. In twenty years, that percentage had increased more than tenfold to 95 percent. Since then, its household penetration has remained identical to that of radio at 99 percent. Yet even with the launching of two new broadcast television networks in the 1990s—the United Paramount Network (UPN) and the Warner Bros. Network (WB)—fewer than half of all television viewers watch the major networks. Instead, viewers are turning to cable television.

Driven by poor reception of traditional broadcast network television and relaxed regulation, the relatively dormant cable television systems that originated in the late 1940s and early 1950s saw explosive growth in the 1970s, the decade when cable was first present in at least 10 percent of American homes. By 1980, cable penetration had doubled to 20 percent, and by the end of the 1990s, cable penetration as measured by subscribership was approximately two-thirds of all households, although 97 percent of all households in the United States were wired for cable. If the newer Direct Broadcasting Satellite (DBS) services are included, virtually all households in the United States are capable of receiving network or cable television programming; close to 1 in 10 households have DBS service, often coupling their satellite offerings with standard cable service that provides local news and programming. All in all, home television viewers on average watch more than four hours of television-based programming a day. For those who are under eighteen years of age and over sixty-five years of age, that number jumps significantly to more than six hours.

Coupled with the explosion of cable programming in the 1970s and the interest of home consumers in watching theater movies at home, the time was ripe for the introduction of the home videocassette recorder (VCR). In 1975, Sony introduced the first commercial VCR, dubbed the Betamax. Its format was soon replaced by the VHS standard, and by 1982, close to 10 percent of homes had VCRs. After the U.S. Supreme Court ruled that taping commercial broadcasts from a television to a VCR within the confines of one's home was legal, promotion of and use of VCRs skyrocketed, reaching more than 50 percent of U.S. households by the mid-1980s. By 1999, that percentage had jumped to 90 percent. Alongside this trend of VCR use was a similar one for the use of a camcorder (portable video camera), which has resulted in one in five households owning a camcorder.

Video games also drew people, especially those under eighteen years of age, who were looking for hands-on electronic entertainment that was not being offered by broadcasting technologies. David Sheff, author of *Game Over* (1993), describes the rise of the video game industry beginning with the first commercially successful game. Pong, the first commercial video arcade game, was introduced outside of the home in 1972. Two years later, it was officially inside the home. A little more than a decade later, in 1986, Japan's Nintendo officially introduced the Nintendo Entertainment System (NES) to the United States. Led by a strong marketing effort and enchanted young users, its popularity soared. In 1990 alone, one in three households owned a Nintendo Entertainment System, at the time the most popular home game console ever created. Subsequent home video game consoles sport CD-ROMs and other technologies that rival those of personal computers. However, it is the Internet (an ever-newer technology that involves elements of video games, radio, television, and even traditional text media) that has taken the American home by storm.

In 1991, only 500,000 homes were connected to the Internet—less than 1 percent of the total homes in the United States. Yet by the end of 1999, more than half of all homes in the United States were connected to the Internet. Two main reasons for this gigantic increase in Internet penetration were the World Wide Web (WWW) and the fixed monthly rate subscription fees offered by Internet Service Providers (ISPs). The WWW, the graphical icon-based interface used by people to access the Internet easily via graphics and icons, was invented in 1989 and became popular with the introduction of the first web browser, Mosaic, in 1993. The web browser simplified "browsing" or "surfing" the Internet for items of interest. Low-wage overseas labor markets, improved production methods, faster product development cycles, and frenzied competition among the major home computer manufacturers are likely to keep the home penetration of the Internet on the rise.

Of note regarding penetration rates of IT in the home is that the rate of adoption depends on whether home users make a one-time purchase or whether they must commit to subscription pricing. For example, the gap between those who owned a radio and/or television (one-time purchases) and those who did not quickly closed, while the gaps for telephone and cable television (subscription services) have not. In other words, the penetration rates of the telephone and cable television have remained lower than their broadcasting counterparts. Moreover, while personal computer ownership and modem usage have skyrocketed among all sectors of the population, minority households still trail their white counterparts in online access. This phenomenon is partly a result of income, but it is also due to geography, ethnicity, housing, marital status, and a multitude of other personal demographics. One striking example is that the 314 U.S. Native American reservations and trust lands have an average telephone penetration rate of 46.6 percent—less than half of the national average. Only six of the forty-eight reservations with five hundred or more Native American households had telephone penetration levels that were above 75 percent—none exceeded 85 percent.

In short, IT devices—goods—penetrate households more quickly than services, even holding constant the total yearly cost of obtaining the good or service and the advertising levels of corporate advertisers. This goods-services dichotomy is arguably the result of households on the margin. In these households, the decision to pay a monthly fee is a difficult one that has to be made each month, which results in a condition that is not conducive to uninterrupted media services for those with limited or fixed resources.

Thus, in the American home, IT breeds IT. As a new technology is developed, marketed, and accepted by people in the homes, it does not replace a previous technology, even if it serves a similar function. For example, the telephone provided a simple way for people to communicate. While it did much to reduce daily traffic from one house to another for social calls, the telephone itself was not replaced by Internet e-mail, which in many cases serves the same function. Likewise, the introduction of television, while hurting the motion picture industry outside of the home, did not eliminate the use of the radio within the home. The personal computer has not sunk the home

video game industry, even while similar game titles are available on both IT devices. Network television survives despite aggressive growth in the cable television and the DBS industries. From the historical record, it is clear that Americans layer their home IT technologies, favoring abundance and choice of IT over pure efficiency, cost, or aesthetics.

Trends of Information Technology in the Home

The traditional media, such as broadcast television and radio, have a limited array of contents and a fixed rigid schedule to which users must conform. These characteristics exist partly because early IT devices were more concerned about functionality than about aesthetics. New media, such as the Internet, offer a wide range of content and greater flexibility for user customization, and home consumers are flocking to technologies that offer this customization.

The telephone is a representative example of this customization trend. Unlike the numerous color options and designs that exist for modern telephones, the original telephone design was available in exactly one color: black. Furthermore, the black telephone could not be bought; it had to be rented from the telephone company, which also numbered but one: AT&T. Specialized cords and adapters, now common, were not options until well into the latter half of the twentieth century. The modern telephone can be had in dozens of shapes and sizes, from numerous distributors. Those people who wish to make a telephone call can do so with the traditional desktop telephone, with cellular or satellite-based telephones, and even over the Internet—all for prices that are, even accounting for inflation, lower than ever. And the wonders continue.

From William Gibson's science fiction cult classic *Neuromancer* (1984), to more recent writings such as *What Will Be* (1997) by futurist Michael Dertouzos, to Erik Davis's media-studies-inspired *Techgnosis* (1998), writers have had little difficulty devising future IT devices and services for the home. According to these authors and the popular press, smaller, more personal devices that merge user and interface will likely dominate the IT environment of the home into the future. Function, as always, will be important, as will the ever-present concerns of privacy, security, and ease of use. Aesthetics, too, will play a more significant role than they have in the past as multinational conglomerates vie for the eyes, ears, and pocketbooks of household consumers. After all, if a company cannot differentiate its product from competitors, it will have difficulty becoming or remaining a successful company. The most frequently mentioned characteristics of future IT items for the home include the following:

1. ability to safeguard personal information using specialized security features,

2. ability to personalize received information depending on user-define preferences,

3. voice and data transmission using traditional and higher bandwidth networks,

4. entertainment capabilities such as electronic games and hyperlinked text documents,

5. customizable visual interface,

6. control of household appliances and timing devices,

7. datebook-type functions, including calendar, to do lists, and alarms for scheduled events,

8. location-neutral functionality, so the device can be used throughout the world,

9. low power consumption and the ability to recharge for repeated and prolonged uses, and

10. affordable cost both in time to learn and cost to buy.

The shaping of the American home is a continuous process. Innovation in home-based IT is rapid and will likely become more so in the future. The available IT provides nearly instantaneous access to the workings of a home and its associated systems. For example, a home user can start the dishwasher, turn on the oven, monitor children and pets, and even open the garage door using simple IT devices. While such features may seem common in the modern home IT environment, they were fantastic ideas even in the 1950s. Much of the modern IT ideas are equally farfetched, but they will likely produce tangible results. Either way, the evolution of information technology will continue, and American consumers will continue to experiment and accept many, if not most, of the new devices and services that are created and offered to the public.

See also: CABLE TELEVISION; CABLE TELEVISION, HISTORY OF; INFORMATION INDUSTRY; INTERNET AND THE WORLD WIDE WEB; RADIO BROADCASTING; RADIO BROADCASTING, HISTORY OF; TECHNOLOGY, ADOPTION AND DIFFUSION OF; TELEPHONE INDUSTRY; TELEPHONE INDUSTRY, HISTORY OF; TELEVISION BROADCASTING; TELEVISION BROADCASTING, HISTORY OF; VIDEO AND COMPUTER GAMES AND THE INTERNET.

Bibliography

Belinfante, Alexander. (1998). *Telephone Subscribership in the United States*. Washington, DC: Federal Communications Commission.

Campbell-Kelly, Martin, and Aspray, William. (1996). *Computer: A History of the Information Machine*. New York: Basic Books.

Davis, Erik. (1998). *Techgnosis*. New York: Three Rivers Press.

Dertouzos, Michael. (1997). *What Will Be: How the New World of Information Will Change Our Lives*. New York: HarperCollins.

Fischer, Claude S. (1992). *America Calling: A Social History of the Telephone to 1940*. Berkeley, CA: University of California Press.

Gibson, William. (1984). *Neuromancer*. New York: Ace.

Hafner, Katie, and Lyon, Matthew. (1996). *Where Wizards Stay Up Late: The Origins of the Internet*. New York: Touchstone.

Lin, Carolyn A. (1998). "Exploring Personal Computer Adoption Dynamics." *Journal of Broadcasting and Electronic Media* 42:95-12.

Marvin, Carolyn. (1988). *When Old Technologies Were New*. New York: Oxford University Press.

National Telecommunications and Information Administration (NTIA). (1995). *Falling Through the Net: A Survey of the "Have Nots" in Rural and Urban America*. Washington, DC: NTIA.

Rogers, Everett M. (1995). *Diffusion of Innovations*, 4th edition. New York: Free Press.

Rogers, Everett M., and Larsen, Judith K. (1984). *Silicon Valley Fever: Growth of High Technology Culture*. New York, NY: Basic Books.

Schement, Jorge Reina, and Curtis, Terry. (1995). *Tendencies and Tensions of the Information Age*. New Brunswick, NJ: Transaction Publishers.

Schement, Jorge Reina, and Forbes, Scott C. (1999). "The Persistent Gap in Telecommunications: Toward Hypothesis and Answers." In *Competition, Regulation, and Convergence: Current Trends in Telecommunications Policy Research*, eds. Sharon Eisner and Ingo Vogelsang Gillett. Mahwah, NJ: Lawrence Erlbaum.

Sheff, David. (1993). *Game Over*. New York: Random House.

Silverstone, Roger, and Hirsch, Eric, eds. (1992). *Consuming Technologies: Media and Information in Domestic Spaces*. New York: Routledge.

SCOTT C. FORBES

▌▨ HOMOSEXUALITY IN THE MEDIA

See: Gays and Lesbians in the Media;
Sex and the Media

▌▨ HUMAN-COMPUTER INTERACTION

Human-computer interaction (HCI) is the study of how people use computers, with the aim of making them easier to use. It has grown in importance as a topic as computers have become less expensive and, thus, are now used by many more people. In the early years of computers (the 1950s to the 1970s), computers were expensive and generally only used by skilled people, often computer scientists. The aim in writing programs was to squeeze the most power from a very limited memory and processing speed. It made sense to pay little attention to the usability of the system when the computer cost millions of dollars and could barely perform the task required. Since the 1980s, as computers have become less expensive and particularly as they have become more widespread, the problems of usability have become more intense. Systems developers can no longer assume that the user of a computer has a degree in computer science or is willing to spend considerable time learning to use it. At the same time, falling hardware costs mean that it has become feasible to allocate computational resources to an interface that is easier to use. But what makes an interface easier to use? That is what researchers in HCI attempted to find out, and it remains the challenge of current research and development.

Research and Development

In addition to computer science, psychology has played a significant role in HCI research. Early work on the design of aircraft cockpits focused on the problems of designing complex displays so that pilots could quickly and accurately make use of many sources of information and act on them. Researchers carefully studied other time-critical and safety-critical applications such as nuclear power stations. Although using a word processor is rarely a life-and-death affair, it can seem overwhelmingly complicated, considering that it should be a simple task. Cognitive psychologists draw on their experience of understanding human learning and problem-solving practices to explain the factors that make a problem easier or harder for a person to solve. This can be used to help to understand the difficulties that people have with using computer programs and to generate recommendations for the design of better interfaces (i.e., how the user will interact with the computer). It involves the application of the traditional scientific method—proposing a hypothesis about user behavior under a certain set of circumstances and then designing a controlled experiment to test the hypothesis. Work in this tradition may also be called "human factors" or "ergonomics."

In parallel with the analytic approach of psychologists, computer scientists explore the development of new computer interfaces in an attempt to solve the problems identified by these analyses. One major development has been the creation of graphical user interfaces such as the Macintosh user interface and Microsoft Windows. Instead of typing commands in order to manipulate, copy, and organize files, users can move small graphical representations ("icons") of the files and folders. They can make the computer carry out tasks by clicking on buttons that may contain text and/or an icon to illustrate what the button will do. Users may also choose commands from lists of names ("menus") that may be on a particular screen or that can drop down or pop up when the user clicks on a particular area. Different contexts for working, such as word-processing a document and working on a spreadsheet, can be provided by rectangles on the screen that can be overlapped ("windows"). To people who use computers on a regular basis, this discussion may sound rather odd. They might even wonder why there is any need to try to explain exactly what icons, menus, and windows are. However, a key point in HCI is the fact that users of computer systems can become so familiar with an interface that they find it normal forget that such an interface initially seemed strange and needed explanation. This was the problem with many of the early designs of computer applications for popular use. Since the designers were familiar with computers and found the designs easy to use, they often forgot that users who were new to computers would need a different, clearer design.

There are several reasons why graphical interfaces are popular. For example, one of the findings from cognitive psychology is that human beings are much better at recognizing something familiar (e.g., by choosing a command from a list) than they are at recalling it (e.g., remembering the exact name for a command without being given any clues). Thus, if computers provide a menu of commands to choose from, rather than requiring users to recall a command and type it into the computer, many more users are likely to be able to make the correct choice.

There is, however, a problem with this approach. If there are only ten things that can be done, then a menu of ten items is fine. If there are one hundred, it gets more complicated, requiring submenus with a resulting problem of whether the user will be able to guess the right submenu in which to look. If there are one thousand items, things are much more complicated. That explains in part why, despite the popularity of graphical user interfaces, text-based interfaces are still used. The Unix operating system is still mostly used with such a complex interface. Unix is a powerful system and there are many commands. It is popular with expert computer users who want access to these commands and are willing to take the time to learn them. Once learned, typing in a powerful command can be much faster than choosing a combination of menu items and doing a sequence of clicking and dragging of icons. It is also possible to program sequences of commands to automate many complex tasks. This is a classic design trade-off. The graphical interface may be easier to learn and faster to use for beginners, but the text-based interface may be much more efficient for experts.

Good introductory overviews of HCI are available in the form of textbooks (e.g., Preece et al., 1994; Dix, 1998) as well as books written by practitioners reflecting on their design experience and the general lessons that can be learned (e.g., Tognazzini, 1992, 1995; Cooper, 1995). The Association for Computing Machinery (ACM) publishes an accessible magazine in the area, called *interactions,* as well as providing numerous resources via its website. Research in HCI examines both the theory of how people reason about and with computer systems, as well as the development and testing of new kinds of interfaces. Some researchers also study how to integrate interface design and efficient evaluation of computer use into the cycle of product development.

Much can be learned from watching someone and noting their confusion as they try to use a computer system. Often, by careful analysis, it is possible to explain why the person was confused, to predict other likely areas of confusion, and to propose ways of redesigning the system to eliminate or at least reduce the chances of that confusion. People often reason by analogy. If the new computer application that they are currently using reminds them of another application that they already know, they will guess that doing something in this new application will do the same thing as in the old application. For example, if they are used to filling in an online form by hitting the tab key to get from one field to another, they will try and do the same thing in the current form. If it does not work (or worse, does something different, such as inserting a tab character into the form), they may not notice at first and will be all the more confused when they eventually do notice. Consistency in interfaces greatly increases their usability. Consistency can be external (i.e., it is similar to other, familiar interfaces) and also internal (i.e., two different parts of the system are similar). For example, imagine how confusing an internally inconsistent interface would be if, after filling in one form, the user must click on the "enter" button at the top of the form, while on the next form, the user, after filling in the form, must click on the "submit" button at the bottom of the form.

Metaphor can be useful in helping someone to understand a new application. Thus, the way a person can organize his or her computer files into folders can use the metaphor of a physical desktop, as in the Windows and Macintosh operating systems. However, metaphors can become confusing if they are used inconsistently. Other techniques to test an interface can be employed prior to doing a usability study. One can use a checklist of desirable interface features to include, or one can use a checklist of common interface errors. The interface can be assessed by comparison with such a list. In this way, certain problems can be detected in a very quick and cost-effective manner. For example, a checklist of desirable features might include the question "Does the interface provide consistent ways of doing similar actions?"

Usability and Design

The usability of a system depends on both textual and graphical aspects. In graphical user interfaces, icons are often used. A poorly designed icon may mean that the user cannot guess what it will do. If the image seems arbitrary, people may forget the meaning of an icon from one use to the next,

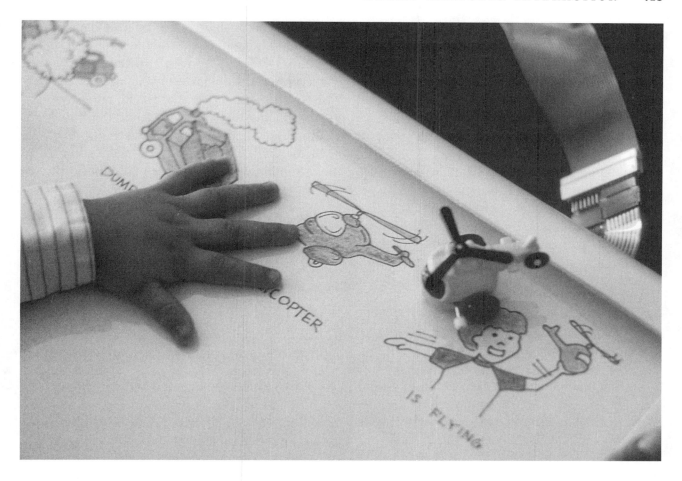

To accommodate the limited capabilities of toddlers, computer learning aids must use software that is designed to simplify the interactions that are necessary to obtain a goal, such as, in this case, a child being able to just touch a picture and have the computer provide the name of the object. (Lowell Georgia/Corbis)

greatly reducing their efficiency. Edward Tufte (1990) has explored many issues that are of importance to the design of comprehensible graphical interfaces. Similarly, textual design—choosing the names of menu options, actions, words on buttons, and so on—is harder than it might first appear. In designing a system and choosing those names, what should a certain option be called? Is it a technical term? If so, will the intended users know what it means? Is it ambiguous? It may not be to the interface designer, but it may be to the user. The selection of names is complex, and again there are ways of testing the usability of ideas, even before a system is actually built. One method is known as participatory design, in which the intended users of a new system are included in the design process.

It can be tempting when reading about the problems that users have, or even when observing a user test, to react in words like the following: "Well, they ought to read the manual or go on a training course. It's not my fault if they can't be bothered to learn to use my system." However, few users read the manual. People are too busy, they want to learn by doing, and often they have had such unproductive experiences with poorly written manuals that they are unwilling to take that route. Thus, designers must strive to make systems as easy to use as possible, so users can guess the most likely action that they should try. The difficulty of learning to use computer applications is a major problem. If designers could improve interfaces, they could create substantial productivity gains for the users of computer systems. Furthermore, designers need to justify why a company should bother to invest scarce resources in improving the usability of its products, and they need to show that such an investment yields substantially greater profits through greater sales of a more usable product.

It has already been noted that designers are tempted to think that all users are similar to them.

Thus, it is important in design to consider the likely background of the intended users. Often, there will be several different kinds of user all with slightly different needs. The design challenge is to cater to as many of those needs as possible, within the budget constraints. Trade-offs are inevitable. Including a given feature may help one group of users but confuse another, so should it be included or not? Users vary by what they may want to do with the software, and also by their background. They may be computer novices or experts. The needs of someone who is new to the system are different from the needs of someone who frequently uses the system. The former may want help and explanation, along with features to make it easy to learn how to use the application. The latter may be much more concerned with doing their tasks as quickly and accurately as possible and be irritated by "helpful" features that slow them down. For example, many graphical interfaces allow the user to carry out actions by a sequence of menu selections, where each stage of the process is explained in a series of text and graphic boxes that pop up on the screen. This helps a novice to the application to understand what to do and the other options that are possible. There may also be a "keyboard shortcut" available for experts who know exactly what they want to do and want to do it quickly. The shortcut is often an obscure combination of keys that must be pressed in a certain order. This is hard to learn (which is bad for the newcomer) but very fast to execute (which is good for the expert). Including the shortcut in the menu option creates an interface that benefits both groups.

As well as experience with computers, there are other ways in which the intended users of systems may be different in some way from their designers, and these differences should also be explicitly taken into account in the design process. People with disabilities have a particular set of needs. They may use special hardware or software configurations to enable them to use a computer application. It is important to check that an interface design is compatible with these different kinds of use. For example, a color display that conveys vital information only by whether a certain area on the screen is red or green will be confusing for a user with red-green colorblindness. The solution, as in other cases, is to provide additional ways of conveying the information: use color and shape, or color and text, for example. Other kinds of potential users who may need special design attention include children and people from countries and cultures different from that of the designer. This means that the designer must consider issues such as choice and style of language, alternative versions of the same language (such as British and American English), whether icons will be meaningful, the effect of graphics, and various other conventions. The format for dates is a classic convention problem—4/5/01 can mean either the 4th of May 2001 or the 5th of April 2001, depending on where in the world you are.

The design of interfaces involves both hardware and software. When certain kinds of input and output hardware become available or inexpensive enough for the intended task, new kinds of interfaces (designed in software) become possible. For example, color monitors and the mouse make it possible to design the kinds of graphical user interfaces that are now common. As handheld computers become more prevalent, particularly as they become networked, new opportunities for innovative interfaces will arise, along with commercial pressures that they should become as easy to use as other domestic appliances. Work on immersive virtual reality looks at how hardware such as very large monitors, wall projectors, or special goggles can be used to give users the illusion of actually traveling in a fabricated three-dimensional world as opposed to manipulating small images on a flat screen. People frequently use images to help them interact with computers, but why not use sound as well? At the moment, most computers only use sound in primitive ways, such as beeping when something is wrong, or for entertainment. Some researchers are working on more advanced ideas, such as being able to hear data as well as, or instead of, seeing it. This is known as "sonification." In addition, researchers are working on ways for a user to talk to a computer and for the computer to talk back. Such sound-based interfaces would be especially useful for people who have visual disabilities or for interacting via a mobile telephone or while driving.

In addition to applications that run on computers, such as word processors and databases, interface design is important for Internet use. Designing web pages, including interactive pages for shopping, pose whole new challenges for HCI. Online customers can be impatient, and if a website is difficult to use, they will very rapidly move on to a competitor's site and make their purchases there. Consequently, design for ease of use is a significant competitive advantage.

Conclusion

HCI is growing in importance as the number of people who interact with computers grows. The explosive growth of the Internet and of e-commerce has served to focus attention on the usability of websites as yet another kind of computer interface. HCI involves both fundamental theoretical research, experimentation, the creation of radically new ways of interacting with computers, and the practical development of computer applications that are easier to use.

See also: ARTIFICIAL INTELLIGENCE; COMPUTER LITERACY; COMPUTER SOFTWARE; ELECTRONIC COMMERCE; INTERNET AND THE WORLD WIDE WEB; SYSTEMS DESIGNERS.

Bibliography

Association for Computing Machinery. (2000). "Association for Computing Machinery." <http://www.acm.org>.

Baecker, Ronald M.; Buxton, William; and Grudin, Jonathan, eds. (1995). *Readings in Human-Computer Interaction: Toward the Year 2000*, 2nd edition. San Francisco: Morgan Kaufmann.

Bias, Randolph G., and Mayhew, Deborah J., eds. (1994). *Cost-Justifying Usability.* San Diego, CA: Academic Press.

Brice, Richard. (1997). *Multimedia and Virtual Reality Engineering.* Oxford, Eng.: Newnes.

Card, Stuart K.; Moran, Thomas P.; and Newell, Allen. (1983). *The Psychology of Human-Computer Interaction.* Hillsdale, NJ: Lawrence Erlbaum.

Cooper, Alan. (1995). *About Face: The Essentials of User Interface Design.* Foster City, CA: IDG Books Worldwide.

del Galdo, Elisa M., and Nielsen, Jakob, eds. (1996). *International User Interfaces.* New York: Wiley.

Dix, Alan J., ed. (1998). *Human-Computer Interaction.* Englewood Cliffs, NJ: Prentice-Hall.

Druin, Allison, ed. (1998). *The Design of Children's Technology; How We Design, What We Design and Why.* San Francisco: Morgan Kaufmann.

Furnas, George W.; Landauer, Thomas K.; Gomez, L. M.; and Dumais, Susan T. (1987). "The Vocabulary Problem in Human System Communication." *Communications of the ACM* 30(11):964–971.

Greenbaum, Joan, and Kyng, Morten, eds. (1991). *Design at Work: Cooperative Design of Computer Systems.* Hillsdale, NJ: Lawrence Erlbaum.

Landauer, Thomas K. (1995). *The Trouble with Computers: Usefulness, Usability, and Productivity.* Cambridge, MA: MIT Press.

Nielsen, Jakob. (1993). *Usability Engineering.* London: Academic Press.

Nielsen, Jakob, and Mack, Robert L., eds. (1994). *Usability Inspection Methods.* New York: Wiley.

Norman, Donald A. (1988). *The Psychology of Everyday Things.* New York: Basic Books.

Norman, Donald A. (1999). *The Invisible Computer: Why Good Products Can Fail, the Personal Computer Is So Complex and Information Applicances Are the Solution.* Cambridge, MA: MIT Press.

Preece, Jenny; Rogers, Yvonne; Sharp, Helen; and Benyon David, eds. (1994). *Human-Computer Interaction.* Reading, MA: Addison-Wesley.

Raman, T. V. (1997). *Auditory User Interfaces: Toward the Speaking Computer.* Boston: Kluwer Academic.

Shneiderman, Ben. (1997). *Designing the User Interface: Strategies for Effective Human-Computer Interaction.* Reading, MA: Addison-Wesley.

Tognazzini, Bruce. (1992). *Tog on Interface.* Reading, MA: Addison-Wesley.

Tognazzini, Bruce. (1995). *Tog on Software Design.* Reading, MA: Addison-Wesley.

Tufte, Edward. (1990). *Envisioning Information.* Cheshire, CT: Graphics Press.

MICHAEL TWIDALE

HUMAN INFORMATION PROCESSING

Because human information processing has to do with how people receive messages, it is a critical topic in communication study. Message reception consists of paying attention to particular messages in the environment and then using them as a guide to behavior. This is a very active process that consists of three separate but related activities: information selection, interpretation, and retention.

Information Selection

Humans operate in an environment that is filled with signals of various kinds. These may be in the form of sights (visual cues), sounds (auditory cues), touch (tactile cues), taste (gustatory cues), or smell (olfactory cues). The number of such cues that are available to individuals at any instant is almost limitless, and were individuals to try to pay attention to all these, they would immediately find themselves in a total information overload situation. It is therefore necessary for people to select and use some of these cues, while ignoring others. This is an extremely important and complex activity, one that people perform repeatedly every waking moment. At the same time, it is a process that occurs in the background of individuals' experiences, and in a manner of which they are often only minimally aware. For example, consider what happens when a person arrives at an unfamiliar airport terminal at the end of a flight. The person exits the plane through the jetway and walks through the door into the terminal. At that instant, the person is bombarded with any number of visual and auditory messages that compete for his or her attention—far more than the person could possibly fully attend to at one time. There are signs, people talking, people moving this way and that, messages being announced over the speakers in the building, vendors, stores, newspaper racks, and so on. Depending on the person's goals—to find luggage, for example—and his or her prior experience in similar situations, the person begins to attend selectively to the messages in the environment, taking particular note of those that are appropriate to the successful accomplishment of the goal. Appropriate messages in this situation might include signs and the direction in which other people getting off of the same flight are walking. The person must ignore other messages that seem less vital in terms of meeting the immediate goal. If the person's intentions were different, he or she might well tune into and use a completely different set of messages. For example, if the person were going to have a two-hour layover while waiting for a connecting flight and had not eaten in several hours, he or she might tune into and use a set of visual, auditory, and olfactory messages that would help in locating a place to purchase a meal or snack.

Information Interpretation

Interpretation consists of attaching meaning to the messages to which individuals selectively attend. Whenever people take note of any message, they make some basic interpretations; they decide if the message is amusing or alarming, true or untrue, serious or humorous, new or old, or contradictory or consistent. When a person decides to watch a television program or movie, for example, he or she makes all of these determinations as a viewer, often without thinking all that much about the process. Similarly, in the case of the airport example mentioned above, noticing

various signs was one component of message reception. However, to be useful, the messages on the signs must also be interpreted. People must know what exactly the words or arrows mean.

In all situations, people's actions will ultimately be based on the meanings they attach to the messages that they have selected. While the above examples may imply that selection, interpretation, and action are simple "1-2-3" activities, this is clearly not the case. Individuals cycle through each of these three activities in such a rapid-fire manner, that it is really quite difficult to identify which component is occurring and in what order. With the airport signs, for example, the person must determine that these were, in fact, signs (and therefore appropriate places to look for messages about directions) even before he or she selectively attended to them and began to interpret the specific words and drawings..

Information Retention

Retention (i.e., memory) plays an indispensable role in selection and interpretation, as the previous examples imply. An individual's memory of previous message-reception activities tells the person how to approach any new message-reception situation. Even though the person may be in an airport that he or she has never been in before, memories about airports in general help guide that person through the new situation in terms of previous experiences in circumstances that are judged to be similar. Thus, for example, through message retention, the person knows what signs look like and he or she knows that they usually provide information that is helpful for navigation.

The ease with which remembered information is available to people seems so natural that it is easy to overlook the complexity of the underlying processes that are involved. People have little difficulty recalling the information that they need in order to go about their daily routines. This includes such information as where to locate things in the home, how to start and operate an automobile, how to travel from home to work, how to perform duties at work, and so on. Morton Hunt (1982, p. 6) provided an excellent description of this complex retention process:

> Although every act of thinking involves the
> use of images, sounds, symbols, meanings,
> and connections between things, all stored

in memory, the organization of memory is so efficient that most of the time we are unaware of having to exert any effort to locate and use these materials. Consider the ranges of kinds of information you keep in, and can easily summon forth from, your own memory: the face of your closest friend . . . the words and melody of the national anthem . . . the spelling of almost every word you can think of . . . the name of every object you can see from where you are sitting . . . the way your room looked when you were eight . . . the set of skills you need to drive a car in heavy traffic . . . and enough more to fill many shelves full of books.

Because of the information retention process, individuals can answer in a split second, and with great accuracy, questions such as "Who was the first president of the United States?" or "What was the address of the house in which you grew up?" Moreover, individuals can perform these operations in far less time than it would take to retrieve the information from any other source, including the fastest computer.

Factors That Influence Message Reception

Many factors influence message selection, interpretation, and retention. A number of these factors have to do with the individual receiver. Others are related to the nature of the message and the source, as well as to the media and environment.

Receiver Influences

Physical, social, and psychological needs play an important role in human information processing behavior. When an individual is hungry, for example, this need will be likely to influence the cues to which he or she attends and the way in which those cues are interpreted. Pretzels in a food stand in the airport are not nearly as likely to be noticed or purchased by a passenger who has just eaten a meal as they are by one who has not.

Attitudes, beliefs, and values are also important influences on how individuals select, interpret, and retain messages. For example, a prime rib dinner that is seen as a mouth-watering delight by some people will be viewed very differently by a vegetarian or by someone whose religious beliefs suggest that the cow is a sacred animal.

In any situation, goals have a great influence on message reception. One example was provided earlier in the airport illustration. A person with the goal of proceeding to the baggage claim area engages in much different message-reception behavior than does a person in a similar environment who has two hours to "waste" while waiting for a connecting flight. One's goals—whether related to specific short-term activities or long-term personal or occupational agendas—are very influential factors in message reception.

Differing capabilities lead to differing message-reception patterns. Most obvious is the example of language capability. The message-reception possibilities and probabilities of a bilingual individual are considerably more extensive than those of someone who speaks only one language. For the same reasons, people who are trained in particular professional and technical fields have access to materials and documents that others do not. Having a specific use for messages also influences selection, interpretation, and retention. For example, reading a book over which one will be tested is generally a quite different information processing experience from reading a book for pure enjoyment.

Individuals differ in their styles of communication, and these differences often lead to differences in message reception. Generally, those people who have highly verbal communication styles (i.e., who talk extensively about their own thoughts and opinions) are likely to have exposure to less information produced by others in interpersonal situations, simply because of the limitations that their style places on the contributions of others. As another example, if that highly verbal person generally uses a questioning style in interactions with others, this will elicit more information from others, and, in turn, the availability of more information becomes an influence on message reception.

Experience and habit are powerful forces in message reception. Once learned, information-reception patterns are likely to be repeated, and hence, habit and prior behavior are important influences and predictors of future information-reception behavior.

Message Influences

Most of the messages that individuals attend to have other people as their source. However, some messages come from the physical environment, and there are other messages for which the individuals themselves are the source. In many situations, people have choices as to which type of messages to attend to and use, and the presence or absence of alternatives is a significant influence on message reception. In the airport scenario, for example, the person could seek the necessary directions by looking at a sign, by watching the flow of pedestrian traffic, or by asking someone. These alternative messages may be more or less easy to attend to, interpret, and retain. A person having a preference for one approach over another is affected by personal style, past experience, and other factors. Messages also vary in their form—in the communication modality involved—and this often influences the likelihood that they will be noticed and acted on. For example, the smell of rotten and decaying garbage is generally more attention-getting that a picture of rotten garbage. Signals may also vary in their physical characteristics (e.g., their color, brightness, size, or intensity), and these factors may well influence message reception. In terms of getting attention, large headlines in a newspaper, for example, are generally more effective than small headlines, and color pictures are generally more effective than black-and-white pictures.

How elements of a message are organized and how novel a particular message is are two additional factors that influence message reception. The way in which information is presented in newspapers is a good illustration of how message organization can influence message reception. Newspaper articles usually begin with a lead paragraph that summarizes all key facts and then provide subsequent paragraphs that provide supporting details. This organization permits and encourages readers to get the general themes of articles without having to read through all of the details. If another organizational approach were used (e.g., if the first section of the article included a variety of details without highlighting key issues), the change would probably have a substantial influence on selection, interpretation, and retention. Novel messages stand out and gain attention simply because they are unfamiliar. Advertisers and marketers make frequent use of this insight by including novel images and approaches in the hope of increasing the amount of attention that is paid to their messages. An advertising message that has text and images printed upside down is one example of a device

being used to increase attention. Opening the hoods of all cars in a car lot as a means of gaining attention is another.

Source Influences

Proximity can be an important factor in communication. Generally speaking, the closer individuals are to a particular information source, the more likely that source is to become an object of attention. This is one explanation for the generally influential role played by family members, neighbors, peer group members, friends, and the community. In the most literal view, proximity refers to physical distance, but in an age when technology so permeates the lives of individuals, the limitations of physical distance are sometimes less significant that those of virtual, or electronic, distance. That is, in some sense, a person who is easily available on e-mail, in a chat room, or through a "buddy list" may have as much or more proximity—and hence as much influence—as someone who is quite close physically.

The way in which individuals process messages often has a good deal to do with how attractive—physically or socially—they find a message source to be. Simply said, individuals who are perceived as being attractive have the good (and sometimes not so good) fortune of having their presence and their messages taken account of more than other people do. The influence of attraction often extends beyond selection; it can influence interpretation and retention as well. What is often referred to as to the "magnetism" or "charisma" that is attributed to celebrities, athletes, or political leaders who capture public favor probably has its foundation in a factor as basic as attraction. Also important to message reception is similarity. Generally speaking, people are drawn to—and hence are more likely to engage in communication with—others who are similar to them. Sometimes, these similarities have to do with factors such as gender, level of education, age, religion, race, occupation, hobbies, or language capacity. In other circumstances, the similarities that are important are needs, beliefs, goals, or values.

When sources are considered to be credible and authoritative, their messages are likely to attract more attention than the messages of people who are not considered to be credible or authoritative. These characteristics are also likely to influence the interpretation and retention of messages. Sometimes, the credibility of a source is associated with particular topics about which the source is considered to have special expertise. For example, an individual who is a stockbroker may be regarded as a good source of information on the stock market industry. In other cases, an individual's credibility might span a number of subjects because of the combination of his or her occupation, education, and celebrity. The intentions and motives that people associate with a sender in a particular situation are also important message-reception influences. If people believe an individual has their best interests at heart, their response to the individual's messages is likely to be quite different from what it would be if they assume that the individual's intentions or motives are simply to sell or deceive.

The manner in which messages are delivered also influences message selection, interpretation, and retention. In the case of spoken messages, volume and rate of speaking, pitch, pronunciation, accents, and the use of pauses and nonfluencies (such as "ummm" or "you know" or "like") can all influence communication. Visual cues such as gestures, facial expressions, and eye contact may also be significant factors.

Status—position or rank—can also be a factor in message reception. Power and authority refer to the extent to which a source is capable of dispensing rewards or punishment for selecting, remembering, and interpreting messages in a particular manner. These factors may come into play in communication situations with a parent, teacher, supervisor, or any other person who occupies a position of authority. The significance that people attach to the positions that are occupied by these individuals or to the power that they have over valued resources (e.g., grades, salary, praise) often has a dramatic influence on message reception.

Media and Environmental Influences

Media can account for significant differences in the selection process and in the nature of interpretation and retention. A message may well be reacted to quite differently depending on whether it arrives in the receiver's environment through a newspaper, the television, the Internet, a videotape, an e-mail, or face-to-face interaction. Of all media, television has received the most attention from researchers. Newspapers are probably second in line in terms of the amount of attention that they have attracted from researchers. As the relatively newer media—such as computers, the Internet, e-mail, teleconferencing, and wireless telephones—have risen in popularity, the amount of research dedicated to these topics has increased. This is a trend that will no doubt continue.

Environmental considerations, such as whether one is at home or at work, alone or with a group, crowded into an overheated movie theater or watching an outdoor concert on a rainy day can and do influence human information processing. These factors are examples of influences that are associated with what might be termed the "setting" or "context" of a communication event. Other environmental influences have to do with factors such as repetition, consistency, and competition. If a particular message is presented just once or twice, such as when a telephone number is provided when someone calls an operator for "information," it is unlikely to have a lasting influence on message reception. On the other hand, if it is a message that is presented over and over, as with a telephone number that is used on a regular basis, the effect is quite different. Repetition can and does affect the way in which people select, interpret, and retain messages.

Closely related to repetition is the concept of consistency. The consistency of messages is often an important factor in message processing. If a person repeatedly heard the phrase "Spain is a wonderful place to live" from a variety of different sources, for example, the consistency is likely to influence the person's message reception. However, if the person also heard a number of people saying that "Spain is a horrible place to live," this competition, or inconsistency, would have a different influence on the person's message reception. For this reason, if individuals hear only good things about a political candidate about whom they had little prior knowledge, the effect on information processing will be quite different from that of individuals who hear an equal number of positive and negative messages. In the former instance, the individuals would be influenced by message consistency; in the latter instance, they would be influenced by message competition.

Conclusion

Communication scholars and professionals recognize that human information processing is a vital part of communication. People who lack familiarity with communication theory tend to assume that communication outcomes are simply the result of what is said or done by a sender and how it is said or done. However, as is apparent from the above discussion, message reception is an extremely complex process—one for which it is very difficult to predict results.

It is certainly the case that the sender and message are important to message reception as it is commonly understood. However, the most significant factors—both because of their number and importance—are probably the factors that have to do with the receiver. An extreme example would be a situation where a receiver cannot understand the language or concepts of a message, has little need or concern about the part of the message that he or she can discern, and has little or nothing in common with the sender. The receiver is unlikely to take much away from the communication situation other than frustration, despite the best efforts of a persuasive speaker and careful attention to the planning and execution of the message. A less extreme example, but one with the same outcome, would be a situation where the receiver does not like the sender, the sender is trying to convince the receiver to support a political candidate whose views are inconsistent with the receiver's beliefs, and the discussion is taking place in an environment in which the receiver is surrounded by friends who share his or her views about the sender and the candidate. How likely is it that the receiver will be influenced in the direction that the sender intends? Not very. It is also because of the complexity of message reception that simple messages such as "just say no" or "smoking can be hazardous to your health" are seldom as influential as senders hope they will be.

Because of the complexity of reception—and the resulting difficulty in predicting communication outcomes—being mindful of these dynamics and the influences that are involved provides the best available assistance for improved communication understanding and effectiveness.

See also: ADVERTISING EFFECTS; COMMUNICATION STUDY; CULTURE AND COMMUNICATION; MODELS OF COMMUNICATION.

Bibliography

Cohen, Gillian. (1989). *Memory in the Real World.* Hillsdale, NJ: Lawrence Erlbaum.

Hoffman, Donald D. (1998). *Visual Intelligence: How We Create What We See.* New York: W. W. Norton.

Hunt, Morton. (1982). *The Universe Within.* New York: Simon & Schuster.

Katz, Elihu; Blumler, Jay G.; and Gurevitch, Michael. (1974). *The Uses of Mass Communication.* Beverly Hills, CA: Sage Publications.

Loftus, Geoffrey R., and Loftus, Elizabeth F. (1976). *Human Memory: The Processing of Information.* Hillsdale, NJ: Lawrence Erlbaum.

Maslow, Abraham. (1943). "A Theory of Human Motivation." *Psychological Review* 50:370–396.

National Institute of Mental Health. (1982). *Television and Behavior: Ten Years of Scientific Progress and Implications for the Eighties,* Vol. 1. Rockville, MD: Author.

Ramachandran, V. S., and Blakeslee, Sandra. (1998). *Phantoms in the Brain: Probing the Mysteries of the Human Mind.* New York: William Morrow.

Ruben, Brent D., and Stewart, Lea P. (1998). *Communication and Human Behavior,* 4th edition. Needham Heights, MA: Allyn & Bacon.

BRENT D. RUBEN

I

∎ INDUSTRY

See: Cable Television; Culture Industries, Media as; Film Industry; Globalization of Media Industries; Information Industry; Magazine Industry; Newspaper Industry; Publishing Industry; Radio Broadcasting; Recording Industry; Telephone Industry; Television Broadcasting

∎ INFORMATION

Millions of people around the world live surrounded by information and information technologies. They expect to hear the news on the radio, enjoy entertainment programming on the television, purchase any book in print, and find a website on the Internet. They expect their homes to contain televisions, cable, videocassette recorders, compact discs, answering machines, fax machines, telephones, personal computers, and satellite dishes. Many work in occupations where they produce and distribute information that is of value to consumers and businesses. In other words, the lives of hundreds of millions—perhaps even billions—of people depend on information. On a typical morning, families around the world will turn on the radio to hear the news, read the morning paper, watch the weather channel on cable, make a telephone call, and gather office reports and schoolbooks—all before anyone leaves the house. In fact, they are so used to this way of living that they take information for granted.

What Is Information?

Many information users might find it hard to respond to the question "What is information?" To begin to form an answer, some basic observations are necessary. First of all, many words convey the idea of information—words such as "data," "knowledge," "writing," "speaking," "sign," and "symbol," to name just a few. Second, a name, a poem, a table of numbers, a novel, and a picture all contain a shared quality called "information." Third, most people will acknowledge that a message passed between two friends contains information. And, fourth, it is evident that many people put a high value on some information but not all information. Each of these four characteristics offers clues to answering the question "What is information?"

One clue can be found in an everyday behavior. People make decisions on a daily basis about all sorts of situations; and, when they do, they often seek information to help them make those decisions. When confronting a choice, people often find that they need more information in order to make a decision. For example, when considering the purchase of an automobile, a potential buyer might ask a neighbor for advice, read a consumer magazine, or take a car for a test drive. Each of these actions provides information to help the person decide which car to buy. Individuals who are confronting important decisions often seek as much information as they can obtain. In contrast, when facing a decision with little or no available information, individuals may hesitate to make a choice. Therefore, the human need to make decisions creates a demand for information and leads to the interest in understanding information.

Information scientists generally emphasize that individuals mostly use information to reduce uncertainty—that is, to clarify something of interest in order to make a decision. Most modern information scientists agree with a popular definition of information such as the following: "Information is a coherent collection of data, messages, or cues organized in a particular way that has meaning or use for a particular human system" (Ruben, 1988, p. 19). This definition may seem vague, but that is because information comes in so many forms.

Humans are always trying to make sense of the world around them, and for that they need data. In fact, anything can provide data because data are the raw stimuli that human brains use to produce information. An ocean, a thunderstorm, and a crowd all become data as soon as someone tries to make sense of them. A thunderstorm, for example, might be just so much noise and water to one person, but to a meteorologist, that same noise and water might form the beginning of an understanding of weather patterns. By observing the direction of the storm and measuring its force, the meteorologist is producing data. If the data is then organized into statistical tables, or into a weather report, the meteorologist will have transformed data into information. The weather report on the evening news, thus, conveys information that had its beginning in data. However, data only become information when organized into a form that can be communicated, such as the weather report. Data are the observations or cues collected in order to produce information, and information is what individuals share with each other when they communicate.

Humans build ideas from information. All humans convert data into information and then use information to reduce the uncertainty they face when making decisions—from simple decisions such as choosing a cereal for breakfast to complex decisions such as choosing a college. Furthermore, that same mental versatility gives humans the power to perform a truly remarkable feat. Every person can enter a room, close the door, shut off the lights (along with other stimuli), and emerge later with a new idea—that is, with new information. No old information was lost or consumed, yet new information is added, and for no additional expenditure of energy beyond the energy expended when thinking. In other words, the same amount of information can produce many new ideas without being used up.

Similarly, two individuals can receive the same information, think about it, and produce new information with opposing interpretations. What is remarkable is that the information each received was the same, while the new information produced was different: same input, different outputs because each brain is unique. Each human takes data as input, organizes the input into a form that produces new information, and then makes sense of it by relating it to other ideas, thus bringing forth individual knowledge. The brain can expend a quantity of energy and think no new thoughts, or it can expend that same quantity of energy and invent a new cure for cancer. Brains are so capable of manipulating information that they can recombine the same information into an infinite number of new ideas. Nothing in the world of physical things behaves this way.

The Idea of Information in the Sciences

Information has become a useful concept in the sciences. For example, cellular biologists speak of deoxyribonucleic acid (DNA) as a library that contains information; they consider genes to be information that is communicated to a new cell through mitosis. Economists discuss money as information that is increasingly transmitted across the Internet as electronic commerce. And, computer scientists consider each bit on a hard disk to be the smallest quantity of data. Each of these fields of inquiry has achieved advances by applying the idea of information to the problems that they study. However, whether they are actually describing information or employing the concept of information as a metaphor remains controversial. For example, some information scientists argue that when biologists describe DNA as a library that contains information, they are using the concept of information as a metaphor; some biologists, in contrast, argue that DNA is actually information. No one has yet developed a theory to explain this controversy. Nevertheless, in these fields and in others, the idea of information has been a useful concept for solving scientific problems. As a useful word in the English language, "information" has a very long history.

Information in Historic Language

The word that English speakers recognize as "information" has its origins in the Latin word *informare*. The Latin *informare* meant to give form to, to shape, to form an idea of, or even to describe, so the seed of the modern meaning can be discerned in the use of *informare* to mean the shaping of an idea in one's head—that is, to inform.

Geoffrey Chaucer introduced the word "information" into the English language in the "Tale of Melibee," one of his *Canterbury Tales*: "Whanne Melibee hadde herd the grete skiles and resons of Dame Prudence and hire wise informaciouns and techynges." The "Tale of Melibee" was probably written sometime between 1372 and 1382. Chaucer's use of the word "informaciouns" (informations) would roughly fit the meaning that contemporary English speakers give to the word "sayings." However, as time went by, other meanings gained greater popularity.

In *Gulliver's Travels* (1727), Jonathan Swift applied a meaning to the word "information" that appears as early as the mid-fifteenth century and sounds more familiar: "It was necessary to give the reader this information." Thomas Jefferson, in an 1804 letter, used "information" as if it referred to a physical object: "My occupations . . . deny me the time, if I had the information, to answer them."

In the twentieth century, scientists began to write as if information were a quantifiable variable, as in the following passage from the November 1937 issue of *Discovery*: "The whole difficulty resides in the amount of definition in the [television] picture, or, as the engineers put it, the amount of information to be transmitted in a given time." By the beginning of the twenty-first century, English speakers had adopted the senses of information as a physical object and quantifiable variable. Taken together, these uses facilitate communicating in an information society.

Information Versus Physical Objects

It seems so simple, but to make full use of the idea of information, people play a curious game with words. To create a language of information, people must adapt the language of the real world. In everyday conversations, individuals speak about information as though it were something made from physical materials. For example, a teacher might decide that one report contains more information than another. Such a comparison implies that information is a quantity that can be measured in terms of more and less. That same teacher might describe the reports as if they were jars filled with

information, so that one report might be filled with more information than the other.

Of course, information does not fill jars, nor can it be easily determined when one has more or less information. Questions that are applicable to physical objects make less sense when applied to forms of information. What color is information? Is one idea bigger than another? Does one idea weigh more than another? When information is lost, where does it go? These questions seem illogical when asked of information because information is symbolic, not physical; that is, information exists as meaning in the minds of humans, whereas objects of the physical world take up space and exist whether or not anyone thinks about them. As a result of this difference, communicating about information poses a challenge because the English language has a limited vocabulary for representing the symbolic realm of information. English speakers solve this problem by employing words that are meant to describe the physical world. In other words, when members of the English-speaking world discuss information, they pretend that information is similar to a physical object. This makes sense even though information does not behave in the same way as a physical object.

Consider that if a person gives a sweater as a gift, the recipient gains the sweater, while the gift giver no longer has it; an exchange has resulted, and resources have moved from one place to another. The gift recipient has gained a sweater, while the gift giver has lost a sweater. One might even see this as a kind of law of nature—for an exchange to occur, someone must gain something and someone must lose something. This "law" applies to all physical objects from soup to nuts. However, information is different.

If, for example, someone writes a manuscript for a book, that person possesses a new manuscript—information—that did not exist before. If the manuscript is sold to a publisher, that publisher possesses the manuscript and may print it as a book. Clearly, an exchange has taken place; the publisher owns the information as a manuscript and the writer has money from the publisher. However, even though the writer sold the manuscript, he or she still has the information. The information remains in the writer's computer or perhaps in a folder; he or she can still read it out loud and even give a copy of the text to a friend. Unlike the example of the sweater, the writer has not lost the information by exchanging it for money.

This paradox of the physical world applies to all kinds of information. Whether the information in question is a manuscript or a piece of software or a movie or a poem, when it is given away, it still remains with the creator of the information. For unlike physical objects, information can be easily copied, and nearly always, it is the copy that is exchanged. Indeed, the ongoing revolution in information technology is all about exponential increases in the ease and fidelity with which information can be copied and transmitted. A person can experience this phenomenon by creating and copying a software file for a friend. The friend can use the file, though the original remains with the creator of the file. Once the friend has the file, he or she can copy it and distribute it to others. In this way, the potential spread of the file is unlimited. The file will continue to disperse as long as someone will copy it and pass it on to another person. Thus, whereas the exchange of a physical good, such as a sweater, requires the giver to relinquish it so the receiver can have it, information can be duplicated and exchanged with ease so both giver and receiver can have it at the same time. It would seem that information is without limits, unlike physical objects in the material world.

However, information can be treated as a physical object. The fact that a person can read from a book while physically holding it in his or her hands proves that information can be configured to the characteristics of a physical object. When information is recorded onto a physical medium, such as paper, tape, celluloid, plastic, or metal, the medium allows the information to be treated as a physical object. After all, a book can be shipped from New York to San Francisco in the same box with a sweater. Similarly, a compact disc (CD) can be transported thousands of miles away from the studio where it was cut. People make lists and carry them around in their pockets, in the same way that they carry keys, pens, and coins—all physical objects. People's daily lives are full of instances where they treat information as though it were a physical object. Nevertheless, regardless of how tangible the form, it is still information—an encyclopedia retains all of the information printed in it no matter how much one copies from it.

The packaging of information, which confers on it the characteristics of a physical object, also helps its transformation into an economic good. The facility with which information can be distributed, in part because of its remarkable ease of duplication, encourages entrepreneurs to explore the commercial possibilities. And, because information can be exchanged for profit, there can emerge markets for information of any kind for which there is a buyer and a seller. Increasingly, the production and distribution of information dominates the U.S. economy. The largest corporations generate information as their product and trade it around the world. Here, then, is the basis for the vast information economy that binds together the economic systems of the world.

Even so, the very ease of duplication that makes information so potentially profitable marks its own Achilles' heel. Information can be duplicated so easily that others can take the information being sold, copy it, and sell it too, whether it belongs to them or not. All sellers of information must contend with the possibility that the information they hope to sell can easily be copied and resold by others. The more illegal copies sell, the less incentive there is for the legitimate producer to offer information for sale. A software company may decide to take a program off the market because it is losing too much money as a result of illegal copying. When too many illegal copies circulate, the legal seller loses the incentive to sell because he or she is not making a profit from the sale of that information. In this way, the selling of illegal copies threatens the legal sale of information and discourages legal sellers from offering their goods. As a result, valuable and interesting information may be kept off the market. When that happens, everyone suffers.

Because information is valued so highly, solutions have emerged to reconcile the vulnerability of information to the characteristics of the physical world. In the world of physical economic goods, producers, sellers, and buyers maintain order through contracts. The same can be applied to the intangible world of information. When the writer in the example above sells the manuscript to the publisher, he or she has agreed to a very important limitation. Even though the writer still possesses the information, the publisher controls the distribution of it. In effect, though the writer may still have the text of the manuscript stored in his or her computer, the writer cannot offer it for sale; whereas, the publisher may bring the information in the manuscript to market with the exclusive right to sell it. As a result, the ability to control the availability of goods, which is so critical to physical markets, can be artificially created for information.

The menace to the orderly functioning of information markets is so threatening that governments have also stepped in and legislated protections for the sale and purchase of information. These laws generally fall under the legal class of copyrights and patents. By registering a text such as a song, or a design such as an invention, with the proper government agency, an individual or organization receives an exclusive right to sell and distribute that information for a fixed period of years. Should anyone else attempt to distribute the same information without permission, then the government is obligated to protect the owners by prosecuting those people who are guilty of illegal use. Without legal protections, no commercial producer of information could expect to profit from his or her product because anyone could take it and reproduce it. Fortunately, legal protections against unlawful copying function well enough that information markets thrive.

If the easy duplication of information poses a threat to the orderly functioning of markets, that same attribute offers an advantage to another group of enterprising producers. These individuals write software and then make it available as shareware and freeware. These two unusual kinds of software take advantage of the remarkable ease with which information can be copied and distributed. The author of a shareware program says in effect, "Here is my product. If you like it pay me for it. If you don't want to pay me, then keep it anyway." Surprisingly, software authors who introduce shareware can be quite successful; their product may take off, or they may be hired by a software firm that is impressed with their code-writing abilities. Clearly, the success of shareware depends both on distribution within the market and on distribution outside of the market, because it is both sold and given away. Yet, even in this strange hybrid of selling and giving, the heart of the strategy lies in the essential feature of information, the fact that the producer retains the information after distributing it to others.

Clearly, the way in which individuals think about information influences the way in which they act. People are so comfortable imagining all manner of possibilities for the uses of information that new information applications are invented with ease. However, no two people interpret information in exactly the same way, nor do they place the same value on it. If the first major feature of information is its ease of duplication, then its second major feature is its subjective value. Information conveys a different meaning to each person and, consequently, a different value to each person. Take, for example, a reading of the *Iliad*. One person might read it to learn about the culture of preclassical Greece. A second person might read it as an allegory of the role of the hero in Western literature. A third person might read it as a mighty adventure story. The text remains identical in every reading, but each reader takes fully different meanings from it. This occurs because the meaning of the information in the *Iliad*, as with any piece of information, rests not in the text or content but in the mind of the reader. Every person's brain contains a unique configuration of knowledge, and it is within that context that new information receives its special meaning.

Ultimately, the meaning and value of information is subjective. The progression whereby humans convert data into information and then frame it within their previous thoughts and experiences results in knowledge. Information is produced from data, and then knowledge is produced from information. Thus, knowledge is an attribute of an individual. When individuals seek to communicate knowledge, they have to transform it back into information that can be communicated. All knowledge, then, is derived from information and grounded in the ideas that humans have previously communicated to each other; even new ideas derive from the accumulation of previous ideas. Were it not so, humans would find it even more difficult to communicate with each other than is already the case because in that situation the basis for understanding would be harder to achieve. Without information, there could be no individual consciousness; and without communication, there would be no society.

Conclusion

Information possesses an amazing capacity for duplication; with information technology, people possess an ever-increasing capacity to duplicate and transmit information. Moreover, each individual derives a personal subjective meaning from any piece of information. However, the fundamental condition that characterizes the Information Age is the ease with which people think of information as a physical object. By describing, selling, storing, and transporting information as though it were a physical object, modern individuals achieve the tremendous accomplishment of an information economy. Economic innovations (e.g., new markets for information) and social perspectives that are derived from this attitude (e.g., judging a newspaper by the "amount" of information contained in it) have become so common that they are taken for granted. This idea of information—treating information as though it is a physical thing—stands as the base of the information society, because it directs thinking in such a way as to encourage the information economy, as well as the language with which individuals make sense of the information society.

See also: COMPUTER SOFTWARE; COPYRIGHT; ECONOMICS OF INFORMATION; ETHICS AND INFORMATION; HOME AS INFORMATION ENVIRONMENT; HUMAN INFORMATION PROCESSING; INFORMATION INDUSTRY; INFORMATION SOCIETY, DESCRIPTION OF; LANGUAGE AND COMMUNICATION; LANGUAGE STRUCTURE; PRESERVATION AND CONSERVATION OF INFORMATION; REFERENCE SERVICES AND INFORMATION ACCESS; RESEARCH METHODS IN INFORMATION STUDIES; RETRIEVAL OF INFORMATION; STANDARDS AND INFORMATION; SYMBOLS; USE OF INFORMATION; VISUALIZATION OF INFORMATION.

Bibliography

Artandi, Susan. (1973). "Information Concepts and Their Utility." *Journal of the American Society for Information Science* 24(4):242–245.

Braman, Sandra. (1989). "Defining Information: An Approach for Policymakers." *Telecommunications Policy* 13(3):233–242.

Brown, John Seely, and Duguid, Paul. (2000). *The Social Life of Information.* Boston: Harvard Business School Press.

Buckland, Michael K. (1991). "Information as Thing." *Journal of the American Society for Information Science* 42(5):351–360.

Negroponte, Nicholas. (1995). *Being Digital.* New York: Vintage Books.

Ruben, Brent D. (1988). *Communication and Human Behavior*, 2nd edition. New York: Macmillan.

Schement, Jorge R. (1993). "An Etymological Exploration of the Links between Information and Communication." *Information and Behavior* 4:173–189.

JORGE REINA SCHEMENT

▌■ INFORMATION INDUSTRY

The information industry comprises a group of enterprises and organizations whose purpose is to produce and process information and to develop the infrastructure and delivery mechanisms to distribute information. For the individuals and companies that implement these functions, it is important to understand the nature of the industry and the issues that affect its activities. For the people and organizations that use information, it is helpful to develop an understanding of the larger picture of the industry as a whole so they know where to find the information they need and how it is being made available.

Information as Product

The definition of "information" that will be used in this entry is that of Michael Buckland (1991), which regards information as objects. Information objects include things such as databases, electronic documents, newspapers, books, and calendars. Information is thus something that can be produced, sold, delivered, and used. In order for these activities to happen, however, some aspects of the nature of information objects must be properly understood.

Information as a product must be used in some way (e.g., read, understood, and applied) in order for its value to be realized. Unlike goods such as food, information cannot be consumed; once it is used, it can still be used again. Information also has a lifecycle; it moves from new to old, from specialized to general, and from contested to accepted. All of these aspects of information affect its value as a product, from the perspectives of both the information buyer and seller. The value of information is sensitive to time; new information may cost more to deliver than old. For a buyer, information that is needed by the end of the day may be worth nothing if it is delivered the following day. Value is also affected by the strength of the need for information; finding an emergency room patient's medical history may have a different perceived value to the customer than answering a crossword puzzle clue. The value of information is also related to a number of factors such as its scarcity or proprietary nature, the cost to produce or assemble the information, and the effect it will have when used. All of these factors affect how the information industry creates, prices, and delivers information to consumers. These factors also affect the willingness of the consumer to purchase and use the information. For a clearer understanding, though, it is useful to examine the specific functions that are required for industry to handle information as a product.

Functions of the Information Industry

The functions of the information industry can be separated broadly into four categories: production, processing, distribution, and the building of infrastructure.

Many of the producers of information fall outside the bounds of the information industry proper; these include authors, illustrators, inventors, and so on. However, information is also produced within the industry itself; for example, companies specializing in data mining use large collections of data to create usable information products such as customer profiles or product purchasing trends. Also, some of the products generated in the processing of information are sufficiently novel that processing becomes a form of production.

Information processing comprises a large portion of the activities within the information industry; processing transforms information into products that can be packaged and sold as usable goods. For example, publishing a journal involves processing a number of articles into an edited and integrated package. Creating an electronic database of journal articles involves assembling citations and abstracts for articles from a carefully selected group of journals and integrating them into a large, usable database system.

Distribution of information also comprises a large part of industry activity; distribution includes marketing the information products that were processed and delivering the products to the customers who purchase them. For example, once an electronic database of journal articles has been assembled, proper distribution ensures that potential customers know it exists and that they can access it after purchase. When the product is delivered to the customer, that individual might be a librarian or other information professional. This person, who then distributes information to specific information users, is often called an "intermediary." For nonprofit segments of the information industry, such as libraries, this may be referred to as "access"; rather than delivering information products to customers, they are making them available to people for their use.

Finally, information industry organizations must build a robust infrastructure in order to support their activities. Such an infrastructure may include, for example, computer hardware and software, database systems, telecommunications systems, marketing channels, and other technological and social structures. An important piece of infrastructure that has had a great effect on the information industry is the Internet; this widely available and standardized means of transferring electronic information (including text and graphics) has allowed organizations to move away from proprietary, dedicated delivery systems and toward integrated, multiproduct, multivendor access to electronic information products.

The four activities of the information industry do not operate in a vacuum; rather, they are the means by which information companies provide goods and services that meet customer needs. In doing so, the information industry plays a number of roles. For example, the information industry attempts to reduce information overload; people and companies that use information perceive that they receive too much information. To compensate, the information industry processes large amounts of information, reducing it to smaller, categorized packages that can be distributed to information users. The information industry also helps facilitate access to information; information users often have difficulty in obtaining information, whether they know what information they need or not. To make getting information easier, the information industry processes information into packages that people will understand and want to use, makes users aware of the existence of these efficient packages, and ensures that information products work properly and are timely and accurate.

The variety and complexity of the functions undertaken by the information industry lead one to wonder about who performs such tasks. Successful accomplishment of these activities requires specific kinds of organizations and specialized jobs.

With the growing use of computers in libraries, such as this library in Newport, Washington, librarians have had to adapt to become not only information managers but also technology managers in order to provide the best possible assistance to the library patrons. (Bob Rowan; Progressive Image/Corbis)

Roles within the Information Industry

Individuals and companies that perform production functions work primarily to change large amounts of raw data into information. In data mining, for example, very large stores of data are manipulated and examined in order to generate reports and profiles that identify and explain broad trends. Surveys, censuses, and other types of data collection do similar things on a smaller scale; numerical data are gathered and the results tabulated. In addition, data are changed into information by being arranged into databases. There are other kinds of information production such as authoring and illustrating; these creative processes generate information objects such as books and journal articles.

Those people who are involved in information processing perform tasks that change information objects into organized collections or packages that are suitable for distribution. One important task is publishing, which can mean aggregating articles

together to form a coherent journal or editing and assembling a book. Once information has been published, a second level of processing takes place, which places documents or their representations into organized forms. For example, indexers and abstracters generate standardized citations of documents and write summary abstracts of the content. These citations and abstracts can then be assembled in large, searchable document repositories. To help make these repositories easy to use, catalogers or subject analysts use standardized methods of arranging documents by subject and describing their content.

Once information has been packaged for distribution, many different people help transfer information from the producer to the customer. Marketing lets customers know that information resources exist, how they may be useful for the customer, and in what ways one product may be more suitable than another. Suppliers and database resellers act as "wholesalers"; for example, they may repackage a number of databases from different producers into one new product or provide a gateway to electronic journals from a variety of publishers.

The form of distribution in which an information professional acting as an intermediary uses the packaged product to provide information to end users can take several forms. A library is a repository where information is collected, organized, and made accessible to users; the librarian is responsible for selecting items, organizing them within the library's own collection, or helping people with information needs to find answers. Some distributors do not collect items; they pay to access a wide variety of resources and employ people who are expert in using them. For example, information consulting or information-on-demand services are hired by customers who have specific information requests. Such companies fulfill the requests, using perhaps many libraries and database services, and sell the results to the customers. Similarly, document delivery services do not collect materials; they use a number of information resources to provide articles or books on request.

Many different individuals and companies are involved in creating information infrastructures. In building the technical components, telecommunications companies provide the wiring and the communication systems that allow for the transfer of data. Internet service providers (ISPs) provide the means for individuals to access telecommunication systems. Software programmers, software engineers, systems analysts, and database designers build databases and other information systems that provide a framework for information objects and their representations. Finally, interface designers ensure that customers can interact successfully with the electronic information systems.

Equally important is the sociological infrastructure. For the sharing, transferring, and repackaging of information to occur, it must be in standardized electronic forms that move over standard communication channels. Standards must be designed and developed, but they must also be implemented when systems are built. The sociological infrastructure also provides help and support to people who are using information products and may need assistance in operating the system. Usually, telephone technical support

workers and technical manual writers provide this assistance.

The information industry also includes people who manage these functions, whether or not the sole product of the organization is information. Knowledge managers, information technology managers, and other types of information managers work in organizations ranging from manufacturing companies to universities to hospitals to banks. These roles combine business knowledge with an understanding of the functional processes of information management to provide an in-house information industry for the organization.

Given the wide variety of people and organizations that are working in the information industry, along with the profound shift caused by electronic information and telecommunications systems, it is inevitable that the information industry should face many issues. An examination of some of these issues will provide a greater understanding of the state of the industry and its future.

Issues and the Future

As the information economy becomes increasingly global, there are a number of factors that affect the use and transmission of information. The global environment is characterized by extreme fluidity; contexts of information use change continually. The information to be shared is heterogeneous in language and in content; people save, organize, and use information in different language and cultural contexts. Increasing numbers of information sources lead to information overload. In addition, developing global standards for large-scale information sharing is made difficult by the different languages, content, and contexts of global information.

The increase in electronic information gathering, packaging, and selling highlights several kinds of rights management issues. First, personal rights of privacy may be stretched or violated as information-gathering behavior both online and offline is tracked and aggregated. Second, ease of transmission and copying of electronic information makes copyright enforcement difficult. In a global context where copyright laws vary between countries, it is difficult to know what laws should apply. Finally, electronic information objects are subject to different kinds of ownership than are physical objects. While objects can be owned in perpetuity, electronic information is often sold on an access or "right to use" basis, creating difficulty in archiving the information.

Finally, the business models associated with selling information are constantly changing. For example, new payment methods have led to systems where information is paid for not with cash but by the user's willingness to view advertising. The availability of small pieces of electronic information (such as single journal articles or graphics) has led to the development of small transaction aggregation and payment systems. Information companies have been developing joint ventures, strategic alliances, and government partnerships to help adjust to a global information context; often, these alliances are between companies who maintain separate and competing businesses. Finally, as new technologies are developed inside and outside the information industry, those new technologies drive the creation of new information products.

The information industry is in a state of flux in which the only guarantee is constant change. While the functions required to handle information as a product have not changed, the technologies, jobs, and products are quite different than they used to be. Understanding the future of the information industry is to understand the constancy of the functions required, to be aware of the issues that are affecting the progress of the industry, and to realize that the industry flourishes by staying abreast of changes in technology and information use.

See also: CATALOGING AND KNOWLEDGE ORGANIZATION; CHIEF INFORMATION OFFICERS; COMPUTER SOFTWARE; COMPUTING; COPYRIGHT; DATABASE DESIGN; DATABASES, ELECTRONIC; ECONOMICS OF INFORMATION; INTERNET AND THE WORLD WIDE WEB; KNOWLEDGE MANAGEMENT; KNOWLEDGE MANAGEMENT, CAREERS IN; LIBRARIES, DIGITAL; PRIVACY AND ENCRYPTION; PUBLISHING INDUSTRY; STANDARDS AND INFORMATION; SYSTEMS DESIGNERS.

Bibliography

Basch, Reva, ed. (1995). *Electronic Information Delivery: Ensuring Quality and Value.* Brookfield, VT: Gower.

Brown, John Seely. (2000). *The Social Life of Information.* Boston: Harvard Business School Press.

Buckland, Michael K. (1991). "Information as Thing." *Journal of the American Society for Information Science* 42:351–360.

Huang, Kuan-Tsae; Lee, Yang W.; and Wang, Richard Y. (1999). *Quality Information and Knowledge.* Upper Saddle River, NJ: Prentice-Hall.

Marchionini, Gary. (1995). *Information Seeking in Electronic Environments.* New York: Cambridge University Press.

Rowley, Jennifer. (1998). "Information Pricing Policy: Factors and Contexts." *Information Services & Use* 18:165–175.

Shapiro, Carl. (1999). *Information Rules: A Strategic Guide to the Network Economy.* Boston: Harvard Business School Press.

MICHELLE M. KAZMER

INFORMATION PROCESSING, HUMAN

See: Human Information Processing

INFORMATION SOCIETY, DESCRIPTION OF

"Information society" is a broad term used to describe the social, economic, technological, and cultural changes associated with the rapid development and widespread use of information and communication technologies (ICTs) in modern nations societies, especially since World War II. Information societies are thought to differ from industrial societies because they treat information as a commodity, especially scientific and technical information; because they employ large numbers of "information workers" in their economies; because information and communication technologies and channels are prolific and are widely used; and because using those technologies and channels has given people a sense of "interconnectedness."

The term is somewhat controversial. Some experts believe that new media and computing technologies have produced a fundamentally new kind of society; others think that the technologies may have changed but that the basic social, cultural, and economic arrangements continue to look much as they have since the industrial era. Others criticize the idea on the grounds that "information" is a vague concept, used in different ways by different people (e.g., to mean documents, systems, ideas, data, knowledge, belief, statistical certainty, or any of a dozen other notions). Therefore, as Frank Webster points out in *Theories of the Information Society* (1995), it is difficult to observe or measure what it is that might make an information society different from other types of societies. Is France an information society because it has extensive, advanced telecommunications networks? Is Japan an information society because it produces more documents now than it did in 1950? Is the United States an information society because its companies employ more "information workers" than "industrial workers"?

Despite these difficulties, most observers would agree that many aspects of everyday life, including the workplace, family life, leisure and entertainment, teaching and learning, and earning and spending, have been affected in one way or another by the availability of new technologies and the ways people use them. "Information society" may be an imperfect label, but it is the most widely used one to talk about these complex changes.

Between the 1950s and the 1970s, economists, sociologists, and other researchers began to study the influences of telecommunications and computing technologies in advanced industrial societies. Two concepts from that period, the "information economy" and "postindustrial society," are still important aspects of the information society idea. More recent research has focused on whether the information society is a real departure from industrial society and on the cultural consequences of ICTs.

The Information Economy

Economists typically divide a nation's economy into three parts or "sectors": (1) primary or extractive (e.g., agriculture, mining, fishing, forestry), (2) secondary or manufacturing (e.g., production of goods manufactured from raw materials), and (3) tertiary or services (e.g., education, health care, law and government, banking and finance, sales, maintenance and repair services, entertainment, tourism, and so on). Only the primary and secondary sectors are traditionally considered to be "productive," that is, to contribute to material stocks of resources and goods that can be bought and sold. Service activities in the tertiary sector only "add value" or help produce or distribute the real products, rather than being valuable in and of themselves. Communication and information, from this perspective, do not have monetary value in themselves because they are not material goods—except when they are transformed into physical products such as movies, books, or computers.

The sheer numbers of television sets, wired and cellular telephones and pagers, radios, computers and modems, print publications, satellite dishes, and so on in homes and workplaces are often cited as evidence of an information society. Certainly, the media, telecommunications, and computing industries all grew dramatically in the twentieth century. However, the sale of telecommunications and computing equipment and supplies such as film, videotape, floppy disks, or paper stock is only part of the picture. "Value-added" information and communication services (e.g., entertainment cable channels, Internet access, or telephone dial tone) are often more profitable than the manufactured goods that carry them (e.g., compact disc players, videocassette recorders, computers, or telephones).

Such basic measurement problems have encouraged economists to begin thinking differently about both services and information. In the United States, experts noted that employment levels declined in the primary and secondary sectors after World War II. Employment in the tertiary service sector, which had been rising since the 1860s, increased sharply after about 1945. Between the 1950s and the 1970s, the American economy grew at the fastest rate in its history, creating huge increases in income and the growth of a large and affluent middle class. By the 1970s, services comprised about half of the economy and 30 to 40 percent of the workforce in some industrialized nations. This sector seemed to be contributing much more to wealthy economies than analysts had previously thought it could. Compared to manufacturing industries, services employed more white-collar, well-educated, and well-paid workers, whose main tasks involved the creation and management of information and interaction with other people.

In his landmark work, *The Production and Distribution of Knowledge in the United States* (1962), Fritz Machlup of Princeton University was among the first economists to recognize and document the increasing numbers of these "knowledge workers" and their contribution to the American economy in the postwar period. He found that the number of "knowledge-producing" occupations grew faster than any other occupational group between 1900 and 1958 and that they made up about one-third of the workforce in 1958. Peter Drucker (1969) also described what he called the "knowledge economy" and "knowledge industries," "which produce and distribute ideas and information rather than goods and services."

The sociologist Daniel Bell (1973) was so impressed by the growing size and economic power of white-collar professionals, a class "based on knowledge rather than property," that he proposed splitting the service sector into three parts, thus creating five economic sectors that would more accurately reflect the variety and importance of service activities. In place of the traditional tertiary sector, he suggested a different tertiary sector made up of transportation services and utilities, a fourth quaternary sector including trade, finance, insurance, and real estate, and a fifth quinary sector comprised of health, education, research, government, and recreation services.

In 1977, Marc Porat published a nine-volume study for the U.S. Department of Commerce entitled *The Information Economy*. He and his colleagues refined Machlup's framework of occupational categories and found that about 40 percent of the American workforce could be defined as information workers. He produced the first input-output table of the U.S. information economy, showing both the employment changes and the amount of the gross national product that was attributable to the "primary and secondary information sectors." Porat's primary information sector included firms whose main business is the production of information and information technology; firms in the secondary information sector use information and information technology to support other types of production.

Using similar definitions of information work and information industries, the Organization for Economic Cooperation and Development (OECD) found that information workers comprised about one-third of the workforce in many of its member countries, mainly in Europe. Other researchers questioned Machlup's and Porat's assumption that only workers who produce informational "goods" could be classified as "information workers." Instead, they said, the definition should be based on the amount of information creation and use required on the job, rather than the products of the job alone.

In Japan, information society is translated as *joho shakai*. According to Youichi Ito (1981),

researchers there took a different approach to documenting the growth of the information economy in the 1960s, focusing on the measurement of information production and consumption. The information ratio used by the Research Institute of Telecommunications and Economics (RITE) in Tokyo measured household spending on information-related activities as a proportion of total household expenditures. That group also developed the johoka index, ten measures that together provided an estimate of a country's degree of "informatization." The RITE researchers defined *johoka shakai* (informationalized society) in terms of per capita income, the proportion of service workers in the workforce, the proportion of university students in the appropriate age group, and a national information ratio of more than 35 percent.

In light of these and other research findings, economists have reconsidered the value of information and communication and developed theories of the economics of information. They have examined tangible forms of information such as books or tape recordings, as well as intangible intellectual property such as the movie rights to a novel, a patent on an industrial process, or employment contracts that prohibit employees from using for another employer what they learn in one job. Increasingly, knowledge or information itself, apart from its physical form, is considered to have an economic value or price—some argue that it can and should be treated like any other commodity or "raw material." Others point out that information does not behave as other physical commodities do. It is the only commodity, it is said, that one can sell and still have. Nonetheless, most economists and other researchers agree that information- and communication-related activities account for an unprecedented proportion of economic investment and output in wealthy societies.

Postindustrial Society

By the 1960s and 1970s, the spread of media and information technologies, increasing demands for information work, and the expanding information economy led some analysts to wonder whether a large-scale social change was underway that would be as important as the Industrial Revolution had been. Industrial society developed in the eighteenth and nineteenth centuries as agricultural, craft-based, local subsistence economies were supplanted by national economies that were based on factory work and assembly-line methods of mass production of manufactured goods. Similarly, some researchers suggested that industrial society might now be giving way to a whole new form of a postindustrial society based on the production and circulation of knowledge rather than manufactured goods.

The term is usually credited to Bell, who in his influential book, *The Coming of Post-Industrial Society* (1973), contended that new technologies had produced profound changes in everyday social life and culture. Bell contrasted the dominant economic sectors and occupational groups in preindustrial, industrial, and postindustrial societies, respectively. He also argued that they differ in terms of the kinds of knowledge that they value, their perspectives about time, and what he called their "axial principles." Preindustrial societies, Bell said, have an axial principle of traditionalism, an orientation to the past, and rely on common sense or experience as the best type of knowledge. Industrial societies' axial principle is economic growth; they are oriented to the present and they believe that empiricism—knowledge gained from observation—is most valuable. The new postindustrial societies have an axial principle of centralizing and codifying theoretical knowledge. They are oriented toward the future and forecasting, and they consider abstract theory to be the best type of knowledge. These different orientations, according to Bell, affect social organization and processes differently in each type of society.

Bell was not the only observer to comment on the changes he saw. In the 1960s, Marshall McLuhan used the term "global village" to describe and critique the effects of worldwide electronic communications on culture, and his ideas certainly seem to have influenced the early visions of the information society. Drucker (1969) declared the era to be the "age of discontinuity" and said that changes associated with information technology constituted a major break with the past. Jean-Jacques Servan-Schreiber (1968) warned Europeans of the "American challenge" of technological dominance. Simon Nora and Alain Minc (1980) wrote a report for the president of France in which they described the convergence of telecommunications and computing technologies—"télématique"—and its potential effects on national sovereignty, social conflict, and human interaction.

In the United States, Alvin Toffler and John Naisbitt wrote popular books that predicted an inevitable tide of technological growth that would sweep away every aspect of traditional life; societies and people that did not adapt would be left behind. By the 1980s, scholars, the media, and laypeople alike took it for granted that they were in the midst of a "technology revolution" that would radically change society and culture forever. The social "impacts" of technology were detected everywhere; the belief that new technology was driving human action was rarely questioned.

An important perspective emerged in the 1980s to challenge the widespread view of a new society driven by the imperatives of technological development, the prospect of ever-growing productivity, and swelling ranks of affluent white-collar knowledge workers. Proponents of this critical view argued that new information and communication technologies tend to reinforce rather than break down established relations of power and wealth. Indeed, the critics said, new technologies were being built and used in ways that extended industrial work organization and processes to industries and workers that had previously seemed immune to assembly-line control, such as health care, education, and the professions. Information technologies gave owners and employers the same kind of control over white-collar professional workers as mass production had given them over blue-collar workers.

Led by notable critics including Herbert Schiller, the advocates of this "continuity" perspective said that industrial capitalism was not dead; it had just taken on a new form. They pointed out that industrial-era ideas about private ownership, market economics, Western-style politics and mass culture were being exported throughout the world via global information and communication networks. The collapse of the Soviet Union in 1989 was widely regarded as a triumph of American-style capitalism and culture. Postindustrial society had preserved industrial institutional structures (e.g., law, education, finance) and organizational arrangements (e.g., private corporations), which critics said would ensure that political and economic power would remain concentrated in the wealthiest nations, firms, and social groups.

In fact, as Porat and others had found, the dramatic rise in white-collar employment in the service sector had flattened out by the 1980s. It appeared that even the most developed economies could use only about 45 to 50 percent "knowledge workers" in their workforces. Of that figure, the greatest demand for information workers was in relatively routine back-office jobs, such as programming, technical support, telephone sales, clerical work, and lower-level management. In the 1980s and early 1990s, despite a strengthening economy, well-educated American white-collar workers were laid off or replaced by temporary workers in record numbers as employers sought to cut costs.

Looking Ahead

In the 1990s, "information society" became a commonplace idea, though major disagreements remain in research and policy circles about its significance. Is it a revolutionary new phase of society driven by unprecedented innovation and the ubiquitous spread of new technologies? Or is it just the latest incarnation of late-stage capitalism, with information instead of raw materials and telecommunications and computing technologies replacing the assembly line? In an attempt to overcome this stalemate, Peter Shields and Rohan Samarajiva (1993) conducted a comprehensive review of information society research. They concluded that four main research perspectives had emerged: postindustrialists, industrialists, longwave theorists, and power theorists.

Other researchers have taken a sociocultural perspective, examining how people use and understand information technologies in the whole fabric of everyday life. Both the continuity and discontinuity views, they say, are technologically deterministic—that is, they assume that technology drives what people do, rather than assuming that people control technologies and decide what to do with them. In contrast, the social shaping of technology view says that technologies are constantly influenced by human actions and social needs, as well as being society-shaping.

Mark Poster (1990) suggests that the "mode of information" has become a defining characteristic of contemporary culture. Social relations and interaction, he says, are being changed by the introduction of electronic communications and information technologies, so to understand the information society, researchers should study people's language and discourse. In a three-volume

work entitled *The Information Age: Economy, Society and Culture* (1996–1998), Manuel Castells surveys the economic, social, and cultural changes of the twentieth century. He proposes that advanced societies are shaped by a "space of flows" of information rather than physical space. Nations, organizations, social groups, and individuals can link together, separate, and reorganize themselves into networks as needed according to their interests and the availability of information.

Key Social Issues

Clearly, many different perspectives have developed for understanding the information society. The implications for broad social change are complex and far-reaching. However, research also suggests that everyday life in information societies is changing. Several characteristics that affect interaction and sociality seem to distinguish what is most "social" about the information society: equitable access to information, privacy and surveillance, and new forms of social organization and community fostered by technology networks.

Equitable Access to Information

If information is the principal resource or commodity in an information society, then equitable access to information technologies and services is crucial if that society is to be a fair and just one. Though one might assume that "everyone" uses new technologies and services, such innovations are often too complicated for some people to use, or too expensive for disadvantaged households to afford. Uneven access has led to a growing concern about the rise of a digital divide between information "haves" and "have-nots," based on race, income, family structure, literacy, national or regional origin, or other factors. The introduction of a new communication medium can create an information gap between the best-positioned members of a society and the less fortunate, excluding many people from educational and economic opportunities.

For example, policymakers, regulators, industry, and the public alike have debated for many years whether universal service can or should be extended for other technologies such as the Internet or cable systems. Universal service originated in the 1920s in the United States as a way to ensure that most households would have inexpensive access to telephone service. More recently, the U.S. e-rate policy has required telephone companies to bill their customers a small amount each month that is passed along to pay for computer equipment and Internet access for public schools and libraries. The policy was intended to help promote fair access to online resources, but it has been strongly opposed by the telephone industry because it subsidizes some users and sets prices for services.

Though the number of computer users is growing rapidly in the United States and around the world, a large proportion of the public still does not have Internet access and may not for years to come. Use of online services is particularly low among non-whites, the poor, and single-parent, female-headed households. Only 60 percent of American households have cable service, and about 60 percent do not have Internet access. The number of households with basic telephone service declined after the AT&T divestiture in the 1980s, due to increased rates for local telephone service.

Access is not only a matter of technology. Literacy is often assumed to be universal in the industrialized nations. Yet data gathered by the Organization for Economic Cooperation and Development (OECD) show that as recently as 1995, anywhere from one-third to one-half of adults in twelve of its wealthiest member states had literacy skills that were below the level considered necessary to function effectively at home and at work (Healy, 1998). In a policy paper for the 1999 National Literacy Forum, the National Institute for Literacy reported similar figures for the United States. In the developing world, literacy is a serious problem among rural populations and in traditional cultures where educational opportunities for girls and women are limited. Language barriers create a different literacy problem. Non-English speakers and readers throughout the world are at a distinct disadvantage when it comes to online information services because there is relatively little online content in local languages.

Equity problems arise in many other ways. Minority or unpopular views may not find wide audiences if substantially all of the major media and information services are owned by a handful of large international firms. The International Telecommunications Union has long been criticized because it allocates the majority of orbital satellite "slots" to the United States and Western Europe, whose telephone and entertainment companies dominate markets throughout the world.

Intellectual property rights such as copyright are being extended, and fair use provisions are being restricted, so that copyright holders can keep works out of the public domain for decades longer than they once could.

Equity is a concern across societies as well as within them. It is often observed that most people in the world have never placed or received a telephone call, much less used online information services or e-mail. Even in affluent areas such as the European Community, subtle regional differences in the distribution of new media and information technologies have been documented. It is doubtful that systems and services will be distributed in poorer parts of the world as evenly as they have been in developed nations.

Privacy and Surveillance

In most developed nations, people enjoy a certain degree of privacy, both the classic "right to be left alone" (in Justice Louis Brandeis's words) and the control of information about their personal affairs and property. However, as more and more information about individuals and their activities has been gathered, stored, analyzed, and traded electronically, people have begun to sense that they are losing control over their personal information and their privacy. New media and information technologies make it much easier for anyone—with or without a legitimate interest or right—to gain and use personal information about others. Some researchers and policy analysts wonder if one of the characteristic features of the information society is a loss of personal privacy resulting from extensive uses of information and communication technologies for record keeping and surveillance.

Concerns about the privacy of electronic networks are not new. Early party-line telephones in rural American communities encouraged eavesdropping among subscribers who shared the same line. In the early 1900s, stockbrokers and bankers adopted telephones quickly when they realized that they could thereby interact without leaving a written record of the conversation or being seen together in meetings or in public. Before the divestiture of AT&T in the 1980s, Americans regarded "Ma Bell" to be almost as powerful as the government. Telephone wiretapping was a staple of detective novels and gangster movies. In the 1960s, the phrase "do not fold, spindle, or mutilate" inscribed across IBM punch cards became a

436 • INFORMATION SOCIETY, DESCRIPTION OF

cultural commentary on the inhumanity of new computerized systems for billing and credit, educational, and government records.

Since the 1990s, however, practically every type of information about individuals has been gathered and kept electronically. U.S. data privacy laws are fairly weak compared to those in Europe and other areas of the world. Private firms and law-enforcement agencies in the United States have lobbied hard to retain their right to access and share all types of data about individuals; indeed, differences in data privacy laws have been a major obstacle in U.S.-European trade talks.

It is no wonder, then, that people may be reluctant to send credit card numbers over the Internet or that they wonder who has access to their medical records. Some have started using "privacy technologies" of their own to thwart intruders.

Changing Social Structures and Community

Researchers, beginning in the early 1990s, have examined the ways that information and communication technologies, especially computer-mediated communication such as e-mail and the World Wide Web, may support new kinds of social relationships and communities. People who communicate online share special types of language, take on new social and professional roles, share community "standards," participate in special events or "rituals," and develop rules of "netiquette". Research has shown that people using new technologies develop extensive networks of personal contacts, including a large proportion of indirect relationships to others.

Such findings suggest that in an information society, communities might be based more on shared interests or background than on physical geography or proximity. "Virtual" communities may be more temporary than geographic communities. Data from the U.S. General Social Survey show that, since 1980, a major shift has occurred away from the "nuclear family" that has been typical in modern industrial societies. About one-third of Americans live in households of only one person, and another one-third live in households with two adults and no children. Perhaps the social support that has been traditionally provided by immediate family, neighbors, and local community groups can now be found online, or by using technologies that allow people to stay in touch with loved ones and friends wherever they are.

Summary

By any measure, life in modern nations is inextricably tied up with the use of networked information and communication systems that link places, data, people, organizations, and nations. By using these systems, people can share information and interact more quickly with more people in more places than ever before. However, the question of whether fundamentally new types of social relationships, work organization, or institutional forms have developed is still open. The information society, like industrial society before it, will depend not just on technologies that people use but on the social arrangements and beliefs that make them part of everyday life.

See also: COMMUNITY NETWORKS; COPYRIGHT; INTERNET AND THE WORLD WIDE WEB; MCLUHAN, HERBERT MARSHALL; PRIVACY AND COMMUNICATION; PRIVACY AND ENCRYPTION.

Bibliography

Agre, Philip E., and Rotenberg, Marc, eds. (1997). *Technology and Privacy: The New Landscape.* Cambridge, MA: MIT Press.

Bell, Daniel. (1973). *The Coming of Post-Industrial Society: A Venture in Social Forecasting.* New York: Basic Books.

Beniger, James R. (1986). *The Control Revolution.* Cambridge, MA: Harvard University Press.

Branscomb, Anne W. (1994). *Who Owns Information? From Privacy to Public Access.* New York: Basic Books.

Castells, Manuel. (1996–1998). *The Information Age: Economy, Society, and Culture,* 3 vols. Cambridge, MA: Blackwell.

Cawkell, A. E., ed. (1987). *Evolution of an Information Society.* London: Aslib.

Drucker, Peter. (1969). *The Age of Discontinuity: Guidelines to Our Changing Society.* New York: Harper & Row.

European Commission. (1997). *Building the European Information Society for Us All: Final Policy Report of the High Level Expert Group.* Brussels: European Commission.

Fischer, Claude. (1997). *America Calling: A Social History of the Telephone to 1940.* Berkeley: University of California Press.

Healy, Tom. (1998). "Counting Human Capital." <http://www.oecd.org/publications/observer/212/Article8_eng.htm>.

Ito, Youichi. (1981). "The 'Johoka Shakai' Approach to the Study of Communication in Japan." In

Mass Communication Review Yearboook, Vol. 2., eds. G. Cleveland Wilhoit and Harold de Bock. Beverly Hills, CA: Sage Publications. [Originally published in *Keio Communication Review* 1 (March 1980): 13–40.]

Jones, Steven G., ed. (1998). *Cybersociety 2.0: Revisiting Computer-Mediated Communication and Community*, 2nd edition. Thousand Oaks, CA: Sage Publications.

Lamberton, Donald E., ed. (1971). *The Economics of Information and Knowledge*. Middlesex, Eng.: Penguin Books.

Machlup, Fritz. (1962). *The Production and Distribution of Knowledge in the United States*. Princeton, NJ: Princeton University Press.

McLuhan, Marshall. (1964). *Understanding Media: The Extensions of Man*. New York: Mentor.

Naisbitt, John. (1982). *Megatrends: Ten New Directions Transforming Our Lives*. New York: Warner Books.

National Institute for Literacy. (1999). "Adult and Family Literacy in the United States: Key Issues for the 21st Century." <http://www.nifl.gov/policy/whpap.html>.

National Telecommunications and Information Administration. (1998). "Falling Through the Net II: New Data on the Digital Divide." <http://www.ntia.doc.gov/ntiahome/net2/falling.html>.

Nora, Simon, and Minc, Alain. (1980). *The Computerization of Society: A Report to the President of France*. Cambridge, MA: MIT Press.

Porat, Marc Uri. (1977). *The Information Economy*, 9 vols. Washington, DC: U.S. Government Printing Office.

Poster, Mark. (1990). *The Mode of Information: Poststructuralism and Social Context*. Chicago: University of Chicago Press.

Schement, Jorge Reina, and Lievrouw, Leah A. (1984). "A Behavioural Measure of Information Work." *Telecommunications Policy* 8:321–334.

Schement, Jorge Reina, and Lievrouw, Leah A., eds. (1987). *Competing Visions, Complex Realities: Social Aspects of the Information Society*. Norwood, NJ: Ablex.

Schiller, Herbert I. (1981). *Who Knows: Information in the Age of the Fortune 500*. Norwood, NJ: Ablex.

Schiller, Herbert I. (1987). "Old Foundations for a New (Information) Age." In *Competing Visions, Complex Realities: Social Aspects of the Information Society*, eds. Jorge Reina Schement and Leah A. Lievrouw. Norwood, NJ: Ablex.

Servan-Schreiber, Jean-Jacques. (1968). *The American Challenge*, tr. Ronald Steel. New York: Atheneum.

Shields, Peter R., and Samarajiva, Rohan. (1993). "Competing Frameworks for Research on Information-Communication Technologies and Society: Toward a Synthesis." *Communication Yearbook* 16: 349–380.

Slack, Jennifer Daryl, and Fejes, Fred, eds. (1987). *The Ideology of the Information Age*. Norwood, NJ: Ablex.

Toffler, Alvin. (1980). *The Third Wave*. New York: HarperCollins.

Webster, Frank. (1995). *Theories of the Information Society*. London: Routledge.

LEAH A. LIEVROUW

INFORMATION STUDIES, RESEARCH METHODS IN

See: Research Methods in Information Studies

INNIS, HAROLD ADAMS (1894–1952)

Harold Adams Innis was a Canadian political economist who turned to the study of communication in the last years of his career and life, publishing two important works on the media, *Empire and Communications* (1950) and *The Bias of Communication* (1951). These two difficult and expansive scholarly books have provided a foundation for Canadian political economy of communication studies since their publication, but in the United States and elsewhere, Innis's legacy primarily has been the influence his work had on Marshall McLuhan, who was a controversial colleague at the University of Toronto from the late 1940s until Innis's death and who became a well-known media theorist in the 1960s. Before he died, Innis was a professor and head of the Department of Political Economy and dean of the School of Graduate Studies at the University of Toronto. Innis College is now named after him.

Considered by Canadian cultural theorists to be one of a triumvirate that also includes McLuhan and George Grant, Innis presented in *Empire and Communications* an encyclopedic interpretation of the influence of communication on Western civilization as he pursued the thesis that communication occupies a crucial position in the political organization of empires, suggestive of the general role of communication in historical change. His studies of each civilization and its dominant media center on concepts of time and space. Durable media such as stone, parchment, and clay emphasize time and favor decentralized and hierarchical institutions. Light media such as papyrus and paper emphasize space and favor centralization and less hierarchy. Empires survive

Harold Adams Innis. (University of Toronto Library)

by managing the bias of dominant media toward either time or space and by balancing media with different biases. Innis also divides history into writing and printing periods, noting the influence of clay, papyrus, parchment, and paper on the writing period, as well as the influence of machinery and wood pulp on the printing period. In a caveat, Innis is careful to guard against suggesting that writing or printing has determined the course of civilization, and also warns against overlooking the importance of the oral period, which has left little record. Reflected in the literature of Greece, in the sagas of northern Europe, as well as in music and poetry, the oral tradition can be too easily forgotten. In many essays included in *The Bias of Communication*, Innis pleads for a return to the balance of eye and ear and the balance of writing and speech, all of which were hallmarks of Greece at its best and of the oral tradition.

In both of his major works, Innis turned from his economic studies of cod fisheries, the fur trade, and railways in Canada to communication as a central productive force in history. As an eco-

nomics historian, Innis brought to communication studies a focus on the rise and fall of civilizations and the dialectical relationships between metropolitan centers and peripheral margins. Primarily studying ancient civilizations, but writing with a grand historical sweep that included comments up to the mid-twentieth century as well, Innis developed the idea that the dominant form of communication, whether it was time-biased or space-biased, fostered different types of social power and control in creating a monopoly on the knowledge of a society. As new forms of communication appeared on the horizon and were developed by competing power groups, those emerging monopolies of knowledge, under the right social conditions, could present powerful forces of change leading to the fall of previous civilizations and the rise of new ones. For example, the use of stone and hieroglyphics in Egypt tended toward a time-biased empire of divine kingship that sustained itself over time with the elite's access to a secret script. When papyrus came along, it enabled Egypt to expand its control over space but it also required the priestly class to share power with an emerging administrative bureaucracy.

Often interpreted as a soft technological determinism within a critical framework similar to or a variant of Marxist analysis, Innis's writing on communication exhibited a strongly stated preference for civilization based on oral communication as existed in ancient Greece at the time of the advent of the phonetic alphabet. Innis traced the shift from the time-biased nature of oral culture, which was adept at creating a rich culture over long periods of time but not over wide expanses of space. Oral societies were more democratic because of the dialogic and conversational character of orality. The spread of writing systems and the introduction of the printing press and movable type in Europe in the mid-1400s gave rise to increasingly dominating forms of empire. The social and institutional organization made possible by writing and printing were space-biased, which are good at extending power and control over space, but more vulnerable to disintegrating in a shorter period of time.

Although the monopolies of knowledge fostered by print technology cultures were threatened, or checked, as Innis often wrote, by the emergence of the electronic media of radio and film, Innis argued that these new media intensified rather than challenged the reach of modern empires to a global scale. The inherent attack against the democratic spirit of oral cultures is amplified by electronic media monopolies of knowledge, Innis argued, in contrast to McLuhan's central argument that electronic media were inherently more decentralizing and democratizing because they represented a return to orality.

Innis's death in 1952 prevented his historical analysis of communication from including the effect of the widespread penetration of television throughout the world, not to mention the proliferation of computer and satellite technology that has occurred since his death. However, given the range of his study of communication media (from stone tablets to the printing press to electronic media) and the media's effect on the rise and fall of the empires of Egypt, Rome, Greece, Babylon, Europe, and America, among others, his legacy provides such a pervasive theory of the relationship between communication media and social organizations that his work can be predictive of many future changes in communication. David Godfrey, for example, in his introduction to the 1986 edition of *Empire and Communications,* ponders Innis's reaction to word processors, which Innis would have regarded as being similar to paper mills, printing presses, and the written alphabet. All are a threat to the oral tradition of human conversation based on speech, hearing, and direct experience in a democratic exchange. Also, as James Carey (1989) predicts, based on Innis's work, the proliferation of new technologies will intensify the speed and spread of empire over both space and time.

Innis's work has appeared in the shadow of McLuhan outside of Canada; however, while Innis has been identified as a member of the Toronto school of communication theorists, the turn of his work toward culture and critical theory makes his scholarship of increasing interest in contemporary American research, which is more open to humanistic and interdisciplinary media studies than in the past ascendancy of media-effects research. Recognized as a founding figure of technology and culture studies, Innis is included, with Lewis Mumford and Jacques Ellul, as one of the key figures in the media ecology approach developed at New York University by Neil Postman and his colleagues. The attention of cultural studies thinker and prominent media researcher Carey also has kept Innis's work from receding. Canadian research continues to be receptive to Innis's work through such contemporary scholars as political scientist Judith Stamps and cultural theorist Jody Berland, as well as through the earlier work of Arthur Kroker.

See also: CULTURAL STUDIES; LANGUAGE AND COMMUNICATION; MCLUHAN, HERBERT MARSHALL; MODELS OF COMMUNICATION; TECHNOLOGY, ADOPTION AND DIFFUSION OF; TECHNOLOGY, PHILOSOPHY OF.

Bibliography

Babe, Robert E. (2000). *Canadian Communication Thought: Ten Foundational Writers.* Toronto: University of Toronto Press.

Carey, James. (1968). "Harold Adams Innis and Marshall McLuhan." In *McLuhan: Pro and Con,* ed. Raymond Rosenthal. Baltimore, MD: Penguin.

Carey, James. (1989). *Communication as Culture: Essays on Media and Society.* Boston: Unwin Hyman.

Crowley, David, and Heyer, Paul. (1999). *Communication in History: Technology, Culture, Society,* 3rd edition. New York: Longman.

Czitrom, Daniel J. (1982). *Media and the American Mind: From Morse to McLuhan.* Chapel Hill: University of North Carolina Press.

Innis, Harold A. ([1950] 1986). *Empire and Communications,* ed. David Godfrey. Victoria, BC: Press Porcepic.

Innis, Harold A. ([1951] 1991). *The Bias of Communication.* Toronto: University of Toronto Press.

Kroker, Arthur. (1984). *Technology and the Canadian Mind: Innis/McLuhan/Grant.* Montreal: New World Perspectives.

Rosenthal, Raymond, ed. (1968). *McLuhan: Pro and Con.* Baltimore, MD: Penguin.

Stamps, Judith. (1995). *Unthinking Modernity: Innis, McLuhan, and the Frankfurt School.* Montreal: McGill-Queen's University Press.

Stevenson, Nick. (1995). *Understanding Media Cultures: Social Theory and Mass Communication.* London, Eng.: Sage Publications.

PAUL GROSSWILER

■ INNOVATIONS

See: DIFFUSION OF INNOVATIONS AND COMMUNICATION; TECHNOLOGY, ADOPTION AND DIFFUSION OF

■ INSTRUCTIONAL COMMUNICATION

The ability to speak clearly, eloquently, and effectively has been recognized as the hallmark of an educated person since the beginning of recorded history. Systematic written commentary on how to develop this ability goes back at least as far as *The Precepts of Kagemni and Ptah-Hotep* (3200–2800 B.C.E.). This document, the oldest remnant of the Egyptian Wisdom Books of the Middle and New Kingdoms (used as a manual of advice to train individuals headed for positions as scribes and officials), contains forty-five maxims, one-third of which are related to effective communication, such as (1) keep silent unless there is something worth saying, (2) wait for the right moment to say it, (3) restrain passionate words when speaking, (4) speak fluently but with great deliberation, and (5) above all, keep the tongue at one with the heart so the truth is always spoken.

Under the label of "rhetoric," the theory and practice of oral discourse was a central concern of Greek, Roman, medieval, Renaissance, and early modern education. In the United States, teachers of communication, from the beginning, devoted considerable intellectual effort to the development of theory and research that was supportive of effective communication instruction—efforts focused on the strategies, techniques, and processes that teachers could use to facilitate the acquisition and refinement of communication competence.

Communication instructors sought to share this knowledge with their colleagues in other classrooms. Donald K. Smith (1954) suggests that speech courses for teachers were offered at Indiana University in 1892; within two decades, the appearance of such courses at other universities was general.

Early efforts applied communication theory and research generated in noninstructional contexts to the tasks of the classroom teacher. What had been learned, for example, about the principles of effective speech making or group discussion was applied to the tasks of preparing a lecture or leading a class discussion. More recently, and largely in conjunction with the development of the International Communication Association's Division 7 (the Instructional and Developmental Communication Division, founded in 1972), communication educators have focused on developing communication theory based on empirical research that is conducted in the instructional context.

This entry explores the subset of communication studies known as communication education. Communication education is the study of communication in instructional (pedagogical) contexts. It is concerned with the study of three categories of phenomena: (1) oral communication skills—instructional strategies that communication instructors use to facilitate the acquisition of communication competence (e.g., What can *communication* teachers do to help students learn how to be more effective in job interviews?), (2) instructional communication—communication skills and competencies that are used by all instructors in the process of engaging in teaching and learning (e.g., How can *all* teachers communicate in ways that help their students learn?), and (3) communication development—the normal developmental sequence by which children acquire communication competence (e.g., Are there certain stages that individuals go through as they learn how to detect deception?).

The primary focus here will be on the second component of the phenomena covered by the term "communication education"—that is, on what communication scholars have learned about the process of communication as individuals interact in instructional settings.

The development of instructional communication theory and research in the United States has been guided by two primary forces: the nature of the communication discipline and the broader context of academia's social and behavioral science research traditions.

Robert Craig (1989) suggests that communication is a discipline wherein the essential purpose is to cultivate communication as a practical art through critical study. The defining characteristic of the discipline is, in his view, "the intimate tie that exists between the discipline's work and practical communicative activities" (p. 97). As a result, the discipline seeks to understand the structure, patterns, and effects of human communication and to use this knowledge to facilitate a higher quality of communication for both individuals and for society. For instructional communication scholars, this has produced a primary focus on the communication skills of teachers—that is, on how teachers can be helped to become more effective communicators in instructional contexts. A focus on the communication skills of students-as-learners exists, but this emphasis has been secondary.

In their research, communication scholars have operated within the broader context of teacher effectiveness research. This context was generated out of the social and behavioral science research traditions of academia. Jonas F. Soltis (1984) suggests that instructional research has emerged from the perspective of roots in three dominant twentieth-century philosophical traditions: logical empiricism (positivism), interpretive theories (analytical, phenomenological, and hermeneutic), and critical theory (neo-Marxist). Soltis argues that "empirical (causal), interpretive (meaningful), and critical (normative) dimensions characterize pedagogy and hence all need to be studied if pedagogical research is to be honest to its subject matter" (p. 5).

One of the first descriptions of instructional communication research was provided by Ann Staton-Spicer and Donald Wulff (1984) who identified, categorized, and synthesized 186 empirical studies of communication and instruction reported in the national and regional communication journals during the years 1974 through 1982. This overview of instructional communication research was updated in 2000 by Jennifer H. Waldeck and her colleagues.

Empirical Inquiry

Since at least 1896, scholars have used empirical research methodology to shed light on what it means to be an effective teacher. As have their colleagues in other social and behavioral sciences, these researchers have operated largely within the language and logic of logical empiricism—a perspective that some have called "the orthodox consensus." Modeled after the approach of the natural sciences, logical empiricism has produced a variety of approaches to instructional communication research ranging, for example, from naturalistic descriptions of teacher classroom behaviors to tightly controlled experiments that manipulate such variables as teacher clarity and teacher humor in order to assess their effect on student learning. Underlying the many varieties of positivist logic are several assumptions:

1. Reality exists independent of both the research and the flux of sensory experiences. The knower and the known are separate entities.

2. There is a deterministic order to reality-for people as well as for natural objects. Reality is neither random nor chosen.

3. The major function of the researcher is to construct general laws or principles that govern the relationship among classes of observable phenomena.

4. The general laws or principles composing scientific knowledge should be consistent with empirical fact. Scientific investigation is properly concerned with establishing an objective grounding for systematic theory.

5. Through continued empirical assessment of theoretical propositions and their deductions, scientific understanding can progress. Scientific knowledge is cumulative.

Operating from the assumptions of logical empiricism, instructional communication researchers have, with overlap, worked within five major research traditions: trait-rating, trait-observation, structure, process-product, and mediating-process. While each has been a dominant tradition at some point in history, all still contribute to instructional communication research.

Trait-Rating Tradition

The earliest attempts to identify effective communication strategies of teachers used students as observers. H. E. Katz (1896), for example, asked large numbers of students to describe the "best" teachers they ever had and subjected the list to a form of content analysis that yielded lists of the behaviors of "good" teachers (e.g., they care about students; they are clear when they lecture; they are fair in their grading). Beginning in about 1917, researchers began to ask these questions of "experts"—school administrators, professors of education, and others—whose opinions were presumed to have greater validity than those of students. A popular, related approach consisted of examining rating scales in an attempt to locate elements considered important enough to be used to rate teacher performance. Communication scholars have focused their interest largely on asking students for their views of the communication traits of effective instructors.

While early work explored the application of the speaker credibility construct to the role of teacher (e.g., expertise: teachers know what they are talking about; trustworthiness: teachers care about students and want to help them; and dynamism: teachers are good storytellers), more recent work has explored both broad, general categories (e.g., communicator style and sociocommunicative style) and narrower traits (e.g., teacher immediacy, teacher argumentativeness,

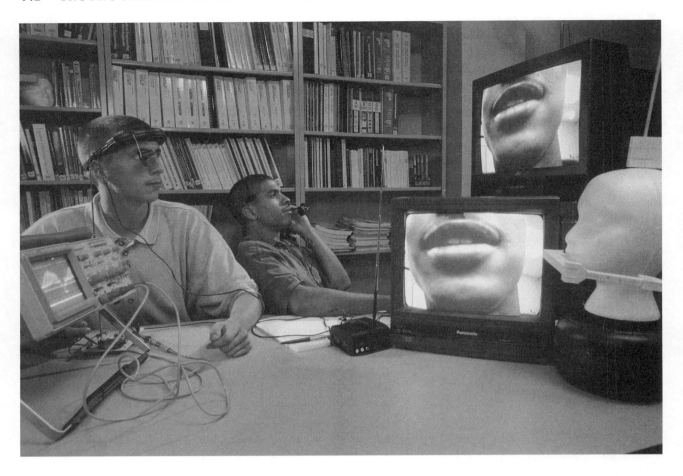

Video can be a valuable source of instruction and is being used here to help students at the Alfred I. duPont Institute learn to read lips. (Richard T. Nowitz/Corbis)

and verbal receptivity). Among the significant programs of research in this domain are ones generated by Robert Norton's conceptualization of communicator style, Janis Andersen's adaptation of teacher immediacy, and Dominic Infante's formulation of argumentativeness.

Trait-Observation Tradition

Dissatisfaction with using someone's opinion (whether a student or an "expert") as a criterion measure of good teaching is not new. The empirical basis for this dissatisfaction was provided by Arvil S. Barr and others as early as 1935, when they demonstrated that correlations between ratings of teachers and mean pupil gains on achievement tests were low (ranging from –0.15 to +0.36, with a mean of +0.16). These findings led researchers to explore the possibilities of systematic observation of teachers, and they turned to the child study movement of the 1920s for their methodology. Because they were studying children who were too young to be tested or interviewed, and because the most convenient place to

work with such children was the classroom, child study movement researchers pioneered the use of direct observation of classroom behaviors. The earliest teacher effectiveness study that used this approach (attempting to describe what a teacher does rather than how well he or she does it) was Romiett Stevens's 1912 study of questioning behavior. Based on four years of observation, she discovered, for example, that teachers talk 64 percent of the time; 80 percent of classroom talk is devoted to asking, answering, or reacting to questions; and teachers ask one to four questions per minute, with an average of two. While a number of developments prevented this research tradition from becoming immediately popular, in 1954 Barr was able to devote an entire issue of the *Journal of Experimental Education* to a review of seventy-five relevant studies done in Wisconsin under his direction. Within the communication discipline, Jon Nussbaum and his students and colleagues have been responsible for focusing attention on the observation of such teacher classroom behaviors as use of humor, self-disclosure, and narratives. Other variables that have received attention include teacher clarity, teacher explanation, teacher affinity-seeking, and teacher fashion.

Structure Tradition

Scholars in the late 1940s began to focus their attention on ways of structuring the classroom environment in such a fashion as to minimize the effect of teacher differences and maximize student learning. The method of classroom discussion, for example, was compared with the method of lecturing, while programmed instruction was compared with stimulation and games. Predictably, in retrospect, because this body of research ignored the complexity and dynamics of the classroom environment, a great deal of research failed to show that one approach was superior to others for any grade level.

A major exception was the use of the personalized system of instruction, as set forth by Fred Keller (1968). In this approach, students are helped to master course content by breaking that content down into smaller units and then helping them master those units with one-on-one tutoring from students that have successfully completed the course. A wide variety of additional instructional strategies have been explored, including use of videotapes, textbooks, interactive distance-learning networks, collaborative learning, and e-mail message strategies.

Process-Product Tradition

Researchers in the 1960s began to isolate and examine elements of teaching behavior that could be used to compare various methodologies (e.g., level of question asking is a variable appropriate to both discussion and programmed instruction). They ultimately isolated more than one thousand such variables. This approach produced an explosion of both descriptive and experimental systematic observation research that centered on identifying links between instructional strategies (processes) and learning outcomes (products).

While early summaries of research within this tradition were largely negative, more recent summaries have been more optimistic. The best-developed program of such research within instructional communication is the "power in the class" series produced by James McCroskey and his colleagues. In the seven essays that compose the original series (and multiple additions), the authors report studies that explore a wide variety of issues related to teacher use of and student reactions to behavior alteration techniques employed in the classroom. In summarizing this body of research, Virginia Richmond and K. David Roach (1992) conclude that instructor compliance-gaining strategies have a potent influence on learning factors in the classroom, from the elementary school to the university. Power bases and compliance-gaining strategies that emphasize positive relationship and relevant knowledge experience (e.g., "because it's fun," "because it will help you later in life," "because you will feel good about yourself if you do") are far superior in overall effects on student learning than are those that have a coercive and rules-oriented flavor (e.g., "because I will punish you if you don't," "because your parents will feel bad if you don't," "because I had to do this when I was in school").

Mediating-Process Tradition

Adapting to the cognitive emphasis (i.e., a concern for what individuals are thinking rather than what they are doing) that is used in other social and behavioral sciences, instructional communication researchers have studied the cognitive processes that mediate instructional stimuli and learning outcomes. For these researchers, process-product relationships are of interest primarily as a basis for reasoning about the kinds of mediating responses that make such relationships possible. Thus, learning that certain kinds of teacher questions lead to certain kinds of student behaviors is treated as a stimulus to explore the thought processes of students and teachers that might produce this relationship.

While some of this work has focused on the pedagogical judgments, plans, and decisions of teachers, most has focused on student perceptions and information-processing responses (e.g., student perceptions of differential treatment by teachers, perceptions of abilities of peers, use of an attribution framework for studying achievement, perceptions of the academic climate). In the teacher domain, for example, Staton (1990) and her colleagues have studied a construct labeled "teacher concerns." Within this body of research, teachers become socialized to the role of teacher in a process that can have three stages: concern for self ("Will the students like me?"), concern for task ("How many tests should I give this semester?"), and concern for effect ("Will students learn more about this topic if

I lecture or if I have them work in groups?"). Teachers begin to master the role of teacher with a concern for self and, it is hoped, move quickly through concern for task to concern for effect.

Interpretive Inquiry

Despite the fact that logical empiricism has been (and continues to be) the most widely espoused and employed epistemology and methodology in instructional communication research, a number of criticisms against the position have led researchers to develop alternative methodologies. While the language used to describe these methodologies varies with orientation, interpretive researchers who focus on the classroom share several assumptions:

1. Face-to-face interaction is a rule-governed phenomenon (i.e., if a teacher asks a question, it is expected, but not required, that students will provide an answer). Rule-governed means that culturally determined expectations for performance exist and that these expectations guide participation and act to constrain the options for what will or can occur. These expectations do not, of course, predict with certainty the exact form of the participation or even the occurrence of participation.

2. The contexts of interaction are constructed by people as they engage in face-to-face interaction. Thus, contexts are not given in the physical setting (e.g., "doing seatwork"); they are constructed by the participants' actions as part of the interaction.

3. Meaning is context specific. Closely related to the concept of context as constructed, this assumption suggests that what a behavior "means" is determined by considering how it is used, what precedes it, and what follows. All instances of behavior are not considered functionally equivalent.

4. Comprehension is an inferencing process. Meaning is viewed as a process of extracting the verbal and nonverbal information so that a person can "make sense" of the evolving events and gain access to the cognitive, social, procedural, contextual, and communicative knowledge that is provided during face-to-face interaction.

5. Classrooms are communicative environments, and the teachers are the only natives.

That is, the teachers know the rules for behaving in this environment because they create the rules; the students do not start with a knowledge of these rules and must learn them. Therefore, emphasis needs to be focused on identifying communication strategies that enable students to adjust to environmental complexity and learn "from" the classroom.

While interpretive inquiry starts with a different view of what it means to be human (active as opposed to reactive—that is, an assumption that individuals make real choices about their behavior as opposed to being shaped by nature and nurture) and while it disagrees with many of the underlying assumptions of logical empiricism, it shares with logical empiricism the view that inquiry should be objective. Individuals who study classrooms from an interpretive perspective are concerned with collecting and analyzing human behavior in natural settings and with exploring what is learned from (and how people learn through) interacting with others. In other words, interpretive research is concerned with how people learn language, learn through language use, and learn about language in educational settings.

Staton (1990) and her students have conducted research that is representative of this work being done in instructional communication. They have undertaken qualitative research in natural settings to explore issues of how students and teachers learn their respective roles. In terms of students, their research examines how people learn the role of "student" across the span of the child and adolescent student career. The central questions addressed are (1) What does it mean to be a new student?, (2) What is the nature of the communication process by which these individuals take on new student roles in new school environments?, and (3) What are the critical dimensions of the particular status passage?

Critical Inquiry

Critical theorists view both empirical inquiry and interpretive inquiry as ideologies (i.e., based on arbitrary belief systems rather than on observable facts) that focus on finding effective means to achieve educational ends that are taken for granted, that preserve the status quo, and that reinforce the power of the dominant class without regard for what kind of social and human life the current forms of schooling produce. They argue, for example, that researchers who use empirical inquiry and interpretive inquiry are studying how teachers can be helped to be more effective in getting students to learn rather than asking whether or not they might better explore how to help students be more effective learners. Critical theorists reject as a myth the idea of value-free research into human social, political, and educational phenomena; they stress instead the need for inquiry that takes into account the historical-ideological moment in which people live and the influence it has on them. Critical scholars, in short, are interested in making people aware of and helping people challenge the values that are inherent in the status quo of the educational enterprise. Research that focuses on creating an awareness of the role of sexism in classroom interaction is an example of this type of inquiry.

Summary

Having explored instructional communication research within empirical, interpretive, and critical perspectives, it is possible to find representative studies for each and every category. Nevertheless, it is striking that the vast majority of the work done by instructional communication scholars involves survey research conducted within the empirical tradition; that is, the majority of instructional communication research explores the dynamics of the college classroom by asking students to report what happens there. In addition to a narrow methodological focus, the focus is narrow in that the emphasis is on the teacher (rather than the student) in the college classroom (rather than in the lower academic levels or in the world of work).

Instructional communication is an exciting and active area within the communication discipline. It has generated a dedicated core group of scholars who are producing quality, programmatic work of methodological sophistication. Much of that work has focused on establishing relationships between paper-and-pencil reports of teacher characteristics and student learning. While successes in these efforts have been and continue to be important, the usefulness of instructional communication research is likely to be enhanced by encouraging a greater diversity of research emphases and traditions—especially within the interpretive and critical frameworks.

See also: ACADEMIA, CAREERS IN; COMMUNICATION STUDY; LANGUAGE AND COMMUNICATION; PUBLIC SPEAKING; RHETORIC.

Bibliography

Andersen, Peter, and Andersen, Janis. (1982). "Nonverbal Immediacy in Instruction." In *Communication in the Classroom*, ed. Larry L. Barker. Englewood Cliffs, NJ: Prentice-Hall.

Barr, Arvil S. (1935). "The Validity of Certain Instruments Employed in the Measurement of Teaching Ability." In *The Measurement of Teaching Efficiency*, ed. Helen M. Walker. New York: Macmillan.

Barr, Arvil S. (1961). *Wisconsin Studies of the Measurement and Prediction of Teacher Effectiveness: A Summary of Investigations*. Madison, WI: Dembar Publications.

Craig, Robert T. (1989). "Communication as a Practical Discipline." In *Rethinking Communication*, Vol. 1, eds. Brenda Dervin, Lawrence Grossberg, Barbara J. O'Keefe, and Ellen Wartella. Beverly Hills, CA: Sage Publications.

Friedrich, Gustav W. (1982). "Classroom Interaction." In *Communication in the Classroom*, ed. Larry L. Barker. Englewood Cliffs, NJ: Prentice-Hall.

Friedrich, Gustav W. (1987). "Instructional Communication Research." *Journal of Thought* 22:4–10.

Gray, Giles W. (1946). "The Precepts of Kagemni and Ptah-Hotep." *Quarterly Journal of Speech* 32:446–454.

Infante, Dominic A. (1988). *Arguing Constructively*. Prospect Heights, IL: Waveland Press.

Katz, H. E. (1896). "Characteristics of the Best Teachers as Recognized by Children." *Pedagogical Seminary* 3:413–418.

Keller, Fred S. (1968). "Goodbye Teacher, . . . " *Journal of Applied Behavior Analysis* 10:165–167.

Norton, Robert. (1983). *Communicator Style: Theory, Applications, and Measures*. Beverly Hills, CA: Sage Publications.

Nussbaum, Jon F. (1992). "Effective Teacher Behaviors." *Communication Education* 41:167–180.

Richmond, Virginia P., and McCroskey, James C., eds. (1992). *Power in the Classroom: Communication, Control, and Concern*. Hillsdale, NJ: Lawrence Erlbaum.

Richmond, Virginia P., and Roach, K. David. (1992). "Power in the Classroom: Seminal Studies." In *Power in the Classroom: Communication, Control, and Concern*, eds. Virginia P. Richmond and James C. McCroskey. Hillsdale, NJ: Lawrence Erlbaum.

Rodriguez, Jose I., and Cai, Deborah A. (1994). "When Your Epistemology Gets in the Way: A Response to Sprague." *Communication Education* 43:263–272.

Rubin, Rebecca B.; Palmgreen, Philip; and Sypher, Howard E. (1994). *Communication Research Measures: A Sourcebook*. New York: Guilford.

Smith, Donald K. (1954). "Origin and Development of Departments of Speech." In *History of Speech Education in America: Background Studies,* ed. Karl R. Wallace. New York: Appleton-Century-Crofts.

Soltis, Jonas F. (1984). "On the Nature of Educational Research." *Educational Researcher* 13:5–10.

Sprague, Jo. (1992). "Critical Perspectives on Teacher Empowerment." *Communication Education* 41:181–203.

Sprague, Jo. (1992). "Expanding the Research Agenda for Instructional Communication: Raising Some Unasked Questions." *Communication Education* 41:1–25.

Sprague, Jo. (1993). "Retrieving the Research Agenda for Communication Education: Asking the Pedagogical Questions that Are 'Embarrassment to Theory.'" *Communication Education* 42:106–122.

Sprague, Jo. (1994). "Ontology, Politics, and Instructional Communication Research: Why We Can't Just 'Agree to Disagree' about Power." *Communication Education* 43:273–290.

Staton, Ann Q. (1990). *Communication and Student Socialization.* Norwood, NJ: Ablex.

Staton-Spicer, Ann Q., and Wulff, Donald H. (1984). "Research in Communication and Instruction: Categorization and Synthesis." *Communication Education* 33:377–391.

Stevens, Romiett. (1912). "The Question as a Measure of Efficiency in Instruction: A Critical Study of Classroom Practice." *Contributions to Education, No. 48.* New York: Teachers College, Columbia University.

Waldeck, Jennifer H.; Kearney, Patricia; and Plax, Timothy G. (1999). "Assessing Technology Use for Instructional Purposes in the Organization." Paper presented to the Instructional and Developmental Division of the International Communication Association Annual Meeting, San Francisco, CA.

Waldeck, Jennifer H.; Kearney, Patricia; and Plax, Timothy G. (2000). "Instructional and Developmental Communication Theory and Research in the 90s: Extending the Agenda for the 21st Century." In *Communication Yearbook*, Vol. 24, ed. William B. Gudykunst, Thousand Oaks, CA: Sage Publications.

GUSTAV W. FRIEDRICH

INTELLECUTAL FREEDOM AND CENSORSHIP

A climate of intellectual freedom is one where any individual may express any belief or opinion regardless of the viewpoint or belief of any other individual, organization, or governmental entity. These expressions range from private communications to speeches, essays, plays, or websites.

Censorship may broadly be defined as any action that works against a climate of intellectual freedom. Censorship affects both written and oral communication. Its span can encompass not only books but also newspapers, magazines, movies, plays, television, radio, speeches, recorded music, e-mail, government documents, and information communicated electronically. Censorship is both the process and the practice of excluding material that is deemed by someone to be objectionable. In theory, any person or organization may, for what they consider appropriate political, social, economic, social, or sexual reasons, set themselves up in the role of censor. Individuals and organizations ferret out that which they consider immoral, profane, objectionable, or offensive and try to impose their will on society by trying to prevent others from having access to the ideas. Censorship is the most powerful nonmilitary tool that is available to governments.

In every society in every age—from ancient Rome to modern America—the climate of intellectual freedom has been constantly threatened by acts of censorship. Examples of censorship in the United States range from banning the inclusion of certain books in library collections to enacting legislation (such as the Communications Decency Act) that infringes on First Amendment rights. The history of humankind's struggle for intellectual freedom reveals much about the conflict between tolerance and intolerance.

Censorship in History

Censorship has existed almost since the beginning of time, and its history is filled with individual authors and publishers who were intent on expressing ideas that others found to be offensive, indecent, or controversial. As early as the fifth century B.C.E., Greek and Roman orators and writers expressed principles of individual liberties. The playwright Euripides wrote, "This is true liberty when free-born men, having to advise the public, may speak free." The Greeks in ancient times did not, however, allow free expression of ideas that went against state religion, and in 399 B.C.E., Socrates was sentenced to death (to be carried out by his drinking of poison hemlock) after having been found guilty of degrading public morals. Socrates, known for his democratic teachings, argued his own defense, which outlined the importance of freedom of expression and is still extensively quoted in modern court cases.

Rome appointed its first censors in 443 B.C.E. The job of the Roman censor was not only to record demographic information about Rome's citizens but to assess moral behavior. Those who performed noble needs were honored. Those who violated the accepted rules of conduct lost status and privileges, including citizenship.

After the fall of the Roman Empire in the fifth century C.E., the Roman Catholic Church controlled freedom of expression in the Western world for the next one thousand years. In the Middle Ages, religious and political censors protected the Church and state from both written and verbal attacks. The Church suppressed views with which it did not agree, and people were branded as heretics when they expressed ideas or opinions that went against Church doctrine. The Church silenced heretics through exile, torture, or death.

The tradition of individual liberties can be traced by to 1215 and the guarantees included in Britain's *Magna Carta*. In spite of the ideals expressed in that important document, the world's earliest censorship statute came from English Parliament in 1275.

The world changed in 1459 when Johannes Gutenberg began to work with movable type. By 1477, England had its first printing press. For the next two hundred years, from the early 1500s until 1694, licensing played a major role in publishing in England. Each publisher was required to get a formal license from the government before publishing works. If material was objectionable, no license was granted. (This was a most powerful example of what is called *a priori* censorship.) Unlike political censorship and church censorship, censorship for obscenity is a relatively recent development. Its roots can be traced to the seventeenth century and the advent of literacy among the masses. The term "obscenity" comes from the Latin *ob* (ideas) and *caenum* (towards dearth of filth).

Censorship of the press continued during the Reformation, until censorship by licensing ended in 1694. John Milton began arguing for the abolishment of licensing for printing about fifty years before Parliament finally acted. In his *Areopagitica* (1644), Milton argues for abolishment of printing licenses. Freedom of expression was very short lived, however. Shortly after 1694, Parliament enacted sedition laws that made it a crime to publish material that expressed hatred of or contempt for the government or the king.

Regardless of the laws and restrictions, people have always found ways to express their ideas and opinions. Since Gutenberg's time, the secret, underground printing of pamphlets has been common throughout Europe.

Censorship in the United States

People think of the United States as the freest country in the world in terms of expression, but during the Colonial period, printing in America was strictly regulated by the government in England. Boston was the site of the first book burning—of Thomas Pynchon's *The Meritorious Price of Our Redemption* (1650)—performed by the public executioner. Newspapers were commonly suppressed in terms of their information content.

When the states voted on the U.S. Constitution in 1789, there was a growing concern being expressed that the Constitution did not guarantee human rights. On December 15, 1791, the states ratified the Bill of Rights (the first ten amendments to the Constitution). The liberties granted with the Bill of Rights make citizens of the United States among the freest in the world. Americans often take those liberties for granted, but they did not happen by accident. The founding fathers carefully planned for the rights of nation's citizens.

Of the ten amendments ratified as part of the Bill of Rights, the most famous has always been the First Amendment: "Congress shall make no law respecting an establishment of religion or prohibiting the free exercise thereof; or abridging the freedom of speech, or of the press; or of the right of the people peaceably to assemble, and to petition the Government for redress of grievances."

The First Amendment requires citizens to protect unpopular speech, minority opinion, and the right of a speaker even when they do not agree with the message being conveyed. In spite of the First Amendment, the human inclination to prevent speech has given America a long history of censorship, intolerance, and repression. In 1885, Mark Twain's *Huckleberry Finn* was banned in Concord, Massachusetts. To this day that same novel continues to be one of the most challenged and banned books ever published.

Anthony Comstock, one of America's most famous self-appointed guardians of public morality, had a long and ardent career as a censor. A grocer by trade, Comstock, as a young man, founded

On November 12, 1936, policemen in New York City participated in a book burning to destroy "obscene" publications. (Bettmann/Corbis)

and was active in the New York Society for the Suppression of Vice. Comstock was instrumental in getting legislation passed to make it illegal to send obscene literature though the mail. The Comstock Law and Comstock's work to outlaw obscene, lewd, lascivious and filthy books and pamphlets set a moral tone in the United States that lasted until the 1950s. Dawn Sova (1998a) has remarked that "Comstock believed that erotic literature was a trap designed by Satan expressly to detour pure and decent young people from the path of righteousness to the road to depravity."

During the twentieth century, particularly during World War I and World War II, censorship was widely practiced and, in fact, accepted by the government and other bodies. In general, during periods of war and unrest, the government and the public are often inclined toward more, not less, control of information and toward suppression of information for security reasons. Following the passage of the Espionage Act of 1917, freedom of speech was more narrowly defined by the courts.

In 1947, Senator Joseph R. McCarthy was elected to the U.S. Senate and became a central figure in the Cold War era. In the early 1950s, McCarthy claimed that there were more than two hundred card-carrying communists in the U.S. State Department but refused to produce evidence of his charges or identify his informers. He used the media to make unfounded accusations and was instrumental in a Supreme Court decision that ruled that speakers could be punished for advocating the overthrow of government, even when it was unlikely that such an occurrence would occur.

The debate about obscene material in previous decades resulted in the 1957 *Roth v. United States* decision, in which the Supreme Court changed the definition of the term "obscenity" to mean works that had sexual content but "no redeeming social importance." Samuel Roth had been charged with sending obscene material through the mail. Found guilty at the lower court level, the Supreme Court upheld Roth's conviction. Justice William J. Brennan Jr. stated that obscenity did not enjoy the protection of the First Amendment because obscenity is "utterly without redeeming social importance."

In 1967, the U.S. Congress created the Commission on Obscenity and Pornography. The report of the commission and its recommendations were rejected by the Senate and by President Richard Nixon. Thus, the 1957 definition of obscenity stood until the Supreme Court's 1973 decision in *Miller v. California*. Marvin Miller, like Roth, had been convicted for sending obscene publications though the mail.

In upholding the decision of the State of California, the Supreme Court's opinion created a new three part test for obscenity: (a) whether the average person, applying contemporary community standards, would find that the work, taken as a whole, appeals to prurient interests, (b) whether the work depicts or describes, in a patently offensive way, sexual conduct specifically defined by the applicable state law, and (c) whether the work, taken as a whole, lacks serious, literary, artistic, political, or scientific value.

Censorship in the United States is not limited to the spoken or written word. Visual arts, including photography, and music lyrics have been the focus of censorship efforts, often by well-organized and well-funded community or national groups. The battles over Robert Mapplethorpe's photographs and the "Sensations" exhibit (which featured works from the Saatchi Collection) at the Brooklyn Museum of Art are but two examples.

Censorship in U.S. schools began after World War II. Textbooks, library books, and material used in classrooms as part of the curriculum have all been the targets of well-meaning parents, community organizations, and even school boards that govern school districts. In 1975, the school board of the Island Trees Union School District ordered nine books removed from the school library. After a 1982 decision by the Supreme Court in *Board of Education v. Pico*, the books were returned. Justice William Brennan, in his opinion, stated, "local school boards may not remove books from school library shelves simply because they dislike the ideas contained in those books and seek by their removal to prescribe what shall be orthodox in politics, nationalism, religion, or other matters of opinion."

Even the power of the U.S. Supreme Court, though, seems insufficient to quell society's yearn

to censor. The American Library Association's list of the ten most challenged books between 1990 and 1999 (out of the 5,600 challenges that were reported) includes many titles that Brennan's landmark words would seem to protect:

1. *Daddy's Roommate,* by Michael Willhoite (96 attempts to ban)
2. *Scary Stories* (series), by Alvin Schwartz (92)
3. *I Know Why the Caged Bird Sings,* by Maya Angelou (60)
4. *The Adventures of Huckleberry Finn,* by Mark Twain (53)
5. *The Chocolate War,* by Robert Cormier (48)
6. *Bridge to Terabithia,* by Katherine Paterson (45)
7. *Of Mice and Men,* by John Steinbeck (45)
8. *Forever,* by Judy Blume (40)
9. *Heather Has Two Mommies,* by Leslea Newman (36)
10. *The Catcher in the Rye,* by J. D. Salinger (32)

Censorship in the 1990s expanded its reach to an ongoing censorship battle over what is acceptable for adults and children to see on the Internet, particularly in public settings. Constitutionally protected sexually explicit material is widely available on every computer hooked to the Internet. Parents, legislators, the government, and industry have rushed to restrict access to what they classify as violence, hate speech, and unacceptably graphic sexual material in cyberspace.

In 1996, the U.S. Congress passed a sweeping telecommunications reform bill—the Telecommunications Act of 1996, which included the Communications Decency Act (CDA). When this bill was passed and thereby made a law, it made it a criminal act to allow minors to see indecent material on the Internet. The CDA was immediately challenged by the American Civil Liberties Union and a coalition of organizations that included the American Library Association. In 1997 the Supreme Court heard oral arguments in *Reno v. American Civil Liberties Union*, the first case regarding the Internet to be brought before the Court. The Court struck down provisions of the CDA that regulated "indecent and patently offensive speech". While the CDA was intended to protect minors, the Court declared it unconstitutional because it would have reduced "the adult population (on the Internet) to reading only what is fit for children."

The Internet has become a battleground that sets the right to free speech against the interests of protecting minor children. The ongoing struggle to control what both children and adults read, view, and hear on the Internet will not be solved soon.

Censorship in Other Countries

Just as censorship has occurred from early history in the Western world, censorship has been prevalent in the history of many of the world's countries for centuries. Citizens in many countries still live in a culture of fear and secrecy, where information is suppressed and access is restricted. Without a commitment to freedom of expression, governments can and do act as they please in denying access to information. In 1948, the Commission on Human Rights completed its work under the leadership of Eleanor Roosevelt, and the United Nations adopted the Universal Declaration of Human Rights without dissent. This living document has been adopted by nations throughout the world. Article 19, the section that deals with freedom of expression and opinion states: "Everyone has the right to freedom of opinion and expression; this includes freedom to hold opinions without interference and to seek, receive and import information and ideas through any media and regardless of frontiers."

These ideals are difficult to live up to even in countries where there are no formal censorship laws. The culture of many countries does not guarantee that freedom of expression will flourish, even in the emerging democracies. Therefore, censorship persists with both formal and informal mechanisms.

Information Freedom and Censorship (1991) reported on freedom of expression and censorship in seventy-seven of the world's countries at a time shortly after the liberation of Eastern Europe and the end of emergency rule in South Africa. In a majority of the countries covered by the report, individuals remained in jail or detention for expressing their opinions and works continued to be banned. At that time, twenty-seven countries operated under State of Emergency or Prevention of Terrorism legislation that allowed those governments to suspend arbitrarily the right to freedom of expression. In many countries, journalists continued to be tortured or killed, and the government retains control or ownership of the press/and or the Internet.

The international transfer of information via the Internet has made information more accessible to some and less accessible to others. Events such as ethnic and religious conflicts are reported around the globe almost instantaneously, and electronic information is not as easily suppressed. Via e-mail, individuals can report on world events, form their own opinions, and express them to others. Still the Internet is controlled or restricted in many parts of the world. In 1999, Reporters Sans Frontieres (RSF), a French-based organization of international journalists, named twenty countries that were enemies of the Internet and reported that forty-five countries restricted their citizens' access to the Internet. Most of these counties restricted access by forcing citizens to use state-run Internet Service Providers (ISPs). The twenty "enemies" protected the public from "subversive ideas" or used the rationale of national security. In some countries, no citizens were allowed access to the Internet. In other countries, users were forced to register with authorities. Some countries used blocking software, and still others used government-run or approved ISPs. The twenty countries that were selected in 1999 as enemies of the Internet included the Central Asian and Caucasus countries of Azerbaijan, Kazakhstan, Kirghizia, Tajikistan, Turkmenistan and Uzbekistan, as well as the countries of Belarus, Burma, China, Cuba, Iran, Iraq, Libya, North Korea, Saudi Arabia, Sierra Leone, Sudan, Syria, Tunisia, and Vietnam.

RFS (1999) also reported that "the Internet is a two-edged sword for authoritarian regimes. On the one hand, it enables any citizen to enjoy an unprecedented degree of freedom of speech and therefore constitutes a threat to the government. On the other hand, however, the Internet is a major factor in economic growth, due in particular to online trade and exchange of technical and scientific information, which prompts some of these governments to support its spread."

Each month RSF publishes a press freedom barometer. In November 1999, 2 journalists were killed, 19 were arrested, and 85 were in jail. An additional 42 had been threatened. Of the 188 member countries of the United Nations, 93 make it difficult or very difficult to be a journalist. This accounts for almost half of the world.

Modern Censorship

Censorship crosses all political and cultural boundaries but can often be classified into one of five categories: political, religious, economic, social, or sexual censorship. Who chooses to censor, why they do it, and the methods they employ vary depending on the country, the situation, the culture, and its history.

Any person or organization can set oneself up in the position of a censor. Generally, censorship comes from state, local, or federal governments, churches and religious institutions, religious zealots, and well-funded organizations across the political spectrum from right to left. Anyone can become a censor and work to restrict access to speech when they seek to control what materials are available to another person or another person's children.

Censorship can target print, electronic, or visual information. Common targets of censorship include materials with sexually explicit content (called "pornography" by some), violence (particularly in film, television, and video games), hate speech, profanity, information that threatens governments or criticizes government officials, and works that contradict or mock religious beliefs. Racist materials, sexist materials, religious materials, and materials that involve witchcraft and Satanism also make the list of things that some people want banned. In short, any material that someone, somewhere deems to be offensive, indecent, or obscene may be a target of the censor.

There are many forms of censorship. Some are obvious, some are subtle, and some are violent. Censorship methodologies include suppression; prohibition; formal book banning; pressure not to acquire works; proscription; removal; labeling to warn consumers about the content of movies, books, videos, television programs, and music lyrics; suspension of publication; and restriction of access to electronic materials (e.g., by filtering).

The use of legislation, lawsuits, licensing, registration requirements, filtering software, or codes of behavior may all constitute censorship. The same is true of the dismissal of employees who speak out against their employers' policies—particularly in the public arena. In authoritarian regimes that substantially restrict or eliminate most or all civil liberties, terror and violence are common ways of ensuring that access to information is restricted and that people are not free to speak or hold beliefs openly.

In the Western world, other methods of censorship include citizens removing materials from libraries and school curricula, Churches condemning publications, authors voluntarily rewriting their works, and governments requiring a formal license to print in advance of publication. Physical abuse, police interrogation, book burning, and bans on travel are more often employed as means of censorship in other parts of the world (though they have been employed in the United States as well). People, not just materials, can also be the targets of censorship. This could include writers and academics, defenders of human rights, those who work in the media, and political opponents.

Much of the censorship seen outside Europe and North America results from a desire to preserve traditional values and to stop what conservative civil and religious authorities view as the "invasion" of Western culture. Many people first seek to censor things because of what they believe to be a well-intentioned desire to protect children, or because of the desire to maintain political stability and security and to decrease influence from foreign governments. Censorship can also occur in an attempt to maintain moral standards and cultural norms, to maintain respect for religious teachings, to protect government and industry secrets, or to respond to community pressure. This motivation is not dissimilar to that which was present in Europe around the time of Galileo's conviction as a heretic. In fact, throughout history, whenever a society experiences a rapid influx of new ideas and beliefs, those who seek to avert change employ censorship as a primary tool.

Conclusion

The tension between intellectual freedom and censorship is as alive in the modern world as it was more than twenty centuries ago. Many censorship attempts, particularly in the United States, fail because information about the censorship attempt is shared and vigorous debate usually ensues.

While the zeal of the censor often brings fame, this fame is often not long lasting. The battle for public opinion often ends with people recognizing that censorship incidents are about control of others. Freedom from censorship is a precious national resource, often taken for granted until challenged. Censorship sometimes brings fortune, particularly when media attention promotes the sale of books that are targeted for removal. Michel Eyquem de Montaigne said it best: "To forbid us anything is to make us have a mind for it."

See also: COMMUNICATIONS DECENCY ACT OF 1996; FIRST AMENDMENT AND THE MEDIA; GUTENBERG, JOHANNES; INTERNET AND THE WORLD WIDE WEB; PORNOGRAPHY; PORNOGRAPHY, LEGAL ASPECTS OF; PRINTING, HISTORY AND METHODS OF; RATINGS FOR MOVIES; RATINGS FOR TELEVISION PROGRAMS; RATINGS FOR VIDEO GAMES, SOFTWARE, AND THE INTERNET; TELECOMMUNICATIONS ACT OF 1996.

Bibliography

American Civil Liberties Union Freedom Network. (2000). "Free Speech." <http://www.aclu.org/issues/freespeech/hmfs.html>.

American Library Association, Office of Intellectual Freedom. (1996). *Intellectual Freedom Manual*, 5th edition. Chicago: American Library Association.

American Library Association. (1999). "Office for Intellectual Freedom." <http://www.ala.org/oif.html>.

Bald, Margaret. (1998). *Banned Books: Literature Suppressed on Religious Grounds*. New York: Facts on File.

Center for Democracy & Technology. (2000). "Free Speech." <http://www.cdt.org/speech/>.

Doyle, Robert. (1999). *Banned Books: 1999 Resource Guide*. Chicago: American Library Association.

Electronic Frontier Foundation. (1999). "Protecting Rights and Promoting Freedom in the Electronic Frontier." <http://www.eff.org>.

Freedom Forum Online. (2000). "Free!" <http:// www.freedomforum.org>.

Foerstel, Herbert N. (1998). *Banned in the Media: A Reference Guide to Censorship in the Press, Motion Pictures, Broadcasting, and the Internet*. Westport, CT: Greenwood Press.

Frohnmayer, John. (1995). *Out of Tune: Listening to the First Amendment*. Golden, CO: North American Press.

Global Internet Liberty Campaign. (1999). "Free Speech." <http://www.gilc.org/speech/>.

Gold, John Coppersmith. (1994). *Board of Education v. Pico (1982)*. New York: Twenty-First Century Books.

Hentoff, Nat. (1992). *Free Speech for Me—But Not for Thee: How the American Left and Right Relentlessly Censor Each Other*. New York: HarperCollins.

Information Freedom and Censorship: World Report, 1991. (1991). Chicago: American Library Association.

International Federation of Library Associations and Institutions. (1999). "Free Access to Information and Freedom of Expression." <http://www.faife.dk>.

Jones, Barbara M. (1999). *Libraries, Access, and Intellectual Freedom: Developing Policies for Public and Academic Libraries*. Chicago: American Library Association.

Karolides, Nicholas J. (1998). *Banned Books: Literature Suppressed on Political Grounds*. New York: Facts on File.

National Coalition Against Censorship. (1999). "Censorship News." <http://www.ncac.org/cen_news/cnhome.html>.

Peck, Robert S. (2000). *Libraries, the First Amendment, and Cyberspace: What You Need to Know*. Chicago: American Library Association.

Peleg, Ilan, ed. (1993). *Patterns of Censorship Around the World*. Boulder, CO: Westview Press.

People for the American Way. (2000). "Freedom of Expression." <http://www.pfaw.org/issues/expression/>.

Reichman, Henry. (1993). *Censorship and Selection: Issues and Answers for Schools*. Chicago: American Library Association.

Reporters Sans Frontieres. (1999). "The Enemies of the Internet." <http://www.rsf.fr/uk/home.html>.

Sova, Dawn B. (1998a). *Banned Books: Literature Suppressed on Sexual Grounds*. New York: Facts on File.

Sova, Dawn B. (1998b). *Banned Books: Literature Suppressed on Social Grounds*. New York: Facts on File.

Symons, Ann K., and Gardner Reed, Sally, eds. (1999). *Speaking Out! Voices in Celebration of Intellectual Freedom*. Chicago: American Library Association.

Symons, Ann K., and Harmon, Charles. (1995). *Protecting the Right to Read: A How-To-Do-It Manual for School and Public Librarians*. New York: Neal-Schuman Publishers.

Williams, Claire Louise, and Dillon, Ken. (1993). *Brought to Book: Censorship and School Libraries in Australia*. Port Melbourne, Australia: D. W. Thorpe.

ANN K. SYMONS
CHARLES HARMON

INTELLIGENCE, ARTIFICIAL

See: Artificial Intelligence

INTERCULTURAL COMMUNICATION, ADAPTATION AND

Millions of immigrants and refugees change homes each year—driven by natural disaster and economic need; seeking better hopes of freedom, security, economic betterment; or simply looking for a more desirable environment in which to live. Numerous others temporarily relocate in a foreign land in order to serve as diplomats, military personnel, or as employees on overseas assignments for other governmental and intergovernmental agencies. Peace Corps volunteers have worked in more than one hundred nations since the inception of that organization in 1960. Researchers, professors, and students visit and study at foreign academic institutions, and missionaries travel to other countries to carry out their religious endeavors. An increasing number of the employees of multinational corporations work overseas, while individual accountants, teachers, construction workers, athletes, artists, musicians, and writers seek employment in foreign lands on their own.

Individuals such as those mentioned above face drastic, all-encompassing challenges as they attempt to construct a new life in a foreign country. They find themselves straddled between two worlds—the familiar culture from their homeland and the unfamiliar culture of their new host society. Despite having varied circumstances and differing levels of engagement and commitment to the host society, all resettlers begin a new life more or less as strangers. They find that many of their previously held beliefs, taken-for-granted assumptions, and routinized behaviors are no longer relevant or appropriate in the new setting. As a result, they must cope with a high level of uncertainty and anxiety. The recognition of verbal and nonverbal codes and the interpretations of the hidden assumptions underlying these codes are likely to be difficult.

Acculturation, Deculturation, and Stress

Once strangers enter a new culture, their adaptation process is set in full motion. Some of the old cultural habits are to be replaced by new ones. Most strangers desire and seek to achieve necessary adaptation in the new environment, especially those whose daily functions require them to establish what John French, Willard Rodgers, and Sidney Cobb (1974) referred to as a relatively stable person–environment fit. The adaptation process unfolds in two subprocesses, acculturation and deculturation, and involves the accompanying experience of stress. As they gradually establish some kind of working relationship with a new culture, these uprooted people are com-

pelled to learn (acculturation) at least some of the new ways of thinking, feeling, and acting, as well as the linguistic and other elements of the host communication system. As new learning occurs, unlearning (deculturation) of some of the old cultural habits has to occur—at least in the sense that new responses are adopted in situations that previously would have evoked old ones.

The acculturative and deculturative experiences, in turn, produce a substantial amount of internal stress caused by temporary internal disequilibrium. Researchers such as Kalervo Oberg (1960) and Adrian Furnham and Stephan Bochner (1986) have examined the stress phenomenon and employed, in doing so, the term "culture shock" and other similar terms such as "transition shock," "role shock," "language shock," and "cultural fatigue." In varying degrees, the phenomenon of culture shock is a manifestation of dislocation-related stress reactions. The manifestations include irritability, insomnia, and other psychosomatic disorders, as well as an acute sense of loss, insecurity, impotence, loneliness, and marginality. Such a state of flux is also met by defense mechanisms such as selective attention, cynicism, denial, avoidance, and withdrawal. The concept of culture shock is further extended by researchers such as Judith Martin (1984) and Bettina Hansel (1993) to include reentry shock—the difficulties, psychological and otherwise, that an individual may experience upon returning home.

As difficult as they may be in some cases, culture shock experiences serve as the very force that drives strangers to learn and adapt. It is through the presence of stress that strangers are compelled to strive to achieve the level of learning and self-adjustment that is necessary in order to meet the demands of the environment and to work out new ways of handling their daily activities. In a study of Canadian technical advisors (and their spouses) who were on two-year assignments in Kenya, Brent Ruben and Daniel Kealey (1979) found that the intensity and directionality of culture shock was unrelated to patterns of psychological adjustment at the end of the first year in the alien land. Of particular interest is the finding that, in some instances, the magnitude of culture shock was positively related to the individuals' social and professional effectiveness within the new environment (i.e., the greater the culture shock, the greater the effectiveness). Based on this finding, Ruben (1983) conjectured that culture shock experiences might, in fact, be responsible for (rather than impede) successful adaptation. Peter Adler (1987) echoed this point when he stated that culture shock is a traditional learning experience that facilitates a psychological change from a state of low self-awareness and cultural awareness to a state of high self-awareness and cultural awareness.

Host Communication Competence

At the heart of the experiences of acculturation, deculturation, and adaptive stress is what Young Yun Kim (1988, 1995) identifies as the stranger's host communication competence, or the ability to communicate in accordance with the communication codes, norms, and practices of the host culture. For the natives, such competence has been acquired from so early in life and has been so internalized in their personal communication system that, by and large, it operates automatically and unconsciously. For strangers, however, many elements of the same competence must be newly acquired, often painstakingly, through trial and error. Until they have acquired an adequate level of host communication competence, they are handicapped in their ability to function in the host environment. The degree to which a given stranger acquires the host communication competence, in turn, reflects his or her overall functional fitness, while the lack of such competence manifests itself in various forms of miscommunication, social inadequacies, and, in some cases, marginalization.

In explaining host communication competence, Kim identifies three dimensions of elements—cognitive, affective, and operational. Cognitively, a competent communicator is knowledgeable in the host language and culture, including the history, institutions, laws and regulations, worldviews, beliefs, norms, and rules of social conduct and interpersonal relationships. The knowledge of the host language, in particular, means not just the linguistic knowledge (e.g., phonetics, syntax, and vocabulary) but also the knowledge about the pragmatic uses of the language in everyday life (e.g., the many subtle nuances in the way the language is used and interpreted by the natives in various formal and informal social engagements). The verbal and nonverbal codes and rules of the host culture define the local communication rules about "correct" behavior. These rules enable the natives to make sense of events, activities, and actions that occur within their society. Communication rules function as directives that govern the flow of messages from one person to another and limit the possibilities of actions of the participants. Such rules identify how a given social goal may be achieved and render the behavior of each person more or less predictable and understandable to others. Communication rules apply to all levels of behavior, both verbal and nonverbal, as well as formal and informal. Some rules are explicitly coded within the written or spoken language, as in the case of grammatically correct writing or organizational rules and regulations. Most other rules, however, are implicit, and these deal largely with the nature of interpersonal relationships such as involvement and intimacy, dominance and status, and cooperation and accommodation. In each situation, from asking a friend for help to seeking to resolve a conflict in a relationship, nonverbal behaviors reflect the cultural rules and elicit specific responses that often have measurable social consequences. The affective (i.e., emotion) dimension of host communication competence involves what Maureen Mansell (1981) referred to as the "expressive response" that engages strangers in personally meaningful interactions with the natives. The affective competence allows strangers to co-participate in the emotional and aesthetic experiences of the natives—from the experiences of joy, excitement, humor, triumph, and beauty, to sadness, boredom, sarcasm, and despair. The affective competence thus leads to an empathic capacity and a sense of belonging in the host environment. Conversely, strangers who lack affective competence are likely to feel distant and alienated because they lack the genuine interest in experiencing the local culture and in developing close relationships with the natives. Underpinning this affective competence is an attitudinal readiness toward the host environment that is affirming and respectful. Affective competence further helps strangers to understand the often subtle and hidden meanings embedded in various messages from the host environment, thereby enriching their intercultural experiences.

Closely linked with cognitive and affective competence is operational (or behavioral) competence, or the ability to express one's ideas and thoughts externally in accordance with the host cultural communication system. No matter how competent someone may be cognitively and affectively, his or her interactions with the host environment cannot be successful without a corresponding operational competence. Operational competence thus enables a stranger to choose a right combination of verbal and nonverbal actions to meet the demands of everyday interactions—such as managing face-to-face encounters, initiating and maintaining relationships, seeking appropriate information sources, and solving various problems they may encounter. Ultimately, it is such operational competence, along with cognitive and affective competence, that makes strangers' life activities effective in the host environment.

Host Social Communication

Host communication competence is vitally and reciprocally linked to participation in social communication activities of the host society. On the one hand, strangers' social communication activities are directly constrained by the level of their host communication competence. On the other hand, each intercultural encounter offers the strangers an opportunity to cultivate the ability to communicate with the natives. The primary mode of social communication is face-to-face interpersonal communication, through which strangers obtain information and insight into the mindsets and behaviors of the local people as well as their own taken-for-granted cultural habits. Interpersonal communication activities often provide strangers with needed emotional support and points of reference for checking, validating, or correcting their own thoughts and actions.

In addition to experiencing interpersonal communication processes, strangers participate in the social processes of the host environment via a wide range of communication media, including radio, television, newspapers, magazines, movies, art, music, and drama. By engaging in these forms of communication, strangers interact with their host culture without having direct involvement with specific individuals, and thereby expand the scope of their learning beyond the immediate social context with which they come into contact. In transmitting messages that reflect the aspirations, myths, work and play, and issues and events that are important to the natives, the various public communication media explicitly or implicitly

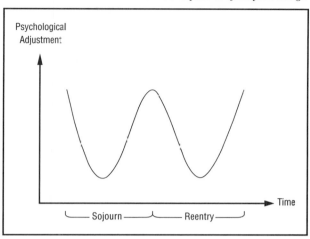

FIGURE 1. *The U-curve and W-curve patterns of adaptive change.*

convey the worldviews, myths, beliefs, values, mores, and norms of the culture. The adaptation function of mass communication is particularly significant during the initial phase of resettlement. During this phase, many strangers have not yet developed a level of host communication competence that is sufficient to forge meaningful interpersonal relationships with local people. The direct communication experiences with the natives can be intensely frustrating or intimidating to many strangers, as they feel awkward and out of place in relating to others and the immediate negative feedback they receive from the natives can be too overwhelming. Under such circumstances, the strangers naturally tend to withdraw from direct contacts and, instead, prefer media as an alternative, pressure-free communication channel through which they can experience the host culture.

Adaptive Change over Time

The cumulative and extensive engagements in the host communication processes bring about a gradual change in strangers over time. The learning and adaptation function of culture shock has been indirectly supported by other studies that have attempted to describe the stages of the adaptation process. Oberg (1979), for example, described four stages: (1) a honeymoon stage characterized by fascination, elation, and optimism, (2) a stage of hostility and emotionally stereotyped attitudes toward the host society and increased association with fellow sojourners, (3) a recovery stage characterized by increased language knowledge and ability to get around in the

FIGURE 2. *Young Yun Kim's model of the stress-adaptation-growth dynamic.*

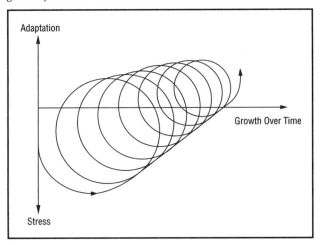

new cultural environment, and (4) a final stage in which adjustment is about as complete as possible, anxiety is largely gone, and new customs are accepted and enjoyed. This four-stage model of adaptive change is depicted by researchers such as Adrian Furnham (1988) and Michael Brein and Kenneth David (1971) in the form of the U-curve hypothesis (see Figure 1). Focusing on temporary sojourners' psychological satisfaction in the host culture, this hypothesis predicts that strangers typically begin the adaptation process with optimism and elation, undergo a subsequent dip or trough in satisfaction, and then experience a recovery. Researchers such as John Gullahorn and Jeanne Gullahorn (1963), as well as Brein and David (1971), have extended the U-curve hypothesis into the W-curve hypothesis by adding the reentry (or return-home) phase to illustrate the fact that the sojourners go through a similar process when they return to their original culture.

Research findings on the U-curve process have been mixed. In a study of groups of Swedes who had spent time in foreign countries, Ingemar Torbiorn (1982) reported that the subjects' satisfaction level followed a pattern similar to the U-curve. After about six months in the host country, satisfaction was significantly lower than it had been at arrival. Toward the end of that year, satisfaction slowly started to increase. Other studies have reported, however, that sojourners do not always begin their life in a new cultural environment with elation and optimism as described by the U-curve. Colleen Ward and her colleagues (1998) conducted a longitudinal study of Japanese students in New Zealand and found a more or less

linear, progressive process of psychological adaptation; that is, adjustment problems were greatest at entry point and decreased over time.

Building on psychological models such as these, Kim (1988, 1995) has created a model in which the adaptation process is explained in terms of a stress–adaptation–growth dynamic—a push-and-pull of competing psychological forces that leads to a gradual transformation of the individual (see Figure 2). This model highlights the continuous draw-back-to-leap nature of the psychological movement that underlies the adaptation process, which is at once progressive (i.e., an increase in integration of previously distinct subunits) and regressive (i.e., a weakening or even a breakup of a previously integrated entity). To the extent that stress is responsible for frustration, anxiety, and suffering, then, it is also credited as a necessary impetus for new learning and psychic growth. In this process of transformation, large and sudden adaptive changes are more likely to occur during the initial phase of exposure to a new culture. Such drastic changes are themselves indicative of the severity of adaptive difficulties and disruptions, as has been demonstrated in culture shock studies. At the same time, the higher the level of stresses stemming from resistance against change, the more powerful the fluctuations that eventually break through in the unfolding of adaptation and growth. The fluctuations of stress and adaptation diminish over time, and a calming of the overall life experiences takes hold. Accompanying this dynamic process are gradual increases in the stranger's overall functional fitness and in the person's psychological health in relating to the host environment. Also emerging in this process is a gradual shift in the stranger's identity orientation from a largely monocultural identity to an increasingly intercultural identity—one with a deepened self-awareness and an expanded capacity to embrace the conflicting demands of differing cultures and form them into a creative and cohesive whole.

Ideology and Adaptation

Traditionally, studies of cross-cultural adaptation in the United States have been largely grounded in the premise that it is a natural phenomenon and that at least some degree of successful adaptation is a goal that most, if not all, individuals who cross cultural boundaries want to achieve. This affirmative view of adaptation, reflected in the theoretical ideas described so far, results from the so-called assimilationist (or melting-pot) ideology, a mainstream American social philosophy that advocates the fusion of diverse cultural elements into a unified system of ideas and practices. In this perspective, adaptation is a matter of practical necessity for people who live and work in a new environment and who are at least minimally dependent on the local culture to achieve some level of psychological and social proficiency in their daily activities.

The assimilationist view and its expectation of cultural convergence, however, have been questioned since the 1970s, when the "new ethnicity" movement began as part of the civil rights movement in the United States. During this time, discussions have increasingly centered on the value of pluralism, leading many scholars to advocate the importance of ethnic and cultural minorities maintaining their cultural and linguistic identities. For example, the conceptualization by John Berry (1980, 1990) suggests the pluralistic nature of adaptation by focusing on the differing "acculturation modes" or identity orientations of individual immigrants rather than on the process in which they strive for a better fit in the host environment. Individuals' acculturation modes are assessed by Berry based on responses to two simple questions: "Are [ethnic] cultural identity and customs of value to be retained?" and "Are positive relations with the larger society of value and to be sought?" As depicted in Figure 3, Berry combines the response types (yes, no) to these two questions, and proposes four identity modes: integration (yes, yes), assimilation (no, yes), separation (yes, no), and marginality (no, no).

A more drastic departure from the traditional assimilationist perspective on adaptation has been taken by a number of "critical" (or "postcolonial") analysts. In sharp contrast to the premise of adaptation as a practical necessity and as a goal for individual strangers, critical analysts tend to view the stressful nature of cross-cultural adaptation as a consequence of power inequality that exists between the dominant group of a society and its ethnic minorities. Likewise, critical analysts such as Radha Hedge (1998) and Robert Young (1996) regard the stressful nature of the adaptation process as a form of oppression. Instead of viewing adaptation as a natural and practical necessity

FIGURE 3. *John Berry's model of four adaptation models.*

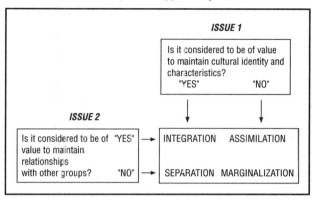

for non-natives, critical analysts tend to place a spotlight on the politics of identity and the perpetual struggle on the part of nondominant group members, including new arrivals, as victims. Based on interviews, for example, Hedge (1998) characterizes the experiences of a small group of Asian-Indian immigrant women in the United States in terms of their displacement and their struggling to deal with the contradictions between their internal identity and external "world in which hegemonic structures systematically marginalize certain types of difference" (p. 36).

It appears, then, that the pluralistic and critical interpretations of cross-cultural adaptation deviate from the traditional assimilationist perspective by suggesting that adaptation is, or should be, a matter of choice rather than a practical necessity. Pluralistic models accentuate variations in the psychological acceptance or rejection by individuals of the host society. Critical analysts move away further from the assimilationist perspective by advocating that cultural minorities must question the merit of adaptation or even reject the legitimacy of adaptive pressures under which they find themselves. These ongoing ideological disagreements, however, lose their relevance and significance in light of the extensive empirical evidence documenting the fact that most individuals do recognize and accept the reality of having to make adaptive changes in themselves when crossing cultural boundaries. To them, the driving force is not an ideological aim but a practical necessity to meet everyday personal and social needs. Instead of engaging in the abstract question about the nature of their relationship to the host society, their primary concern is to be able to function well in that society.

It is in this sense that the theories, concepts, and related research evidence highlighted in this entry serve as an intellectual template for individual immigrants and sojourners who strive to help themselves for their own adaptive ends. People learn, for example, that stressful experiences of learning cultural habits (i.e., acculturation) and unlearning cultural habits (i.e., deculturation) are unavoidable if people are to achieve a level of fitness in the new milieu. To accelerate this goal, people need to recognize the host environment as a partner and engage themselves in its interpersonal and mass communication activities. People also must recognize the tremendous adaptive capacity within themselves. This internally driven motivation is essential for anticipating and withstanding the challenge of culture shock, so as to undertake the task of developing a sufficient level of host communication competence. Such has been the case for many people who have ventured through new experimental territories and achieved a new formation of life. Their individual accomplishments bear witness to the remarkable human capacity for adaptation and self-renewal.

See also: INTERCULTURAL COMMUNICATION, INTERETHNIC RELATIONS AND; INTERPERSONAL COMMUNICATION; NONVERBAL COMMUNICATION.

Bibliography

Adler, Peter. (1987). "Culture Shock and the Cross-Cultural Learning Experience." In *Toward Internationalism*, eds. Louise Luce and Elise Smith. Cambridge, MA: Newbury.

Berry, John. (1980). "Acculturation as Varieties of Adaptation." In *Acculturation: Theory, Models, and Some New Findings*, ed. Amado Padilla. Washington, DC: Westview.

Berry, John. (1990). "Psychological Acculturation: Understanding Individuals Moving Between Cultures." In *Applied Cross-Cultural Psychology*, ed. Richard Brislin. Newbury Park, CA: Sage Publications.

Brein, Michael, and David, Kenneth. (1971). "Intercultural Communication and the Adjustment of the Sojourner." *Psychological Bulletin* 76(3):215–230.

French, John, Jr.; Rodgers, Willard; and Cobb, Sidney. (1974). "Adjustment as Person-Environment Fit." In *Coping and Adaptation*, eds. George Coelho, David Hamburg, and John Adams. New York: Basic Books.

Furnham, Adrian. (1988). "The Adjustment of Sojourners." In *Cross-Cultural Adaptation*, eds. Young Yun Kim and Willim Gudykunst. Newbury Park, CA: Sage Publications.

Furnham, Adrian, and Bochner, Stephan. (1986). *Culture Shock: Psychological Reactions to Unfamiliar Environments*. London: Mathuen.

Gullahorn, John, and Gullahorn, Jeanne. (1963). "An Extension of the U-Curve Hypothesis." *Journal of Social Issues* 19(3):33–47.

Hansel, Bettina. (1993). "An Investigation of the Re-Entry Adjustment of Indians Who Studied in the U.S.A. " *Occasional Papers in Intercultural Learning, No. 17.* New York: AFS Center for the Study of Intercultural Learning.

Hedge, Radha. (1998). "Swinging the Trapeze: The Negotiation of Identity among Asian Indian Immigrant Women in the United States." In *Communication and Identity across Cultures*, eds. Dolores Tanno and Alberto Gonzalez. Thousand Oaks, CA: Sage Publications.

Kim, Young Yun. (1988). *Communication and Cross-Cultural Adaptation: An Integrative Theory*. Clevedon, England: Multilingual Matters.

Kim, Young Yun. (1995). "Cross-Cultural Adaptation: An Integrative Theory." In *Intercultural Communication Theory*, ed. Richard Wiseman. Thousand Oaks, CA: Sage Publications.

Martin, Judith. (1984). "The Intercultural Reentry: Conceptualization and Directions for Future Research." *International Journal of Intercultural Relations* 8(2):115–134.

Mansell, Maureen. (1981). "Transcultural Experience and Expressive Response." *Communication Education* 30:93–108.

Oberg, Kalervo. (1960). "Culture Shock: Adjustment to New Cultural Environments." *Practical Anthropology* 7:170–179.

Oberg, Kalervo. (1979). "Culture Shock and the Problem of Adjustment in New Cultural Environments." In *Toward Internationalism: Readings in Cross-cultural Communication*, eds. Elise Smith and Louise Luce. Cambridge, MA: Newbury.

Ruben, Brent. (1983). "A System-Theoretic View." In *International and Intercultural Communication Annual, Vol. 12: Intercultural Communication Theory*, ed. William Gudykunst. Beverly Hills, CA: Sage Publications.

Ruben, Brent, and Kealey, Daniel. (1979). "Behavioral Assessment of Communication Competency and the Prediction of Cross-Cultural Adaptation." *International Journal of Intercultural Relations* 3(1):15–27.

Torbiorn, Ingemar. (1982). *Living Abroad: Personal Adjustment and Personnel Policy in the Overseas Setting*. New York: Wiley.

Ward, Colleen; Okura, Yutaka; Kennedy, Anthony; and Kojima, Takahiro. (1998). "The U-Curve on Trial: A Longitudinal Study of Psychological and Sociocultural Adjustment During Cross-Cultural Transition." *International Journal of Intercultural Relations* 22(3):277–291.

Young, Robert. (1996). *Intercultural Communication: Pragmatics, Genealogy, Deconstruction*. Philadelphia: Multilingual Matters.

YOUNG YUN KIM

■ INTERCULTURAL COMMUNICATION, INTERETHNIC RELATIONS AND

Polyethnicity, the side-by-side existence of people with varying ethic backgrounds, has become the norm for most of the human community around the world. As a result, concerns about interethnic relations have increased. Even as individuals of differing ethnic backgrounds live and work in closer proximity than ever before, issues of ethnicity and ethnic identity frequently bring about volatile responses in many people. Indeed, hardly a day passes without reports of some new incidents of ethnic conflict in some part of the world. Of course, each society, each locale, and each incident involves a unique set of historical, situational, and psychological twists, making it difficult to generalize about the nature of interethnic relations. In the case of the United States, interethnic relations has been at the forefront of public consciousness and a source of social unease and struggle ever since the Reconstruction era of the late nineteenth century when debates about civil rights began. Today, the traditional American ideology rooted in the primacy of the individual is challenged by the ideology of pluralism, a conflict that has galvanized many Americans into us-against-them posturing in the form of what is commonly referred to as "identity politics" or "politics of difference."

Social scientists have attempted to find systematic ways to understand the nature of interethnic relations in general, and interethnic communication behavior in particular. The literature created by these individuals presents a wide array of concepts, theories, and research findings that offer insights into how and why different ethnic groups and individuals interact with one another. Psychologists have tried to identify factors within individuals and the immediate social situations that help explain ingroup communication behaviors (i.e., between people of the same background) and outgroup communication behaviors (i.e., between people from different backgrounds). Sociologists have examined interethnic relations mainly from the perspective of society, focusing on macro-structural factors such as social stratification and resource distribution. Anthropologists have provided case studies of interethnic relations in specific societies, while sociolinguists and communication scholars have focused on the processes and outcomes of face-to-face interethnic encounters.

Key Terms and Definitions

The word "ethnicity" is employed in the field of sociology primarily as a label to designate a social group and to distinguish it from other social groups based on common indicators of national origin, religion, language, and race. In this group-level definition, ethnicity becomes the objective (i.e., externally recognizable) character, quality, or condition of a social group as well as an individual's membership in an ethnic group. Likewise, anthropological approaches to ethnicity emphasize the group-level collective cultural patterns including language, norms, beliefs, myths, values, and worldviews, as well as symbolic emblems, artifacts, and physical characteristics—from foods, flags, folk songs, folk gestures and movements, and folk dances to skin colors and facial features. Such features associated with an ethnic group are commonly referred to as ethnic markers that connote a common tradition linking its members to a common future. In contrast, psychological studies have defined ethnicity primarily in terms of ethnic identity, that is, an individual's psychological identification with, or attachment to, an ethnic group. Social identity theory, originally proposed by Henri Tajfel (1974), provides a systematic account of the significant role that membership in an ethnic group plays in shaping an individual's self-image and how that person behaves in relation to members of ingroups and outgroups. Other scholars, such as J. Milton Yinger (1986), see ethnic identity as a primordial "basic identity" that is embedded in the deep core of personhood. For others, such as George de Vos (1990), ethnic identity provides "a sense of common origin—as well as common beliefs and values, or common values" and serves as the basis of "self-defining in-groups" (p. 204).

Interethnic communication occurs whenever at least one involved person takes an ingroup–outgroup psychological orientation. As explained by Tajfel (1974), John Turner and Howard Giles (1981), and Marilynn Brewer (1979, 1986), the participants in interethnic communication tend to see themselves and their interaction partners along ethnic categories. The degree to which ethnic categorization influences communication, according to Rupert Brown and John Turner (1981) and Tajfel and Turner (1986), varies on the "intergroup–interpersonal continuum." At one end of this continuum are communication encounters between two or more individuals whose behaviors are fully determined by their respective ethnic group categorization. At the other end are those encounters in which the participants are not at all affected by ethnic categories and, instead, communicate with each other based entirely on the personal relationship that exists between them.

Associative and Dissociative Communication Behaviors

Young Yun Kim (1997) has conceptually integrated various interethnic communication behaviors along a bipolar continuum of association and dissociation. Associative and dissociative behaviors are not two mutually exclusive categories but vary in the degree of associative social meaning that is being communicated. Behaviors that are closer to the associative end of this continuum facilitate the communication process by increasing the likelihood of mutual understanding, cooperation, and convergence or the coming-together of the involved persons. Participants in an interethnic encounter behave associatively when they perceive and respond to others as unique individuals rather than as representatives of an outgroup identified by an us-and-them orientation. Such a cognitive tendency to perceive others as unique individuals is variously labeled in social psychology as "differentiation," "particularization," "decategorization," "personalization," and "mindfulness." The associative orientation is expressed outwardly in what Cynthia Gallois and her colleagues (1995) refer to as "convergent" verbal and nonverbal encoding behaviors. Among such behaviors are attentive and friendly facial expressions and complementary or mirroring body movements, as well as personalized (rather than impersonal) speech patterns that focus on the other person as a unique individual.

Conversely, dissociative behaviors tend to contribute to misunderstanding, competition, and divergence (or the coming-apart) of the relationship between the participants in the communication process. A communication behavior is dissociative when it is based on a categorical, stereotypical, and depersonalized perception that accentuates differences. Dissociative behaviors also include many forms of divergent verbal and nonverbal behaviors that indicate varying degrees of psychological distance and emotional intensity–from the subtle expressions in what Teun van Dijk (1987) has referred to as prejudiced talk (e.g., "you people") to blatantly dehumanizing name-calling, ethnic jokes, and hate speeches. Nonverbally, dissociative communication occurs through covert and subtle facial, vocal, and bodily expressions that convey lack of interest, disrespect, arrogance, and anger. More intense dissociative expressions of hatred and aggression include cross-burnings, rioting, and acts of violence.

Dissociative communication behavior is not limited to observable verbal and nonverbal acts. It also includes intrapersonal communication activities. One of the widely investigated intrapersonal communication activities in interethnic encounters is the categorization or stereotyping of information about members of an outgroup based on simplistic preconceptions. Such is the case whenever one characterizes any given ethnic group in a categorical manner, failing to recognize substantial differences among its individual members. This stereotypical perception is accompanied by a tendency to accentuate differences and ignore similarities between oneself and the members of the outgroup and to judge the perceived differences unfavorably. Robert Hopper (1986) explains such an ethnocentric tendency when he focuses on "Shiboleth schema" as the way in which people consider the dialects and accents that are displayed by non-mainstream groups to be defects and therefore objects of discrimination.

The Communicator

Associative and dissociative interethnic communication behaviors are directly linked to the internal characteristics of the communicator. An often-investigated psychological attribute is the communicator's cognitive complexity, or the mental capacity to process incoming information in a differentiated and integrated manner. As explained by George Kelly (1955) and by James Applegate and Howard Sypher (1988), individuals of high cognitive complexity tend to use more refined understanding of incoming messages and to display more personalized messages. Other researchers such as Marilynn Brewer and Norman Miller (1988) have linked low cognitive complexity to ignorance, erroneous generalizations, biased interpretations, and stereotype-based expectations.

Another characteristic that is important for understanding interethnic behaviors is the strength of the communicator's commitment to his or her ethnic identity. Commonly referred to as ingroup loyalty, ethnic commitment often supports dissociative behaviors such as ingroup favoritism and outgroup discrimination. Ingroup loyalty tends to increase when the communicator experiences status anxiety about his or her ethnicity in the face of a perceived threat by a member or members of an outgroup. In contrast, communicators tend to act associatively when their identity orientations reach beyond an ascribed ethnic identity and embrace members of an outgroup as well. Kim (1988, 1995), refers to such an orientation as an intercultural or interethnic identity—a psychological posture of openness and accommodation that reflects a level of intellectual and emotional maturity.

The Situation

In addition to the communicator characteristics, situational factors influence the way communicators behave in interethnic encounters. Each encounter presents a unique set of conditions. One of the key situational factors is the level of homogeneity (i.e., similarity) or heterogeneity (i.e., dissimilarity) that exists between the participants, based on ethnic differences such as distinct speech patterns, skin colors, and physical features. A high level of homogeneity is likely to encourage associative behaviors, whereas a high level of heterogeneity is likely to increase a sense of psychological distance between the participants and block them from noticing any underlying similarities that they might share. Heterogeneous encounters are also likely to increase the perceived incompatibility between the participants and inhibit their ability to form a consensus on topics of communication. However, while certain distinct features of communication behavior are strongly related to dissociative behaviors, not all ethnic differences are incompatible.

Interethnic communication behaviors are further influenced by the structure that organizes the way in which interactions are carried out. The structure of an interaction provides each communicator with guidelines for his or her behavior. One such structural guideline is provided by a shared higher goal that transcends each party's own personal interest. Groups with this type of shared goal would include military combat units, sports teams, and medical teams fighting an epidemic. The presence of the shared goal provides a structure of interdependence and mutuality that is geared toward cooperation, thereby creating a climate that promotes associative behaviors. On the other hand, a competitive, task-oriented structure for interactions tends to accentuate ethnic differences rather than similarities, engender mistrust, and discourage the building of interpersonal relationships across ethnic lines. According to Brewer and Miller (1984), people also tend to exhibit more dissociative behaviors when they find themselves in an organization that is governed by an asymmetric power structure that has been created along ethnic lines. For example, if few ethnic minorities occupy leadership positions in an organization, this power differential is likely to foster separateness and divisiveness between members of differing ethnic groups in that organization.

The Environment

The social environment is the broader background against which a particular interethnic encounter takes place. One environmental factor that is crucial to understanding associative and dissociative communication behaviors is the history between the ethnic groups represented in the communication process. Dissociative communication behaviors, for example, are more likely to occur in an environmental context that has had the history of subjugation of one ethnic group by another. Often, subjugation has taken the form of political, economic, or cultural domination through slavery, colonization, or military conquest. Members of a group that has been subjugated in the past may feel that they have the right to live on or possess territory that the group has traditionally claimed as its own. Many historical accounts have been written on the topic of colonization and the subsequent influences on interethnic discrimination and mistrust. In the case of the West Indian immigrants living in England, for example, the traditional colonial history and the domination tendencies of Whites over non-White immigrants have been observed to play out in interethnic encounters even today. Similar historical influences on contemporary interethnic power relationships can be found in many other societies, including the situations of Native Americans and African Americans in the United States, Koreans in Japan, Palestinians in Israel, and French-speaking Canadians in Quebec.

This inequality is further reflected in patterns that separate ethnic groups by socioeconomic class. Some investigators such as Harold Wolpe (1986) have argued that capitalistic economic systems exploit ethnic minorities. Michael Hechter (1975) used the term "internal colonialism" to explain a structural (or institutionalized) discrimination in which the imposed division of labor allows the core or dominant group to keep for themselves the major manufacturing, commercial, and banking roles while delegating the least profitable kinds of work to the peripheral groups (such as the ethnic minorities). Under conditions of inequality, the ethnic actions of subordinate groups serve as an outlet for the expression of comparative feelings of dissatisfaction, thereby increasing the likelihood of divergent interethnic behaviors.

By and large, inequities among ethnic groups in a given society are reflected in the laws and rules of the society. In contemporary democratic societies, laws and rules generally mirror the ideological climate and the values and opinions that are held by the majority of the citizens. Over time, changes in institutional inequity in interethnic relations in a given society tend to accompany corresponding changes in judicial actions as well as governmental and other institutional policies. Since the 1950s, countries such as the United States and Canada have undergone a significant transformation toward an increasing equity among their majority and minority ethnic groups. There has been a series of legal actions such as the U.S. Supreme Court's 1954 ruling against racial segregation in public schools. However, some formal barriers persist, as demonstrated by the continuing patterns of intense racial discrimination in housing. Nevertheless, significant progress has been achieved in some institutions, notably in education and employment, to promote equal treatment of individuals of all ethnic categories, thereby fostering a social environment that is more conducive to associative behaviors at the level of the individual.

Interethnic communication behaviors are further influenced by the collective strength of the communicator's ethnic group. As Raymond Breton and his associates (1990) have theorized, a strong ethnic group with a high degree of "institutional completeness" is likely to encourage its members to maintain their ethnicity and discourage them from assimilating into the society at large. Individuals in a well-organized ethnic community, such as the Cuban community in Miami, Florida, are likely to adhere more strongly to their Cuban identity and maintain their ethnic heritage more than their German-American counterparts, whose ethnic community is not cohesively organized. The same Cuban Americans tend to place less emphasis on embracing the mainstream American culture at large. The extent of interethnic contact across different ethnic groups is also an environmental factor that influences individual communication behaviors. Arrangements such as integrated schools and neighborhoods in urban centers allow for maximum contact and interaction, while other arrangements such as segregated ethnic neighborhoods provide the least amount of potential for interethnic interaction, which results in the cementing of any existing hostilities or prejudice. Accordingly, the classical approach to reducing interethnic dissociative behaviors—the contact hypothesis originally articulated by Yehuda Amir (1969)—has been to increase equitable and cooperative interethnic contact so as to increase mutual understanding and cooperation. This approach has not always been successful. Research has shown that, at least in the short run, interethnic contact is just as likely to heighten conflict as it is to reduce it.

Conclusion

The communicator, the situation, and the environment are all important elements to consider when examining the specific contextual factors related to understanding the associative and dissociative behaviors of individual communicators in interethnic encounters.

Associative communication is more likely to occur when the communicator has a high degree of cognitive complexity and an inclusive identity orientation that embraces individuals of differing ethnic backgrounds as members of the ingroup. Communicators are more likely to engage in associative behaviors when there are minimal ethnic differences between them. In addition, associative behaviors are more likely to occur in a situation where there is a shared higher goal, where there is a spirit of mutuality, and where there is a power structure that is minimally differentiated along ethnic lines. Associative behaviors also tend to occur in a social environment where there has not been a strong historical legacy of one group dominating another, where there is minimal socioeconomic stratification along ethnic lines, and where legal and other social institutions are based on the principle of equal rights for all individuals without regard to their ethnic backgrounds.

Dissociative communication is more likely to occur when communicators categorize members of an outgroup based on simplistic and rigid stereotypes and an exclusive ethnic identity that engenders ingroup favoritism and outgroup discrimination. Communicators are more likely to engage in dissociative behaviors when there are salient ethnic differences between them, when there is no common goal that binds them together in a cooperative relationship, and when there is a clear power differential along ethnic lines. Dissociative behaviors are further encouraged in a social environment that is steeped in a history of conflict and subjugation, where there exists systematic ethnic differences in socioeconomic status, and where various institutions favor a certain ethnic group while discriminating against another.

Each interethnic encounter presents a unique circumstance in which some factors may be of greater relevance and play a more prominent role than others. Even a single factor, such as an individual's strong loyalty to the ingroup or a prejudice against an outgroup, may be so powerful as to overshadow all favorable situational factors that are operating in a given encounter. Such would be the case when two individuals respond to an identical set of situational and environmental conditions in vastly different manners. Yet, a serious consideration of the factors related to the communicator, the situation, and the environment can lead to an understanding of the hidden constraints that may potentially lead to dissociation and the conditions that facilitate association between individuals of differing ethnic backgrounds.

Much work is still needed to refine the understanding of how interethnic communication plays out in a specific real-life setting. Detailed questions need to be raised, for example, about how each layer of factors simultaneously influences the way people communicate in an interethnic encounter. There also needs to be a better understanding of the long-term interaction and the significance of associative and dissociative communication behaviors at the grass roots. Clearly, associative communication is vitally important to the cohesion and continued evolution of a society as a single entity. At the same time, it is essential to develop a clearer and more systematic articulation of the role of certain forms of dissociative communication (e.g., nonviolent protests) that can be important forces in the defense of society against stagnation and for the reinforcement of new learning, self-renewal, and growth for all sides involved.

See also: INTERCULTURAL COMMUNICATION, ADAPTATION AND; INTERPERSONAL COMMUNICATION; SOCIOLINGUISTICS.

Bibliography

Amir, Yehuda. (1969). "Contact Hypothesis in Ethnic Relations." *Psychological Bulletin* 71:319–342.

Applegate, James, and Sypher, Howard. (1988). "A Constructivist Theory of Communication and Culture." In *Theories in Intercultural Communication*, eds. Young Yun Kim and William Gudykunst. Newbury Park, CA: Sage Publications.

Breton, Raymond. (1964). "Institutional Completeness of Ethnic Communities and the Personal Relations of Immigrants." *American Journal of Sociology* 70(2):193–205.

Breton, Raymond; Isajiw, Wsevolod; Kalbach, Warren; and Reitz, Jeffrey. (1990). *Ethnic Identity and Equality: Varieties of Experiences in a Canadian City*. Toronto: University of Toronto Press.

Brewer, Marilynn. (1979). "Ingroup Bias in the Minimal Intergroup Situation: A Cognitive-Motivational Analysis." *Psychologicla Bulletin* 86:307–324.

Brewer, Marilynn. (1986). "The Role of Ethnocentrism in Intergroup Conflict." In *Psychology of Intergroup Relations*, 2nd ed., eds. Stephen Worchel and William Austin. Chicago: Nelson-Hall.

Brewer, Marilynn, and Miller, Norman. (1984). "Beyond the Contact Hypothesis: Theoretical Perspectives on Desegregation." In *Groups in Contact: The Psychology of Desegregation*, eds. Norman Miller and Marilynn Brewer. New York: Academic Press.

Brewer, Marilynn, and Miller, Norman. (1988). "Contact and Cooperation: When Do They Work?" In *Eliminating Racism*, eds. Phyllis Katz and Dalmas Taylor. Newbury Park, CA: Sage Publications.

Brown, Rupert, and Turner, John. (1981). "Interpersonal and Intergroup Behavior." In *Intergroup Behavior*, eds. John Turner and Howard Giles. Chicago: University of Chicago Press.

De Vos, George. (1990). "Conflict and Accommodation in Ethnic Interaction." In *Status Inequality: The Self in Culture*, eds. George de Vos and Marcelo Suarez-Orozco. Newbury Park, CA: Sage Publications.

Gallois, Cynthia; Giles, Howard; Jones, Elizabeth; Cargile, Aaron; and Ota, Hiroshi. (1995). "Accommodating Intercultural Encounters: Elaborations and Extensions." In *Intercultural Communication Theory*, ed. Richard Wiseman. Thousand Oaks, CA: Sage Publications.

Hechter, Michael. (1975). *Internal Colonialism: The Celtic Fringe in British National Development, 1536–1966*. Berkeley: University of California Press.

Hopper, Robert. (1986). "Speech Evaluation of Intergroup Dialect Differences: The Shibboleth Schema." In *Intergroup Communication*, ed. William Gudykunst. London: Edward Arnold.

Kelly, George. (1955). *The Psychology of Personal Constructs*. New York: W. W. Norton.

Kim, Young Yun. (1988). *Communication and Cross-Cultural Adaptation: An Integrative Theory*. Clevedon, England: Multilingual Matters.

Kim, Young Yun. (1995). "Identity Development: From Cultural to Intercultural." In *Information and Behavior, Vol. 5: Interaction and Identity*, ed. Harmut Mokros. New Brunswick, NJ: Transaction.

Kim, Young Yun. (1997). "The Behavior-Context Interface in Interethnic Communication." In *Context and Communication Behavior*, ed. James Owen. Reno, NV: Context Press.

Pettigrew, Thomas, and Martin, Joanne. (1989). "Organizational Inclusion of Minority Groups: A Social Psychological Analysis." In *Ethnic Minorities: Social Psychological Perspectives*, eds. Jan van Oudenhoven and Tineke Willemsen. Berwyn, PA: Swets North America.

Tajfel, Henri. (1974). "Social Identity and Intergroup Behavior." *Social Science Information* 13:65–93.

Tajfel, Henri, and Turner, John. (1986). "The Social Identity Theory of Intergroup Behavior." In *Psychology of Intergroup Relations*, eds. Stephen Worchel and William Austin. Chicago: Nelson-Hall.

Turner, John, and Giles, Howard, eds. (1981). *Intergroup Behavior*. Chicago: University of Chicago Press.

Van Dijk, Teun A. (1987). *Communicating Racism: Ethnic Prejudice in Thought and Talk*. Newbury Park, CA: Sage Publications.

Wolpe, Harold. (1986). "Class Concepts, Class Struggle, and Racism." In *Theories of Race and Ethnic Relations*, eds. John Rex and David Mason. New York: Cambridge University Press.

Yinger, J. Milton. (1986). "Intersection Strands in the Theorisation of Race and Ethnic Relations." In *Theories of Race and Ethnic Relations*, eds. John Rex and David Mason. New York: Cambridge University Press.

YOUNG YUN KIM

INTERNET, RATINGS FOR

See: Ratings for Video Games, Software, and the Internet

INTERNET, VIDEO GAMES AND

See: Video and Computer Games and the Internet

INTERNET AND THE WORLD WIDE WEB

In the 1980s, if someone had asked a friend how they kept in touch with a classmate, that friend would have responded "by phone" or "by mail" or perhaps "not often enough." In the 1980s, if someone wanted to find a movie review, they looked in the newspaper; a recipe, they looked in a cookbook; the sports scores, they turned their television to ESPN. Today, the way people do some or all of these things is likely to be drastically different, yet all are variations on a theme: "used e-mail," "looked it up on the Internet," "did a search on Yahoo," or "went to ESPN.com to get the score." The common theme, "the Internet" or "the web," is arguably one of the most potent political, economic, and social forces created in the twentieth century.

Definitions

What is the Internet? Wendy Lehnert (1998, p. 21) calls it "a global assemblage consisting of over 19 million computers in rapid interconnection," while Douglas Comer (1991, p. 493) describes the Internet as "The collection of networks and gateways . . . that use the TCP/IP [transmission control protocol/Internet protocol] . . . suite and function as a single, cooperative virtual network." These definitions differ in their specificity, yet both are still correct. While the roots of the Internet can be traced to a research project sponsored by the U.S. government in the late 1960s, the Internet today bears little resemblance to the Internet of the early 1970s or even the early 1980s. Drastic increases in computer power, network capacity, and software capability, accompanied by similar reductions in cost, have put Internet capability into an ever-growing set of hands. Access that was limited to a few research universities in the United States in the early 1980s has now expanded to libraries, schools, businesses, and especially private homes. In 1997, the *Computer Industry Almanac* estimated that more than 200 million people worldwide would be "Internet connected" by the year 2000. The Internet defies simple definition in part because it changes so rapidly. For example, Lehnert's mention of nineteen million computers was correct in July 1997, but by the same month three years later, according to the Internet Software Consortium (2001), her statement needed to be amended to "ninety-three million computers" in order to be accurate.

The World Wide Web (WWW or web) also defies simple definition. Tim Berners-Lee and his colleagues (1994) defined it generally as "the idea of a boundless information world in which all items have a reference by which they can be retrieved." It is interesting to note that in almost the next sentence they describe it much more narrowly as the body of data accessible using specific addressing mechanisms and access technology. Thus, no less of an authority than one of the founders of the web speaks of it specifically and narrowly, and also very generally as a vision or "idea." Both are reasonable ways to think about the web.

Only one-third the age of the Internet, the web is nonetheless inextricably interwoven with the Internet. For many people there is essentially no difference between the two, because their sole interface to the Internet is through the "web browser," the software that runs on a home computer and is the mechanism through which a person reads e-mail, chats with friends, or surfs the web. While the Internet and the web are technically separate entities, with separate histories and attributes, they also now have an almost symbiotic relationship. The web takes advantage of Internet services, standards, and technology in order to request, find, and deliver content. The governance, engineering, and growth of the Internet are largely enabled through the use of web technologies.

History

As noted by Comer (1997) and Daniel Lynch (1993), the Internet has its roots in a networking research project that was started in the late 1960s

Tim Berners-Lee. (Henry Horenstein/Corbis)

by the U.S. government's Advanced Research Project Agency (ARPA). The original ARPANET comprised only four sites, three academic and one industrial. As work progressed, more sites were added, and by the mid-1970s the ARPANET was operational within the U.S. Department of Defense.

By the late 1970s, it was becoming clear that a major barrier to expanding the ARPANET was the proprietary nature of the communication protocols used by computers that would need to be connected. This observation sparked the creation and deployment of an open set of communication standards that came to be known as the TCP/IP suite. In the mid-1980s, the National Science Foundation (NSF), interested in providing Internet access to a larger number of universities and researchers, built the NSFNET, which augmented the ARPANET and used the same common set of communication standards. By 1990, ARPANET had been officially disbanded, replaced by the NSFNET and a set of other major networks all running TCP/IP. Collectively, this was the Internet. In the mid-1990s, NSF got out of the network management business entirely, leaving the administration of the current set of physical networks that comprise the Internet to a small set of commercial concerns.

Web Beginnings

In 1989, Berners-Lee, a computer scientist at CERN, the European Particle Physics Laboratory in Switzerland, proposed a project to help that organization manage the vast quantities of information and technical documents that it produced. The fundamental idea was to create an information infrastructure that would allow separate departments within the laboratory to make documentation electronically accessible, to allow decentralized maintenance of the information, and to provide a mechanism for linking between projects and documents. That infrastructure, originally called "Mesh" and later the "World Wide Web," received internal funding in 1990, and Berners-Lee developed a prototype that ran on a computer called the NeXT. In 1991, Berners-Lee demonstrated the prototype at a conference in San Antonio, Texas. As related by Joshua Quittner and Michelle Slatalla (1998), by late 1992 the web had piqued the interest of Marc Andressen and Eric Bina, two programmers at the National Center for Supercomputing Applications (NCSA). In short order they wrote the first widely available, graphics-capable web browser, called Mosaic.

The Web Takes Off

Mosaic was free and available to anyone to download from NCSA. It initially only ran on machines running the Unix operating system, but by late 1993, versions developed by other programmers at NCSA were available for both the Apple MacIntosh and the International Business Machines (IBM) personal computer (PC). In the space of months, the World Wide Web went from essentially having academic interest to having mass-market appeal. By mid-1994, the team of programmers at NCSA had parted en masse for California to help form what soon became Netscape Communications. By the end of that year, they had built the first version of Netscape Navigator, and in 1995, they quickly captured more than 75 percent of the browser market. Both Quittner and Slatalla (1998) and Jim Clark (1999) provide details on this exciting time in Internet history as viewed from the Netscape perspective.

The late 1990s has been characterized by continued explosive growth, the introduction of important technologies such as the Java programming language, live video and audio, the widespread use of secure connections to enable online commerce, and continually more elaborate methods to describe web content. The emergence of Microsoft as a major influence has also had a large effect on the growth of the Internet.

Technical Underpinnings

There is a core set of technical capabilities and standards that allow the Internet to function effectively. It is useful to discuss the technical infrastructure of the "net" by trying to answer the following questions. What does the network actually look like? How does data get transferred from one computer to another? How do computers communicate with each other and "agree" on a communication language?

The Internet Is Packet Switched

When a person calls someone on the telephone, the telephone company sets up a dedicated, person-to-person circuit between the caller and the person being called. The physical infrastructure of the telephone company is set up to provide such a circuit-switched network—it means that before connecting the call, the company must reserve network resources along the entire connection path between the two individuals. On the other hand, as described by Larry Peterson and Bruce Davie (2000), a packet-switched network, of which the Internet is the most well-known example, is composed of links and switches (also called routers). A router can have multiple incoming links and multiple outgoing links. Data is encapsulated as a series of packets, each marked with a source and destination address. Each packet is passed along from link to link through a series of switches, where each switch has a table that indicates, by destination address, which outgoing link a packet should be sent along. Unlike a circuit-switched network, a packet-switched network such as the Internet provides no end-to-end reservation of resources. This means that packets from the same source machine can travel different paths in the network, they can be lost along the way, and they can arrive at the destination in a different order than the order in which they were sent.

The standard for the interchange of packets on the Internet is called the Internet protocol (IP). The standard describes exactly what an IP-compliant packet should look like. For example, each packet must contain control information such as which computer sent the packet, which machine is supposed to receive it, and how long the packet has been "in the network." Of course, the packet also contains data as well. IP also describes how adjacent links on the packet-switched network should communicate, what the error conditions are, and many other details. It is important to note that IP is about packets and not about end-to-end connections.

Reliable Delivery

By definition, a circuit-switched network provides a reliable, end-to-end communication channel between two parties. With the possibility of lost data and out-of-order delivery, a packet-switched network such as the Internet must have some other method of providing a reliable channel that runs "on top of" IP. As noted by Comer (1991), this is the function of the transmission control protocol (TCP). TCP software running at both ends of a communication channel can manage all of the details of chopping a large outgoing message into IP packets and of putting the packets back together at the other side. By using TCP software, higher-level services such as e-mail, file transfer, and web data are shielded from the messiness associated with packet transfer.

Names and Addresses

If an individual writes a letter to a friend, it is easy to remember the name of the recipient, but it is typically harder to remember the full address. That is why address books exist. What is more, the postal service needs the right address to deliver the letter. If an individual puts a friend's name on the letter with nothing else, then the postal service will not know what to do with it, unless the friend's name is Santa Claus or "President of the United States." The situation on the Internet is not much different. The TCP/IP layer of the Internet does not know directly about names; rather, it needs a specific address in order to determine how to route data to its eventual destination.

Every computer that is attached to the Internet must be addressable. That is, it must have a unique identifier so that data destined for that computer can be tagged with the proper address, and routed through the network to the eventual destination. The "Internet address," also called an "IP address" or "IP number," is typically expressed as a sequence of four numbers between zero and 255, for example, <152.2.81.1> or <209.67.96.22>. If a person could examine any set of arbitrary packets being routed on the Internet, then every single one of them would have a destination and source IP number as part of the control information.

In theory, there are more than four billion IP addresses. In reality, there are vastly fewer addresses than that available because of the way that addresses are distributed. In order for the network to function efficiently, IP addresses are given out in blocks. For example, if a new company needs a bunch of IP numbers, then the company asks for one or more sets of 256 number blocks, and these are assigned to the company, although the company may ultimately use fewer blocks than have been allocated. As noted by Lyman Chapman (1993), distribution of IP addresses was even more inefficient in the past. An organization could ask for a 256-number block (a category "C" number) or a 65,536-number block (a category "B" number) but nothing in between. This led to many organizations owning a category B number but using only a fraction of the available range.

In general, humans do not deal with Internet addresses. For one thing, they are much harder to remember than names such as <www.espn.com> and <www.unc.edu>. However, the IP layer of the network, the place where all the data gets packetized and transported, does deal with IP addresses. Thus, there must be (and is) a translation service available that allows a human-readable name such as <ruby.ils.unc.edu> to be mapped to a particular IP address, such as <152.2.81.1>. This service is called the domain name service (DNS). When a person sends an e-mail message to a friend at <email.cool_u.edu>, the mail service must first consult a DNS server in order to get the Internet address of <email.cool_u.edu>. Once this is done, the mail software can establish a connection with a mail server at <email.cool_u.edu> by using the DNS-supplied address.

As Paul Albitz and Cricket Liu (1997) describe it, the "names" in the DNS server are arranged in an inverted tree structure, starting with a relatively small number of top-level domains, for example, <com>, <edu>, <org>, and <net>. There are considerably more second-level domains within a single top domain. For example, there are thousands of college and university domains that end in .edu, including <unc.edu> (University of North Carolina, Chapel Hill), <evergreen.edu> (Evergreen College), and <vt.edu> (Virginia Tech). The process continues with different departments at a university receiving third-level domains, such as <ils.unc.edu> and <chem.unc.edu>. Machines in those departments then receive names such as <ruby.ils.unc.edu> or <www.chem.unc.edu>.

FIGURE 1. *Typical stacking of service use on the Internet, with services that use other services appearing higher in the stack. Protocols that each service uses are also given.*

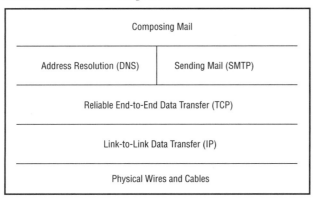

Composing Mail	
Address Resolution (DNS)	Sending Mail (SMTP)
Reliable End-to-End Data Transfer (TCP)	
Link-to-Link Data Transfer (IP)	
Physical Wires and Cables	

One important feature of the DNS system is that it allows for distributed zones of control. Put simply, this means that if a university wants to connect a new department to the Internet, the new department need only get the university to establish a new administrative zone and assign a subblock of IP addresses to the new zone. The new department would then be free to choose their own computer names and assign particular addresses from their subblock to those machines, all without consulting the university or any higher-level authorities. DNS also has easy mechanisms handling new and changed names.

The importance of having separate names and addresses cannot be overstated. It makes it easier for individuals to remember the name of a website or the e-mail address of a friend. Just as important, it allows flexibility in assigning a name to a computer. For example, an organization can keep its brand name (<www.nike.com>), but as necessity dictates, they can change the machine that hosts and serves web content.

Clients, Servers, and Protocols

A fundamental concept that is important for understanding how the Internet works is that of the client and the server. Client-server computing revolves around the provision of some service. The user of the service is the client, and the provider of the service is the server. Client and server communicate using a prescribed set of interactions that together form a protocol (i.e., the rules for interaction). To illustrate, consider a person who enters a favorite fast-food restaurant to order fries and a hamburger. Typically, the person (the client) waits in line, makes an order to the cashier (the server), pays, waits for the food, and

has the food served to him or her on a tray. Optionally, the person may choose to leave before ordering or decide to ask for extra ketchup. This set of required and optional interactions together form the protocol. On the Internet, the client and server are typically computer programs. Accordingly, the protocol itself is very prescriptive because computers are not tolerant of subtle errors that humans can easily accommodate.

One way to think about the Internet is as a set of services provided to both humans and computers. For example, consider a simple interaction such as sending an e-mail. There are several services needed to accomplish this task. First, because the friend has an e-mail address such as <jamie@email.cool_u.edu>, a service is needed to figure out the location of <email.cool_u.edu>. A DNS provides this. Second, once the e-mail software has the location of <email.cool_u.edu>, it must send the message to some entity that has access to Jamie's inbox. This entity, a program running on <email.cool_u.edu>, is called the mail server. Finally, the message itself is transported using the service that provides reliable in-order delivery of data: TCP software. If one were to build a stack of Internet services that illustrated this example, it would look much like Figure 1, with the basic services at the bottom (wires and cables) and the high-level services (the software used to compose the e-mail message) at the top.

Web browsers such as Netscape's Navigator and Microsoft's Internet Explorer are multipurpose clients. An individual can send e-mail, read news, transfer files, and, of course, view web content all by using a single browser. These programs understand multiple protocols and are thus clients for all of the corresponding services.

Growth

The growth of the Internet and of the World Wide Web has been nothing short of explosive. In fact, the number of host computers on the Internet (essentially, the number of computers that have an Internet address), doubled every fourteen months between 1993 and 1999 (Internet Software Consortium, 2001; Netcraft Ltd., 2001).

Data on the growth of the web is less reliable and involves culling information from multiple sources. One reasonable measure of growth is the number of available web servers. Data through 1996 were obtained from Mathew Grey, a student at the Massachusetts Institute of Technology (MIT), who built software that specifically tried to count the number of servers. Later numbers are available from Netcraft Ltd. (2001) in England. The number of servers rose from thirteen in early 1993 to an estimated seven million in July 1999. Over those six years, the number of servers doubled every three and one-half months.

Governance

The Internet is governed by the Internet Society (ISOC), a nonprofit organization. Members of the society include companies, government agencies, and individuals, all with an interest in the development and viability of the Internet. Within the society, there are subgroups that manage the technical infrastructure and architecture of the Internet, as well as several other areas.

One of these subgroups, the Internet Engineering Task Force (IETF), manages the short- and medium-term evolution of the Internet. Through various working groups within the IETF, new standards are drafted, examined, prototyped, and deployed. The process is geared toward selecting the best technical solutions to problems. The output of these various efforts are technical documents called "Requests for Comments" (RFCs). As noted by Comer (1997), "Request for Comments" is a misnomer, as an approved RFC is much more akin to a standard than to something open for debate. For example, there are RFCs that describe all of the various common protocols used on the Internet, including TCP, IP, Mail, and the web's data transfer protocol, hypertext transfer protocol (HTTP). The IETF does most of its business through e-mail and online publishing. All RFCs are available online at a number of places, including the ITEF website.

Web Basics

The discussion so far in this entry has assumed some basic terminology and concepts. It is now time to be more specific about things such as "hypertext" and "website."

Hypertext and Web-Pages

The notion of hypermedia was first suggested by Vannevar Bush (1945) when he described his idea of a "Memex"—a machine that would allow a person to organize information according to their personal tastes and provide for linkages between pieces of information. In the mid-1960s, Douglas Englebart and Ted Nelson further developed the notion of "hypertext," the idea that pieces of text could be linked to other pieces of text and that one could build these linkages to arrange information in different ways, not in just the traditional left-to-right, top-to-bottom method.

A web-page is a single document that can contain text, images, sound, video, and other media elements, as well as hyperlinks to other pages. A website is a group of pages organized around a particular topic. Typically, all pages connected with a website are kept on the same machine and are maintained by the same individual or organization.

The structure of a typical web-page reflects the influences of all of this earlier work. The hypertext markup language (HTML), the web's content description language, allows content developers to specify links between different pieces of information very easily. The hyperlink can refer to information in the same document or to information that physically resides on another page, on another machine, or on another continent. From the user's perspective, all such links look and function the same. The user clicks on the link and the referred page is displayed, which itself may have links to other pieces of information in other places. This is one of the fundamental ideas behind the web.

Uniform Resource Locators

A uniform resource locator (URL, pronounced either by spelling out the letters U-R-L or by making it a word that rhymes with "pearl") is the closest thing a user has to the address of an information item. When a user clicks on a link in a web-page, the web browser must determine which Internet-connected computer to contact, what resource to ask for, and what language or protocol to speak. All of these pieces are represented in the URL.

Consider the following typical URL: <http://www.ils.unc.edu/viles/home/index.html>. The first part of the URL, <http> in this case, represents the protocol the browser should speak—hypertext transfer protocol (HTTP) in this case. HTTP defines the set of interactions that are possible between web servers and web browsers. The next piece of the URL, <www.ils.unc.edu>, is the domain name of the machine that is running the information server that has access to the resource. The last piece, </viles/home/index.html>, is the address of the resource on that machine. In this case, this is the path to a particular file on that machine. Other protocols are possible, including <ftp>, <telnet>, and <mailto>, but the vast majority that an individual encounters during searching or "surfing" the web are ones accessed using the web's native data-transfer protocol, HTTP.

Unfortunately, as anyone who has bookmarked a "stale" page or done a search that yielded "dead" links knows, URLs are not guaranteed to be permanent. They are truly addresses in the sense that the item can move or be destroyed or the server can "die." There is considerable effort in the WWW community to create permanent URLs (PURLs) or uniform resource names (URNs) for those items that are truly supposed to last, but there had been no widespread deployment as of the year 2000.

Search Engines

As the web grew, it quickly became apparent that finding information was becoming increasingly difficult. One early method used to organize information was the web directory, an organized list of new and interesting sites that a person could use as a jumping-off point. The web soon grew too large to keep up with in this fashion. In 1994, the first search engines started to appear. As Lehnert (1999) notes, a search engine is a website that provides searchable access to a large number of web-pages. Search engines work using automated web-page harvesters called robots or spiders. The robot starts with a set of pages and fetches these from their locations. Each fetched page has links to other pages. By successively harvesting pages and following links, a search engine can build a very large set of web-pages. With appropriate database and search capability, these pages form a searchable archive of web-pages.

As anyone who has ever performed the same search on multiple search engines knows, the results can vary tremendously, both in the identity of the documents returned as the "hit list" and in the usefulness of the hits in satisfying the user's information need. There are many reasons for this, all of which can contribute to variability in results. First, search engines use different methods for deciding how to include a web-page in their indexes. For example, Yahoo (<www.yahoo.com>) provides a human-categorized list of websites with both search and directory capability, while AltaVista (<www.altavista.com>) has automated methods for building their searchable database of

pages. Second, search engines index vastly different numbers of documents, so documents in some engines are simply not available in others. In data compiled by Lehnert (1999), Infoseek (<www.infoseek.com>) includes about thirty million pages, while AltaVista includes almost five times that number. Third, each engine uses different information-retrieval techniques to build their searchable databases. Some sites weigh certain parts of the document higher than other sites: for example, one search engine may use descriptive HTML meta tags that have been assigned by the author of the page, while another engine will ignore them. Some search engines give higher weight to a page that has lots of links to it, so-called link popularity, while other engines do not consider this at all. Finally, some search engines will consider the entire text of the document when they build their indexes, while others may only consider the title, headings, and first few paragraphs.

While search engines are extremely important and useful, they do not contain all of the information available on the Internet or even on the World Wide Web. For example, newly created pages do not appear because it can take a long time for search-engine spiders to find the pages, if in fact they are ever found. Information contained in web-accessible databases is not included either. This includes the millions of items available in online stores such as Amazon.com. For businesses trying to get visibility or to make money through online sales, being able to be found by new customers is very important. This means that getting ranked highly in a search engine is very desirable. Knowledgeable businesses create their websites with detailed information on how the main search engines work.

Browser Wars

The success and effect of the Internet and the web initially caught the Microsoft Corporation flat-footed, though as related by Paul Andrews (1999), the company was starting to develop a vision for modifying their software products to embrace the Internet. By late 1995, Microsoft responded and started releasing versions of Internet Explorer that eventually rivaled Netscape's Navigator in ease of use and features. Thus started the famous browser wars. As noted by Ian Graham (1997), one tactic that both companies used was to introduce HTML extensions that only worked in their own browsers. As market share for both browsers approached equality, these tactics left content providers in a quandary, as they needed to describe their content in a way that worked in both browsers. As of late 1999, standards organizations such as the World Wide Web Consortium had remedied some of the incompatibilities, but accommodating differences in browsers continued to occupy a considerable amount of time for content developers.

One feature of the computer landscape at this time was that Microsoft enjoyed huge penetration into the installed base of computers. According to data compiled by Michael Cusumano and David Yoffie (1998), more than 85 percent of all computers in the world ran versions of Microsoft's operating system, the software that controls the computer. One part of the Microsoft strategy was to enter into agreements with computer manufacturers to preload new computers with Internet Explorer. At the same time, Microsoft was developing versions of the browser that were more tightly coupled with the operating system. According to some observers, these tactics went too far in that computer manufacturers were required to preload Internet Explorer or suffer unwanted consequences. Microsoft denied the charges of attempting to exert such leverage, stating in part that the tighter integration of the browser with the operating system was part of their business strategy and to forbid this was to limit their ability to provide innovative products.

On May 18, 1998, the U.S. Department of Justice and the attorneys general from twenty states filed suit against Microsoft, alleging first that Microsoft was a monopoly under the Sherman Antitrust Act of 1890 and second that Microsoft had engaged in unfair business practices (including illegal tying of products, in this case tying the use of Internet Explorer with the use of the computer's operating system). In November 1999, Judge Thomas Penfield Jackson found that the Department of Justice had proved that Microsoft was indeed a monopoly and that it had used that power to the disadvantage of American consumers. Accordingly, on April 28, 2000, the Department of Justice filed a proposal in federal court to split Microsoft into two separate companies, one to make and sell the Windows operating system, the other to handle the company's other software products. Judge Jackson accepted this decision on June 7, 2000. Microsoft vigorously pursued an overturning decision through the U.S. Court of Appeals. In support of this strategy, on September 26, 2000, the U.S. Supreme Court ruled 8–1 against a Department of Justice request to bypass the appeals court, effectively extending the case for at least a year.

The Future Internet

It is difficult and probably fruitless to speculate on what the Internet will look like in the future. In December 1995, no less an authority than Robert Metcalfe, an Internet pioneer and the inventor of Ethernet, predicted that the Internet would collapse in 1996. At a conference in 1997, Metcalfe literally ate his words, putting his written comments in a blender and drinking them like a milkshake as his audience cheered. It is safe to say that the Internet and World Wide Web will continue to grow, probably at the same breakneck speed. If Charles Goldfarb and Paul Prescod (1998) are to be believed, HTML, the workhorse of content description, will be at least augmented, if not replaced, by the more powerful families of languages defined by the extensible markup language (XML). Advances in wireless technology and portable computing devices mean that web browsing will no longer be relegated to the desktop. Greater network capacity pushed all the way to the home means that more interactive, multimedia capability may realistically be available to the typical consumer. One safe prediction is that the future promises to be exciting.

See also: COMMUNITY NETWORKS; COMPUTER LITERACY; COMPUTER SOFTWARE; WEBMASTERS.

Bibliography

Albitz, Paul, and Liu, Cricket. (1997). *DNS and BIND*. Cambridge, MA: O'Reilly.

Andrews, Paul. (1999). *How the Web Was Won*. New York: Broadway Books.

Berners-Lee, Tim; Cailliau, Robert; Groff, Jean-Francois; and Pollermann, Bernd. (1992). "The World Wide Web: The Information Universe." *Electronic Networking: Research, Applications, and Policy*. 1(2):52–58.

Berners-Lee, Tim; Cailliau, Robert; Luotonen, Ari; Nielsen, Henrik F.; and Secret, Arthur. (1994). "The World Wide Web." *Communications of the ACM* 37(8):76–82.

Bush, Vannevar. (1945). "As We May Think." *Atlantic Monthly* 176(July):101–108.

Chapman, A. Lyman. (1993). "The Billion-Node Internet." In *Internet System Handbook,* eds. Daniel C. Lynch and Marshall T. Rose. Reading, MA: Addison-Wesley.

Clark, Jim. (1999). *Netscape Time: The Making of the Billion Dollar Start-Up that Took on Microsoft.* NewYork: St. Martin's Press.

Comer, Douglas E. (1991). *Internetworking with TCP/IP, Volume I: Principles, Protocols, and Architecture.* Englewood Cliffs, NJ: Prentice-Hall.

Comer, Douglas E. (1997). *The Internet Book.* Upper Saddle River, NJ: Prentice-Hall.

Cusumano, Michael A., and Yoffie, David B. (1998). *Competing on Internet Time: Lessons from Netscape and Its Battle with Microsoft.* New York: Free Press.

Engelbart, Douglas C., and English, William K. (1968). "A Research Center for Augmenting Human Intellect." In *AFIPS Conference Proceedings of the 1968 Fall Joint Computer Conference,* Vol. 33. San Francisco, CA: Thompson Book.

Goldfarb, Charles F., and Prescod, Paul. (1998). *The XML Handbook.* Upper Saddle River, NJ: Prentice-Hall.

Graham, Ian S. (1997). *The HTML Sourcebook,* 3rd edition. NewYork: Wiley.

Internet Engineering Task Force. (2001). "IETF: The Internet Engineering Task Force." <http://www.ietf.org/>.

Internet Society. (2001). "Welcome to ISOC. " <http://www.isoc.org/>.

Internet Software Consortium. (2001). "Internet Domain Survey." <http://www.isc.org/ds/>.

Lehnert, Wendy G. (1998). *Internet 101: A Beginner's Guide to the Internet and the World Wide Web.* Reading, MA: Addison-Wesley.

Lehnert, Wendy G. (1999). *Light on the Internet.* Reading, MA: Addison-Wesley.

Lynch, Daniel C. (1993). "Historical Evolution." In *Internet System Handbook,* eds. Daniel C. Lynch and Marshall T. Rose. Reading, MA: Addison-Wesley.

Metcalfe, Robert. (1995). "From the Ether: Predicting the Internet's Catastrophic Collapse and Ghost Sites Galore in 1996." *InfoWorld* 17(49):61.

Netcraft Ltd. (2001). "The Netcraft Web Server Survey." <http://www.netcraft.com/survey/>.

Persistent Uniform Resource Locator. (2001). "PURL." <http://www.purl.org/>.

Peterson, Larry L., and Davie, Bruce S. (2000). *Computer Networks: A Systems Approach.* San Francisco, CA: Morgan Kaufmann.

Petska-Juliussen, Karen, and Juliussen, Egil, eds. (1997). *Computer Industry Almanac,* 8th edition. Dallas: Computer Industry Almanac, Inc.

Quittner, Joshua, and Slatalla, Michelle. (1998). *Speeding the Net: The Inside Story of Netscape and How It Challenged Microsoft.* New York: Atlantic Monthly Press.

World Wide Web Consortium (2001). "W3C." <http://www.w3.org/>.

CHARLES L. VILES

■ INTERNET WEBMASTERS

See: Webmasters

■ INTERPERSONAL COMMUNICATION

Interpersonal communication can be defined broadly as "communicating between persons." As Arthur Bochner (1989, p. 336) points out, though, that definition can be made more specific:

The anchor points [for a narrower and more rigorous conceptualization] are: 1) at least two communicators; intentionally orienting toward each other; 2) as both subject and object; 3) whose actions embody each other's perspectives both toward self and toward other. In an interpersonal episode, then, each communicator is both a knower and an object of knowledge, a tactician and a target of another's tactics, an attributer and an object of attribution, a codifier and a code to be deciphered.

In attempting to apply this narrower definition to research in interpersonal communication published in a leading communication journal (i.e., *Human Communication Research*), Glenn Stamp (1999) found that very few articles met all of the definition's rigid criteria. The definition embodies particular perspectives regarding the character of interpersonal communication. By including articles that met some of the criteria of the definition and incorporating only those that were readily classifiable as interpersonal communication and not organizational communication, mass media, rhetorical, and so on, Stamp found that, during its first twenty-five years of publication, *Human Communication Research* published 288 articles on interpersonal communication. This indicates that interpersonal communication is a well-established research tradition in the communication field. Stamp also noted the difficulty of defining interpersonal communication. This difficulty extends to its study—because interpersonal communication is often private, fleeting, and complicated.

History of the Study of Interpersonal Communication

The study of interpersonal communication began during the 1970s, at a time when many people saw successful interpersonal relationships as being a key to happiness. The (speech) communication field has its origins in the study of rhetoric, or public speaking, especially in political settings. Therefore, in grade schools, high schools, and universities, communication scholars were teaching public speaking. The influence of these origins for the study of interpersonal communication is evident in the emphasis on persuasion in interpersonal contexts. This emphasis characterizes much of the early work in the field and continues to persist. In addition to having roots in the study of rhetoric, the studies related to interpersonal communication—published in most of the mainstream communication journals (e.g., *Human Communication Research*, *Communication Monographs*, *Communication Quarterly*)— are characterized by the use of hypothesis testing, which is a traditional feature of social-scientific hypothetico-deductive research methods. This reflects the heavy application of social psychological approaches to the communication field as it struggled to become a recognized social science discipline like experimental psychology. In addition to these influences, in reading interpersonal communication work it becomes evident that the work of Paul Watzlawick, Janet Beavin, and Don Jackson (1967), Gregory Bateson (1972), and Erving Goffman (1967, 1971) also influenced both what scholars of interpersonal communication examined and how they examined it.

Major Approaches to Interpersonal Communication

Four predominant approaches to interpersonal communication are summarized here: the developmental approach, the situational approach, the rules approach, and the covering law approach. It should be noted that each of these approaches has difficulties with regard to how adequately it captures the phenomenon of interpersonal communication. This is informative about the character of interpersonal communication, underlining the fact that it is a complex and multifaceted activity.

Developmental Approach

Some scholars suggest that interpersonal communication should be understood as a developmental phenomenon. That is, interpersonal relationships go through a discernible set of steps or "stages." While many different stage models of relationships exist, particularly in psychology,

Mark Knapp's model offers a clear example of how relationships may develop from a state in which individuals are unacquainted to a state in which they are intimate (at which point the relationships may remain stable or they may disintegrate). Knapp (1978) shows how interpersonal communication is crucial to these stages, suggesting that each stage is characterized by a particular way of speaking. Gerald Miller and Mark Steinberg (1975) suggest that relationships are interpersonal to the extent that they are based on one partner's psychological knowledge of the other partner. They suggest that relationships progress along a continuum from "noninterpersonal" to "interpersonal." Noninterpersonal relationships are those in which communicators base their predictions about another person on sociological or cultural knowledge. That is, these predictions are not based in specific, individualized knowledge of that person but on generalized assumptions about that person's social or cultural group. As the relationship progresses, the ability of communicators to make predictions about the other people comes to be based to a greater extent on psychological or individualized knowledge. In this way, Miller and Steinberg suggest, the relationship becomes more interpersonal. While these models capture the evolving character of relationships and the extent to which this evolution may involve different types of communication, it represents interpersonal communication as somewhat static. Relationships are seen to be locatable at a particular stage of development because of discernible ways of talking. This contrasts with the view that relationships are organic and constantly shifting in character. The developmental approach can be summarized as being concerned with the quality of the communication that goes on between people.

Situational Approach

The situational approach suggests that factors particular to social situations determine the extent to which an encounter involves interpersonal or, alternatively, intrapersonal, small group, organizational, public, or mass communication. This approach suggests that situations may determine the character of the communication that takes place. According to this approach, some relevant features of situations include how many people are involved, whether the situation is formal or informal, private or public, and face-to-face or mediated (see Table 1).

TABLE 1.

Types of Communication According to Situational Approach

Type of Communication	Number of Communicators	Formal/Informal	Private/Public	Face-to-Face/Mediated
Intrapersonal	1	Informal	Private	N/A
Interpersonal	2	Informal	Private	Face-to-Face
Group	3–12	Semi-informal	Semi-public	Either
Organizational	12+	Formal	Public	Either
Public	Many	Formal	Public	Either
Mass	Many	Formal	Public	Mediated

This approach suggests that interpersonal communication occurs between only two people in informal settings, in private, and face-to-face. Additional dimensions that could be tabulated as factors in the situational approach include the degree of physical proximity between communicators (ranging from close in interpersonal communication to distant or mediated in public or mass communication), the available sensory channels (ranging from many in interpersonal communication to just visual and auditory in mass communication), and the immediacy of feedback (ranging from immediate in interpersonal communication to asynchronous and comparatively rare in mass communication). Both intuition and scholarship suggest that difficulties with this approach stem from the fact that communication often is not constrained by settings. Rather, communication may shape the setting as well as being shaped by it. It is possible to have a party in a classroom or a conversation between friends in a doctor's office. Thus, the situational approach tends to be characterized by issues of quantity.

Rules Approach

The rules approach suggests that interpersonal communication is a rule-governed activity. According to this approach, there are rules for social life that individuals use to structure their communication with others. While much work in interpersonal communication appears to subscribe to this view, it is usually done implicitly rather than explicitly. That is to say, findings about interpersonal communication often assume that there is a "regular" way of doing things that has some normative value attached to it, but findings are rarely, if ever, couched in terms of "rules for doing X." W. Barnett Pearce (1976) describes rules for managing meaning in interpersonal communication. While the rules approach recognizes the orderliness of much of social interaction, beyond appealing to socialization and education, it is often not able to get at the specifics of where rules "are" and how individuals learn them.

Covering Law Approach

Some work in interpersonal communication takes as its goal the formulation of universal rules for interpersonal communication, along the lines of laws that pertain to the natural world. For example, it is taken as axiomatic that water boils at 212°F (100°C). A covering law approach looks for laws of communication that have the same ability to explain, predict, and control behavior. One such proposed "law" is uncertainty reduction theory. Charles Berger and Richard Calabrese (1975) suggest that in situations where individuals meet new people, they may experience high uncertainty. This results in a drive to reduce uncertainty, often accomplished by engaging in self-disclosure (Jourard, 1971; Petronio, 1999). Because self-disclosure is subject to a norm of reciprocity, the self-disclosure of one party encourages self-disclosure from the other. Finding out more about another person enables an individual to predict more accurately their communication behavior, thereby reducing the uncertainty. Research has explored this concept in various settings, including interculturally. However, the complexity of factors involved in understanding what is happening in a communication situation often results in doubts regarding the status of the concept as a covering law.

Much of the research published in the mainstream journals of the communication field proceeds according to traditional hypothetico-deductive social scientific strictures. This often involves experimental or survey research aimed at testing a hypothesis. Robert Craig (1995) offers a threefold explanation for this. First, at the time when interpersonal communication emerged as an area of study, communication departments were divided between "humanists" and "scientists." Rhetoricians typically took a humanistic position, regarding the study of communication as a liberal art that could not become a science. Scholars studying interpersonal communication took the position that in order for it to be rigorous, experimental research was necessary. Craig suggests that a second explanation for the turn to scientific methods by scholars of interpersonal communication was an effort to offset the "academically disreputable, anti-intellectual, 'touchy-feelie' image" (p. vi) that was associated with it as a legacy of the human potential movement in the 1960s. A third explanation was the field's initial reliance on theories from such cognate fields as experimental social psychology. Borrowing theories from related fields that used these methods may have resulted in appropriating their methods also.

Social scientific work of this kind has sometimes been criticized for overusing as subjects the convenience sample of college sophomores. While college sophomores may be better educated and more "elite" than much of the population, nonetheless a large percentage of the population in the United States attends college. Furthermore, between the ages of eighteen and twenty-two, individuals may be looking more actively for companions and/or mates than at other times in their lives and thinking seriously about their interpersonal communication. These could be considered advantages of studying this population. Clearly, using this approach, it is difficult to get a sense of how relationships develop over time and just what moment-by-moment communication looks like. This issue has been addressed in a line of work that is gaining increasing prominence in the field—work that comes from the perspective of social constructionism (Gergen, 1985). This approach sees selves and relationships as having a dynamic, interactive character, in which they are constructed moment-by-moment through communication. Working from this perspective, researchers have taken a more descriptive approach to their object of study, often enabling them to describe specific methods through which relationships are constructed. Work using social approaches contrasts in various ways with traditional approaches to interpersonal communica-

tion. Wendy Leeds-Hurwitz (1995, p. 5) summarizes the differences as follows. Social approaches emphasize the social, organic, ritual, and interpretive aspects of interpersonal communication, while traditional approaches emphasize its psychological, mechanistic, transmission, and scientific aspects. Although not all scholars of interpersonal communication would agree with these contrasts, they summarize some of the key dimensions along which more traditional approaches and social approaches to interpersonal communication differ.

Some Important Interpersonal Communication Concepts

The influence of the traditional approach to interpersonal communication can be seen in some of the key concepts and findings that have been developed since the early 1970s. These include stage theories of relationships, factors that move couples through relationships (uncertainty reduction, self-disclosure, social exchange theory), persuasion strategies, the role of nonverbal communication, and communication-related personality constructs (e.g., cognitive complexity, self-monitoring, Machiavellianism, communication apprehension).

Stage Theories of Relationships

Relationships are typically seen to develop through a series of stages. According to these theories, each stage in a relationship is characterized by distinctive forms of communication. Mark Knapp and Anita Vangelisti (2000) lay out ten stages from "greeting to goodbye," as follows:

1. Initiating: The stage that involves all of the processes that occur when people first come together.
2. Experimenting: The "small talk" stage, which further uncovers common topics.
3. Intensifying: Partners come to perceive themselves as a unit.
4. Integrating: Relaters are treated as a unit by outsiders.
5. Bonding: The relationship is formalized by some kind of institutionalization.
6. Differentiating: Disengaging or uncoupling emphasizes individual differences.
7. Circumscribing: Communication is constricted or circumscribed.

8. Stagnating: Many areas of discussion between the members of the couple are cut off and efforts to communicate effectively are at a standstill.

9. Avoiding: Communication is specifically designed to avoid the possibility of communicating face-to-face or voice-to-voice.

10. Terminating: The relationship ceases, which can happen immediately after initiating or after many years.

Stage theories represent an inventory of the progress of relationships from inception to stabilization and sometimes to termination. Each stage is characterized by particular ways of talking. While these stages are logically and intuitively acceptable, there are two difficulties with stage theories. First, they might seem to suggest that relationships are easily characterized as falling into a given stage. Yet it is known that even in the course of a brief conversation, several stages may be represented. This suggests that stage theories may present a rather static view of relationships, which does not take full account of their dynamic, interactively constructed character. Second, many of the stages do not differentiate the development of romantic relationships from the development of friendships. It is likely that in many cases there is a substantive difference between how the two are initiated, developed, maintained, and terminated.

Factors that Move Couples through Relationship Stages

The drive to reduce uncertainty so as to make the other person, and ultimately the relationship, more predictable may result in communicators engaging in self-disclosure that may be reciprocated, resulting in the interactants coming to know one another better. These communication activities may move interactants through stages of relationships. Another motivational force may be social exchange. According to this theory, based on assumptions drawn from economics, relationships can be described in terms of the rewards, costs, and profits that partners offer each other. For example, Uriel Foa and Edna Foa (1974) describe a model whereby couples negotiate for resources such as love, status, information, money, goods, or services. These are located along continua of concreteness and particularism. The theory suggests that a relationship will develop or fail to develop according to the costs or rewards that intimates are able to provide each other.

Persuasion Strategies

Communication scholars have given extensive attention to strategies for persuading, or "interpersonal influence." Perhaps reflecting the field's roots in the study of rhetoric, communicators are taken to be strategic players. For example, Robert Clark and Jesse Delia (1979) suggest that communicators are engaged with three simultaneous concerns: instrumental (trying to achieve specific goals), relational (the effect on the relationship in which the communication occurs), and identity (how an individual is being perceived by others). Researchers have described many different strategies communicators use in the process of persuasion. These are commonly referred to under the umbrella of compliance-gaining strategies. This line of research originates in the work of George Marwell and David Schmitt (1967). More recent works describe the range of strategies communicators may use in trying to get others to do things (cf. Dillard, 1989; Siebold, Cantrill, and Meyers, 1994).

Role of Nonverbal Communication

Nonverbal communication is often studied in isolation from verbal communication. However, it is widely accepted that the two are intimately connected. It has been suggested that nonverbal communication may regulate verbal communication (providing one of the indications that a turn may be complete and that speaker transition could occur, for example), complement it (as when someone says they are sorry and flushes red), accent it (as when the hand is brought down hard on the table when someone is saying "Come here NOW"), repeat it (as when a person says "North" and then points in that direction), substitute for it (nodding instead of saying "Yes"), or contradict it (as when someone says "I love you too" in a sarcastic or nasty voice). Scholars of nonverbal communication often divide it into a number of distinct areas. These include proxemics (the study of the communicative use of space), kinesics (the study of the use of the body), haptics (the study of the use of touch), chronemics (the study of the use of time), and vocalics (the study of the use of the voice). Studies of nonverbal communication have emphasized the importance of understanding nonverbal communication in understanding how communication works.

Communication-Related Personality Constructs

Personality constructs are generally derived from psychology, focusing on measurable aspects of individuals that can be used to characterize and understand them, and possibly to explain and predict their conduct in certain situations. In this way, they tend to be cognitive in nature. However, some communication-related personality characteristics have been described. A person's cognitive complexity is determined by the number, abstraction, differentiation, and integration of constructs that they have about the social world and others in it (Delia, 1977). Those who are high in each of these constructs are said to be more cognitively complex than those who are lower in them. There is some controversy regarding how cognitive complexity is to be measured. Frequently, it is measured by seeing how many constructs can be coded in a subject's response to a particular question, raising the concern that cognitive complexity and loquaciousness might be conflated. Self-monitoring is the process through which a person adapts to a particular social situation. A "high" self-monitor is someone who assesses the social situation and adjusts conduct to meet the needs of that situation. A "low" self-monitor is someone who does not adapt to the social situation, but rather tends to present a consistent self (Snyder, 1974). Machiavellianism is a person's propensity to manipulate others. This concept, like communicator characteristics in general, raises the question of whether someone who measures "high" in a characteristic will demonstrate it on all occasions, or whether it may vary from communication situation to communication situation. Studies of communication apprehension have shown that feelings of anxiety about communication situations may be traits, (actual persistent characteristics of a communicator) or states (which arise only in certain conditions, such as public speaking).

Conclusion

An understanding of interpersonal communication processes offers both researchers and lay practitioners insight into the complexity of coming together in everyday interpersonal communication situations. Interpersonal communication is complex, private, and ephemeral. Yet, because it is so important in people's everyday lives, many native theories exist about its character. Despite the difficulty of studying it, significant progress has been made in the attempt to describe how interpersonal communication works in a variety of settings. The findings described above suggest that a scholarly understanding of how communication works for individuals, couples, groups, organizations, and families contrasts with native theories about it, and can be very important. For example, if it is understood that while individuals have discernible characteristics, a person's identity or "self" can be seen to emerge in and through interpersonal communication—constructing what Kenneth Gergen, (1991) calls a "relational self"—then individuals can have a sense of participation in the creation (through interpersonal communication) of who they are. This allows individuals to develop the sense that if they are not content with "who they are," this conception of self could be changed in and through communication. Similarly, understanding that relationships are constructed, maintained, and dismantled through particular ways of talking makes clear to communicators that relationships can be seen as "works in progress." This can help couples to overcome problems in all phases of relationships.

Understanding the processes of interpersonal communication in groups enables group members to see that group roles, relationships, and decision-making processes are not fixed. Because they are constructed through various ways of communicating, there can be some flexibility. Here again, scholarly theories may contradict native theories about interpersonal communication and may provide ways of solving problems that may have seemed insoluble. In organizations, understanding the processes of interpersonal communication is crucial. The recognition that, even in formal organizations, task-related relationships are managed through interpersonal communication can have important consequences for how successfully these relationships are managed. Interpersonal communication in families brings together the complexities of managing selves, relationships, and tasks through communication. A scholarly understanding of the nature of communication in families can help family members avoid such communication problems as role assignment, stereotyping, repeated blame, and others that may result in family difficulties. If families realize that difficulties of this kind are often constructed through communication, possible ways of remediating them become clearer.

See also: APPREHENSION AND COMMUNICATION; GROUP COMMUNICATION; INTERPERSONAL COMMUNICATION, CONVERSATION AND; INTERPERSONAL COMMUNICATION, ETHICS AND; INTERPERSONAL COMMUNICATION, LISTENING AND; INTRAPERSONAL COMMUNICATION; NONVERBAL COMMUNICATION; ORGANIZATIONAL COMMUNICATION; PUBLIC SPEAKING; RELATIONSHIPS, STAGES OF; RELATIONSHIPS, TYPES OF; RHETORIC.

Bibliography

Bateson, Gregory. (1972). *Steps to an Ecology of Mind.* New York: Ballantine Books.

Berger, Charles, and Calabrese, Richard. (1975). "Some Explorations in Initial Interaction and Beyond: Toward a Developmental Theory of Interpersonal Communication." *Human Communication Research* 1:99–112.

Bochner, Arthur. (1989). "Interpersonal Communication." In *International Encyclopedia of Communications,* eds. Erik Barnouw, George Gerbner, Wilbur Schramm, and Larry Gross. New York: Oxford University Press.

Clark, Robert, and Delia, Jesse. (1979). "Topoi and Rhetorical Competence." *Quarterly Journal of Speech* 65:197–206.

Cody, Michael, and McLaughlin, Margaret. (1990). "Interpersonal Accounting." In *The Handbook of Language and Social Psychology,* eds. Howard Giles and W. Peter Robinson. London: Wiley.

Craig, Robert. (1995). "Foreword." In *Social Approaches to Communication,* ed. Wendy Leeds-Hurwitz. New York: Guilford.

Delia, Jesse. (1977). "Constructivism and the Study of Human Communication." *Quarterly Journal of Speech* 63:68–83.

Dillard, James. (1989). "Types of Influence Goals in Personal Relationships." *Journal of Social and Personal Relationships* 6:293–308.

Drew, Paul, and Heritage, John. (1992). *Talk at Work.* Cambridge, Eng.: Cambridge University Press.

Fitch, Kristine. (1998). *Speaking Relationally: Culture, Communication, and Interpersonal Connection.* New York: Guilford.

Foa, Uriel, and Foa, Edna. (1974). *Societal Structures of the Mind.* Springfield, IL: Thomas.

Gergen, Kenneth. (1985). "Social Constructionist Inquiry: Context and Implications." In *The Social Construction of the Person,* eds. Kenneth J. Gergen and Keith E. Davis. New York: Springer-Verlag.

Gergen, Kenneth. (1991). *The Saturated Self.* New York: Basic Books.

Giles, Howard, and Street, Richard. (1994). "Communicator Characteristics and Behavior." In *Handbook of Interpersonal Communication,* 2nd edition, eds. Mark L. Knapp and Gerald R. Miller. Thousand Oaks, CA: Sage Publications.

Goffman, Erving. (1967). *Interaction Ritual.* Garden City, NY: Doubleday.

Goffman, Erving. (1971). *Relations in Public.* New York: Harper & Row.

Jourard, Sidney. (1971). *Self-Disclosure: An Experimental Analysis of the Transparent Self.* New York: Wiley.

Knapp, Mark L. (1978). *Social Intercourse from Greeting to Goodbye.* Boston: Allyn & Bacon.

Knapp, Mark L., and Vangelisti, Anita. (2000). *Interpersonal Communication and Human Relationships.* Boston: Allyn & Bacon.

Leeds-Hurwitz, Wendy. (1995). *Social Approaches to Interpersonal Communication.* New York: Guilford.

Mandelbaum, Jenny. (1987). "Couples Sharing Stories." *Communication Quarterly* 35:144–171.

Mandelbaum, Jenny. (1989). "Interpersonal Activities in Conversational Storytelling." *Western Journal of Speech Communication* 53:114–126.

Mandelbaum, Jenny. (1993). "Assigning Responsibility in Conversational Storytelling: The Interactional Construction of Reality." *Text* 13:247–266.

Marwell, George, and Schmitt, David. (1967). "Dimensions of Compliance-Gaining Behavior: An Empirical Analysis." *Sociometry* 30:350–364.

McCroskey, James, and Daly, John. (1984). *Personality and Interpersonal Communication.* Beverly Hills, CA: Sage Publications.

Miller, Gerry R., and Steinberg, Mark. (1975). *Between People.* Chicago: Science Research Associates.

Pearce, W. Barnett. (1976). "The Coordinated Management of Meaning: A Rules Based Theory of Interpersonal Communication." In *Explorations in Interpersonal Communication,* ed. Gerald R. Miller. Beverly Hills, CA: Sage Publications.

Petronio, Sandra, ed. (1999). *Balancing the Secrets of Private Disclosures.* Mahwah, NJ: Lawrence Erlbaum.

Shimanoff, Susan. (1980). *Communication Rules.* Beverly Hills, CA: Sage Publications.

Siebold, David; Cantrill, James; and Meyers, Renée. (1994). "Communication and Interpersonal Influence." In *Handbook of Interpersonal Communication,* 2nd edition, eds. Mark L. Knapp and Gerald R. Miller. Newbury Park, CA: Sage Publications.

Snyder, Mark. (1974). "The Self-Monitoring of Expressive Behavior." *Journal of Personality and Social Psychology* 30:526–537.

Stamp, Glenn. (1999). "A Qualitatively Constructed Interpersonal Communication Model: A Grounded Theory Analysis." *Human Communication Research* 25:431–547.

Watzlawick, Paul; Beavin, Janet; and Jackson, Don. (1967). *Pragmatics of Human Communication: A Study of Interactional Patterns, Pathologies, and Paradoxes.* New York: W. W. Norton.

JENNY MANDELBAUM

INTERPERSONAL COMMUNICATION, CONVERSATION AND

Linguists have long studied the properties of language as an organized system, focusing especially on syntax (i.e., grammatical organization) and semantics (i.e., how meaning works). J. L. Austin (1962) noticed that linguists tend to assume that language is used "constatively" (i.e., to describe the world). Austin contested this, suggesting that language is used to accomplish actions. That is, in his words, "Speech Acts." Coming together with Ludwig Wittgenstein's (1953) notion of "language games," the notion of language use as a way through which humans enact their everyday business with one another has been very influential. The interest of communication scholars in language is then a pragmatic one. That is, such scholars are interested in language-in-use. While in the communication field language and nonverbal communication are frequently treated as separable, the argument that they are in fact part of the organic whole of everyday conversation is a strong one. The to and fro of language that orchestrates nonverbal behavior through which everyday actions get done is what constitutes conversation. It has been suggested that conversation can be regarded as the "primordial site of sociality" (Schegloff, 1987). That is, it is in and through conversation that humans come together to construct and coordinate their daily lives. Thus, a detailed knowledge of how conversation works is central to understanding how interpersonal communication works.

Within the communication discipline, the study of conversation has developed out of the study of language. Language studies have focused on the attitudes of communicators toward language, on language and culture, and on psycholinguistic and sociolinguistic questions such as how language use is related to aspects of character and how it is related to aspects of social class, race, gender, and so on. Since the early 1980s, increasing attention has been paid to the organization of naturally occurring conversation and its role in interpersonal communication.

Much work in discourse analysis, sequential analysis, and conversation analysis has attended to the role of ordinary conversation in interpersonal communication. Conversation analytic work focuses on the workings of naturally occurring conversations in everyday life and therefore provides a useful resource for inspecting how everyday conversation affects, and may even be taken to constitute much of, interpersonal communication.

Conversation analytic study of interaction began in the early 1960s when Harry Sacks began to notice that systematic description of conversations was possible. Specifically, he described a systematic method by which a caller to a suicide hotline could avoid giving a name. His work with Emanuel Schegloff, Gail Jefferson, Anita Pomerantz, David Sudnow, and others started with the observation that "The talk itself was the action, and previously unsuspected details were critical resources in what was getting done in and by the talk" (Schegloff, 1992, p. xviii). Sacks (1984) indicates that the initial interest was not in conversation itself, but rather in social order. Starting from the ethnomethodological premise that everyday life is constructed in an orderly fashion and treated by interactants as being orderly, Sacks and his colleagues took the position that anywhere they looked in naturally occurring social life they could find that orderliness. Taped conversations had the advantage that they were preserved and could be played repeatedly and transcribed. However, as study of conversation proceeded, it became clear that it played a crucial role in everyday social life. Subsequently, the field has laid out features of the organization of naturally occurring interaction, as well as descriptions of the methodical ways in which a wide range of interpersonal actions are conducted.

Content

Regular methods for taking turns at talk, for constructing sequences, for repairing difficulties in talk are described by conversation analysts. Drawing on these resources, the overall structure of conversation is laid out. Each aspect of the structure of conversation is important because variations in the regularities have implications for the relationships that exist between people. This is further evidenced in a range of interpersonal conversational activities, including joke-telling, complimenting, blaming, inviting and turning down invitations, accounting, and complaining. Patterns of conversation in professional settings (e.g., medical and legal) reveal that the setting and the talk that goes on within it have a reciprocal influence. A brief description of how these activities are accomplished in talk shows how their enactment has implications for interpersonal communication.

Joke-Telling

Sacks (1974, 1978) has described the orderliness of joke-telling and the interpersonal activities that it may be designed to accomplish. He suggests that joke-telling is tightly and economically structured and that it may function as a kind of "newsletter" for the audience of early teenage girls for whom it appears to be designed. Sacks further suggests that because the joke that he describes is about oral sex, its tellability was limited to its intended audience—early teenage girls. The joke that he examines concerns three sisters who marry three brothers. The mother of the three girls "leads" the joke recipients through the joke, listening through the doors of her daughters' rooms on their wedding night and then asking them about the strange sounds she heard. In the punchline of the joke, the youngest daughter gets the better of the mother, disobeying one maternal rule in the observance of another. Sacks suggests that the joke serves as a newsletter for its early teenage audience in the following ways. First, by featuring three sisters marrying three brothers it may address the target group's concern about being separated from their friends when they get married. He notes that young adolescent girls tend to "travel in packs." Second, listening at the door and hearing inexplicable sounds may be something young teenagers have experienced and wondered about. Raising it in this joke format may be a way of addressing this concern *sub rosa*. Third, trumping the mother by flouting one rule while observing another may appeal to adolescent girls who struggle with their mothers and with the often conflicting and confusing parent-imposed rules of childhood. In these ways, then, Sacks sees the joke as serving an interpersonal function. Observing joke-telling in a variety of settings indicates that jokes are often tailored to serve interpersonal functions of this type.

Complimenting

According to Pomerantz (1978a), compliments have two simultaneous functions. First, they are positive assessments—offering a positive evaluation of some aspect of another person. Second, they are supportive actions—something nice someone may do for another. In general, there is an empirical skewing in conversation in favor of agreeing with positive assessments and accepting supportive actions (Pomerantz, 1984). Pomerantz (1978a) observes that despite this, compliments frequently are turned down in ordinary conversation. She points out that there is a widespread preference in conversation for avoiding engaging in self-praise and that a conflict with this preference would be encountered by individuals who agree with the positive assessment and accept the supportive action embodied in a compliment. Thus, compliments may be turned down or deflected in order to avoid violating the norm of not engaging in self-praise. In this way, Pomerantz shows how offering and responding to compliments are activities that are discernibly influenced by interpersonal communication considerations. While psychological reasons, such as low self-esteem, are often offered to explain turning down compliments, as this conversation structural explanation shows, close examination of details of conversation can offer an alternative explanation based in the structure of conversation.

Blaming

Pomerantz (1978b) notes that blaming can be accomplished interactively. A speaker may take the first step in indicating that something blameworthy has happened, without officially laying blame. A speaker reports an "agentless, unhappy event"—some "negative" circumstance for which the agent is not officially designated. This puts the recipient in the position of inferring from the reported circumstance that someone is to blame. In the next turn, the speaker can assign responsibility or report some other circumstance that shows he or she is not to blame. Pomerantz (p. 118, instance 4) provides the following example:

R: Liddle has been eating pudding.

C: You've been feeding it to him.

R reports an agentless unhappy event (i.e., the baby eating pudding). In the recipient's turn, C transforms the unhappy event into a consequent event by describing an another event (i.e., R feeding pudding to the baby) that is chronologically prior to the unhappy event. If an unhappy event can be turned into a consequent event, then an agent for it (i.e., a person to blame) can be specified. In this example, C, the recipient of the report of the agentless unhappy event thus attributes blame for the event by describing the preceding event. In this way, reporting provides a method for a speaker to make attributing responsibility relevant, without actively engaging in blaming. This puts the recipient in the position of claiming or attributing responsibility. Thus, blaming becomes voluntary and collaborative. In blaming, the technique of presenting a neutral brief story or report, which puts the recipient in the position of inferring the "upshot" or consequences, provides a method for undertaking a delicate activity. A similar mechanism operates in the organization of conversational complaints.

Inviting

Reportings may be used in a bipartite technique for managing invitations (Drew, 1984). By reporting a possible upcoming social event, such as, "Uh, next Saturday night's surprise party here for Kevin," the speaker can put the recipient in the position of inferring that this social event could be available for them to participate. The recipient could then treat the report simply as news. If this occurs, the potential inviter could take it as an indication that the recipient is not interested in attending the party. Alternatively, the recipient can respond by self-inviting, or at least indicating some interest in attending the party. Similarly, the invitee may turn down the invitation by reporting circumstances that the inviter could hear as precluding the invitee from taking up the invitation. This can put the inviter in the position of either modifying the invitation in an attempt to achieve acceptance of it or abandoning the invitation without the invitee having to give, and the inviter having to receive, an outright "no." Thus, reporting provides a collaborative method for managing invitations without explicitly engaging in an activity that could result in the inviter getting turned down. Like blaming, then, inviting can be managed interactively by making information available that puts the recipient in the position to advance the action or not take it up. In this way, both inviting and blaming, activities that both have some interpersonal delicacy associated with them, can be managed in a collaborative fashion.

Accounting

Managing issues of responsibility is often dealt with under the rubric of "accounts." While the term "accounts" is used to characterize a variety of actions, in its strongest sense it refers to stories with which communicators attempt to remediate some wrong. Marvin Scott and Sanford Lyman (1968, p. 46) examined "talk that shore[s] up the timbers of fractured sociation." Often, they found,

this shoring up involves telling about some specific aspect of an event in order to provide an explanation or justification for its having happened. A great deal of work in a number of fields has examined this phenomenon.

Richard Buttny (1993) has identified four different ways in which the concept of accounts has been taken up. First, the telling of accounts in conversation can be seen as being strongly related to remediating social wrongs, especially as this activity relates to matters of face-preservation. Work in the communication field has focused in this domain. Second, accounts focus on explanation of everyday activities, with less of a focus on remediating social wrongs. Third, accounts form part of the attribution theory literature. In this line of work, accounts as explanations of actions (whether the actions are problematic or not) are not limited to verbal accounts; they may form part of private cognitions. Fourth, for ethnomethodologists, social actors treat their everyday activities as "accountable" (i.e., sensible, normal, and proper). Accounting processes offer one method by which everyday people treat and come to see their actions as being ordinary. Rather than being a feature only of remediation, for ethnomethodologists, accounts are part of the everyday work of constructing the social fabric of everyday life, even though they are often "seen but unnoticed."

For practical reasons, much work on accounts relies on reconstructed or remembered accounts, or accounts that are produced in response to hypothetical situations. As they occur in interaction, though, accounts are often found in narrative structures. They may be found in the psychotherapeutic setting as part of justifications for actions. Kenneth Gergen and Mary Gergen (1983) found them being used to explain failed relationships. Buttny (1993, p. 18) points out, "Narratives as a discourse genre work as accounts when tellers re-present past events in such a way to defend their conduct. Narratives allow the teller to offer explanations at a greater length."

Complaining

A story may be told in such a way as to provide for the delicate management of a complaint. Here, a structure is used that is similar to the structure used in constructing blame, where the story is told neutrally, leaving the recipient to infer what is being done. However, in complaints, tellers may first set up a frame that allows the recipient to infer the negative or problematic character of the neutrally recounted events. The frame puts the recipient in the position of collaborating with the teller to discern, and show the appropriate reaction to, the complainable events the teller recounts. Jenny Mandelbaum (1991) describes how one teller set up a frame for the events she was about to tell: "He really doesn't know where he is. He always gets mixed up." This puts the recipient in the position of listening to and understanding the events of the story with this frame in mind. Whether or not such a story is treated as a complaint or simply as an account of an activity may be shaped by considerations related to the relational delicacy of becoming involved with the complaint or not.

Context

Studies of conversation have shown that it is both a context-shaped and a context-renewing phenomenon (Drew and Heritage, 1992). That is to say, talk in social and professional settings is constructed by the interactants, rather than by the setting, but conversation may also show the sensitivity of interactants to the fact that the talk is taking place in a given setting. Schegloff (1987) suggests that one aspect of what makes talk into institutional talk is how turn-taking is organized. In institutions, there is often a variation on the system for exchanging turns that exists in ordinary talk. Studies of talk in the medical and legal contexts show that other features of language may also be involved in how professionals and lay people work together through conversation.

Medical Setting

Studies of conversation in the medical setting show that although it is a professional setting, how talk unfolds has important implications for interpersonal communication. For example, John Heritage and Sue Sefi (1992) have studied health visitors with new parents in Great Britain. They contrast the responses that each parent makes when a health visitor comments that the baby is enjoying a bottle:

1. Health Visitor: He's enjoying that, isn't he.
2. Father: Yes, he certainly is.
3. Mother: He's not hungry because he just had his bottle.

The father agrees with the health visitor's remark, indicating that he understands it as an assessment of how the baby is taking the bottle. The mother's response indicates defensiveness regarding whether or not the baby is hungry, which could implicate a failure on her part. In this way, she shows that she takes the health visitor's comment to have institutional relevance regarding her competence as a mother. It is thus seen that the same remark can be understood to have interpersonal relevance or to have institutional relevance and that the recipient of the remark plays a part in constituting its possible institutional character.

Legal Setting

Paul Drew (1985) has studied how talk in a court of law can be constructed to display institutional concerns. Specifically, this talk is designed in such a way as to be partly for the benefit of non-participating overhearers (i.e., the jury and judge). Also, this talk is designed to be responsive to the context of both prior and anticipated testimony. Participants' awareness that talk is overheard by the jury and judge is demonstrated in a particular vigilance with regard to word selection. For example, a prosecuting attorney in a rape trial asks a witness (the victim) if she went to a "bar." In responding, the witness responds that she went to a "club." The shift from "bar" to "club" can be attributed to the witness's understanding that "bar" may sound more disreputable than "club," which may influence how she is perceived by the jury and judge. With regard to talk being designed with prior and anticipated testimony in mind, Drew has shown how, in responding to an attorney's question, a witness may proceed from descriptive to explanatory accounts that show that he or she anticipates the negative case that the attorney is trying to build. Thus, particular aspects of language have significant interpersonal and institutional consequences in the legal setting.

Conclusion

Recognizing the centrality of conversation in interpersonal communication can have important consequences for communicators. Language (and the associated nonverbal conduct that is part of its production) may be a medium through which relationships are created, maintained, and dismantled. A detailed understanding of how language works in interpersonal communication shows that it is orderly, not random. Once communicators understand the structure, they can know what to expect in communication. This can lead them to become more effective communicators. Furthermore, as is shown by the example of complimenting described above, a structural explanation of conduct may emphasize the communicative character of an action and may differ markedly from the native theory explanation, which may emphasize individual psychology. As the discussion of blaming shows, understanding some of the different interactional methods that are available to interactants can give them a choice between pursuing blame in a collaborative or a confrontative manner. Similarly, awareness of different methods for inviting makes interactants aware of the possibility of providing for voluntary coparticipation in shared activities. In the professional setting, the effect of different ways of talking on how institutions and institutional roles are produced can also have an important effect on interpersonal communication in the workplace.

Understanding the role of conversation in how relationships are enacted and managed can empower communicators to go beyond the stereotypes that they may hold with regard to themselves, others, relationships, and institutions by re-creating them anew in and through different ways of communicating.

See also: INTERPERSONAL COMMUNICATION; INTERPERSONAL COMMUNICATION, ETHICS AND; INTERPERSONAL COMMUNICATION, LISTENING AND; INTRAPERSONAL COMMUNICATION; LANGUAGE AND COMMUNICATION; LANGUAGE STRUCTURE; NONVERBAL COMMUNICATION; RELATIONSHIPS, TYPES OF; SOCIOLINGUISTICS; WITTGENSTEIN, LUDWIG.

Bibliography

Austin, J. L. (1962). *How To Do Things with Words.* Cambridge, MA: Harvard University Press.

Buttny, Richard. (1993). *Social Accountability in Communication.* Newbury Park, CA: Sage Publications.

Drew, Paul. (1984). "Speakers' Reportings in Invitation Sequences." In *Structures of Social Action: Studies in Conversation Analysis,* eds. J. Maxwell Atkinson and John C. Heritage. Cambridge, Eng.: Cambridge University Press.

Drew, Paul. (1985). "Analyzing the Use of Language in Courtroom Interaction." In *Handbook of Discourse Analysis, Vol. 3: Discourse and Dialogue,* ed. Teun A. van Dijk. London: Academic Press.

Drew, Paul, and Heritage, John, eds. (1992). *Talk at Work.* Cambridge, Eng.: Cambridge University Press.

Gergen, Kenneth, and Gergen, Mary. (1983). "Narratives of the Self." In *Studies in Social Identity,* eds. Theodore R. Sarbin and Karl E. Scheibe. New York: Praeger.

Harvey, John H.; Weber, Ann L.; and Orbuch, Terri L. (1990). *Interpersonal Accounts.* Oxford, Eng.: Basil Blackwell.

Heritage, John, and Sefi, Sue. (1992). "Dilemmas of Advice: Aspects of the Delivery and Reception of Advice in Interactions between Health Visitors and First-Time Mothers." In *Talk at Work,* eds. P. Drew and J. Heritage. Cambridge, Eng.: Cambridge University Press.

Mandelbaum, Jenny. (1991). "Conversational Non-Co-Operation: An Exploration of Disattended Complaints." *Research on Language and Social Interaction* 25:97–138.

Pomerantz, Anita M. (1978a). "Compliment Response: Notes on the Co-operation of Multiple Constraints." In *Studies in the Organization of Conversational Interaction,* ed. Jim N. Schenkein. New York: Academic Press.

Pomerantz, Anita M. (1978b). "Attributions of Responsibility: Blamings." *Sociology* 12:115–121.

Pomerantz, Anita M. (1984). "Agreeing and Disagreeing with Assessments: Some Features of Preferred/Dispreferred Turn Shapes." *In Structures in Social Action: Studies in Conversation Analysis,* eds. J. Maxwell Atkinson and John C. Heritage. Cambridge, Eng.: Cambridge University Press.

Sacks, Harvey. (1974). "An Analysis of the Course of a Joke's Telling in Conversation." In *Explorations in the Ethnography of Speaking,* eds. Richard Bauman and Joel Sherzer. Cambridge, Eng.: Cambridge University Press.

Sacks, Harvey. (1978). "Some Technical Considerations of a Dirty Joke." In *Studies in the Organization of Conversational Interaction,* ed. Jim N. Schenkein. New York: Academic Press.

Sacks, Harvey. (1984). "Notes on Methodology." In *Structures in Social Action: Studies in Conversation Analysis,* eds. J. Maxwell Atkinson and John C. Heritage. Cambridge, Eng.: Cambridge University Press.

Schegloff, Emanuel A. (1987). "From Micro to Macro: Contexts and Other Connections." In *The Micro-Macro Link,* eds. Jeffrey Alexander, Bernhardt Giesen, Richard Münch, and Neil Smelser. Berkeley: University of California Press.

Schegloff, Emanuel A. (1992). "Harvey Sacks: An Introduction and Memoir." In *Lectures on Conversation* [by Harvey Sacks], ed. Gail Jefferson. Oxford, Eng.: Basil Blackwell.

Scott, Marvin. (1993). "Foreword." In *Social Accountability in Communication,* by Richard Buttny. Newbury Park, CA: Sage Publications.

Scott, Marvin, and Lyman, Sanford. (1968). "Accounts." *American Sociological Review* 33:46–62.

Wittgenstein, Ludwig. (1953). *Philosophical Investigations*, tr. G. E. M. Anscombe. New York: Macmillan.

JENNY MANDELBAUM

▣ INTERPERSONAL COMMUNICATION, ETHICS AND

In 1984, on behalf of more than 130 petitioners, James Jaksa from Western Michigan University submitted a request to the administrative committee of the Speech Communication Association—now known as the National Communication Association (NCA)—to establish a Communication Ethics Commission. In the petition, Jaksa noted that "ethics is central to [the communication] field and has been an indispensable part of our tradition since our beginnings." Jaksa went on to add the following:

[The] search for truth, truthfulness in communication, and the moral obligations of speakers, listeners, third persons, and society as a whole are concerns of scholars in communication. However, events in contemporary society have presented a real threat to confidence in "the word." . . . The tendency to accept lies and deception as the norm in parts of our society is increasing. Yet truthfulness must be the norm for communication to exist and for society to survive. This includes private and public settings across the entire spectrum of our discipline: interpersonal, business and professional, organizational, mediated and mass communication, political and intercultural communication, and other specialized areas.

In 1985, the Communication Ethics Commission was officially established.

The NCA Communication Ethics Commission

The NCA Communication Ethics Commission continues to be an active hub for scholarly activity in the field of ethics and interpersonal communication as well as in other areas of interest to its members (e.g., ethics in contexts such as the media, the classroom, and in organizations). The commission distributes the quarterly newsletter *ethica* and cosponsors (with the Western Michigan University Department of Communication, Western Michigan University Center for the Study of Ethics in Society, and Duquesne University) a biannual National Summer Conference on Communication Ethics. This conference, held in Gull Lake, Michigan, draws together scholars from around the country to discuss issues of scholarly and pedagogical importance in communication ethics.

In 1999, after a year-long process of extensive examination, comment, and discussion (with numerous contributions from members of the Communication Ethics Commission), the NCA adopted the following "Credo for Ethical Communication":

Questions of right and wrong arise whenever people communicate. Ethical communication is fundamental to responsible thinking, decision making, and the development of relationships and communities within and across contexts, cultures, channels and media. Moreover, ethical communication enhances human worth and dignity by fostering truthfulness, fairness, responsibility, personal integrity, and respect for self and others. We believe that unethical communication threatens the quality of all communication and consequently the well-being of individuals and the society in which we live. Therefore we, the members of the National Communication Association, endorse and are committed to practicing the following principles of ethical communication:

- We advocate truthfulness, accuracy, honesty, and reason as essential to the integrity of communication.

- We endorse freedom of expression, diversity of perspective, and tolerance of dissent to achieve the informed and responsible decision making fundamental to a civil society.

- We strive to understand and respect other communicators before evaluating and responding to their messages.

- We promote access to communication resources and opportunities as necessary to fulfill human potential and contribute to the well-being of families, communities and society.

- We promote communication climates of caring and mutual understanding that respect the unique needs and characteristics of individual communicators.

- We condemn communication that degrades individuals and humanity through distortion, intimidation, coercion, and violence, and through the expression of intolerance and hatred.

- We are committed to the courageous expression of personal convictions in pursuit of fairness and justice.

- We advocate sharing information, opinions, and feelings when facing significant choices while also respecting privacy and confidentiality.

- We accept responsibility for the short- and long-term consequences for our own communication and expect the same of others.

Additional Rules, Guidelines, and Perspectives

In his book *Ethics in Human Communication* (1996), Richard Johannesen built on the work of John Condon and set out the following guidelines for interpersonal communication:

1. Personal beliefs and feelings should be shared in a candid and frank manner.

2. Keeping social relationships harmonious may be more ethical than speaking one's mind in groups or cultures where interdependence is valued over individualism.

3. Communicate information accurately, with minimal loss or distortion of the intended meaning.

4. It is generally unethical to deceive someone intentionally.

5. There should be a consistency in the meanings that verbal and nonverbal cues, words, and actions communicate.

6. It is usually unethical to block the communication process intentionally with behaviors such as cutting off people before their point has been made, changing the subject when another person obviously has more to say, or using nonverbal behaviors to distract people from the intended subject.

Lana Rakow (1994) proposes an interpersonal communication ethic that emphasizes norms of trust, mutuality, justice, and reciprocity. She suggests three ethical rules for achieving healthy relationships: (1) inclusiveness or being open to multiple perspectives on truth, an encouragement of them and a willingness to listen, (2) participation or ensuring that all people must have the means and ability to participate, to be heard, to speak, to have voice, to have opinions count in public decision making, and (3) reciprocity so participants are considered to be equal partners in a communication transaction and there is a reciprocity of speaking and listening.

Many scholars of ethics and interpersonal communication offer a dialogic perspective in which sustaining and nurturing dialogic interaction is one of the most important values in a communication encounter. In a dialogic perspective, both participants in an interaction are considered to be worthy of respect and should be allowed to express their own points of view. Theorists such as Ronald C. Arnett (1992) explore the value of dialogue in maintaining interpersonal communication encounters. Extending philosopher Martin Buber's analysis of the need for dialogue, Arnett does not call for a "perfect dialogue"; instead, he discusses the importance of a position of humility in which the interactants argue for their own ideas while respecting the rights of others to do the same. Johannesen (1996) lists the following six characteristics of a dialogue: authenticity, inclusion, confirmation, presentness, a spirit of mutual equality, and a supportive climate. Authenticity refers to being direct, honest, and straightforward but not necessarily saying everything that comes to mind. Inclusion refers to trying to see other people's viewpoint without sacrificing one's own convictions. Confirmation occurs when people express positive warmth for each other. Presentness occurs when people concentrate completely on the encounter and demonstrate that they are willing to be completely involved in the interaction. A spirit of mutual equality exists when the participants view each other as people and not as objects to be manipulated or exploited. A supportive climate exists when the participants avoid value judgments that stifle understanding and instead encourage each other to communicate freely.

Feminist and Interethnic Scholarship

Feminist scholarship has had a great influence on the theorizing about ethics and interpersonal communication. One of the major contributions of these scholars has been to highlight and explicate the concept of care. Carol Gilligan, in *In a Different Voice* (1982), proposes that women are more likely to base their decisions on an "ethic of care" in which relationships with others and responsibility for them is paramount and that men are more likely to use an "ethic of justice" that emphasizes hierarchical principles and issues of right versus wrong. Julia Wood (1994) has criticized this perspective for promoting the stereotype of women as nurturers, and Nel Noddings (1984) contends that any person (female or male) is capable of being either the caring one or the cared for. Rita C. Manning (1992) maintains that a reciprocal web of caring is created in day-to-day interactions with others and that although one may be free to choose who to care for at what point in time, roles and responsibilities (such as parenthood) set up an obligation to respond in a caring manner. Nevertheless, Gilligan made a major contribution to theory in the field of interpersonal communication ethics by (1) emphasizing that neither the care perspective nor the justice perspective is a more morally developed perspective and (2) including the voices of women in an area in which they were not well represented previous to her theorizing.

In extending the consideration of ethics in interpersonal communication beyond the bounds of Anglo-American culture, Anthony Cortese argues in *Ethnic Ethics: The Restructuring of Moral Theory* (1992) that morality based on justice cannot be purely subjective (derived from the principles of individuals alone) nor purely objective (based, for example, on universal rules). Instead, he calls for "communication without domination":

> [R]elationships, not reason nor justice, are the essence of life and morality. . . . Relationships provide the context and the basis for any type of justice, any code of moral principles for which we live. Relationships provide the context for all of our sets of belief, value systems, and behavioral norms. Justice must always refer to some type of relationship; justice is meaningless without its application to relationships. If we do not comprehend the social fabric of our relationships with others, then justice is merely a set of empty mathematical, reified formuli. Justice then hangs dangerously devoid of meaning, like a trapeze artist without a safety net. That is, without relationships justice contains no system of checks and balances. It becomes primary and an end itself without regard to the purpose of morality [pp. 157–158].

Questions for Further Study

In a 1997 presentation to the NCA, Johannesen raised several questions that are faced by scholars who study ethics. First, can communication ethics survive the devastating critique posed by postmodernism (i.e., the contemporary idea that life is fragmented in many ways and there is no ultimate moral authority guiding ethical action in all contexts)? Can interpersonal communication ethics survive if there is no individual moral agent, there is no autonomous self that can decide ethical questions objectively, there are no absolute moral values, and there is only fragmentation and alienation? After reviewing several approaches to the notion of self, Johannesen concluded that even in a postmodern context it is possible to have a self that is unique and individual, capable of acting responsibly. Second, do transcultural ethical values block the search for minimum ethical standards for communication? Johanessen points to *Ethics in Intercultural and International Communication* (1997) by Fred Casmir and *Communication Ethics and Universal Values* (1997) by Clifford Christians and Michael Traber as examples of works that successfully identify universal ethical principles. Third, can people recognize the roles that diversity and marginalization (i.e., people who do not have equal access to political and other types of power in a society) play in developing communication ethics? Johanessen responded that, as other scholars have noted, honoring diversity must also include respect for common values and respect for all human beings.

See also: FEMINIST SCHOLARSHIP AND COMMUNICATION; INTERPERSONAL COMMUNICATION.

Bibliography

Anderson, Kenneth E. (2000). "Developments in Communication Ethics: The Ethics Commission, Code of Professional Responsibilities, Credo for Ethical Communication." *Journal of the Association for Communication Administration* 29:131–144.

Arnett, Ronald C. (1992). *Dialogic Education: Conversation About Ideas and Between Persons.* Carbondale: Southern Illinois University Press.

Arnett, Ronald C., and Arneson, Pat. (1999). *Dialogic Civility in a Cynical Age: Community, Hope, and Interpersonal Relationships.* Albany: State University of New York Press.

Arnett, Ronald C.; Arneson, Pat; and Wood, Julia T. (1999). *Dialogic Civility in a Cynical Age: Community, Hope, and Interpersonal Relationships.* Albany: State University of New York Press.

Casmir, Fred L., ed. (1997). *Ethics in Intercultural and International Communication.* Mahwah, NJ: Lawrence Erlbaum.

Christians, Clifford, and Traber, Michael, eds. (1997). *Communication Ethics and Universal Values.* Thousand Oaks, CA: Sage Publications.

Cortese, Anthony. (1992). *Ethnic Ethics: The Restructuring of Moral Theory.* Albany: State University of New York Press.

Gilligan, Carol. (1982). *In a Different Voice: Psychological Theory and Women's Development.* Cambridge, MA: Harvard University Press.

Jaksa, James A., and Pritchard, Michael S. (1994). *Communication Ethics: Methods of Analysis,* 2nd edition. Belmont, CA: Wadsworth.

Jaksa, James A., and Pritchard, Michael S. (1996). *Responsible Communication: Ethical Issues in Business, Industry, and the Professions.* Cresskill, NY: Hampton Press.

Jensen, J. Vernon. (1997). *Ethical Issues in the Communication Process.* Mahwah, NJ: Lawrence Erlbaum.

Johannesen, Richard L. (1996). *Ethics in Human Communication,* 4th edition. Prospect Heights, IL: Waveland.

Makau, Josina M., and Arnett, Ronald C., eds. (1997). *Communication Ethics in an Age of Diversity.* Urbana: University of Illinois Press.

Manning, Rita C. (1992). *Speaking from the Heart: A Feminist Perspective on Ethics.* Lanham, MD: Rowman & Littlefield.

Noddings, Nel. (1984). *Caring: A Feminine Approach to Ethics & Moral Education.* Berkeley: University of California Press.

Pritchard, Michael S. (1991). *On Becoming Responsible.* Lawrence: University of Kansas Press.

Rakow, Lana. (1994). "The Future of the Field: Finding Our Mission." An address presented at Ohio State University, May 13.

Wood, Julia T. (1994). *Who Cares? Women, Care, and Culture.* Carbondale: Southern Illinois University Press.

LEA P. STEWART

▉ INTERPERSONAL COMMUNICATION, LISTENING AND

Listening is a fundamental part of the process of communication. Adults spend about 42 percent of their time in listening activities, and children spend about 58 percent of the time in the same activity (Lederman, 1977). Listening is a complex facet of the communication process, and it is considered by some communication researchers to be a more difficult activity than speaking. While the word "listening" is used interchangeably with some other words, such as "hearing," it is a unique process, unlike any other.

Definition

To define "listening" entails comparing and contrasting it with some other similar activities: "perception," "attention," and "hearing."

"Perception" has been defined as a process of extracting information from the world outside oneself, as well as from within. When perceiving something, a person is able to note certain stimuli and draw some kind of information from them. One type of perception is listening, the process by which one selectively attends to certain auditory stimuli. Listening is selective perception and attention to auditory stimuli.

In the selective process of listening, stimuli are filtered. Hearing is related to listening. Hearing is a nonselective process. If one has hearing that is not impaired, he or she hears every audible sound that occurs in his or her presence. Thus, hearing is a prerequisite for listening. While words such as "listening" and "hearing" are often used interchangeably in everyday speech, listening is a process that includes selective attention and the assignment of meaning. Physiologically, listening involves the use of hearing organs to receive those acoustic vibrations that are converted into signals that can be understood by the brain. It is the brain that gives meaning to those vibrations. The brain decodes these vibration patterns that are known as "words." Physiologically, listening occurs in waves. There are natural peaks and valleys in the listener's processing of auditory stimuli, and listeners can only comprehend some of the stimuli that they are able to hear.

Just as listening has a physiological basis, it also has a psychological basis. The psychological aspects have to do with interest and attention. A person listens to what interests him or her and does not listen to what is found to be boring or dull or irrelevant. Listening is an activity that involves the skills of paying attention, making sense of what is being said (interpretation), and providing feedback or response to the speaker. These skills are learned, and they can be improved. Improvement of listening involves correcting the five most frequently found psychological interferences to effective listening: habitual inattention, selective perception, selective inattention, inaccurate inference making, and the inability to frame concepts. Habitual inattention occurs when listeners regularly and consistently find their attention wandering. Selective perception occurs when listeners only perceive some of the things that are being said to them. Selective inattention occurs when listeners listen only to those things to which they want to pay attention. Inaccurate inference making occurs when listeners draw conclusions incorrectly about the meanings of what they have heard. The inability to frame concepts happens when listeners are unable to comprehend or understand what has been said.

Reasons for Listening

People listen for a variety of reasons. The most fundamental reasons for listening are to learn something, to be informed, to be entertained, or to form relationships. When people listen to learn, be informed, be entertained, or to form relationships, they are motivated by the prospect of gaining something for themselves. As a result of listening, they know more, are more informed, or are more entertained.

When it comes to forming relationships, people listen for some other reasons. In many ways, communicators act as sounding boards for others when they function as listeners. People continually address verbal messages to each other. People listen if there is some reason to do so; if not, while they may look as if they are paying attention, they simply do not really do the work that it takes to listen to the person who is speaking.

There are several reasons to listen to someone who is speaking. One reason one person listens to another is because he or she knows that at times he or she needs the other person to listen to him or her. Everyone is at one time or another in need of good listeners. A second reason that anyone listens to anyone else is because he or she cares about that

other person or about what that other person has to say. A third reason for listening is because one feels he or she must listen. There are many other reasons for listening, including to pass time, to enjoy a joke, to get directions, to add to one's knowledge, and to share another's experience.

The Role of the Listener

Just as there are many reasons to listen, the role of the listener is more than just passively taking in sounds and making sense of them. In interpersonal communication, listening includes providing reactions and responses for the person who is speaking. These reactions and responses are called feedback. It is feedback to the speaker that makes listening a more active process. Feedback is any form of response to the speaker's message. It is verbal and/or nonverbal and/or silent. Any response or lack of response is the listener's message to the original speaker. Thus, verbal (words) and/or nonverbal (sounds, gestures, facial expressions) communications are the ways in which feedback is provided. The skillful listener is continuously paying attention, evaluating what is being said and what it means, and deciding on what are the best choices to make about selecting the most appropriate feedback or response.

Feedback serves two functions. First, it indicates the listener's understanding or misunderstanding of the speaker's intended meaning. Second, it shows the listener's willingness or resistance to proceed as requested and/or directed by the speaker. Viewed as feedback, responses or lack of responses are the listener's tools for indicating to the speaker how effectively he or she has expressed himself or herself. Feedback that is other than what is desired, either in form or content, would be an indication that the speaker has not been effective.

Active Listening

Because of the importance of the feedback from listeners, and because that feedback takes the form of some active response, listening is at times referred to as "active listening." "Active listening" is a term that is used to refer to listening activity that includes providing the speaker with feedback. The speaker talks. The listener listens. The listener reacts: nods, says something, utters subvocalizations (e.g., "ohh," "uh huh"). Active listening, therefore, goes beyond the attention and interpretation of stimuli. Active listening involves verbal and nonverbal response. Active listeners work at letting the people who talk to them know that they are listening. Active listeners work at letting those people know that they are being attended to—that the listener is working at understanding what the speaker is trying to say.

As an active participant in interpersonal communication, the listener attempts to see, hear, and understand all that is said or done by the speaker who is attempting to communicate. One of the hallmarks of the good listener is that he or she is empathetic and supportive. In other words, the listener tries to understand what is being said both emotionally and intellectually. The listener works to try to understand what is meant, or the meaning of what is being said, by the speaker. In trying to understand, the listener may even be helping the speaker to understand better the message that is being sent. In this sense, the listener is an active responder. While listening is being discussed separately from speaking, in conversations or interpersonal communication, speaking and listening are roles that are exchanged almost imperceptibly.

It is often said that a good listener is a good conversationalist. What this means is that the person who is quiet and listens thus allows the other person to speak. However, beyond allowing another to speak, a good listener really is a good conversationalist, because the listener provides feedback that is needed by the speaker, and the listener actively takes a turn in engaging in conversation. In essence, feedback is a message that the listener directs toward the original speaker in response to the original speaker's message. It occurs in response to the original message maker rather than as the initial message in a given conversation or verbal interaction. Thus, feedback is both a response and the listener's message.

As a responder, the listener has choices to make about the ways in which to frame the message and how to convey it. First, the listener must decide the timing: when will he or she respond. Second, the listener must decide how to respond. The listener can respond either verbally by saying something or nonverbally by gestures, facial expressions, or vocalizations. In fact, listeners usually provide a combination of these responses. The verbal response is what is left until the speaker has completed his or her thoughts. The nonverbals—facial expressions, nods of the head, gestures, vocalizations—may take place while the speaker is talking.

Being More than an Active Responder

Feedback can be more than just a response to a speaker or a speaker's message. Feedback can be seen as the listener's exertion of control over the communication. In this instance, feedback is not a measure of ineffectiveness on the speaker's part. It is the listener's way of expressing how the conversation must proceed if the listener is going to continue to participate in the conversation. The listener responds to the speaker by indicating either verbally or nonverbally that the conversation needs to take a turn in order to keep the listener involved. A deep yawn while a speaker goes on at length would be an example of a nonverbal expression that the conversation needs to be changed.

To view feedback only as the response to the speaker violates the activeness principle of listening. It makes the listener a less-than-equal partner, one who passively functions only to assist the speaker in accomplishing his or her ends. In any interpersonal exchange, however, all participants must be accomplishing some sort of personal ends, or they may have no reasons to participate, actively or passively.

Feedback is more effective when it is descriptive, specific, timely, and about behaviors that can be changed. In offering feedback, the listener is attempting to let the speaker know how he or she responds to the speaker and the speaker's message. For example, feedback that is descriptive is report-like rather than judgmental and includes details that explain what the listener needs for the speaker to be understood clearly. Its timeliness is significant. If it is offered as an interruption or before the speaker has completed his or her thought, it is either not of value to him or her or it may be perceived as being an attempt to redirect the conversation. Feedback, to be effective, must also be reflective of something about which the listener thinks the speaker can take some action.

See also: INTERPERSONAL COMMUNICATION; INTERPERSONAL COMMUNICATION, CONVERSATION AND; INTERPERSONAL COMMUNICATION, ETHICS AND; NONVERBAL COMMUNICATION; RELATIONSHIPS, STAGES OF; RELATIONSHIPS, TYPES OF.

Bibliography

Fergus, Robert H. (1966). *Perception.* New York: McGraw-Hill.

Kelly, Lynne; Lederman, Linda C.; and Phillips, Gerald M. (1989). *Communicating in the Workplace: A Guide to Business and Professional Speaking.* New York: HarperCollins.

Lederman, Linda C. (1977). *New Dimensions: An Introduction to Human Communication.* Dubuque, IA: W. C. Brown.

Lederman, Linda C. (1995). *Asking Questions, Listening to Answers, and Talking to People.* Dubuque, IA: Kendall Hunt.

Petrie, Charles R., Jr. (1966). "What Is Listening?" In *Listening: Readings,* ed. Sam Duker. New York: Scarecrow Press.

Miller, Gerald, and Steinberg, Mark. (1975). *Between People.* Chicago: Science Research Associates.

Nicols, Ralph, and Stevens, Lawrence. (1957). *Are You Listening?* New York: McGraw-Hill.

Smith, Vance. (1986). "Listening." In *A Handbook of Communication Skills,* ed. Owne Hargie. New York: New York University Press.

Trenholm, Sarah, and Jensen, Arthur. (1996). *Interpersonal Communication.* Belmont, CA: Wadsworth.

Wolvin, Andrew D., and Coakley, Carolyn G., (1985). *Listening.* Dubuque, IA: W. C. Brown.

LINDA COSTIGAN LEDERMAN

▧ INTERVENTION

See: Antiviolence Interventions; Parental Mediation of Media Effects

▧ INTRAPERSONAL COMMUNICATION

Intrapersonal communication, or communication within the individual, is an area of study that is fundamental to the study of all communication. Communication can be thought of as beginning with the self. When a person talks of communication with others, he or she speaks of interpersonal communication, or communication between one individual (the self) and another. Intrapersonal communication limits itself to communication within the individual. It is communication that takes place within the individual when he or she is communicating with others, or simply, when he or she is alone and thinking to himself or herself. When a person says to himself or herself, "way to go," he or she is engaging in intrapersonal communication. Intrapersonal communication, how-ever, has been less studied than many other areas of communication.

Studying Intrapersonal Communication

While the literature on communication has included the area of intrapersonal communication since the 1980s, it has been a problematic area of study for researchers. One of the most often discussed problems among communication researchers in the last part of the twentieth century was how to study intrapersonal communication—and how to understand it.

The "self" has long been acknowledged as an integral part of any communication interaction between people. It is defined in a variety of ways, all of which try to establish the self as something that is unique and separate from any other individual or entity. From a systems perspective, the self is viewed as an entity that interacts with and processes information or data from its environment. The self (individual) affects the environment and is affected by it in a dialectic relationship in which the self is a socially constructing and constructed reality. Explanations of the derivation of the sense of self tend to emphasize social interaction as a profound influence. Symbolic interactionists argue that it is in social interaction that the self is created, with individuals taking roles in response to the feedback that they receive from others. Charles Cooley (1902) identified the "looking-glass self" as the view of self that arises in response to the opinion of others. George Herbert Mead (1934) extended the looking-glass self, proposing that the structure of the self is a reflection of the entire social process—the self as a complex and multiple structure that arises from all social experience.

As early as the work of William James (1890), the notion of multiple selves has been part of the literature on communication between people. Eric Berne (1964) depicted three ego states of the self, and Mead (1934) differentiated between the "I," the impulsive, unorganized, unpredictable self, and the "me," the generalized other who provides direction and guidance. The construct of self as being a composite of multiple selves derives from psychoanalytic theory, based on the concept of internalization, or the incorporation into the self of that which was before external to the self.

The self, similar to any other multifaceted system, is made up not only of parts but also of relationships between those parts, referred to hereafter as "intrapersonal relationships." An enhanced understanding of the dialectic between intrapersonal and interpersonal communication is made possible by examining the intrapersonal relationships that exist between the multiple selves that constitute each participant in a dyad.

Defining "Intrapersonal Relationships"

"Intrapersonal relationships" were first defined in the literature on communication by Linda Lederman (1996). She based her conceptualization of intrapersonal relationships on the literature on interpersonal relationships. A review of the literature on interpersonal relationships suggested to Lederman that whatever is known of relations between people that is useful in understanding their communication can be applied and examined as it sheds light on the concept of intrapersonal relationships and communication.

In interpersonal communication, defining what is meant by "relationship" is difficult. The difficulty lies in identifying what a relationship is and when one exists. The same holds true for intrapersonal relationships. Generally, it is agreed that two or more people are in a relationship if they have an effect on each another—if they are "interdependent" in the sense that a change in one person causes a change in the other person and vice versa. Harold Kelley and his colleagues (1983, p. 135) define relationships as two chains of events, one for P (person) and one for O (other) that are on the same time dimension and that are causally interconnected. For two people to be in a relationship with each other then, some of the events in P's chain of events must be causally connected to some of the events in O's chain. This definition of "relationship" applies to the interface of chains of events in multiple selves as readily as in two-person systems. Given the physical reality that the self shares with itself, it is self-evident that the chains of events that are experienced by any one of an individual's multiple selves is on the same time dimension and is causally interconnected with the experiences of the other selves. In fact, the psychopathological state of multiple personalities exists when the selves become so detached from each other that they have "separate lives." This does not mean that the multiple selves all experience any given event in the same way, but it does indicate that there are connections between the chains of events and causal connections.

Interpersonal relationships are not observable; instead, what can be observed are cues that can be interpreted to determine the nature of the relationships between two people. Erving Goffman (1959) notes that the tie signs between people, such as hand holding, provide clues as to the nature of the connection (relationship). Jerome Manis and Bernard Meltzer (1967) explore how people attempt to determine when other people are "with" each other (i.e., connected, related) based on their behaviors, verbal as well as nonverbal. These interpretations are based on culturally determined cues, such as bonding signals, in the form of nonverbal behaviors and/or explicit descriptive labels that are produced by the two people or are applied by other to them. The labels and behaviors can be either mismatched or correctly matched. The relationships themselves between the communicators are never visible; they are the products of inference and interpretation.

Intrapersonal relationships, too, are invisible. The connections between multiple selves are not visible to outsiders. Instead, inferences are drawn based on the interpretations of verbal and nonverbal behaviors. For example, when observing the way a person is dressed, it is possible to draw inferences, such as "She takes good care of herself" or "He neglects himself," which makes a statement about the interpretation of the self in relation to itself, or about an intrapersonal relationship. This is not unlike statements of the self in relation to another (e.g., "John and Mary are going together," "She's so involved with him"). When someone responds to a compliment about his or her attire by saying, "Oh, it was on sale, I got it for almost nothing," inferences can be drawn about the way in which the individual engages verbally with others in relating to himself or herself. Inference making is necessary in understanding any relationship; the invisibility of a relationship does not preclude one's ability to infer a relationship intrapersonally any more than interpersonally.

Because relationships cannot themselves be made visible in either interpersonal or intrapersonal communication, the nature of those relationships must be derived by examining evidence of them in terms of what goes on between the participants: the manifestations of their interdependence. Thus, when, for example, Ralph and Vinnie wear the same tee-shirts, the shirts become the manifestation of some relationship that exists between them. They may be friends or family members or members of the same team. The shirts provide evidence of some connection. In intrapersonal relationships, it is the manifestations of the interrelationships between multiple selves that indicate a relationship. A person gives self-congratulations for getting a good grade or provides self-criticism for making a wrong turn.

Intrapersonal relationships, then, can be defined as those connections between multiple selves, albeit invisible, that determine the interdependence of those selves and the effect of that interdependence as it affects and is affected by any part of the self that makes up one's being. By using the same kinds of considerations to examine intrapersonal relationships that are used to explore interpersonal relationships, intrapersonal communication can be seen to encompass more than simply one's self-concept or its derivation—more even than one's talk with oneself. Intrapersonal relationships are a rich field for examination as they potentially affect communication, be it intrapersonal or interpersonal.

The Importance of Intrapersonal Relationships

One's relationship with oneself interacts with one's relationships with others, just as an individual's relationship with a spouse affects that individual's romantic relationships with others, or as an individual's relationship with his or her child affects his or her relationships with others. One's relationship with oneself affects and is affected by one's relationships with others. One's attitudes, feelings, and thoughts about self can intervene in communication just as possibly as one's attitudes, feelings, and thoughts about the other. Thus, for example, when one is very critical of oneself, it is harder to accept compliments from others than when one feels pride in oneself. Or, what one thinks someone else means by a compliment may be related to how one thinks about oneself. If, for example, Jack is self-conscious about his looks, and Bob tells him he likes Jack's haircut, Jack may take Bob's comments as sarcasm. To the extent that the purpose of communicating is to be understood, it is important to examine the role of intrapersonal communication in the understanding of interpersonal interactions.

Intrapersonal communication is a complex and complicated system of symbols and meanings. It is

part of everyday life. By including communication with the self in the study of communication, the understanding of the complex set of symbolic interactions that take place in communication is increased. It also has very practical applications. Just as one can learn to communicate better with a coworker or family member, one can learn to communicate more effectively with oneself. One can learn to listen to oneself, to note the ways in which one talks to oneself, and to change that self-talk in order to improve one's relationship with the self.

See also: INTERPERSONAL COMMUNICATION; MEAD, GEORGE HERBERT; NONVERBAL COMMUNICATION; RELATIONSHIPS, TYPES OF.

Bibliography

Berne, Eric. (1964). *Games People Play: The Psychology of Human Relationships*. New York: Grove Press.

Blumer, Herbet. (1975). "Symbolic Interactionism." In *Approaches to Human Communication*, eds. Richard W. Budd and Brent D. Ruben. Rochelle Park, NJ: Hayden.

Cooley, Charles H. (1902). *Human Nature and the Social Order*. New York: Scribner.

Freud, Sigmund. (1933). *New Introductory Lectures on Psychoanalysis*. New York: W. W. Norton.

Gergen, Kenneth J. (1982). "From Self to Science: What Is There to Know?" In *Psychological Perspectives on the Self*, Vol. 1, ed. Jerry Suls. Hillsdale, NJ: Lawrence Erlbaum.

Goffman, Erving. (1959). *Presentation of Self in Everyday Life*. New York: Doubleday.

James, William. (1890). *The Principals of Psychology*. New York: Holt.

Kelley, Harold H.; Berscheid, Ellen; Christensen, Andrew; Harvey, John H.; and Huston, Ted L., eds. (1983). *Close Relationships*. New York: W. H. Freeman.

Lederman, Linda C. ([1996] 1998). "Internal Muzak: An Exploration of Intrapersonal Communication." Reprinted in *Communication Theory: A Reader*, ed. Linda C. Lederman. Dubuque, IA: Kendall Hunt.

Manis, Jerome G., and Meltzer, Bernard N. (1967). *Symbolic Interaction: A Reader in Social Psychology*. Boston: Allyn & Bacon.

Mead, George Herbert. (1934). *Mind, Self and Society*. Chicago: University of Chicago Press.

Millar, Frank E., and Rogers, L. Edna. (1976). "A Relational Approach to Interpersonal Communication." In *Explorations in Interpersonal Communication*, Vol. 5, ed. Gerald R. Miller. Beverly Hills, CA: Sage Publications.

LINDA COSTIGAN LEDERMAN

▮ JOURNALISM, HISTORY OF

Some form of "news packaging," defined as tailoring news for sale, has likely existed since the first newspapers were published. This entry, however, examines the history of journalism in terms of four basic American eras: the 1830s, the Civil War era, the Watergate era, and the 1980s and beyond. News packaging (not to be confused with distribution techniques of print media) has three crucial definitional elements:

1. arrangement of news in formats to make it more appealing, accessible, and readily available while facilitating the ability of consumers to "make sense of" it—that is, making news easier to grasp, absorb, digest, understand, and use,

2. efforts to market news as a product, and

3. the notion of news as a commodity.

When the term "packaging" was first used in this sense is not clear, but a 1971 book by James Aronson may have been the first with the concept in the title: *Packaging the News: A Critical Survey of Press, Radio and Television*. Since the late 1980s, the term has been widely used, but it must be distinguished from "framing"—also used increasingly interchangeably with "packaging." Framing, however, instead of referring to overt efforts to sell news, concerns how the "packaging" or "framing" of subjects in news accounts shapes the way in which people think about events and issues. Generally not considered a conscious effort, framing is assumed to result from the beliefs and values of content producers as absorbed via cultural heritages.

Over time, the emphasis in news packaging has evolved from helping readers find news quickly to presenting news in ways that help consumers make sense of it. Important impetuses to developments include: (1) the drive to gain readers or viewers—to profit; (2) new technologies; and (3) new media, new ways of conveying news, or reinvented media forms.

The 1830s and the Penny Press

Beginning in the 1830s, a shift occurred away from a partisan press and toward the penny press, which brought profitability to the field and laid the foundation for later news packaging developments. As part of this shift, the interest in news events overtook interest in political essays. Pre-1830s newspapers served political parties and seem to have been aimed at an educated elite—especially political leadership. Dominated by political content, they had small circulations (averaging approximately 1,000), were expensive, and, with estimated life spans averaging three years, were rarely profitable. Advertising was sold by the square, newspapers were delivered by mail, and unpaid subscriptions caused serious financial problems.

Seeking profits, the first successful penny newspaper editor, Benjamin Day, beginning in 1833, introduced structural changes and news packaging techniques. On the structural level, he established new advertising sales and circulation systems, thereby assuring profits through both. He sold advertising by the line and created street sales of newspapers, charging carriers less when they paid in advance. Solving the deadbeat subscriber problem and establishing a new advertising sales system put newspapers on a solid financial foundation. The first penny newspapers were small enough to be easily carried around, so they could be read as opportunities arose during the day; thus, Day made news more accessible to readers through newspaper price, size, and content.

Day's approach to content especially fits the definition of news packaging. The items were concise and easy to read, and thus they were more accessible to the less educated than were the publications that featured political essays. Day is credited with establishing core news values that have endured, including prominence, proximity, and human interest. Among wittily written and deliberately amusing items, some "stories," such as the great moon hoax, were fabricated for sheer entertainment.

The Civil War and News Innovations

The Civil War era marks a significant turning point in news packaging history. The format became crystallized (in a version that is very similar to the modern newspaper), and several wartime changes consolidated the commercial value of newspapers. Organized business techniques for handling demand, supply, and costs of producing war news increasingly shaped the press, leading to a well-defined business model. People's need to know what might be happening to loved ones away at war and whether the nation might endure created an insatiable demand for news. This unprecedented value attached to newspapers meant news was treated distinctly as a product, as, in the effort to meet demand, more newspaper space was given to war news than had been given to any subject previously.

A style that has come to be called the inverted pyramid was created to standardize the presentation of information. By beginning with summary leads (that explained who, what, when, where, why, and how), an item could quickly provide the readers with the most important elements of news accounts. Some, including J. Cutler Andrews (1970), say the summary lead developed from the use of the telegraph by Civil War correspondents, who had to transmit essential details quickly before sending fuller reports. However, at least

one scholar, David Mindich (1998), has attributed the summary lead to a model found in U.S. Secretary of War Edwin Stanton's writing.

Related to the summary lead, multideck headlines (i.e., headlines with multiple divisions, creating subheadlines under the main headline) were used during the war. Prewar headlines were one column wide, and many were "standing heads" (e.g., "By Telegraph") that revealed little if any information about the content to follow. However, headlines became increasingly tailored to stories during the war, and multideck headlines—used on occasion in the *New York Herald* before 1860— became common packaging techniques. The decks gave readers the gist of elements about events being reported, thus making news readily accessible and digestible. As with the summary lead, some have credited these developments to the use of the telegraph by correspondents. Because telegraph lines were unreliable during the war, due to underdevelopment, vulnerability to weather conditions, and to being cut by enemy troops, reporters developed the practice of transmitting the most important details first, followed by full accounts as access to the telegraph permitted. Editors built multideck headlines of those details, packaging the information for readers to absorb quickly.

Other news packaging advances that occurred during the Civil War period include interviews, direct quoting of sources, descriptive techniques adapted from fiction and poetry, use of multiple sources, expansion of eyewitness accounts, and illustration. While these were used before the war, none was common, but illustration and interviews became irreversibly integral to news packaging. Before 1860, newspapers had little display material and virtually no cartoons or illustrations, except small woodcuts that were commonly restricted to advertisements. However, to help package war news, magazine publishers hired artists to draw pictures of battles. (Soon after the war, the first illustrated newspaper, the *New York Daily Graphic,* began, and, in 1880, the first photograph appeared in a newspaper.) Also, interviews, rare before the war, became a fad soon after.

News packaging advanced also as journalists focused on the commodity qualities of news. That is, marketing involves emphasizing the most salable qualities, and the most salable quality of Civil War news was timeliness. Prewar accounts com-

A group of Civil War correspondents gather at the mobile headquarters of James Gordon Bennett's New York Herald. *(Corbis)*

monly reported events in chronological order, and some were two to three years old, especially those from abroad. One had to read to the end of a story to learn the latest developments of the events that were being reported. During the war, however, demand for the most recent accounts entrenched timeliness as a permanent value, along with factual accuracy. One of the first editors to create a set of written rules to govern the work of journalists was George C. Childs. After purchasing the *Public Ledger* (in Philadelphia) in 1864, Childs listed twenty-four rules to govern the conduct of the journalists who were working for that newspaper.

Following the Civil War, news packaging escalated, especially in an environment influenced by Joseph Pulitzer's successes in the 1880s. Among the many news-selling techniques associated with him are the staging of events to report, undercover reporting, and visuals. The physical appearance of newspapers was changing as well. Departmentalizing content into labeled sections made it easier for the readers to find the subjects that were of the most interest to them, and this approach advanced

significantly by the 1890s. Indeed, the notion of news as a commodity was so common that discussions through the last thirty years of the nineteenth century focused on newspapers as businesses. An 1897 article by Lincoln Steffens likened a newspaper to a factory or department store—alluding to the many departments that were by then established in newspapers to separate various kinds of content. Excesses in using gimmicks to sell news turned more attention to the qualities of the product being sold, which in turn provoked efforts to create and maintain "quality control." Such efforts encompassed development of professional organizations, codes of ethics, and journalism education. The latter was especially assisted by Pulitzer's 1904 article that suggested a journalism curriculum and his 1911 endowment of the Columbia University School of Journalism, which opened in 1912. While that packaging stage in newspapers seemingly peaked by 1900, a new media genre two decades later epitomized news packaging. *Time* magazine was first published in 1923 with a purpose to present weekly digests of the most important news from the nation and the world. Other news magazines soon followed the success of this packaged news medium.

Watergate and the Mass Media

Several factors in the second half of the twentieth century culminated in the late 1970s and early 1980s in an environment that propelled news packaging to an unprecedented degree. One very important factor was the development of image manufacturing to sell political candidates to voters. This practice, which began at least as early as the 1952 presidential campaign, was, by the mid-1980s, entwined with news packaging to a degree that blurred lines between image and news in such events as presidential press conferences, political campaigns, and interviews. Television has so pervasively influenced news packaging as to be perhaps still undistillable. However, one must note at least (1) the power of the television ratings system to compel ever-more enterprising efforts to package news to sell and (2) the creation and perpetuation of the "sound bite" as a packaging technique. These bites, which are snippets of interviews with "experts," are used to distill reports into the most compact form possible and "enhance" the quality of opposing sides. Other factors that propelled news packaging in these years included new media, the spread of communication technologies, and efforts of traditional media to remain competitive in a changing popular culture environment.

A catalyst for consolidating these as an impetus to modern news packaging was a "let-down" in the mid-1970s as the Watergate scandal subsided. The drama of this episode, which led to the first resignation of a U.S. president (in this case, to avoid impeachment over abuse of power), so riveted attention to news reports that its end brought a clear public sense of a news vacuum (ironically, in an era of information overload). Media personnel sought ways to sustain (or recapture) what some have called an almost addictive attention of consumers to the media throughout the Watergate episode. For newspaper journalists, an added perceived need to continue trying to compete with television intensified the search for ways to sell news, and by the spring of 1983, scholar Ben H. Bagdikian referred to a "passion for an unholy trinity sweeping all American media—packaging, marketing, and graphics."

The 1980s and Beyond

A newspaper intended to present news as a package appeared in 1981. *USA Today*, called a "new medium" and "experimental little newspaper," came with a promise that it "would be easy and fun to read." Advance research, called the most thorough ever on behalf of a newspaper, had sought how, where, and what length to publish stories for optimum sales. The resulting news package included short items; no jumps; lots of charts, graphs, and color; and information presented so it could "be absorbed quickly." A departmental managing editor described the aim as simple presentations that communicate a sense of urgency; clear, straightforward writing; photographs of "what has happened today or what's coming"; "fact-filled" and "vibrant" graphics; and "urgency" in headlines (Seelye, 1983). By the late 1990s, these packaging elements were commonplace in newspapers across the nation.

Criticism has probably always accompanied news packaging. James Parton wrote in 1866 of watching a "respectable New Yorker" observe a penny newspaper for the first time: "[H]e gazed at it . . . with . . . mingled curiosity and contempt." However, modern trends may have produced more criticism than did past developments. By 1990, news packaging, which has always seductively flavored information with ingredients to amuse, aroused strong criticism for mixing information and entertainment in televised magazines. These shows came to be derisively called "infotainment," as current-affairs programmers, in an attempt to compete with "melodramatic pseudo-documentary and talk shows," borrowed the theme music of television programs and used simulations and reenactments—too often without identifying the latter as such. Furthermore, as Rae Corelli (1989) has pointed out, the appearance of television magazine journalists in situation comedies and dramatic series (to enhance the salability of both genres) blurred even further the lines between informational and noninformational programs. A statement by Bagdikian (1983) distilled enduring concerns as he spoke (referring to *USA Today*) of "the primacy of packagers and market analysts in a realm where the news judgment of reporters and editors has traditionally prevailed." And Lynn Staley, in 1998, complaining about an increasingly blurred line between hard and soft news, said "packaging the news is getting trickier as words and pictures have to be balanced carefully to reflect what is substantial [versus what is] sensational."

With the expansion of the Internet, online publishing capabilities are still being defined and assessed, but John Pavlik (1997) has already referred to the work as involving "repackaging" information. Doug Underwood (1992), who said that modern news packaging trends made "news into just another commodity," predicted that, as newspapers joined "electronic competition," reporters would be "ever more subject to the forces of technological change, the demands of perpetually updating the news for electronic services, and the pressure to think of their work in marketing terms." Thus, news packaging appears certain to reach new levels in cyberspace.

See also: BLY, NELLIE; HEARST, WILLIAM RANDOLPH; INTERNET AND THE WORLD WIDE WEB; JOURNALISM, PROFESSIONALIZATION OF; MAGAZINE INDUSTRY; MAGAZINE INDUSTRY, HISTORY OF; MURROW, EDWARD R.; NEWS EFFECTS; NEWSPAPER INDUSTRY; NEWSPAPER INDUSTRY, HISTORY OF; NEWS PRODUCTION THEORIES; PULITZER, JOSEPH.

Bibliography

Abrahamson, David. (1996). *Magazine-Made America: The Cultural Transformation of the Postwar Periodical.* Cresskill, NJ: Hampton Press.

Andrews, J. Cutler. (1970). *The South Reports the Civil War.* Princeton, NJ: Princeton University Press.

Aronson, James. (1971). *Packaging the News: A Critical Survey of Press, Radio, TV.* New York: International Publications.

Bagdikian, Ben H. (1983). "Fast-Food News: A Week's Diet." *Columbia Journalism Review* 21(6):32–33.

Bennett, Lance. (1988). *News: The Politics of Illusion,* 2nd edition. New York: Longman.

Carter, Edward L. (1971). "The Revolution in Journalism During the Civil War." *Lincoln Herald* 73 (Winter):229–241.

Corelli, Rae (1989). "Packaging the News: Racy Talk Shows Masquerade as News Programs." *Maclean's* 102(44):82.

DePalma, Anthony (1982). "Survival Journalism, Allbritton Style." *Columbia Journalism Review* 21(May/June):47–50.

Dicken-Garcia, Hazel. (1989). *Journalistic Standards in Nineteenth-Century America.* Madison: University of Wisconsin Press.

Emery, Michael; Emery, Edwin; and Roberts, Nancy L. (2000). *The Press and America: An Interpretive History of the Mass Media,* 9th edition. Boston: Allyn & Bacon.

Harding, Ken. (1999). "Trends That Are Reshaping Newspapers." *Editor & Publisher* 127(45):22–25.

Hart, Gary. (1987). "Why Media Miss the Message." *The Washington Post,* Dec. 20, Sunday Final Edition, p. C1.

Hudson, Frederic. (1873). *Journalism in the United States from 1690 to 1872.* New York: Harper and Brothers.

Jones, Alex S. (1985). "Libel Suits Show Differing News Approaches of Papers, TV, and Magazines." *The New York Times,* Jan. 31, p. B9.

McKibben, Gordon. (1991). "Packaging the News." *The Boston Globe,* June 24, City Edition, Op-Ed, p. 11.

Mindich, David. (1998). *Just the Facts: How "Objectivity" Came to Define American Journalism.* New York: New York University Press.

Parton, James. (1866). "The New York Herald." *North American Review* 102(April):373–418.

Pavlik, John V. (1997). "The Future of Online Journalism: Bonanza or Black Hole." *Columbia Journalism Review* 36(2):30–36.

Pulitzer, Joseph. (1904). "The College of Journalism." *North American Review* 178(May):190–199.

Schoonmaker, Mary Ellen. (1983). "The Color Craze: It's Not Just USA Today—Papers Everywhere Are Chasing Rainbows. What's This Doing to the News?" *Columbia Journalism Review* 21(6):35–37.

Seelye, Katharine. (1983). "Al Neuharth's Technicolor Baby: USA Today! Give 'em What They Want!" *Columbia Journalism Review* 21(6):27–35.

Shope, Dan. (1995). "Producing, Packaging News and Ads Tests Skill, Machines Against the Clock." *The Morning Call,* Feb. 26, Outlook Section, p. E6.

Soley, Lawrence. (1992). *The News Shapers: The Sources Who Explain the News.* New York: Praeger.

Staley, Lynn. (1998). "More Tabloid than High Minded." *Design,* Fall Issue, p. 4.

Steffens, Lincoln J. (1897). "The Business of a Newspaper." *Scribner's Magazine* 22(Oct.):447–467.

Swanberg, W. A. (1967). *Pulitzer.* New York: Scribner's.

Underwood, Doug. (1988). "When MBAs Rule the Newsroom." *Columbia Journalism Review* 26(6):23–30.

Underwood, Doug. (1992). "The Newspapers' Identity Crisis: Reinventing the Media." *Columbia Journalism Review* 30(6):24–27.

HAZEL DICKEN-GARCIA

JOURNALISM, PROFESSIONALIZATION OF

Contemporary mass communication scholars, as well as some journalists themselves, still debate whether journalism is, or even whether it should be, a profession. But certainly, during the past 250 years, journalism in America has evolved toward professional values, from the one-person printing operations of the Colonial period to the division of labor of the antebellum newsroom and the emergence of reporters in the mid-1860s to the more sophisticated understanding of the social role and responsibility of mass media of the early twentieth century.

To qualify as a profession, an occupation should be founded on a body of specialized knowledge over which the professional gains authority through specialized education and training; furthermore, a professional has a large degree of autonomy from outside censure and is regulated by an internal code of ethics and by the sanction of fellow professionals through professional associations. On a moral level, a profession provides society with a service that no others can. These defining characteristics are based on those of classic professions such as medicine and law. Many critics claim that journalism hardly fits them, because of the lack of educational requirements and licensing, among others. These critics also point out that unionization of such journalists as daily newspaper reporters, which is commonplace, limits autonomy in the sense that unionized employees are not free as individuals to set their own workplace rules. Other critics respond that journalists possess the most important professional feature—a higher calling to work fundamentally not for personal pecuniary gain but for public service.

By the 1830s, journalism in the United States had become a full-time occupation and the "professional communicator" developed—someone whose thoughts have no necessary relation to the message. The professionalization of journalism emerged visibly after the U.S. Civil War, with the establishment of professional associations, standards and codes of ethics, and education programs. For example, Cornell University was offering a "certificate of journalism" in 1873, and Joseph Pulitzer, founder of the *New York World,* endowed Columbia University in 1903 to found a journalism school. The Missouri Press Association was formed in 1876, and it established its own ethical code. Edwin Shuman published perhaps the first comprehensive journalism textbook, *Steps into Journalism,* in 1894.

Unquestionably, the most evident sign of change toward more professional journalism was the parallel emergence in the late nineteenth century of the ultimate journalistic value: objectivity. Partly in reaction to the sensationalistic excesses and the blunt commercialism of yellow journalism in the 1890s, journalists sought professionalization, and its norm of objectivity, as a way to make their occupation more respectable and socially responsible. The reforming impetus of progressivism also spurred journalists to detach themselves from crass circulation battles and fight for social enlightenment. Michael Schudson, in *Discovering the News* (1978), argues that professionalism was a way to strive for more objective reporting. According to Dan Schiller (1979), objectivity also helped commercial newspapers legitimate their function as watchdogs of the public good. While allowing journalists to be independent from the self-interests of business and politicians, objectivity has also come under attack for thwarting the autonomy of journalism—a critique attached to professionalism itself. While some envision professionalism as the opposite of bias, others charge professionalism with serving as a method of control by management over reporters and editors (a co-opting of labor unrest) that ultimately standardizes news content and protects the status quo. In this view, Douglas Birkhead (1984) argues that the professionalization of journalism is so opposed to independence in favor of business interests as to be "a perversion of the ideal."

Somewhat paradoxically, other critics of professionalism and objectivity who also follow the "power approach" charge that the autonomy of journalists functions as a profit- and prestige-seeking device, which makes journalists detached from the public and socially irresponsible. They accuse objectivity of downgrading the journalist from critic to mere reporter of facts, a "communication technician." This criticism found voice in the social responsibility theory of the press early in the twentieth century; the theory, best expressed by the Hutchins Commission Report in 1947, holds that there is no freedom apart from responsibility, so a free press should perform a certain service for society and some institution (the government) must make it do so. Attacking objectivity, this theory holds that the public is served not only by facts but by context that can point to conclusions (i.e., interpretation). While journalists had been instrumental in developing a socially responsible press to give credibility to their occupation, most balked at the Hutchins Report because of its hint at governmental censorship and disregard for the prevailing libertarian view of press freedom. (Some consider it a sign of professionalism that journalists have been active in "political agitation" over a free press.) The contemporary product of this theory—public journalism—can also be seen as both a development and a threat to professionalism. If professionals have as their ultimate goal serving and improving society, then public journalism follows quite naturally. But some see it as the opposite of professionalism and objectivity, which they criticize for shielding journalists from true public service. Other critics of professionalism argue that it stifles diversity and even that the "institutionalized mentality" it breeds restricts press freedom.

Finally, the question remains whether journalists see themselves as professionals; several scholars tend to agree that journalists do indeed. Penn Kimball, in the defining article "Journalism: Art, Craft, or Profession?" (1965), claimed journalists are "pros" because of their higher calling, their special role in society, and the need they have for both schools and associations to develop a professional ethic outside of a formal code. While journalism might not be a classic profession in the organizational sense, journalists are found to espouse professional values such as commitment to public service, autonomy, and a sense of "calling." In their germinal study, "Professionalization Among Newsmen" (1964), Jack McLeod and Searle Hawley Jr. concluded that professional journalists gave much importance to objectivity and responsibility in newspapers. Slavko Splichal and Colin Sparks (1994) noted a shared positive attitude toward professionalization (especially as occupational autonomy) in aspiring journalists across twenty-two countries worldwide. Whether this global trend will create a corps of independent-minded, socially responsible, and useful professional journalists, or whether it is an indication of cultural imperialism in the interests of big business, remains open to debate.

See also: Cultural Studies; Culture Industries, Media as; Democracy and the Media; First Amendment and the Media; Functions of the Media; Globalization of Media Industries; Journalism, History of; News Production Theories; Pulitzer, Joseph; Social Change and the Media; Society and the Media.

Bibliography

Allison, Marianne. (1986). "A Literature Review of Approaches to the Professionalism of Journalists." *Journal of Mass Media Ethics* 1(2):5–19.

Banning, Stephen A. (1998). "The Professionalization of Journalism: A Nineteenth-Century Beginning." *Journalism History* 24(4):157–164.

Birkhead, Douglas. (1984). "The Power in the Image: Professionalism and the Communications Revolution." *American Journalism* 1(2):1–4.

Johnstone, John W. C.; Slawski, Edward J.; and Bowman, William W. (1976). *The News People: A Sociological Portrait of American Journalists and Their Work*. Urbana: University of Illinois Press.

Kimball, Penn. (1965). "Journalism: Art, Craft, or Profession?" In *The Professions in America*, ed. Kenneth Lynn. Boston: Houghton Mifflin.

McLeod, Jack M., and Hawley, Searle E., Jr. (1964). "Professionalization Among Newsmen." *Journalism Quarterly* 41:529–538.

Mindich, David T. Z. (1998). *Just the Facts: How "Objectivity" Came to Define American Journalism*. New York: New York University Press.

Schiller, Dan. (1979). "An Historical Approach to Objectivity and Professionalism in American News Reporting." *Journal of Communication* 29(4):46–57.

Schudson, Michael. (1978). *Discovering the News: A Social History of American Newspapers*. New York: Basic Books.

Soloski, John. (1989). "News Reporting and Professionalism: Some Constraints on the Reporting of the News." *Media, Culture and Society* 2:207–228.

Splichal, Slavko, and Sparks, Colin. (1994). *Journalists for the 21st Century*. Norwood, NJ: Ablex.

Weaver, David H., and Wilhoit, G. Cleveland. (1996). *The American Journalist in the 1990s*. Mahwah, NJ: Lawrence Erlbaum.

Nancy L. Roberts
Giovanna Dell'Orto

▎■ KNOWLEDGE MANAGEMENT

The basic challenge in knowledge management is learning how to design an organization's strategy, structure, and systems so that the organization can use what it knows to innovate and adapt. Although the field of knowledge management is still evolving, its terrain may be surveyed by focusing on two themes: the structure of organizational knowledge (i.e., the nature of knowledge in organizations and what makes it distinct from other forms of knowledge) and the processes by which organizations turn knowledge into action and results (i.e., how organizations create, share, and use knowledge).

Data, Information, Knowledge

Information and knowledge are the outcomes of human action and cognition that engage signs, signals, and artifacts in social and physical settings. Knowledge builds on an accumulation of experience. Information depends on an aggregation of data. Consider a document that contains a table of numbers that indicate product sales for the quarter. As they stand, these numbers are data. An employee reads these numbers, recognizes the name and nature of the product, and notices that the numbers are below last year's figures, indicating a downward trend. The data has become information. The employee considers possible explanations for the product decline (perhaps using additional information and personal judgment) and comes to the conclusion that the product is no longer attractive to its customers. This new belief, derived from reasoning and reflection, is knowledge. Thus, information is data that is given context and vested with meaning and significance. Knowledge is information that is transformed through reasoning and reflection into beliefs, concepts, and mental models.

Types of Organizational Knowledge

Knowledge in organizations is not monolithic, nor is it homogenous; knowledge evolves from different origins and is engaged in different ways. Research suggests that organizational knowledge may be divided into tacit knowledge, explicit knowledge, and cultural knowledge.

Tacit Knowledge

In organizations, tacit knowledge is the personal knowledge used by members to perform their work and to make sense of their worlds. It is learned through extended periods of experiencing and doing a task, during which time the individual develops a feel for and a capacity to make intuitive judgments about the successful execution of the activity. Examples of tacit knowledge at work would be the technician who can tell the health of a machine from the hum it generates, or the bank manager who develops a gut feeling that a client would be a bad credit risk after a short conversation with the customer. Because tacit knowledge is experiential and contextualized, it cannot be easily codified, written down, or reduced to rules and recipes.

Despite its being difficult to articulate, tacit knowledge can be and is regularly transferred and shared. Tacit knowledge can be learned through observation and imitation. Thus, apprentices learn their craft by following and copying their masters, professionals acquire expertise and norms through periods of internship, and new employees are immersed in on-the-job training. According to Donald Sch^n (1983), professionals reflect on what they know during the practice itself (e.g., when they encounter an unusual case) as well as afterward (e.g., in a postmortem) and, in doing so, test and refine their own tacit knowledge. Tacit knowledge can also be shared. Although not completely expressible in words or symbols, tacit knowledge may be alluded to or revealed through rich modes of discourse that include the use of analogies, metaphors, or models and through the communal sharing of stories. Storytelling provides channels for tacit learning because narratives dramatize and contextualize knowledge-rich episodes, allowing the listener to replay and relive as much of the original experience as possible.

Ikujiro Nonaka and Hirotaka Takeuchi (1995) emphasize that tacit knowledge is vital to organizations because it is an important source of new knowledge. New knowledge in the form of discoveries and innovations is often the outcome of creative individuals applying their tacit insights and intuitions to confront novel or difficult problems. Because tacit knowledge resides in people's minds, it is lost when employees leave the organization.

Explicit Knowledge

Explicit knowledge is knowledge that is expressed formally using a system of symbols and can therefore be easily communicated or diffused. Explicit knowledge may be object based or rule based. Object-based knowledge may be found in artifacts such as products, patents, software code, computer databases, technical drawings, tools, prototypes, photographs, voice recordings, films, and so on. Knowledge is object based when it is represented using strings of symbols (e.g., words, numbers, formulas) or is embodied in physical entities (e.g., equipment, models, substances). In the first case, the symbols directly represent or codify the explicit knowledge. In the second case, explicit knowledge may be extracted from the physical object by, for example, disassembling equipment, inspecting software code, or analyzing the composition of a substance. Explicit knowledge is rule based when the knowledge is codified into rules, routines, or operating procedures. A substantial part of an organization's operational

knowledge about how to do things is contained in its rules, routines, and procedures. Although all organizations operate with standard procedures, each organization will develop its own repertoire of routines, based on its experience and the specific environment in which it functions.

Patrick Sullivan (1998, p. 23) discusses an organization's explicit knowledge that takes the form of "intellectual assets," which he defines as "the codified, tangible, or physical descriptions of specific knowledge to which the company can assert ownership rights." Examples of intellectual assets may include plans, procedures, drawings, blueprints, and computer programs. Intellectual assets that receive legal protection are intellectual property. Five forms of intellectual property are entitled to legal protection in the United States: patents, copyrights, trade secrets, trademarks, and semiconductor masks.

Explicit knowledge codified as intellectual assets is valuable to the organization because it adds to the organization's observable and tradable stocks of knowledge. Moreover, because they have been committed to media, ideas may be communicated more easily. Explicit knowledge serves a number of important purposes in an organization. It encodes past learning in rules, coordinates disparate organizational functions, and signifies competence and rationality. Because explicit knowledge has been codified, it remains with the organization even after its inventors or authors leave the organization.

Cultural Knowledge

An organization's cultural knowledge consists of the beliefs it holds to be true based on experience, observation, and reflection about itself and its environment. Over time, an organization develops shared beliefs about the nature of its main business, core capabilities, markets, competitors, and so on. These beliefs then form the criteria for judging and selecting alternatives and new ideas, and for evaluating projects and proposals. In this way, an organization uses its cultural knowledge to answer questions such as "What kind of an organization are we?" "What knowledge would be valuable to the organization?" and "What knowledge would be worth pursuing?"

Cultural knowledge includes the assumptions and beliefs that are used to describe and explain reality, as well as the criteria and expectations that are used to assign value and significance to new information. These shared beliefs, norms, and values form the sense-making framework in which organizational members recognize the saliency of new information. Although cultural knowledge is not written down (but is conveyed in stories, histories, and reward or evaluation systems), it remains with the organization even after employee changes and staff turnover.

There are well-known accounts of organizations in which cultural knowledge is misaligned with its efforts to exploit tacit and explicit knowledge. For example, Xerox PARC (Palo Alto Research Center) in the 1970s pioneered many innovations that later defined the personal computer industry but which Xerox itself did not commercialize. PARC had invented or developed the bit-mapped display technology that was required for rendering graphical user interfaces, software for on-screen windows and windows management, the mouse as a pointing device, the first personal computer (Alto), and an early word-processing software (Bravo) for the Alto. Xerox was not willing to realize the application potential of these inventions because its identity and business strategy was still focused on the photocopier market. Many of the researchers working on these projects subsequently left PARC, taking their knowledge with them.

Knowledge Creation

Nonaka and Takeuchi (1995, p. 59) suggest that the production of new knowledge involves "a process that 'organizationally' amplifies the knowledge created by individuals and crystallizes it as a part of the knowledge network of the organization." Two sets of activities drive the process of knowledge amplification: (1) converting tacit knowledge into explicit knowledge and (2) moving knowledge from the individual level to the group, organizational, and interorganizational levels. An organization creates knowledge through four modes: socialization, externalization, combination, and internalization.

Socialization is a process of acquiring tacit knowledge through sharing experiences. As apprentices learn the craft of their masters through observation and imitation, so do employees of a firm learn new skills through shared activities such as on-the-job training. Externalization is a process of converting tacit knowledge into explicit concepts through the use of abstractions, metaphors, analogies, or models. Combination is a process of creating explicit knowledge by bringing together explicit knowledge from a number of sources. For example, individuals exchange and combine their explicit knowledge through conversations, meetings, and memos. Computerized databases may be "mined" to uncover new explicit knowledge. Finally, internalization is a process of embodying explicit knowledge into tacit knowledge, internalizing the experiences that are gained through the other modes of knowledge creation in the form of shared mental models or work practices.

Knowledge Sharing

Promoting the effective sharing and transfer of knowledge is often the centerpiece of knowledge management initiatives. Unfortunately, there are significant cognitive, affective, and organizational barriers to knowledge sharing. Cognitively, the individual who is transferring knowledge must put in mental effort to explain new concepts, demonstrate techniques, answer questions, and so on. Affectively, the individual may experience regret or reluctance about losing ownership of hard-earned expertise. Organizationally, individuals are not rewarded for solving another person's problems, nor are they usually given the time or support needed to share information. There are also cultural factors in most organizations that inhibit knowledge sharing. Thomas Davenport and Laurence Prusak (1998) consider the most common inhibitors to be lack of trust, different frames of reference, lack of time and opportunity, rewards going to those who own knowledge, lack of capacity in recipients to absorb new knowledge, the not-invented-here syndrome, and intolerance for mistakes.

Max Boisot (1998) points out that diffusion of organizational knowledge is increased and accelerated by the codification and abstraction of personal knowledge. Codification is the process that creates perceptual and conceptual categories that facilitate the classification of phenomena. Whereas codification groups the data of experience into categories, abstraction is accomplished by revealing the structure and cause-and-effect relationships that underlie phenomena. It leads to knowledge that is based on abstract thought and is mainly conceptual and broadly applicable. The more codified and abstract an item of knowledge becomes, the larger the percentage of a given population it will be able to reach in a given period of time.

Knowledge Use

The use of knowledge is a social activity. Whenever organizational knowledge is put in use, its tacit, explicit, and cultural facets bind together in a flow of practice and social interaction. Work groups form around these practices, creating communities of practice. Communities of practice emerge of their own accord and tend to self-organize; people join and stay because they have something to learn and to contribute. By sharing and jointly developing practice, communities of practice evolve patterns of relating and interacting with one another. Over time, they develop a common understanding of the meaning and value of their work, as well as a shared repertory of resources that include both the tacit (e.g., "war stories," workarounds, heuristics) and the explicit (e.g., notebooks, tools, communication devices). Communities of practice therefore constitute historical and social settings that embrace all three categories of organizational knowledge.

Knowledge Management in Practice

A thorough understanding of knowledge management can best be obtained by examining specific examples of the process being put into practice. Two good examples are the Xerox Eureka project and the consulting firm of PricewaterhouseCoopers.

Xerox Eureka

The Eureka project at Xerox is an example of how an organization can tap into the tacit knowledge of its employees, codify that knowledge, and facilitate its diffusion and use. Eureka is also an illustration of how an organization can balance the need for looseness and improvisation with the need for structure and control when managing its knowledge.

In the early 1990s, Xerox was employing approximately twenty-three thousand technicians around the world to repair copiers at client sites. Some of the repair solutions existed only in the heads of the experienced technicians, who had found ways of dealing with tough machine-repair problems. Xerox developed Eureka as a system of practices, procedures, and tools that would allow the personal knowledge of technicians to be vali-

dated and shared. Eureka was initially developed by Xerox PARC and deployed in 1992 for service representatives in Xerox France. By the end of 1999, more than five thousand tips had been entered, and they were available to Xerox service representatives worldwide via their laptop computers.

The following is how Eureka works. Customer service representatives who are on site visits discover solutions to difficult repair problems. They submit these tentative solutions into a "pending tips" database. Pending tips are voted and commented on by other technicians when they try these tips to solve customer problems. Tips that are validated by product leaders or specialists are then edited and entered into the "validated tips knowledge base." Service representatives are motivated to use Eureka because of its problem-solving benefits. They are motivated to contribute to it by personal recognition (e.g., their names are attached to the tips they submit) and by prizes for frequently used tips.

Priscilla Douglas (1999, pp. 217–218) of Xerox described the effect of Eureka as follows:

> Technically, Eureka is a relational database of hypertext documents available online via the Intranet. It can also be viewed as the distributed publishing of local community know-how. In practice, Eureka is an electronic version of war stories told around the water cooler—with the added benefits of a user-friendly search engine, institutional memory, expert validation, and corporate-wide availability. It is a way to simultaneously grow both intellectual capital and social capital.

Eureka saves Xerox about 5 percent on labor and another 5 percent in parts costs in field customer service. It is being used by 15,000 Xerox technicians worldwide. Tom Ruddy, Xerox's director of knowledge management for worldwide customer services, estimates that Xerox will eliminate approximately 150,000 calls per year with Eureka—worth $6 million to $8 million. Savings should actually be higher, since Xerox has implemented the system in its call centers, increasing the expected number of users to more than 25,000.

PricewaterhouseCoopers

Consulting firms recognize that their products and services are based almost exclusively on knowledge, and many are active in implementing strategies that leverage their internal knowledge. Organizationally, the approach of PricewaterhouseCoopers (PwC) is based on a four-level structure for managing knowledge:

1. The Global KM Management Team coordinates the overall PwC approach to knowledge management and implements specific, key enterprise-wide initiatives.

2. The KM Council (composed of the Global KM Core Team, lines of service chief knowledge officers, and representatives from stakeholders throughout the firm) coordinates global efforts with those of lines of business and industry clusters.

3. The KM Action Committees are responsible for areas such as content architecture, best practices, knowledge management technologies, professionalism, and people information.

4. The KM Communities of Interest (which comprise approximately one thousand professionals, knowledge managers, researchers/analysts, information specialists, and extranet owners) share innovative thinking in the knowledge management area.

To promote knowledge management as a professional career, the firm has developed a competencies framework and a set of professional principles. Thus, the primary mission of a knowledge management professional is to harvest, share, and build PwC's intellectual capital. Bonuses, promotions, and partner admissions are linked to knowledge sharing. For example, partners are formally assessed on their ability to foster knowledge sharing, and everyone from new hires to partners are encouraged and recognized for their knowledge creation and sharing activities. The firm encourages knowledge sharing by including the names of contributors on documents in knowledge stores, by providing publicity on individuals who make the extra effort to share knowledge, by sending thank-you notes from partners and peers to personnel files, and by awarding "Knowledge Bucks" prizes and spot bonuses (Hackett, 2000).

PwC sees its investment in knowledge management as highly strategic; knowledge sharing increases customer satisfaction and revenues while providing the firm with a competitive advantage. Brian Hackett (2000, p. 66) relates the following example:

In one instance, PwC was providing auditing work to a global client. PwC became aware that the client was dissatisfied with an electronic commerce project that was being conducted by another consulting company. Asked to develop a proposal in one week, this auditing team had to quickly locate PwC's expertise in another area, find expertise pertinent to the client's industry, and develop a responsive proposal. Using PwC's vast network of internal databases, KnowledgeCurve, and other sources, the team located a partner who specialized in e-commerce, another partner with the appropriate industry expertise, database experts, and a change management expert. In less than a week, PwC effectively maximized its internal talent and produced a winning proposal.

Both Xerox and PwC are finding ways to use tacit, explicit, and cultural knowledge to improve corporate performance. In each case, knowledge management is a formal activity.

See also: CHIEF INFORMATION OFFICERS; KNOWLEDGE MANAGEMENT, CAREERS IN; MANAGEMENT INFORMATION SYSTEMS.

Bibliography

Boisot, Max. (1998). *Knowledge Assets: Securing Competitive Advantage in the Information Economy.* New York: Oxford University Press.

Brown, John Seely, and Duguid, Paul. (1998). "Organizing Knowledge." *California Management Review* 40(3):90–111.

Bukowitz, Wendi, and Williams, Ruth. (1999). *Knowledge Management Fieldbook.* New York: Prentice-Hall.

Choo, Chun Wei. (1998). *The Knowing Organization: How Organizations Use Information to Construct Meaning, Create Knowledge, and Make Decisions.* New York: Oxford University Press.

Davenport, Thomas H., and Prusak, Laurence. (1998). *Working Knowledge: How Organizations Manage What They Know.* Boston: Harvard Business School Press.

Douglas, Priscilla. (1999). "Xerox: Documents Convey Knowledge." In *Smart Business: How Knowledge Communities Can Revolutionize Your Company,* by Jim Botkin. New York: Free Press.

Edvinsson, Leif, and Malone, Michael S. (1997). *Intellectual Capital: Realizing Your Company's True Value by Finding Its Hidden Brainpower.* New York: Harper Business.

Hackett, Brian. (2000). *Beyond Knowledge Management: New Ways to Work.* New York: The Conference Board.

Leonard-Barton, Dorothy. (1995). *Wellsprings of Knowledge: Building and Sustaining the Sources of Innovation.* Boston, MA: Harvard Business School Press.

Nonaka, Ikujiro, and Takeuchi, Hirotaka. (1995). *The Knowledge-Creating Company: How Japanese Companies Create the Dynamics of Innovation.* New York: Oxford University Press.

Roos, Johan; Roos, Goran; and Dragonetti, Nicola Carlo. (1998). *Intellectual Capital: Navigating in the New Business Landscape.* New York: New York University Press.

Schön, Donald. (1983). *The Reflective Practitioner.* New York: Basic Books.

Sullivan, Patrick H., ed. (1998). *Profiting from Intellectual Capital.* New York: Wiley.

Sveiby, Karl Erik. (1997). *New Organizational Wealth: Managing & Measuring Knowledge-Based Assets.* San Francisco, CA: Berret-Kohler.

Von Krogh, Georg; Ichijo, Kazuo; and Nonaka, Ikujiro. (2000). *Enabling Knowledge Creation: How to Unlock the Mystery of Tacit Knowledge and Release the Power of Innovation.* New York: Oxford University Press.

Zack, Michael H. (1999). *Knowledge and Strategy.* Boston: Butterworth-Heinemann.

CHUN WEI CHOO

KNOWLEDGE MANAGEMENT, CAREERS IN

Once upon a time an article about careers might well have described a "career ladder." The concept was a useful one when organizations were hierarchical in nature and one might progress step by step ever higher in the management hierarchy. Many research studies of such diverse careers as college presidents, career army officers, directors of academic libraries, and chief executive officers concluded that successive positions followed a predictable upward pattern (i.e., a career ladder).

At the beginning of the twenty-first century, however, the comfortable clarity and stability that the hierarchy offered is gone. David Skyrme (1999), a frequent writer on knowledge management (KM) topics, summarizes the transformation in business and society that has taken place in the "networked knowledge environment." The defining characteristics of networked organizations, according to Skyrme, are not so much particular organizational structures as they are informal human networking processes with the information technology that "underpins and enhances human networking" (p. 15). New ways of working in these environments include self-managed teams, virtual teams, flexible offices, and teleworking. The transition from a hierarchical organization to a postmodern environment can be characterized as "a series of interwoven projects defined by the sense-making and learning of its participants" (Addleson, 2000, p. 151).

The learning organization places less emphasis on rules, detailed specification of tasks, and error avoidance than on creative chaos, risk-taking, and error detection and correction. Organizations that tend to have knowledge management initiatives also usually have (1) senior management who believe that organizational learning and knowledge management are critical success factors, (2) an organizational culture focused on rapid growth, often driven by outside competitors, (3) internal trust, leading to a willingness to share knowledge, and (4) a strong customer orientation.

An IBM-supported study of twenty chief knowledge officers (CKOs) in North America and Europe sought to determine commonalities in the roles and to explore current and evolving knowledge management practices. The model CKO in this study is both a technologist and an environmentalist. He or she (many are female) has a responsibility "to encourage and initiate investment in information technology (IT) and also in the social environment" (Earl and Scott, 1999, p. 6). Most of the CKOs interviewed lacked formal IT training but had past involvement with IT projects. The first initiative for a CKO is often technological—building knowledge-sharing tools such as groupware projects, knowledge directories, and intranets. In the organizational domain, the CKOs create social environments and initiate events and processes to encourage knowledge creation and exchange—for example, through the design of space and by sponsoring events that bring people together to create communities with common interests. Part of the CKO's job as environmentalist involves a radical redesign of performance measurement systems in order to encourage collective, rather than individual, performance. The CKO also works with any educational or organizational development opportunities as a means of encouraging knowledge creation.

CKOs are change agents and entrepreneurs. They have a broad view of the organization and the ability to think strategically. Most CKOs have held a variety of jobs; no one professional background is dominant. They usually have had a number of years of experience in the organization (typically about ten years) and have established a reputation for credibility. Knowledge of the organization and its culture "yield advantages in the consulting and influencing aspects of the job" (Earl and Scott, 1999, p. 8).

CKO positions are new. All those who held the title in the IBM study were the first incumbents in the role. They operate with small budgets and staff. Most view their roles as temporary because once the goal of "embedded knowledge capacity" has been achieved, a knowledge management office and implementation team may not be needed. It is not clear, however, what would mark the attainment of the goal as objective measures of performance are often lacking, despite the demand for measures of knowledge and intellectual capital.

Another study, commissioned by the Library and Information Commission of the United Kingdom and undertaken by TFPL (1999), sought to determine the routes available to people wishing to develop knowledge management skills. Rather than studying the CKO, the emphasis in this study was on knowledge management facilitation roles. As is true of the appointment of a CKO, the first members of the knowledge management team are usually internal, perhaps for two reasons: (1) those who are already members of the firm are more apt to have important tacit knowledge about the organization and how it works and (2) personnel needs in this area are difficult to define and classify. As the concept of knowledge management has become more accepted and pervasive, external recruitment procedures have been established.

One search company, KnowledgeJobs (2001), specializes in knowledge jobs and provides a classification of them. In a similar manner, Nigel Oxbrow (2000) identifies a number of special roles such as knowledge management consultant, intranet manager, content manager, extranet manager, communities coordinator (to identify and stimulate communities of interest and communities of practice), and knowledge architect (to design structures for information resources, taxonomies for more accurate retrieval of information, and expertise databases).

These categories appear to be influenced by past experience, education, and job titles, rather than by identifying new knowledge, skills, and attitudes. The TFPL study identified a knowledge management skill set to include the following: business process identification and analysis; knowledge asset identification, creation, maintenance, and exploration; knowledge mapping and flows; the ability to leverage information and communication technology to create knowledge management enablers; project management; an understanding of information management (IM) and awareness of technology opportunities. To this list, Skyrme (1999) would add financial management skills, knowledge of how people learn, and how knowledge is developed, shared, and reviewed.

Information management skills are important, but people who demonstrate these skills do not necessarily come from the information profession. No one profession or function comprehends the whole picture of corporate information flows. Historically, different types of information have been treated as discrete entities, with the library/information profession focusing largely on external information and records management focusing on internal information. Other functions with information management capability include market research, strategic planning and competitive intelligence, customer relations, sales, technical support, research and development, and information technology.

For people to take advantage of knowledge management opportunities means they must develop a wide horizon and focus on the business objectives of the organizations that employ them. Jo Cates (2000), a knowledge manager for the Ernst and Young Center for Business Knowledge, offers tips for those people who are seeking career positions in the knowledge management field. She points out that most positions require industry experience, but she also notes that no field has a lock on these positions. She encourages attention to the presentation of skill sets on resumes; for example, she suggests adding "synthesis" to research skills and "taxonomy management" to cataloging skills.

Certainly, visibility and operational (or organizational) knowledge are important. Temperament probably plays a role in most successful careers as well. The need for a "match" between the person and the job is commonly discussed. The typical profile of a knowledge manager seems to include an outgoing personality, strong interpersonal skills, a high level of energy, a pragmatic and flexible cast of mind, high tolerance of ambiguity, and a sense of, and commitment to, business imperatives. Given the apparent growth of the knowledge management function within organizations, the number and kinds of positions below the CKO is expanding, although probably not indefinitely. For those people who are willing to take the leap, opportunity awaits.

See also: CHIEF INFORMATION OFFICERS; KNOWLEDGE MANAGEMENT; ORGANIZATIONAL COMMUNICATION.

Bibliography

Addleson, Mark. (2000). "Organizing to Know and to Learn: Reflections on Organization and Knowledge Management." In *Knowledge Management for the Information Professional*, eds. T. Kanti Srikantaiah and Michael E. D. Koenig. Washington, DC: American Society for Information Science.

Cates, Jo. (2000). "Managing a Knowledge Management Career Search." *Business & Finance Bulletin* 113(Winter):17–21.

Earl, Michael J., and Scott, Ian A. (1999). "Opinion: What Is a Chief Knowledge Officer?" <http://mit-sloan.mit.edu/smr/past/1999/smr4022.html>.

KnowledgeJobs. (2001). "The KnowledgeJobs Classification System." <http://www.knowledgejobs.com/strategy/system.htm>.

Oxbrow, Nigel. (2000). "Skills and Competencies to Succeed in a Knowledge Economy." *Information Outlook* 4(10):18–22.

Skyrme, David J. (1999). *Knowledge Networking: Creating the Collaborative Enterprise.* Oxford, Eng.: Butterworth Heinemann.

TFPL, Ltd. (1999). "Skills for Knowledge Management." <http://www.lic.gov.uk/publications/executivesummaries/kmskills.html>.

EVELYN H. DANIEL

KNOWLEDGE ORGANIZATION

See: Cataloging and Knowledge Organization

L

LANGUAGE ACQUISITION

Human language is a remarkable symbolic means of communication that makes it possible for individuals to convey their thoughts and feelings to others. Although babies are born completely without language, by the time they are three or four years old, children have acquired thousands of vocabulary words, complex grammatical and sound systems, and the ability to speak appropriately in many different social situations. Although societies around the world differ in many ways, language is a universal phenomenon, and children around the world acquire their native language in very similar ways.

The Structure of Language

All human languages include a number of systematic features that the young learner must master. Languages are organized hierarchically and include a number of subsystems. The systems of language include phonology, morphology, the lexicon and semantics, syntax, pragmatics, and discourse. Children begin to acquire some aspects of their language during their first few months of life.

The phonology of a language is its sound system. This system includes all of the significant sounds that are used in the language, as well as the ways in which they can be combined to make acceptable-sounding new words. For example, a new cereal in English might be called "Crunchix," but not "Kshicrun," because acceptable English words cannot begin with "kshi." Across the world, languages use many hundreds of different sounds, from trills on the tongue to scrapes in the throat, but each language employs only a small subset of these possible sounds. The sounds that the speakers of a language regard as different from one another are its phonemes. In English, for example, people make slightly different "p" sounds in words such as pool, where the "p" is followed by a puff of air (aspiration), or in words such as spool, where there is no puff of air following the "p." English speakers perceive these as just one sound, the phoneme "p." In the Hindi language spoken in India, however, the "p" without the puff of air and the "p" with the puff of air are different phonemes. The Hindi language has words such as *phal* ("fruit") and *pal* ("moment") that differing only in that puff of air. Some languages have many more phonemes than others, but it is typical for a language to have about twenty-six consonant and nine vowel phonemes. In written English, the alphabet does not always represent the sounds of the language clearly or consistently, but in Spanish or Russian, the sounds of the language and the letters used to represent them correspond quite well.

The morphology of a language is a set of rules for word formation and variation. (The term "rules" is used to refer to the way things are regularly done in a language by speakers of that language, not to a set of formal regulations that are taught in school.) Morphemes are the smallest units in a language that carry definable meaning or grammatical function (the word "hat," or the plural ending "-s," for example.) Addition of a morpheme can change a word from singular to plural or indicate the tense of a verb. Other morphological rules allow one word to be changed

509

into another word (e.g., "fit" into "unfit") or into another part of speech (e.g., "fit" into "fitness").

The lexicon and semantics of a language are its vocabulary words and the meanings that go with them. Speakers of a language have a remarkably large and complicated mental lexicon or dictionary. English-speaking adults can recognize more than 50,000 different words, and in common speech, they can come up with or produce anywhere from 20,000 to 50,000 of those words.

The syntax of a language includes the ways that words can be combined or rearranged in order to produce different kinds of utterances (e.g., questions, negatives, imperatives, and passives). Children soon learn to understand syntax—such as the difference between "The tiger chases the girl" and "The girl chases the tiger." In English syntax, meaning depends on word order. Typically, the first noun in a sentence is the subject, and the next is the object. Subjects are often followed by verbs. All sentences do not follow this pattern in English, however, and children must learn to interpret passives and other complex constructions. Complex syntax is not mastered until well into the school years.

Pragmatics is the appropriate use of language in various social situations. People all know how to talk in different ways, depending on the situation they are in, or the person they are addressing. People speak differently to babies, to informal acquaintances, and to people in authority, for example. If people are called into court, they do not say "Hi, sweetie" to the judge, although they might say this to their neighbor's little girl; people's knowledge of pragmatics leads to their choice of words and their interpretation of the language that they hear in social situations. Depending on their own roles, the person they are addressing, and the situation they are in, speakers vary their language according to a complex set of pragmatic conventions. Parents stress the importance of pragmatics when they teach very young children social routines, such as when to say "hello," "thank you," and "bye-bye."

Children must gain an understanding of how connected sentences are related to each other. In English, people must use a noun before a pronoun referring to the same thing can be used. Thus, "My dog ate it" is not a good way to begin a conversation with one's teacher, but saying "it" makes sense if the teacher has just asked where the student's homework is, since, in this case, the "it" refers to the homework. How to make a conversation or engage in other spoken or written activities that last longer than a single sentence requires knowledge of the discourse conventions of a language. After children enter school and begin to gain literacy skills, learning to use all of the discourse rules that are involved in expository writing is a particularly difficult task.

Stages of Language Acquisition

Understanding how children acquire language makes it possible to identify instances where they may not be developing language in an age-appropriate way, and may need intervention or remediation. It also allows people to know when immature-sounding language is part of normal language acquisition (such as when a two-year-old says "top" instead of "stop," since it is normal for a child of this age to simplify the pronunciation of consonant clusters). Knowing what stage of language development a child has reached also makes it possible for people to interpret what the child says and to tailor their own language so that communication is effective.

At birth, infants are prepared to learn any language. For example, an American baby adopted by an Inuit-speaking Eskimo family would grow up speaking fluent Inuktitut and have no trouble saying words such as *qikturiaqtauniq* ("mosquito bite"). However, even before their first birthdays, babies begin to lose the ability to hear the distinctions among phonemes in languages other than their own. By around the age of six months, babies have already begun to hear the sounds of their own language in the same way that adult speakers do, as Patricia Kuhl and her associates (1992) have shown in their research.

Human infants are intensely social; even in the first few days of life, they look into the eyes of their mothers and are sensitive to the emotional tone of the human voice. Long before they say their first words, babies begin to acquire the communicative skills that underlie language. As they get a little older they begin to take their turn in little "conversations" with their caregivers. The adult speaks, and the baby's turn can be something as simple as a sneeze or a burp. As they near their first birthday, many babies understand fifty or more words and can point out the right person when asked "Where's mommy?" They show that they are intentional communicators even before they begin to talk, by using gestures, by using con-

A sixteen-month-old child learns body part terms by touching the part of a stuffed lion that corresponds to the mother's "Where is . . . ?" questions. (Laura Dwight/Corbis)

sistent word-like sounds, and by becoming insistent when they are not understood.

As their communicative skills grow, the ability of infants to produce speech sounds also develops. They begin to babble, or play with sounds, midway through the first year. At first, babbling may consist of just a few sounds. Soon, the infant begins to babble repeated syllables, such as "dada" and "baba." A little later, many babies babble long sequences of syllables that resemble the sentences of their language. Communicative development in the first year has universal features and occurs in this way in all parts of the world, regardless of the degree of sophistication of the culture or complexity of the language being learned. First words emerge during the babbling stage and are produced by many infants at about the same age when they take their first steps, around their first birthday or a little later.

Once babies have begun to produce a few words, they begin to use them for a number of purposes. The earliest words children acquire refer to things in their immediate world that are important to them. They learn the names of their relatives (e.g., their mommy or daddy) and words referring to food, to games, toys, animals, body parts, and simple actions (e.g., eat, sit, up, down). Babies tend to learn the names of things that move or that they can act on (e.g., a mitten or ball) rather than something that is not related to their everyday activities (e.g., the sky or a floor). Early words represent different parts of speech, such as nouns, verbs, and adjectives, although nouns tend to make up the largest category. These words are also simple in terms of their pronunciation and generally not more than two syllables long. Infants use their single words in fairly complex ways. They may say "cookie," meaning "I want a cookie" or "that is a cookie" or "another cookie." In this one-word stage of language acquisition, children are restricted to the here-and-now. They do not talk about the future or the past.

Late in the second year, after they have acquired about fifty words, children begin to put the words together into little two-word sentences. Children's early two-word utterances also have universal characteristics. Children around the world are trying to get across very much the same kinds of ideas. They want to ask for more of something ("more cookie"), to reject something ("no sock"), to notice something ("hi, doggie!"), or point out that something has disappeared ("all-gone milk"). These early word combinations are called telegraphic utterances, because the child makes them without articles, prepositions, inflections, or other little grammatical words, and they sound like telegrams. The child can now say such things as "That kitty," meaning "That is a kitty," and "Mommy sock," meaning "Mommy's sock" or "Mommy, give me my sock" or "Mommy is putting on her sock." The telegraphic utterances become longer as the child gains language ability and becomes able to say even more things. Although the language of toddlers is similar across all languages during the telegraphic stage, what is acquired next depends on the structure of the language that the child is learning.

As the child's utterances grow longer, grammatical forms begin to appear. In English, children begin to add articles, prepositions, and inflections to their language. English-speaking children learn the articles "a" and "the," but in languages such as Chinese or Russian, which do not have articles, they learn other things. One remarkable discovery has been that children acquiring a given language follow essentially the same order of acquisition. As the vocabulary of young children continues to grow they gain a knowledge of morphology even before they enter kindergarten that allows them to make plurals or past tenses of words they have never before heard. In fact, when a young child says "mouses" instead of "mice," this is good evidence that the child is learning the regular forms of the language and knows how to make plurals, even if he or she has not yet learned the irregular forms. Almost all preschool children produce regularized plurals and past tenses such as "gooses" and "ringed" as they acquire the systematic aspects of their language. By the time they enter school, children also know how to make all of the basic sentence types of their language, and they can use them in connected discourse.

Although the basics of the language are acquired in the first few years of life, there is much to be accomplished during the school years as well. By the age of six, children have acquired approximately fourteen thousand words, as the linguist Eve Clark (1993) points out in her book *The Lexicon in Acquisition*. As children grow older, the words that are related to each other become associated in the mental lexicon, so that a word such as "doctor" becomes linked to words such as "nurse," "hospital," and "stethoscope." This growing vocabulary is necessary for success in school.

School-age children begin to use language in a variety of new ways. Children develop pragmatic skills as they interact with others, and they learn how to use language appropriately in many different situations. Their language becomes decontextualized, in the sense that they can now talk about things that are not in their immediate environment (e.g., ancient history, events in other countries). Another new development is the ability to think about language itself, to know what a word is and even what their favorite words are. This new skill, called metalinguistic awareness (awareness of language), contributes to their ability to make jokes and riddles and to engage in other kinds of wordplay with their peers. It also helps them to acquire literacy skills. Learning to read and write are, of course, essential developments in the school years.

Although it is evident that the major aspects of language acquisition are complete by the time an individual has finished formal schooling, language skills continue to develop throughout the life span. Individuals are continually adding new vocabulary and learning new pragmatic and discourse skills.

Theories of Language Acquisition

Although many researchers have described what happens during the course of language development, there is much debate over just how children are able to acquire such a complex system in such a short time. Several major theories have attempted to explain the mechanisms of language acquisition:

Learning theory explanations of language development are based on the work of B. F. Skinner and other behaviorists, who view language as just one kind of human behavior that is learned. According to this theory, children learn to imitate adults, who also actively teach the children the language. For example, when babies begin to babble, adults reinforce or reward the babbling. A little later, the adults are thought to reward systematically the utterances that become closer and closer approximations of the target language until, eventually, children are speaking like the adults around them.

Many linguists, including Noam Chomsky and Steven Pinker, believe that the basic principles of language are innate, or present at birth, and that only human beings are capable of language. According to this view, adults' role in children's language development is minimal; all that is necessary is for the infant to be exposed to language. A built-in mechanism in the brain—referred to as a "language acquisition device" (LAD)—allows the child to develop language skills in a very short time without explicit teaching. These theorists believe that language is a unique and separate ability and that acquisition is possible only during a brief critical period during early childhood.

Jean Piaget was a major proponent of cognitive developmental theory. According to this theory, language is not a separate capacity; rather, it is just one facet of children's general intellectual ability. Cognitive theorists believe that infants use their senses and motor skills to begin to learn about the world—for example, that cats are furry and say "meow"—and that once they have gained such knowledge, they map words such as "kitty" onto the concepts that they have already attained.

Social interactionists, including Jerome Bruner and Catherine Snow, view language as a facet of communicative behavior that develops through interaction with other human beings. They agree that humans have special linguistic abilities that are not shared by other animals, but they hold that children acquire language in part through the help of others, rather than purely through their own mental activity. Thus, interaction, rather than exposure, is seen as necessary. These researchers have found that there are special ways of talking to young language learners the world over that are tailored or fine-tuned to children's cognitive and communicative needs. They believe that the clear and simple child-directed language that adults use helps children to figure out how language works.

Understanding Language Acquisition

All of the components of language are important for communication, and disruption at any level can lead to miscommunication or even fail-

ure to communicate. For example, an individual who has not correctly acquired the sound system will not be able to make important distinctions between similar-sounding words (e.g., the difference between "ship" and "sheep"). Morphology and syntax are needed to convey meaning. A rich, shared lexicon, or vocabulary, is needed in a complex society in order to make reference to people, places, and concepts. The pragmatic system is particularly important in communication because even slight misuses or inappropriate uses of pragmatics can have quite disastrous interpersonal results, particularly if pragmatic conventions that govern politeness are violated. Finally, everyone must learn how discourse works in order to communicate about any connected set of ideas or events. If people understand how language is structured, they gain insight into what the basic building blocks of messages are and into what may have gone awry when communication fails.

See also: ALPHABETS AND WRITING; INTERPERSONAL COMMUNICATION; LANGUAGE AND COMMUNICATION; LANGUAGE STRUCTURE; SOCIOLINGUISTICS; SYMBOLS.

Bibliography

Bruner, Jerome. (1983). *Child's Talk: Learning to Use Language.* New York: W. W. Norton.

Chomsky, Noam. (1965). *Aspects of a Theory of Syntax.* Cambridge, MA: MIT Press.

Clark, Eve. (1993). *The Lexicon in Acquisition.* New York: Cambridge University Press.

Gleason, Jean Berko, ed. (2000). *The Development of Language.* Boston: Allyn & Bacon.

Kuhl, Patricia K.; Williams, Karen A.; Lacerda, Francisco; Stevens, Kenneth; and Lindblom, Bjoern. (1992). "Linguistic Experience Alters Phonetic Perception in Infants by 6 Months of Age." *Science* 255(5044):606–608.

Piaget, Jean. (1926). *The Language and Thought of the Child.* New York: Harcourt Brace Jovanovich.

Pinker, Steven. (1994). *The Language Instinct: How the Mind Creates Language.* New York: Morrow.

Skinner, Burrhus F. (1957). *Verbal Behavior.* Englewood Cliffs, NJ: Prentice-Hall.

Snow, Catherine E. (1989). "Understanding Social Interaction and Language Acquisition: Sentences Are Not Enough." In *Interaction in Human Development,* eds. Marc Bornstein and Jerome Bruner. Hillsdale, NJ: Lawrence Erlbaum.

JEAN BERKO GLEASON
ELENA ZARETSKY

LANGUAGE AND COMMUNICATION

For the communication field, language can be understood as an organized system of symbols used for creating and transmitting meaning. Language involves the meaningful arrangement of sounds into words according to rules for their combination and appropriate usage. James Bradac (1999, p. 12) captured the multiplicity of conceptions of language when he noted three ways of defining it:

Language$_1$: "[The] communicative agency [. . . that] allows speakers to accomplish routinized purposes (e.g., exchange greetings) and other purposes that are completely novel. . . . It is highly flexible and adaptable."

Language$_2$: "[The] biologically based, hierarchical system studied by linguists. It has multiple levels, each complexly structured and interrelated with the others. The structures at each level can be represented by construction rules [. . . and] constitute part of the tacit knowledge of speakers."

Language$_3$: "[A] collection of verbal features that are often influenced or even determined by environmental, physical, or psychological variables that are not under the conscious control of speakers."

A variety of aspects of language are studied in the communication field. These include consideration of the origins of language, language acquisition, phonetics, phonology, syntax, semantics, pragmatics, language and culture, language and diversity, and language and relationships.

Approaches to Language Study in the Communication Field

A variety of different methodological perspectives have been brought to bear on the study of language. Psycholinguists study the psychological principles that are involved in how language is processed and represented. Noam Chomsky's theory of transformational generative grammar emphasized cognitive aspects of language use, theorizing that linguistic competence (i.e., the ability to produce proper sentences in any language) is innate in all humans. This led linguists to study linguistic performance (i.e., actual sentences) in order to infer what may be going on in the brain. That is, the study of surface structure provides information about the deep structure of language.

Some scholars in the communication field take a cognitive approach to language, examining perceptions of and attitudes toward a speaker based on the language they use.

Sociolinguists in the communication field couple the social characteristics of communicators with features of how they communicate. One example of this is the search for a gender-linked language effect. That is, scholars have examined language to see if particular features of it can be tied to the gender of the speaker.

Other researchers employ a descriptive approach (i.e., ethnography of speaking) to examine how culture may influence different aspects of language use. "Discourse analysis" can be thought of as an umbrella term that refers to a range of different approaches, including speech act theory, interaction analysis, and critical approaches. Stephen Levinson (1983, p. 286) describes discourse analysis as "a series of attempts to extend the techniques so successful in linguistics beyond the unit of the sentence."

Harvey Sacks (1984) recognizes that the study of the language used in poetry, literature, and rhetoric often seems to be given priority over the study of the language used by individuals in their everyday talk. However, he makes the case that the language of everyday talk is in fact an immensely important field of study because it is the fundamental medium through which social life is enacted. It is for this reason that conversation analysts focus on the seemingly mundane talk that is used in everyday and institutional settings. Using videotapes and audiotapes (of conversations that would have happened whether or not they were taped) as data, conversation analysts describe in detail the practices that communicators use for enacting a wide range of activities in a variety of settings.

The Origins of Language

There is much speculation about the origins of language. Two theories exist regarding the evolution of language in humans. First, it is claimed by some that language was the result of a pivotal development in the human brain, at which point humans gained the capacity for language. Chomsky (1957) is an important proponent of this theory. Others suggest that language developed gradually as humans developed. It is thought by some, such as Philip Lieberman (1998), to be a result of the evolution of the brain, nervous system, and vocal cords. Regarding the character of language itself, some propose that language "expresses" the character of nature itself, in the manner that an onomatopoeic word such as "whoosh" captures the character of the sound it is designed to name. Others suggest that languages are largely conventionalized, with the relationship between the object and the word that names it being arbitrary. Animals also use symbolic forms of communication to signal one another. For example, bees may dance in a particular pattern to signal to other bees the location of a food source. The different songs of birds may have different meanings. The major difference between animal language and human language is that humans can create new messages for new situations, while animals cannot.

Language Acquisition

Most children have acquired spoken language by the time they are five years of age. This suggests that children are born with the neural prerequisites for language. On the basis of the fact that feral children (i.e., children who have grown up separated from any human contact) do not speak any sort of language when they are found, it has been suggested that social stimulation of language is essential. Victoria Fromkin and Robert Rodman (1993) have identified the following stages in language acquisition:

1. Babbling Stage. At around six months of age, infants begin to babble. Many of the sounds they make resemble the sounds of human language. This babbling occurs in deaf children and in the hearing children of deaf parents who do not speak, so it is thought not to depend on auditory input. However, for language to develop, children appear to need either auditory input or sign language.

2. Holophrastic Stage. At approximately one year of age, children begin to produce apparently meaningful words that often stand as "sentences." At first, these words may be used simply to label ("cheerio"), but as the children develop, these words may provide such communicative functions as asking for

Symbolic language in the animal world is illustrated by the bee dance, where a bee (number 37) "dances" to communicate a feeder location to other members of the swarm during an experiment at Michigan State University. (James L. Amos/Corbis)

things (e.g., indicating "I want a cheerio"). At this stage, words may also be used to convey emotion.

3. Two-word Stage. At about twenty-four months of age, children may begin to produce two-word combinations. At first, these appear to be two holophrastic utterances—two isolated words produced together. Soon though, children begin to produce the appropriate intonation contours for the two words to be heard as a grammatically and semantically connected "sentence."

4. Telegraphic Speech. As children continue to mature, they begin to build strings of words that may be longer than three words. The name for this type of speech comes from the fact that the strings are often missing such "function" words as "to," "the," "is," and "can."

There are various theories about how children acquire language. Some suggest that it is acquired through imitation. Others suggest that it is acquired through positive reinforcement (i.e., acceptance of "correct" sentences and "correction" of incorrect ones). Children appear to acquire the rules of grammar in stages that become increasingly complex. The mechanism that enables this process is thought to be a process of generalizing or overgeneralizing grammatical rules ranging from simple to complex.

Language is made up of various components. These have been studied under the rubrics of phonetics, phonemics, syntax, semantics, and pragmatics.

Phonetics

Phonetics is the study of the sounds of language. This involves determining the discrete sounds that can be made in a language and assigning a symbol to each sound. The International Phonetic Alphabet is a compilation of symbols that represent the sounds that are made in all languages. For each language, the collection of sounds that are unique to that language can be represented by symbols from the International Phonetic Alphabet. Sounds may be distinguished according to how they are made—which airstream mechanisms are used and whether the sounds are voiced, voiceless, nasal, oral, labial, alveolar, palatal, velar, uvular, glottal, and so on. Pitch, tone, intonation, and stress are also important features of phonetics.

Phonology

Phonology is the study of the sound patterns that are found in language. It may also be used to refer to a speaker's knowledge of the sound patterns in their specific language. While humans can make an almost infinitely wide variety of spoken sounds, the regularity of the sounds that are made in a given language represent some agreement as to which sounds are meaningful in a consistent way. Fromkin and Rodman (1993, p. 35) point out that "[phonetics] provides the means for describing speech sounds; phonology studies the ways in which speech sounds form systems and patterns in human language." It is on the basis of phonological knowledge that individuals are able to produce sounds that form meaningful utterances, recognize foreign accents, make up new words, and so on. Individuals recognize different sounds on the basis of their difference from other sounds. For example, the words "pill" and "bill" are distinguished by the difference between "p" and "b," making them "distinctive" sounds in English. Distinctive sounds are phonemes, and pairs of words of this sort are minimal pairs. Studying phonology involves laying out the sets of minimal pairs that make up a language, or the phonological rules that make different sounds meaningfully discriminated.

Syntax

The basic unit of grammar is the morpheme. A morpheme is a minimal linguistic sign: "a phonological form which is arbitrarily united with a particular meaning and which cannot be analyzed into simpler elements" (Fromkin and Rodman, 1993, p. 114). Thus, the word "lady" consists of one morpheme, while the word "ladylike" consists of two—"lady" and "-like". In order for language to be used for communication, though, morphemes must be organized in a particular order. Strings of morphemes are organized according to the rules of grammar (i.e., syntactic rules). The grammar of English, for example, results in "The car drove on the street" having a different meaning from "The street drove on the car." The placement of a word in a sentence influences whether it is understood as the subject or object of the sentence. The study of syntax involves laying out the grammatical structures that are meaningful and permissible in a given language (i.e., the phrase-structure rules).

Semantics

While the phrase "Colorless green ideas sleep furiously" is grammatical, it is conventionally contradictory and meaningless. This suggests that knowing the syntactic rules of a language is not sufficient. It is also necessary to know how meaning works. The study of meaning is complex. On the one hand, a "dictionary" approach to meaning suggests that all words have objective definitions. This approach, structural semantics, is based in formal logic. In contrast, lexical semantics is concerned with explaining "how people understand words and what cognitive processes interact with this understanding to produce meaningful communication" (Ellis, 1999, p. 60).

Pragmatics

Even with an understanding of syntax and semantics, the crucial feature of language is its appropriate use. The distinction between the abstract knowledge of language and its actual use is captured in the distinction that Ferdinand de Saussure (1960) drew between *langue* (i.e., the formal language) and *parole* (i.e., the actual use of language to communicate). In order to be able to use language competently, communicators must have knowledge of the norms for appropriate usage.

As Levinson (1983) points out, delineating the parameters of the field of pragmatics is complex. The term is used in many different ways. Examining notions of language structure without considering the context in which it is used may result in a compelling formal study with little practical application. Pragmatics attempts to explain language in use. This involves coming to an understanding of the complex concept of context. Teun Van Dijk (1997, p. 11) suggests that context is what "we need to know about in order to properly understand the event, action or discourse." Karen Tracy (1996) shows that context is a complicated, illusive phenomenon. Paul Drew and John Heritage (1992) point out that people tend to think of context as a "bucket" in which things take place. Those things are often taken to be shaped by the bucket. Heritage (1984) has also demonstrated that while context may shape communication, communication often shapes context, providing for a reciprocal relationship in which talk is both context shaped and context renewing.

Other aspects of pragmatics that have received extensive scholarly attention include speech acts. This theory, described by J. L. Austin (1962), asserts that language is performative rather than being merely constative or descriptive. That is, when individuals use language, they do so in order to perform an action, not merely to describe some state of affairs. Thus, when the Queen says "I name this ship . . . ," she is actually performing the action of naming the ship. John Searle (1969, 1975) elaborated on Austin's Speech Act Theory, explaining some of the felicity conditions that must pertain for an utterance to have illocutionary force, or social and communicative purpose. Furthermore, utterances may have perlocutionary force if the attempted action of the speech act is accomplished. Saying "Pass the salt" has the illocutionary force of a directive. If interactants are in a situation where this can actually be done, and the salt is passed, the utterance has perlocutionary force. Indirect speech acts involve saying, for example, "It's cold in here" as a way of requesting that the door or window be closed. Conversation analysts have discussed utterances of this kind as the first turn in a presequence—an exchange that is designed to precede some other action. This view that language is active in the social world comes together with Ludwig Wittgenstein's (1953) theories about language consisting of language games (i.e., the regular ways in which individuals use language to perform activities in everyday life). This active view of language feeds into social constructionist theory, which suggests that much of the social life of individuals—their selves, relationships, and even cultures—are constructed through language and communication.

Another aspect of pragmatics addresses the question of how people are able to understand what a person may be doing with specific utterances. H. Paul Grice proposed the following cooperative principle: "Make your contribution such as is required, at the stage at which it occurs, by the accepted purpose or direction of the talk exchange in which you are engaged" (Grice, 1976, p. 45). This involves four aspects that Grice formulated as "maxims":

1. Quantity: A contribution should be just enough, not too much and not too little.
2. Quality: A contribution should be true.
3. Relation: A contribution should be relevant.
4. Manner: A contribution should be brief, orderly, and not ambiguous, overly verbose, or obscure.

Grice suggested that individuals attempt to understand talk according to this principle and these maxims. Even if an utterance appears to be elliptical or obscure, an individual will try to understand it, but with the assumption that something "special" is going on. That is, an individual will make assumptions beyond the semantic content of the utterance. These assumptions are referred to as "conversational implicature," which Donald Ellis (1999, p. 78) defines as "an interpretive procedure that operates to figure out what is going on." Levinson (1983. p. 102) gives the following example:

A: Where's Bill?

B: There's a yellow VW outside Sue's house.

The semantic content of B's utterance would suggest a failure in cooperation. Yet interpreting the utterance at a deeper level, assuming that it is in fact cooperative, an individual might come to the conclusion that there is a connection between where Bill is and where the yellow VW is. Therefore, the answer to A's question, if Bill has a yellow VW, is that he is likely to be found at Sue's house. Thus, inference is used to preserve the assumption of cooperation. This is the process referred to as "conversational implicature."

Discussion of pragmatics indicates that its concern with competent use of language as a means of doing action in the social world makes it a central concern for communication.

Language and Culture

Culture and language are thought to be intimately connected. As with theories of context, there is debate regarding whether culture shapes language or language shapes culture. Language use is widely thought to be strongly related to culture. Sociolinguists and ethnographers of language and communication have devoted significant attention to the interplay between language and communication. The Sapir–Whorf hypothesis suggests that language shapes the thinking of individuals to the extent that it constrains the kinds of thoughts and ideas people can have (linguistic determinism). Furthermore, a strong version of the Sapir–Whorf hypothesis takes the position that because different cultures have different grammatical and lexical structures (i.e., use different languages), it is virtually impossible for members of different cultures to understand one another fully (linguistic relativity). Other researchers have shown that culture may play an important role in shaping norms of conduct. For example, Gerry Philipsen (1975) showed that, in certain social circles in a working class neighborhood in a large industrial town, speaking instead of using one's fists was considered a sign of weakness. Thus, it seems that language and culture are mutually elaborating. A study of one may increase the understanding of the other.

Language and Diversity

Communication scholars have given extensive attention to linguistic markers and their effect on how people are perceived. Linguistic markers are those features of speech that are taken as an indicator of a person's social identity. For example, Robin Lakoff (1975) suggested a number of features that some take to characterize women's speech. This includes markers of uncertainty, such

as tag questions (ending an utterance with "isn't it?," "don't you think?," and so on), qualifiers (such as "maybe," "perhaps"), disclaimers (such as "I may be wrong but"), hypercorrection (using "correct" features of speech rather than colloquial usages), and use of a wide range of color words (such as "chartreuse," "aqua"), instead of standard primary color words (such as "red," "green"). Lakoff suggested that these usages may result in women being perceived as powerless speakers in contrast to men. Here, Lakoff connected specifics of language use with social power. Subsequent research has struggled to document the claim that men and women speak differently, but the researchers have had very varied degrees of success. Some suggest that it is stereotypes and prejudice that cause men and women to be seen differently. It has been proposed that use of sexist language may reinforce negative stereotypes of women. For example, certain usages may have the effect of making women invisible. When a woman marries and takes her husband's name, the change from "Miss Jane Smith" to "Mrs. Michael Jones" may have the effect of making her invisible. Use of generic terms such as "man" and "he" (which has declined significantly since the 1970s) may also have the effect of making women invisible.

Other research has asked similar questions with respect to whether certain cultures are marked by particular ways of talking and whether certain social groups are perceived more positively than others.

Language and Relationships

It has been suggested that different stages in the development of relationships are marked by distinct ways of talking. However, there is debate regarding whether being at a particular stage of a relationship produces a particular way of talking or whether talk constructs relationships. Work on linguistic idioms suggests that couples may use "private language" in public and in private as a way of both displaying and creating special integration or "togetherness."

Conclusion

Clearly, language is a highly complex and multifaceted phenomenon. Understanding its various aspects may enable communicators to go beyond stereotypes that are often unwittingly based in unspoken attitudes that individuals may hold about language. Recognizing the various components of language (i.e., phonetics, phonology, syntax, semantics, pragmatics) may help communicators to understand not just the complexity of language, but also its orderliness. Understanding semantics helps communicators see that there is a shared responsibility between interlocutors for meaning making; it is not simply a matter of one participant speaking clearly. Pragmatics elucidates the fact that appropriate use of language can be thought of as a rule-bound activity, where rules may apply differently in different situations. Its rule-bound character means that rules can be learned and applied in new settings. Finally, understanding that using language is a way of doing actions, rather than merely describing the world, demonstrates that language can be a form of political action. For example, using sexist and racist language may do more than reflect a person's views; it may actively engage in creating or perpetuating sexism and racism. The study of language brings to light features of a system that is a key part of the basic currency of human collective life but that is often overlooked precisely because it is so basic.

See also: ANIMAL COMMUNICATION; GENDER AND THE MEDIA; INTERCULTURAL COMMUNICATION, ADAPTATION AND; INTERCULTURAL COMMUNICATION, INTERETHNIC RELATIONS AND; INTERPERSONAL COMMUNICATION; INTERPERSONAL COMMUNICATION, CONVERSATION AND; LANGUAGE ACQUISITION; LANGUAGE STRUCTURE; NONVERBAL COMMUNICATION; SOCIOLINGUISTICS; SYMBOLS; WITTGENSTEIN, LUDWIG.

Bibliography

Austin, J. L. (1962). *How To Do Things with Words.* Cambridge, MA: Harvard University Press.

Bradac, James. (1999). "Language$_{1...n}$ and Social Interaction$_{1...n}$: Nature Abhors Uniformity." *Research on Language and Social Interaction* 32:11–20.

Capella, Joseph. (1990). "The Method of Proof by Example in Interaction Analysis." *Communication Monographs* 57:236–240.

Chomsky, Noam. (1957). *Syntactic Structures.* The Hague: Mouton.

Drew, Paul, and Heritage, John C., eds. (1992). *Talk at Work.* Cambridge, Eng.: Cambridge University Press.

Ellis, Donald. (1999). *From Language to Communication.* Mahwah, NJ: Lawrence Erlbaum.

Fromkin, Victoria, and Rodman, Robert. (1993). *An Introduction to Language,* 5th edition. Fort Worth, TX: Harcourt Brace Jovanovich.

Grice, H. Paul. (1975). "Logic and Conversation." In *Syntax and Semantics 3: Speech Acts,* eds. P. Cole and J. L. Morgan. New York: Academic Press.

Heritage, John C. (1984). *Garfinkel and Ethnomethodology.* Cambridge, Eng.: Polity Press.

Labov, William, and Fanshel, David. (1977). *Therapeutic Discourse.* New York: Academic Press.

Lakoff, Robin. (1975). *Language and Women's Place.* New York: Harper & Row.

Levinson, Stephen. (1983). *Pragmatics.* Cambridge, Eng.: Cambridge University Press.

Lieberman, Philip. (1998). *Eve Spoke: Human Language and Human Evolution.* New York: W. W. Norton.

Millar, Frank, and Rogers, Edna. (1976). "A Relational Approach to Interpersonal Communication." In *Explorations in Interpersonal Communication,* ed. Gerald R. Miller. Beverly Hills, CA: Sage Publications.

Philipsen, Gerry. (1975). "Speaking 'Like a Man' in Teamsterville: Culture Patterns of Role Enactment in an Urban Neighborhood." *Quarterly Journal of Speech* 61:13–22.

Sacks, Harvey. (1984). "Notes on Methodology." In *Structures in Social Action: Studies in Conversation Analysis,* eds. J. Maxwell Atkinson and John C. Heritage. Cambridge, Eng.: Cambridge University Press.

Saussure, Ferdinand de. (1960). *Course in General Linguistics.* London: Peter Owen.

Schegloff, Emanuel A. (1984). "On Some Questions and Ambiguities in Conversation." In *Structures in Social Action: Studies in Conversation Analysis,* eds. J. Maxwell Atkinson and John C. Heritage. Cambridge, Eng.: Cambridge University Press.

Searle, John. (1969). *Speech Acts: An Essay in the Philosophy of Language.* London: Cambridge University Press.

Searle, John. (1975). "Indirect Speech Acts." In *Syntax and Semantics 3: Speech Acts,* eds. Peter Cole and John Morgan. New York: Academic Press.

Tracy, Karen. (1996). *Colloquium: Dilemmas of Academic Discourse.* Norwood, NJ: Ablex.

van Dijk, Teun A. (1991). *Racism and the Press.* New York: Routledge.

van Dijk, Teun A. (1997). "Discourse as Interaction in Society." In *Discourse as Social Interaction,* ed. Teun A. van Dijk. London: Sage Publications.

Wittgenstein, Ludwig. (1953). *Philosophical Investigations.* Oxford: Basil Blackwell.

JENNY MANDELBAUM

■ LANGUAGE STRUCTURE

Both scholars and communicators operate on the premise that language is structured in an orderly fashion. An alternative view is that language is organized in a random fashion. Clearly, however, communicators treat language as tightly structured. A source of debate centers around whether the structure of language is innate in humans or is learned through socialization processes.

Research History

Noam Chomsky (1957, 1965) suggests that children are born with knowledge of a universal grammar (i.e., a set of principles that are common to all languages) that can be applied to any language. This fundamental knowledge of languages is an individual's linguistic competence. The ability to use a given language in a particular situation is an individual's linguistic performance. Scholars can use linguistic performance as a resource for inferring the character of linguistic competence.

Chomsky observed that while there are a fixed number of phonemes (i.e., meaningfully discriminated smallest units of sound) and morphemes (i.e., meaningfully discriminated blocks of phonemes), humans can construct an infinite number of sentences. This suggests that in learning a language, individuals are learning rules for producing sentences, rather than learning sentences themselves. Actual sentences are referred to as "surface structures." From them, linguists can infer deep structures (i.e., the basic rules of grammar that are part of a speaker's innate knowledge and are the same across languages). Chomsky, therefore, was concerned with inferring a theory of abstract sentence structure that could account for and generate grammatically correct sentences. In this sense, the grammar that Chomsky was seeking to describe was a generative one. Chomsky's grammar is also referred to as "transformational" because the few rules that operate to create an infinite number of sentences perform transformations on deep structure.

Some linguists and communication scholars examine the structure of suprasentential units. Their interest is to see how it is that a larger unit of discourse may be coherent and "hang together," or have cohesion. Karen Tracy (1985, p. 30) defines conversational coherence as "the fact that comments produced in conversation seem connected to each other in meaningful orderly ways." In this sense, conversational coherence is strongly related to topic organization. A "text" that is "coherent" is one in which topic is successfully managed. Different schools of thought take differ-

ent positions with regard to how coherence works. For example, John Searle (1969, 1975) takes a speech act theory perspective. He sees conversation as being made up of series of speech acts that have rules for when and how a particular utterance is to be understood to perform a particular action. These rules provide for the recognizability of a particular turn as doing a particular action, and the have been called "felicity conditions." Michael Halliday and Ruqaiya Hasan (1976) describe different linguistic devices that provide for connection within discourse. Their focus is on written texts, but their work has been applied to oral communication as well. The cohesive devices they describe include, for example, references, conjunctions, ellipsis, substitution, and pronomial reference. Each of these requires connecting with something earlier in the text to be understandable and thus provides for the text to be seen as a coherent whole.

Conversation analysts have described many aspects of the structure of language as it is used to conduct the mundane business of everyday communication. Harvey Sacks (1984) observes that the structured character of everyday social life is a dominant feature. He suggests that one could examine almost any aspect of society to find its locally structured character. Conversation analysts examine tapes of naturally occurring conversations. At first, taped conversation was examined simply because it was easy to obtain. Subsequently, it was realized that because taped conversations can be replayed, they can be transcribed and examined in great detail. Thus, by examining audio and video recordings of naturally occurring interaction, conversation analysts have been able to discover a range of structural features of conversation that are part of the infrastructure through which a wide range of activities are conducted in and through conversation.

Basic Structures

Some of the most important conversational structures are turn-taking, sequence organization, and repair.

Sacks, Emanuel Schegloff, and Gail Jefferson (1974) describe how turn-taking in conversation can be seen as a locally managed system. They point out that many different systematic processes for taking turns could be envisioned; for example, Starkey Duncan and Donald Fiske (1977) propose that turn-taking is based on the exchange of cues in talk. Sacks, Schegloff, and Jefferson describe the organization of turn-taking as communicators' organized solutions to the practical problem of who should talk when and for how long, and how speaker change should be arranged. They show how conversation proceeds in minimal units that could consist of a word, a clause, a phrase, or a sentence. These minimal units of talk (i.e., turn constructional units) are produced in such a way that it is hearable whether or not they are complete. One speaker produces such a unit. At its point of possible completion, a next speaker may take the conversational floor. If this does not happen, the current speaker could continue until the possible end of the next turn constructional unit, when there is another opportunity for speaker change to occur. These speaker change opportunities are called "transition relevance places." A speaker may bid for a longer turn at talk (i.e., one consisting of multiple turn constructional units) by starting his or her turn as a list (e.g., "First. . . . "). In this way, the interlocutor can project that the upcoming turn will consist of multiple items that are contained in multiple turn constructional units. This may also be done by projecting that there is a story to tell. Thus, turn-taking is locally managed, and it proceeds on a turn constructional unit by turn constructional unit basis.

A fundamental observation regarding turn-taking is that, ordinarily, one speaker speaks at a time, and speaker change recurs. While this is the canonical organization for turn-taking, variation can occur. For example, it is possible for overlap to occur if a speaker begins to take a turn when another person is at or near a point of possible turn completion. As Jefferson (1986) has shown, overlaps are often precisely placed, and they display one speaker's close monitoring of another's talk. It is also possible for a speaker to talk interruptively, coming in at a point that is not at or near a point of possible turn completion. Don Zimmerman and Candace West (1975) have suggested that interruption is practiced disproportionately by men interrupting women and therefore may be a way of enacting power. Schegloff (1987) calls this into question, pointing out that taking the floor via an interruption is tantamount to winning a battle but that the war is won only if the interruptive turn is actually taken up in subsequent talk. Nonetheless, other more subtle interpersonal activities—such as monopolizing the conversational floor or preventing the other speaker from taking an extended turn—can be accomplished by overlap and interruption.

Often, subsequent turns at talk are related to prior ones by a relationship that is stronger than just a serial relationship. That is, a next turn may be specifically "implicated" by a prior one, such that it can be heard to be officially "missing" if it does not occur. This strong relationship may be apparent in the way in which turns are structured. A strong relationship between turns is often referred to as "sequence organization." Schegloff and Sacks (1973) refer to pairs of turns of this kind as "adjacency pairs." Examples of adjacency pairs include summons/answer, question/answer, greeting/greeting, and compliment/response. According to Schegloff and Sacks (pp. 295–296), adjacency pairs have the following features:

1. They are two utterances in length (i.e., a first "pair part" is followed by a second "pair part").
2. The two utterances are adjacently placed (i.e., the second pair part must come right after the first pair part).
3. Different speakers produce each utterance.
4. First pair parts precede second pair parts.
5. The pair type of which the first pair is a member is relevant to the kind of second pair part that is selected (e.g., if the first part is a question, the second pair part must be an answer and not a greeting).

If a second pair part is not produced after a first pair part is uttered, it will be heard as officially "missing." Delaying a second pair part, or postponing it through such items as "um" or "well," may be heard to foreshadow upcoming disagreement (Sacks, 1987). Thus, sequence organization is another environment in which subtle interpersonal dramas can be enacted.

Problems in talking together are generally resolved very soon after they happen. Schegloff, Jefferson, and Sacks (1977) describe how repairs can be made when problems occur. The first opportunity for a problem to be resolved is through "self-initiated" repair, where a speaker offers a correction or substitution to something that has been said (e.g., "She was giving me all the people that were gone this year, I mean this quarter, you know."). If the speaker does not correct the problem in or just after the turn in which the problem occurred, another speaker can initiate repair with a next turn repair initiator (i.e., a turn that can be heard to indicate a problem of some sort in the prior turn), thus putting the speaker of the problem in the position to remediate it. Schegloff, Jefferson, and Sacks (p. 368) provide the following example:

B: Well I'm working through the Amfat Corporation.

A: The who?

B: Amfat Corporation. It's a holding company.

Here, A produces a turn that calls into question, or initiates repair on, an item mentioned in B's first turn. Next B offers a redoing and explanation of the problematic item. If this type of repair does not occur, the second speaker can complete the repair, as the following example from Schegloff, Jefferson, and Sacks (p. 378) illustrates:

A: Listen to the pigeons.

B: Quail, I think.

Thus, the possibilities for repair include self-initiated self-repair, other-initiated self-repair, and other-initiated other-repair. The organization of repair is also a rich site for interpersonal activities, since it is a method through which intersubjectivity is negotiated. Repeated use of repairs may constitute an inability to understand one another, for instance (Ragan and Hopper, 1984).

Overall Structural Organization

Two general features of the overall structure of a conversation are how it is begun and how it is ended. Schegloff (1968, 1986) describes how conversations on the telephone are opened. He shows that although there is a canonical order of adjacency pairs enacted by interactants (e.g., summons/answer, identification/recognition, greeting/greeting, "how are you"/"how are you," reason for the call), these should not be thought of as the enactment of a script. The series of sequences can be deviated from at any point in the conversation. For example, the answer to the summons may be a "Hello" instead of an expected corporate identification. A caller may take this up. Problems in recognizing one another may occur. The response to "How are you?" may be "Oh, okay, I guess" and

thus may indicate that there might be some trouble that could become elaborated. Both following and deviating from the canonical format may have implications for the relationship between the interactants.

Schegloff and Sacks (1973) describe a canonical way that telephone calls may be brought to a close. They show how the orderliness of methods for closing telephone calls (and, by implication, the orderliness of other features of conversation) represents the interactants' solutions to the technical problem of how to suspend the relevance of speaker exchange. That is, once a conversation has begun, speaker exchange recurs. Speakers are thus faced with the problem of working together to agree to suspend the relevance of exchanging turns. This is accomplished by producing a preterminal sequence in which it is possible for interlocutors to recognize that the conversation is possibly complete, but that previously unmentioned mentionables could be inserted. Thus, for example, after the apparent completion of some previous spate of talk, an "Okay" shows that the current speaker is not advancing the talk at this point and yields the floor to the other speaker. If the other speaker passes up this opportunity by producing a reciprocal "Okay," then the conversation may be treated as closed. This will be indicated by an exchange of "Goodbye." Thus, sequence organization can provide a structure for the closing of a conversation.

Because talk is organized on the basis of speakers taking minimal turn constructional units, with the potential for speaker exchange recurring after each next turn constructional unit, special work must be done if, for example, a speaker is to take the floor for an extended turn at talk to tell a story. In this case, the prospective storyteller produces a story preface in which he or she indicates that he or she may have something to tell. These turns vary with regard to how strongly they project an upcoming story. First pair part turns such as "You wanna hear a story my sister told me last night" (Sacks, 1974) or "You'll never guess what happened to me today" strongly project a story. They also make a forwarding response strongly relevant, putting the prospective recipient(s) in the position of aligning as recipients of an extended turn by saying "Okay" or "What?" Alternatively, a turn may simply announce some news, such as "Shawn ate lobster this afternoon." Recipients could treat this as the news and offer some assessment such as "Wow," or they could treat it as projecting a story, in which case they could solicit further talk about it with a turn such as "He did?" Thus, the temporary suspension of turn-by-turn talk for the taking of an extended turn to tell a story is interactively worked out at the possible beginning by interactants.

In the body of the story, recipients can become passive recipients, producing continuers such as "mm hm" or "uh huh" (which show them to be attending but do not shape the story by showing what they make of it). Alternatively, recipients may produce assessments, such as "Wow" or "How terrible" that show what they are making of the story-so-far. Turns of this kind are considered to be more "active" recipiency because they may influence the course of the storytelling, particularly if they display an understanding of the storytelling that is not in line with that of the teller. The most active kind of recipiency (i.e., the kind of turns that may have the most effect on how the telling unfolds) are first pair part turns that actively require the teller to take a particular kind of turn next. According to Jenny Mandelbaum (1989), a first pair part recipient turn, placed just at the point where the teller is apparently about to make fun of one of the recipients, can (by actively influencing what the teller says next) divert the storytelling from making fun of a recipient and convert it into a storytelling in which something good happened. Recipients of storytellings can show different kinds of understanding of the point that the storyteller is trying to make. When a recipient goes along with the point the teller appears to be making, he or she is aligning with the teller. The recipient is affiliating when he or she shows support for the action or perspective apparently espoused by the teller. While alignment and affiliation are not limited to storytelling, storytelling is an environment in which alignment and affiliation often become observable issues for interactants. The recipients' alignment and/or affiliation, or lack of them, are primary ways in which interpersonal work can be undertaken in the storytelling environment.

Collaboration between teller and recipients is also necessary at the possible end of the storytelling. When the teller produces turns that suggest that the storytelling is possibly complete, the recipient must show a realization of the possible completion in order for turn-by-turn talk to resume. Thus, conversational storytelling is interactively constructed throughout its course. This demonstrates that the normative structures for conversation that have been described above are just that—normative structures that are constructed and enacted by interactants. That is to say, they are not fixed rules, but rather, they are the communicators' organized solutions to the structural problems that are embodied in the activity of interacting.

See also: GROUP COMMUNICATION; INTERPERSONAL COMMUNICATION; INTERPERSONAL COMMUNICATION, CONVERSATION AND; LANGUAGE AND COMMUNICATION; STORYTELLING.

Bibliography

Chomsky, Noam. (1957). *Syntactic Structures.* The Hague: Mouton.
Chomsky, Noam. (1965). *Aspects of a Theory of Syntax.* Cambridge, MA: MIT Press.
Duncan, Starkey, and Fiske, Donald W. (1977). *Face to Face Interaction: Research, Methods, and Theory.* Hillsdale, NJ: Lawrence Erlbaum.
Ellis, Donald. (1999). *From Language to Communication,* 2nd edition. Mahwah, NJ: Lawrence Erlbaum.
Fromkin, Victoria, and Rodman, Robert. (1993). *An Introduction to Language,* 5th edition. Fort Worth, TX: Harcourt Brace Jovanovich.
Goodwin, Charles. (1984). "Notes on Story Structure and the Organization of Participation." In *Structures of Social Action: Studies in Conversation Analysis,* eds. J. Maxwell Atkinson and John C. Heritage. Cambridge, Eng.: Cambridge University Press.
Halliday, Michael A. K., and Hasan, Ruqaiya. (1976). *Cohesion in English.* London: Longman.
Jefferson, Gail. (1986). "Notes on 'Latency' in Overlap Onset." *Human Studies* 9:153–184.
Mandelbaum, Jenny. (1989). "Interpersonal Activities in Conversational Storytelling." *Western Journal of Speech Communication* 53:114–126.
Ragan, Sandra, and Hopper, Robert. (1984). "Ways To Leave Your Lover." *Communication Quarterly* 32:310–317.
Sacks, Harvey. (1974). "An Analysis of the Course of a Joke's Telling." In *Explorations in the Ethnography of Speaking,* eds. Richard Bauman and Joel Sherzer. Cambridge, Eng.: Cambridge University Press.
Sacks, Harvey. (1984). "Notes on Methodology." In *Structures in Social Action: Studies in Conversation Analysis,* eds. J. Maxwell Atkinson and John C. Heritage. Cambridge, Eng.: Cambridge University Press.
Sacks, Harvey. (1987). "On the Preference for Agreement and Contiguity in Sequences in Conversation." In

Talk and Social Organization, eds. Graham Button and John Lee. Clevedon, Eng.: Multilingual Matters.

Sacks, Harvey; Schegloff, Emanuel A.; and Jefferson, Gail. (1974). "A Simplest Systematics for the Organization of Turn-Taking for Conversation." *Language* 50:696–735.

Schegloff, Emanuel A. (1968). "Sequencing in Conversational Openings." *American Anthropologist* 70:1075–1095.

Schegloff, Emanuel A. (1986). "The Routine as Achievement." *Human Studies* 9:111–152.

Schegloff, Emanuel A. (1987). "From Micro to Macro: Contexts and Other Connections." In *The Micro-Macro Link,* eds. Jeffrey Alexander, Bernhardt Giesen, Richard Münch, and Neil Smelser. Berkeley: University of California Press.

Schegloff, Emanuel A.; Jefferson, Gail; and Sacks, Harvey. (1977). "The Preference for Self-Correction in the Organization of Repair in Conversation." *Language* 53:361–382.

Schegloff, Emanuel A., and Sacks, Harvey. (1973). "Opening Up Closings." *Semiotica* 7:289–327.

Searle, John. (1969). *Speech Acts.* New York: Academic Press.

Searle, John. (1975). "Indirect Speech Acts." In *Syntax and Semantics, Vol. 3: Speech Acts,* eds. Peter Cole and Jerry L. Morgan. New York: Academic Press.

Tracy, Karen. (1985). "Conversational Coherence: A Cognitively Grounded Rules Approach." In *Sequence and Pattern in Communicative Behavior,* eds. Richard Street and Joseph Capella. Baltimore, MD: Edward Arnold.

Zimmerman, Don, and West, Candace. (1975). "Sex Roles, Interruptions and Silences in Conversation." In *Language and Sex: Difference and Dominance,* eds. Barrie Thorne and Nancy Henley. Rowley, MA: Newbury House.

JENNY MANDELBAUM

■ LAZARSFELD, PAUL F. (1901–1976)

During the 1940s and 1950s, the Department of Sociology at Columbia University was dominant such department in the United States. It owed this distinction mainly to Paul F. Lazarsfeld, an investigator of mass communication effects and a research methodologist, who collaborated with his colleague Robert K. Merton, a sociological theorist. Lazarsfeld pioneered the university-based research institute, first in Europe at the University of Vienna and later in the United States at the University of Newark, Princeton University, and Columbia University. His Bureau of Applied Social Research at Columbia was famous in the 1940s and 1950s for conducting the most important investigations of mass communication effects.

Lazarsfeld was born in Vienna and grew up there, highly involved in socialist politics. He organized and led the Red Falcon youth organization of the Socialist party. He earned his Ph.D. in applied mathematics at the University of Vienna, and taught research methodology in the Department of Psychology there. In 1925, Lazarsfeld founded the Research Center for Economic Psychology (*Wirtschafts-psychologische Forschungsstelle*), which engaged in market research, to provide jobs for his unemployed Socialist party friends. The most noted study by Lazarsfeld's research institute was an investigation of Marienthal, a small community near Vienna in which everyone was unemployed during the Great Depression. His opportunities for advancing his career at the University of Vienna were blocked by anti-Semitism.

From 1933 to 1935, Lazarsfeld traveled among several American research universities on a Rockefeller Foundation fellowship and decided to migrate, given Adolf Hitler's increasing dominance of Austria. In 1937, Lazarsfeld founded and became the director of the Research Center of the University of Newark, which mainly conducted research on the unemployment of youth. The Rockefeller Foundation funded the Radio Research Project on the effects of radio through Princeton University, with Lazarsfeld as director of the project from his base at the University of Newark.

In 1939, Lazarsfeld moved with the Radio Research Project to Columbia University, where he became a faculty member in the Department of Sociology. There he joined forces with Merton and began the next thirty-five years of their academic collaboration, in which they formed a fruitful merger of theory and empirical research. The Rockefeller Foundation project on radio effects became the Bureau of Applied Social Research in 1944. This research institute was regarded as the most important center for the empirical study of mass communication problems for the next several decades. Funded by government, foundations, and private companies, the bureau provided research training opportunities for doctoral students at Columbia University and an outlet for

Lazarsfeld's numerous research ideas. He presided over the bureau with a rather chaotic management style, stealing funds from one project in order to conduct other research, in a process that one bureau researcher called "Robin Hooding."

Among the most noted of the studies conducted by the bureau was the Erie County (Ohio) investigation of the role of the mass media and of opinion leaders in the two-step flow of communication. The 1944 book that resulted from this study, *The People's Choice* (written by Lazarsfeld, Bernard Berelson, and Hazel Gaudet), helped establish the specialty of political communication and ushered in a scholarly era of the minimal effects of mass communication. Contrary to their expectations, Lazarsfeld and his colleagues found that the mass media of radio and print had relatively minor direct effects on how people voted in the 1940 presidential election in the United States. Mainly, people decided for whom to vote on the basis of interpersonal communication with peers.

Another famed bureau study followed, the Decatur (Illinois) research in which Lazarsfeld sought further understanding of the two-step flow of communication—in which ideas move from the media to opinion leaders and then to their followers through interpersonal networks. The results of the Decatur study appeared as a 1955 book, *Personal Influence* (written by Lazarsfeld with Elihu Katz), and illustrated the importance of media-stimulated interpersonal communication between opinion leaders and their followers as they made consumer decisions about movies, fashions, and so on.

Lazarsfeld's methodological contributions were many and varied: the focus-group interview, which he pioneered with Merton in 1941; panel surveys, a research design that he used in the Erie County study; and important qualitative data-analysis techniques. In fact, Lazarsfeld saw himself mainly as a methodologist or toolmaker, one who could study mass communication, unemployment, or any other social science topic. Nevertheless, Lazarsfeld was one of the four main forefathers of communication study, along with the political scientist Harold Lasswell, and the social psychologists Kurt Lewin and Carl Hovland. Lazarsfeld's research dealt centrally with individual actions, such as voting, consumer purchases, and so on, taking place in a social context. He sometimes described himself as a mathematical sociologist and was quite proud of being named the Quetelet Professor of Social Science at Columbia University in 1962. (Adolphe Quetelet was a nineteenth-century Belgian statistician.)

Lazarsfeld was ideally located for his research since New York City was the hub for the rising industries of radio and television broadcasting, advertising, and public relations during the 1930s and thereafter. Media-related companies needed to know the size of their audiences and their sociodemographic composition, a type of market research that Lazarsfeld helped create at the Bureau of Applied Social Research. In fact, Lazarsfeld is acknowledged to be one of the forefathers of market research. His investigations of the effects of mass communication also fit with the needs of media industries.

When Lazarsfeld was once asked about the seeming paradox between his leftist beginnings in Vienna and his capitalistic actions in America, he remarked that he was just "a socialist on leave" in the United States.

See also: ELECTION CAMPAIGNS AND MEDIA EFFECTS; MODELS OF COMMUNICATION; SCHRAMM, WILBUR.

Bibliography

Katz, Elihu, and Lazarsfeld, Paul F. (1955). *Personal Influence: The Part Played by People in the Flow of Mass Communication*. New York: Free Press.

Lazarsfeld, Paul F.; Berelson, Bernard; and Gaudet, Hazel. (1944). *The People's Choice: How the Voter Makes Up His Mind in a Presidential Campaign*. New York: Duell, Sloan and Pearce.

Rogers, Everett M. (1994). *A History of Communication Study: A Biographical Approach*. New York: Free Press.

EVERETT M. ROGERS

■ LESBIANS IN THE MEDIA

See: Gays and Lesbians in the Media; Sex and the Media

■ LIBRARIANS

Librarians connect people with information and ideas by organizing and facilitating the retrieval of information in all formats. Dictionaries have long

Although librarians are becoming increasingly responsible for technology in the library, they are still responsible for the accumulation and distribution of the cultural heritage, including items such as this scroll, which is being handled by a librarian in San Francisco. (Phil Schermeister/Corbis)

tended to define the word "librarian" as the person in charge of a library. Library users tend to associate the word with anyone who works in a library. Professional associations and those people who work in libraries tend to reserve the appellation for one who holds a master's degree in library and information studies.

The work librarians perform, how and where they do it, and how they are perceived have all evolved in a manner that parallels changes in the way information is produced and stored. Technology fueled this evolution in the twentieth century. Three different library educators, each writing about thirty years apart, defined "librarianship" as follows. In 1933, Pierce Butler wrote that "the fundamental phenomenon of librarianship . . . is the transmission of the accumulated experience of society to its individual members through the instrumentality of the book" (p. 84). In 1964,

another acclaimed library educator, Carl White, wrote that librarianship was concerned with the retention, organization, and use of the accumulated heritage in all its forms, with books and journals being just a part of that heritage (see pp. 10–11). Thirty-four years later, a third library educator, Richard Rubin (1998, p. 379), wrote that "librarians support fundamental democratic values by emphasizing equality of access to knowledge. . . . Underlying the special character of librarianship is not its techniques, but its underlying values. The significance of librarianship lies not in its mastery of sources, organizational skills, or technological competence, but in *why* librarians perform the functions they do. The fact that librarianship tends to encompass the vast body of print, audiovisual, and electronic information increases the importance of these underlying values further and differentiates it from other, even kindred, professions such as museum curators or historical society professionals."

Librarians today use an astonishing array of resources as they connect people with information and ideas. In a single working day, a librarian is likely to help a user select a novel for pleasure reading, use the Internet to answer reference questions, help someone learn to retrieve information from CD-ROM databases, and teach a small class how to use World Wide Web search engines. The twenty-first century also finds librarians performing a wide range of work in a variety of exciting settings. The majority of librarians work in traditional school, public, academic, and special libraries (such as corporate, law, or medical libraries). Other librarians bring their specialized knowledge and skills to bear in ventures such as serving as information architects who design intranets, information brokers who retrieve and analyze information on a freelance basis out of their homes or offices, and researchers who work for international consulting firms.

Never before has the librarians' ability to understand and use a wide variety of methods to organize and retrieve information been so much in demand. As more and more information is produced daily, and as instant access to that information becomes vital, the need for technologically savvy librarians will continue to grow. Information literacy (teaching people how to access and interpret information in all formats) is an increasingly significant part of thelibrarians' charge. For the first time ever, the librarians' ability to analyze users' needs to determine what information is appropriate and then to select, acquire, organize, and retrieve information that meets those needs is considered *chic* in many circles.

Like all professions, librarianship offers specialties and subspecialties. The primary demarcations in the field are set by the type of library one works in (i.e., public, academic, school, or special). Other specialties are formed by the type of work, such as catalogers, systems librarians, children's librarians, or collection development librarians. According to the *Occupational Outlook Handbook* (2000) of the U.S. Department of Labor, librarians held about 152,000 jobs in 1998. Most were in school and academic libraries, while others were in public and special libraries. A small number of librarians worked for hospitals and religious organizations, while others worked for governments at all levels. About one-third of all librarians held part-time positions in 1996.

In order to become a librarian, one needs a master's degree in library and information studies. Most professional positions in public and academic libraries require that the degree be from a program accredited by the American Library Association. School library media specialists must be certified by the state in which they are employed. Certification requirements vary, but most states require a master's degree. Special librarian positions also usually require a master's degree with additional education or significant experience in the subject area. For example, most law librarians hold a law degree as well as a master's in library and information studies (MLIS) and engineering librarians might hold a bachelor's degree in a scientific area as well as an MLIS degree.

Career paths vary widely. Since many libraries are small, they might only employ one professional librarian. Other libraries are huge, employing thousands of people, and thus offer considerable opportunity for administrative advancement. According to the U.S. Department of Labor Statistics (2000), the median annual salary of all professional librarians was $38,470. Librarians employed by the federal government received an average annual salary of $56,400 in 1999.

Librarianship is primarily a service profession, but one that requires an increasingly broad technological base. Because of this, librarianship is one of the more unusual professions in the twenty-first century. Librarians can be found connecting people with information in settings such as branch libraries serving large urban housing projects, bookmobiles equipped with Internet workstations connected by satellite or cellular modems, and ultramodern health sciences libraries on university research campuses. While the setting and the clientele vary, the mission of each librarian is the same today as it was at the dawn of the printed word: to connect people with the information and ideas they need and want.

See also: LIBRARIES, FUNCTIONS AND TYPES OF; LIBRARIES, HISTORY OF; LIBRARY AUTOMATION; REFERENCE SERVICES AND INFORMATION ACCESS.

Bibliography

American Library Association. (2001). "Welcome to the American Library Association." <http://www.ala.org>.

Butler, Pierce. (1933). *An Introduction to Library Science.* Chicago: University of Chicago Press.

Rubin, Richard E. (1998). *Foundations of Library and Information Science.* New York: Neal-Schuman.

U.S. Department of Labor. (2000). *Occupational Outlook Handbook, 2000–2001.* Indianapolis, IN: JIST Publishing.

U.S. Department of Labor, Bureau of Labor Statistics. (2001). "Occupational Outlook Handbook: Librarians." <http://stats.bls.gov/oco/ocos068.htm>.

White, Carl M., ed. (1964). *Bases of Modern Librarianship.* New York: Macmillan.

CHARLES HARMON
ANN K. SYMONS

LIBRARIES, DIGITAL

A library must have a collection of materials that carry information. In addition to its collection, a library must have some kind of organizational rules and some kind of finding mechanisms, collectively known as its "technologies" (e.g., catalogs, search engines). Finally, every library serves one or more identifiable communities of users. A library becomes digital as the collection, the technologies, and the relation to the users are converted from printed formats (i.e., books and paper) to electronic formats. First, the collection itself must be made machine readable. Next, the technologies must be converted to computer-based forms. Finally, an interface to members of the user community must be provided in computer formats. A digital library may be as small as the set of files on one person's computer, organized into a hierarchical directory structure and supplemented by the owner's personal scheme for naming files and directories. In such a system, the meaning of the path name "c:/documents/personal/smith.david/to/2000April24" is clear to the owner of the system. However, if the owner wished to locate the letter in which "I wrote to David Smith about Aunt Martha," this naming scheme might not be adequate. If the system were used by many people, the problem would be complicated further by the possibility of there being more than one David Smith. The problem of indexing or organizing by content exists for every digital library, from the smallest to the largest. The key technology for solving this problem is called "information retrieval."

The purpose of a library, viewed in the broadest sense, is to facilitate communication across space and time by selecting, preserving, organizing, and making accessible documents of all kinds. Digital libraries provide many opportunities to improve upon paper libraries. For example, methods of information retrieval make it possible to index books at the level of chapters, or even at the level of sections and paragraphs. However, just as a paper library can provide too many books, digital libraries can provide an even greater overabundance of documents, chapters, and passages. This calls for improvements at the micro level (e.g., better identification of relevant passages) and at the macro level (e.g., effective organization of vast networks into useful and usable logical collections). In addition, the old problem of preserving fragile paper materials is replaced by the problem of maintaining usability, given the potential transience of particular modes of storage (e.g., magnetic tape, diskette, CD-ROM, DVD). Libraries must plan for unending migration of their collections to new modes of storage.

Digital Library Collections

The materials in a collection may be found in a single group, or they may be contained in multiple, nonoverlapping subcollections, which may be housed at physically and logically distinct locations. This raises the problem, which is new to digital libraries, of combining documents found in several distinct collections into a set that will be most useful to the user of the library. This problem is commonly known as "collection fusion."

In the world's libraries, most volumes are text, in some human language. These form a major part of digital libraries as well. Along with texts, libraries contain other texts about those texts. Data added to a collection, or to an object in the collection, for the purpose of identification is called "metadata" (i.e., "data about data"). An early example of metadata is the catalog card in a mid-twentieth-century library. In a digital library, some metadata are prepared by hand (i.e., "cataloging"). Metadata may also be generated automatically from machine-readable text that has been analyzed to support indexing and retrieval of passages and documents by subject.

Some digital library collections contain images or graphics that have been created by human effort (e.g., sketches, oil paintings, hand-designed maps). The object in the collection may, alternatively, be a mechanically produced (i.e. photographic) representation of a human product or artifact. Other images may be photographic or tomographic representations of naturally occurring scenes or objects. Each kind of image poses specific problems for the digital library. For a humanly produced artifact, information about the author and the date and place of production are both useful and (in principle) knowable—although there can be identification and attribution problems with older artifacts. Newly produced artifacts can be labeled or "tagged" with this information. Typically, the added information is permanently linked to the information object (e.g., by placing both in a single machine-readable file).

Metadata about images may also include more technical descriptions of the imaged object and of the imaging process itself—for example, "church in northern New Brunswick, imaged at 4:30 P.M. on April 13, 1999, in infrared light of wavelength 25 microns." Part of this information (that the object is an image of a church) must be provided by a human analyst. On the other hand, the wavelength of the infrared light, the time at which the image was made, and the precise geographic location of the imaged object (which may be determined by a global positioning system device built into the digital camera) can all be automatically included in the machine-readable record.

Is the World Wide Web a digital library? Strictly speaking, it is not; it is better regarded as an interconnected set of different libraries that contain different kinds of collections and serve

An international initiative was started on February 24, 2000, when King Juan Carlos of Spain and James Billington of the U.S. Library of Congress "clicked" to launch a collaborative digital project between the Library of Congress and the National Library of Spain. (Reuters NewMedia Inc./Corbis)

different communities of users. In fact, a given person may belong to several communities of users (e.g., a dentist may, on the one hand, may search the web for information about dental procedures and, on the other hand, for information about a gift for his or her son). Most digital libraries are best regarded as being made up of several related collections or subcollections. Users access these collections through two kinds of technologies: engines and interfaces. The engine is the collection of computer programs that locate documents for indexing and the programs that build indexes. The interface is the collection of computer programs that lets a user "see" the organization, the contents of the index, and often the documents themselves.

Digital Library Technologies

Indexing of texts by the words that they contain is an example of generating metadata from features. In this approach, the features of the document are simply the words that it contains.

Indexing is based on things such as the frequency of words, which is taken to be an indication of what the document is about. In a sense, there becomes a "library catalog card" for every occurrence of a meaningful word and every book in which it occurs. Of course, the technology is more efficient, but the access provided has the same power that a huge card catalog would.

Machine-readable records of sounds are difficult to index automatically. If the sound is a human voice speaking some natural language, voice recognition tools may be used to create an approximate transcription of the speech, which becomes a powerful basis for the creation of metadata for retrieval purposes. For naturally occurring sounds, such as birdcalls, the first line of classification is based on an analysis (using waves and wavelets) of the physical properties of the sound.

For texts themselves, the distribution of words in the text forms the basis for defining many kinds of features. These include the frequency with which a given term occurs in the document, the presence or absence of terms, the location of terms within the document, the occurrence of two- and three-word phrases, and other statistically defined properties of the text.

National Initiatives

As a shared national priority, the development of digital libraries is addressed both by existing libraries and by programs created by the national government and by philanthropic organizations. The National Science Foundation, the National Institutes of Health, and the U.S. Department of Defense, among others, joined temporarily in the early 1990s to solicit and fund projects to develop key technologies for digital libraries. This program was later subsumed into the broader Information Technology Research initiative, which addresses both key technologies and the building of collections.

In addition, organizations such as the private Getty Foundation and the Andrew W. Mellon Foundation encourage, with their funding, efforts aimed at building specific collections of images or texts in digital form. These projects often have a major research component, such as the Columbia University Digital Library initiative. In general the goal of these initiatives is to "manage the revolution" by ensuring that each major experiment in digital libraries is conducted and documented in a way that will ease the path for those who come later.

Management and Policy Issues

Digital libraries pose new problems related to management and policy. For example, rapid advances in technology make most forms of digital storage either obsolete or difficult to support after a period of about ten years. Therefore, digital libraries must provide for a continual process of "preservation" or "conservation" of the content of its collections by moving them from soon-to-be obsolete media to more contemporary media. Since the price of media is generally highest when they are new and falls sharply as they reach the end of their periods of market dominance, this poses difficult economic policy issues for digital libraries. This "migration" problem stands in sharp contrast to the ease with which one can still read a paper book printed more than two hundred years ago.

Policy issues also arise in the protection of authors, publishers, and readers from various kinds of exploitation. The methods (i.e., web-based browsers) that are used to deliver the contents of digital libraries require that a separate physical copy of the document reside on the computer (either in the volatile random access memory or on the more permanent hard drive storage). This copy might then be appropriated, adopted, modified, and used in other documents, thereby depriving the author and the publisher of revenue, credit, or both. For materials that are essentially images, there are methods, called "digital watermarking," for embedding a unique identifier in the image. While this does not prevent misappropriation of the material, it does support *post facto* discovery of that activity and the search for legal remedies. However, standard text processing tools can convert some kinds of page descriptions—for example, those made available in the Adobe postscript format or the portable data format(pdf)— into pure text, which carries no watermark.

Protection of readers is also an issue because, even in an open political system, some materials are deemed inappropriate and potentially harmful to some groups of readers, particularly the young. There are both technical and policy problems related to identifying and tagging such materials automatically, as well as to knowing which readers should be permitted access to materials of each identified class. Efforts to resolve this problem legislatively are ongoing in the United States.

Costs and Benefits of Digital Libraries

While digital libraries represent an exciting new technology, they carry costs as well as benefits. As both technological and social entities, digital libraries compete for scarce resources, so they must be evaluated. The evaluation process must serve a diverse group of stakeholders, including individuals (e.g., readers, authors, librarians), corporate entities (e.g., libraries, host institutions, publishers), and national entities with shared interests (e.g., health, science, education).

The economics of digital libraries is still in its infancy, but it seems to be characterized by several key features: (1) observation of the library system in use, as opposed to a simple assessment of its size or collections, is essential to evaluation, (2) observations must be reduced both to numerical measures of some kind (e.g., statistics) and to comprehensible narrative explanations, and (3) the resulting measures and narratives must make sense to various groups of stakeholders in order to support decisions.

While much library material is ephemeral (e.g., newspapers), much of the value of libraries lies in the works of art and of scholarship that they contain. With regard to scholarship, colleges and universities are still developing the policies that will encourage (or discourage) the publication of digital works by their faculties. Unless such work is recognized, scholars will not produce in the new formats. There are challenging issues related to ownership of digital collections. The effort expended in digitizing collections must be paid for either by concurrent funding (e.g., government-sponsored programs) or with borrowed funds that must be repaid by sale of access to the materials. In a nation committed to equal access to information, many of whose leaders in science and industry obtained much of their basic knowledge in the public libraries of the twentieth century, issues of ownership and access will be among the pressing national policy problems of the twenty-first century.

Prospect

Overall, it seems likely that libraries in digital form will become the norm. Systems for duplication and migration will be needed to ensure the permanence of the cultural heritage in this form. Sound economic frameworks will be needed to ensure that access is provided in ways that benefit the society as a whole rather than only those who can afford to pay for the newest technology. All in all, an ever-accelerating technology will make the digital library an increasingly effective servant and collaborator for the society that develops and maintains it.

See also: CATALOGING AND KNOWLEDGE ORGANIZATION; COMMUNICATIONS DECENCY ACT OF 1996; DATABASES, ELECTRONIC; INTERNET AND THE WORLD WIDE WEB; LIBRARIES, FUNCTIONS AND TYPES OF; LIBRARIES, NATIONAL; LIBRARY AUTOMATION; PRESERVATION AND CONSERVATION OF INFORMATION; RETRIEVAL OF INFORMATION.

Bibliography

Andrew W. Mellon Foundation. (2000). "Programs." <http://www.mellon.org/awmpd.html>.

Columbia University Libraries. (2001). "Columbia University Digital Library Initiative." <http://www.columbia.edu/cu/lweb/projects/digital/>.

Defense Advanced Research Projects Agency. (2001). "Information Technology Office." <http://www.darpa.mil/ito/research/im/>.

Faloutsos, Christos. (1996). *Searching Multimedia Data Bases by Content*. Boston: Kluwer Academic.

Getty Foundation. (2000). "Research at the Getty." <http://www.getty.edu/research/index.html>.

Kluwer Academic Publishers. (2001). "Information Retrieval." <http://www.wkap.nl/journals/ir>.

Lesk, Michael. (1997). *Practical Digital Libraries: Books, Bytes, and Bucks*. San Francisco: Morgan Kaufmann.

National Institute of Standards and Technology. (2001). "Text REtrieval Conference (TREC)." <http://trec.nist.gov/>.

National Science Foundation. (2000). "Information Technology Research." <http://www.itr.nsf.gov/>.

National Science Foundation. (2001). "Digital Libraries Initiative." <http://www.dli2.nsf.gov/>.

Salton, Gerard, and McGill, Michael. (1983). *Introduction to Modern Information Retrieval*. New York: McGraw-Hill.

Springer Verlag. (2001). "International Journal on Digital Libraries." <http://link.springer.de/link/service/journals/00799/index.htm>.

University of California, Berkeley. (2001). "SunSITE: The Berkeley Digital Library." <http://sunsite.berkeley.edu/>.

Van Rijsbergen, C. J. (1979). *Information Retrieval*, 2nd edition. London: Butterworths.

PAUL B. KANTOR

LIBRARIES, FUNCTIONS AND TYPES OF

The word "library" was originally drawn from the Latin term *liber*, which means book. Historically, the libraries of the world have been closely identified with the books that came to fill their respective shelves. As recent as the 1980s, it would have been possible to define the nature and future of libraries in terms quite similar to those used in the description of libraries in the fifteenth, the eighteenth, and the mid-twentieth centuries. For it is apparent to even the most casual of students that the character of libraries has remained remarkably stable throughout some four millennia. Across those four thousand years, librarians constructed libraries large and small that were designed to effectively collect, organize, preserve, and make accessible the graphic records of society. In practical terms, this meant that librarians, the managers of these ever-growing libraries, collected large numbers of books and periodicals, arranged them for relatively easy use, and made these collections accessible to at least part of the community (if not the whole community). This broad definition of the nature and function of libraries served quite nicely until recently.

What shattered this timeless consistency, of course, was the emergence of information technology (IT) and the onset of the "information era." The emergence of the e-book, the e-journal, and hypertext writing systems appears to be rapidly undermining previous commitments to the print-on-paper communication system that played such a fundamental part in constituting the libraries of the world. Authors and publishers are increasingly recognizing IT as the new "core" or "defining" technology of the information era. It is apparent that knowledge production is being rapidly shifted to this new medium in an attempt by authors and publishers to amplify intellectual capacity through the enlightened adoption of a new medium that promises to enhance productivity, while concomitantly lowering the costs of knowledge production. It is also clear that librarians are being asked to devote ever-larger proportions of their limited resources to the provision of digital information services, and are being required to devote ever-smaller proportions of their budgets to the traditional print-on-paper materials.

The dramatic and accelerating development of the digital communication system and its rapid adoption by large segments of society has forced a wide-ranging revision of the notion of "library" and a reconsideration of the role of the librarian within the context of the now-dominant information economy. Initially, this development was viewed by library interests in much the same contradictory fashion as it was by society at large. For some, the idea of using IT to eliminate the print-on-paper system was a positive and exciting new development, while for others it promised an intensely unappealing future. Many librarians viewed the emergence of the information revolution as the long-sought opportunity to transcend the limitations imposed on libraries by the print-on-paper system, while to others the much celebrated "death of the book" heralded little more than cultural decline. As a result, the last decade of the twentieth century was marked by heated and highly polemical arguments about the nature and extent of the information revolution and its implications for the future of libraries.

Types

While the digital revolution has forced an intensifying debate about the future of libraries, much, nevertheless, remains the same. For example, for several centuries the principal types of libraries have remained unchanged. What differentiates these library types is the nature of their clienteles; and thus governmental, public, academic, school, and special libraries are found, serving information-seeking patrons throughout the world.

The first of these types to emerge in time was the library serving government. From the beginnings of centralized civilizations some five thousand years ago, it was necessary for governments to collect and organize for efficient use, large (and eventually huge) amounts of information. Then as now, some of the largest libraries in any country are government libraries serving special clienteles of civil servants, legislators, or members of the judicial and executive branches of the government, and are supported with public resources. For example, in Washington, D.C., there are literally hundreds of governmental libraries ranging in size from the mammoth Library of Congress, generally considered the largest library in the world, to small libraries containing only a few thousand volumes and serving only a few individuals. The same could be said for each of the most sophisticated world capitals such as Moscow, Paris, London, and Berlin. The government library category would also include thousands of libraries serving state, provincial, and municipal governments.

Another large and extremely diverse group of libraries can be categorized as special libraries that serve a wide variety of business enterprises. In any developed nation, thousands of special libraries serving companies large and small offer sophisticated information services to the employees of their respective companies. These libraries are funded with corporate resources and thus consider their collections and services to be proprietary and accessible only to those who work for the company. Special libraries offer a wide range of services to company employees but focus on two: preserving and organizing vital records relating to the opera-

Special academic libraries are often designed to meet collection and facility needs, which is the case with this fifteen-thousand-volume academic library on the Universe Explorer, a floating campus for college students who are participating in a "Semester at Sea Voyage" on the Atlantic Ocean. (Dave G. Houser/Corbis)

tion of the company, and providing a resource from which the research staff of the company can mine ideas for new products and services.

Equally significant are the public libraries of the world; that is, those libraries established as public trusts, administered with public funds, and open to every element of the citizenry, from children to adults. Free and readily accessible to local inhabitants, these libraries constitute the very cornerstone of information access for citizens, and virtually every community in the developed countries, from Great Britain to Sweden to the United States, proudly boasts the existence of significant numbers of public libraries that are open to all of their citizens. While these libraries offer many services, the emphasis on recreational or leisure reading is a unique characteristic of public library service.

Academic libraries are those libraries that serve the students and faculty of the colleges and universities of the world. The collections of these academic libraries can range from a few thousand

well-chosen volumes in the library of a small community college to the approximate ten million volumes found in the complex system of libraries serving Harvard University in Cambridge, Massachusetts. Unlike their public library counterparts, the academic library is little concerned with recreational or leisure reading and is devoted almost exclusively to the collection, preservation, and preparation for use of scholarly research materials that may never be widely used but are viewed as having research significance.

School libraries complete our categorization of library types. The school library is devoted to the support of the educational programs of elementary and secondary schools in countries throughout the world. Heavily oriented toward didactic material viewed as useful by schoolteachers, and smaller than academic libraries, the school library is an integral part of the education of children.

Perhaps it would be appropriate to end this section on contemporary libraries by noting the great variations in the number and nature of libraries that exist from country to country and continent to continent. The most extensive system is that found in the United States, which boasts some 8,500 public libraries, over 3,500 academic libraries, and literally tens of thousands of government, school, and special libraries. This massive library system is managed by some 250,000 professional librarians. Most of the Western European countries also have large and well-supported systems, but Eastern Europe, Africa, and most of Asia lag far behind. Thus, it should be no surprise to find that American and Western European libraries have also taken the lead in deploying information technologies in the service of their diverse clienteles.

Functions

While the information revolution has placed enormous pressure on libraries as they try to find their way across this dramatic technological divide, librarians continue to carry out a series of basic functions in the service of their overarching goal of making information readily available to their clienteles.

Perhaps first and foremost in the functions carried out by libraries is the never-ending collection of recorded information deemed of value to the users of libraries. Hundreds of thousands of librarians have devoted millions of hours to the assembly of the tens of thousands of library collections found throughout the world. Such collection development requires special awareness of the nature of knowledge production and the nature and extent of user needs, and remains one of the most important functions of the librarian. The glorious fruits of the labors of those responsible for the collection development function over the years can be seen in the magnificent book collections to be found in the great national libraries of the world, such as the Library of Congress, with nearly twenty million volumes, and the national libraries of England, France, Germany, and Russia, with nearly as many volumes. Such collections, painstakingly assembled, represent a virtually complete memory of the cultural history of their respective nations, and as such remain invaluable. These print-on-paper resources are, of course, now being joined by massive amounts of digital information stored in the computers of the libraries.

Once such large and valuable collections were assembled in countless libraries across the world, it next fell to the library profession to preserve those collections across time. Thus, librarians have pioneered techniques for restoring old books to usable states, and are leaders in the project to ensure that all future books will be printed on materials designed to last for hundreds of years. Librarians have also been in the forefront of the discussion of the most effective ways to collect, organize, store, and preserve digital communications.

Another enormously costly aspect of the effort to preserve library collections has been the construction of library buildings specially designed to conserve the priceless contents of the libraries of the world. These libraries have become ever more expensive, and, depending on the size of the collection, can run to hundreds of millions of dollars to build. Many people hope this huge cost can be eliminated in the future as digital communication comes to replace traditional books and periodicals in the knowledge production system. Then, a computer might well become the library, but it must be noted that it would be many years before the accumulated knowledge of the world, stored in millions of books, periodicals, and manuscripts, could be translated onto the new digital medium. Thus, it appears that librarians will be faced with the daunting task of managing yet one more medium in the future.

Large collections of books are virtually unusable without careful attention to organization for ready access. As a result, the cataloging and classification of library materials remains a central function of the libraries of the world. Using various classification schemes such as the Library of Congress Classification scheme or the Dewey Decimal Classification scheme, librarians have prepared detailed catalogs that act as efficient guides to the contents of their ever-larger collections. Providing author, title, and subject access to library collections, these catalogs remain essential to the proper utilization of any library. Librarians have also been working to develop search engines that will facilitate searching the multitude of databases available to library patrons via the Internet.

Finally, libraries must be interpreted for effective use. This library function is implemented by librarians who are prepared to answer user requests for specific information related to research projects and classwork. Librarians also prepare a wide variety of reference and bibliographic tools designed to provide library patrons with guidance in the use of specific elements of the collections of a library, such as periodical holdings, book reviews, or biographies of prominent individuals. Librarians are particularly committed to providing extensive formal and informal instruction to users who are seeking guidance in navigating their way through complex library collections and gaining what librarians refer to as "information literacy."

Information Technology and Libraries

Thus, while the types and the functions of libraries have remained much the same as they have been for several millennia, it is essential to note that the revolutionary spread of integrated digital communication systems has dramatically complicated and influenced the way in which libraries function in modern society. Perhaps an initial glance at several of the largest national libraries of the world—the Library of Congress and the Bibliotheque de France—will make this point clear. The Library of Congress, located in Washington, D.C., is housed in two expansive and expensive buildings and contains more than twenty million volumes in its collections. It is charged with a multitude of roles, including providing extensive reference and research services to the U.S. Congress, serving as the largest scholarly research library in the world, and offering a widely praised books-for-the-blind program. Even at the beginning of the twenty-first century, the Library of Congress receives a book every five seconds and has a massive number of unprocessed items waiting to be cataloged. At the same time, the Library of Congress has taken a leadership role in the deployment of IT in libraries. Perhaps the most dramatic venture is the American Memory Project, which is designed ultimately to translate a vast amount of the collection of the library into a digital format that will be accessible via the Internet from all over the world. In attempting to transfer such huge amounts of printed material to digital formats, the Library of Congress has been forced to deploy the most sophisticated and expensive IT available today, and most experts estimate that it will still cost millions of dollars and take decades for the American Memory Project to encompass any significant portion of the vast holdings of the Library of Congress.

The tremendous controversy surrounding the architectural design of the Bibliotheque de France illustrates the problems associated with the construction of library buildings in the information era. When the plans were first presented to the French public in 1991, there was a huge public outcry because it appeared that the Bibliotheque de France had been designed by architects who seemed to think that the book was "dead" in the digital era. Thus, very little provision was made for the preservation and use of books and periodicals in the new French national library. Many critics railed against the design, suggesting that it threatened the "collective memory" of the French people as represented by the millions of books in the library. The architects were urged to plan for the deployment of the latest technology for reproducing and storing information without gambling on the survival of the traditional book collection that represents the "collective memory" of the nation. The outcry in the early 1990s was so great that the French architects were forced to return to the drawing board and develop a design for a building that would be more friendly to the print-on-paper materials in the collection.

College and university libraries throughout the world should face a quite similar if less extensive set of problems as they enter the information era. Ever-larger amounts of the material they acquire is being produced in digital formats, and college and university students are especially sophisticated users of the new IT and are increasingly insistent that coursework and course readings be accessible via the Internet. Such demands have forced university administrators, faculty, and academic librarians to invest substantial amounts of money in IT and e-books and e-journals. At the same time, librarians must constantly attempt to stay abreast of the rapidly changing information environment so that they can adequately interpret the emerging "electronic library" for students and faculty.

Indeed, it appears that students and their parents are pushing the IT revolution at all levels of education as they demand ever-wider access to a growing array of IT. Students throughout the world are increasingly aware of the burgeoning information economy and the kinds of job opportunities available in that sector. Thus, their demands for ready access to e-mail, Internet services, online coursework, and digital reading materials and research resources are at least in part intensely pragmatic as they rush to qualify for the new employment opportunities in the information economy.

Virtually all libraries have been significantly influenced by the emergence of the new IT and the widespread development of the Internet. For instance, a vast majority of the libraries in the United States, and many more libraries throughout the world, have eliminated the old library card catalog and replaced it with an Online Public Access Catalog (OPAC). Almost as many libraries now provide Internet access to library patrons via dozens of computer terminals available to the general public.

Far fewer libraries have been able to completely replace their print-on-paper collections with e-journals and e-books, but nevertheless, there are many libraries worldwide, especially in the special library sector, which have gone virtually digital where in a very real sense the whole library is contained in a computer. An example of a totally digital and commercial library would be Microsoft's Corbis.com. This huge database comprises the largest collection of digital art and photography in the world, and half a million individuals visit this digital art library each day via the Internet. Those who discover art or photography that they want to own on the site can purchase these materials from Corbis.com.

Thus, by the beginning of the twenty-first century, every aspect of human existence has been influenced by the new IT. However, two particularly pressing information-era issues emerged to trouble all of those who were charged with planning library development.

Commodification of Information

In 1973, Daniel Bell, the distinguished Harvard University sociologist, published his now-famous book titled *The Coming of Post-Industrial Society*, in which he forecast, with amazing accuracy, the coming of the information revolution, an era he predicted would mark a complete break with our industrial past. Central to his work was the notion that the information society would be characterized by a changeover from a goods-producing to an information-producing society. He went further to insist that, in time, information would come to represent the most important commodity sold in the new electronically linked world marketplace. Two decades later, Bell's prediction was confirmed when Bill Gates, the president of Microsoft (and by then the wealthiest man in the world), noted in his 1995 book titled *The Road Ahead* that digital information had indeed become a central commodity in a massive global information marketplace, and that brash and uncivilized market forces were definitely at play in the public sector of the economy as well. Virtually everyone now concurs with this conclusion, but many remain troubled by the implications of the dramatic and relentless commodification of information.

One concern is essentially political. That is, many students of the notion of "democracy" in the Western world have pointed out that a key characteristic of the democratic model is the insistence that the success of democratic systems depends on the extensive and enlightened participation of citizens in the political process. An important corollary, and a central justification for the public library systems of the world, is the belief that enlightened participation by the citizenry is dependent on widespread and easy access to "free" information defined as a public good and provided with public tax funds.

Librarians and others remain skeptical of the idea that the commodification of information and the privatization of information delivery systems is conducive to the democratic process. They fear that such a process, if left unchecked, would actually lead to the restriction of access to information for those citizens who lack the financial resources necessary to buy significant amounts of digital information in the information marketplace. That is, many fear that the commodification of information, and the abandonment of the idea of information as a public good, would lead to an ever-larger gap between the "information rich" and the "information poor" in society and have the ultimate effect of undermining the democratic process. Thus, it should come as no surprise to find that the librarians of the world are at the forefront of the effort to provide widespread access to information to all of the citizens of a nation via a system of public, school, government, and academic libraries defined as public goods and supported by the state.

Many other critics, many of them librarians, see grave cultural implications in the insistence that all information of value will come to be defined as a commodity and that all information sales and services should be privatized. These critics are also troubled by the suggestion that all valuable information will come to be seen as practical or instrumental. And they insist that this notion would undermine the cultural value of books and reading, where great books are viewed as "priceless," and are often quite "unpopular" with the mass reading audience. The aggressive and instrumental commodification of information is seen as a recipe for cultural decline and the destruction of not just the book, but more importantly, the "great books." Librarians insist that the provision of public tax support for libraries has guaranteed the existence of a culture of great writing, because librarians have always attempted to purchase and preserve only the best that had been thought and written in their respective societies. In a real sense, librarians argue, they have acted as subsidies for the high-culture industry, and thus they fear that the commodification of information and the privatization of information delivery systems could ultimately undermine the cultural life of the nation.

It must be noted that advocates of the e-book and the commodification of cultural production insist that the information revolution does not threaten literacy, but rather simply promises to undermine the old print literacy. What will emerge, they insist, is a new hypertext writing system that will significantly alter the way people write and read as individuals create "texts" that are no longer linear and that tend to empower readers, who will be able to manipulate books in ways rarely imagined before the information era.

The Library as Place

Michael Levy, writing for the January 1, 2000, issue of *Newsweek*, concluded that by the year 2020 some 90 percent of books sold would be published as e-books. It is assessments such as these, widely endorsed by many experts, that lead librarians to wonder what "place" they will occupy in the new millenium. Richard Lanham sums up this dilemma in his book *The Electronic Word* (1993) when he notes that "the library world feels *dépaysé* today. . . . Both of its physical entities, the buildings and the books they contain, can no longer form the basis for planning" (p. 134).

Library buildings are hugely expensive to build and operate, and at present virtually all of the libraries in the developed West, at least, are filled to capacity. In the minds of many this situation will slowly, and happily, disappear as more and more of the books that currently stand in ordered rows on library shelves are digitized and transferred to a computer system located "somewhere" on the Internet. And as virtually everyone agrees that more and more new books will be published as e-books, it follows that society is rapidly approaching the time when it will no longer be necessary to build any new libraries, and some would go so far as to insist that society may well be able to close those buildings still operating by the beginning of the twenty-second century. These concerns and developments are forcing librarians to carefully analyze the role of the library in the information era and explicitly attempt to imagine a completely new library landscape where large traditional library buildings are slowly replaced by computers holding massive numbers of e-books and e-journals. Where will librarians work, what will they do, and how should they be trained when the library is no longer a "place"?

In the past, librarians could focus on the collection and preservation of books, and because access to books and periodicals depended on ownership, libraries could offer a valuable service to a select group of users by simply buying and housing as many books as possible. The new IT promises to break the linkage between ownership and access, and information seekers can now "access" information in a wide range of information markets. These users are extremely sophisticated consumers of information services and demand ever-more effective delivery systems. Librarians are struggling to define new programs that will effectively compete with the vast array of information services available through the Internet. The ability of the library profession to successfully fit into the new information environment will dictate the future of the library.

While it seems certain that libraries of the twenty-first century will appear quite different than those of the twentieth century, the precise direction and speed of the change remain murky. What seems likely is that answers to such questions will emerge over the course of the new century as librarians and communication specialists experiment, investigate, and analyze developments in countless libraries throughout the world. It also seems obvious that the pace of change will vary widely from country to country, and even from region to region within individual countries.

Perhaps the most responsible way to conclude would be to say that most interested parties seem to agree that society cannot simply walk away from the collective fruits of the intellect as represented in the untold millions of words-on-paper so thoughtfully housed and made accessible in the libraries of the world. And at the same time, almost everyone is equally certain that IT and the e-book must be effectively deployed by a profession that boasts three thousand years of sustained commitment to the responsible collection, preservation, and effective organization for use of the recorded knowledge of civilization—no matter in what format that knowledge may come.

See also: ARCHIVES, PUBLIC RECORDS, AND RECORDS MANAGEMENT; ARCHIVISTS; COMMUNITY NETWORKS; INTERNET AND THE WORLD WIDE WEB; LIBRARIANS; LIBRARIES, DIGITAL; LIBRARIES, HISTORY OF; LIBRARIES, NATIONAL; LIBRARY AUTOMATION; PRESERVATION AND CONSERVATION OF INFORMATION; REFERENCE SERVICES AND INFORMATION ACCESS.

Bibliography

Bell, Daniel. (1973). *The Coming of Post-Industrial Society: A Venture in Social Forecasting*. New York: Basic Books.

Berring, Robert C. (1995). "Future Librarians." In *Future Libraries*, eds. R. Howard Bloch and Carla Hesse. Berkeley: University of California Press.

Bloch, R. Howard, and Hesse, Carla, eds. (1995). *Future Libraries*. Berkeley: University of California Press.

Bolter, J. David. (1991). *Writing Space: The Computer, Hypertext, and the History of Writing*. Hillsdale, NJ: Lawrence Erlbaum.

Buckland, Michael. (1992). *Redesigning Library Services: A Manifesto*. Chicago: American Library Association.

Buschman, John, ed. (1993). *Critical Approaches to Information Technology in Librarianship*. Norwood, NJ: Ablex Publishing.

Crawford, Walt, and Gorman, Michael. (1995). *Future Libraries: Dreams, Madness, and Reality*. Chicago: American Library Association.

De Gennaro, Richard. (1987). *Libraries, Technology, and the Information Marketplace: Selected Papers*. Boston: G. K. Hall.

Drucker, Peter F. (1999). "Beyond the Information Revolution." *The Atlantic Monthly* 284(4):40–59.

Gates, Bill. (1995). *The Road Ahead*. New York: Viking.

Hannah, Stan A., and Harris, Michael H. (1999). *Inventing the Future: Information Services for the New Millenium*. Greenwich, CT: Ablex Publishing.

Harris, Michael H. (1999). *History of Libraries in the Western World*, 4th edition. Lanham, MD: Scarecrow Press.

Harris, Michael H.; Hannah, Stan A.; and Harris, Pamela C. (1998). *Into the Future: The Foundations of Library and Information Services in the Post-Industrial Era*, 2nd edition. Greenwich, CT: Ablex Publishing.

Harris, Roma M. (1992). *Librarianship: The Erosion of a Woman's Profession*. Norwood, NJ: Ablex Publishing.

Landow, George P. (1992). *Hypertext: The Convergence of Contemporary Theory and Technology*. Baltimore: Johns Hopkins University Press.

Lanham, Richard A. (1993). *The Electronic Word: Democracy, Technology, and the Arts*. Chicago: University of Chicago Press.

Levy, Steven. (2000). "It's Time to Turn the Page." *Newsweek*, Jan. 1, pp. 96–98.

Lubar, Steven. (1993). *InfoCulture: The Smithsonian Book of Information Age Inventions*. New York: Houghton Mifflin.

NRENAISSANCE Committee. (1994). *Realizing the Information Future: The Internet and Beyond*. Cambridge, MA: MIT Press.

Nunberg, Geoffrey, ed. (1996). *The Future of the Book*. Berkeley: University of California Press.

O'Donnell, James J. (1998). *Avatars of the Word: From Papyrus to Cyberspace*. Cambridge, MA: Harvard University Press.

Peek, Robin P., and Newby, Gregory B., eds. (1996). *Scholarly Publishing: The Electronic Frontier*. Cambridge, MA: MIT Press.

Radway, Janice. (1994). "Beyond Mary Bailey and Old Maid Librarians: Rethinking Reading." *Journal of Education for Library and Information Science* 35:275–296.

Schwartz, Charles A., ed. (1997). *Restructuring the Academic Library in the Wake of Technological Change*. Chicago: Association of College & Research Libraries.

Van Deusen, Gerald C. (1997). *The Virtual Campus: Technology and Reform in Higher Education*. Washington, DC: George Washington University.

Winter, Michael. (1988). *The Culture and Control of Expertise: Toward a Sociological Understanding of Librarianship*. Westport, CT: Greenwood Press.

Wresch, William. (1996). *Disconnected: Haves and Have-Nots in the Information Age*. New Brunswick, NJ: Rutgers University Press.

Young, Arthur P., and Peters, Thomas A. (1996). "Reinventing Alexandria: Managing Change in the Electronic Library." *Journal of Library Administration* 22:21–41.

MICHAEL H. HARRIS

LIBRARIES, HISTORY OF

As places that preserve written evidence, libraries existed as early as the third millennium B.C.E. Those from Mesopotamia featured baked clay tablets with cuneiform writing, and those from Egypt featured papyrus rolls. Great collections from this time are still being uncovered, such as the one at Ebla in modern Syria. They tell mostly of record-keeping agencies. In the centuries just before the birth of Christ, their records also came to be viewed as religious, political, and literary texts, and as this happened, the modern library emerged. It was a place, but it was also a center of the society's thought.

The most impressive library of antiquity was in Egypt at Alexandria, the city named for Aristotle's most famous pupil, Alexander the Great. The *Pinakes* ("tablets") of Callimachus listed its holdings, and probably also the titles that needed to be found and added to the library, since the collection was meant to grow. This work cites texts (not mere factual information but writings that were seen as permanent, and thus stable in meaning so they could be cited, criticized, and revised) and thus it also records a literary "canon" of the important writings of civilization. The destruction of the Alexandrian library is one of the great tragedies of human history, and the suggested assailants have included Marc Antony, the early Christians, and the early Muslims. It is likely that what precisely happened to that library will never be known because there is no existing evidence. This is ironic considering that evidence is exactly what libraries seek to preserve.

Libraries were sustained through the Middle Ages as writings were preserved by monastic copyists. The original Benedictine scriptorum at Monte Cassino in southern Italy was recreated in Ireland, and eventually throughout much of Europe. A heritage of antiquity thus survived alongside biblical and early Christian writings, as humanist poets and scholars sought out the evidence of a lost antiquity preserved in surviving manuscripts. If the loss of the Alexandrian library symbolically represents the decline of classical civilization, Boccaccio's visit to Monte Cassino symbolically represents the Renaissance of modern Western history.

Rediscovery of the past inspired the passions of many book collectors, including the Medicis, many the Popes, the Duke of Urbino, King Mathias Corvinus of Hungary, and Humphrey, Duke of Gloucester. Prominent book collectors of more recent times include John Rylands in England and J. Pierpont Morgan, Henry Clay Folger, and Henry L. Huntington in the United States. Less famous, but just as important, were the countless book owners who, as readers, collectors, and patrons, maintained personal libraries. The instinct to build and use collections thus reflects and fosters the personal and social responsibilities of inquiring minds.

Johannes Gutenberg's printing press (ca. 1450) obviously fostered the growth of libraries. The Renaissance may have cherished its books, but it was the later age of reason, enriched by the blessings of the printing press, that cherished its libraries. Francis Bacon's vision of the advancement of learning proposed three mental faculties: reason (naturally the foremost), memory, and imagination—a conception that still underlines most modern library classification schemes. The faculty of reason, celebrated by RenÈ Descartes, also inspired the first great treatise on library method, Gabriel Naudé's *Advis pour dresser une bibliothèque* (1623).

Of the institutional libraries that still survive, few date from before 1600. Among the oldest is the Bodleian Library in Oxford, which was opened in 1602. The library was founded when Sir Thomas Bodley, on learning that Duke Humphrey's private collection had been ignored, boldly vowed to provide funds, along with rules and purposes. As other institutional collections emerged, libraries slowly became a public good. Tall single-room libraries emerged during the seventeenth century and were lavishly decorated in the eighteenth century. However, their aim slowly changed, from places of beauty and personal enrichment to ones that also addressed a social mission. In 1650, John Dury's *The Reformed Librarie Keeper* introduced the idea of a "publick stock of Learning." A half-century later, Jonathan Swift, in his satire "Battle of the Books" staged a mock battle between the Ancient Books and the Modern Books in the Library of St. James in London. Swift's satirical conflict, which presented scholarly skirmishes over several decades, had profound implications for the search for the best evidence. In simple terms, humanists were seen as readers who used libraries for both primary and secondary sources, while scientists used empirical laboratory work for their primary

This 1813 print depicts the interior of the Bodleian Library in Oxford, England. (Historical Picture Archive/Corbis)

sources and libraries mostly for secondary sources. The "Battle of the Books" also foreshadowed the decline of the aristocracies, both intellectual and political. Libraries were an homage to tradition, but in the new modern political states that arose out of the democratic revolutions, libraries also reflected the rights and responsibilities of the newly enfranchised citizens. National literatures were canonized through source materials acquired by and maintained in libraries, and national bibliographies were established to record the output of the national press. In democratic societies, libraries were a civic necessity.

Public libraries date from the late sixteenth century, but only in the nineteenth century were they first widely supported by tax funds. The models were the many "social" libraries, joint-stock or subscription institutions that allowed members loan privileges or access to noncirculating ("reference") collections. In his *Autobiography* (1784), Benjamin Franklin discussed the tribulations and successes of his small reading group that attempted to formalize its activity under the name of the "Junto." Other

social libraries were designated to reflect special readerships (e.g., mercantile, apprentices, mechanics), conditions of access (e.g., free, subscription, joint-stock), or ideals (e.g., lyceum, Athenaeum).

Tax support for school libraries began in 1835 in the state of New York; municipal support for public libraries soon followed and led to the landmark founding of the Boston Public Library in the 1850s. In England, the work of Edward Edwards had promoted the Library Act of 1850. Tax-supported public libraries soon began to multiply in the industrial Midlands of England and in the New England region of the United States. Emerging urban centers were prime locations for the new public libraries.

Public libraries thus came to reflect the same democratic instincts that led to a free press. They would serve enlightened citizens who would produce even more enlightened citizens. As printing technology improved during the industrial revolution, more reading matter was available. Thus emerged the classic ideology of libraries: a commitment to public literacy, intellectual freedom, and the dialectic processes that define and enhance the common good of the societies that support the libraries and which they served. It was assumed during the early days that libraries in a liberal society must provide freedom of access to the totality of civilization, in reliable forms. The classic adage about "the right book for the right reader at the right time" incorporates the vision of personal betterment that commits librarians to public service and to the never-ending battle against censorship. Out of the ambiguities arose other bold adage: "Librarians have opinions, libraries do not." Values, contexts, and commitments, such as result from the interaction between the text and the mind of the reader, remain the primary objective of libraries.

The public library movement in the United States faltered before the Civil War but quickly resumed afterward and encouraged the founding of the American Library Association in 1876. National practices for cataloging and classification were high on the agenda of the new profession. Public libraries comfortably shared their concerns with other libraries. Academic libraries, then still mostly symbols of learning and repositories for alumni bequests, slowly grew in support of the new German-style seminars that would in time lead to the modern research university. Scientific libraries soon found their focus in their own organization, the Special Libraries Association (founded in 1901). The public library, however, has remained an ideal, benefiting from the vast patronage of Andrew Carnegie in the early years of the twentieth century. During the years of the Great Depression in the 1930s, Carnegie's support of public libraries offered hope and enlightenment to a discouraged populace. In the 1950s, federal support for libraries of all kinds began to grow.

Originally, the title of "librarian" had been given out to caretakers of no or dubious distinction. Librarianship began developing into a recognized profession when formal educational programs became available and were required for employment. One of the earliest such programs was founded in 1884 by the brilliant, outrageous, and legendary Melvil Dewey in New York. Dewey's quirky egalitarianism, mixed with the widespread vision of library service, led to the strongly feminine character of libraries that emerged around 1900.

Sanctioned by the values of their mission, libraries continued to grow. Much as manufacturing and sales were separated in the flourishing American corporation, however, so in libraries was work with readers (public service) separated from processing activities (technical service). Concerns for efficiency often confronted concerns for the professional agenda and standards, so when computers and telecommunications systems arrived, libraries were understandably quick to take full advantage of them. Early work in systems design may have been frustrated by the vast holdings and intellectual complexity of libraries, which were always expanding, and by the unpredictable needs of readers, which were always being redefined. Viewed as engines of a sort, however, librarians are clearly exhilarated by the prospects of improving their mechanisms for making their resources available to readers.

See also: CARNEGIE, ANDREW; CATALOGING AND KNOWLEDGE ORGANIZATION; DEWEY, MELVIL; FRANKLIN, BENJAMIN; GUTENBERG, JOHANNES; LIBRARIANS; LIBRARIES, DIGITAL; LIBRARIES, FUNCTIONS AND TYPES OF; LIBRARIES, NATIONAL; LIBRARY ASSOCIATIONS AND CONSORTIA; LIBRARY AUTOMATION; PRINTING, HISTORY AND METHODS OF.

Bibliography

Harris, Michael H. (1995). *A History of Libraries in the Western World*, 4th edition. Metuchen, NJ: Scarecrow.
Hobson, Anthony R. A. (1970). *Great Libraries*. New York: Putnam.
Jackson, Sidney. (1974). *Libraries and Librarianship in the West*. New York: McGraw-Hill.
Krummel, D. W. (1999). *Fiat lux, fiat latebra: A Celebration of Historical Library Functions*. Champaign: University of Illinois, Graduate School of Library and Information Science, Occasional Papers 209.
Lerner, Fred. (1998). *The Story of Libraries*. New York: Continuum.

D. W. KRUMMEL

LIBRARIES, NATIONAL

National libraries collect, preserve, and organize materials that document the intellectual capital of their respective countries. Because the political histories, intellectual and cultural traditions, and attitudes toward libraries vary considerably from country to country, there is much variety among such institutions and only the most general of definitions applies to them all. According to the International Federation of Library Associations and Institutions (IFLA), there are almost 175 institutions serving the functions of national libraries, including those not officially so designated.

Functions of National Libraries

In the context of the history of library and information science, national libraries are a relatively recent phenomenon. There have been collections of books and archives associated with nations for thousands of years, and large-scale libraries in the modern sense have been associated with imperial or other royal courts since the sixteenth century. It is generally agreed that the first national library took form when, in 1795, the French National Convention decreed that the royal collections would become national property and form the basis of a depository of all printed publications in France. During the nineteenth century, more than twenty such national collections were formed worldwide, with that of the British Museum Library serving as the most prominent model. Under Anthony Panizzi, that library aimed to become the most comprehensive collection of English literature in the world and the most comprehensive collection of international literatures outside of their respective countries.

From the earliest years to the present, national libraries have served as research institutions rather than lending institutions, and their users have traditionally been advanced researchers rather than the general public. As the nineteenth century progressed, national libraries because resource centers for the deposit of periodicals, official government publications, works published in the respective countries, works published abroad by nationals of the respective countries, and works about the respective countries regardless of where they were published. A major function of national libraries toward the end of the century and the beginning of the twentieth century became that of bibliographic control and bibliographic cooperation, which necessitated the establishment of standards of bibliographic records. Perhaps more easily visible in national libraries than anywhere was the gradual shift in the nineteenth and early twentieth centuries from collecting literature to establishing comprehensive records of literature in the sci-

ences, technology, and business. Because of the growing importance of such literatures to wide audiences, national libraries served as coordinating institutions for resource sharing and the cooperative use of bibliographic records.

National libraries have been criticized at various times as being stagnant, unwieldy general collections and excessively specialized collections serving relatively elite populations. Proponents of such collections have argued that the institutions have large and complex roles. Their attempt to preserve their respective cultural traditions, to be exhaustive in several collecting areas, and to be comprehensive in as many others areas as possible constitutes the very nature of modern national libraries.

The various purposes of modern national libraries include the following (with considerable variation from country to country):

1. collect (acquire, organize, preserve, and provide access to) national literature on all subjects exhaustively,

2. collect literature on all subjects comprehensively, regardless of national origin,

3. coordinate bibliographic activities of a country,

4. provide bibliographic access to the nation's literature in the form of a national bibliography,

5. coordinate national bibliographic services, including resource sharing and the sharing of bibliographic data,

6. provide technical and training expertise for libraries and other information agencies nationwide,

7. lead in international bibliographic cooperation efforts,

8. educate the general public about a nation's historical, literary, and scientific traditions,

9. coordinate national policies of intellectual property, especially copyright,

10. establish a system of legal deposit of published material,

11. provide research assistance to government entities, and

12. provide access by means of in-house consultation or lending to researchers as well as the general public.

Being icons of information policy for their respective countries, national libraries are perhaps the most visible manifestations of information dis-

The facilities that accommodate national libraries vary greatly; the Austrian National Library, for example, is housed in the Hofburg Palace in Vienna. (Bob Krist/Corbis)

tribution that can be observed by the outside world. While national information policies are not promulgated in such institutions, but rather in the countries' legislative bodies, the libraries do play symbolic roles beyond the practical ones of organizing and providing access to information. They demonstrate that the country in question is cognizant of the need to preserve a past, to document the country's intellectual capital, and to provide its citizens with access to information. Some national libraries do indeed house specialized departments that are enabled by legislation to protect intellectual property; the Library of Congress is one prominent example of this. Such departments can be charged with the task of writing the specific details required by broad legislation, and they can play central parts in the development of laws that together constitute a country's information policy.

Library Growth and the Related Problems

Because of the comprehensive nature of many national libraries, they have faced growth problems on a larger scale than have any other library types. The growth of institutions such as the French National library, the British Museum Library, and the Library of Congress was due to the rapid expansion of scientific and other research literature after the eighteenth century and because of the effects of changing printing technologies in the nineteenth and twentieth centuries. By the end of the nineteenth century, most of the countries of Europe, North America, and South America had established national libraries, and the major countries of Asia and Africa were to follow in the twentieth century. There are fewer than two hundred national libraries, but it is remarkable that most of them were established in the last 150 years and that they grew so rapidly that they assumed the roles of major cultural institutions throughout the world.

There is no question that printed resources grew at faster than expected rates in the nineteenth and early twentieth centuries. The largest and most comprehensive national libraries have also been leaders in the acquisition and storage of materials in other formats, most notably including microforms from the 1930s onward and digital information from the 1950s onward (but especially since the mid-1980s). The major national libraries of European countries, including especially those of Austria, Romania, Hungary, France, and Great Britain, established centers of documentary reproduction to preserve microformats of materials that faced threats of war and natural disaster. The National Archives of the United States was one of the world's leaders in microphotography for the purpose of preserving the intellectual content of records. The Library of Congress and other major national institutions have alternately struggled to keep up with advances in such information technologies and provided leadership to their respective countries in areas such as documentation (especially large-scale microform projects) and electronic information storage and retrieval. These institutions have become leading storehouses of data in all formats, and they have provided leadership to other libraries for their own microform and electronic preservation efforts and as consultants for digitization programs.

Because national boundaries are impermanent, national libraries attempt to adjust to boundary shifts when they occur. With such circumstances as the reunification of Germany and the breakup of the Soviet Union, Yugoslavia, and Czechoslovakia, issues beyond those of general collecting strengths and chronology come into sharper focus. Countries with very definite cultural identities desire that their characteristics be reflected in the living cultural monuments called national libraries; however, changes in such large-scale institutions take much time and can be complicated by competing ideologies. The Slovak National Library in Matica slovensk has very old roots in the nationalist movement in the area and is now the major library of the Slovak Republic, as well as its bibliographic center. The National Library of the Czech Republic in Prague has a centuries-old history that closely reflects the history of the Czech people. An economic factor provides yet another disincentive for the formation of comprehensive national collections. New countries, especially those created by wars, are in no financial position to create large retrospective collections, especially when they have many higher priorities. In some cases, as with the National and

University Library Ljubljana, the library reassumed the function of a national library (when Slovenia became an independent country in 1991) to complement its role as the leading academic library. This particular institution has added and dropped functions to coincide with the political changes that occur in Slovenia.

U.S. Institutions

Because national libraries vary considerably in purpose, it is difficult to find one that can represent them all. However, the Library of Congress illustrates many of the collections and services that are found in the national libraries of other countries. Complemented by prominent specialized national institutions, including the National Archives, the National Library of Medicine, and the National Agricultural Library, the Library of Congress is the de facto national library of the United States. It is the largest library in the world and preserves 115 million items on all subjects, in all existing formats, and in several hundred languages. It has offices throughout the world to acquire, process, and organize materials, and it has more than fifteen thousand formal agreements with other libraries and foreign governments to address material purchases, gifts, deposits, and other issues. Its primary stated purpose is to serve the legislature of the United States, but for more than 150 years, it has also served the international research community and the general public.

The Library of Congress maintains some of the world's most prominent materials within some of the most comprehensive subject collections anywhere. These subjects include maps, artwork, music, literature, and scientific materials. While the Library of Congress occupies several large historic buildings, it has evolved to become more than just a physical collection of materials; it provides nationwide services for researchers, publishers, teachers, the blind, and the physically handicapped. It works with other federal libraries and information centers and provides technical consulting. The Library of Congress is well known for its digitization projects, which provide access to library materials of high interest on a variety of topics to readers worldwide via its extensive Internet website. The Library of Congress is home to the Copyright Office of the United States, and like other national libraries, it is the most important national resource center for issues of intellectual property. It has developed an informational and educational presence on the Internet that has been emulated by other national libraries. This relatively recent development has changed the direction of public awareness of the institution and has provided a new means of access to its collections and services for the library world and the general public. The Library of Congress website is a source for information about the library's holdings, its programs, its services, and its history. The website has also become an educational resource for American history and culture because of the American Memory project. A related website, "Thomas" is a comprehensive portal to information about federal legislation. Both sites are sufficiently sophisticated for use by advanced researchers, yet they are appropriate for school-age researchers who are seeking authoritative information. The Library of Congress is not typical of the world's national libraries, but it does exemplify their major functions.

Conclusion

As conservative institutions that are concerned primarily with preserving their nations' intellectual culture, national libraries have reacted to technological developments in the printing and publishing world. As leaders in the library community, they have led the field in programs for preservation of library materials and the adoption of information technologies.

See also: ARCHIVES, PUBLIC RECORDS, AND RECORDS MANAGEMENT; BIBLIOGRAPHY; LIBRARIES, DIGITAL; LIBRARIES, FUNCTIONS AND TYPES OF; LIBRARIES, HISTORY OF; LIBRARY AUTOMATION; MUSEUMS.

Bibliography

Chandler, George. (1982). *International and National Library and Information Services: A Review of Some Recent Developments*. New York: Pergamon.

International Federation of Library Associations and Institutions. (2001). "National Libraries of the World: An Address List." <http://www.ifla.org/VI/2/p2/natlibs.htm>.

Library of Congress. (2001). "The Library of Congress." <http://lcweb.loc.gov>.

Library of Congress. (2001). "Thomas: Legislative Information on the Internet." <http://thomas.loc.gov>.

Line, Maurice. (1988). "National Libraries in a Time of Change." *IFLA Journal* 14(1):20–28.

Line, Maurice. (1990). "Do We Need National Libraries, and If So What Sort?" *Alexandria* 2(2):27–38.

THOMAS D. WALKER

LIBRARIES, REFERENCE SERVICES OF

See: Reference Services and Information Access

LIBRARY ASSOCIATIONS AND CONSORTIA

Library associations and library consortia in the field of library and information science are two related, but very different, membership organizations. It may be possible for an association to be a member of a consortium, but that is not common. It is much more likely that a consortium may become a member of one or more professional library associations. The distinction between associations and consortia is often found in their missions and membership criteria.

Associations usually have much broader missions, such as the promotion of the welfare of librarians and the institutions in which they work. Associations usually accept membership from individuals as well as organizations, with individual membership making up the bulk of their membership support. Consortia, on the other hand, often have narrower missions, usually very specific in scope, such as the sharing of books, journals, and other materials (resource sharing). Consortia nearly always restrict membership and participation to institutions and organizations. Given the interrelationship of library associations and consortia, and the potential for confusion between the two, it is worth spending some time looking at detailed definitions.

Definition and Typology of Associations

A common dictionary definition of an association is "an organization of persons having a common interest." Most dictionaries link the term "association" to the term "society," which is sometimes defined as "an organized group working together or periodically meeting because of common interests, beliefs, or profession." For library associations, the definition of a society fits well. Most library associations can be characterized as organized groups (often under charters approved by state or national governments) consisting of individuals and institutions that share interests in libraries and librarianship. Usually, library associations are concerned with principles and standards for services and sometimes for certification of professional personnel or accreditation of programs that provide education for library professionals. They are also concerned with support of professional principles and ethics that are related to access to information and intellectual freedom, especially in countries where there is a tradition of open access to information. In some cases, the organization may function more as an extension of government policy, especially in the countries that are formally associated with the former Soviet Union. However, as time goes on, library associations even in those countries are focusing more on professional principles and less on being an extension of government agencies.

In the United States, there are national library associations that represent the interests of medical, law, music, and art libraries, to name a few. There are also local, state, or regional chapters of these national associations. These chapters meet separately from the national association meetings, and they have as their mission the provision of services and communications at the local or regional level. Thus, the law, special, and medical library associations, for example, may have regional or state chapters that serve the state of Illinois or the city of Chicago or the Midwest region. In the United States, states have their own state library associations that represent libraries of all types. In some states, there are separate associations for elementary and secondary school librarians, often indicated by having "school library media specialist" or similar terminology in the name of such associations to contrast their mission and membership from the more general state library associations that include academic, public, and special librarians within their membership.

Definition and Typology of Consortia

The dictionary definition of a consortium often includes references to an association or society, noting that the word comes from Latin for "fellowship or company." However, in library and information science, the term "consortium" refers more specifically to a group of institutions, rather than persons, that join together for the mutual benefit of all the members of the group. Often, there is a formal legal compact among the institutions that agree to join the consortium. Thus, in the professional terminology of librarianship, consortia are usually groups of institutions joined together, while associations are more likely to represent individuals and institutions or just individuals who form a society based on mutual interest. There are exceptions to this generalized definition, of course. One of the most notable is the Association of Research Libraries, a group that has membership open only to institutions (libraries) that meet the specified criteria for membership. Even here, however, the Association of Research Libraries exists to assist the member institutions in communicating and sharing research reports and so on, as opposed to the generally more specific compacts of consortia, which focus on sharing resources, joint acquisitions, or coordinated cooperative projects.

Consortia follow categories similar to those of associations. There are international and national consortia, as well as regional, state, and local consortia. The term "network" is often used as a synonym for "consortium." Some people have noted that academic, special, and research libraries seem to favor the more Latin-based word "consortium," while public, school, and library groups that consist of many different types of libraries tend to favor the word "network." When the term "consortia" is used, the group often has a more focused or single-purpose mission, such as sharing periodical resources or seeking joint bids on expensive digital databases, while groups of libraries using the term "network" to describe themselves are more likely to have a mission that includes broader, more encompassing, multiple cooperative activities and to include public as well as academic, research, and special libraries.

Library Associations in the United States

The largest and the oldest of the library associations in the United States is the American Library Association (ALA). The ALA includes Divisions, Sections, and Roundtables that cover all types of libraries, including public, academic, research, school, and institutional libraries. Nearly every function and type of material that libraries are involved with are also covered, ranging from information services to technical and computer services and from multimedia to government information sources. The ALA, which was founded in 1876 by

Melvil Dewey (the developer of the Dewey Decimal Classification) and others, has grown to have more than fifty-five thousand members in the United States and nearly two thousand international members. Both individuals and institutions may be members of the ALA. In 1999, there were nearly four thousand organizations and institutions that held memberships in ALA. Many of the units within the ALA hold separate conferences at sequenced intervals to supplement the ALA's annual summer and midwinter meetings.

There are a number of specialized associations that do not focus on the institution of librarianship exclusively. One is the American Society for Information Science (ASIS), which is the national society for those people who are involved in information science. It grew out of the American Documentation Institute, which was established in 1937 to promote interest in scientific and technical information transfer. In 1999, ASIS had more than three thousand personal members and more than two hundred institutional members.

The Association for Library and Information Science Education (ALISE) is an organization directed at educators in graduate schools of library and information science in North America. As such, it might be considered to be an example of a specialized educational association because of its focus on specific issues that are related to the education of librarians and information scientists.

Most states have state associations that represent libraries of all types within the state. While these individual associations are separate from the ALA, they generally maintain a liaison by having representatives within the ALA governing structure.

There are a number of national umbrella associations that encompass diverse interests in subjects and in types of libraries. The Special Libraries Association includes a wide variety of interests in specialized libraries, ranging from libraries that serve science and technology research organizations to those that serve business and commercial organizations.

Library Associations Outside of the United States

Numerous associations exist at the multinational, national, regional, state, and local levels worldwide. While the ALA was the first national library association to be established, library associations were established in other countries in the latter part of the nineteenth century and in the early twentieth century. The Library Association, which is the British association of librarians and is comparable to the ALA, was established a year in 1877. In the period between 1892 and 1922, Japan and most of the major European countries established national library associations with missions that were similar to those of the American and British associations. While Canada did not establish a separate library association until 1946, Canadian librarians were and continue to be active participants in the ALA from its inception.

International Library Associations

The International Federation of Library Associations and Institutions (IFLA) is the umbrella association that provides a venue for librarians to meet and communicate internationally. As its name implies, IFLA is an organization of library associations (international, national, and multinational), but it also accepts membership applications from libraries, library schools, research organizations, and other institutions. There is also a personal membership category for individuals. In 2000, there were 17 international association members, 137 national association members, and more than 1,000 institutional members worldwide. Personal affiliates accounted for 300 memberships. Thus, IFLA serves as both an umbrella organization for national and international library associations throughout the world and a place for institutions and individuals to come together over shared interests in international issues that are related to librarianship.

There are many international associations that are related to special library interests. The International Association of School Librarianship (IASL), the International Association of Law Libraries (IALL), the International Association of Agricultural Information Specialists (IAALD), and the International Association of Technological University Libraries (IATUL) are four such examples. These, and similar groups, are international association members of IFLA.

Library Consortia in the United States

Consortia are usually formed when two or more institutions realize that they can more effectively solve a problem or meet a need by working together with other institutions but still maintaining their own autonomy and most of their independence. While there may be informal cooperative efforts among libraries and related information institutions, they are unlikely to take the name "consortium" without some sort of formal charter or agreement in writing. The formal groups are the focus of this discussion.

Examples of library consortia in the United States range from regional consortia in one state, such as the Triangle Research Libraries Network in North Carolina, to regional consortia covering several states, such as the Committee on Institutional Cooperation (which represents the states of the Big Ten University System) and the Big 12 Plus Libraries Consortium (which covers university libraries in the Midwest and in southwestern states).

The Triangle Research Libraries Network in North Carolina was created in 1933 by the University of North Carolina, Chapel Hill, and Duke University. North Carolina State University and North Carolina Central University have since joined the cooperative program of coordinated collection development and resource sharing. The Chicago Public Library, the Newberry Library, and John Crerar Library also formed a consortium in the 1930s in Chicago to cooperate on acquisitions and purchasing materials.

Many consortia in the 1930s and 1940s were established to develop regional union catalogs of holdings. The Bibliographic Center for Research (established in Denver in 1934) and the Pacific Northwest Bibliographic Center (established in Seattle in 1948) are two such examples. Both have since been integrated into or replaced by the national electronic databases that list the catalog holdings of individual libraries in one database, but resource-sharing consortia still are built on the concepts of these early union catalogs. One such database is the VEL (Virtual Electronic Library), established in the 1990s by the Committee on Institutional Cooperation (CIC), which maintains a library consortium within the "Big Ten" university libraries plus the University of Chicago. The VEL catalog, which can be accessed through the World Wide Web, lists the holdings of all of the university libraries that participate in the consortium and permits borrowing by the faculty and students of those institutions.

International Consortia

Most consortia are regional or national in scope. Some are multinational and include membership in a number of organizations. However, there are comparatively few consortia that are truly international in scope and membership.

For example, the International Coalition of Library Consortia (ICOLC) was formed in 1997 from an informal group known as the Consortium of Consortia (COC). ICOLC had become an international group by 1998, with seventy-nine North American library consortia joining consortia from around the world. The mission of the coalition is to inform participants "about new electronic information resources, pricing practices of electronic providers and vendors, and other issues of importance to directors and governing boards of consortia." A review of the membership of this coalition reveals a wide variety of cooperative organizations that range from state or university agencies to state and national libraries. The most common function of these international consortia involves electronic content licensing. Resource sharing is a close second.

As noted above, the major benefits of a consortia agreement is that resources may be shared through interlibrary loan or digital transmission and that more cost-effective contracts for acquisition of print and digital resources can be negotiated as a result of the bargaining power of a critical mass of libraries joining together in negotiation. This latter advantage seems to be contributing to the interest in consortia worldwide. In addition, consortia often provide both training for the staffs of member organizations and discounts on continuing education opportunities. As the trend of concentrating the business of distribution of information resources into fewer and fewer separate publishers and distributors continues, consortia are developing as a viable option for libraries to counter the increases in costs of information. They provide libraries with a mechanism for negotiating with an ever-increasing concentration of information providers. Therefore, as long as the trend toward consolidation of publishing and distribution sources continues, the formation of consortia by libraries in order to gain better negotiation positions will continue as well.

Nearly all library associations and consortia are actively involved in planning for the future. Some have special committees and projects that have been established specifically to project future trends and events and to determine the appropriate responses for the members of the associations and consortia. Both library associations and library consortia must be oriented toward the future as libraries respond to the changing technological and social environment of the twenty-first century.

See also: DEWEY, MELVIL; LIBRARIANS; LIBRARIES, DIGITAL; LIBRARIES, FUNCTIONS AND TYPES OF; LIBRARIES, HISTORY OF; LIBRARIES, NATIONAL.

Bibliography

International Federation of Library Associations. (2000). *IFLA Directory, 2000–2001*. The Hague: The Netherlands

R. R. Bowker. (2000). *American Library Directory, 2000–2001*. New Providence, NJ: R. R. Bowker.

TERRY L. WEECH

LIBRARY AUTOMATION

Modern libraries are complex systems that consist of many procedures and functions. Traditionally, these functions (subsystems) have included acquisition of materials, cataloging and classification, circulation and interlibrary loan, serials management, and reference services. The most important function, however, has been the provision of service to the users. For centuries, librarians have managed warehouses of documents by acquiring, cataloging, and classifying books, journals, and other materials, and circulating them to their clients. Computer and telecommunication technologies have empowered the new breed of information professionals to select, organize, retrieve, and transfer (SORT) the actual information effectively and efficiently to the users.

In the Beginning

Historically, the most labor-intensive operation of a library has been circulation, the main goal of which is to retain a record for each item that is borrowed from the library. This transaction record usually contains information about the material (e.g., call number, title, and author), as well as information about the borrower (e.g., name, address, telephone numbers). The record also includes two other important items: the borrowing date and the due date. Up until the mid-1970s,

the library staff, or in some cases the user, would enter the circulation transaction information on a special card for each borrowed item and then file the card in a prespecified sequence (e.g., by call number, title, or date due back to the library). When the book was returned, the appropriate circulation card would be pulled from the file, and the book would be returned to the shelves. Maintaining the circulation file, however, was a time-consuming task. Every day, the file would have to be updated, which involved merging and sorting the new transaction cards with the master file, locating overdue books, and identifying items that were requested by other users. In addition, individual overdue notices had to be written and sent, fines had to be calculated, and library users who had outstanding fines had to be identified.

To reduce the cost and increase the efficiency of the subsystem, library managers sought new approaches. While a few libraries used microfilm technology to record transactions and thereby reduce labor expenses, most libraries directed their attention to computers to automate their circulation operations. Using the batch-processing technology of the mid-1960s, the staff would record the transactions on punch cards, which would then be processed overnight, resulting in a printed master list of all the items borrowed from the library. Although the automated circulation systems were primitive by modern standards, they were a cost-effective solution that allowed a library to provide a better service to its clients.

Meanwhile, librarians were embarking upon another venture, which proved to be a pivotal point in the history of library automation. One of the most important functions in a library is cataloging and classifying individual items. Creating such a bibliographic record is time consuming because it requires professional librarians to apply the *Anglo-American Cataloging Rules* to each item. To curtail the costs and raise the productivity of the system, librarians and library technicians have copied the cataloging information for individual documents from the Library of Congress and other institutions. In the early 1960s, a few libraries formed informal networks to exchange their printed book catalogs to decrease the amount of original cataloging that their staffs had to perform. Toward the end of the 1960s, the Library of Congress took a leading role in using computer technology to establish a project for exchanging cataloging information. Under the leadership of Henriette Avram, MARC (Machine-Readable Cataloging) was developed as a protocol for storing bibliographic information in a standard format to facilitate exchange of cataloging records. In the ensuing decade, MARC computer tapes allowed many libraries in the United States and Canada to exchange cataloging information. It also facilitated the production of other products such as catalog cards and microfiche. The Library of Congress experiment was so successful that many other countries embraced the MARC record structure (with minor local variations), and eventually it was adopted by the International Organization for Standardization (ISO).

In the early 1970s, another important development shaped the future of library automation. Lockheed Missiles and Space Company introduced Dialog, an online information service that provided access to a variety of bibliographic databases. Many large academic libraries began to offer specialized services for scientists who required literature searches for their projects. As the demand for online access to information grew, so did the number and the size of databases. Between 1975 and 1999, the number of databases grew from 301 to 11,681, and the number of records in these databases increased from 52 million to 12.86 billion.

Progress

The technological progress occurring in the last half of the 1960s and in the early 1970s led to the introduction of turnkey systems in libraries. Computer hardware and software were combined to provide libraries with an exclusive and dedicated system to automate circulation operations. Turnkey systems usually consisted of a minicomputer, dumb terminals (i.e., stations without a central processing unit), and software to manage check-in and check-out of documents and to issue overdue lists.

By the end of the 1970s, many libraries had automated some of their functions, mainly circulation, cataloging, and, to a lesser extent, reference services. This was also the era of the development of the Ohio College Library Center (OCLC), known as a "bibliographic utility." OCLC was one of the first computer-assisted library cooperatives, in which fifty-four college libraries joined to share their cataloging records. OCLC, which was later renamed the Online Computer Library Center,

Inc., provided online access for more than thirty thousand libraries in sixty-five countries to its vast MARC database and produced millions of catalog cards for libraries around the world. Shared cataloging, though relatively expensive, enabled many large libraries to begin transferring cataloging and classification duties from professional librarians to library technicians.

Libraries also began to convert their old card catalogs into machine-readable records. Many large-scale retrospective conversion (RECON) projects, while costly, were underway or had been completed by the mid-1980s. Academic institutions were in the forefront of RECON projects, creating millions of MARC records based on their holdings in their main and branch libraries.

These first automated library systems required a different type of bibliographic record for each function (e.g., cataloging, circulation, and acquisitions), which resulted in inefficiencies and delays in entering data and in a lack of quality-control standards. Technological advances and market demands required the vendors of library automation systems to develop a new generation of powerful integrated systems. These systems were designed to use a single bibliographic record for all the library functions. A unique MARC record allows every book (or any item) to be tracked from the moment that it is chosen for acquisition by a library to the time that it is available on the shelf for the user. At each subsystem, the MARC record is enhanced and augmented with the additional information that becomes available about the book (e.g., when the order is placed). Libraries, which have completed their RECON projects, can transfer their large bibliographic databases to the new integrated systems and automate all their operations.

Acquisitions and serials management were the last modules to be incorporated into the integrated systems. Procurement of library materials involves complex functions such as online ordering, invoicing, accounting, and claims for unfulfilled orders. When a book is considered for selection, the automated system allows library staff to enter minimal bibliographic information about it. The incomplete record is then augmented with new information to form a MARC format record as soon as the item is acquired and received by the library. Some bibliographic utilities offer libraries time-sharing access to their large databases for acquisition purposes. Among these is the Research Libraries Information Network (RLIN), which supports a number of functions such as preordering, standing orders, and in-process information. Serials management is one of the most complex operations in an online environment. Tracking publication patterns of individual journals, automatic claiming of late arrivals or missing issues, and maintaining binding information are a few examples of the activities performed by the automated serials management subsystem.

Perhaps the greatest effect that automation had in the 1980s (certainly the most visible) was the introduction of online public-access catalogs (OPACs). The new online catalogs quickly gained wide acceptance among the public, who preferred them to traditional card catalogs. The first generation online catalog was simply an extension of the card catalog and had limited capabilities. These OPACs provided users with a few access points (i.e., ways to find library materials), generally the traditional author/title/subject headings, using character-by-character matching to retrieve bibliographic records. Despite the limitations of the early OPACSs, library patrons preferred them to the card catalog, since these online systems provided patrons with information about circulation status (e.g., whether books were checked out or in the library).

Another significant technological development was the introduction of CD-ROM technology. Although the first bibliographic database on CD-ROM only appeared in the mid-1980s, by the end of the decade, hundreds of titles on CD-ROM were available in the marketplace. Libraries were among the first organizations to adopt the new technology, since librarians and information professionals realized the potential of the CD-ROM as a storage medium for vast amounts of information. This technology was used to provide access to a variety of bibliographical records, including MARC cataloging information. Many libraries used CD-ROMs to supplement or even replace the online utilities as a cost-saving measure.

Standards

As library functions became increasingly automated, libraries encountered problems in linking different computer systems, interoperability of systems, and implementing the client/server computer architecture. To alleviate these problems,

ISO developed the Open Systems Interconnection Reference Model (OSI) in the early 1980s. This model consists of protocols for a layered communication system, which simplifies the movement of data between various computers. ISO also developed another set of protocols, referred to as Search and Retrieve Service Definition and Protocol Specification, to facilitate search and retrieval of information.

At the same time in the United States, the American National Standards Institute (ANSI) and the National Information Standards Organization (NISO) proposed the Information Retrieval Protocol for managing bibliographical records. This protocol was later modified and became known as the Z39.50 standards.

Z39.50 uses the client/server model to send messages or protocol data units (PDUs). The Information Retrieval Protocol has eleven "facilities": Initialization, Search, Retrieval, Result-Set-Delete, Browse, Sort, Access Control, Accounting/Resource Control, Explain, Extended Services, and Termination. This elaborate scheme, in conjunction with an abstract database model, has been developed to accommodate the differences among server databases. The client may specify the record structure and data elements to be retrieved, preferred syntax (e.g., different MARC formats), naming of the result set, and subsequent deletion of the set. The server should be able to provide access and resource control for the client. The standard also has provisions for security passwords, charging and billing, scanning terms in lists and indexes within the browsing facility, and sorting.

Several other standards that facilitated the management and communication of the digital information were proposed and drafted by the end of the 1980s. Along with information retrieval standards, new MARC communication standards were introduced (i.e., MARC 21) to include not only traditional bibliographic fields but also information about computer files, music, maps, and multimedia materials. In addition, the Unicode project, which began in 1988, responded to the lack of a consistent international character set and led to a set of standards for encoding multilingual text. Unicode is modeled on ASCII coding but uses a 16-bit schema rather than an 8-bit encoding system.

Standard Generalized Markup Language (SGML), initiated by ANSI in 1978, was designed as a way to separate content from style and as a means of marking up any type of text so it can be effectively handled and managed by any type of computer. SGML identifies and names digital information to be used in a variety of products and services, such as indexing, typesetting, hypertext manipulation, and CD-ROM distribution. SGML, which was approved and ratified in 1986 by ISO as an international standard, formed the basis for other markup languages such as Hypertext Markup Language (HTML) and Extensible Markup Language (XML).

The Internet

Although computer networks were first developed in the 1960s and the first e-mail was sent in the early 1970s, it was not until the late 1980s that computer communication systems were widely used in libraries. File Transfer Protocol (FTP) was used for transfer of large data files, and e-mail service was used for fast and efficient interlibrary loans. Telnet, however, had the greatest effect on information services by allowing users to have remote access to libraries. Researchers no longer had to rely on librarians to find information in distant libraries or even travel to many locations to search library catalogs.

As telecommunication technology progressed at a rapid rate, so did computer hardware and software technologies. The introduction of graphical user interfaces (GUIs), particularly the Windows operating system, had a profound effect on library automation. Vendors promptly converted their character-based systems designed for the older generation mainframe computers to Windows-based GUI systems that used client/server architecture. Librarians began hastily to write request for proposals (RFPs) and seek funding to upgrade their outdated automated systems. The users were the real benefactors of the new systems, since they would no longer need to learn and memorize long commands to search, retrieve, and display the desired bibliographic records.

Throughout the 1990s, the pace of development in libraries matched the changes fueled by the introduction of the World Wide Web. Many library automation vendors adopted the Z39.50 standards and created web-based catalogs. New products included features of the previous generations of online catalogs, such as author/title/subject or keyword searching, Boolean operators, and truncation capabilities, but they also provided users with new ways to search for and display the requested information. The implementation of Z39.50 standards ensured uniformity among web interfaces in incorporating these features.

While web-based systems were being developed, the Library of Congress, OCLC, and other organizations sought new methods for enhancing the contents of millions of cataloging records in their databases. MARC format was augmented by adding a new field in its record structure to reflect the availability of information resources on the web. The Electronic Location and Access field was added to contain the Uniform Resource Locator (URL) of the item, linking the record to any type of digital unit. The unit may be a full-text document, still image, audio and video segment, or a software program.

The instability of URLs, however, poses a serious problem for maintaining large bibliographic databases while assuring high-quality control standards. Through the establishment of new systems, protocols, and standards, such as Persistent Uniform Resource Locator (PURL), Uniform Resource Name (URN), Uniform Resources Identifier (URI), OpenURL, and Digital Object Identifier (DOI), many of these obstacles may be overcome. Another approach to providing access to the varied items on the web is the development of metadata standards, introduced in the mid-1990s as a way to describe the attributes and contents of digital items. Metadata describe the content of a document in a formalized way and have been used in different contexts. The Dublin Core Metadata Element Set, for example, outlines fifteen elements to identify a web-based document. The Resource Description Framework (RDF) is another example of metadata used to describe web resources to accommodate interoperability between various applications.

The Digital Library

The terms "electronic library," "e-library," "virtual library," and "digital library" have been used interchangeably to describe a new phenomenon—the development of digital information warehouses. The digital library, encompassing many concepts, was best defined by Christine Borgman (1999, p. 233) as "(1) a service; (2) an architecture; (3) a set of information resources, databases consisting of text, numbers, graphics, sound, video, etc., and (4) a set of tools and capabilities to locate, retrieve and [use] the information resources available."

In 1993, a consortium of several institutions, including the National Science Foundation and the National Aeronautics and Space Administration, funded the first Digital Library Initiative. The consortium sponsored a few large-scale projects to investigate the technological feasibility of developing digital libraries to contain information sources that can be accessed through the Internet. Digital Library Initiative-2 (DLI-2), which involved ten sponsoring organizations and more than twenty projects, was launched in 1998. The focus of DLI-2 was on the social, behavioral, and economic aspects of digital libraries.

Libraries have automated their subsystems to provide better service to their users. At the same time, advances in computer and telecommunication technologies, new standards for storage and retrieval of documents, and the World Wide Web have dramatically changed the functions performed by librarians. Automating libraries now signifies the transfer of digital information, regardless of the medium, shape, size, or form, from the producer to the consumer. Library automation has been transformed to information automation.

See also: COMMUNITY NETWORKS; DATABASES, ELECTRONIC; INTERNET AND THE WORLD WIDE WEB; LIBRARIANS; LIBRARIES, DIGITAL; LIBRARIES, FUNCTIONS AND TYPES OF; LIBRARIES, HISTORY OF; LIBRARY ASSOCIATIONS AND CONSORTIA; PRESERVATION AND CONSERVATION OF INFORMATION; RETRIEVAL OF INFORMATION.

Bibliography

Barber, David. (2000). "Internet-Accessible Full-Text Electronic Journal & Periodical Collections for Libraries." *Library Technology Reports* 36(5):3–111.

Barry, Jeff. (2000). "Delivering the Personalized Library." <http://www.libraryjournal.com/automated-marketplace/2000/delivering.asp>.

Borgman, Christine L. (1999). "What Are Digital Libraries? Competing Visions." *Information Processing and Management* 35:227–243.

Boss, Richard W. (1997). *The Library Administrator's Automation Handbook.* Medford, NJ: Information Today.

Boss, Richard W. (2000). "Information Technology Standards." *Library Technology Reports* 36(4):3–110.

Breeding, Marshall, ed. (2001). "Library Technology Guides: Key Resources and Content Related to Library Automation." <http://staffweb.library.vanderbilt.edu/breeding/ltg.html>.

Cibbarelli, Pamela, ed. (2000). *Directory of Library Automation Software, Systems, and Services,* 2000–2001 edition. Medford, NJ: Information Today.

Cooper, Michael D. (1996). *Design of Library Automation Systems: File Structures, Data Structures, and Tools.* New York: Wiley.

Crawford, Walt, and Gorman, Michael. (1995). *Future Libraries: Dreams, Madness, and Reality.* Chicago: American Library Association.

Dzurinko, Mary, and Platt, Nina, eds. (2001). "Integrated Library System Reports." <http://www.ilsr.com>.

Evans, Peter, ed. (2001). "Biblio Tech Review: News, Analysis, and Comment." <http://www.biblio-tech.com>.

Healy, Leigh Watson. (1998). *Library Systems: Current Developments and Future Directions.* Washington, DC: Council on Library and Information Resources.

Leiserson, Anna Belle, ed. (2001). "AcqWeb." <http://acqweb.library.vanderbilt.edu>.

Library of Congress. (2001). "Z39.50: Gateway to Library Catalogs." <http://lcweb.loc.gov/z3950/gateway.html>.

Lloyd, Naomi, ed. (2000). "Library Automation Resources." <http://www.escape.ca/~automate/resource.html>.

Meghabghab, Dania Bilal. (1997). *Automating Media Centers and Small Libraries: A Microcomputer-Based Approach.* Englewood, CO: Libraries Unlimited.

Osborne, Andres, ed. (2001). "Library Automation Pages." <http://www.escape.ca/~automate/resource.html>.

Saffady, William. (1999). *Introduction to Automation for Librarians,* 4th edition. Chicago: American Library Association.

Scott, Peter, ed. (2000). "LibDex: The Library Index." <http://www.libdex.com>.

SOLO Librarian's Listserve. (2001). "Survey of Library Automation Systems in Use at Various Libraries." <http://www.alrc.doe.gov/library/autosurv.html>.

Williams, Martha E. (2000). "The State of Databases Today: 2000." In *Gale Directory of Databases,* Vol. 1, ed. Marc Faerber. Detroit: Gale Group.

JAMSHID BEHESHTI

■ LICKLIDER, JOSEPH CARL ROBNETT (1915–1990)

J. C. R. Licklider, born on March 11, 1915, was first and foremost a psychologist. He received his B.A. and M.A. degrees from Washington University in 1937 and 1938, respectively, and his Ph.D. in psychology from the University of Rochester in 1942. In 1941, he joined the faculty at Harvard University, where he was a researcher in the Psycho-Acoustics Laboratory until 1946 and then a lecturer at the Psychology Laboratories until 1949. At that point, he joined the faculty at the Massachusetts Institute of Technology (MIT).

At MIT in the 1950s, Licklider was first exposed to computers while working in human factors engineering. He immediately realized their potential for transforming society, but he also realized that this transformation could only be achieved by improving the usability of computers. It was during this period that he did some of his most seminal and influential work.

"Man-Computer Symbiosis"

Published in 1960, "Man-Computer Symbiosis" was one of Licklider's most influential and widely read papers. Although more inclusive language is now used, this idea struck Licklider as having great potential for profoundly transforming the way people do their work. Based, by his own admission, on a completely unscientific evaluation of his own technical thinking, Licklider discovered that he spent most of his time on clerical or mechanical tasks that only served as preparation for thinking. Tasks such as searching, calculating, plotting, and determining the logical consequences of hypotheses or assumptions obstructed the flow of thoughts and insights that ideally should be the sole occupation of a scientist. Moreover, Licklider found to his own embarrassment that his selection of a scientific problem was often based on the feasibility of the necessary clerical work rather than his capacity to do the intellectual work involved. This indicated that further progress in science would be impeded without some way to reduce the clerical load inherent in scientific research.

The answer, Licklider knew, was to have computers do the clerical and mechanical tasks, thereby freeing researchers to concentrate on the intellectual aspects of their work and to perform the decisions that required human judgment rather than accurate calculation. However, it was imperative that the use of computers was a seamless part of research rather than a process that halted when software had to be written to handle particular problems. In this sense, computers had to be inter-active, with sophisticated, flexible software that could be used in a large number of situations.

Licklider referred to this complementary division of work between humans and computers as "symbiosis," where the close union and cooperation of two dissimilar organisms benefits both. While in fact humans benefit from this arrangement far more than computers, the analogy nonetheless helps to illustrate Licklider's vision.

Libraries of the Future

Perhaps Licklider's grandest vision was the "Library of the Future," which consisted of large, interconnected, distributed knowledge bases organized and subdivided by fields of knowledge. As conceived, it was far more organized than the World Wide Web that developed in the 1990s and would have offered its users advanced analysis that went far beyond mere text indexing and retrieval.

Although Licklider found the conventional library to have shortcomings, most of which had to do with the physical nature of the printed book and the arrangement of books on library shelves, he still favored the printed page for display. More significant, he favored retaining most "component-level schemata" of current bibliographic practice, including concepts such as titles, authors, abstracts, body text, footnotes, lists of references, catalogs, indexes, and thesauri. These, when combined with the speed of access provided by networked computers and with interactive computing, would have provided some of the components of the online library he envisioned.

While not planned as a centralized, monolithic system, the "Library of the Future" still would have required widespread cooperation to make its various services work in a unified way. Licklider described it as a "procognitive system" that would offer its users access to the actual knowledge contained in the library rather than merely its collection of publications. This proved to be an elusive goal, as it involved somehow extracting and encoding the essence of meaning contained within the literature it encompassed and then allowing the user to have the system execute chains of logical reasoning to test hypotheses. While some expert systems have demonstrated such functionality within limited domains of knowledge, no one as of the year 2000 has succeeded in demonstrating a system that does this in a generalized way.

Other Influential Ideas

In 1962, Licklider joined the Advanced Research Projects Agency (ARPA) of the U.S. Department of Defense. While there, he served as director of information processing techniques and behavioral sciences, and he played a significant role in the development of the ARPANET, which demonstrated the usefulness and reliability of high-speed packet-switched networks over large geographical areas and laid the foundation for the Internet. Licklider is also credited with establishing concepts such as time sharing and resource sharing, making it possible for multiple users to access a single large computer.

In 1968, Licklider, along with Robert W. Taylor, published a paper titled "The Computer as a Communication Device," which outlined how networked computers could improve the quality and effectiveness of long-distance communication and support online interactive communities. They described in detail what is essentially the infrastructure of the Internet, with computers interconnected by "message processors" that pass messages between computers and handle such tasks as packet routing and error detection and correction. They also described a number of networked devices that would act as user liaisons in the demanding online world, addressing such issues as e-mail filtering, network security, and even electronic commerce, years before their time.

From 1968 to 1970, Licklider directed project MAC at MIT, the first university-based, large-scale experimental computer science project, which later became the MIT Laboratory for Computer Science. His work at ARPA also set the precedent for the establishment of the first graduate programs in computer science, located at the University of California at Berkeley, Carnegie Mellon University, MIT, and Stanford. These programs, which remain among the best graduate computer science programs available, have served as role models for other programs that have since been developed.

Licklider retired from the faculty at MIT in 1985, but he remained a professor emeritus until his death on June 26, 1990.

See also: COMPUTER SOFTWARE; COMPUTING; ELECTRONIC COMMERCE; INTERNET AND THE WORLD WIDE WEB; LIBRARY AUTOMATION.

Bibliography

Hafner, Katie, and Lyon, Matthew. (1996). *Where Wizards Stay Up Late: The Origins of the Internet.* New York: Simon & Schuster.

Lee, John A. N., ed. (1992). "MIT Time-Sharing and Interactive Computing." *Annals of the History of Computing* 14:1.

Lee, John A. N., ed. (1995). *International Biographical Dictionary of Computer Pioneers.* Chicago: Fitzroy Dearborn Publishers.

Licklider, J. C. R. (1960). "Man-Computer Symbiosis." *Institute of Radio Engineers Transactions* HFE-9:4–11.

Licklider, J. C. R., and Taylor, Robert W. (1968). "The Computer as a Communication Device." *Science and Technology* 76(April):21–31.

Taylor, Robert W. (1990). *In Memoriam: J. C. R. Licklider, 1915–1990.* Palo Alto, CA: Digital Equipment Corporation.

ERIC JOHNSON

■ LISTENING

See: Interpersonal Communication, Listening and

■ LITERACY

The word "literacy," which was first used in the nineteenth century to mean the opposite of the more easily defined term "illiteracy," has come to be a widely accepted term. In most cases, literacy means the ability to read and write, to understand what is written, and to be able to communicate in the written form. Within this framework, however, there are many aspects to its meaning. Scholars and researchers debate the context and intent of the uses of literacy in many disciplines, ranging from psychology to sociology to linguistics. It is the purpose of this entry to consider the history and development of reading and writing, to consider the need for a literate society, and to examine briefly some programs and activities that have been undertaken in an attempt to provide a reasonable literacy standard for all people.

Early History

Human beings first began to record activities in a recognizable way as early as 10,000 B.C.E. Cave paintings were used in many different parts of the world (especially in France and Spain) to record herds of animals that the artists had seen. These rough drawings were probably meant to indicate that a band of animals had passed that way or to record some other event or activity, although there is no actual account to indicate very specific meanings. It is thought that communication between people increased as the level of social development increased. As a community grew, it was necessary to keep a record of transactions between members—who traded so many animals to someone else or how much grain was produced in one harvest. Some of the earliest forms of recordkeeping involved the use of stones or pebbles, notched sticks, or knotted cords to represent a transaction.

From these early efforts, attempts at writing tried to be more systematic by using small separate pictures to tell connected stories. The hieroglyphics of ancient Egyptians, cuneiform, and scripts from Mayan and Aztec cultures are examples of this type of picture-writing. Most historians agree that there was probably one alphabet from which all others followed, but many details about these developments are still a mystery. This early writing was used to record the sophisticated dialogues of Plato and the logic of Aristotle, for example, but the system of writing was primarily used to record oral speech. There was little use of vowels, and letters, words, and sentences were not separated. Most scholars agree that this form of writing and reading was only marginally related to literacy, which required the development of language with rules of grammar and punctuation to make it intelligible in silent or private reading.

Toward the end of the seventh century, monks in Ireland and England introduced word separation and punctuation into Greek and Latin texts in order to isolate units of meaning. This made it possible for a reader to consider a text silently, an innovation that was exclusive to the British Isles until the tenth century. Writing in the vernacular—Middle English, French, Italian, and German, for example—was still largely used for oral reading. Although the clergy in the early Roman Church conducted schools for clerics and some sons of noblemen, the use of books was limited, and those books were primarily copied by hand. Even in university towns, reading was limited, and much of the learning that occurred was the result of "learned discourse." The scholarly reading of Greek and Latin was limited to only certain segments of the population.

In other parts of the world, the use of language was not associated with writing; the oral tradition was the most common method of instruction. In the early Middle Ages (through the twelfth and thirteenth centuries), monastic orders spread throughout Europe and Great Britain, and the production of manuscript books became the occupation of many monks. Texts were produced by hand with elaborate decoration of everyday things as well as fantastic and imaginary beasts—often depicted with gold leaf and in rare colors. These books were highly valued and were kept chained to cabinets and lecterns in monastic libraries because they were so rare. Even with these manuscripts available, oral reading was still a major source for learning, praying, and governing.

Outside of books of prayers and texts for learning, writing continued to be primarily a matter of importance in the legal field—keeping track of births and deaths, property ownership, deeds, agreements, and the like. In reality, literacy was initially important only to the governing class, the Church, and the legal community. In fact, it was of great concern that reading and writing be limited to these groups for fear that the "lower classes" would use such abilities to assert themselves and destabilize the community as a whole. Although the Church hierarchy was opposed to popular literacy as a possible challenge to authority, some clergy, as early as the twelfth century, favored the use of the vernacular for reading the Bible. Guglielmo Cavallo and Roger Chartier (1999, p. 34) point to the change in reading patterns from monastic, "which assigned to writing a task of preservation and memory that was in great part disassociated with reading," to "the scholastic model of reading, which made the book both the object and the instrument of intellectual labor" as a major revolution in reading.

In the late Middle Ages, with the rise of universities, libraries became a part of the scholarly process. By the end of the thirteenth century, library architecture and furnishings changed dramatically. Reference libraries were opened at Merton College, Oxford, in 1289, and a similar one was established at the Sorbonne in Paris in 1290. The library of the university was seen as a common good and that the books were there for scholarly use by professor and student alike. The restraints that were placed on the use of these books, however, restricted scholars and set the stage for the remarkable change that was brought about by the invention of printing.

The Printing Press and Its Importance

The invention of moveable type in the sixteenth century coincided with the Reformation that was started by Martin Luther and the posting of his theses. Luther and those who followed him stressed the necessity of reading the Bible to find true salvation. With the printing press, the potential for making such material available to a wide audience could be realized. At first, many of the printed works were more related to manuscripts than to books, but as the craftsmen became more familiar with the new invention, the printed book gained a distinct personality. The role of the individual author became more significant, a title page was included, and print characters were more standardized. One of the more important innovations was the distribution of these works through networks that were developed by the printers themselves and later by independent entrepreneurs in publishing houses.

The rise of the middle class and the spread of the use of vernacular language (instead of the Latin of the Church) increased a need for "common people" to read. As the Reformation swept over Europe, translating the Bible into the language of the people became a priority. Even with this proliferation of material, however, oral language was still at the center of most communication. Scholars have debated the degree of literacy that existed in Western Europe throughout the sixteenth and seventeenth century, and the estimates of the number of readers range from the low 1 percent for women to the high 30 percent for some regions of Germany. It was not until the later half of the eighteenth century, however, that what some have called a "reading revolution" occurred. Conservative bookseller Johann Georg Heinzmann expressed a sentiment shared by many of his contemporaries in 1795: "[It] was not the Jacobins who dealt the fatal blow to the *ancien regime* in Germany, it was readers" (Wittmann, 1999, p. 285). Although historians debate the extent to which reading had spread in the latter half of the eighteenth century, there is no doubt that factors such as the growth in book production, proliferation of newspapers, and lower book prices among others encouraged a growth in the general interest in reading.

The Spread of Literacy

By the beginning of the nineteenth century, conditions in Western Europe were conducive to the spread of literacy. Public education was available in both the United States and Europe, although it was not until the middle of the century that most industrialized countries had legislation that provided for the firm establishment of formal schooling. In France, the Guizot Law of 1833 suggested the need for education, but basic education was not mandated until reform laws were passed in the 1880s. The literacy rate in Great Britain in 1850 was approximately 70 percent for men and 55 percent for women, but it was only with the enactment of the Education Act of 1870 that the basis for mandatory education was created in the British Isles. Although the Massachusetts Bay Colony passed a law in 1647 to "establish and maintain schools," attendance was not mandatory. It was not until 1852 that Massachusetts established a compulsory attendance law. Within the following fifty years, many states established universal public education as a standard. Public education in the United States was originally based on three assumptions: that all citizens could be taxed to support education, that parents must provide opportunities for basic education, and that free public education must be secular. In some places, factory schools allowed children and workers to attend classes for part or all of a day. Parents could choose to send their children to a school other than one supported by public monies, but that did not relieve them of their responsibility to provide support for the public schools. This general establishment of a basic, compulsory education system set up the possibility for educating a literate public. There was still a great discrepancy in readers between rural and urban communities, but with the rise of the Industrial Revolution, the shorter workday provided more opportunities for reading.

This shift in literacy led to many changes. One of the first was a withdrawal of both teachers and children from the work force. Learning took place away from the family; it was given over to an established system for both socialization and education. This profound revolutionary development is still prevalent in modern educational systems. Another development was that the availability of and market for reading materials (including newspapers and "cheap" fiction) blossomed. Publishers became established as distributors of the printers'

Andrew Carnegie, shown here in a 1902 political cartoon, was one of the early supporters of creating public libraries to increase the literacy of the general population. (Bettmann/Corbis)

work. Books that had originally been printed in quantities of 1,500 to 2,000 copies in a first run were being issued in editions of 30,000 by 1850. The novel, which was not highly regarded as an art form, came into its own by the middle of the nineteenth century. Publishers began to expand the market for these new favorites by issuing chapters for newspapers and magazines to print in installments. In fact, there are accounts of American readers crowding the docksides to obtain the latest installment of the trials and tribulations of Charles Dickens's Little Nell in *The Old Curiosity Shop*. This is similar to the modern phenomenon of lines of readers waiting to buy the latest book of the Harry Potter series.

Although public education initially catered primarily to young boys, girls were still part of the public education system, and they were a major part of the reading population by the 1890s. Novels were in great demand and magazines flour-

ished. For women, *Godey's Lady's Book* was eagerly awaited for its tips on housekeeping and current fashion. Children read *St. Nicholas Magazine*, which was published between 1873 and 1939 and featured young writers and illustrators such as Louisa May Alcott and Winslow Homer.

In the transition from a largely non-reading population to one in which primary education provided a rather large mass of literate individuals, oral tradition still persisted. Street cries of peddlers hawking wares, song-sellers chanting ballads, and the reading of the Bible to families or workers was still very much a part of the everyday life of an ordinary citizen. In schools, children's recitations of Bible passages, poetry, or other forms of oratory often gathered large groups of adults to listen and applaud. Families shared the serialized adventures (such as those written by Dickens or Jules Verne) in a group as avid listeners—even though each member of the group might well have been able to read on his or her own.

Libraries also were important in the spread of reading in the nineteenth century. With Boston leading the way in 1852, tax-supported public libraries were organized in cities in the northeastern and midwestern parts of the United States. Public libraries were seen by community leaders as educational agencies, supporting and supplementing the newly formed public primary schools (although some public libraries posted "No children or dogs allowed" signs). Libraries were considered a public good, a necessity to support an expanding market and worthy of public support. State laws enabled public libraries to exist, rather than mandating them, and left ambiguities in the concept of just who was to be served. Well into the twentieth century, certain groups of people (e.g., African Americans and young people who were under fourteen or sixteen years of age) were excluded from being able to use some public libraries.

Although the idea that most communities should have a tax-supported public library was widely recognized, it was primarily the largess of Andrew Carnegie that spread the public library from major urban cities to smaller cities and towns across the United States and throughout the world. Carnegie's libraries represented a partnership with government—with Carnegie funding the buildings and the community providing the land and the upkeep of the facilities and collections. In England, public lending libraries were also widely distributed, helped by an 1850 law that allowed local authorities the right to levy support for a public library. As Martyn Lyons (1999, p. 332) points out, libraries in Great Britain and Europe were seen as "instruments of social control, designed to incorporate a sober working class elite into the value system of the ruling classes." Public taste did not necessarily conform to this concept, but the possibilities for self-education and life-long learning were goals that existed early in the public library movement.

Literacy in the Twentieth Century

In the early part of the twentieth century, some educators believed that the problem of literacy was settled, especially with the establishment of compulsory education in many parts of the United States and Western Europe. Many countries that were less developed were also still under colonial rule. As part of that social structure, literacy was considered to be a skill of the occupying powers and therefore available to only a small segment of the population. In the United States, however, it was quickly discovered that some groups of people had decidedly lower or relatively nonexistent literacy levels. African Americans and large groups of immigrants both had problems in literacy and learning. African Americans had consistently been denied access to materials and sometimes even instruction; immigrant groups had problems because of language differences. So although the basic pattern of public education was fairly well set at the beginning of the twentieth century and it was assumed that each child had an equal opportunity to learn to read and write, the actual implementation of public education programs varied greatly. Brave new experiments in learning (exemplified by the teachings of John Dewey, which, for example, held sway for some thirty years) did not touch the learning lives of children in rural and urban poverty. Beset by two world wars and a worldwide economic depression, the first fifty years of the twentieth century saw some major increases in literacy rates, with equally dismal rates for other segments of the population.

The actual definition of "literacy" has been the subject of some intense discussion. On an operational level, definitions have ranged from the ability to sign one's name, to pronouncing words, to comprehending paragraphs. In 1994, the Organization for Economic Co-operation and Development (OCED) conducted the International Adult Literacy Survey. The second in a series of related reports (Darcovich et al., 1997) identified three "domains" of literacy, defining literacy along a continuum of skills rather than limiting the definition to a distinction of those who were literate and those who were not. The domains include "prose literacy," "document literacy," and "quantitative literacy." Prose literacy was used to describe the knowledge and skills that are needed to understand and use information from texts such as news stories, brochures, and instruction manuals. Document literacy identified the knowledge and the skills that are necessary to use information in a variety of formats, from job applications to bus schedules, from payroll information to charts, tables, or maps. Quantitative literacy was used to refer to such operations as balancing a checkbook or completing an order form or understanding other types of numerative material that is embedded in text. This categorization of adult literacy skills along a continuum has provided a more realistic way of assessing literacy for both adults and children as learners.

The way in which reading has been taught has also been the subject of heated debates in both the popular press and academia. The early studies of reading instruction concentrated on what was wrong with instruction. Since then, researchers have tried to identify those factors that were predictive of success in reading. David Wray (1997) has offered a clear overview of the many differences of opinion about the teaching of reading. He has identified two streams of thought: one that focused on a code-based approach to reading and another that emphasized the place of meaning. Wray contends that, although some aspects of the argument have shifted from whether teaching should focus on whole language or phonics to whether written language should be acquired naturally or through more formal means, most researchers and practitioners rely on a balanced approach to reading instruction. Research by Shirley Brice Heath (1983), for example, concentrated on the social context of literacy in her widely cited study of three communities in the Carolina Piedmont region. Brian Street (1999) notes that debates about literacy have shifted from teaching methods (i.e., phonics versus whole language) to literacy practice in a social context, which clearly sets an agenda for research, policy, and curriculum. Street further contends that this shift in direction extends "the clarification of the key concepts in the field, the analysis of the underlying assumptions and theories, and development of practical applications" (p. 39).

Preschool children and their families have also been the subjects of interest to those who are concerned about relatively low levels of literacy, especially among poorer families with less education. Some researchers have concentrated on literacy for younger children, not teaching reading but creating a "climate for reading." Terms such as "family literacy" or "emergent literacy" are generally associated with efforts to link early literacy efforts to success in school for poor children, while at the same time offering some sort of adult education program to parents, grandparents, or caregivers of these poor families. Family literacy programs may share a common goal, but the programs vary greatly from country to country, depending on funding, family culture within the country, and the political priority for literacy. While these programs have various goals, many other researchers have suggested that planning is a significant factor in the success of these programs. Short-term goals with very specific outcomes must be matched with long-term planning that takes into account the needs and successes of both child and family. Factors that are of major importance in determining the strength and direction of family literacy programs and plans include (1) a conceptual framework that identifies the cultural and social structures of families and (2) careful consideration of the measures used to assess the program.

Another area of controversy has been ways in which literacy programs for both children and adults are evaluated. Methods of assessing programs have altered as critics argue that traditional assessments are based on outdated and inappropriate models. The debates regarding children of school age have taken place within a larger discussion of the quality of education in the United States. Studies and publications—including *A Nation at Risk*, by the National Commission on Excellence in Education (1983)—have pointed to continuing arguments about literacy and its measures in society. Both the popular press and academia seem to disagree about the meaning and usefulness of some approaches to literacy. While some studies point to the fact that literacy rates have risen steadily since the end of the nineteenth century, others argue that simply reading and writing is not enough. Reading and writing well enough to function in an increasingly complex environment is the challenge.

By the end of the twentieth century, academics, employers, policymakers, and parents had begun to realize that the ability to organize, understand, and use language is essential to a creative, productive life. Many scholars who work with literacy programs, plans, and policy have come to agree that there can be no single, uniform approach to literacy. Rather, programs on a local or regional level are often the result of a national or international attempt to solve the problem. Several agencies are key players in this arena internationally and can serve as examples of how such agencies often directly affect lives on levels beyond that of acquiring skills in reading and writing.

The United Nations has a network of agencies, functioning on a practical level to address global concerns, guided by principals of peace, progress, and the setting of standards. In 1945, the United Nations charged one agency in particular with the responsibility of literacy provision: the United Nations Educational, Scientific, and Cultural Organization (UNESCO). By the end of the 1990s, several other agencies of the United Nations that had mandates for assistance to poorer countries saw education as a target for development. Chief among these agencies are the World Bank, the United Nations Development Program (UNDP), and the United Nations Children's Fund (UNICEF).

From the beginning, UNESCO's task was to persuade governments that universal literacy should be a priority. By identifying literacy as a basic human right, UNESCO set about analyzing needs, demonstrating the best practices, setting up pilot or experimental projects, and fostering cooperation between governments, the academic community, and practitioners. For nearly four decades (from its founding in 1945 through the mid-1980s), for example, UNESCO had a strategy of funding that emphasized basic education in African countries, which was shaped largely by British Colonial Office philosophy from the 1920s and 1930s. However, politics within the United Nations itself often stymied implementation of policies, including those related to literacy. When the Soviet Bloc in the 1960s proposed a World Campaign for Universal Literacy as part of the

Development Decade, the proposal was opposed by the United States. The United States was much more interested in education as a part of economic growth, especially when connected with worker productivity, an approach that led to a rapid expansion of formal schooling in most newly independent nations. By the mid-1970s, however, UNESCO had begun to recognize that universal application of policy was not effective and instead adopted a more flexible and diversified approach to literacy policy, with an emphasis on culture as an organizing principal. UNESCO's policy stressed the social and economic consequences of literacy instead of the political and consciousness-raising implications. At the national government level, UNESCO argued for a balance between formal schooling and out-of-school strategies for literacy acquisition.

The World Bank is an agency that is concerned with lending, and projects are often developed to create systemwide change, along with reforms, training programs, policy advice, or other such arrangements. The World Bank, which is one of the major sources of funding (in the form of loans) for educational programs around the world, accounts for nearly 25 percent of educational assistance. One policy approach is to support universal primary education. The World Bank rejects adult literacy education, however, insisting that there is little evidence to support the link between adult programs and worker productivity, therefore economic growth.

UNDP is the largest provider of grant aid (as opposed to loans). Its programs attempt to foster partnerships between public and private agencies in order to enhance living standards and economic growth. In the literacy field, the UNDP's lack of commitment to adult literacy programs in the mid-1960s kept such efforts at a minimum. In 1990, however, UNDP was a co-convener of the World Conference on Education for All. This conference, held in Jomtien, Thailand, featured considerable rhetoric about the need for literacy programs for adults and young people. In addition, the participants in the conference pledged that the world illiteracy rate would be cut in half by the year 2000. Funding realities suggest, however, that UNDP remains more in line with the World Bank policy of favoring formal education programs rather than the balanced approach of UNESCO.

UNICEF is primarily concerned with the welfare of children, and it has always considered this commitment to include the mothers of these children. At first, UNICEF was careful to avoid conflict with UNESCO and declined any involvement with formal school programs. As UNESCO's influence shifted and waned, UNICEF incorporated both formal education as well as out-of-school programs for mothers and young women, hoping to elevate the level of the care being provided to children. UNICEF accomplishes much of its work through country-based programs for literacy.

In spite of the funding provided by these intergovernmental agencies, the promise made at Jomtien to cut the world illiteracy rate in half by the year 2000 was not realized. Oxfam International, a long-time leader in international development aid, refused to participate in the planning for the year 2000 follow-up to the Jomtien conference because of lack of progress, leadership, and commitment to literacy from the more developed countries. Mohamed Maamouri (2000) has identified several reasons for the failure to meet the goals of the Jomtien conference. He asserts that "basic education" is too often restricted to primary, formal schooling and that, in spite of a major emphasis in funding, the results of work concentrated in that area are not satisfactory. Economic restructuring, wars, falling amounts spent on basic education per capita, and high demographic growth rates have contributed to an increase in illiteracy and the continuation of low literacy rates among out-of-school youths and young adults. Maamouri points to three problems (in addition to monetary concerns) that have created such declines. First, mass literacy programs are often political in nature, making claims that cannot be fulfilled. Second, both teachers and students lose motivation when learning is not associated with positive, identifiable results. Third, he suggests that while adult literacy classes are often taught in local languages, formal primary schooling uses an official language (often that of the former colonial power). This barrier between formal and nonformal educational efforts can sow confusion and create problems for learners.

The number of illiterate people in most developing countries represents more than half of their total populations of youths and adults—with girls and women accounting for nearly two-thirds of the illiterate population. This gender imbalance reflects the growing "feminization of poverty." A number of programs attempt to offer practical solutions to the low literacy rate by suggesting activities that produce income and employment and foster good parenting skills. Other programs suggest a link between adult learning and the education of children and youths, encouraging the use of materials related to nutrition, primary health, and HIV-AIDS education as learning tools.

Conclusion

The problems for those who struggle with the basic skills of reading and writing and meaning are exacerbated by intensive technological expansion. The Internet and the World Wide Web have created even more demands on learners at every level, and the term "computer literacy" now vies with other forms of literacy for programs of education. Those who work with the poorest nations find themselves debating issues about which language or dialect to teach. Libraries, which were a force in the spread of literacy and life-long learning in the nineteenth century, struggle with problems of identity and survival in the twenty-first century. Those who set policy and create priorities find themselves faced with choices much like the clerics of the fifteenth and sixteenth centuries, who were afraid of the results of offering the "lower classes" access to reading the word on their own.

See also: ALPHABETS AND WRITING; CARNEGIE, ANDREW; COMPUTER LITERACY; LIBRARIES, FUNCTIONS AND TYPES OF; LIBRARIES, HISTORY OF; PRINTING, HISTORY AND METHODS OF.

Bibliography

Cavallo, Guglielmo, and Chartier, Roger. (1999). "Introduction." In *A History of Reading in the West*, eds. Guglielmo Cavallo and Roger Chartier. Amherst: University of Massachusetts Press.

Darcovich, Nancy, et al. (1997). *Literacy Skills for the Knowledge Age*. Ottawa: Human Resources Development Canada.

Flesch, Rudolf. (1955). *Why Johnny Can't Read—And What You Can Do About It*. New York: Harper.

Freire, Paulo. (1972). *Pedagogy of the Oppressed*. New York: Herder and Herder.

Gadsden, Vivian. (1998). "Family Cultures and Literacy Learning." In *Literacy for All: Issues in Teaching and Learning, ed.* Jean Osborn and Fran Lehr. New York: Guilford Press.

Heath, Shirley Brice. (1983). *Ways with Words: Language, Life, and Work in Communities and Classrooms*. Cambridge, Eng.: Cambridge University Press.

Jones, Phillip. (1997). "The World Bank and the Literacy Question: Orthodoxy, Heresy, and Ideology." *International Review of Education* 43:367–375.

Lyons, Martyn. (1999). "New Readers in the Nineteenth Century: Women, Children, Workers." In *A History of Reading in the West*, eds. Guglielmo Cavallo and Roger Chartier. Amherst: University of Massachusetts Press.

Maamouri, Mohamed. (2000). "World Literacy: What Went Wrong?" *UNESCO Courier* 3:31–33.

National Commission on Excellence in Education. (1983). *A Nation at Risk: The Imperative for Educational Reform*. Washington, DC: Government Printing Office.

Nickse, Ruth. (1990). "Family and Intergenerational Literacy Program: An Update of 'The Noises of Literacy.'" ERIC Document Reproduction Service. ED327726.

Resnick, Daniel P., and Gordon, Jay L. (1999). "Literacy in Social History." In *Literacy: An International Handbook*, eds. Daniel A. Wagner, Richard L. Venezky, and Brian V. Street. Boulder, CO: Westview Press.

Saenger, Paul. (1997). *The Space Between Words: The Origins of Silent Reading*. Stanford, CA: Stanford University Press.

Shanahan, Timothy, and Neumann, Susan B. (1997). "Literacy Research That Makes a Difference." *Reading Research Quarterly* 32:202–212.

Stedman, Lawrence C., and Kaestle, Carl F. (1987). "Literacy and Reading Performance in the United States, from 1880 to the Present." *Reading Research Quarterly* 22:59–78.

Street, Brian V. (1999). "The Meanings of Literacy." In *Literacy: An International Handbook,* eds. Daniel A. Wagner, Richard L. Venezky, and Brian V. Street. Boulder, CO: Westview Press.

Wittmann, Reinhard. (1999). "Was There a Reading Revolution at the End on the Eighteenth Century?" In *A History of Reading in the West*, eds. Guglielmo Cavallo and Roger Chartier. Amherst: University of Massachusetts Press.

Wray, David. (1997). "Reseach into the Teaching of Reading: A 25-Year Debate." In *Educational Dilemmas, Vol. 4: Quality in Education*, eds. Keith Watson, Celia Modgil, and Sohan Modgil. London: Cassell.

MARGARET MARY KIMMEL

■ LITERACY, COMPUTER
See: Computer Literacy

■ LUMIÈRE, AUGUSTE (1862–1954)

■ LUMIÈRE, LOUIS (1864–1948)

The Lumière brothers, Auguste and Louis, were French inventors and artists who were involved in the early development of the film industry. They are usually mentioned together rather than individually because they always worked together. However, some people suggest that it was Louis who possessed the real talent that led to their tremendous successes.

Antoine Lumière, the father of Auguste and Louis, was a successful photographer. He and Louis invented a photographic plate that became a commercial success. The family employed more than three hundred workers in their factory to create these photographic products. With the invention of Thomas Edison's Kinetoscope (which used George Eastman's new flexible film), however, Antoine was concerned that the family's invention was going to become obsolete.

After viewing a Kinetoscope, which displayed the image inside the machine and allowed for only one viewer at a time, Antoine returned home to instruct his sons that they should develop a device that would get the picture outside of the machine. While Edison had worked on such an invention at one point, he had shelved the project to work on other things.

The brothers worked on the invention for several months, but Auguste said that Louis invented the final device during a single night when he was suffering from feverish dreams and a migraine. The Cinématographe, as they called it, served as both camera and projector, and the brothers patented it in February 1895. The machine also featured a significant improvement in the claw device that regulated the movement of the film.

The Lumières began demonstrating their device to private groups, such as the societies for national industry and for photography, as early as March 1895. However, it was on December 28, 1895, that they first presented (in Paris) a motion picture for the general public. One possible reason for the long delay in making their first public presentation could be that they were preparing for the onslaught that would follow. It is certainly true that they had several Cinématographe machines created and photographers and projectionists trained and ready

to go by early 1896. This proved essential since their invention quickly attracted worldwide attention. Film parlors opened in London, Geneva, Vienna, Brussels, Berlin, Bordeaux, Madrid, Belgrade, and New York within six months. Demand was so great in New York that twenty-one operators were not enough to keep pace. The Lumières' army of photographers had soon shot 1,200 short films on a wide range of subjects.

The effect that the Lumières' invention had on history is not insignificant. Barriers related to language and national custom were overcome by this means of communication. The world began to seem smaller as viewers saw films of people from many other nations. It was an intentional decision on the part of the Lumières to let people see sights from around the world as their crews filmed almost every continent and major culture. Fashions and fads began to spread with the films, contributing to a reduction in the cultural uniqueness of different nations. In addition to the Cinématographe, the Lumières worked to develop wide-gauged film, 360-degree projection that encircled the audience, and three-dimensional effects. They also made contributions to the development of color-plate photography.

Beyond their mechanical inventions, the Lumières contributed in new ways to the art of the motion picture. Their first film, *Workers Leaving the Lumière Factory* (1895), featured just what the title suggests, along with a dog, a bicycle, and a horse exiting the building. Capturing real-life events was central to most of the films that were made by the Lumières and their hired crews. These films have since become increasingly valued for their documentation of life at the end of the nineteenth century.

The Cinématographe was much more portable than the Kinetoscope, which allowed the Lumières to make most of their films outside while Edison had to bring acts into his studio to film. This gave much more variety to the Lumière films, which included subjects such as children at different stages of development, family members engaged in various activities (the first "home movies"), working-class people, military regiments from many nations, and fire and police personnel.

Some of the Lumière films are important for reasons other than the reality that they showed. For example, *The Arrival of a Train at the Station* (1895) impressed audiences because the locomotive was

Louis Lumière (left) and Auguste Lumière work together in their laboratory in Lyon, France. (Bettmann/Corbis)

filmed as it moved toward the camera—giving audience members (who were obviously new to the cinema experience) the impression that the train was going to crash through the screen and into the audience. This film, one of the most remembered of the brothers' films, also shows wonderful photographic skill in the lighting and composition of the piece. The Lumières developed ways to display more depth of field and sharpness in their photography than any other early filmmaker. Another film, *Tables Turned on the Gardner* (1895), was the first farcical film, as well as the first film to tell a story. In it, a gardener is watering a flowerbed with a very large hose when a boy comes up behind and steps on the hose, stopping the flow of water. As the gardener looks into the dried-up hose, the boy steps off of the hose, causing water to spray into the gardener's face. While this narrative type of film was more the exception than the rule, it was followed by at least a few other attempts at telling short stories.

The Lumière brothers and their photographers were involved in many important innovations during the early years, including product placement, tracking shots, and trick photography. The most basic form of product placement was when some of their films showed the cinemas where the public could see the films. Other films featured specific products, such as beer produced by a brewer who was a family friend. Tracking shots are those films that are created while the camera is moving. The first use of a moving camera for a Lumière film occurred when one of their photographers in Venice shot footage while riding through the waterways by boat. Upon seeing the film, the brothers asked that more such tracking films be made. Trick photography, close-up shots, and editing were novel devices that the Lumières employed on occasion in their early films, but the techniques never became regular features. As a result, other people (such as Georges Méliès, who is known for his early use of trick photography) are usually credited with their development.

Overall, the mechanical devices that were created by the Lumière brothers turned motion pictures into an entertainment medium for the masses. The brothers also helped to define cinematography by introducing the elements of artistic photography to the composition of their films. Through these technical and artistic accomplishments, the Lumières were able to bring together both people and images from around the world.

See also: EDISON, THOMAS ALVA; FILM INDUSTRY, HISTORY OF; FILM INDUSTRY, TECHNOLOGY OF; MÉLIÈS, GEORGES.

Bibliography

Ceram, C. W. (1965). *Archaeology of the Cinema.* New York: Harcourt, Brace & World.

Ellis, Jack C. (1979). *A History of Film.* Englewood Cliffs, NJ: Prentice-Hall.

Rhode, Eric. (1976). *A History of the Cinema from Its Origins to 1970.* New York: Hill and Wang.

STEPHEN D. PERRY

■ MACHLUP, FRITZ (1902–1983)

Fritz Machlup was born in Vienna, Austria, and began his career there as an entrepreneur and businessman. He did not pursue a scholarly career until after he moved to the United States in 1933. In the United States, Machlup's career encompassed work in many fields, including capital, monetary, and business-cycle theory, along with work on knowledge creation and dissemination.

Career Highlights

During his career, Machlup was a visiting professor at more than fourteen American universities, including Harvard University, Cornell University, the University of California at Berkeley, and Stanford University. He was the Abram G. Hutzler Professor of Political Economy at Johns Hopkins University in Baltimore, Maryland, from 1947 to 1960 and the Walker Professor of Economics and International Finance and Director of the International Finance Section at Princeton University in New Jersey between 1960 and 1971. He was on the faculty of the School of Economics at New York University from 1971 until his death in 1983. In addition, Machlup was a Visiting Professor at Osaka University in Japan (1970), at the University of Melbourne (1970) and at the University of Vienna (1972–1973).

Among his non-academic accomplishments, Machlup was a council member of the Austrian Cardboard Cartel in Vienna, Austria (1929–1931), a Special Consultant to the Post War Labor Problems Division, Bureau of Labor Statistics, U.S. Department of Labor (1942–1943), Chief of the Division of Research and Statistics, Office of Alien Property Custodian, Washington, D.C. (1943–1946), and a consultant to the U.S. Department of Treasury (1965–1977).

Areas of Study

In 1950, Machlup began his groundbreaking work on the role of knowledge and its economic influence and continued to research and publish on the topic for more than thirty years. Through his work, Machlup was instrumental in developing the scholarly subfield of knowledge creation, diffusion, and utilization. In 1980, in the first volume of *Knowledge* (his series on knowledge creation, distribution, and economic significance), Machlup provided a classification of five major types of knowledge: (1) practical knowledge, (2) intellectual knowledge, (3) small talk or pastime knowledge, (4) spiritual knowledge, and (4) unwanted knowledge. Practical knowledge is the knowledge that is instrumental or central to one's work or profession. Intellectual knowledge satisfies one's "intellectual curiosity." Small talk knowledge satisfies one's "nonintellectual curiosity and one's desire for light entertainment and emotional stimulation." Spiritual knowledge is related to one's religious beliefs. Unwanted knowledge is outside of one's interests—"usually accidentally acquired, aimlessly retained" knowledge.

Before he arrived at this scheme, Machlup had reviewed and considered several distinctions—such as basic and applied knowledge, theoretical and historical knowledge, general/abstract and particular/concrete knowledge, nomothetic and ideographic knowledge, analytical and empirical knowledge, enduring and ephemeral knowledge, knowledge for many and for only a few, as well as social and private knowledge. Machlup reserved his most critical discussion for the most widely used classification: mundane knowledge, scientific knowledge, humanistic knowledge, social science knowledge, and artistic knowledge.

It should be remembered that each type of knowledge has a "claim" on how one establishes what is "known" as "true knowledge." Each offers a set of rules or understandings for the inquiry to establish acceptable evidence. Scientific knowledge, in the sense of controlled experiments in the natural sciences, has come to be viewed, by many, to be a unique and superior form of knowledge because it offers a set of rules for inquiry that promises precision and the hope for overcoming systematic bias and human error.

Machlup went beyond some rather traditional distinctions between data, information, and knowledge. Data is meant to be the most rudimentary unit of analysis (i.e., raw material). Information goes beyond data. Information is thought of as refined data, which provides some added value to the user. Knowledge, which goes beyond information and provides added value, must be able to withstand being subjected to some validation or "truth test."

The type of knowledge may well have an effect on how one views utilization and how one thinks about relevant and appropriate outcomes. Not only have some types of knowledge assumed more importance than others in potential users' perceptions, but past studies also often refer to use as if there are no significant differences among various types of knowledge that might be used.

Publications

Over the years, Machlup authored more than twenty-two books, including *The Political Economy of Monopoly* (1952), *An Economic Review of the Patent System* (1958), *The Production and Distribution of Knowledge in the United States* (1962), and *Education and Economic Growth* (1970). His later works on information and knowledge include *Information Through the Printed Word* (1978) and the *Knowledge* series (of which he completed three volumes: *Knowledge and Knowledge Production*, 1980; *The Branches of Learning*, 1982; *The Economics of Information and Human Capital*, 1983).

His numerous contributions to international economic theory include *International Trade and the National Income Multiplier* (1943), *International Payments, Debts, and Gold* (1964), *Remaking the International Monetary System: The Rio Agreement and Beyond* (1968), and *The Alignment of Foreign Exchange Rates* (1972). He was also a major contributor to the literature on the methodology of economic research, which work appeared in two volumes, *Essays on Economic Semantics* (1963) and *Methodology of Economics and other Social Sciences* (1978).

Machlup's papers—"Register of the Fritz Machlup Papers, 1911–1983"—are available through the Hoover Institution on War, Revolution, and Peace Archives at Stanford University. These papers contain correspondence, writings, reports, memoranda, notes, questionnaires, data, financial records, grant proposals, instructional materials, and other printed matter related to economic theory and to information systems and the creation and dissemination of knowledge.

See also: ECONOMICS OF INFORMATION; KNOWLEDGE MANAGEMENT.

Bibliography

Dreyer, Jacob S. (1978). *Breadth and Depth in Economics: Fritz Machlup—The Man and His Ideas*. Lexington, MA: Lexington Books.

Kregel, J. A., ed. (1989). *Recollections of Eminent Economists*. New York: New York University Press.

Ludwig von Mises Institute. (2001). "Fritz Machlup." <http://www.mises.org/aboutmachlup.asp>.

ROBERT F. RICH

■ MAGAZINE INDUSTRY

To understand the scope of the magazine industry, it is necessary to define the term "magazine." And while the translation of the word "magazine" may simply be "a storehouse," technological advances constantly challenge how people define the word in their own minds. In the modern world, online websites and television broadcasts are considered to be magazines, but in the traditional sense, a magazine is printed on paper. At the most basic level, a magazine provides information that may be more in depth but less timely than that of, for example, a newspaper. A magazine can typically focus on trends or issues, and it can provide background information for news events.

Magazines have the luxury of focusing on a smaller target audience, which means they do not have to try to please all of the people all of the time. Instead, they can narrow their audience to a very specific population—such as the sports enthusiasts or amateur gourmet chefs. By focusing on a specific target audience or niche, magazines know what their readers want to see in the magazine, and advertisers know more about the target audience for their advertisements.

Types of Magazines

In general, there are three categories of magazines: consumer, trade, and organization. A consumer magazine is what comes to mind most readily for most people when the term "magazine" is mentioned. Consumer magazines are on newsstands and in grocery store aisles everywhere. They can be bought as single issues or by subscription, and they are marketed like any other product (using advertisements and special promotions). There are actually fewer consumer magazines than any other type, but the consumer magazines generally have the largest audiences. Consumer magazines can be broken down into a large variety of specialized categories, such as men's, women's, entertainment, regional, political, general interest, and so on.

A trade magazine specializes in a particular business, so its content is focused on job-related subjects and its readers have specific occupations. Many of these magazines are provided at no cost to a controlled audience. Because trade magazines are able to deliver a highly desirable audience to advertisers, they are able to charge higher advertising rates.

Organization magazines can be divided into three categories: association and society, public relations, and custom. The association and society magazines are often provided as part of the membership in the organization. The purpose of these magazines is mainly to enhance the organization. They can provide unity and a forum to discuss issues and to draw members closer to one another. Association and society magazines may carry advertisements, and they may be sold through reader subscriptions (which may be incorporated into membership dues). Regardless, the basic purpose of these publications is still to enhance their organization rather than make a profit.

Organizations and companies publish public relations magazines for self-promotion, and they may each have more than one such magazine to do this. For example, an internal publication may target the employees of a company (to keep them abreast of the progress of the company and help them to feel a part of it), while an external publication may target the same company's clients (to explain how the company works and to provide a better understanding of the company's philosophy or mission). Traditionally these magazines do not have advertisements and are provided at no cost to the readers.

The third type of organization magazine is the custom or sponsored magazine. A client may receive a magazine of this type as a result of purchasing a particular product or using a particular service. Typically, custom magazines are provided free of charge, but they may be also be sold on newsstands or through subscriptions. The purpose of a custom magazine is to promote or enhance the use of a company's products. For example, the in-flight magazines that are provided by airlines are designed to keep the passengers occupied and to make the flight more pleasant. It may be obvious who the sponsor is, or a company may team up with a consumer magazine to create a more subtle approach. Advertisements are usually part of these magazines, and advertisements from other companies may be included as well.

Basic Staff Structures

With such a wide variety of magazines, it is almost impossible to estimate the number of magazines that are published each year. The counts completed by various agencies vary so significantly that it becomes difficult even to put together rough numbers. In addition, most counts do not include the organization magazines. So, while it is difficult to estimate the actual numbers of magazines, it is certain that the magazine industry holds a prominent place in the economy. It provides an important outlet for advertisers to reach a very specific target audience, which helps their companies to continue to grow and succeed.

In the United States, many of the consumer magazines are published in New York City, but Illinois, California, and Pennsylvania are also responsible for a large number of titles. It is common for one company to own many magazines. This allows them to shift money around and take chances on launching new titles. The largest magazine producers include Conde Nast, Hearst, Meredith, Hachette Fillipachi, and Time Warner. A small number of consumer magazines make up most of the industry's total revenues, but there are many small magazines and small businesses in the industry, too.

Whether a magazine is published by a small company or by a huge conglomerate, it is still possible to discuss a "typical" structure of a magazine. This is because, regardless of the scale, there are basic principles that lead to the success of a magazine. In most cases, a magazine is divided into two parts, the creative side (i.e., the editorial and art departments) and the business side (i.e., the advertising, circulation, and general management departments). All of these divisions must work very closely to ensure the stability of the magazine and to deliver the publication on schedule.

Often overseeing the entire process is the president or chief executive officer. This person may have an extensive background in the publishing industry, but in the case of large media companies, it is possible that the president may not have any experience in the industry. Typically, this person reports to the board of directors of a company and is held responsible for the profits and losses, direction, and reputation of the magazine. At smaller companies, this person may also be responsible for the development of new products, the management of personnel, and other financial aspects of the magazine. The duties of this position may even be combined with those of the publisher.

The publisher traditionally has an advertising background, although this is not always the case. For example, magazines that depend heavily on circulation as a source for revenue may be more likely to have a publisher who has experience in the circulation department. For the majority of magazines, however, the main source of revenue is advertising. A publisher typically ensures the visibility of the magazine in the marketplace and helps define the audience of the magazine for advertisers.

The publisher and the advertising director often work closely. It is the advertising director's job to convince companies to advertise with the magazine. Often, magazines will advertise to potential advertisers by placing advertisements in trade publications that reach the media buyers or those people who are in charge of advertising for

their companies. Advertising directors may also create printed brochures and media kits about the magazine and send them to the advertising departments of companies. An advertising director may also work with the publisher to ensure that they reach potential readers. For those magazines that rely on subscriptions and sales rather than advertisements, guaranteeing that the publication reaches the potential readers would be the main focus of the advertising director's job. Instead of advertising to companies, the advertisements would be directed at target readers.

The circulation director keeps a close eye on just who is reading the magazine. When a magazine's revenue depends heavily on advertising, it is important to be able to identify the type of audience an advertiser can reach by placing and advertisement in the magazine. Most important, the circulation director maintains the rate base, or the number of readers the magazine is guaranteed to reach. This is the number that the advertising rates for the magazine are based on. When a magazine's revenue is based on sales of the magazine alone, the circulation director provides the crucial measurement of the magazine's performance. This person can help to identify trends, such as what type of magazine covers sell more on the newsstand; for example, a food magazine may or may not sell more magazines when a dessert is featured on the cover. The information provided by the circulation department guides the publisher and advertising director as well as the editor.

The editor is responsible for the content of the magazine, which includes the visual elements as well as the written elements. Thus, this position requires a strong sense of the overall editorial message of the magazine. A good editor is both creative and a good manager. He or she must work closely with the magazine designers and department editors or writers to ensure continuity. The editor focuses on delivering the kind of magazine that the core readers and subscribers want to see. If a magazine fluctuates too much from this core design, readers will be lost, which results in a loss of revenue from advertising and magazine sales

Bringing the advertisements and the editorial content together in one finished, printed piece is the job of a production director. The production director ensures that the magazine is in the proper format for the printer, and he or she then oversees the printing. This can include finding the most feasible paper stock and negotiating prices, as well as monitoring the quality of the printing job. The production director may also be responsible for the distribution of the printed magazine. Otherwise, the circulation department is responsible for the distribution.

Many magazines use outside companies to handle the mailings to subscribers, and the circulation director oversees this process to ensure that it is being correctly executed. For newsstand sales, publishers may work with a distributor to determine the number of magazines that should be sold on the newsstand. The distributor also finds wholesalers who will receive magazine shipments and deliver them to retailers. Distributors keep track of the number of magazines that are sold, and they collect the unsold magazines.

While the specific roles performed by the people who hold the above positions vary according to the size of the magazine staff and the type of magazine that is being produced, the basic structure and functions are all necessary for the efficient production of a magazine. These positions have evolved with the development of the magazine. Education, technology, and distribution are important factors that have shaped the growth of the magazine industry.

Historical Changes in the Industry

When the first magazines were published in the United States in the eighteenth century, the majority of the population could not read. The magazines targeted the elite and were quite expensive. They were packed full of information, often gathered from British magazines, with little or no artistic embellishment. The publications were printed by hand-set type on hand-operated presses, which was time consuming and labor-intensive. Often, the only illustration for a magazine was the cover art. These were usually made from crude woodcuts, although a few magazines used the more expensive copperplate engravings. Later in the eighteenth century, magazines were used for distributing political essays and ideas. Typically, the publisher was also the editor, printer, and main writer. In many cases, the articles were all unsigned.

The distribution of the early magazines was difficult. Either by hand, horse, or carriage, they were delivered to subscribers. Since postmasters decided whether or not magazines could be mailed through the formal postal system, many magazines employed their own carriers. It was not until improved roads and railway systems were in place in the nineteenth century that the distribution of magazines became easier.

In the nineteenth century, the number of magazines increased, as did the rate of literacy. Women became targeted audiences for the first time, and they devoured magazines that discussed leisure activities and homemaking. Magazines began to have paid editors, and writers signed their articles and essays. Content expanded to include literary essays, short stories, and poetry. By the middle of the century, the types of magazines had expanded to include trade, professional, and corporate magazines. The look of the magazine also improved tremendously during the nineteenth century. Copperplate and steel engravings became more feasible, and some magazines even hired watercolorists to hand-tint the engravings. Woodcuts were much less expensive and had improved from the crude eighteenth-century prints. As a result of their increased quality, magazine illustrations began to be used to decorate homes. By the end of the century, printing presses were able to print both sides of a continuous roll of paper, which made the process of creating a magazine more cost efficient.

Magazines, at the beginning of the twentieth century, began to appear in households that did not even contain books. Content became more concise. The essays became shorter to accommodate the increasingly fast-paced society. While photography had been invented in the nineteenth century, it was not until halftone printing was invented in the twentieth century that magazines were able to reproduce photographs easily and inexpensively. Artists and engravers found themselves no longer in demand, and art directors became part of magazine staffs that had previously consisted of only writers and editors. Since the early 1980s, computers have significantly changed the production process for magazines. When *Scientific American* published its January 1995 issue, which highlighted "The Computer in the 21st Century," it became the first magazine to publish without the use of film. While these technological advancements could reduce the time and cost of producing a magazine, the postal costs did not follow suit. In fact, postal rates increased dramatically during the twentieth century, making it difficult for many magazines to survive.

The growing relationship between the magazine industry, other media industries, and the Internet is typified by the February 2001 announcement by the Disney Company chairman, Michael D. Eisner (right), and the chairman and owner of US magazine, Jann S. Wenner, that Disney had acquired a 50 percent interest in US magazine and that the magazine will have several tie-ins to broadcast and Internet activities owned by the Disney Company. (AFP/Corbis)

Technology and Trends

Magazines are everywhere. They are easily accessible and geared toward all facets of the population. Clearly, the magazine industry has gone through many changes that reflect the evolutions in society and in the technology that is used to produce magazines. Technology, such as television was first thought to be a great competitor for the magazine, but many magazines now have television shows as counterparts, and vice versa. In addition, specialized cable channels resemble magazines in many ways, including the fact that both formats attempt to serve specific targeted niches. As with television, the Internet was initially considered to be a major foe for the magazine. However, many magazines have already developed a "new media" staff to produce an online version of the magazine. The people in charge of these magazines realized that the Internet provides a viable way to maintain a close rela-

tionship with readers and offers another forum in which to sell advertising. Also, because there are no real production costs, the Internet is a very practical way for magazines to reach potential new subscribers.

A stronger emphasis on visual design is a continuing trend in the magazine industry. Television and computers have strongly influenced this trend. Journalists need to be able to think in terms of visual communication as well as written communication. Magazine art departments are growing larger in order to encompass online design as well as print design. They understand that a strong, effective design is increasingly crucial if they are to continue attracting readers.

With increased outlets to promote magazines and their advertisers, strong branding of a magazine is becoming increasingly important. Audiences need to recognize instantly a magazine's masthead on various products, television shows, and the Internet, and they need to associate it with quality and integrity. All of this means that editors need to continue working closely with publishers and advertising departments to develop a strong marketing strategy.

See also: MAGAZINE INDUSTRY, CAREERS IN; MAGAZINE INDUSTRY, HISTORY OF; MAGAZINE INDUSTRY, PRODUCTION PROCESS OF; NEWSPAPER INDUSTRY; PRINTING, HISTORY AND METHODS OF.

Bibliography

Cowles Business Media. (1996). *Handbook of Magazine Publishing,* 4th edition. Stamford, CT: Cowles Business Media.

Daly, Charles P.; Henry, Patrick; and Ryder, Ellen. (1997). *The Magazine Publishing Industry.* Boston: Allyn & Bacon.

Johnson, Sammye, and Prijatel, Patricia. (1999). *The Magazine from Cover to Cover.* Lincolnwood, IL: NTC/Contemporary Publishing Group.

Mogel, Leonard. (1998). *The Magazine: Everything You Need to Know to Make It in the Magazine Business,* 4th edition. Pittsburgh: GATF Press.

STACEY BENEDICT

■ MAGAZINE INDUSTRY, CAREERS IN

A variety of careers are available in the magazine industry, from the obvious jobs in editorial and advertising to work in supporting areas such as circulation and marketing. The majority of consumer magazines are published in New York City; however, many career opportunities exist elsewhere, particularly at magazines published for city, state, or regional audiences and at magazines that serve trades and associations.

While staff positions vary from one magazine to the next, most have the same basic staff roles. Editorial functions are carried out by people who work with words and images to create the editorial product. The editor or editor-in-chief is the top editorial position at a magazine and is responsible for directing all content and implementing the mission of the magazine. The editor's right-hand person, the managing editor, is responsible for following the day-to-day operations of a magazine, and the duties of that position include enforcing deadlines, overseeing the quality of the work, managing the editorial staff, and serving as the liaison between writers, artists, and production personnel. The production manager, along with production assistants, work closely with the managing editor to track the progress of each issue, helping the staff meet printing deadlines and making sure that each page is formatted correctly for the printer.

Some magazines also have an executive editor who may fulfill some of the managing editor's duties but who is usually more focused on content issues than on production. The editor and executive editor work with a staff of senior editors and/or section editors as they oversee particular areas of a magazine by planning content, assigning articles, and writing stories. Associate and assistant editors may have similar duties with smaller magazine departments or may assist the senior editor on a magazine's larger sections. Staff writers handle specific story assignments without managerial and planning functions. Entry-level positions in the writing area of the editorial department usually fall under the title of editorial assistant. The duties for a person in this position can be wide ranging and often include basic administrative functions, but they may, in some cases, include short writing assignments.

Once articles are written, copy editors read them to correct errors in fact, grammar, spelling, and punctuation; to eliminate problems in organization, clarity, and style; and to ensure that the piece reflects the content and tone of the mission of a magazine. The copyediting staff, often referred to by the traditional newspaper term "the copy desk," is managed by the copy chief. Entry-level positions on the copyediting staff include proofreaders and fact checkers.

The visual side of the editorial department is supervised by the art director, who works closely with the editors to carry out the unique look of a magazine. The art director makes all assignments to photographers, photo stylists, and illustrators and manages the designers who lay out editorial pages. The more experienced staffers in the art department may carry titles such as senior designer; while the entry-level positions may include staff artist, junior designer, or art assistant.

Many careers are available on the business side of magazines. The top position is generally the publisher, who has usually worked up through the ranks of advertising sales. An advertising sales director manages a team of advertising sales representatives who are responsible for selling space in the magazine to advertisers. These "ad reps" or "sales reps" not only maintain long-standing relationships with current advertisers but must generate business by securing new accounts. Entry-level positions that assist the advertising sales team include advertising sales coordinators, advertising production assistants, and sales assistants.

The advertising sales staff is also supported by people who provide expertise in both business and creativity. The marketing director designs a sales strategy to attract advertisers. The research director gathers information about a magazine's readership to help advertisers better understand and appreciate the audience they will be reaching. The public relations director works to promote a magazine's image among its various constituents—readers, advertisers, and others in the magazine industry. The promotion director prepares sales materials such as board presentations, brochures, and videos that sales representatives use to help sell advertising. The merchandising director develops and implements "value-added" programs to enhance the marketing programs of advertisers. All of these sales support directors employ assistants to help carry out their jobs; the promotion and merchandising directors also manage artists and copywriters to prepare materials related to their work.

Other careers at magazines can be found in the circulation, distribution, technical support, and finance and accounting departments. A new position that is rapidly being included on many staffs is an online editor who oversees the content and design of the website of a magazine.

Many people who supply creative talent for magazines do so as self-employed freelancers, working from their home or private studios. These writers, photographers, photo stylists, artists, and designers may work predominantly for one magazine, which may earn them the title of "contributor" on the masthead, or they may work for a variety of magazines, sometimes specializing in one content area such as food or travel.

People seeking positions in writing and editing for magazines must possess a firm command of the language, which can be developed through college programs in the liberal arts, journalism, and other communication fields. Many section editors and staff writers have education and/or

experience working in a secondary area that is related to the editorial content of a magazine (e.g., in politics, fashion, or horticulture). Potential magazine artists should have experience not only in graphic design but in the latest design software and in the prepress and printing processes. College students who are planning on having writing or art careers at magazines are encouraged to seek experience in the media industry, preferably at publications; internships offer valuable training and often provide opportunities for permanent employment after graduation.

Those individuals who plan to pursue a career on the sales side of magazines must be able to persuade effectively. A college degree in business, marketing, advertising, or another communication field is helpful, but many advertising sales representatives begin in an entry-level position and gain the experience they need as they work their way up the ladder. People who are interested in sales and promotion must be able to persevere, accept rejection, and thrive on competition. Strong negotiation and presentation skills are helpful. College students are wise to seek experience in business situations that will help them learn about advertising sales, such as preparing research and presentations and otherwise assisting sales representatives.

Anyone pursuing a career at a magazine, regardless of the position, should be dependable, efficient, and organized in order to meet deadlines. Computer literacy is also a must, as is the ability to communicate effectively, both through writing and speaking. Creativity, the ability to juggle multiple tasks, and a passion for magazines will help ensure a fulfilling career.

See also: EDITORS; MAGAZINE INDUSTRY; MAGAZINE INDUSTRY, HISTORY OF; MAGAZINE INDUSTRY, PRODUCTION PROCESS OF; PUBLIC RELATIONS, CAREERS IN; WRITERS.

Bibliography

Daly, Charles P.; Henry, Patrick; and Ryder, Ellen. (1997). *The Magazine Publishing Industry*. Boston: Allyn & Bacon.

Goldberg, Jan. (1999). *Careers in Journalism*, 2nd edition. Lincolnwood, IL: VGM Career Horizons.

Johnson, Sammye, and Prijatel, Patricia. (2000). *Magazine Publishing*. Lincolnwood, IL: NTC/Contemporary Publishing Group.

Magazine Publishers of America and American Society of Magazine Editors. (1995). *Guide to Careers in*

Magazine Publishing. New York: Magazine Publishers of America and American Society of Magazine Editors.

Mogel, Leonard. (1998). *The Magazine: Everything You Need to Know to Make It in the Magazine Business,* 4th edition. Pittsburgh, PA: GATF Press.

TRACY LAUDER

MAGAZINE INDUSTRY, HISTORY OF

The first two publications to be categorized as magazines were created in England by Richard Steele and Joseph Addison. Steele began publishing the *Tatler* in 1709 and then joined with Addison (who had written for the *Tatler*) to begin publishing the *Spectator* in 1711. These publications differed from newspapers because they carried more of an emphasis on entertainment and enlightenment than on pure information and news. Magazines in America began with a similar concept.

The Eighteenth Century

American magazines were chiefly born out of the need to voice political opinions and ideals as the Colonies evolved into a democratic nation. The first magazines in America debuted in 1741: Benjamin Franklin's *The General Magazine, and Historical Chronicle, For all the British Plantations in America,* which published six issues; and Andrew Bradford's *American Magazine, or a Monthly View of the Political State of the British Colonies,* which ran for three issues. Both folded quickly, some say, because America was not yet ready for this new type of publication, showing a general lack of interest.

Another reason there were few magazines in America is because there were few who could read them or afford them. Most literate people were wealthy males, and because it was expensive to produce and distribute a magazine, they were the primary readership. Few women of that time were educated; therefore, magazines carried what was then thought to be male-oriented content such as politics, business, and science.

America's early magazines were filled with reprints of essays and information that was originally published in British magazines, books, and pamphlets. Very little of the work was attributed

The General Magazine, and Historical Chronicle, For all the British Plantations in America, *which was printed and sold by Benjamin Franklin in 1741, was the first magazine to be published in the British Colonies, and it carried the crest of the Prince of Wales.* (Bettmann/Corbis)

due to the lack of copyright laws. As the Revolutionary War approached, magazine content became more persuasive and political, and the words of some of the great statesmen of the time were frequently published. Magazine writers, however, did not work for money or fame; no payments were made and bylines were rarely given. In many cases, the publisher of a magazine also edited materials, wrote content, *and* ran the press.

Much time and labor were needed to produce a magazine before the 1800s. Printing presses had not evolved much past the movable type created by Johannes Gutenberg in 1448. Type was set by hand—letter by letter, page by page—and printed by hand using wooden presses. The stiff rag paper and oil-based ink were also made by hand, unless the printer was fortunate enough to afford imported printing supplies from England. The design of early magazines was bland, and the small type was difficult to read. Illustrations, which typically were found only on the cover or title page, were generated from rough woodcuts, although some publishers could afford the more detailed images of engraved copperplate.

Because magazines were larger and heavier than newspapers, postal stagecoaches often would refuse to deliver magazines because they took up precious space. If the postmaster accepted magazines on board, they were charged a much higher rate than that of other mail. The Postal Act of 1792 provided even lower rates for newspapers and subjected magazines to the higher rates assessed on letters. Two successful magazines of the day, *The Columbian Magazine* and *The American Museum,* soon died under the high postal rates. Two years later, the U.S. Congress saw the need to support magazine publishing and lowered postal rates for them, resulting in more new start-ups—a trend that continued into the 1900s. Rates were still high enough, however, to be a burden on the reader, because at that time delivery charges were paid in addition to the subscription price.

The Nineteenth Century

In the 1800s, literacy increased, and by the end of the U.S. Civil War, the majority of Americans could read. Magazines began to seek larger readerships—including the growing middle class that had more disposable income. From 1825 to 1850, approximately 5,000 magazines were launched (although not all of them succeeded), most from the Northeast, with New York replacing Philadelphia and Boston as the magazine-publishing capital. After the Civil War, the magazine industry boomed, increasing from 700 titles in 1865 to 3,330 in 1885. Circulation had grown also, but readerships of 100,000 were still considered huge. By the 1830s and 1840s, paid editors and bylined writers were common, and a new writing professional, the "magazinist," was born.

Magazines published in the nineteenth century sought to broaden their appeal. Meanwhile, magazines that targeted large groups such as religious denominations and trades began to take off during the latter part of the century. Notable mass-market magazines of the 1800s include *Atlantic Monthly, Century Magazine,* and *Scribner's Magazine.* Two of the greatest mass-circulation successes that appealed to the growing middle class were *Ladies Home Journal* and *Saturday Evening Post.* Cyrus H. K. Curtis developed the former in 1879, and when circulation reached the 500,000 mark in 1889, Edward Bok took over the editorship and was the first to cover many new areas of interest for women. In 1904, *Ladies Home Journal* was the first magazine to reach a circulation of more than one million. Curtis achieved additional success when he acquired *Saturday Evening Post,* which was struggling, in 1897. Under the editorship of Horace Lorimar, the magazine eventually grew to be regarded as the most successful magazine of the first half of the twentieth century. Curtis is known for recognizing the importance of readership to advertisers and for capitalizing on the increasing demand to place national brand-based advertising.

By the end of the century, magazines owners began to discover that advertising revenue could pay for the actual production, thereby making magazines more affordable for the reader. Frank A. Munsey was one of the first to experiment with this new idea. In 1893, he reduced the annual subscription rate of *Munsey's Magazine* from $3 to $1 and circulation grew from 40,000 to 500,000 by 1895. As a result, the magazine attracted more advertisers who were developing national advertising campaigns based on brand recognition.

One of the most successful startups of the era was *Harper's Magazine,* created by Harper & Brothers in 1850. These book publishers used their magazine as a way to make money with their book press during down time and as a vehicle in which to promote their book titles. The elegant publication featured biographies, essays, and articles on travel, leisure, and science. Throughout its successful history, *Harper's Magazine* attracted a wealthy, educated, upper-class audience. Other magazines that spun off from book businesses include *Collier's Weekly, Atlantic Monthly,* and *Putnam's New Monthly Magazine.* In a similar way, the highly successful women's magazine *McCall's* originated in 1873 when pattern maker James McCall saw it as a viable way to sell his dressmaking designs.

The best known of the early magazines targeting women was *Godey's Lady's Book* (1830–1898), which emphasized fashion and manners. Sara Josepha Hale, who served as the editor of the magazine for more than forty years, was known for shaping women's magazines of the day. She encouraged publisher Louis Godey, who hired her in 1837, to help educate women by providing articles about subjects other than fashion, such as history, art, music, travel, childcare, and important women. *Godey's Lady's Book* eventually grew to a circulation of 150,000.

New technology changed the look of magazines through the 1800s. In the early part of the century, magazines began to enhance text with illustrations and engravings. Copperplate engravings were often individually painted by hand with watercolors, such as those found in *Godey's Lady's Book,* but these engravings were obviously labor-intensive and costly to produce. Woodcuts were a less expensive option than steel or copper plates and were gradually improved to provide durability and detail. Illustrations became more popular as the century progressed, but by the late 1800s, with new engraving technology, photographs began to be more common.

New printing techniques made publishing magazines quicker and easier. The old flatbed press could only print one sheet at a time; in 1822, the steam-powered press accelerated the process, and in 1847, the rotary press made printing even faster. The greatest press advancements appeared in 1871, with the advent of the web perfecting press, which could simultaneously print both sides of a single roll of paper, and in 1886, when the invention of the Linotype machine by Ottmar Mergenthaler virtually dispensed of hand-set type, thereby speeding up the typesetting process nearly eightfold. Meanwhile, handmade linen papers were replaced with wood pulp papers, lowering the cost of the product. All of these new developments saved time and money, which resulted in lower magazine prices for the consumer.

Postal rates, however, continued to be a major monetary concern for magazines. In 1825, Congress enacted rates based on distance traveled, which resulted in magazine circulation being concentrated in the northeastern United States. In 1845, Congress eliminated the distance factor and set rates based on weight alone. Magazine publishers continued to push for better rates, and in 1852, postal rates for magazines dropped again. At this time another significant change was made when publishers were allowed to pay postage on magazines at the mailing office—absorbing costs

themselves and eliminating the need for subscribers to prepay postage on magazines at their own post offices. Finally, in 1879, Congress passed the Postal Act, which allowed magazines a lower second-class rate.

The Twentieth Century

Magazine readership flourished in the 1900s. More people were able to read, more people found leisure time in which to read, and more people had discretionary income to spend on magazines. Early in the century, magazines carried over the content focus from the nineteenth century, providing general interest articles and advice; however, this editorial style soon gave way to specialized content that met the needs of specialized audiences. Magazines began to move toward shorter articles, more concise writing, and more service-oriented journalism. Although mass circulation leaders such as *Saturday Evening Post* and *Life* remained popular through the early part of the twentieth century, they eventually folded when magazines with uniquely focused editorial concepts began to dominate the industry.

Reader's Digest, created by DeWitt Wallace and his wife Lila Acheson Wallace in 1922, was one of the first notable successes of the twentieth century. The couple tried to meet the needs of busy readers by condensing and reprinting a variety of articles published in other magazines and by printing them in a small magazine format that was easily transported. Henry Luce and Briton Hadden founded *Time* in 1923 with similar goals of educating busy readers, and their publication broke ground as a weekly news magazine. Meanwhile Harold Ross's *New Yorker* provided another unique editorial product with its individualistic criticism, sarcastic wit, and slanted profiles.

Other special-interest magazines, such as *Sports Illustrated* and *Modern Maturity,* became so popular that they eventually gained large circulations. *Sports Illustrated* was founded by Time, Inc., in 1954. Although it was hugely popular from the start, it took ten years to turn a profit. *Modern Maturity,* founded in the 1980s by the American Association of Retired People (AARP), became one of the nation's top-circulating magazines due to the organization's growing membership. A wide variety of special-interest magazines created in the twentieth century were so popular that they eventually gained mass appeal, including such titles as

In 1971, the Volunteers of America presented DeWitt Wallace and Lila Acheson Wallace (cofounders of Reader's Digest*) with the Ballington and Maud Booth Award for Distinguished Service to Humanity. (Bettmann/Corbis)*

Playboy (1953), *TV Guide* (1953), *Rolling Stone* (1967), *Travel and Leisure* (1971), and *Ms.* (1972).

At the end of the nineteenth century, photography became an important part of magazine content. With the invention of the halftone in the 1880s, a photograph could be transferred onto a sensitized printing plate, eliminating the need for an artist and engraver—thereby cutting the cost of providing visual images. At the beginning of the twentieth century, a halftone cost $20, compared to a wood engraving at $300. Many magazines such as *McClure's* and *Munsey's* began to use photographs to enhance articles, and *Collier's* became noted for its news photography after its coverage of the Spanish–American War in 1898. It was other magazines, however, such as *National Geographic, Life,* and *Look* that took full advantage of this new technology, basing their content on the image before the word. In addition, fashion magazines in the 1920s such as *Vogue, Vanity Fair, Town & Country,* and *Harper's Bazaar* embraced photographic content.

As readers began to see more photographs and color in magazines, they became more demanding of magazine appearance. Art directors joined the staffs of writers and editors in the 1930s and 1940s. Two of the noteworthy groundbreaking art

directors were Alexey Brodovitch at *Harper's Bazaar* and Mehemed Fehmy Agha at *Vogue* and *Vanity Fair.* They led the way for magazines to gain distinctive visual styles.

In the latter half of the twentieth century, advancements in computers and satellite technology decreased the time needed to place advertising and deliver fast-breaking news. Enhanced computer technology also had an effect on magazine production—first in design and production and later in editorial. Gradually, many magazines moved to computer-to-plate (CTP) production, where no film is shot, decreasing the amount of time necessary to get raw content to the press. At the same time, magazines began to accept digital art from advertisers, further streamlining the production process.

Postal rates remained a concern for magazine publishers throughout the twentieth century. In the early 1900s, transportation systems enhanced methods for delivering magazines, but postal rates became increasingly higher and more complicated. In 1917, editorial material was charged a single rate, while advertising was zoned and assessed fees accordingly. After the 1960s, some publishers actually found it cost-effective to cut circulation. In 1970, the Postal Reorganization Act took the rate-setting power from Congress and turned it over to the U.S. Postal Service. By 1980, postal rates had increased more than 400 percent, which led some publishers to begin experimenting with alternative carriers to combat the cost.

The Twenty-First Century

Despite the prolific use of personal computers to gain access to information and entertainment via the Internet, print magazines have retained popularity in the United States. Newsstands feature new titles regularly, creating competition within even the most narrowly focused niche markets. New technology should continue to make production of magazines faster and easier, while the interests of readers will continue to drive editorial content and garner advertising for one of America's favorite mediums.

See also: EDITORS; GUTENBERG, JOHANNES; MAGAZINE INDUSTRY; MAGAZINE INDUSTRY, CAREERS IN; MAGAZINE INDUSTRY, PRODUCTION PROCESS OF; PRINTING, HISTORY AND METHODS OF; WRITERS.

Bibliography

Click, J. William, and Baird, Russell N. (1994). *Magazine Editing and Production,* 6th edition. Madison, WI: Brown and Benchmark.

Folkerts, Jean, and Teeter, Dwight L., Jr. (1998). *Voices of a Nation: A History of Mass Media in the United States,* 3rd edition. Boston: Allyn & Bacon.

Johnson, Sammye, and Prijatel, Patricia. (2000). *Magazine Publishing.* Lincolnwood, IL: NTC/Contemporary Publishing Group.

Mott, Frank Luther. (1939, 1957, 1968). *A History of American Magazines,* 5 vols. Cambridge, MA: Harvard University Press.

Nourie, Alan, and Nourie, Barbara, eds. (1990). *American Mass-Market Magazines.* New York: Greenwood Press.

Peterson, Theodore. (1964). *Magazines in the Twentieth Century.* Urbana: University of Illinois Press.

Sloan, Wm. David, and Startt, James D., eds. (1996). *The Media in America: A History,* 3rd edition. Northport, AL: Vision Press.

Tebbel, John, and Zuckerman, Mary Ellen. (1991). *The Magazine in America, 1740–1990.* New York: Oxford University Press.

Wood, James Playsted. (1971). *Magazines in the United States.* New York: Ronald Press.

TRACY LAUDER

▌■ MAGAZINE INDUSTRY, PRODUCTION PROCESS OF

The production process of a magazine involves several steps that are often carried out simultaneously by all who contribute to the final product, including the editorial and advertising departments, the printer, and the circulation department. For this reason, communication, planning, and organization are vital in the process of turning ideas into a magazine. While every magazine varies in this process, a basic formula does exist.

Planning and Preparing Content

The process often begins with the end. The editor and the publisher determine a date that a magazine will reach the reader, and the printer and the circulation department provide deadlines that must be met to accomplish this. Once these dates are established, the scheduling and planning of the magazine can proceed.

With most magazines, the stories for each issue are planned several months, even one year, in advance. An idea for a story can come from several sources: the editor, the staff, queries from freelance writers, and, occasionally, unsolicited manuscripts. The content of each issue is ultimately the responsibility of magazine editors. The staff is typically expected to submit ideas to the editor. They are often the best source of story ideas because they have a more developed understanding of the focus of a magazine. Queries from freelance writers are also sent to the editor. A query should clearly outline the story idea and any special knowledge or the sources to be used by the writer. A finder's fee may be paid to the author of a query if the idea is used but assigned to another writer. While many magazines do not read any unsolicited manuscripts, some magazines have found it worthwhile to sort through these works. Regardless of its origin, once an idea is approved by the editor, it is assigned to either staff or freelance writers.

When a manuscript is completed by a writer, it is usually given to a magazine in electronic format along with a hard copy. Depending on the size of the staff, an editor may route a manuscript through what is called a "reading line" of senior editors for their comments and evaluation. Often, a manuscript will need some repair to be usable. The writer is provided with suggestions for necessary changes and asked to make the revisions. After this step, if only minor changes are needed, the magazine staff may make the revisions themselves. The magazine will then officially accept or reject the manuscript.

If a manuscript is officially accepted, it enters the copyediting phase. It will be thoroughly checked for accuracy. Every fact used in the manuscript must be verified, including names, quotes, and statistics. A writer is commonly asked to provide his or her sources, so a fact checker may retrace every step. The reputation of a publication is at risk because its readers expect the publication to be a reliable source, and advertisers do not want to be associated with poor-quality product. Fact checking also helps guard against lawsuits. While larger magazines have an entire department of fact checkers, other magazines rely on editors or copy editors to verify the accuracy of each manuscript.

A copy editor then critically reviews the manuscript for any grammatical errors or misspelled words, rewrites any awkward phrasing, and solves any organizational problems. A manuscript must also comply with the style adopted or developed by a magazine, which governs the treatment of things such as abbreviations, punctuation, names, titles, and spelling preferences. The copy editor is responsible for the overall polishing of the manuscript for publication. Once the copyediting is complete, the manuscript is ready to be laid out by the art department.

By the time a manuscript leaves the copy desk, the art director and the editor or assigning editor have made decisions about illustration or photography to accompany the piece. A freelance photographer may have been hired for a photo shoot or the rights to print an image may have been purchased by a stock photography agency. Low-resolution scans of these images, text, and any captions or pull quotes written by the assigning editor are given to a designer in the art department to lay out. The art director and the editor will then review the design and send it back to the copy desk for proofreading and any minor trimming necessary. Once a layout is approved by the copy editor, editor, and art director, it is ready for printing.

Production, Printing, and Distribution

Deciding what articles and advertisements will run in an issue and where they will be placed is called the break of the book. The size of an issue and the ratio of advertisement to editorial must be determined. Once these variables are established, a production manager begins mapping out the magazine, usually making a thumbnail of each page. The editor and the art director provide an outline of stories they want to include in the issue. Most publications have departments and special sections that run in the same place each issue, which aids in planning the magazine. Regardless, the map will undergo several revisions throughout production—to accommodate any changes in advertisements and stories scheduled to run.

The production manager oversees the final preparations made for the printer. While the editorial pages are coming together, the production manager collects materials for the advertising pages. Because most of these pages are created by other advertising agencies and design houses, the production manager must be sure that each advertisement arrives on time and conforms to the specifications of the publication. Advertisements are often sent to the magazine as film or in electronic format, but they can also be sent as preprinted pages that will be bound into the publication.

Before the production manager gives the materials to the printer, the printer has already scheduled press time, ordered paper, and made any other preparations possible. As soon as the printer receives the materials, the prepress process begins. If low-resolution images have been used, they will be replaced with high-resolution files. Any final color adjustments to the images will also be made at this time. The magazine is now ready to go to film.

A printer will not run the press without final approval from the publisher. Therefore, a proof is pulled from the film so the magazine can sign off on it. Printers have several ways of making proofs, from blue lines to digital color proofs. At this point, the order of the pages is checked, and the entire publication is reviewed one last time for any errors. While the printer will charge for any changes that are made at this point, it is the last opportunity to make corrections without spending a great deal of money. Once this proof is approved, the magazine is ready to go to press.

The production manager or the art director may be present at the beginning of a press run for quality control purposes. This process is called a press check, and it involves working with the press operators to ensure that the pages will run in register with acceptable color quality. When the representative of a magazine is satisfied with the press sheet, it is signed and used as a reference throughout the press run.

After the magazine pages are printed and dried, they will be folded, trimmed, bound, and made ready for distribution. A circulation director is responsible for getting the magazine into the hands of the reader. Larger magazines have in-house circulation departments that physically prepare the magazines for distribution. They also maintain records of subscribers and their subscription status and are responsible for fulfilling the agreement. Magazines are typically labeled with mailing addresses and bar codes and presorted for second-class mail. A circulation department must know the requirements of the U.S. Postal Service and meet these specifications to ensure a cost-efficient and timely delivery.

For single-copy sales, the circulation department may work with a national distributor to get the printed issues to retailers. A large magazine

A key issue in the production of a magazine is the creation and perpetuation of an editorial focus, such as the political focus that John F. Kennedy Jr. chose when he decided to create George magazine in 1995. (Reuters NewMedia Inc./Corbis)

will ship copies to wholesalers throughout the country provided by the national distributor. A wholesaler will record the quantities that they send to retailers such as supermarkets and convenience stores in their region. Any unsold copies will be returned to the wholesaler, who notifies the national distributor. The national distributor is able to provide sales figures for the publisher.

Maintaining Editorial Focus

The publisher and the editor must be in tune with their target audience to create a successful magazine. The publisher relies on sales figures and subscriptions as a source to track the progress of the publication. A magazine may also conduct or commission reader surveys, and it is the editor's job to use this information to ensure that the editorial content reflects the preferences of readers. Throughout the production process, the editor is responsible for keeping the big picture in sight, and ensuring that the decisions made will uphold the mission of the magazine.

Most magazines are classified as either consumer or trade publications. Hundreds of categories exist in the consumer classification. Each targets readers by where they live, their interests, age, sex, income level, race, or any other defining characteristics. A consumer magazine finds a niche that allows advertisers to reach a target market that is relevant to their product. Advertising is a large portion of consumer magazine revenue, and these magazines are readily available to consumers. Trade magazines target specific professions, and while advertising is an important source of revenue, trade magazines can charge much higher subscription rates than consumer magazines.

The nature of a magazine is an important variable to consider in the production process. Scheduling is the most obvious factor that is affected by the focus of a magazine. For example, a news magazine does not have the predictability of other magazines. Special reports and investigations must be put together quickly if they are going to remain newsworthy by the time the publication is distributed. Fashion magazines have a little more predictability in that, typically, fall and spring issues are larger to accommodate the fashion shows and new styles of the season. Many photo shoots for fashion, lifestyle, and outdoor magazines must be completed one year in advance due to the change of seasons. For example, if a fall issue requires outdoor scenes, the photographer cannot capture the changing leaves with a photo shoot in May.

Editorial scheduling is just one of the many factors that are influenced by the type of magazine being produced. The size of a magazine staff, and the process a manuscript must go through, can also vary. For example, a cooking magazine typically has a test kitchen staff. Their job is to test any recipe for publication to ensure that it is usable and tasty. They also develop recipes for stories and contribute to story ideas. Thus, while a manuscript is being scrutinized by editors and copy editors, the accompanying recipes are being analyzed by the test kitchen. Other magazines may require a manuscript to be checked for accuracy and relevance by a field expert before it is officially accepted by for publication. Fitness magazines, for example, often have medical experts that review manuscripts for accuracy.

A magazine that has a heavy concentration of photography and images, such as an art magazine, caters to a more visual audience. Having a target audience with discriminating eyes makes the production and printing quality of the utmost importance, and it may require more color proofs and extensive press checks. Many art magazines use a higher quality of paper, which affects the size of the production cost per issue.

Technological Advancements

The magazine production process has changed tremendously since the mid-twentieth century because of technological advances. Most magazines have become digital, using personal computers and page layout software. This has eliminated several positions and steps in the production process. Prior to the desktop revolution, the production process was a closely linked chain, in which each person performed a specific duty without variation in a sequence without deviation. With the advent of desktop publishing, these specific duties became blurred as every staff member became more closely involved in the production process. Now, an editor can place copy in a layout while an art director can perform tasks that were normally left to the production staff. Therefore, it has become necessary for people working in a desktop publishing system to resolve these issues of responsibility in order to prevent conflict among the members of the staff and to avoid confusion in the production process.

Magazine staffs have also been reduced as computer software has simplified tasks that once required specialized training. Magazines enjoy the economic benefit of producing magazines with a smaller staff, yet members of the staff find themselves performing more duties than ever before. One person can edit text, format it, and perform pagination simultaneously, speeding up the process and eliminating the bottlenecks of the old process.

As technology has provided a faster, more efficient way of putting together a magazine, editorial and advertising deadlines have been pushed back. News magazines can add timely stories as they broke, and all magazine advertising departments enjoy the extra time to pull in more advertising. Yet this puts added pressure on the production staff to meet the tight deadlines. Constantly changing technology has also become an issue. As new software and systems are constantly being introduced and used in the publishing industry, production staffs must train and learn to use new tools, often for job security. Despite the new gray areas presented by technological developments, magazines have enjoyed the benefits of a faster, more streamlined production process.

The technological explosion has also contributed to the development of an entirely new category of magazine. Several computer magazines have been successfully established, while other magazines have added new sections that relate their editorial focus to computers, such as online shopping, guides to useful Internet websites, and reader e-mails. It is only natural that this new computer culture makes its way into editorial content as it becomes a part of the everyday lives of the readers.

Just as magazines cannot ignore this growing computer culture editorially, publishers have found themselves faced with questions about the future of printed medium versus electronic format. Most magazine professionals have realized that electronic media should be seen as another form for distribution of their information, rather than as a threat to their magazine. While most publishers have not rushed to embrace an electronic format completely, they have begun to take advantage of the technology in one way or another.

The CD-ROM became one of the avenues explored by magazines in the mid-1990s. The capacity of the compact disc (CD) to store not only text and large images but animation, video, and sound provides a new challenge editorially. An entirely new world became the realm of possibility for magazines. Readers can navigate through text and images with greater freedom—with cross-references and indexes that literally lead the readers to whatever information they seek. Readers can interact with the electronic pages. Despite these advantages, computer compatibility and slower hard drives remain a challenge. Magazine publishers have found this a useful way to provide special one-shot publications or software that act as companions to their magazines. For example, cooking magazines have used the CD-ROM to provide recipe software that allows readers to access an entire database of recipes as well as to add their own recipes to the archived material.

Online magazines offer even more advantages to communicating ideas. While the World Wide Web offers more options for content than a printed magazine, such as sound and video, the immediacy of the web is perhaps its most powerful asset. The production process requires fewer steps than the printed magazine. This allows editors to update a page as quickly and as often as they choose, meaning that there are no "old issues" or obsolete stories. Magazines can finally have the same relevancy that only television and radio possessed in the past. Editors are also able to communicate directly with readers, responding to their questions and suggestions as quickly as they wish. An online magazine can set up a forum or "chat room" where readers can communicate with each other as well as with the editorial staff. While these advantages are undeniable, most printed magazines are not switching over to online formats. Instead, the magazines are expanding to include the online formats.

See also: EDITORS; MAGAZINE INDUSTRY; MAGAZINE INDUSTRY, CAREERS IN; MAGAZINE INDUSTRY, HISTORY OF; PRINTING, HISTORY AND METHODS OF; WRITERS.

Bibliography

Cowles Business Media. (1996). *Handbook of Magazine Publishing*, 4th edition. Stamford, CT: Cowles Business Media.

Daly, Charles P.; Henry, Patrick; and Ryder, Ellen. (1997). *The Magazine Publishing Industry*. Boston: Allyn & Bacon.

Johnson, Sammye, and Prijatel, Patricia. (2000). *Magazine Publishing*. Lincolnwood, IL: NTC/Contemporary Publishing Group.

Mogel, Leonard. (1998). *The Magazine: Everything You Need to Know to Make It in the Magazine Business*, 4th edition. Pittsburgh: GATF Press.

Patterson, Benton Rain, and Patterson, Coleman E. P. (1997). *The Editor in Chief: A Practical Management Guide for Magazine Editors*. Ames: Iowa State University Press.

STACEY BENEDICT
TRACY LAUDER

MANAGEMENT INFORMATION SYSTEMS

What are management information systems? A simple answer would be that management information systems are systems that are used to deliver management information. It could also be said that these systems might or might not be implemented by means of computing technology. They might be very formalized (i.e., explicit) or more informal (i.e., implicit). The real problem in understanding management information systems comes with what is defined as management information, as well as the particular view taken on how managers actually go about engaging with this information and these systems in doing managerial work on a day-to-day basis. Generally, the controversy with these systems is not about what they are but rather about why they are necessary or not and how they are actually used or not. It is in addressing these questions that a particular view of management information systems will tend to come to the fore.

Most contemporary authors would agree that it is useful to define management information as essential information extracted or filtered from the transactional or primary organizational activities to support management in identifying and solving problems as well as in making decisions to ensure the efficient and effective management of the organization. Again, this seems quite easy and intuitive to understand. It may be this intuitive need and the possibilities presented by computing technology that made H. Igor Ansoff claim, in his 1965 paper "The Firm of the Future" that "man-computer decision making is potentially the most powerful competitive tool which will be available to the firm of tomorrow." Was it? Is it still? The answer must be yes and no. The history of management information systems, especially formalized computer-based systems, has been rather disappointing. Many of the promises of efficient and effective decision making and problem solving through real-time and accurate information has not materialized. Managers continue to talk of information abundance, even overload, but argue they often lack what is really relevant—this is mostly expressed by the phrase, "we are drowning in data but we are starving for information."

Is it that these systems are not real-time enough, or that they are collecting the wrong data, or perhaps that they are presenting it in inappropriate ways? All of these may be possibilities. However, it may also be more fundamental. If a look is taken back to the 1960s and early 1970s, it is seen that controversy surrounded the idea of computer-based management information systems from its inception. The two most prominent detractors were Russell Ackoff, with his paper "Management Misinformation Systems" (1967), and John Dearden, with his paper "MIS Is a Mirage" (1972). Both of these authors felt that the management decision-making processes were much more complex than suggested by the proponents of computer-based management information systems. They also argued that the proponents did not have an adequate understanding of the way in which managers used information in actual decision-making processes. The extensive studies by Henry Mintzberg in the early 1980s of managerial work seemed to confirm that managers were indeed much less structured, informal, and intuitive in their use of information in decision-making processes. By the end of the 1980s and in the beginning of the 1990s, it became evident that management information systems were not the "grand solution" to the management problem its proponents thought it would be. Nevertheless, there were many benefits indirectly derived from these efforts, especially an understanding of how mangers actually go about making decisions and solving problems.

Historical Roots

The logic that would make management information systems a self-evident need in the second half of the twentieth century started long before the first computer was applied in a business context. In fact, one could trace the origin of this logic back to the very inception of the modern period and the work of the seventeenth-century philosopher René Descartes. Descartes, considered the father of the modern worldview, was struck by the large number of competing, and often contradictory, systems of knowledge about the world that had been presented to him as part of his education. He believed that humanity will only progress if they establish an absolutely certain basis to separate true statements from false statements—that is, to secure knowledge on a trustworthy foundation. This principle forms the implicit basis from which the father of modern management, Frederick Winslow Taylor, two hundred years later shaped its essence.

Taylor, akin to Descartes, was struck by the unsystematic manner in which factory work was being conducted and the lack of systematic knowledge on how to achieve results with a required degree of certainty. With this in mind, Taylor developed standardized techniques and methods to measure work. Tasks were divided into the smallest possible unit—the rational division of labor. Every unit was then rationalized according to available knowledge provided by detailed study of workers' movements, actions, and techniques for executing work. Every unnecessary technique, movement, or action was illuminated until only that which can no longer be doubted remained. A similar procedure was then applied to the workers themselves. The optimized work and worker were then placed under detailed monitoring to ensure compliance and to provide feedback for improving the work process. The improvements that Taylor achieved were phenomenal—even for very basic work such as shoveling things. He reported improvements of hundreds, and sometimes even thousands, of percent.

There is no doubt that Taylor's scientific management (often referred to as "Taylorism") was spectacularly successful. It was rapidly adopted by many factories and became the self-evident model for managing work in that organizational setting. However, this success masked the implicit outcome of the scientific management logic. This outcome must be carefully considered because it helps reveal the logic for management information systems and shows why management information systems never realized the potential that was anticipated by its original proponents.

The important implicit outcome of scientific management was the separation of cognition and action—in other words, "thinking about work" and "doing the work" became separated. Thinking was transferred from the worker to the management function or process. Thus, through scientific management, thinking and worker action became separated for the sake of absolute efficiency, and the need for an information system to act as a bridge for this gap came about—initially messengers and telephones, later computer-based information systems.

In Taylorism, management becomes conceived of as the brain that moves the body (work processes) in a planned and coordinated way. The information system becomes viewed as the system that connects the brain with the body—the nervous system as it were. From this separation of work and thought about work, established by scientific management, management information systems emerged as a self-evident need. As organizations grew in size and complexity, this need became more and more acute. Likewise, the problem of allocating resources—workers, machines, material, and so on—could no longer simply be solved on "diagrams and maps," which acted as models for the reality. As organizations became more complex than can be represented on diagrams and maps, more sophisticated models were needed to act as representations of reality, where different possible allocations, or scenarios, could be developed and evaluated. Thus emerged the need for decision-support systems. Likewise, more and more detailed information about work in progress and work completed were needed so that the planning horizon could be up to date.

Evolving Role

It is therefore not surprising that Henri Fayol, in his seminal work *General and Industrial Management* (1949), concluded that the essential management activities were planning, organizing, controlling, and leading. These activities flow logically from the way management became articulated in scientific management. As these management activities became more clearly articulated, they became supported by an increasingly complex set of techniques for gathering data and reporting results. In this regard, the development of managerial accounting was significant, with the first work on budgeting appearing in 1922 and the development of "responsibility accounting" in the early 1950s. However, the development of computer-based management information systems to support management activities was not yet evident, as the first electrical computers, the ENIAC (1946) and the UNIVAC 1 (1951), were seen as primarily mathematical machines.

In 1954, the UNIVAC 1 was installed at General Electric as a business application to do payroll processing. The business community rapidly appropriated the computer as a business tool, with its use growing to 100,000 business computers by 1974. In its first decade of application, the computer was essentially used as a more efficient technology for automating work that involved laborious calculation, such as payroll calculations. The focus was on its speed and accuracy as a mathematical tool. However, it soon became evident that the capturing or recording of data required for the calculations could also be used to create reports for managers. As such, computer-based management information became an unintended consequence of the automation of calculating operations.

The automation of more and more work processes generated increasing amounts of data for the manager to consider. Herbert Simon, the Nobel laureate, realized that managers would need systematic methods to use this, now increasingly abundant, data. Simon produced the first systematic account of managerial decision making in his seminal work *The New Science of Management Decisions* (1960), wherein he makes the distinction between structured and unstructured decisions. In a structured decision, the nature of the problem and the data required to consider a solution for the problem are known in advance. In an unstructured decision, the problem needs to be structured before it can be considered. It is therefore not possible to know in advance exactly what information will be required. Together with this work, a number of other works started to appear that had a particular influence on the way management information systems was conceived.

Framework for Definition

The most widely used, and undoubtedly the most influential, framework for management information systems was the framework presented by Anthony Gorry and Michael Scott Morton in 1971. This framework rapidly became the blueprint for the development of management information systems and is still used in most textbooks as the basis for discussing management information systems.

Gorry and Scott Morton proposed that the type of decisions and, therefore, information needs would vary according to the level of management control. Based on this idea, they suggested a framework for identifying the type of information required by each level of management. They concluded that operational management needed largely internal information, which is well defined, detailed, and narrow in scope. Furthermore, their information need tends to be current, usually referring to the most recent period—day, week, or month. They normally require a high level of accuracy and a structured and well-defined format of presentation. Typical examples of these would be the daily sales or production reports that provide detailed functional information such as sales per units, sales per salesperson, or sales per region. On the other end of the spectrum, they concluded that strategic management required general information that is broad and far-reaching in scope—mostly from external sources. Their information tended to be aggregated and summarized with an emphasis on forecasting, prediction, and future scenarios. The presentation of their information often varied to accommodate the diversity of formats used by the variety of sources—both internal and external. Typical examples of these would be internal strategy documents, government and central bank economic forecasts, market analyst commentaries, and share price predictions. From this initial framework, they proposed different types of systems to support the three management levels in the organization. The operational control process—first line or supervisory management—tend to be supported by frequent, detailed reports on the most recent work completed or in progress. The systems implemented to automate the basic operational business activities (e.g., payroll systems)—referred to as transaction processing systems—provide the data for this management reporting. The management control level—referred to as middle management or tactical management level—is supported by some form of decision-sup-port system. These systems implement the decision process as defined by Simon, using modeling techniques that were developed by the emerging management science field—as explained by Ralph Sprague and Eric Carlson (1982) and, more recently, by George Marakas (1999).

Management science field emerged out of the operations research field of study, where mathematical models were being developed to solve complex resource allocation problems. (Operations research was itself an outcome of resource allocation problems encountered in World War II.) It was only in the latter half of the 1980s that the concept of an executive information system for strategic planning emerged. As the organizational hierarchies increased, the senior managers felt increasingly isolated from the basic business operations; the management separation of scientific management affected them the most. Thus, one had a contradiction in which the operational managers had the direct experience and knowledge of the business and the senior managers had the authority to allocate resources but not the knowledge to do so effectively. The executive information system was seen as the solution to this problem. Robert Thierauf (1991) proposes that an executive information system would provide the executive access to information about the operations in an easy to use, aggregate format with the ability to "drill down" and look at the detail data behind the aggregate presentations. With the coming of the executive information systems, the three management levels were associated with three distinct types of systems: management reporting systems, decision-support systems, and executive information systems. These systems are best summarized in the following manner. Operational managers are mostly supported by management reporting systems that provide specific, detailed, and current information about operations in the form of regular management reports. These systems act as the essential feedback for operational control and short-term problem solving. Middle managers are mostly supported by decision support systems. They are interactive computer-based systems intended to help decision-makers use data and mathematical models (such as cash flow or scheduling models) to identify and solve unprogrammed, semistructured problems. The system supports, rather than replaces, managerial judgment. Its objective is to improve the effectiveness of the decisions and not necessarily the efficiency with which decisions are being made. Strategic managers are supported by a variety of internal and external sources. One such internal source is the executive information system. It provides, in a useful and navigable format, direct online access to relevant, timely, accurate, and actionable information about aspects of an organization that are of particular interest to the senior managers. It allows the senior managers to identify broad strategic issues and then explore the information through increasing layers of detail, until they are able to explore the root causes of the issues.

From this discussion, it is evident why management information became viewed as essential information filtered from the transaction processing systems or primary organizational activities and processed, or structured, by the management information system to support management—in an appropriate manner for each level of management—in identifying and solving problems or making decisions to ensure the efficient and effective management of the organization. Gordon Davis and Margrethe H. Olsen, in the second edition of the influential text *Management Information Systems: Conceptual Foundations, Structure, and Development* (1985, p. 6), define management information systems as follows: "Management information systems are integrated, user-machine systems for providing information to support operations, management, and decision-making functions in an [organization]."

Unrealized Promise

These conceptual frameworks are useful to think through how management information systems could and ought to be designed and developed, but what about the actual implementation of these systems in organizations? With these conceptual models in mind, and based on the expected value of management information systems, organizations proceeded to invest huge amounts of resources in their design, development, and implementation. The management information systems project was the major concern for organizations in the 1970s and the 1980s. Even the functional unit responsible for information systems in the organizations was often referred to as the "Management Information Systems Department." Management reporting systems quickly became the backbone to support

operational control in organizations—and could be said to be the most successful and enduring element of management information systems. Data capturing became more real-time (at the moment when it happens) and end users became more proficient at creating their own reports, queries, and so on. Decision-support systems have been relatively successful in small and specific areas of application. However, it has become evident that modeling organizational processes is much more complex than anticipated and that the most important factors considered by managers in decision making are often part of their tacit and intuitive understanding of the particular situation at hand. The field of decision support systems has grown to include support for group decision making, embedding artificial intelligence technology into these systems. However, effective decision support in areas that really matter still remains elusive. Relatively recent developments include data warehousing and online analytical processing. Executive information systems also have been moderately successful and continue to be used to a lesser or greater degree.

As with decision-support systems, the intuitive and unstructured nature of executive work remains the Achilles' heel of executive information systems. Neither decision-support systems nor executive information systems have become pervasive in any sense of the word. There appears to be a consensus that management information systems have not quite delivered on the promises heralded in the early 1970s. Studies of the investment in this technology have shown high levels of investments with rather low, or even negative, returns on investment, as reported by Paul Strassman in his book *The Business Value of Computers* (1990).

Management information systems have become much less of a concern for organizations—as reflected in research agendas, development priorities, and general business discourse. Some of the concerns about management information have shifted to other areas, such as enterprise resource planning systems. The most important factor for this change in emphasis is the shift in organizational thinking and development. By the second half of the 1980s and the early 1990s, organizational theorists and practicing managers realized that the standardized and stable production processes assumed by scientific management were simply no longer feasible. Organizations needed to be more flexible and able to respond to the increasingly sophisticated, interconnected, and dynamic environment. The only way to gain this flexibility was to reconnect "thinking about work" with "doing work"—thereby reversing the ill effects of scientific management. This attempt has led to the development of new models for managing organizations. To name but a few, these new models include learning organizations (where employees are encouraged to think about and improve their own work), quality circles (where quality problems are solved through collaborative consultation), empowerment of workers (through authority and resources), and multiskilling (where the widening of the skill base of all employees is encouraged). The design of computer-based information systems has responded to these changes. Thus the development of information technology to support learning, collaboration, and sharing of knowledge occurred, rather than the development of technologies for management control. The new technologies included initiatives such as computer-supported cooperative work systems in the form of groupware (to support collaboration), intranets (i.e., Internet technology that is available to an organization for sharing data on an internal basis), and knowledge repositories (to share knowledge through the organization).

Although management information systems will undoubtedly remain in some form as an integral part of the information systems infrastructure of organizations, it will not perform the central role that was once envisaged by its early proponents. In the new (i.e., postscientific management) organizational climate, new technological solutions are needed and are being developed. There is no doubt that they will also disappoint, because the problem of information and information systems is always, in the final analysis, a social problem rather than merely a technical one.

See also: ARTIFICIAL INTELLIGENCE; CHIEF INFORMATION OFFICERS; GROUP COMMUNICATION; GROUP COMMUNICATION, DECISION MAKING AND; KNOWLEDGE MANAGEMENT; KNOWLEDGE MANAGEMENT, CAREERS IN; ORGANIZATIONAL COMMUNICATION; SYSTEMS DESIGNERS.

Bibliography

Ackoff, Russell L. (1967). "Management Misinformation Systems." *Management Science* 14:147–156.

Ansoff, H. Igor. (1965). "The Firm of the Future." *Harvard Business Review* 43(5):162–178.

Davis, Gordon B., and Olsen, Margrethe H. (1985). *Management Information Systems: Conceptual Foundations, Structure, and Development.* London: McGraw-Hill.

Dearden, John. (1972). "MIS Is a Mirage." *Harvard Business Review* 50(1):90–99.

Fayol, Henri. (1949). *General and Industrial Management.* London: Pitman.

Gorry, G. Anthony, and Scott Morton, Michael S. (1971). "A Framework for Management Information Systems." *Sloan Management Review* 13(1):55–70.

Introna, Lucas D. (1997). *Management, Information and Power: A Narrative of the Involved Manager.* Basingstoke, Eng.: Macmillan.

Marakas, George M. (1999). *Decision Support Technology for the 21st Century.* Englewood Cliffs, NJ: Prentice-Hall.

Mintzberg, Henry. (1980). *The Nature of Managerial Work.* Englewood Cliffs, NJ: Prentice-Hall.

Simon, Hubert A. (1960). *The New Science of Management Decision.* New York: Harper & Row.

Sprague, Ralph H., and Carlson, Eric D. (1982). *Building Effective Decision Support Systems.* Englewood Cliffs, NJ: Prentice-Hall.

Strassman, Paul. (1990). *The Business Value of Computers.* New Canaan, CT: Information Economics Press.

Taylor, Federick W. (1914). *The Principles of Scientific Management.* London: Harper & Row.

Thierauf, Robert J. (1991). *Executive Information Systems: A Guide for Senior Management and MIS Professionals.* New York: Quorum.

LUCAS D. INTRONA

◼ MARCONI, GUGLIELMO (1874–1937)

Guglielmo Marconi, the originator of wireless telegraph signals, created the means of overcoming many of the hurdles to the commercialization of wireless. In particular, he was the first person to transmit radio signals across the Atlantic Ocean without the use of cables.

Marconi was born in the Italian countryside in somewhat modest circumstances. While he had little formal education (although his mother did tutor him), he loved to read about experiments with electricity that were described in the books in his father's library. Marconi audited courses at

Guglielmo Marconi is shown with his electrical wireless apparatus in an 1896 photograph. (Hulton-Deutsch Collection/Corbis)

the University of Bologna, because he could not gain admittance to the university for credit, and studied under Augusto Righi, a scientist who had worked with electromagnetic waves. Since Righi was also a neighbor, Marconi would often visit him with questions and ideas. Righi rarely encouraged Marconi's ideas about a practical system of transmitting information using these electromagnetic waves. Still, Marconi showed a dogged persistence in trying out method after method in his experiments.

In 1895, after following the experiments of Heinrich Hertz, Marconi (at twenty-one years of age) devised a system that allowed him to ring a bell that was two rooms away in his attic workshop. He was able to do this purely by striking a telegraph key that created electromagnetic waves. Marconi began producing this effect at longer and longer distances, eventually moving outside and sending the signals over a distance of several hundred yards. Initially, distances were overcome simply by using more powerful electrical charges, a condition that would never allow practical wireless

communication to travel very far. Marconi eventually found that if he placed part of the transmitter on the ground, resistance was cut dramatically and the signal would travel much farther. Thus, Marconi invented the grounded antenna and began sending telegraph signals over distances of up to two miles (regardless of hills or other obstacles).

After the Italian Ministry of Post and Telegraph rejected his initial presentation of the invention, Marconi took it to England. After applying for a patent to protect his idea, he began working to gain British support. Since his mother was Irish, he had several family connections in England and was able to arrange a presentation of the invention to William Preece of the British postal system in 1896. Preece became an avid supporter and provided postal system personnel to help Marconi continue to develop his system. By 1899, Marconi had established a wireless link across thirty-two miles of the English Channel.

The wireless system as it then existed allowed for only one person at a time to transmit in a given geographical area. If multiple transmissions were sent simultaneously, they were incomprehensible or canceled each other out. Marconi looked for a way to tune the signal to specific wavelengths. By 1900, he had succeeded in developing a system of tuned multiplex telegraphy, which allowed multiple messages to be sent from the same transmitter simultaneously with each message being received accurately by different receivers in different locations.

Another obstacle to be overcome by Marconi was a belief by many scientists that electromagnetic waves would not be able to follow the curve of the earth and could, therefore, never transmit signals across the vastness of an ocean. In 1899, Marconi had transmitted signals from ship to shore over a span of sixty-six nautical miles, far more than enough to ensure that the waves were somehow bending around or traveling through the ocean to reach the shoreline. Marconi was convinced that the wireless could span the ocean, and he set out to prove it. He had a powerful transmitting station built in Poldhu, on the coast of England, and set sail for St. John's, Newfoundland. Once there, Marconi attached a receiving wire to a kite and flew the kite at a height of four hundred feet. To anyone who expressed interest in what he was doing, Marconi pretended that he was working on contacting passing ships on their transatlantic voyages. On December 12, 1901, he received the letter "S" several times and had an assistant verify the reception. He then announced to the world that he had received a message from England, which was more than twenty-one hundred miles away across the Atlantic.

Still, many people doubted Marconi's claim because of the bias of his only witness and the simplicity of the message. Therefore, Marconi outfitted the ship *Philadelphia* with sophisticated wireless equipment, a telegraph recorder that would mark the signals on paper tape, and a public listening-room so passengers and crew could serve as witnesses to the receptions. The experiment, which took place during a 1902 voyage where the ship sailed from Cherbourg to New York, was a success. Marconi recorded receiving signals from over a distance of more than two thousand miles. As a by-product of his experiment, Marconi also found that the signals traveled best at night, but this was a phenomenon that he was at a loss to explain.

In 1907, Marconi finally perfected the system of transatlantic wireless and began commercial service between Glace Bay, Nova Scotia, and Clifden, Ireland. His work on wireless brought him the Nobel Prize for physics in 1909.

The early 1910s were full of lawsuits in which Marconi was forced to defend his patent rights. He emerged victorious, however, and the results were financially profitable for his British, American, and international companies. In 1916, during World War I, America wanted to avoid foreign control in wireless properties that were being used by the military. As a result, the American Marconi Company was forced by the U.S. government to merge with General Electric. Thus, Marconi lost the influence he had established in wireless communication in America. In his home base of Britain, however, Marconi and his companies were influential in the startup of public radio broadcasting and helped to establish the British Broadcasting Company, which later became the British Broadcasting Corporation (BBC).

Marconi continued to experiment on improving radio broadcasting. He eventually was able to send messages in specific directions and around the globe. He also performed experiments with radar and with microwave, proving that microwaves could also travel beyond the horizon of the earth. In 1924, he set up a system of wireless stations that linked England to the British colonies around the world. He also set up a radio service for the Vatican in Rome in 1931 and created the first microwave link so that the Pope's messages could instantly be sent several miles away to the short-wave transmitter that could then broadcast the message live to the world. Failing health restricted Marconi's activity for much of the last ten years of his life. He died of heart failure in 1937.

See also: EDISON, THOMAS ALVA; MORSE, SAMUEL F. B.; RADIO BROADCASTING, HISTORY OF.

Bibliography

Carter, Alden R. (1987). *Radio: From Marconi to the Space Age*. New York: Franklin Watts.

Dunlap, Orrin E., Jr. (1937). *Marconi: The Man and His Wireless*. New York: Macmillan.

Gunston, David. (1965). *Marconi: Father of Radio*. New York: Crowell-Collier.

Ivall, Tom, and Willis, Peter. (1997). "Making Continuous Waves." *Electronics World*, February, pp. 140–143.

Jensen, Peter R. (1994). *Early Radio: In Marconi's Footsteps, 1894 to 1920.* Kenthurst, NSW: Kangaroo Press.

Jolly, W. P. (1972). *Marconi,* New York: Stein and Day.

Marconi, Degna. (1962). *My Father, Marconi.* New York: McGraw-Hill.

Parker, Steve. (1994). *Guglielmo Marconi and Radio.* New York: Chelsea House.

STEPHEN D. PERRY

■ MARKETING RESEARCH, CAREERS IN

Marketing research, by any name, essentially involves the collection, analysis, and presentation of data to answer some predetermined questions developed jointly by a researcher and a client. Individuals who are planning to engage in a marketing research career have a flexibility of choice that is not always obvious. The range of industries, types of companies, and types of data one can choose from for a marketing research career is surprisingly broad. Almost all industries—nonprofit organizations, multimillion-dollar manufacturing companies ranging from consumer goods to high-end industrial equipment, and even small Internet start-up companies—require marketing research specialists. Joining either an in-house marketing research department within a larger organization such as Kraft or Procter & Gamble, or an independent marketing research firm, which can range in size, is another option. The type of data that a marketing researcher works with is also flexible. One can choose to work primarily with quantitative (numerical) or qualitative data or with a mix of both. The data sets can range from economics and pricing, attitudes and intentions, secondary behavioral data, to management principles.

The advantages of such a selection are clear—more options and greater flexibility. The disadvantages, especially for an individual who is new to the field, are potential confusion and the need to explore widely for opportunities. Career guides usually have a very narrow definition of marketing research. Most refer to the description merely as a marketing function. However, there are many careers with different titles that reflect the responsibilities and challenges of a marketing research career. Therefore, it is helpful to look for jobs with descriptions other than marketing research. For example, terms such as "economists," "management analysts," "sales forecasting," "consultants," or "sales operations" may include many positions in marketing research. Marketing research books may be more helpful than career guides in understanding the functions of a "marketing researcher." Books such as *The Market Research Toolbox: A Concise Guide for Beginners* (McQuarrie, 1997) or *Marketing Research: Methodological Foundations* (Churchill and Churchill, 1998) contain valuable descriptions of the scope and challenges of marketing research.

The process of marketing research proceeds in stages. First, the objectives and questions for which the information is collected must be established. The types of objectives and questions can range widely, encompassing short-term, immediate needs such as, "What promotion should be run for the Christmas holidays?" to long-term strategic questions such as, "When should a new product be launched and how much investment should be made in it?" These objectives and questions will then guide how data is collected. If the objective is to understand better the acceptance of a new product idea by customers, then focus groups might be the right approach. If the objective is to estimate the rate of new product adoption in a target group, then the best data might be secondary data showing past adoptions of similar products by a similar group. The common data-collection methods include focus groups (where individuals come together as a group to share their experiences and perspectives on a particular issue), conjoint studies (which obtain ratings from individuals on different product attributes to quantify the relative utility of each attribute), experiments, and various survey methodologies such as by mail and phone. Internet surveys are gaining popularity and have the advantage of being quicker and cheaper.

Once the data has been collected, the marketing researcher must determine which statistical analyses to perform and what recommendations to present. Both univariate and advanced multivariate analytical techniques are common in marketing research (Rao and Steckel, 1997). Sometimes, qualitative data are also subjected to quantitative analyses, but in general, greater value is placed on quantitative analyses than on qualitative analyses. This preference is largely due to the generalizability of large-sample quantitative studies (assuming that the sample is representative of the market) compared to small-sample nongeneralizable studies. Also, many marketing and management teams like to have strong, "solid" data with which to back their recommendations. As highlighted in the title of the book *How to Lie with Statistics* (Huff, 1982), numbers, however, are not always "solid." It is the ethical responsibility of the marketing researcher to be honest and to present the data and its results without bias. The presentation of the results and recommendations are usually done orally, accompanied by the use of computerized graphics. These are sometimes accompanied by a more detailed, written project report.

Throughout the process of identifying the objectives and questions, data collection, and data analyses, close collaboration with the client is required. In fact, the ability to develop and maintain strong, long-term client relationships is essential for promotion consideration and success at the higher managerial and director levels. Moreover, close client relationships tend to encourage better answers to better questions—the driving force behind marketing research.

To be a successful marketing researcher, one must be able to think broadly and yet pay attention to detail. Breadth of thinking is required when analyzing client business needs and selecting, from a wide range of possibilities, the best questions, the best methodologies, and the key recommendations to make. These decisions require a general knowledge about marketing environmental factors as well as the advantages and disadvantages of many different data collection and analysis methodologies. Once these larger issues have been dealt with, one must be able to organize data collection and analyze the data efficiently and carefully. A seemingly small mistake of forgetting to remove one code from the data set can easily result in erroneous recommendations harming the client, one's division or company, and one's career.

Successful marketing researchers tend to have strong mathematical, statistical, and marketing backgrounds. In addition, the ability to think conceptually, problem-solve, and take initiative are additional valued skills. According to the *1999 Career Guide Management Consulting* (Hunn, 1998), other personality factors such as confidence and the ability to communicate clearly are also important. Most marketing research jobs request at least a four-year degree in math, statis-

tics, operations research, or business. The exact degree, however, depends in large part on the industry. For example, many health-care marketing research firms require degrees not in business or statistics but in the sciences. Similarly, new Internet start-up companies look for individuals who have a strong knowledge of the industry and technology, and look primarily for a computer science or engineering degree. Most companies, however, prefer an M.B.A. or a master's degree in marketing research. In fact, to rise to senior marketing research positions, an M.B.A. is usually required. There is also an increasing push toward hiring individuals who hold a doctoral degree because such individuals are valued for their ability to think conceptually. Most of the individuals who fall into this category also have a strong quantitative background. Without a four-year degree, one would need to enter the marketing research field at the most junior level, as a data-entry operator or interviewer.

The financial returns of being a marketing researcher start for new entrants at slightly higher rates compared to new graduates from business schools and can rise to income levels equivalent to chief executive officers of smaller companies. The social rewards are equally attractive. Many market researchers branch out from established companies to open their own research firms, while some become independent consultants to large corporations. Others who remain in a corporate environment have the option of heading large cross-functional marketing research departments or of transitioning into marketing.

Overall, with the growing need for a better understanding of the needs of customers, the outlook for the marketing research field is very positive. According to Ron Krannich and Caryl Krannich (1998), research analysts and consultants are in one of the most promising career fields. In fact, they expect this field to grow at a higher-than-average rate.

See also: ADVERTISING EFFECTS; PSYCHOLOGICAL MEDIA RESEARCH, ETHICS OF; RESEARCH METHODS IN INFORMATION STUDIES.

Bibliography

Churchill, Gilbert A., and Churchill, Gilbert A., Jr. (1998). *Marketing Research: Methodological Foundations,* 7th edition. Orlando, FL: Dryden Press.

Huff, Darrell. (1982). *How to Lie with Statistics*. New York: W. W. Norton.

Hunn, L. Neil, ed. (1998). *1999 Career Guide Management Consulting*. New York: Harvard Business School.

Krannich, Ron L., and Krannich, Caryl R. (1998). *The Best Jobs for the 21st Century*. Manassas Park, VA: Impact Publications.

McQuarrie, Edward F. (1997). *The Market Research Toolbox: A Concise Guide for Beginners*. Thousand Oaks, CA: Sage Publications.

Rao, Vithala R., and Steckel, Joel H. (1997). *Analysis for Strategic Marketing*. Reading, MA: Addison-Wesley.

EUGENIA YEW-YEN PECK

■ MᶜLUHAN, HERBERT MARSHALL (1911–1980)

Herbert Marshall McLuhan, universally known as Marshall McLuhan, combined Cambridge University's New Criticism of literary textual analysis with the political economy-inspired communication theory of fellow Canadian and University of Toronto colleague Harold Innis. McLuhan was a leading scholar of popular communication media from the mid-1940s until his death in 1980 (which followed a stroke that had left him without his greatest gift, speech). An unconventional, colorful, and controversial professor of English who became the director of the Center of Culture and Technology of the University of Toronto, McLuhan rose to popular culture status himself with a handful of best-selling books and nonbooks published in the 1960s, including *The Gutenberg Galaxy: The Making of Typographic Man* (1962), *Understanding Media: The Extensions of Man* (1964), *The Medium is the Massage: An Inventory of Effects* (1967), and *War and Peace in the Global Village* (1968).

McLuhan created his own iconoclastic mix of observations about media by adapting and popularizing the communication bias theory of Innis and drawing from an interdisciplinary array of humanist thinkers, including T. S. Eliot, I. A. Richards, F. R. Leavis, St. Thomas Aquinas, Lewis Mumford, and a group of scholars at Toronto in the 1950s, such as anthropologist Edmund Carpenter. Considered today to be a member of the loosely knit Toronto school of communication studies, McLuhan's well-turned theoretical aphorisms, including "the medium is the message" and

Herbert Marshall McLuhan. (Bettmann/Corbis)

"the global village," became part of scholarly and popular consciousness in thinking about the media. McLuhan helped create a humanistic, qualitative, cultural, and critical analysis of the complex relationship between technology and culture. He offered an alternative to mainstream mass communication research.

McLuhan contended that all media, or technologies, extend the human body and human functions. All material existence qualifies as media, including wheels, which extend the foot, and clothing, which extends the skin. Numbers, clocks, roads, architecture, and many other material technologies are media, in addition to the traditional communication media of speech, writing, printing, and electronic media. Individuals and societies respond to this extension of human form with a sense of shock and pain, associated with amputation of a limb, thus failing to recognize the ultimately human source of all technology, much as the Greek figure Narcissus failed to recognize his reflection as his own. McLuhan's stated goal was to make people aware of the humanness of technology in order to lead them to exert human control over technology.

Another important concept in McLuhan's thought was that media alter the perceptual or sensory ratios of individuals and cultures, so that all media, but most important the dominant media of a historical period, emphasize either the acoustic or the visual. Ear-based oral culture and multisensory or tactile electronic media culture both emphasize the acoustic. Eye-based literate and print media cultures emphasize sight and the visual, or the sense of vision operating in isolation of the other senses. In this scheme, the three stages of history are (1) the acoustic oral communication stage, from the emergence of speech to the advent of alphabetic writing systems and the rise of literacy, (2) the visual print communication stage, from the advent of movable type and the printing press in 1450s-era Europe to that of the telegraph in 1830s-era America, and (3) the acoustic electronic communication stage, beginning with the telegraph but intensifying with the rise of film, radio, television, satellites, and computers. Acoustic and visual cultures create opposing modes of consciousness and forms of social organization, including religion, politics, economics, and the arts, the last of which interested McLuhan the most deeply. Acoustic cultures are associated with tribal and sacred cultures, participatory local and global politics, noncapitalist economies, and both traditional and nonrepresentational art, music, literature, and media. Visual cultures are characterized by a focus on the individual and the secular, representative democracy and nationalism, socialism and corporatism, and representational art, music, and literature. The message of the medium, McLuhan argued, is the way it changes individual sensory perceptions and the cultures in which one type of medium is always dominant. As mechanization of the media has intensified from the natural forms of speech and ideogrammatic language to the printing press and industrial production, and more recently to the globally integrated field of television and beyond, the media environment now retrieves elements of the tribalism of village culture on a global geographic scale, thus creating a global village.

The style and tone, as much as the substance, of McLuhan's media and social theories drew increasingly sharp reactions from media researchers and educators. His first book, *The Mechanical Bride: Folklore of Industrial Man* (1951), critically and morally protested against the effect of popular culture. Print media advertisements, he argued, degrade culture, destroy individualism, and blur the distinctions between the human and the technological. Reflecting his contact with Innis and others in Toronto, *The Gutenberg Galaxy* (published more than ten years later) offered a humanistic and literary history of the harmful effects of print culture on psychology and society. With the publication of *Understanding Media* in 1964, critics argued that McLuhan was losing his critical stance and embracing technological determinism. Although he achieved widespread recognition in the late 1960s, McLuhan's spirited attacks on the print culture methods of education and social science research in mass communication and other fields made many adversaries, whose criticisms were strengthened by his collaborative turn to unconventional book forms filled mostly with graphic elements and aphorisms and by his confrontational and arrogant demeanor. By the time of his death in 1980, McLuhan had published little new material and had fallen from serious consideration by many media scholars.

In the 1980s, publications by media ecologists Joshua Meyrowitz (1985) and Neil Postman (1985), a biography by Philip Marchand (1989), McLuhan's letters (1987), and two posthumously coauthored books (McLuhan and McLuhan, 1988; McLuhan and Powers, 1989) helped rekindle interest in McLuhan's work. The emergence of a more cohesive and humanistic turn toward studies in culture and communication, and the continuing interest in McLuhan and Innis in Canada (Babe, 2000), also helped initiate what may be considered a renaissance in McLuhan studies, including comparisons of McLuhan to the Frankfurt School (Stamps, 1995) and to an array of critical, cultural, and postmodern theorists (Stevenson, 1995; Grosswiler, 1997). McLuhan has even been characterized as a transitional postmodernist figure (Willmott, 1996). Drawing as he did from many disciplines with a focus on the whole cultural field, McLuhan remains an influential scholar and a fruitful source of study in communication and culture.

See also: CULTURE AND COMMUNICATION; INNIS,
    HAROLD ADAMS; SOCIAL CHANGE AND THE MEDIA.

Bibliography

Babe, Robert E. (2000). *Canadian Communication Thought: Ten Foundational Writers*. Toronto: University of Toronto Press.

Brantlinger, Patrick. (1983). *Bread and Circuses: Theories of Mass Culture as Social Decay*. Ithaca, NY: Cornell University Press.

Carey, James. (1968). "Harold Adams Innis and Marshall McLuhan." In *McLuhan: Pro and Con*, ed. Raymond Rosenthal. Baltimore: Penguin.

Carey, James. (1989). *Communication as Culture: Essays on Media and Society*. Boston: Unwin Hyman.

Czitrom, Daniel J. (1982). *Media and the American Mind: From Morse to McLuhan*. Chapel Hill: University of North Carolina Press.

Grosswiler, Paul. (1997). *The Method is the Message: Rethinking McLuhan Through Critical Theory*. Montreal: Black Rose Books.

Marchand, Philip. (1989). *Marshall McLuhan: The Medium and the Messenger*. New York: Ticknor & Fields.

McLuhan, Marshall. (1951). *The Mechanical Bride: Folklore of Industrial Man*. New York: Vanguard.

McLuhan, Marshall. (1962). *The Gutenberg Galaxy: The Making of Typographic Man*. Toronto: University of Toronto Press.

McLuhan, Marshall. (1964). *Understanding Media: The Extensions of Man*. New York: Mentor.

McLuhan, Marshall. (1987). *Letters of Marshall McLuhan*, eds. Matie Molinaro, Corinne McLuhan, and William Toye. Toronto: Oxford University Press.

McLuhan, Marshall, with Fiore, Quentin, and Agel, Jerome. (1967). *The Medium Is the Massage: An Inventory of Effects*. New York: Bantam.

McLuhan, Marshall, with Fiore, Quentin, and Angel, Jerome. (1968). *War and Peace in the Global Village*. New York: Bantam.

McLuhan, Marshall, with McLuhan, Eric. (1988). *Laws of Media: The New Science*. Toronto: University of Toronto Press.

McLuhan, Marshall, with Powers, Bruce. (1989). *The Global Village: Transformations in World Life and Media in the 21st Century*. New York: Oxford University Press.

Meyrowitz, Joshua. (1985). *No Sense of Place: The Impact of Electronic Media on Social Behavior*. New York: Oxford University Press.

Ong, Walter. (1982). *Orality and Literacy: The Technologizing of the Word*. New York: Methuen.

Postman, Neil. (1985). *Amusing Ourselves to Death: Public Discourse in the Age of Show Business*. New York: Penguin.

Rosenthal, Raymond, ed. (1968). *McLuhan Pro and Con*. Baltimore: Penguin.

Stamps, Judith. (1995). *Unthinking Modernity: Innis, McLuhan, and the Frankfurt School*. Montreal: McGill-Queen's University Press.

Stevenson, Nick. (1995). *Understanding Media Cultures: Social Theory and Mass Communication*. London: Sage Publications.

Theall, Donald F. (1971). *Understanding McLuhan: The Medium Is the Rear View Mirror*. Montreal: McGill-Queen's University Press.

Willmott, Glenn. (1996). *McLuhan, Or Modernism in Reverse*. Toronto: University of Toronto Press.

PAUL GROSSWILER

■ MEAD, GEORGE HERBERT (1863–1931)

Whether they know it or not, nearly every communication scholar today works with ideas that George Herbert Mead helped to develop. It was Mead who urged scholars to think of communication as a collaborative interaction rather than a sequence of thoughts, coded, sent, and received. It was Mead who described the sense of self as social rather than individual, public rather than private, and emergent rather than permanent. And it was Mead who put these new theories of self and communication to work, in the service of social and educational reform.

The American philosopher John Dewey once described Mead as "a seminal mind of the very first order." Yet Mead's contributions went unappreciated for many years after his death in 1931. By that time, philosophy had become absorbed in narrower questions of language and truth, and social psychology had embraced quantitative modes of behaviorist research. By the 1960s and 1970s, however, in sociology, social psychology, and philosophy as well as communication, Mead's work had again gathered appreciative readers. Historians of social science have come to identify him as a key figure in the development of the "Chicago School of Thought." Sociologists view him as the seminal theorist for symbolic interactionism. Pragmatist philosophers study him as an early proponent of their views, a figure of equal importance with Dewey, William James, and Charles Peirce. Phenomenological philosophers praise his interest in human consciousness. Cultural studies scholars appreciate his model of a plural, emergent, dialogical self.

This belated attention is all the more striking given how sporadic and scattered Mead's writings were. The bibliography created by the Mead Project (at the Department of Sociology at Brock Uni-

George Herbert Mead. (Library of Congress)

versity, St. Catharines, Ontario, Canada) lists 116 items, many of them book reviews, editorials, and magazine pieces. Mead himself never published a book. The well-known book-length collections of Mead's work—*The Philosophy of the Present* (1932), *Mind, Self and Society* (1934), *Movements of Thought in the Nineteenth Century* (1936), and *The Philosophy of the Act* (1938)—were all assembled from lectures, unpublished manuscripts, and the class notes of former students after his death.

Like many American social scientists of his generation, Mead had a religious upbringing. He was born in 1863 in South Hadley, Massachusetts, but spent most of his childhood in Oberlin, Ohio. His father was a Congregationalist minister who taught at Oberlin Theological Seminary from 1869 until his death in 1881. Mead's mother was an English instructor who taught at Oberlin College and at Abbot Academy in Andover, Massachusetts, and later became president of Mt. Holyoke College. Mead earned his bachelor's degree at Oberlin in 1883. After graduation, he worked briefly as a schoolteacher and then spent three years as a rail-

road surveyor. In the autumn of 1887, Mead resumed his studies, this time at Harvard University, where he met the philosophers Josiah Royce and William James. A year later, he traveled to Germany for graduate studies, first at Leipzig and then at Berlin, where his teachers would include the physiological psychologist Wilhelm Wundt and the philosopher Wilhelm Dilthey. Mead never wrote a dissertation and thus did not finish his doctorate. In 1891, he took his first university teaching position at the University of Michigan, where he met John Dewey. In 1894, when Dewey was invited to be chair of the Department of Philosophy at the University of Chicago, Mead went with him. Mead remained a professor in Chicago's Department of Philosophy until his death in 1931.

Mead resembled many American intellectuals of his generation in rejecting the idea of a fixed moral order that underlies all human experience. Theologians and philosophers had typically believed that proper human behavior could be deduced from metaphysical or natural principles. Theologians had imagined a world governed by a God-given moral code; philosophers, a world governed by an underlying rational order. But Mead thought that evolutionary biology and the practical success of the scientific method had discredited such formalist beliefs. Evolution revealed a natural world that was constantly changing and adapting. And neither philosophical nor religious dogma seemed able to solve the vexing problems confronting a rapidly industrializing, multicultural, urban society. It was science, not metaphysics, that had provided clean water, vocational education, and vaccination.

Absent any guarantees of truth, Mead thought that humans should apply the experimental methods of science to the study of society. This insistence on studying the world as it presents itself in everyday experience led Mead and others to a philosophical approach that has variously been called pragmatist, instrumentalist, or functionalist. For later generations of communication scholars, this approach would prove invaluable. By the end of the twentieth century, communication would emerge, par excellence, as the study of the specific forms and practices by which humans connect, coordinate, and imagine their relations.

Mead insisted that any analysis of human behavior should start with action rather than thought. For Mead, thinking was a biological process by which humans orient themselves to the world. Though Mead was an early proponent of what was later termed the "social construction of reality," he also was interested in prelinguistic forms of interaction. He argued that, well before they acquire language, humans participate in a "conversation of gesture" that provides their first model of interaction. This description of thought as a social, public act led, in turn, to a radically new way of talking about the self. Philosophy and religion had typically treated the self as an irreducible inner essence—as a soul or mind or power of reason. Mead argued that people should treat the individual self as one outcome of social interaction. Instead of a single, unified self, he proposed a self that contained both subjective and objective aspects, which he called an "I" and a "Me." People are an "I" when they are acting in the present moment; they are a "Me" in retrospect, as they consider the public self that they have performed for others. In short, people become who they are by imagining how others have seen them.

Mead, like Dewey, believed that all these theories would find their richest expression in a democratic society. Pragmatist philosophy encouraged democracy by promoting dialogue and experimentation, and refusing appeals to custom or authority. But the actual experiences of American democracy also shaped pragmatist philosophy. It was in the high school, the settlement house, and the union hall, as much as in the German graduate school, that Mead discerned the arts of human communication.

See also: DEWEY, JOHN; PEIRCE, CHARLES SANDERS; SOCIETY AND THE MEDIA.

Bibliography

Cook, Gary A. (1993). *George Herbert Mead: The Making of a Social Pragmatist*. Urbana: University of Illinois Press.

Dunn, Robert G. (1998). "Self, Identity, and Difference: Mead and the Poststructuralists." *Sociological Quarterly* 38:687–705.

Farr, Robert M. (1996). "George Herbert Mead: Philosopher and Social Psychologist." In *The Roots of Modern Social Psychology, 1872–1954*. Oxford, Eng.: Blackwell.

Joas, Hans. (1985). *George Herbert Mead: A Contemporary Reexamination of His Thought*. Cambridge, Eng.: Polity Press.

Mead, George Herbert. (1932). *The Philosophy of the Present*, ed. Arthur E. Murphy. LaSalle, IL: Open Court Publishing.

Mead, George Herbert. (1934). *Mind, Self and Society: From the Standpoint of a Social Behaviorist*, ed. Charles W. Morris. Chicago: University of Chicago Press.

Mead, George Herbert. (1936). *Movements of Thought in the Nineteenth Century*, ed. Merritt H. Moore. Chicago: University of Chicago Press.

Mead, George Herbert. (1938). *The Philosophy of the Act*, ed. Charles W. Morris et al. Chicago: University of Chicago Press.

Mead Project. (1999). "George's Page." <http://paradigm.soci.brocku.ca/~lward>.

Reck, Andrew J., ed. (1964). *George Herbert Mead: Selected Writings*. Chicago: University of Chicago Press.

Rucker, Darnell. (1969). *The Chicago Pragmatists*. Minneapolis: University of Minnesota Press.

Strauss, Anselm. (1956). *The Social Psychology of George Herbert Mead*. Chicago: University of Chicago Press.

JOHN J. PAULY

MEDIA EFFECTS

See: Advertising Effects; Arousal Processes and Media Effects; Catharsis Theory and Media Effects; Cultivation Theory and Media Effects; Cumulative Media Effects; Desensitization and Media Effects; Election Campaigns and Media Effects; Mood Effects and Media Exposure; News Effects; Nutrition and Media Effects; Parental Mediation of Media Effects; Social Cognitive Theory and Media Effects; Sports and Media Effects; Tobacco and Media Effects

MEDIA INDUSTRIES, GLOBALIZATION OF

See: Globalization of Media Industries

MÉLIÈS, GEORGES (1861–1938)

Born in Paris in 1861, the third child of a successful boot manufacturer, Georges Méliès showed interest in the visual arts of drawing, caricature, painting, and sculpture from childhood. As a young man, he briefly entered the family trade and worked with the shop machinery. He later said, "I was born an artist in my soul, very skilled with my hands, capable of inventing things and a comedian by nature. I was at once an intellectual and a manual worker." His knowledge of mechanics combined with his artistic talents later led him to undertake scenic and machinery design for the theater and films.

During an 1884 stay in London, Méliès was first attracted to the world of stage illusion. He returned to Paris in 1885, but rather than reentering the family business, he continued the study of painting and drawing. He married his first wife, Eugénie Genin, the same year. Their children, Georgette and André, were born in 1888 and 1901, respectively.

When Méliès's father, Louis, retired in 1888, Méliès sold his inherited share of the footwear business to his two older brothers and bought the famous, but run-down, Théatre Robert-Houdin from the widow of the famous magician for whom it was named. Over the next ten years, he created at least thirty illusions for the theater, many of which he later recast into motion-picture effects.

It is likely that Méliès attended the first public film screening in Paris by the Lumière brothers (Auguste and Louis) on December 28, 1895. He bought a projector and began to show films at the Théatre Robert-Houdin in April 1896.

Between 1896 and 1900, Méliès started to develop the film genres and technical approaches that he would explore throughout his filmmaking career, which peaked between 1901 and 1904 and ended in 1912. Unlike the Lumière cameramen, who chose outdoor locations for their documentary style of production, Méliès selected a closed, interior space in which to compose his "artificially arranged scenes." This practice anticipated that of the great studios at the height of the film industry. He built the first permanent film studio and created the first company solely dedicated to producing films, the Star Film Company. He may have been the only filmmaker to use artificial light as early as 1897.

A perfectionist, Méliès worked meticulously on all aspects of production. He devised effects, designed period costumes, and drew backgrounds before writing a scenario to guide the action. In addition to handling logistical details, Méliès often joined with friends and family to act in his own films. His daughter, Georgette, who acted as a child, later became, perhaps, the world's first female camera operator. Although demanding, Méliès was concerned for the well-being of his actors and technicians; he was active in theatrical and motion-picture trade organizations throughout his career.

Shaky finances caused Méliès to return to the stage in 1910 and to leave filmmaking two years later. His wife, Eugénie, died in 1913, after a long illness. In 1917, during World War I, his film studio at Montreuil became a hospital for the war-wounded. Méliès and his family staged variety shows after that in a second studio converted into a theater. He remarried in 1925, to Jehanne d'Alcy, a former actress and Méliès's mistress of many years. The two sold toys and candy at a small shop in the Gare Montparnasse. Méliès published his reminiscences in 1926 and made his last public appearance in 1929 at a gala retrospective of his work at the Salle Pleyel. The following year, his daughter Georgette died. In 1931, Méliès was awarded the Legion of Honor and hailed by Louis Lumière as "the creator of cinematic spectacles." In 1932 he, his wife, and his granddaughter were given lodging at an estate owned by an organization for people who had been involved with motion pictures. He died of cancer on January 21, 1938, and is buried in the Père Lachaise cemetery in Paris.

During his career, Méliès completed some 498 films. Many vanished or were destroyed during his lifetime. Some prints were recycled for their silver content during World War I, with the celluloid made, ironically, into boot heels for soldiers. Other film copies disappeared when the Théatre Robert-Houdin was demolished in 1923. In the 1950s, however, thirty-three lost prints of Méliès films were rediscovered in the U.S. Library of Congress, preserved as rolled paper contact sheets submitted for copyright. A collection sold by Méliès's brother, Gaston, to the Vitagraph Company and privately held for many years added an additional thirty films that had been thought missing. In all, 137 Méliès films are known to have survived.

Méliès is best known for creating a vocabulary of special-effects photography, based on his stage illusions, that manipulates time and space. He first used stop-substitution, his single most important cinematic contribution, in *The Vanishing Lady* (1896); double exposure in *The Cabinet of Mephistopheles* (1897); reversed action in *A Dinner*

The French cinematographer Georges Méliès plays the role of a magician in one of his early films. (Hulton-Deutsch Collection/Corbis)

Under Difficulties (1898); and an early matte shot in *A Mysterious Portrait* (1898).

Méliès refined these techniques in hundreds of short fantasy films; his most famous, *A Voyage to the Moon* (1902), spread his name around the world. He explored other genres from historical recreation to political films. *The Dreyfus Affair* (1899) was probably the first film serial as well as the first film censored for political reasons. He also pioneered the "stag" film by feigning nudity in *After the Ball* (1897). It is possible that *Cinderella* (1899) alerted Cecil B. DeMille to the possibilities of spectacle, which he later became known for in Hollywood.

Early biographers and film historians saw Méliès's contribution to film as primitive and evolutionary toward the style that was later practiced by D. W. Griffith. Méliès's work was criticized for having no developed story line, only a series of scenes; for using only one camera angle; and for the technical impreciseness of mismatched edits. However, less-biased analysis examines Méliès's work from its own singular perspective. For Méliès, story line was always the finishing touch in a creative process, not the core. He started with a series of illusions costumed and set in an appropriate period. His editing process highlighted magical effect or comprehensive point-of-view, not narrative flow. In one instance, Méliès cut film to show a vehicle crashing through a building twice from two different perspectives; that way, his audience could see the reactions of those outside the building as well as those within the building. To Méliès, the stuttering effect of such reiteration on the narrative was not a concern. Although his camera remained physically stationary, Méliès simulated camera movement by shifting the visual perspective of scenes in his background painting. Scholars now acknowledge that Méliès's unique exploration and presentation of cinematic space is essentially different from films of the period that used three-dimensional space.

See also: FILM INDUSTRY, HISTORY OF; GRIFFITH, D. W.; LUMIÈRE, AUGUSTE/LUMIÈRE, LOUIS.

Bibliography

Frazer, John. (1979). *Artificially Arranged Scenes: The Films of Georges Méliès*. Boston: G. K. Hall.

Gaudreault, André. (1987). "Theatricality, Narrativity, and Trickality: Reevaluating the Cinema of Georges Méliès." *Journal of Popular Film and Television* 15(3):110–119.

TED C. JONES

◼ MILLS, C. WRIGHT (1916–1962)

Charles Wright Mills grew up in Dallas in a thoroughly bourgeois family. His father was an insurance agency manager—one of the petty office workers that Mills would later identify as the new proletariat in his book *White Collar* (1951). After graduating from the University of Texas at Austin and flirting with a career as a car salesman, Mills went, in 1939, to graduate school at the University of Wisconsin. There he met his mentor and later collaborator, Hans Gerth, who introduced Mills to the work of classic European sociologists, in particular Max Weber. In addition to Weber, Gerth, as a German émigré and former member of the Frankfurt School, exposed Mills to the latest European neo-Marxist sociological thought. After his first teaching job at the University of Maryland, Mills moved to Columbia University in 1946, where he stayed until his death.

His most important books, in addition to *White Collar*, are *The Power Elite* (1956) and *Sociological Imagination* (1959). The basic theme of Mills's work is how power permeates every aspect of American society and how it is the duty of the critical sociologist to expose how power has compromised individual freedom. Many of his critics and supporters have emphasized the European elements in Mills's work. While it is certainly true that Gerth's influence had a decisive impact on Mills, fundamentally his thought is built on an American foundation, especially the work of Thorstein Veblen, and the American Pragmatists: Charles Peirce, William James, and John Dewey.

The core of Mills's sociological outlook is his concept of a mass society and its relationship to authority. In his book *The Power Elite*, he identified the American power elite as an alliance of political, military, and industrial leaders. Mills did not suggest that this elite acted in a conspiratorial manner. He argued that the members of the elite, because they were raised in similar social circumstances and went to the same privileged schools, were predisposed to think alike. Hence, their exercising of power was inevitably linked, if not explicitly coordinated.

What makes Mills's critique so radical, and powerful, is that he describes the power elite's relationship to the powerless majority by identifying the role of the mass media in maintaining the power structure. The sociologist asserted that the majority of the nation's citizens had been reduced to a politically inactive and uninformed mass, creating a mass society. According to Mills, in the past, America was directed by numerous groups of politically literate and active citizens. He referred to this decentralized society as a community of publics. The arrival of mass communications changed this liberal political culture. Mills admitted that the United State was never an ideal community of publics, nor had the mass society of the mid-twentieth century completely eliminated all vestiges of an informed and active public. Yet, in his view, by the 1950s the balance had shifted decisively toward the mass society.

To illustrate this shift, Mills described four distinguishing characteristics of a mass society. The first was the ratio of opinion givers to receivers. In a mass society, the number of opinion givers was limited while mass communication dramatically increased the number of opinion receivers. Thus, the sociological meaning of mass communication was the ability of authority to centralize and control information distribution. An additional attribute of the mass society was that the ability of the opinion receivers, or the masses, to reply was limited. Mills believed that the technology of mass communications had imposed uniformity upon opinion givers by concentrating them in mass media corporations while simultaneously rendering the opinion receivers mute.

The third characteristic of the mass society was that authority also controlled the institutions (e.g., legislative bodies, corporate boards, and the courts) that translated opinion into policy. Mills further argued that the inability of the mass society to respond to opinion and to influence public policy psychologically affected the individual. This social–psychological trait was highlighted in what he saw as the fourth distinguishing trait of a mass society—the "penetration" of the masses and their total lack of autonomy. By "penetration,"

Mills meant the ability of the elite to control virtually every aspect of the lives of the mass of the people by monopolizing the institutions of society.

Mills used Fascist and Communist societies as extreme examples of penetration. However, he also claimed that the power elite of the United States had penetrated American society and that the elite did not have to rely on crude and violent authoritarian measures. The elite's control of the mass media, combined with the vast scale of modern communications, allowed authority to psychologically manipulate the minds of the masses. In *The Power Elite*, Mills explained that the media of the 1950s—primarily television and radio—created a kind of "psychological illiteracy" where the "man of the masses" became dependent on the media for an understanding of the world. He argued that what was so insidious about this penetration of the minds of the masses was that most Americans developed their "identity and aspirations" from the media, as well as their conceptions of the outside world. Thus, Mills implied that contemporary American political culture was inherently, albeit by relatively subtle means, totalitarian.

There is an ironic nostalgia running throughout Mills's radical critique of modern society. His writings suggest that modern technological developments have enabled the elite to expand their power. Yet Mills did not idealize the past. Like Weber, Mills recognized that the preindustrial world was inefficient and ultimately unsustainable. Although he accepted the inevitably of the development of the modern world of mass industry and culture, Mills hoped that a critical intellectual tradition could point out the dangers that came with this historical progression. With an optimism that contrasted strongly with his pessimistic historical outlook, Mills believed that critical intellectuals like him could speak for the powerless masses.

One could argue that Mills was too optimistic about the ability of the critical intellectual to influence public policy and too pessimistic about the prospects of future technological development. His concept of a mass society was based on the technology of the 1950s. More than fifty years later, it appears that the technology of mass communication may be equalizing the ratio of opinion givers to opinion receivers through innovations such as the Internet. Nevertheless, despite the fact that the technological parameters of mass communication have changed dramatically since Mills's death, his

C. Wright Mills. (Archive Photos)

warnings about the tendency of the elite to concentrate their power institutionally is still very relevant in the era of the multinational corporation.

See also: CULTURE AND COMMUNICATION; CULTURE INDUSTRIES, MEDIA AS; DEWEY, JOHN; GLOBALIZATION OF CULTURE THROUGH THE MEDIA; PEIRCE, CHARLES SANDERS; SOCIETY AND THE MEDIA; WEBER, MAX.

Bibliography

Gerth, Hans. H., and Mills, C. Wright, eds. (1946). *From Max Weber: Essays in Sociology.* New York: Oxford University Press.

Gillman, Richard. (1975). "C. Wright Mills and the Politics of Truth: *The Power Elite* Revisited." *American Quarterly* 27:461–479.

Horowitz, Irving Louis. (1983). *C. Wright Mills: An American Utopian.* New York: Free Press.

Mills, C. Wright. (1951). *White Collar: The American Middle Class.* New York: Oxford University Press.

Mills, C. Wright. (1956). *The Power Elite.* New York: Oxford University Press.

Mills, C. Wright. (1959). *The Sociological Imagination.* New York: Oxford University Press.

Mills, C. Wright. (1963). *Power, Politics and People: The Collected Essays of C. Wright Mills.* New York: Oxford University Press.

Tillman, Rick. (1984). *C. Wright Mills: A Native Radical and His American Intellectual Roots.* University Park: Pennsylvania State University Press.

ROBERT FABER

▣ MINORITIES AND THE MEDIA

The topic of race and ethnicity in the media has generated a wealth of research attention. In general, analyses of media portrayals show a great deal of variability both across time and across types of media content. These variations are reflected in studies of racial differences in use and enjoyment of media offerings, and are also evident in research exploring potential effects that media portrayals may have on the attitudes and beliefs that viewers hold about race.

Portrayals of Race and Ethnicity

In the late 1960s, Cedric Clark (1969) characterized the typical ways that minorities are featured in the media by identifying four distinct stages of portrayals. The first stage, labeled "nonrecognition," referred to the idea that initially, people of color are generally ignored by the media and are rarely seen in any type of portrayal. The second stage, "ridicule," referred to negative and stereotypical media images. The third stage, "regulation," referred to the portrayal of minorities in roles upholding social order or protecting the status quo (e.g., police officers, military). The final stage, "respect," referred to portrayals including a diversity of images, both positive and negative, that parallel characterizations of Caucasians. To what extent do these stages accurately describe images of race and ethnicity in recent media content? The answer to this question largely depends on the racial or ethnic group in question and the type of media content under consideration.

Frequency of Portrayals

The percentages of minority characters on television have increased dramatically over the last several decades, largely due to an increase in the portrayal of African Americans. For example, Bradley Greenberg and Larry Collette (1997) content analyzed the major characters who appeared on new television programs from 1966 to 1992. Across these years, the percentage of African-American characters increased from 6 percent in the 1960s to 14 percent in the 1990s. In contrast, virtually no new Asian or Hispanic characters were introduced in the 1990s. These results parallel those reported by Robert Kubey (1995) in his analysis of character appearance on network and cable stations. In his study, Caucasians accounted for 81 percent of all appearances, African Americans 9 percent, Hispanics 7 percent, and Asians 2 percent—with the remainder being coded as "other." Together, these studies suggest that television content at the beginning of the twenty-first century features a frequency of African-American portrayals that closely approximates population proportions, but continues to underrepresent other minorities including Hispanics, Asians, and Native Americans.

In addition to examining frequencies of portrayals in general, many analyses have also explored representation within specific genres, programs, or networks. For example, content analyses during the 1970s tended to report that although African Americans accounted for almost 10 percent of all characters, these appearances were extremely segregated and were almost entirely confined to situation comedies featuring all-black casts. Similar racial segregation continues to be apparent in television content. Kubey (1995) reported that although African Americans represented 11 percent of all characters appearing on cable television, this figure dropped to 6.6 percent when the Black Entertainment Network (BET) was excluded from the analysis. Similarly, the representation of Hispanic characters was almost entirely confined to Spanish-language channels; when those channels were excluded, Hispanic characters represented less than 3 percent of all appearances.

In terms of specific genres, many researchers have voiced particular concerns about the lack of minority representation in children's television programming. For example, Bradley Greenberg and Jeffrey Brand (1993) noted that only two of the twenty programs they examined contained regularly appearing African-American characters, only one featured a regularly appearing Hispanic character, and none featured Asian or Native American characters. These results parallel the earlier analysis by Francis Barcus (1993) of children's programs, which reported that only 18 percent of programming scenes featured interactions between Caucasian and minority children.

In addition to portrayals in entertainment, depictions of race in news content have received considerable attention by many researchers. For example, the analysis by Robert Entman (1990) of local television news in Chicago found that among all stories featuring African Americans, 41 percent of the air time was devoted to issues of violent crime. In contrast, portrayals of minorities in more-positive roles such as newsmakers appear to be less common. For example, David Dodd, Barbara Foerch, and Heather Anderson (1988) examined the covers of *Time* and *Newsweek* from 1953 to 1987. Of all primary individuals featured on the covers of these magazines, only 6.6 percent were racial minorities, and only one cover featured a Hispanic individual. In addition, among the sixty-one "Man of the Year" awards selected during that period, only two featured racial minorities.

Finally, analyses of minority representation in advertising reveals patterns of portrayals that mirror many of the trends found in programming content. That is, despite increases in the frequency of minority representation over the years, the prominence of the portrayals continues to lag behind that of Caucasians. For example, the content analysis by Robert Wilkes and Humberto Valencia (1989) of advertising during prime-time network programming revealed that approximately 6 percent of all commercials contained Hispanic models, and 27 percent contained African-American models. However, approximately 70 percent of all minority portrayals were contained in minor or background roles as opposed to major roles such as spokesperson. Similar findings were reported by Charles Taylor and Barbara Stern (1997) in their analysis of Asian Americans in network advertising. Although the total proportion of Asian characters in the commercials (8.4%) exceeded population proportions, the majority of Asian characters appeared only in minor or background roles.

Nature of Portrayals

In addition to exploring the frequency of media portrayals, a great deal of research has explored the manner in which minority characters are depicted. Earlier analyses of television content tended to report very negative and stereotypical images of minorities. In general, minority characters were often depicted as younger than Caucasians, as less likely to be employed in high-prestige occupations, and as more likely to be impoverished and from broken families. However, more recent analyses of prime-time programming suggest trends toward more-positive portrayals, at least among African-American characters. For example, the content analysis by Carolyn Stroman, Bishetta Merritt, and Paula

Matabane (1988) of prime-time programming showed that the majority of African-American characters were portrayed as middle- or upper-class (73%), with the most-frequent occupations being professional (22%) or law enforcement (38%) roles. In addition, the majority of African-American characters (60%) were thirty-five years old or older, and most (60%) were characterized as members of families.

Though depictions in fictional program content appear to have shown considerable improvement from earlier decades, recent analyses of nonfiction content continue to report disparities in the portrayal of minorities versus Caucasians, and particularly so for depictions of crime and violence. In contrast to analyses of fictional crime programs that tend to find an underrepresentation of minorities as criminal suspects, analyses of news content tend to report that people of color are overrepresented as criminals. For example, Travis Dixon and Daniel Linz (2000) content analyzed a random sample of local television newscasts in the Los Angeles area for their portrayals of criminal activity and crime victimization. In general, African Americans were more than twice as likely to be portrayed as perpetrators than as victims of crime, whereas Caucasians were more likely to be portrayed as victims than as perpetrators. In addition, comparisons with actual, local crime statistics recorded during the same time period revealed that African Americans were underrepresented as crime victims and overrepresented as crime perpetrators in the news, whereas Caucasians were overrepresented as victims and underrepresented as perpetrators. Latinos were generally underrepresented as both victims and as perpetuators, suggesting a general underreporting of events within the Latino community.

Similar patterns of racial portrayals have also been reported in a related type of entertainment programming; reality-based police shows. These programs such as *Cops* and *America's Most Wanted* blur the distinction between fiction and news, but typically employ video footage or reenactments of actual crimes. The content analysis by Mary Beth Oliver (1994) of these shows revealed that 77 percent of African-American characters and 89 percent of Hispanic characters were portrayed as criminal suspects rather than police officers, compared to only 38 percent of Caucasian characters. In addition, African-American and Hispanic criminal suspects were more likely than Caucasian criminal suspects to be the recipient of police aggression, even after controlling for the type of crime portrayed and the use of aggression by the criminal suspect. Similar patterns of portrayals were also noted by Robert Entman (1992, 1994) in his analyses of national television news and local television news coverage in Chicago. Specifically, Entman reported that African-American suspects were more likely than Caucasian suspects to be shown as poorly dressed and as physically held or restrained by police officers, suggesting that they were more dangerous or "criminal."

Responses by Minorities to Media Portrayals of Minorities

Given that many media portrayals of race feature less-than-flattering images, how might minority viewers react to such depictions? Although at first glance it might seem that minorities would simply "tune out" and consume significantly less media content than would Caucasian viewers, overall viewing frequencies suggest that the reverse is actually the case, particularly among African-American viewers. In general, Nielsen Media Research (1998) reports that African-American households watch approximately two more hours of prime-time programming per week than do all other households combined, and five more hours of daytime programming per week. Similarly, Hispanic households watch approximately seven more hours of total television programming per week than do all other households, though this difference is largely attributable to a larger number of family members in Hispanic homes.

Although African Americans and Hispanics appear to view television more frequently than do Caucasians, these groups tend to view very different types of programming. While top-rated prime time and syndicated programs for non–African American households tend to feature predominantly Caucasian characters (e.g., *Seinfeld, Friends, Home Improvement*), top-rated programs among African-American households tend to feature a greater preponderance of African-American characters (e.g., *Living Single, Martin, Family Matters*). Similarly, Spanish-language programming receives the highest viewer ratings in Hispanic households.

These differences in viewing patterns are consistent with numerous studies examining the responses of viewers to media characters. In gen-

eral, research suggests that viewers attend more-closely to and have more-favorable impressions of characters in their own racial or ethnic group. Similarly, African-American children are more likely than Caucasian children to want to emulate African-American characters featured in the media. For example, Bradley Greenberg and Charles Atkin (1982) reported that while African-American and Caucasian elementary children were equally likely to agree that they wanted to "be like" a variety of white characters, a significantly larger percentage of African-American children (37%) than Caucasian children (11%) identified with black characters. Similar differences have also been reported among adult samples and for other types of media content, such as advertising. For example, the review by Tommy Whittler (1991) of the responses viewers had to commercials suggested that black viewers tended to respond more favorably and to better recall advertisements when the advertisements featured African Americans than when they did not.

Although minorities generally show more interest and more-favorable attitudes toward same-race media portrayals, there has been some concern about the potential harmful effect of overall television viewing on minority viewers and particularly on children. Specifically, given that the more-general media landscape tends to underrepresent people of color and to frequently feature stereotypical portrayals, there may be reason to suspect that frequent viewing could lead to lower levels of self-esteem or feelings of self-worth. However, the review by Sherryl Browne Graves (1993) of related research revealed mixed support for this hypothesized influence, at least among African-American children. While some studies suggested negative impacts of stereotypical images on black children's self-concepts, other studies reported that any portrayal (positive or negative) of African Americans increased favorable attitudes among black children. Similar results were also reported by Federico Subervi-Vélez and Juan Necochea (1990) in their survey of Hispanic elementary school children in California. Contrary to predictions, overall television viewing was marginally associated with more-positive self-concept scores, and viewing of Spanish-language television was unrelated to self-concept.

While the effects of media viewing on self-concept are not clear-cut, these mixed findings should not be interpreted as suggesting that minorities are satisfied with media portrayals. For example, Ronald Faber, Thomas O'Guinn, and Timothy Meyer (1987) surveyed Caucasians, Hispanics, and African Americans in the Chicago area concerning their television viewing habits and their perceptions of media portrayals of race. Hispanic and African-American respondents were significantly more likely than Caucasian respondents to believe that Hispanics and African Americans were underrepresented in the media. In addition, heavier viewing among African-American and Hispanic respondents was associated with more-negative perceptions of racial portrayals. Similar indications of disapproval were reported by Debra Merskin (1998) in her survey of Native American college students. Approximately two-thirds of the respondents in her sample reported dissatisfaction with television programming aimed at both child and adult audiences.

Effects on Caucasian Viewers

In contrast to studies employing minority samples, most media research employing Caucasian samples specifically has focused on the ways in which media images of race may increase negative attitudes and stereotyping. In this regard, some researchers have employed a cultivation perspective to examine the influences of television on the beliefs that viewers hold about racial minorities. For example, Blake Armstrong, Kimberly Neuendorf, and James Brentar (1992) reasoned that exposure to different types of media programming would be related to the perceptions that viewers had of African-American socioeconomic status. Consistent with predictions, viewing of fictional programming was related to estimates that African Americans enjoy higher socioeconomic positions, whereas exposure to news programming was related to estimates that African Americans are relatively worse off economically compared to Caucasians.

This type of cultivation perspective has also been employed to examine nonfiction content and crime-related beliefs about racial minorities. For example, Mary Beth Oliver and Blake Armstrong (1998) surveyed white respondents about their beliefs of the prevalence of African-American and Caucasian involvement in crime. While greater viewing of both reality-based and fictional police programs predicted higher estimates of crime

involvement for both racial groups, reality-based viewing was associated with greater increases in estimates for African-American than Caucasian involvement. These authors interpreted their findings as reflecting the typically more-incriminating portrayals of African Americans in reality-based than fictional crime programming.

In addition to exploring the ways in which media exposure can gradually cultivate attitudes and beliefs about race, other researchers have explored the idea that negative media images of African Americans can prime (or bring to mind) negative thoughts that can, in turn, affect subsequent perceptions of individuals. Thomas Ford (1997) demonstrated this type of priming effect in an experiment in which white participants viewed television comedy skits that featured either neutral portrayals of African-American characters or stereotypical portrayals (e.g., poor, unemployed, and so on). In a subsequent task, participants read a brief description of a crime story that featured either an African-American or a Caucasian suspect. Ratings of the likely guilt of the African-American suspect were significantly higher among those participants who had viewed the stereotyped videos than among those who had viewed the neutral videos, whereas ratings of guilt for the Caucasian suspect were unaffected by the video portrayals.

In addition to suggesting that television viewing can lead to negative racial stereotypes under some conditions, research also suggests that the racial stereotypes held by viewers can influence the ways in which viewers understand, interpret, or react to racial images presented in the media. Research from this perspective typically makes the assumption that the responses that viewers have to media are not uniform, and that much of the variation in responses reflects different attitudes and beliefs that act as a "filter" of media messages. In terms of race-related issues, research from this perspective has examined a variety of attitudinal or belief "filters" that may affect the reactions of viewers, including racial prejudice, punitiveness about crime, and authoritarianism. In general, these studies show that viewers tend to interpret or remember media portrayals in ways that are consistent with or that reinforce their existing attitudes or beliefs about race. For example, Neil Vidmar and Milton Rokeach (1974) examined the responses to the award-winning television program *All in the Family*. Although this program was designed to expose and condemn racism, Vidmar and Rokeach found that viewers had very different perceptions of the program that varied as a function of their racial attitudes. In particular, viewers scoring lower on racial prejudice tended to interpret the program and the primary characters in ways consistent with the intentions of the producers, whereas viewers scoring higher on racial prejudice tended to interpret the program and the characters as more sympathetic to racially prejudiced attitudes.

The aforementioned line of research concerning interpretations of media content implies that attempts to use media to reduce racial stereotyping may meet with considerable challenges. However, some research, particularly with children, suggests that under some circumstances, favorable portrayals of race may lead to beneficial or prosocial outcomes. For example, the review by Robert Liebert and Joyce Sprafkin (1988) of research on the effects of multiracial portrayals in *Sesame Street* suggests that positive portrayals can lead to a host of benefits, including greater acceptance of, identification with, and desire to interact with racial minorities.

Conclusion

The frequency and nature of media images of race has experienced a great deal of positive change since the early days of the television. However, the most noteworthy changes have occurred for fictional portrayals of African-American characters. Other minorities remain largely ignored by the media or cast in minor or often negative roles. These types of portrayals (or lack thereof) are associated not only with differential viewing preferences among racial groups, but also with the potential danger of increasing racial prejudice and stereotyping among Caucasian viewers. Certainly, much additional research is needed to examine how media portrayals can work toward increasing racial harmony rather than creating or sustaining stereotypes.

See also: CULTIVATION THEORY AND MEDIA EFFECTS; NEWS EFFECTS; SESAME STREET.

Bibliography

Armstrong, G. Blake; Neuendorf, Kimberly A.; and Brentar, James E. (1992). "TV Entertainment, News, and Racial Perceptions of College Students." *Journal of Communication* 42(3):153–176.

Barcus, Francis Earle. (1983). *Images of Life on Children's Television.* New York: Praeger.

Clark, Cedric C. (1969). "Television and Social Controls: Some Observations on the Portrayals of Ethnic Minorities." *Television Quarterly* 8(2):18–22.

Dixon, Travis L., and Linz, Daniel. (2000). "Race and the Misrepresentation of Victimization on Local Television News." *Communication Research* 27:547–573.

Dodd, David, K.; Foerch, Barbara, J.; and Anderson, Heather, T. (1988). "Content Analysis of Women and Racial Minorities as News Magazine Cover Persons." *Journal of Social Behavior and Personality* 3:231–236.

Entman, Robert M. (1990). "Modern Racism and the Images of Blacks in Local Television News." *Critical Studies in Mass Communication* 7:332–345.

Entman, Robert M. (1992). "Blacks in the News: Television, Modern Racism, and Cultural Change." *Journalism Quarterly* 69:341–361.

Entman, Robert M. (1994). "Representation and Reality in the Portrayal of Blacks on Network Television News." *Journalism Quarterly* 71:509–520.

Faber, Ronald J.; O'Guinn, Thomas C.; and Meyer, Timothy P. (1987). "Televised Portrayals of Hispanics: A Comparison of Ethnic Perceptions." *International Journal of Intercultural Relations* 11:155–169.

Ford, Thomas E. (1997). "Effects of Stereotypical Television Portrayals of African-Americans on Person Perception." *Social Psychology Quarterly* 60:266–275.

Graves, Sherryl Browne. (1993). "Television, the Portrayal of African Americans, and the Development of Children's Attitudes." In *Children & Television: Images in a Changing Sociocultural World,* eds. Gordon L. Berry and Joy Keiko Asamen. Newbury Park, CA: Sage Publications.

Greenberg, Bradley S., and Atkin, Charles. (1982). "Learning about Minorities from Television: A Research Agenda." In *Television and the Socialization of the Minority Child,* eds. Gorden L. Berry and Claudia Mitchell-Kernan. New York: Academic Press.

Greenberg, Bradley S., and Brand, Jeffrey E. (1993). "Cultural Diversity on Saturday Morning Television." In *Children & Television: Images in a Changing Sociocultural World,* eds. Gordon L. Berry and Joy Keiko Asamen. Newbury Park, CA: Sage Publications.

Greenberg, Bradley S., and Collette, Larry. (1997). "The Changing Faces on TV: A Demographic Analysis of Network Television's New Seasons, 1966–1992." *Journal of Broadcasting & Electronic Media* 41:1–13.

Kubey, Robert. (1995). "Demographic Diversity on Cable: Have the New Cable Channels Made a Difference in the Representation of Gender, Race, and Age?" *Journal of Broadcasting & Electronic Media* 39:459–471.

Liebert, Robert M., and Sprafkin, Joyce. (1988). *The Early Window: Effects of Television on Children and Youth*, 3rd edition. New York: Pergamon Press.

Merskin, Debra. (1998). "Sending Up Signals: A Survey of Native American Media Use and Representation in the Mass Media." *Howard Journal of Communications* 9:333–345.

Nielsen Media Research. (1988). *1988 Report on Television*. New York: Nielsen Media Research.

Oliver, Mary Beth. (1994). "Portrayals of Crime, Race, and Aggression in 'Reality-Based' Police Shows: A Content Analysis." *Journal of Broadcasting & Electronic Media* 38:179–192.

Oliver, Mary Beth, and Armstrong, G. Blake. (1998). "The Color of Crime: Perceptions of Caucasians' and African Americans' Involvement in Crime." In *Entertaining Crime: Television Reality Programs*, eds. Mark Fishman and Gray Cavender. New York: Aldine de Gruyter.

Stroman, Carolyn A.; Merritt, Bishetta; and Matabane, Paula. (1988). "Twenty Years Later: The Portrayal of Blacks on Prime-Time Television." Paper presented at the Annual Conference of the Association for Education in Journalism and Mass Communication, Portland, OR.

Subervi-Vélez, Federico A., and Necochea, Juan. (1990). "Television Viewing and Self-Concept Among Hispanic American Children: A Pilot Study." *Howard Journal of Communications* 2:315–329.

Taylor, Charles R., and Stern, Barbara B. (1997). "Asian-Americans: Television Advertising and the 'Model Minority Stereotype.'" *Journal of Advertising* 16(2):47–61.

Whittler, Tommy E. (1991). "The Effects of Actors' Race in Commercial Advertising: Review and Extension." *Journal of Advertising* 20(1):54–60.

Vidmar, Neil, and Rokeach, Milton. (1974). "Archie Bunker's Bigotry: A Study in Selective Perception and Exposure." *Journal of Communication* 24(1):36–47.

Wilkes, Robert E., and Valencia, Humberto. (1989). "Hispanics and Blacks in Television Commercials." *Journal of Advertising* 18(1):19–25.

MARY BETH OLIVER
DANA R. BROUSSARD

■ MODELS OF COMMUNICATION

Models are representations. There are model airplanes, mathematical models, and models of buildings. In each case, the model is designed to provide a simplified view of some more complex object, phenomenon, or process, so that fundamental properties or characteristics can be high-

FIGURE 1. *Aristotelian view of communication.*

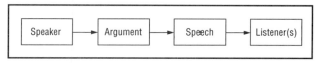

lighted and examined. Models highlight some features that their designers believe are particularly critical, and there is less focus on other features. Thus, by examining models, one learns not only about the object, situation, or process, but also about the perspective of the designer.

In communication study, models function in this same way, allowing for the simplification of complex dynamics to help scholars and students better understand the components and processes that are involved. As with other models, communication models also provide important insights into the perspectives of the designers.

One of the first scholars to examine the communication process in terms of its component parts was Aristotle (385–322 B.C.E.), who characterized communication (then called "rhetoric") in terms of an orator (i.e., a speaker) constructing an argument to be presented in a speech to an audience (i.e., listeners). This view is illustrated in visual form in Figure 1. This Aristotelian view of communication usefully highlighted the perspectives of communication thinkers until the mid-twentieth century.

In the late 1940s, and through the 1950s and 1960s, a number of new communication models were advanced. Many of the new models preserved the basic themes of the Aristotelian perspective. In 1949, Claude Shannon and Warren Weaver published a model that they called the "Mathematical Model of Communication." Based on their research with telephones and telephonic communication, the model also used boxes and arrows to represent the communication process. However, their view was more complex. They began with the "information source" box and then, using arrows as the connections, progressed on to boxes for the "transmitter," the "channel," the "receiver," and, finally, the "destination."

Box-and-arrow models of communication, of which there have been many over the years, emphasize the components of communication (e.g., a sender, message, and receiver) and the direction of influence. Where arrows go from left to right, that is, from a sender to a receiver, the

FIGURE 2. *"Sawtooth" communication model.*

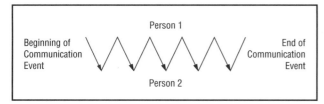

FIGURE 3. *Group communication model.*

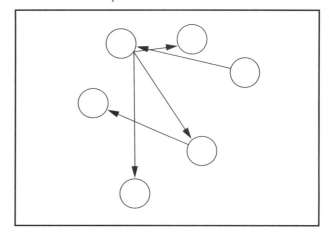

implication is that it is the sender who, through messages or speeches, brings about communication influences on the receiver.

Other models, including a helical–spiral model developed by Frank Dance (1967), a circular model proposed by Lee Thayer (1968), and a "sawtooth" model advanced by Paul Watzlawick, Janet Beavin, and Don Jackson (1967), emphasized the dynamic and evolutionary nature of the communication process rather than the components or the directions of influence.

A "sawtooth" model that is similar to the sort advanced by Watzlawick, Beavin, and Jackson (1967) is shown in Figure 2. The lines represent messages that are exchanged during the course of a communication event. The downward lines with arrows represent messages sent by Person 1, while the upward lines represent messages initiated by Person 2. A model of this sort highlights the communication process, dynamics, and history, while it minimizes the emphasis on direction of influence.

Other types of models that have become popular emphasize communication networks—the flow of messages among individuals in a group or organization, for example. Such a model for a hypothetical group is depicted in Figure 3. Each circle represents an individual, and the arrows denote messages.

Communication models serve to clarify the nature of communication, to provide a guide for research, and to offer a means of displaying research findings. Such models are a tool by which scholars, practitioners, and students can illustrate their thinking about what they consider to be the most important aspects of communication.

See also: EVOLUTION OF COMMUNICATION; GROUP COMMUNICATION; INSTRUCTIONAL COMMUNICATION; INTERPERSONAL COMMUNICATION; NETWORKS AND COMMUNICATION; NONVERBAL COMMUNICATION; ORGANIZATIONAL COMMUNICATION; PARADIGM AND COMMUNICATION.

Bibliography

Aristotle. (1954). *Rhetoric and Poetics*, tr. Robert W. Rhys. New York: Random House.

Dance, Frank E. X. (1967). *Human Communication Theory: Original Essays*. New York: Holt.

Ruben, Brent D., and Stewart, Lea P. (1998). *Communication and Human Behavior*, 4th edition. Needham Heights, MA: Allyn & Bacon.

Schramm, Wilbur. (1954). *The Process and Effects of Mass Communication*. Urbana: University of Illinois Press.

Shannon, Claude E., and Weaver, Warren. (1949). *The Mathematical Theory of Communication*. Urbana: University of Illinois Press

Thayer, Lee. (1968). *Communication and Communication Systems*. Homewood, IL: Irwin.

Watzlawick, Paul; Beavin, Janet H.; and Jackson, Don D. (1967). *Pragmatics of Human Communication*. New York: W. W. Norton.

BRENT D. RUBEN

▮ MOOD EFFECTS AND MEDIA EXPOSURE

Moods are generally considered to be similar to acute emotions but characterized by lower excitatory intensity, longer experiential duration, and greater diffuseness in terms of both causal circumstances and motivational implications. Nico Frijda (1993) considers the motivational nonspecificity of moods to be their primary defining property. Acute emotions, such as fear or anger, tend to be attributed to inducing conditions and are typically associated with specific behavioral objectives. Moods, in contrast, need not be connected to particular causes and are marked by the absence of impulsion toward specific courses of action.

There appears to be little consensus, however, on whether or not the experience of mood requires conscious awareness. William Morris (1989), for example, suggests that moods may be consciously experienced or may manifest themselves without awareness. The stipulation that individuals need be neither conscious of their moods, nor cognizant of potential consequences of these moods, carries with it the assumption that nonconsciously experienced moods are nonetheless capable of influencing cognition and action. Robert Thayer (1989), on the other hand, insists that mood experiences necessitate awareness, and he suggests that this awareness provides vital feedback to individuals about their state of wellness. Thayer highlights the hedonic distinctness of moods, a feature that moods share with acute emotions. Specifically, he distinguishes between moods marked by energetic arousal (i.e., moods linked with sensations of energy, vigor, and peppiness), and tense arousal (i.e., moods associated with feelings of tension, anxiety, and fearfulness). These arousal types are consistent with the hedonic classification of moods into good or pleasant versus bad or unpleasant. Thayer conceives of a depression–elation continuum onto which all moods can be mapped, and he emphasizes that all of these states favor consequences that are in the interest of individuals' wellness.

Morris (1992), in a biopsychological theory of mood functions, similarly stresses consequences for wellness. Specifically, he proposes that good moods express the organism's effective coping with environmental demands, whereas bad moods are manifestations of deficient coping and failure in meeting ecological demands. Individuals in pursuit of wellness thus should be motivated to alter, to the extent possible, depressive states to experiences of elation and to seek courses of action that hold promise of accomplishing this objective.

Mood Management

Dolf Zillmann (1988a, 1988b), in developing a theory of self-administered mood management, accepted the hedonistic premise that individuals, in their continual efforts to improve affective experience, follow an impulse toward pleasure maximization. Specifically, his theory suggests that people tend to arrange their stimulus environment so as to increase the likelihood that (1) bad moods are short-lived and their experiential intensity is reduced, (2) good moods are prolonged and their experiential intensity is enhanced, and (3) bad moods are terminated and superseded by good moods of the highest possible experiential intensity.

The arrangement of stimulus environments may be conscious or nonconscious. It is conscious when people are aware of their moods and engage in deliberate efforts to alter them in accordance with the stipulated management objectives. It is nonconscious when people pursue these objectives without cognizance of moods and intentions to modify them in particular ways. For the presumably prevalent case of nonconscious mood management, Zillmann proposed a mechanism that is primarily based on negative reinforcement (i.e., the removal of negative stimulation). It is thought that people initially sample stimulus conditions in a random fashion. Given that they experience bad moods, the encounter of stimuli that provide relief leaves a trace in memory that makes it likely that the relief-providing stimuli will be sought out during future bad moods. The frequent experience of relief under these circumstances eventually establishes a mood-specific preference for particular stimulus environments. The enhancement of good moods by the encounter of pleasant stimuli functions analogously, except that the preference is mediated by positive reinforcement.

Although mood-management theory applies to the arrangement of stimulus environments generally, the readily manipulable media environment, especially the wealth of choices offered in media entertainment, has been of focal interest in considering the management of moods.

Media Effects on Moods

Mood-management theory entails the assumption that exposure to environmental stimuli, to media displays in particular, is capable of modifying prevailing moods. If this capability did not exist, mood repair through relief and mood enhancement through added pleasure could not happen, and mood-specific preferences for particular displays could not be formed. Fortunately, however, the mood-altering capacity of media portrayals has been amply documented and is not in question (cf. Kubey and Csikszentmihalyi, 1990; Morris, 1989; Thayer, 1989).

By way of illustration, Joseph Forgas and Stephanie Moylan (1987) ascertained the moods of large numbers of theater patrons who had just seen predominantly funny or sad movies. They found postexposure moods to correspond closely with content classifications; that is, comical contents induced good moods, tragic contents induced bad moods. Moods also manifested themselves in a comparatively positive versus negative outlook on various social issues.

Edward Hirt and his collaborators (1992) exposed sports fans to live televised basketball games that involved their favorite teams. Their teams won some of these games and lost others. Moods, and along with them the self-esteem of the fans, were positive after hoped-for wins and negative after feared losses.

News reports were found to induce moods in a similar fashion (Zillmann, Taylor, and Lewis, 1998). Bad news about publicly known people and groups fostered bad moods when the people and groups were liked, whereas it fostered good moods when the people or groups were disliked or despised.

In the elicitation of moods by media content, individual differences along gender and personality lines may be pronounced. Mary Beth Oliver (2000) aggregated evidence suggesting that, among adolescents, males extract more positive moods from violent and horrifying films than do females, whereas females respond more favorably to so-called melodramatic tear-jerkers than do males. Such gender differences derive in part from personality characteristics that transcend gender.

Mood Management through Communication Choices

Mood-management theory has been supported by numerous research demonstrations. In general terms, it has been shown that the stipulated hedonistic objectives are best served by the choice of exposure to material to which the likely reaction (1) is excitationally opposite to prevailing moods that derive from noxiously experienced hypoarousal or hyperarousal, (2) has positive hedonic valence above that of prevailing moods, and (3) during distinctly negative affective experiences, has little or no semantic affinity with the inducers of these moods (cf. Zillmann, 1988b, 2000).

The merits of counterexcitatory exposure choices have been explored experimentally (Bryant and Zillmann, 1984). Respondents were placed into either a state of boredom or stress and then provided with the opportunity to watch television in privacy. Unknown to them, only programs that had been preevaluated as either exciting or calming were available. The viewing choices of the respondents were secretly recorded, primarily in terms of accumulated time dedicated to exciting or calming programs. The findings revealed that bored viewers preferred exciting over calming programs, whereas viewers in acute stress preferred calming over exciting ones. The spontaneous selections of the respondents thus did serve excitatory homeostasis, as expected, in that the return to normal levels of sympathetic excitedness was accelerated for both hypoaroused and hyperaroused people. Their intuitive choices were correct in minimizing aversive experiences, thereby serving wellness.

Similarly conducted selective-exposure research gives evidence that viewers who sample entertaining programs attempt to elude, diminish, or terminate bad moods—such as being disappointed, depressed, frustrated, annoyed, or angry—by consuming comedy or engaging drama with a pleasing and appeasing overall message (e.g., Helregel and Weaver, 1989; Kubey and Csikszentmihalyi, 1990; Meadowcroft and Zillmann, 1987; Zillmann and Bryant, 1986; Zillmann and Wakshlag, 1985). All of these choices are supportive of the proposal that exposure is sought to programs that promise relief from bad moods and the enhancement of mildly pleasant affective states. In more general terms, exposure is sought to programs that appear capable of providing a degree of pleasure above that already manifested in the prevailing mood.

The proposal that the repair of noxious experiential states is best accomplished by seeking exposure to contents with little or no affinity to these moods, as well as by avoiding exposure to contents with such affinity, is directly addressed in an investigation on crime apprehension (Wakshlag, Vial, and Tamborini, 1983). After the respondents' fear of victimization was made salient to them or not, they could choose a drama from a set of crime dramas that differed with regard to the amount of featured violence and the justness of the resolution. It was observed that respondents who were acutely crime-apprehensive showed a stronger tendency than others to avoid drama dwelling on violence. These respondents also showed a stronger interest in drama featuring the triumph of justice in its resolution. It seems that in making such choices it is tacitly understood that diversionary stimulation has a more beneficial effect than mulling over the conditions that fostered the noxious experiential states that are in need of repair, and that exposure to material related to these states could only exacerbate the situation by frequent reminder of the aggravating circumstances.

Nonexperimental research produced further corroboration of mood management through specific and, at times, nonspecific choices of available media offerings. Daniel Anderson and his collaborators (1996), for example, conducted a massive behavior survey of television consumption in the family context. Specifically, these investigators assessed family stress levels and related them to television program choices. High stress levels proved to be associated with increased comedy viewing and decreased news consumption. This accords with mood-management theory in that comedy is considered programming with great absorption potential and high positive hedonic valence—in short, programming with a high capacity for disrupting and alleviating bad moods. News programs, usually laden with reports of threatening events, do not have this capacity and thus are likely to perpetuate bad moods based on troubling experiences. In addition, Anderson and his colleagues observed that stressed women, compared to non-stressed women, watched more game and variety programming as well as more television overall.

This research relates to the work on conflict management, specifically to such management through media choices that affect mood improvements. Rena Repetti (1989) conducted an investigation on the media behavior of air-traffic controllers, a profession known for pronounced daily variation in stress levels. The air-traffic controllers were observed in their homes after normal and highly stressful days at work. Acutely stressed controllers invariably attempted to watch television in order to calm down. When family circumstances allowed such diversionary stimulation, family life proceeded in a comparatively tranquil fashion. When circumstances prevented this relaxation, friction with family members tended to escalate to aggravated conflict, often with destructive results.

Nonexperimental research conducted with the experience sampling method (Kubey and Csik-szentmihalyi, 1990) further substantiates the stress-reducing capability of extended television consumption. In predetermined random intervals during waking hours, large numbers of research participants were contacted by beeper and instructed to record their activities and moods at these times. The findings show that television viewing, across all contents, is primarily a relaxing experience called on when relaxation is in demand. Extended television viewing was invariably preceded by particularly bad moods. When bad moods were more moderate, viewing was less extensive. In this analysis, loneliness emerged as a salient mediator of bad mood. Television viewing thus seems to serve the dual function of providing relaxation and substituting for social interaction. Additional comparisons of elements of mood before and after television viewing corroborate its agitation-diminishing and calming effect, but they fail to give evidence of affect enhancement in terms of increased happiness, cheerfulness, friendliness, and sociability.

All this is to say that a considerable amount of evidence indicates that media offerings are indeed used to manage moods in predictable ways. It also is to say that such mood management is not merely a matter of fostering potentially trivial amusements, amazements, pleasant titillations, and cheap thrills, but that the management of moods can have significant social consequences and even health benefits.

Nonconscious Choices

At times, people are fully aware of seeking mood improvements by selecting particular media environments. At other times, however, they are not cognizant of what it is that guides their selections. This point is compellingly made by research on women's media preferences during the menstrual cycle. It has been shown that women, several days prior to the onset of menstruation as well as during menstruation, are more partial to comedy than at other times throughout the cycle (Meadowcroft and Zillmann, 1987). All indications are that women are unaware of these changes in their entertainment preference. They are similarly unaware of their greater attraction to drama at midcycle. It appears that when hormonal fluctuations place women into a diffuse bad mood, they are intuitively drawn to those entertainments that hold the greatest promise for effective mood repair—that is, for cheering them up, if only for a limited period of time.

A similar relationship between hormonal variation, bad moods, and women's nonconscious preference for light-hearted entertainments has also been observed in connection with pregnancy, with comedy preference being especially pronounced during the so-called postpartum-blues period after delivery (Helregel and Weaver, 1989).

Utilities of Bad-Mood Perpetuation

The evidence concerning mood management through communication choices is not entirely supportive of mood-management theory, however. Nor should this theory be construed as an all-encompassing theory. Findings that are difficult to reconcile with the theory have been reported, and exception-accommodating expansions of the theory have been suggested (Zillmann, 2000). There seem to exist a number of conditions under which people deliberately seek to retain their moods. Retaining good moods does not pose a problem, as the motivation to do so is part of management theory. The perpetuation of bad moods, however, and with it the avoidance of good moods, can be considered to challenge the hedonistic premise of the theory.

Gerrod Parrott (1993) examined the motives for seemingly counterhedonistic behaviors and provided a listing of idiosyncratic pursuits of this kind. He focused on dispositions such as character building and the striving for spiritual betterment. Considering mood management through communication choices, these dispositions certainly can, on occasion, inspire people to forego pleasant stimulation in the interest of retaining their somber moods. However, retaining these moods has its rewards, too, as those who manage to resist the temptation of easy pleasures, entertainment pleasures in particular, can celebrate their accomplishments, thereby gaining access to pleasures they deem superior. Behaviors of this kind, then, are counterhedonistic only if their ultimate end is ignored.

Parrott further enumerated conditions under which bad moods are retained and good moods avoided in a shorter, more mood-specific time frame. Two sets of conditions apply to media choices most directly: (1) people can feel bad about feeling good, when feeling good is situationally inappropriate and (2) people can try to prevent worse moods. Bad moods may thus be tolerated for some time because avoiding them would have punitive consequences. Considered in context, the behavior is again not counterhedonistic. Not knowing the context greatly complicates the prediction of media choices in bad-mood situations, however.

Emotional Utility

The cliché of such a situation is the apparent appeal of love songs whose lyrics bemoan abandonment by a lover to those who suffered a similar abandonment. In agreement with this cliché, it was found that people who had lost their lover declared a preference for sad love music over happy love music (Gibson, Aust, and Zillmann, 2000). In contrast, people who had just experienced romantic success declared the opposite preference. People in acute distress over their loss of love, then, appear to find solace in symbolically commiserating with others. Additionally, hearing about the romantic triumph of others in happy love music seems offensive to them, and avoiding such pleasure music is obviously in the interest of minimizing bad moods.

It can have similar emotional utility to retain a negative mood state if it helps maintain the motivation for mood-resolving actions. People may seek to retain anger, for example, in order to resolve a situation that, if left unresolved, is likely to manifest itself in an extended period of distressing moods. Edgar O'Neal and Levi Taylor (1989) conducted an investigation that demonstrates such emotion maintenance by entertainment choices. Specifically, it was observed that acutely angry men took an exceptionally strong interest in programs that featured hostility and violence, but only if they believed they would have the opportunity to retaliate soon against the person who instigated their anger. In contrast, equally angry men who believed they would never get the opportunity to retaliate showed comparatively little interest in violence-laden drama. They exhibited increased appetite for mood-improving comedy, instead. For those who expected the chance to retaliate, the choice of violent contents apparently prolonged the related adverse experience of anger in the interest of future (retaliatory) behavior believed to be of superior hedonic quality. Temporarily perpetuating a bad mood thus can have emotional utility without challenging the principle of hedonism.

Informational Utility

The limitations of mood management by communication choices are more directly apparent in the selection of nonfictional materials. Exposure to the news and educational material tends to be motivated by curiosity and informational needs whose satisfaction has little, if anything, to do with hedonism. Such messages have informational utility that is essentially independent of gratification in affective terms. Revelations in the news may be elating or depressing. If they are distressing, or if recipients anticipate distress reactions, exposure to the news may nonetheless be accepted, if not actively sought. On occasion, however, even news reports are bypassed in order to prevent bad moods or their exacerbation. This seems especially likely when distressing news revelations are of little consequence for the recipients. The only available investigation on that subject shows that during bad moods, women tend to avoid bad news (Biswas, Riffe, and Zillmann, 1994). Men, however, tend to seek exposure despite the prospect of worsening moods.

Regarding educational material, Marie-Louise Mares and Joanne Cantor (1992) observed that informational utility can readily overpower hedonistic selection motives. These investigators assessed the degree of loneliness experienced by elderly people and then had them evaluate the desirability of viewing various hedonically positive or negative programs. The programs were introduced as documentaries focusing on elderly people. Some were said to feature unhappy, lonely people; others were said to feature happy, successful people. The lonely elderly viewers indicated a preference for seeing programs that featured unhappy people. More contented elderly viewers indicated a preference for seeing programs that featured happy people. The fact that the programs that dealt with the problems that lonely elderly people face were selected by lonely elderly people would seem to suggest that these people hoped to learn from the documentaries how best to cope with the indicated problems. The programs did not have such informational utility for the comparatively contented elderly, who consequently could turn to material with greater propensity for mood enhancement.

Scope and Limitations of Mood Management

Hedonism, the driving force of mood management, defines only one motive in a set of motives that influence the public's selection of media content. Such content may have utilities that are relatively independent of hedonistic considerations. These extrahedonistic motives tend to exert their influence in concert with the hedonistic force. In fact, this confounding in the operation of selection motives can be considered the rule rather than the exception. Domains of dominant influence of competing motives can be specified, however.

Hedonism must be regarded as the dominant choice determinant for entertaining media content, with informational utility being a secondary factor in this domain. The primary object of entertainment choices is, after all, the repair of undesirable moods along with the attainment and enhancement of desirable ones. Mood management may thus be considered as the central model for choices in the realm of media entertainment. Informational utility, in contrast, must be regarded as the dominant choice determinant for informational and educational media content, with hedonism being a secondary factor in these domains. News and education thus define domains of media content in which the application of mood-management considerations may be of limited value.

See also: AROUSAL PROCESSES AND MEDIA EFFECTS; GENDER AND THE MEDIA; NEWS EFFECTS.

Bibliography

Anderson, Daniel R.; Collins, Patricia A.; Schmitt, Kelly L.; and Jacobvitz, Robin S. (1996). "Stressful Life Events and Television Viewing." *Communication Research* 23:243–260.

Biswas, Rahul; Riffe, Daniel; and Zillmann, Dolf. (1994). "Mood Influence on the Appeal of Bad News." *Journalism Quarterly* 71(3):689–696.

Bryant, Jennings, and Zillmann, Dolf. (1984). "Using Television to Alleviate Boredom and Stress: Selective Exposure as a Function of Induced Excitational States." *Journal of Broadcasting* 28(1):1–20.

Forgas, Joseph P., and Moylan, Stephanie. (1987). "After the Movies: Transient Mood and Social Judgments." *Personality and Social Psychology Bulletin* 13:467–477.

Frijda, Nico H. (1993). "Moods, Emotion Episodes, and Emotions." In *Handbook of Emotions,* eds. Michael Lewis and Jeannette M. Haviland. New York: Guilford Press.

Gibson, Rhonda; Aust, Charles F.; and Zillmann, Dolf. (2000). "Loneliness of Adolescents and Their Choice and Enjoyment of Love-Celebrating Versus Love-Lamenting Popular Music." *Empirical Studies of the Arts* 18(1):43–48.

Helregel, Brenda K., and Weaver, James B. (1989). "Mood-Management During Pregnancy through Selective Exposure to Television." *Journal of Broadcasting and Electronic Media* 33(1):15–33.

Hirt, Edward R.; Zillmann, Dolf; Erickson, Grant A.; and Kennedy, Chris. (1992). "Costs and Benefits of Allegiance: Changes in Fans' Self-Ascribed Competencies After Team Victory Versus Defeat." *Journal of Personality and Social Psychology* 63(5):724–738.

Kubey, Robert, and Csikszentmihalyi, Mihaly. (1990). *Television and the Quality of Life: How Viewing Shapes Everyday Experience.* Hillsdale, NJ: Lawrence Erlbaum.

Mares, Marie-Louise, and Cantor, Joanne R. (1992). "Elderly Viewers' Responses to Televised Portrayals of Old Age." *Communication Research* 19:459–478.

Meadowcroft, Jeanne M., and Zillmann, Dolf. (1987). "Women's Comedy Preferences during the Menstrual Cycle." *Communication Research* 14:204–218.

Morris, William N. (1989). *Mood: The Frame of Mind.* New York: Springer-Verlag.

Morris, William N. (1992). "A Functional Analysis of the Role of Mood in Affective Systems." In *Review of Personality and Social Psychology, Vol. 13: Emotion,* ed. Margaret S. Clark. Newbury Park, CA: Sage Publications.

Oliver, Mary Beth. (2000). "The Respondent-Gender Gap." In *Media Entertainment: The Psychology of Its Appeal,* eds. Dolf Zillmann and Peter Vorderer. Mahwah, NJ: Lawrence Erlbaum.

O'Neal, Edgar C., and Taylor, S. Levi. (1989). "Status of the Provoker, Opportunity to Retaliate, and Interest in Video Violence." *Aggressive Behavior* 15:171–180.

Parrott, W. Gerrod. (1993). "Beyond Hedonism: Motives for Inhibiting Good Moods and for Maintaining Bad Moods." In *Handbook of Mental Control,* eds. Daniel M. Wegner and James W. Pennebaker. Englewood Cliffs, NJ: Prentice-Hall.

Repetti, Rena L. (1989). "Effects of Daily Workload on Subsequent Behavior during Marital Interaction: The Roles of Social Withdrawal and Spouse Support." *Journal of Personality and Social Psychology* 57:651–659.

Thayer, Robert E. (1989). *The Biopsychology of Mood and Arousal.* New York: Oxford University Press.

Wakshlag, Jacob; Vial, Virginia; and Tamborini, Ron. (1983). "Selecting Crime Drama and Apprehension about Crime." *Human Communication Research* 10:227–242.

Zillmann, Dolf. (1988a). "Mood Management through Communication Choices." *American Behavioral Scientist* 31(3):327–340.

Zillmann, Dolf. (1988b). "Mood Management: Using Entertainment to Full Advantage." In *Communication, Social Cognition, and Affect,* eds. Lewis Dono-
hew, Howard E. Sypher, and E. Tory Higgins. Hillsdale, NJ: Lawrence Erlbaum.

Zillmann, Dolf. (2000). "Mood Management in the Context of Selective Exposure Theory." In *Communication Yearbook,* Vol. 23, ed. Michael E. Roloff. Mahwah, NJ: Lawrence Erlbaum.

Zillmann, Dolf, and Bryant, Jennings. (1986). "Shifting Preferences in Pornography Consumption." *Communication Research* 13:560–578.

Zillmann, Dolf; Taylor, Kay; and Lewis, Kelley. (1998). "News as Nonfiction Theater: How Dispositions toward the Public Cast of Characters Affect Reactions." *Journal of Broadcasting and Electronic Media* 42(2):153–169.

Zillmann, Dolf, and Wakshlag, Jacob. (1985). "Fear of Victimization and the Appeal of Crime Drama." In *Selective Exposure to Communication,* eds. Dolf Zillmann and Jennings Bryant. Hillsdale, NJ: Lawrence Erlbaum.

DOLF ZILLMANN

MOORE, ANNE CARROLL (1871–1961)

Anne Carroll Moore was a pioneering children's librarian who shaped the profession of children's services in American public libraries. Devoting her career to children's librarianship, Moore touched every aspect of the field–writing, reviewing, lecturing and teaching, training staff, administering children's services at the New York Public Library, and consulting with publishers. Her insistence on quality literature for children stimulated the growth of American children's literature in the twentieth century.

Born and raised in Limerick, Maine, Moore was the only daughter of Luther Sanborn Moore and Sarah Barker Moore. She and her seven brothers lived on a farm named Alderwood in southwestern Maine, in sight of Mt. Washington. Moore's parents were clearly influential in developing her strong personality. Luther Moore was a farmer, lawyer, and politician who brought his daughter along as company in visits and read to her. Anne absorbed her mother's love of beauty, particularly in the form of flowers and gardens. Her educational experiences were particularly positive, both at Limerick Academy, a preparatory school in Maine, and the Bradford Academy in Massachusetts, a two-year college with which she sustained a long association. After her formal education, she returned home to study law under her father's tutelage, despite the unpromising prospects for women in the field.

All her plans drastically changed when her parents died suddenly in 1892 from a severe bout of influenza and then her sister-in-law died later in that same year. She helped her widowed brother raise his two children for several years, her only child-rearing experience. Career options seemed unappealing to her—either missionary work or teaching. One brother, recognizing her kinship with books, suggested the new field of librarianship. She applied to the state library school in Albany, New York, for which she lacked the requisite college degree, and then applied to Pratt Institute Library School in Brooklyn, New York, where she began her professional studies and career.

At Pratt, Moore began a tutelage under Mary Wright Plummer, director of the library. Plummer, a librarian with international stature, was made director in 1894, after which she helped design an expanded facility that included a children's room—the first of its kind in the country to be built. The one-year training course did not yet include the subject of children's librarianship. Moore's intention was to return after graduation in June 1896 to Maine in the new area of county library service, which did not materialize as a prospect. On her way to the American Library Association convention in Cleveland, she met Caroline Hewins, the director of the Hartford Public Library, who pioneered the professional interest in library services to children. After returning from the conference, Moore received a job offer from Mary Wright Plummer to assume responsibilities for the new children's room at Pratt. These two women—Plummer and Hewins—became Moore's mentors in the field.

At Pratt, Moore developed the professional practices that shaped her subsequent career: managing the children's room, participating in professional activities, and writing. Moore's intention, which included methods of the new kindergarten movement, was to open access to books for children, to organize a system of circulation, to create thematic exhibits of pictures and books with accompanying reading lists, and to extend the influence of the library beyond its walls. In 1898, she introduced her well-known register pledge, which pledged the child to take good care of all books, to pay all fines, and to obey all rules. She also began work with schools: making contacts, giving talks, and providing special library services, such as storytelling.

It was during the Pratt years that Moore became a leader in the profession in the new practice of children's services. Moore was chosen as chair of the Club of Children's Librarians, which later became the Children's Services Division of the American Library Association. She presented a landmark paper at the 1898 conference, "Special Training for Children's Librarians," in which she stated for the first time what was needed in this new field. Her leadership role in the American Library Association was instrumental in forming an organizational identity of children's librarians and in raising concerns of critical importance to the field.

Moore was recruited for the position of Superintendent of Work with Children at the New York Public Library in 1906, where she served until her retirement in 1941. Moore developed the Children's Room into a cosmopolitan site of international interest, where foreign visitors often toured, and immigrant populations felt connected to their own native culture. It was here that the expanding children's book community was centered as Moore became a leader in both the publishing and the provision of books for children.

After her first decade at the New York Public Library, Moore's interest began to shift from professional issues to the literature of childhood. Her interest in communities now encompassed the publishing industry, which was just beginning to diversify into the children's book market. These interests emanated from her high standards of selection for branch libraries and her heightened sense of the quality desirable in the content and production of children's books. Her exhibits and reading lists were an economic impetus for publishers to heed her counsel. Moore began writing reviews in *The Bookman*, which was the first ongoing critical column on children's books, and later in the *New York Herald Tribune* and the *Horn Book* magazine.

Moore also wrote two novels for children: *Nicholas: A Manhattan Christmas Story* (1924) and *Nicholas and the Golden Goose* (1932). The books were modeled on a doll, which became for Moore an imaginary companion, whose existence disconcerted colleagues. Her presence was long felt in the New York Public Library and book community even after her retirement. She served as a visiting lecturer, received an honorary doctorate from

Pratt Institute, and was honored with the Regina Medal by the Catholic Library Association.

Moore died on January 20, 1961. Despite subsequent reevaluations of her reputation, she remains one of the most influential figures in the history of children's services in American public libraries.

See also: LIBRARIANS; LIBRARIES, HISTORY OF; STORYTELLING.

Bibliography

Bader, Barbara. (1997). "Only the Best: The Hits and Misses of Anne Carroll Moore." *Horn Book* 73(5):520–528.

Bush, Margaret. (1996). "New England Book Women: Their Increasing Influence." *Library Trends* 44(4):719–735.

Lundin, Anne. (1995). "A Delicate Balance: Collection Development and Women's History." *Collection Building* 14(2):42–46.

Lundin, Anne. (1996). "Anne Carroll Moore: 'I Have Spun out a Long Thread.'" *Reclaiming the American Library Past: Writing the Women In*, ed. Suzanne Hildenbrand. Norwood, NJ: Ablex.

Moore, Anne Carroll. (1924). *Nicholas: A Manhattan Christmas Story.* New York: Putnam.

Moore, Anne Carroll. (1932). *Nicholas and the Golden Goose.* New York: Putnam.

Sayers, Frances Clarke. (1972). *Anne Carroll Moore: A Biography.* New York: Athenaeum.

ANNE LUNDIN

■ MORSE, SAMUEL F. B. (1791–1872)

Samuel Finley Breese Morse is recognized as the most influential figure in the development of the electromagnetic telegraph. It is interesting to note that although Morse is remembered as an inventor, he endeavored most of his life to become a great artist.

Morse was born in Charlestown, Massachusetts, on April 27, 1791, to Elizabeth Breese Morse and Jedidiah Morse. His mother was a strong-willed individual who held tremendous influence over Morse and his two brothers, Sidney and Richard. His father, the town pastor, was also active as an author and geographer.

Morse learned of electricity while attending the lectures of Jeremiah Day at Yale University. Nevertheless, he wanted to become an artist, and

he was fortunate to be acquainted with the American painter Washington Allston. Morse's parents supported his ambition to travel with Allston to London to further his training. There, Morse assumed Allston's practice of sculpting the images of his paintings. His first sculpture, *Dying Hercules* (1812), earned Morse international recognition from the Adelphi Society of Arts in London.

Morse began a prolific career in portraiture after marrying Lucretia Pickering Walker and establishing a residence in Charleston, South Carolina, in 1818. Morse and his brother Sidney dabbled briefly in invention, but their failed attempts motivated Morse to refocus on painting and the New York art community after moving to New Haven, Connecticut, in the early 1820s. In late 1824, Morse received word that the Common Council of the City of New York had chosen him to paint a portrait of the Marquis de Lafayette during his tour of the United States. In February 1825, while Morse was in Washington, D.C., for a sitting for the painting, he received word of his wife's death and quickly returned to New Haven. His father died shortly thereafter, and a distraught Morse moved to New York. In November 1825, he and thirty other artists founded what would eventually become known as the National Academy of Design. Morse, who served as the first president of the academy, completed the painting of Lafayette in 1826. (That portrait now hangs in New York's City Hall, and the related bust is in the possession of the New York City Public Library.)

In November 1829, with his three children entrusted to the care of various family members, Morse decided to leave New York for a three-year tour of Europe. While in France, Morse met with Louis Daguerre. (Morse, impressed with Daguerre's precursor to modern photography, eventually opened his own daguerreotype studio in New York, where he taught Mathew Brady, the famed American Civil War photographer.) While in France, Morse also had seen the Chappe semaphore telegraph, which was a visual signaling device that used movable arms on tall masts. Morse was intrigued still with the signaling device when he boarded the *Sully*, the ship on which he returned to New York from Le Havre, France, in 1832. Aboard ship, Morse met and held long discussions with Charles T. Jackson concerning his ideas for a form of telegraphy that used electricity. Later, each would make claims to the invention of

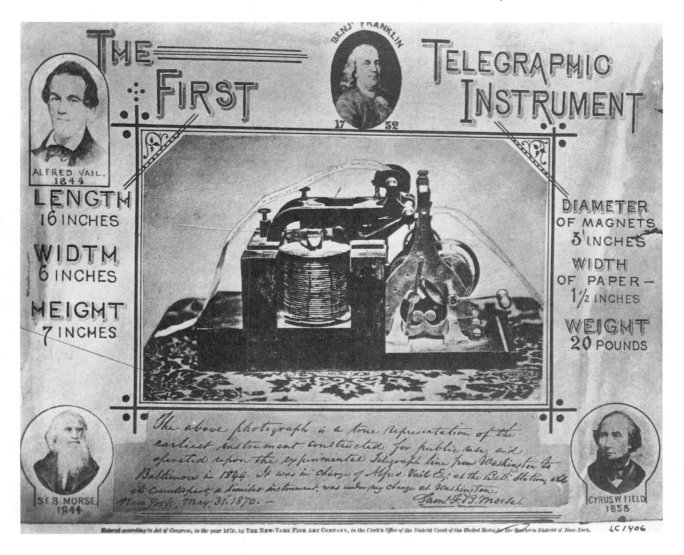

Photographs of Samuel F. B. Morse and Alfred Vail are included with an image and descriptive details of the first telegraphic instrument. (Corbis)

the electromagnetic telegraph. While Morse provided more evidence for his claims than Jackson did, the evidence revealed that neither could claim sole credit for the invention.

Morse began teaching art at New York University in 1835. While there, he began developing his telegraph. Early in 1836, Morse attempted to make the model work through forty feet of wire, but such early attempts failed. Leonard D. Gale, a professor of chemistry at the university, became interested in Morse's work. Gale helped Morse correct many problems in his model. Another important contributor to the Morse telegraph was Alfred Vail (a former art student of Morse), who understood mechanical engineering. Vail provided technical assistance, funds, and facilities in Speedwell, New Jersey, for equipment construction. Although many historians argue that Gale and Vail probably provided most of the innovation for

Morse's final working product, each received small shares of the patent for the telegraph, the caveat of which was filed by Morse on October 3, 1837.

On March 4, 1843, the U.S. Congress provided approximately $30,000 for the construction of a telegraph line between Washington, D.C., and Baltimore. The original idea was to lay telegraph lines underwater and underground, but wire insulation was too unreliable. As an alternate, Vale and Ezra Cornell (the designer of the plow Morse used for burying cable) suggested stringing wire overhead on poles. Finally, on May 24, 1844, the line opened with the message "What hath God wrought!"

Morse had attempted to develop a telegraph code in 1832 using dots and dashes to represent actual words, but that method proved too cumbersome. American Morse Code, which uses dots and dashes to represent letters and numbers directly, was developed in 1844. In 1850, sound reading of Morse code replaced visual reading of telegraph tape. Continental code, which transmits better through undersea cables, was adopted in 1851.

At the age of fifty-five, when he was a superintendent of the Washington–Baltimore telegraph, Morse proposed to finish a panel of art in the rotunda of the U.S. Capitol. Morse ended his art career with the rejection of that proposal. While in his late fifties, Morse married Sarah Elizabeth Griswold, his second cousin, with whom he had four children. Their marriage was overshadowed by intense patent litigation against Morse and his telegraph.

Versions of electric telegraphy had been developed as early as 1774. Several versions of telegraphy appeared almost simultaneously after Hans Christian Oersted's discovery of electromagnetism in 1819. Models were developed in England by Peter Barlow and Charles Wheatstone in 1824 and 1837, respectively. Wheatstone became involved with others in the United States in litigation against Morse, his patent, and his claim to be the inventor of the electric telegraph. Joseph Henry was found to have produced a working model in 1831; Harrison Gray Dyar strung telegraph wires on poles in Long Island for his static electricity model in 1827. While these cases illustrated clearly that other individuals had created working electric telegraphs before Morse had, the courts determined that none of the other innovators had applied for U.S. patents for models that were direct challenges to Morse's design.

Morse died on April 2, 1872, in his winter home in New York. Based on the facts of his life history, it might be more appropriate if Morse were remembered predominantly as the artist who helped to found the National Academy of Design rather than as the inventor of the telegraph. This would certainly have been the view of those people who criticized Morse and alleged that he had claimed the work of others as his own. Nevertheless, his efforts did lead to the worldwide adoption of a common system of telegraphy.

See also: TELEPHONE INDUSTRY, HISTORY OF.

Bibliography

Coe, Lewis. (1993). *The Telegraph: A History of Morse's Invention and Its Predecessors in the United States.* Jefferson, NC: McFarland & Company.

Harlow, Alvin F. (1936). *Old Wires and New Waves: The History of the Telegraph, Telephone, and Wireless.* New York: D. Appleton-Century Company.

Mabee, Carleton. (1943). *The American Leonardo: A Life of Samuel F. B. Morse.* New York: Alfred A. Knopf.

Morse, Edward Lind, ed. (1973). *Samuel F. B. Morse: His Letters and Journals*, 2 vols. New York: Da Capo Press.

MARTIN L. HATTON

MOTION PICTURE INDUSTRY
See: Film Industry

MURROW, EDWARD R. (1908–1965)

Edward R. Murrow's use of word pictures while reporting from London during World War II made him an American hero. He rewrote the rules of broadcast journalism on radio and then wrote most of the rules for television journalism and documentary reporting. For years, he was the most respected voice in broadcast news, and yet, he also hosted the earliest version of the celebrity tabloid show.

Murrow was born into a farming and logging family in North Carolina, but he grew up in Washington state. While attending Washington State College, he studied speech and played the lead in many theater productions.

In 1934, Murrow began arranging, through the International Institute of Education, for the placement of Jewish intellectuals from Germany in institutions of higher learning in the United States. Because it was during the Great Depression, he also had to arrange for financial support for these intellectuals. Some of these leading scientists, including Albert Einstein, participated in interviews that Murrow set up with the radio networks.

As a result of his work with German refugees, Murrow was offered a job with the Columbia Broadcasting System (CBS) as "Director of Talks" in 1935. He was promoted in 1937 and became the head of CBS operations in Europe. In this position, he was not supposed to report news; he was not considered to be a journalist. However, Murrow broke the rules when, in 1938, Adolf Hitler's armies entered Austria. Murrow went to Vienna and filed a report on the invasion. His style was unique, allowing sounds and the words he chose to paint pictures for the listeners. In doing this, he had developed a new type of reporter, the radio correspondent.

Back in London, during the bombing raids by the Germans, Murrow remained above ground, out of the bomb shelters. This made it possible for him to report to an anxious audience every night on the nature and events of the war. These reports, which would always start with his trademark phrase "This is London," made him famous in America and a hero to the British.

Murrow tried to create reports that caused those who listened to live the experience and to be moved by it as he had been moved. In order to do this, he often put himself in great danger against his boss's orders. He flew along on bombing runs over Berlin, and he moved with the troops during the Allied thrust into Europe. One of his most moving broadcasts was of the Allied arrival at the Buchenwald concentration camp, wherein he described the horrors that had been inflicted upon the people who had been interred there.

When the war ended, Murrow returned to America, where he became the vice-president of CBS News. As the most famous radio news voice of World War II, Murrow was not satisfied with the desk job, so he went back to being a reporter in 1947. He then collaborated with Fred Friendly on a series of recorded documentaries called *I Can Hear It Now* (an oral history of the period from 1932 to 1945). After Murrow returned home from reporting on the Korean War, he and Friendly turned their collaboration into a weekly radio program on CBS. It was called simply *Hear It Now,* and it ran from December 1950 to June 1951.

Murrow did not like television, with its natural emphasis on pictures instead of ideas, as a medium for news. However, he could not stop the wheels of progress, so in 1951, he and Friendly created *See It Now,* a television version of their radio series. This program, which ran until 1958, helped to create the television documentary. *Person to Person,* Murrow's more popular television program, was of a completely different nature. Running from 1953 to 1959, this program was a celebrity interview show that featured guests such as Marilyn Monroe, Roy Campanella, Arthur Godfrey, and even then-Senator John F. Kennedy. Through remote hookups, Murrow (in New York) would question the celebrities (in their homes)

Edward R. Murrow. (Bettmann/Corbis)

about their lifestyles. While the program disappointed fans of Murrow's serious work, it made a lot of money for both CBS and Murrow. In addition to these two television programs, Murrow continued to broadcast a nightly radio show.

One of the principles that Murrow lived by was "Tell the truth, and fear no man" (which had been ingrained in him as part of his Quaker upbringing). This principle would play a prominent role in the most important moment of his television career. Senator Joseph McCarthy was heading the House Un-American Activities Committee, which had fostered and exploited a fear of communism infiltrating America. CBS, along with other media organizations, had "black lists" of people who reportedly had Communist connections and were, therefore, unemployable. CBS also had a loyalty oath that employees were required to sign, thereby disavowing any Communist ties and affirming their loyalty to America.

While Murrow signed the oath, he knew the procedures being used by McCarthy were wrong, and he looked for a television story that would be appropriate for *See It Now* and would expose McCarthy's tactics. On October 20, 1953, Murrow chose to air a story that questioned the methods that were used in discharging a lieutenant, Milo Radulovich, from the U.S. Air Force Reserve. Based on sealed evidence and closed hearings, the soldier had been dismissed as a security risk because his father and sister had what were considered to be leftist leanings. After the show aired, the lieutenant was reinstated, but one month later, it became clear that McCarthy was trying to blacklist Murrow in retaliation for his stand in defense of the lieutenant. Murrow, who respected McCarthy's power but refused to fear him, ordered the *See It Now* crew to prepare a show about McCarthy's authoritarian tactics. After three months, he decided on March 9, 1954, that the time was right to go ahead with the program, regardless of the consequences. Fortunately, Murrow was the most respected reporter in America, and the vast majority of people supported his program. Murrow had given voice to a majority view that had been silenced. Finally, it was okay to disagree with McCarthy—because Murrow had done it. When Murrow was criticized for his personal attack on the senator, he said that history would judge whether he or McCarthy had served America better. In 1954, the answer to this question came when the U.S. Senate overwhelmingly censured Senator McCarthy for his actions.

One of Murrow's follow-ups to *See It Now* was *Small World,* which ran from 1958 to 1959 and extended the technology of electronic newsgathering by using simultaneous hookups around the world to present unrehearsed discussions among important international opinion leaders. Murrow then began producing documentaries for another series, *CBS Reports.* His most famous documentaries included *Harvest of Shame* (1960) and *Biography of a Bookie Joint* (1961). Murrow left CBS in 1961 to join the John F. Kennedy administration as the director of the U.S. Information Agency. He received the Presidential Medal of Freedom from Lyndon Johnson in 1964 and was named an Honorary Knight Commander of the Order of the British Empire by Queen Elizabeth II in 1965 (shortly before his death from lung cancer).

See also: JOURNALISM, HISTORY OF; RADIO BROADCASTING, HISTORY OF; TELEVISION BROADCASTING, HISTORY OF.

Bibliography

Finkelstein, Norman H. (1997). *With Heroic Truth: The Life of Edward R. Murrow.* New York: Clarion Books.

Persico, Joseph E. (1988). *Edward R. Murrow: An American Original.* New York: McGraw-Hill.

Ranville, Michael. (1996). *To Strike at a King: The Turning Point in the McCarthy Witch Hunt.* Troy, MI: Momentum Books.

Sperber, Ann M. (1998). *Murrow, His Life and Times.* New York: Fordham University Press.

Winfield, Betty H., and DeFleur, Lois B. (1986). *The Edward R. Murrow Heritage: Challenge for the Future.* Ames: Iowa State University Press.

STEPHEN D. PERRY

▮ MUSEUMS

The word "museum," from the ancient Greek *mouseion,* originally referred to any location sacred to the Muses (*Mousa*). The Muses, who were the ancient Greek goddesses of the arts, were honored and revered by poets, playwrights, and artists. Any place inhabited by the Muses was likewise considered sacred and a source of divine inspiration. The playwright Euripides, for example, in the fifth century B.C.E., described *mouseia* as places of beauty and nature where birds sang and poets were inspired.

In the fourth century B.C.E., a formal sanctuary dedicated to the Muses was established just below Mount Helicon, a mountain in central Greece. According to legend, the Muses first appeared to the poet Hesiod (ca. 700 B.C.E.) on this very hillside, telling him to sing of the gods as he tended his father's sheep. The sanctuary featured an open-air amphitheater, where statues and other works of art were displayed, and supposedly held a manuscript copy of the collected works of Hesiod. This was, perhaps, the first place ever called a "museum."

The History of Museums

Over the centuries, the notion of a museum evolved from any place sacred to the Muses to the multifaceted museums of today. In the modern world, a museum is defined as any institution that maintains a collection of objects to be preserved, studied, and displayed for educational or aesthetic purposes. This is very different from the original definition of a *mouseion.*

The notion of collecting objects is deeply rooted in human history. Collecting is an activity with great symbolic significance. Collections have been used to honor the dead; Neolithic burial sites often show the dead interred with objects of personal or religious significance. Collections of sacred objects honor the gods; sacrificial offerings accumulate at altars and in temples. Collections of plunder signify conquest and domination; plundered artifacts convey a sense of power over the vanquished. Collections of all types can express admiration or fascination with whatever the objects represent; sports fans, for example, collect memorabilia from their favorite teams or players. However, the mere act of collecting things does not make the resulting collection a museum.

Museums in Antiquity

In the classical world of Greece and Rome, sacred objects were often collected and placed in temples or sanctuaries as offerings to the gods. The Parthenon in Athens, for example, contained many valuable objects ranging from gold and silver artifacts to inlaid statues and carved marble reliefs. These works of art, although now scattered in museums around the world, were originally intended as gifts to the gods; they belonged to the divinity to whom they were offered. The treasuries of classical temples, usually filled with a clutter of precious objects, were generally not open to the public, and the objects contained therein were displayed only on rare occasions. Thus, these temples could not be considered museums.

Collections of objects were not restricted to temples and other religious sites in the ancient world. Works of art were also collected by individuals and displayed in public spaces. Individual aristocrats in ancient Rome would fill their urban homes and country villas with exquisite art. Great public arenas in ancient Greece, such as those at Delphi or Olympia, would feature works of art dedicated in commemoration of great accomplishments. Likewise, the Forum in Rome was filled with exquisite statues representing important historic figures. Although the works of art displayed in these settings would all be considered museum artifacts today, none of the original locations would have been referred to as museums.

There were a few locations in the classical world that could possibly have been considered museums. For example, famous schools in Athens, such as the Lyceum or the Academy, maintained collections of objects that were used for educational purposes. Philosophical classes in Athens were often based on empirical observations of natural objects. The philosopher Aristotle, tutor to Alexander the Great, encouraged his students to collect specimens from the natural world for the purposes of examination. During his conquest of Persia, Alexander had exotic specimens captured and sent home to Aristotle for further study.

The Museum at Alexandria

It was not until the early third century B.C.E. when an institution emerged that most closely resembled the modern notion of a museum. This occurred with the creation of the Museum at Alexandria in Egypt, one of the most famous institutions in the ancient world. Established in 290 B.C.E. by Ptolemy I, the Museum was a place devoted to learning and intellectual reflection, where scholars gathered to study collections of objects. Designed by Demetrius of Phaleron, a former student of Aristotle, the institution was destined to become the center for intellectual learning in the classical world.

Funded by the Egyptian Ptolemaic monarchy, the Museum featured extensive collections of objects, an observatory, lecture halls, gardens, living quarters, and a library. The Library, perhaps the most famous branch of the Museum, grew rapidly over the centuries and at its height contained almost half a million volumes. For almost six centuries, scholars from around the world would travel to Egypt to study the resources of the Museum and contribute the fruits of their own knowledge to the Museum's holdings.

The scholars who worked at the Museum formed the world's first academic community. They were governed by a priest and supported by the state. Like scholars in an early university, they lived, worked, and studied within the institution. Their primary activity was research, and they gave few lectures.

Museums in the Middle Ages

The Museum at Alexandria was destroyed during civil warfare around 270 C.E. After this, the collecting of artifacts once again became a private affair. Rich individuals would collect great works of art according to their interests and tastes for their own personal enjoyment. Communities of scholars, such as monks in monasteries, would collect great works of literature or artistic effort for posterity, hiding them from the public in order to protect them for the future. The first university museum, the Ashmolean, was founded in 1683 at Oxford University in England. However, even universities would restrict access to their collections by the general public.

Over the centuries, displaying works of fine art grew into an art itself for individual collectors. These collectors would exhibit their collections in elaborate displays that ranged in size from vast galleries to tiny cabinets. During the seventeenth and eighteenth centuries, a specialized type of collecting emerged and grew in popularity. Referred to as *wunderkammer,* these were cabinets of curiosities. The owners of these cabinets took great pride in gathering together objects that were rarely seen and hard to acquire. They particularly prized rare specimens of natural history, such as butterflies or fossils. Yet these collections existed almost exclusively for the enjoyment of the collectors, their friends, and their families; the collections were rarely opened to the public.

Early Modern Museums

The first true public museums were created as royal collections of art and were gradually made accessible for the public to enjoy. In Paris, for example, galleries of art initially housed in royal palaces and collected by generations of French kings were made available to select members of the public in the 1750s. However, it was not until 1793, during the French Revolution, that these galleries were opened to the public as the Louvre Museum.

The British Museum was founded in 1753 as perhaps the first public museum. In contrast to earlier museums that focused primarily on art, the British Museum emphasized both natural history and cultural heritage materials. However, its resemblance to the modern version of the museum was slight. Prospective visitors had to apply for admission in writing and in advance, and it could take two weeks to receive permission to enter the facility. Groups of visitors were limited to fifteen people or less and visits had to be restricted to two hours in length. Moreover, visitors had to stay together on their tour, and only two such tours were allowed each day.

The idea that museums should be institutions open to the general public gained in momentum with the growing notion that the nation–state could display collections of prestigious works of art for its own glorification. Thus, during the late-eighteenth and early-nineteenth centuries, countries around the world began to open national museums. Well-known examples include the Vatican Museum in Rome, the Royal Danish Museum in Copenhagen, the Hermitage Museum in St. Petersburg, and the Smithsonian Museum in Washington, D.C. These institutions paved the way for the modern museum.

The Modern Museum

Today, many different types of institutions can be called museums. These include zoos, planetariums, aquariums, art galleries, nature centers, historical monuments, botanical gardens, science and technology centers, and so on. The wide range of institutions that consider themselves museums means that it can prove very difficult to classify museums neatly into distinct categories. Museums are thus often classified in many different ways and using many different methods. They can be grouped by the nature of the objects they collect, by the audience they serve, by their intended purpose, by their size, by their source of funding, and so on.

Types of Museums

The most popular method of classifying museums is by the nature of their collections. This can be difficult to determine as collections in various museums often overlap. Some museums have very specialized collections while some have very general ones; most museums fall somewhere in between. Many museums include collections of more than one type. However, despite unavoidable overlaps between categories, this method of classifying museums has the advantage of being based on the collections themselves. This approach arranges museums into categories in a way that seems logical to most museum visitors. Moreover, it provides a way of illustrating some of the key differences in approaches different types of museums bring to their collections and intended audiences.

For the purposes of this entry, museums can be divided into four general types: (1) art museums, (2) science and technology museums, (3) natural history museums, and (4) cultural history museums.

Art museums collect and present a variety of artifacts considered to be of aesthetic value. Artifacts exhibited in art museums include paintings, sculpture, and the decorative arts. Art museums often include historical objects, traditionally drawn from classical antiquity, among their collections. However, most art museums collect artifacts based on their aesthetic merits rather than their cultural or historical importance. Thus, it is usually sufficient for artifacts in art galleries to be exhibited loosely arranged by time period or artist. When displaying artifacts of aesthetic value, the context in which the collections are displayed is less important than in other museums where artifacts might have to be displayed in an appropriate historical context to be understood. In general, art museums tend to be more focused on personal appreciation of art, with the interpretation of artifacts left up to the individual. Exhibits in art museums, therefore, are usually less didactic in nature than in other forms of museums. Modern art museums are often considered experimental; many are designed and constructed in an attempt to show the latest in modern artistic styles. The Guggenheim Museum in New York or the Georges Pompidou Center in Paris are good examples of museums of modern art that attempt to embody modern art conventions in their own construction. Other well-known art museums include the Museum of Modern Art in New York, the San Francisco Fine Arts Museum, the Art Institute in Chicago, the Louvre Museum in Paris, the Tate Gallery in London, and the Guggenheim Museum in Bilbao, Spain.

Museums of science and technology collect objects and design exhibitions that demonstrate scientific principles, illustrate important discoveries in the history of science, or describe important technological innovations. Sometimes these objects are valuable and irreplaceable artifacts of science and technology, such as the Orville and Wilbur Wright's airplane, Galileo's telescope, or Charles Babbage's analytical engine. Often, however, the emphasis in the exhibit is placed not on the artifacts themselves but on the process the artifacts illustrate. In these situations, the museum will collect objects that can be used to demonstrate lessons, processes, or scientific principles to their visitors. For this reason, exhibits in science museums are typically very hands-on, featuring demonstrations and interactive displays with an emphasis on education. Well-known examples of museums of science and technology include the Museum of Science and Industry in Chicago, the Exploratorium in San Francisco, and the Air and Space Museum at the Smithsonian in Washington, D.C.

Natural history museums preserve and present specimens collected from the world of nature. Objects collected by natural history museums include birds, mammals, insects, plants, fossils, rocks, and reptiles. Exhibits within these museums cover such academic fields as botany, geology, paleontology, and zoology. Natural history collections were found among the earliest types of museums, such as the British Museum in London. Natural history was a popular hobby for individuals in the eighteenth and nineteenth centuries, and large collections of interesting specimens were often donated to growing national museums of natural history. From an educational standpoint, museums of natural history have proven useful for scholars and students of all ages and from all disciplines. By providing collections of animals, plants, and minerals, neatly organized and arranged by type or classification, such museums provide an invaluable service to individuals who may not otherwise have access to rare specimens. Well-known examples of museums of natural history include the National Museum of Natural History in Paris, the Natural History Museum in London, the Smithsonian's Museum of Natural History in Washington, D.C., the Field Museum in Chicago, and the American Museum of Natural History in New York.

Cultural history museums cover a variety of topics, cultures, and time periods. They can be found at many different levels in society. They range from museums of local history that illustrate the history of a city or county, to national museums that exhibit the history of an entire country, to museums of world history that display artifacts collected from all cultures throughout history and around the globe. In addition, museums of history often focus on different types of collections. Cultural history museums with a focus on archaeology, for example, gather artifacts from antiquity, such as Greece, Rome, Egypt, or Mesoamerica, to almost present day, such as colonial America. Anthropological or ethnographic museums typically present artifacts arranged by culture and attempt to provide the visitor with a new way of looking at different world cultures. History museums of a general nature often present

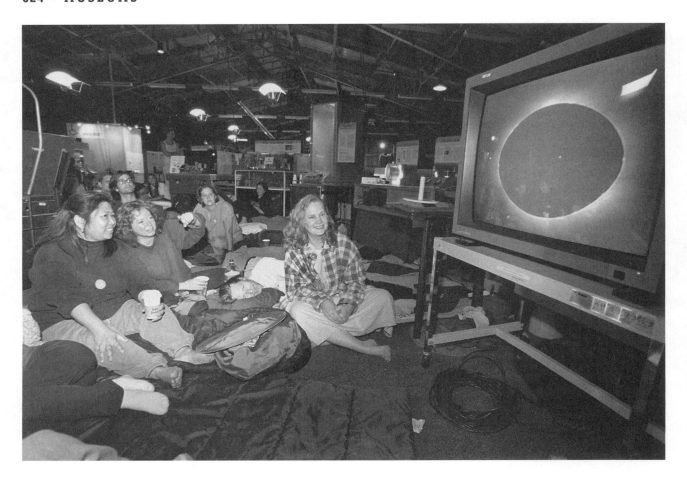

On August 11, 1999, the Exploratorium in San Francisco allowed a select group of participants to stay overnight to view a total solar eclipse by using high-speed Internet connections and live video links from an Exploratorium field station in Amasya, Turkey. (AFP/Corbis)

their collections chronologically, allowing their visitors to follow the evolution of objects in their collections through time. Usually, cultural history museums display artifacts that were once of utilitarian value, not just aesthetically pleasing. Such museums make an effort to situate their artifacts in a historical context; many often use models or simulated environments to provide an appropriate setting for their artifacts. These museums are essentially educational in their exhibit design philosophy; they usually offer more interpretation and explanation than other types of museums. Well-known examples of cultural history museums include the Museum of American History at the Smithsonian in Washington, D.C., and the British Museum in London.

Finally, there are also specialty museums of various miscellaneous types that do not fit neatly into the above classification scheme. These include museums that feature collections of unusual artifacts of a particular type, like baseball cards or Superman memorabilia; museums that cater to a specialized audience, such as children's museums; or museums dedicated to a specialized time period or geographic area, such as a museum of a small town or community.

The Purpose of Museums

All museums collect, preserve, and interpret objects. When working with their collections, modern museum professionals aim to accomplish three goals of equal importance: (1) to preserve the artifacts entrusted to their care; (2) to research and study their collections; and (3) to educate the public about the value, educational or aesthetic, of their holdings. All museums face the same problems in achieving these goals.

A fundamental aspect of collecting is the desire to preserve that which one collects. From the moment an artifact enters a museum's collection, museum professionals must take every precaution to ensure that no further damage or deterioration occurs to the artifact. This is called preventative conservation. Conservation activities form an important part of the artifact lifecycle in the museum. Although many visitors to a museum believe that the only responsibility the museum has is to care for the artifacts on exhibit, usually only 5 percent to 10 percent of a museum's entire collection is displayed to the public at any one time. The vast majority of a museum's collection remains locked away in storage facilities. It is crucial that proper care be taken of those artifacts in storage. This includes careful monitoring of environmental conditions, the storage of artifacts in nonreactive, nonharmful containers, and occasional conservation activities to ensure that artifacts remain undamaged over the years. If museum professionals do not take steps to preserve their collections, then their artifacts will eventually deteriorate beyond repair. Therefore, preservation is an essential goal of the modern museum professional.

For thousands of years, scholars have relied on museums to provide collections of objects worthy of study. Likewise, it is essential that the collection of a museum be properly examined, studied, and researched by the appropriate experts. The role of the curator in the museum is to ensure that the museum's artifacts are identified, made available to experts for study, and the resulting knowledge recorded and preserved for future scholars. In this way, the museum is fulfilling its role as an academic institution that began in Alexandria more than two thousand years ago. Today, many university museums maintain research collections; these collections are usually not displayed to the public and are reserved for academic research only. Such museums pride themselves on having extensive research collections, ranging from rare books to herpetological specimens, which attract researchers from around the world to come and study at their facility. For the museum professional, research is required to create programs for both educational and scholarly purposes. Research is also necessary to learn proper methods of preserving the artifacts in the care of the museum. Some artifacts will require special conservation methods. Other artifacts, such as bones from ancient graves, may be culturally sensitive and require special handling or display. Only with appropriate research can the museum ensure that its collections are being properly handled, treated, and exhibited.

Visitors to a museum today take for granted that their experience will be an educational one, but this was not always the case. The notion that a museum should serve an educational role outside of the academic sphere is a relatively new idea, rooted in the nineteenth century. The Royal Danish Museum in Copenhagen was one of the first museums to present its collections in an instructional manner—metal artifacts, for example, were arranged to illustrate the evolution of the Copper, Bronze, and Iron Ages. Today, virtually all artifacts are displayed in a manner that emphasizes the educational experience of the visitor. Exhibits introduce important themes, label copy keeps the visitor informed of the facts as well as the museum's interpretation of the artifacts, and tour guides emphasize the most important lessons to be learned from any given display. Museums today have different means of reaching their audiences. Most museums maintain education departments that train docents and other volunteers, offer special education programs, or bring educational outreach activities to the schools. Additional items, such as paper guides, booklets, or audiocassettes, allows visitors to delve into exhibit topics of interest to them in more depth without overwhelming other visitors with extraneous labels and displays. In general, museums have found that by educating the public, they increase the public's interest in the collections of the museum, benefiting both museum and museum visitor.

It is important to remember that from the moment an artifact enters a museum, it enters an artificial environment. An artifact on display or in storage in a museum will follow a life very different from its original or intended purpose. A cup that one thousand years ago was used for drinking will sit in a case, be kept for study, or be displayed to schoolchildren. No longer a utilitarian object, its utility lies in its value as an educational or research tool. Once an object becomes a museum artifact, it enters a new environment. The role of the museum professional is to facilitate this transition through preservation, research, and education.

Museum Organizations

The job of the museum professional is complicated, and many organizations exist to help museum professionals in their daily work. The American Association of Museums (AAM) was founded in 1906 to assist museums and museum professionals across the country. The AAM serves as an accreditation organization for museums, offers guidance in maintaining professional standards, and educates museum professionals through annual conferences, journals, and publications. More than sixteen thousand members, both individuals and institutions, are represented by the AAM. The International Council of Museums (ICOM) was founded in 1946 and has more than fifteen thousand members from 150 countries. ICOM is affiliated with the United Nations Educational, Scientific, and Cultural Organization (UNESCO) and provides an international forum for museum professionals to discuss global issues of museum education, responsibilities, and professionalism.

With the assistance of such organizations, the job of the museum professional has steadily evolved from an amateur to more professional status. In addition, museum studies has emerged as an approved field of study in its own right. It is now possible to obtain a master's degree in museum studies at many universities. Museum-studies programs worldwide train future museum professionals in the techniques and methods of the museum field. The establishment of museum studies as an approved academic discipline has helped museums around the world become more professional in managing their valuable resources.

Museums and Information Resources

Museums are responsible for maintaining and preserving many valuable resources, the most important of which are their collections of artifacts. These objects are vital information resources that document the worlds of art, science, nature, or history. By preserving their artifacts, museums are often preserving a direct link to the human past or to the natural world that may no longer exist outside the walls of the museum.

Equally important, however, are the data museums collect about their artifacts through research and study. Knowledge about a collection is accumulated through the efforts of curators, academic scholars, and other museum professionals. This information is then recorded in permanent form. The resulting documents form surrogate records that both describe and represent the artifacts of the museum. Surrogate records provide a valuable service by offering a source of data about artifacts that can be manipulated and accessed far more easily than the actual objects themselves. Thus, when

a curator needs to know how many paintings a museum has collected from a particular artist or a scholar wants to study a certain type of ceramic vessels, these individuals can consult data contained in the surrogate records while the artifacts themselves remain safely in storage. As museums become more professional, there is an increased awareness of the need to keep artifacts safe, secure, and undisturbed. The less frequently a museum artifact needs to be handled, the longer it will remain undamaged. To this end, more museums are limiting access to their collections, and more museums are encouraging research to be conducted using surrogate records. It is essential, therefore, that the data in the records of the museum be accurate and up-to-date.

The task of managing information resources in museums has now become a science. The integration of advanced information technology into museum environments has had a serious effect on the way modern museums manage their data records. Information science professionals worldwide now study the role of information technology in managing museum information resources. This field of study is generally known as "museum informatics."

Information Management in Museums

Museums have always had a need to manage their information resources. They need to know not only what they have but also what they know about what they have. In the past, information about museum collections was maintained in paper and card files. Access to these records was usually restricted to museum employees; moreover, search capabilities in these files were usually limited to only a few key fields. For example, card files may have been sorted by donor name, by accession number, or by title of object. Assuming the cards were kept up-to-date and properly organized, accessing data by any of these fields was usually straightforward. However, locating a set of records sorted by culture or material type would have been a difficult if not impossible task for even the most skilled and knowledgeable museum employee.

Modern information systems in museums offer museum professionals many new methods of organizing and accessing data. Such systems work in conjunction with existing paper records to augment the information-management capabilities of the museum. Electronic database systems allow museum employees to search and sort their computer records by almost any field. In addition, museum professionals are now able to store far more data about their artifacts on the computer than ever before possible on accession cards or ledger files. Also, by maintaining artifact data in electronic format, modern museums now have the capability to share data about their collections with other institutions in ways never before possible. Organizations are currently working to devise standards that will allow museums around the world to collaborate in their efforts to identify and research their collections. By sharing artifact records from one organization to another, museums may be able to advance significantly the state of knowledge in their fields.

However, as museums work to increase access to their information resources, some problems have been exacerbated; especially troublesome are those that concern copyright and intellectual or cultural property. The question of ownership of artifacts has traditionally been a difficult one for museum professionals. Whether or not the British Museum should return the Parthenon Marbles (also known as the Elgin Marbles) to Greece, for example, has been hotly debated since Lord Elgin removed these massive carvings from Athens in the late-eighteenth century. Laws such as the Native American Graves Protection and Repatriation Act (NAGPRA) exist to ensure that the rights of the original owners of museum artifacts are protected. As museums increase their online presence, many of these issues are now returning to the forefront of intellectual debate. Additionally, many museum professionals worry that by making electronic images and data about their collection available online, they are encouraging individuals to violate copyright regulations by making their own digital copies of works of art.

New Opportunities for Digital Museums

Despite these difficulties, the "wired" museum raises all sorts of new possibilities for the museum professional. Within the museum itself, interactive exhibits offer visitors new options for an in-depth exploration of exhibits. Computer displays can provide additional detailed data about each exhibit in the museum and allow visitors to interact with museum displays in ways never before possible. Electronic displays can help museums meet the accessibility needs of their visitors, providing audio, enlarged text, and so on, as needed. Note that electronic systems augment the artifacts

A tourist at the British Museum photographs a portion of the Elgin Marbles, the ownership of which has long been a contentious issue between Great Britain and Greece. (Reuters NewMedia Inc./Corbis)

of a museum, enhancing the experience of visiting a museum but never completely replacing the original collections.

Online, virtual museums offer digital visitors everything from information about the museum's location and hours of operation to virtual tours of the museum's galleries and collections. Many museums have information records about their artifacts linked to their websites in a manner that allows the general public to retrieve digital images and detailed textual descriptions of any artifact in the collection of the museum. Many museum educators create specialized educational outreach programs for schoolchildren. These programs, available online over the museum's website, are often integrated with school curricula and national educational standards. Finally, interactive online exhibits are able to offer virtual visitors specialized access to artifact data. For example, by gathering information about visitor interests online, museums can offer dynamic exhibits over the Internet that are specifically created for each individual patron.

The museum of the future will use technology to connect distant museums, museum professionals, and museum patrons. A scholar from New York who is examining over the Internet the rich collections of the Hermitage will be able to interact, via a three-dimensional virtual display, with a fellow researcher from Berlin who is studying the same collection. Students, teachers, scholars, and members of the general public, armed with only a computer and an Internet connection, will be able to browse the collections of every museum worldwide, including artifacts not currently on display in the museum. Individuals will have immediate access to the accumulated knowledge of a wide variety of experts in every field from every country. Virtual visitors physically located thousands of miles apart will stand next to each other in three-dimensional representations of archaeological sites so realistic as to be indistinguishable from the real thing, will handle three-dimensional virtual representations of priceless artifacts rendered with laser mapping accurate to the micrometer, and will share data and other information resources in ways never before possible.

See also: ARCHIVES, PUBLIC RECORDS, AND RECORDS MANAGEMENT; ARCHIVISTS; CURATORS; DATABASES, ELECTRONIC; INTERNET AND THE WORLD WIDE WEB.

Bibliography

Alexander, Edward P. (1979). *Museums in Motion: An Introduction to the History and Functions of Museums.* Nashville, TN: American Association for State and Local History.

Bearman, David, and Trant, Jennifer, eds. (2000). "Museum Informatics Meets the World Wide Web." *Journal of the American Society for Information Science* 51(1):2–56.

Burcaw, George E. (1995). *Introduction to Museum Work.* Walnut Creek, CA: AltaMira Press.

Chenhall, Robert G. (1978). *Nomenclature for Museum Cataloging: A System for Classifying Man-Made Objects.* Nashville, TN: American Association for State and Local History.

Dudley, Dorothy H., and Wilkinson, Irma B., eds. (1979). *Museum Registration Methods.* Washington, DC: American Association of Museums.

Hooper-Greenhill, Eilean. (1991). *Museum and Gallery Education.* Leicester, Eng.: Leicester University Press.

Hooper-Greenhill, Eilean. (1992). *Museums and the Shaping of Knowledge.* London: Routledge.

Jones-Garmil, Katherine, ed. (1997). *The Wired Museum: Emerging Technologies and Changing Paradigms.* Washington, DC: American Association of Museums.

MacBeath, George, and Gooding, S. James, eds. (1969). *Basic Museum Management.* Ottawa: Canadian Museums Association.

MacDonald, George F. (1991). "The Museum as Information Utility." *Museum Management and Curatorship* 10:305–311.

MacDonald, George F. (1992). "Change and Challenge: Museums in the Information Society." In *Museums and Communities,* eds. Ivan Karp, Christine Mullen Kreamer and Steven D. Lavine. Washington, DC: Smithsonian Institution Press.

Pearce, Susan M. (1994). *Interpreting Objects and Collections.* London: Routledge.

Pettit, Charles, and Orna, Elizabeth. (1998). *Information Management in Museums.* Aldershot, Eng.: Gower.

Thomas, Selma, and Mintz, Ann, eds. (1998). *The Virtual and the Real: Media in the Museum.* Washington, DC: American Association of Museums.

Vance, David, and Chenhall, Robert G. (1988). *Museum Collections and Today's Computers.* New York: Greenwood Press.

Weil, Stephen E. (1995). *A Cabinet of Curiosities: Inquiries into Museums and Their Prospects.* Washington, DC: Smithsonian Institution Press.

Zorich, Diane M. (1999). *Managing Digital Assets: Options for Cultural and Educational Organizations.* Los Angeles, CA: Getty Information Institute.

PAUL F. MARTY

■ MUSIC, POPULAR

Public outcries about possible negative effects of popular music on youths are not new. They accompanied, for example, the emergence of jazz in the 1920s, the shaking of Elvis Presley's hips in the 1950s, and much of the politically influenced rock-and-roll of the 1960s. With few exceptions, however, social scientists began to pay systematic attention to the role of popular music in the socialization of youths only in the 1980s. Increased research on popular music resulted from the extreme, "edgy" nature of the messages that began to appear in songs and music videos near the end of that decade. Popular music regularly draws fire from parents, teachers, and mainstream cultural authorities for reputed sexual explicitness, demeaning of women, violence, racism, and glorification of drugs and alcohol and because the hard-edged music of performers such as Marilyn Manson has been charged with influencing the people who have been responsible for several school shootings. Oversimplified and alarmist as such charges tend to be, they bespeak a growing awareness of the role of popular music in the process of growing up. As European researcher Keith Roe (1987, pp. 215–216) writes, "in terms of both the sheer amount of time devoted to it and the meanings it assumes, it is music, not television, that is the most important medium for adolescents."

Uses and Gratifications

Although many studies report that adolescents spend more time with television than with music, surveys often underestimate young people's total exposure to popular music. Numerous studies base estimates of music listening on radio use, ignoring exposure from other sources, such as CDs, tapes, and music videos. Moreover, music listening is often a secondary, background activity, appearing in the environment of adolescents without any conscious decision to introduce it, and such secondary exposure often goes unreported. Secondary exposure is important, however, and can often be observed when an adolescent is studying, chatting, or doing chores and still reacts if the "background" music is turned off. According to 1990 data gathered by Donald Roberts and Lisa Henriksen, when all popular music listening is counted, whether from radio or other sources and whether in the foreground or the background, preadolescents and adolescents spend somewhere between three and four hours a day with popular music. Girls listen more than boys—substantially more by the high school years—and African-American youths listen more than white youths. Music-video viewing occupies about fifteen to thirty minutes a day for adolescents.

Music matters to adolescents in ways that go beyond the mere filling of time. It can reduce tension, provide escape or distraction from problems, relieve loneliness, ease the drudgery of repetitive chores, fill uncomfortable silence, provide fodder for conversation, energize parties, and delineate the boundaries between subgroups. How important is music to adolescents? One study reported that, when asked what medium they would choose to take with them if they were stranded on a desert isle, junior and senior high school students from northern California chose music ahead of all other media, including television. By eleventh grade, music was selected over television by a margin of two to one (Roberts and Henriksen, 1990).

Research on popular music uses and gratifications suggests "the primacy of affect." That is, for most youths, music use is governed principally by the desire to control mood and enhance emotional states. When teenagers feel lonely or seek distraction from their troubles, music tends to be the chosen medium. The listening experience can be quite intense, often associated with the "peak" experiences of life, both positive and negative. As in many areas related to popular music use, gender makes a difference in terms of mood management. Males are more likely than females to use music as a tool to increase energy level and seek stimulation—to get "psyched up." Females, on the other hand, are more likely to listen in order to lift their spirits when they are down or even to dwell on a somber mood. In the same way that girls often listen to sad songs when they are sad, many male heavy metal fans apparently listen to angry music when they are angry. In one study, a typical heavy metal fan said he sought out "full-blown thrashing metal" when he was "mad at the world" (Arnette, 1991).

Several scholars contend that the social uses and meanings of popular music provide the real key to understanding its place in the lives of youths. Popular music is central to many adolescent social occasions. It accompanies courtship and sexual behavior, offers a basis for friendships, and provides the backdrop at parties and dances. Perhaps the strongest testimony to the importance of music in socializing is the near impossibility of teenagers having a party without music. Music can replace or invoke the presence of absent peers, thus relieving feelings of loneliness. Music listening may also prepare adolescents for future peer interactions and relationships. To a large extent, youths who know little about pop culture or current music trends are consigned to the margins of teenage culture, whereas pop music "experts" tend to enjoy both more friends and enhanced status.

Music Preferences

Many adults tend to lump contemporary popular music into three categories: rock, heavy metal, and rap. Youth culture, however, recognizes a mind-boggling array of genres. An inventory of popular music types might include Top 40, rap/hip-hop, contemporary hits, easy listening, album rock, soft rock, hard rock, classic rock, grunge, alternative, new age, world beat, progressive rock, reggae, protest rock, industrial rock, salsa, house, ska, high life, technopop, synthpop, college rock, alternative rock, death metal, thrash metal, and thrash punk, as well a number of still-popular categories from the past, such as new wave, punk, surfer music, Motown, and psychedelic rock. Many teenagers or college students could probably add another dozen entries to the list.

The important point is that young people do not listen simply to "popular music"; rather, they select a certain type of music, often to the exclusion of most other types. For example, heavy metal fans typically abhor Top 40 songs; rap fans pay little attention to classic rock. Such diversity and selectivity of popular music tastes matter. To the extent that popular music influences adolescent beliefs or behavior, the effect of the music depends on the specific genre. Three hours a day of "death metal" provides different messages than three hours a day of soft-rock ballads, and the effects of the two would be expected to be different.

Music preferences also matter because of their link with individual and group identity. They suggest who adolescents think they are and how they function in their society. Differences in music preference are not random or idiosyncratic; they are related to various background, peer group, and individual differences. Of all the demographic predictors of music taste, race and ethnicity may be the most powerful. Entire genres of popular music are linked unambiguously and proudly with their racial and ethnic roots—R&B, soul, and rap with African-American culture, salsa with Hispanics, reggae with its Jamaican heritage, and so on. In a 1999 study of U.S. youths' media use, Roberts and his colleagues found that more than 70 percent of African-American teenagers cited rap as their favorite music; only 22 percent mentioned either pop rock or "Top 10," and very few cited rock, heavy metal, punk, or country. The preferences of the white youths were distributed much differently; both rock and heavy metal drew a quarter of the responses and only 13 percent mentioned rap.

Gender is also associated with fundamental differences in music preferences. Whatever the historical era and whatever the population being studied, females are more attracted to softer, more romantic, more mainstream forms (pop, disco, soft rock, Top 40). Males gravitate to harder-edged genres (heavy metal, hard rock, punk, grunge, psychedelic rock). Males are also more likely than females to adopt nonmainstream, fringe or "progressive" music affinities.

Music preference is also connected to where youths stand in their peer culture. "Music style" (i.e., the selection of a certain type of music and a personal style to go with it) functions as a powerful identifying marker in the school crowd structure. Some groups, such as "alterna-chicks," "punkers," "metalheads," "rastas," and so on, are labeled primarily on the basis of music choice. Research by Roe (1987) in Europe indicates that the link between school experience and popular music taste springs inevitably from the process of academic evaluation, which creates an "in-group" of people who are popular with other youths and share the dominant values and goals of the school structure, and an "out-group" of people who operate on the margin and harbor antischool, antiadult feelings.

Interpretation and Effects

Much of the criticism aimed at popular music and music videos stems from two assumptions: (1) that a given lyric has a single, relatively evident meaning and (2) that the values and behaviors portrayed in lyrics and music-video images influence how young listeners think and act. It is not surprising that most commentators emphasize the negative. Public anxiety is fueled by trends toward sexual explicitness and a clear increase in lyric treatments of such topics as violence, misogyny, racism, suicide, Satanism, and substance use. The emergence in the early 1980s of music videos, which made it possible for adults ostensibly to "see" what their children were listening to, added to the criticism.

Although most adolescents say it is music's "sound" that attracts them, "content" clearly matters. A significant number of youths mention lyrics as a primary gratification and most cite them as a secondary gratification. For better or worse, young people attend to, process, discuss, memorize, and even take to heart what lyrics and music videos say. The important issues are what meanings accrue from this process, and what influences they exert on the attitudes and behavior of young people.

To assume a single, "correct" meaning for a song ignores the constructive nature of interpretation. Wide variations exist in the sense audiences make of popular lyrics and music videos. For example, some people read a refrain such as "Let's get physical" as an invitation to casual sex, while others see it as a call to aerobic exercise. Such differences, however, are far from random. Different psychological and social experiences influenced by factors such as age, gender, race/ethnicity, and socioeconomic status are related to the meanings that different listeners impute to a given lyric. Younger adolescents and teenagers from lower socioeconomic status backgrounds make more concrete interpretations, often failing to recognize metaphors. Girls focus on different aspects of romantic lyrics than boys. A video image interpreted by white adults as gratuitously violent may be read by African-American youths as an honest political statement. Sexually active teenagers interpret lyrics about teenage pregnancy quite differently from less experienced counterparts (Christenson and Roberts, 1998). Moreover, right or wrong, particular performers and genres become associated with particular themes (e.g., heavy metal with drugs, violence, and suicide; rap with violence and misogyny), leading audiences to develop schemas (i.e., generalized images) that can result in agreement about a song's general themes, if not the particular details. In short, although variant readings of popular songs are more common than many critics assume, the variance is related in predictable ways to group and individual differences and to the degree to which different genres and performers are associated with particular themes.

Peter Christenson and Roberts (1998) have summarized a growing body of experimental research indicating that music content, particularly in music-video form, exerts at least short-term influences on the perceptions and attitudes of adolescents. For example, music videos laced with antisocial or violent images made viewers more antagonistic toward women and more likely to condone violence. Highly gender-stereotyped videos increased acceptance of gender-stereotyped behavior in others. Sexually charged videos influenced viewers to perceive subsequently observed ambiguous behavior as "sexier" and to express more accepting attitudes toward premarital sex. White youths exposed to politically radical rap videos became more racially tolerant and less likely to sympathize with reactionary racial political positions. Although these findings have not been replicated using lyrics only, there is evidence that once young people have seen a music video, the visual images are "replayed" during subsequent exposure to audio-only renditions of that song.

It is a huge leap from the short-term outcomes found in experiments to claims about the role of popular music in suicides and shootings by teenagers. Millions of heavy metal and "gangsta rap" fans spend hours with their chosen music genres and never threaten others or themselves. Most professionals who are concerned with the causes of violence and suicide point to numerous conditions that are unrelated to popular culture (e.g., depression, access to guns, substance abuse, "conduct disorders") as necessary precursors of such drastic acts, and such conditions have been at work in most of the incidents that are cited in the debate. In short, the argument that exposure to popular music can function as a primary cause of such drastic behaviors seems tenuous.

This does not, however, negate the potential role of popular music in at least some suicides and violent incidents. As noted above, music is frequently used for mood control, and its influence on mood suggests an "amplification effect," a strong tendency for music to heighten whatever emotional state a listener brings to a listening situation, including anger and depression. To immerse oneself in angry, depressing music, then, seems a poor strategy for coping with anger and despair. Given substantial evidence that adolescents who are depressed, angry, alienated, abusing drugs, and so on are particularly drawn to the kinds of angry, nihilistic music that celebrates such "troubled" states and traits, there is legitimate cause for concern. While by no means a first cause of suicide or violence, there is good reason to argue that these kinds of music can certainly play a contributory role.

Most of the time, however, popular music is simply a source of pleasure for young people. They listen because they like it. In addition, popular music teaches young listeners about the world, helps them sort out emotions and manage moods, and facilitates social interaction. This is not surprising since popular music is of, by, and for youths, addressing issues that are central to them (e.g., love, sex, loyalty, independence, friendship, authority) with a directness that they seldom get from adults. In other words, popular music is perhaps the primary vehicle of youth culture.

See also: PORNOGRAPHY; SEX AND THE MEDIA; VIOLENCE IN THE MEDIA, ATTRACTION TO; VIOLENCE IN THE MEDIA, HISTORY OF RESEARCH ON.

Bibliography

Arnette, J. (1991). "Adolescence and Heavy Metal Music: From the Mouths of Metalheads." *Youth and Society* 23(1):76–98.

Christenson, Peter G., and Roberts, Donald F. (1998). *It's Not Only Rock and Roll: Popular Music in the Lives of Adolescents.* Cresskill, NJ: Hampton Press.

Roberts, Donald F.; Foehr, Ulla G.; Rideout, Victoria J.; and Brodie, Mollyann. (1999). *Kids & Media @ the New Millennium.* Menlo Park, CA: Kaiser Family Foundation.

Roberts, Donald F., and Henriksen, Lisa. (1990). "Music Listening vs. Television Viewing among Older Adolescents." Paper presented at the annual meeting of the International Communication Association, Dublin, Ireland, June.

Roe, Keith. (1987). "The School and Music in Adolescent Socialization." In *Popular Music and Communication,* ed. James Lull. Beverly Hills, CA: Sage Publications.

DONALD F. ROBERTS
PETER G. CHRISTENSON

NATIONAL LIBRARIES

See: Libraries, National

NATIONAL TELEVISION VIOLENCE STUDY

Violence on television has been the subject of debate for decades in the United States. It seems as though everyone has an opinion on the topic. Many observers argue that there is an excessive amount of bloodshed on television. In fact, a 1999 national poll by the Pew Research Center found that 70 percent of Americans believe that entertainment programs contain too much violence. Others criticize certain types of portrayals that seem overly graphic or gratuitous. Still others defend the use of violence in the media by pointing to movies such as *Schindler's List* (1993) and *Saving Private Ryan* (1998), both of which contain a great deal of physical aggression but have educational value.

Spending an evening with the television remote control can fuel this debate. After the 1999 shooting at Columbine High School in Colorado, Josh Getlin (1999, p. A17), a reporter for the *Los Angeles Times*, described television in the following way:

> Scenes of unspeakable carnage from Columbine High School (click) gave way to images of buildings burning in Belgrade after a NATO attack (click) followed by a hidden-camera video showing a nanny beating a toddler (click), then a Western

shoot-'em-up (click) and more scenes from the suburban campus where students were gunned down like targets at a carnival arcade. It was just another night on American television and a disturbing reminder of how deeply ingrained violence is in our culture.

Is the television landscape truly saturated with violence? Does all violence on television look the same? In 1994, researchers at four American universities set out to answer these questions. The result is the National Television Violence Study (NTVS), a comprehensive, scientific analysis of the nature and amount of violence on American television. The researchers monitored more than eight thousand hours of television across a three-year period, from 1994–1995 to 1996–1997. Three annual reports were released as part of the project (*National Television Violence Study*, 1997, 1998a, 1998b).

The study was a milestone in the history of television research for two reasons. First, it went beyond simple counts of violent behaviors in a program and instead provided an extensive analysis of how violence is portrayed on television. Contextual features such as whether a perpetrator is attractive and whether the violence is rewarded are far more important than the sheer amount of aggression in trying to understand how harmful a portrayal might be for viewers. Second, the study was based on the largest and most representative sample of television programs ever evaluated in a single project.

Background

The NTVS came about during a decade of intense political and public criticism of the media. During the early 1990s, there were numerous bills before Congress that involved some attempt to regulate television content. In a study of newspaper coverage during the time, Cynthia Hoffner (1998) found that 50 percent of the articles about television violence focused on possible solutions to the problem, most notably, government regulation.

In 1993, in the midst of this public scrutiny, Senator Paul Simon (D-IL) and other policymakers called on the entertainment industry to examine more closely the way in which violence is depicted on television. The National Cable Television Association (NCTA), a trade association representing the cable industry, responded to this call by sponsoring a study of television content to be conducted independently of Hollywood. After reviewing proposals from many expert researchers across the country, NCTA commissioned the NTVS, funding the project at a cost of $3.3 million.

The NTVS involved a team of media researchers from four universities. Researchers at the University of California, Santa Barbara, assessed violence in all types of entertainment programming such as drama, comedy, movies, children's shows, and music videos. It is this portion of the study that will be reported here. Researchers at the University of Texas at Austin provided an in-depth analysis of violence in a specific type of programming—reality-based shows, such as real-life police and rescue shows and talk shows. Researchers at the University of Wisconsin, Madison, studied the role of television ratings and advisories, including their effect on the viewing decisions of parents and children. Researchers at the University of North Carolina, Chapel Hill, examined the effectiveness of antiviolence public-service announcements.

In addition to the researchers, NTVS involved an advisory council, whose role was to protect the integrity and independence of the research, especially since the funding was coming from the cable industry itself. The council also provided the researchers with advice and feedback on the design, findings, and implications of the study. The council included representatives from seventeen national organizations concerned with the effect of television on society. Among these were the American Academy of Pediatrics, the Ameri-can Medical Association, the International Communication Association, and the National Parent Teacher Association. In addition, one-third of the members came from organizations representing the entertainment industry, such as the Producers Guild of America and the Caucus for Producers, Writers, and Directors.

Foundations of the Study

The NTVS is a content analysis that is strongly based on what is known about how media violence affects viewers. The following conclusions served as the four basic "foundations" for the project:

1. Television violence contributes to harmful effects on viewers.
2. Three types of effects can occur from viewing television violence: (a) learning aggressive attitudes and behaviors, (b) desensitization to violence, and (c) fear of being victimized by violence.
3. Not all violence poses the same degree of risk of these harmful effects.
4. Younger children are a special audience.

These foundations resulted from an extensive review that the researchers conducted (before beginning the project) of all the scientific studies that had examined the effects of television violence.

Foundation 1

The conclusion that television violence contributes to harmful effects on viewers has been reached by virtually every major professional organization that has reviewed the research, including the American Psychological Association (1993), the American Medical Association (1996), and the National Institute of Mental Health (1982).

Foundation 2

Literally hundreds of studies show that television violence can contribute to aggressive behavior in children. Moreover, this effect can persist into adolescence and adulthood. For example, one study by Rowell Huesmann (1986) found that exposure to television violence at the age of eight years helped to predict criminal behavior in a sample of adults. In addition to increased aggression, there are two other types of harmful effects that can occur. Repeated exposure to violence can cause viewers to become more callous, or desensitized, to the harmfulness of violent behavior. Also,

Content Analysis

A content analysis is a scientific method for studying the features of different communication messages. Researchers can use a content analysis to analyze messages in newspapers, on the radio, on television, and even in people's diaries. Any recorded document can be studied by this method.

As an example, Roger Johnson (1999) was interested in looking at the types of stories featured on television news. He decided to study four different types of news programming: national network news (CBS), local news (a CBS affiliate), cable network news (CNN), and independent superstation news (WWOR, New York). The first step in a content analysis is to draw a representative sample of the documents to be studied. If Johnson had chosen a single night from each type of programming, his sample would have been limited to a certain set of stories or events occurring on that particular day. Instead, he randomly selected one newscast a week over a six-month period for each type of programming, resulting in a total sample of one hundred programs. In this way, Johnson's sample covers a range of time periods and possible news stories.

Next, the researcher must precisely define the measures and categories that will be analyzed within the documents. In this case, Johnson specified six categories of news stories: violent crime, tragedy, nonviolent conflict, social protest, war/military affairs, and all others. Two coders were trained to recognize these themes. Then, working independently, the coders watched the videotaped programs and placed each of the 1,798 separate news stories into one of the six categories. By having the two coders work alone, Johnson made sure that the judgments were as objective as possible. What did he find? Slightly more than half of all news stories (53%) featured violent crime, tragedy, or conflict, leading Johnson to conclude that news programming is dominated by "bad" news.

Content analyses differ in how good or scientifically valid they are. A valid content analysis should include a representative sample of documents, precise definitions of the measures, and independent coders who show a high level of agreement on their judgments. Johnson's study is characterized by all of these elements. As a contrast, compare it to a hypothetical study that looks only at network news during a particular week and that involves a single person judging the content. This may be how viewers themselves draw opinions about the nature of television news, but it is not very scientific or generalizable.

A content analysis can provide information about what is contained in mass-media messages, and it can even be used to compare the mass media with the real world to see how realistic or distorted the messages are. It cannot, however, be used to test the effect of media messages on the audience. Quite simply, it is not a study of how people react to the messages; rather, it is a study of the messages themselves.

---

long-term exposure to violent portrayals can exaggerate people's fear of being attacked by violence in the real world.

Foundation 3

There are many ways to depict violence on television. For example, a fistfight can last only a few seconds and be shot from a distance, or it can persist for several minutes and feature many close-ups of the action. There are also differences in the types of characters who commit violence—some are heroes trying to save lives and others are criminals acting out of greed or anger. There are differences also in the outcomes of violence—some portrayals show the pain and suffering of the victim, whereas others do not. In other words, not all television violence is the same. In fact, the way in which violence is presented helps to determine whether the portrayal poses harm to the viewer. Certain features of violence increase the risk of a harmful effect such as learning aggression or desensitization, whereas others decrease that risk.

NTVS identified eight contextual features that help to predict the likely effect of violence on viewers. First, the nature of the perpetrator must be considered. An attractive perpetrator is a potent role model, especially for children, and can increase the likelihood that viewers will learn aggression from a portrayal. Second, the motive or reason for violence is important. Acts that seem justified or morally correct can increase viewer aggression, whereas unjustified violence can actually decrease the risk of learning aggression. Third, the presence of weapons, especially guns and knives, can enhance aggression because such devices often trigger violent thoughts and memories in the viewer. Fourth, violence that is extensive or graphic can increase the risk of viewers learning aggression from a program. Exposure to extensive graphic violence also produces desensitization and can increase fear among viewers, the other two harmful effects mentioned above. Fifth, portrayals of violence that seem realistic are more likely to increase viewer aggression than are unrealistic scenes. Realistic violence also can increase audience fear. However, this does not mean that cartoon or fantasy violence on television is harmless, as discussed below. Sixth, violence that is explicitly rewarded or that simply goes unpunished increases the risk of learning aggression, whereas violence that is condemned decreases that risk. In addition, violence that goes unpunished can elevate fear, particularly when it appears to be unjust or random. Seventh, the negative consequences of violence for the victim are an important contextual cue. Showing the pain and suffering that result from violence can discourage the learning of aggression among viewers. Finally, violence that is cast in a humorous light can contribute to viewer aggression by making it seem rewarding. Humorous violence also may desensitize viewers to the seriousness of such behaviors.

Given the importance of context, NTVS created measures of all eight of these features so they could be evaluated anytime a violent portrayal was found on television.

Foundation 4

Both children and adults are influenced by the contextual features described above. Nevertheless, some unique concerns arise with regard to young children, particularly those under the age of seven years. Young children's cognitive abilities are still developing, so they often have interpretations of the television messages that are different from the interpretations of mature viewers. For example, studies by Peter Nikken and Allerd Peeters (1988) and by John Wright and his colleagues (1994) show that young children often have difficulty distinguishing reality from fantasy on television. In other words, what seems unrealistic to an older child or adult may be quite real to a preschooler. This helps to explain why researchers such as Lynette Friedrich and Aletha Stein (1973) found that young children will readily imitate violent cartoon characters.

Younger children also are more vulnerable to television violence in general. In a meta-analysis of 217 studies, Haejung Paik and George Comstock (1994) found that compared to older viewers, preschoolers showed the strongest effects of television violence on aggressive behavior. Because of these age differences, NTVS identified younger children as a special audience when monitoring the content of television and reporting the findings.

Definition of Violence

Most people would agree that when a character shoots someone with a rifle, it is an example of violence. But what if they found out that the character tripped over a rock while hunting and the shooting was accidental? Violence can be defined in numerous ways, with each decision about the definition having important implications for the findings of a given study. For example, should verbal assaults be considered as violence? Should physical aggression directed at animals be included? What about humorous depictions of violence, such as slapstick?

Obviously, there are no "true" or correct answers to these questions. Yet researchers must clearly specify what gets "counted" as violence and what does not before embarking on a content analysis. According to NTVS, three key features must be present for a portrayal to qualify as violence: (1) the perpetrator as well as the target of violence must be animate or living beings, (2) there must be a clear intent to harm, and (3) the harm must be physical in nature as opposed to psychological or emotional. The following is an even more precise definition:

> [Violence is] any overt depiction of a credible threat of physical force or the actual use of such force intended to physically harm an animate being or group of beings. Violence also includes certain depictions of physically harmful consequences against an animate being or group that occurs as a result of unseen violent means [National Television Violence Study, 1997, p. 41].

Thus, three forms of violence were included in the study: credible threats, behavioral acts, and harmful consequences of unseen violence.

Sample

One of the hallmarks of the NTVS project is its sample, which is substantially larger than that of any other single content analysis of television violence. Previous studies of television violence typically analyzed anywhere from 80 to 120 hours of programming. In contrast, NTVS videotaped about 2,700 hours of material each year during the three-year period, resulting in a total sample of more than 8,000 hours. Furthermore, most of the earlier studies examined programming on the three major broadcast networks only (ABC, NBC, and CBS). Although this may have reflected American viewing patterns in the past, more than two-thirds of American homes had cable television by 1995. To more fully capture the universe of American television in the 1990s, NTVS looked at programming across twenty-three different broadcast and cable channels.

Another strength of the sample is that instead of choosing intact days or weeks of programming, NTVS selected each individual program randomly from a population of all programs appearing across a nine-month timeframe. This approach ensured that an unusual news event, such as a schoolyard shooting or the breakout of war, would have much less effect on the overall representativeness of the sample. If an entire day or week had been chosen, such atypical news events could have dominated and therefore contaminated the sample.

Each year from October to June, the researchers randomly selected programs on twenty-three television channels to create a composite week of content for each channel. Programs were sampled between the hours of 6:00 A.M AND 11:00 P.M., across all seven days of the week. The twenty-three channels were those most frequently viewed by the American public, with the exception of CNN and ESPN, which were excluded because sports and breaking news were not evaluated in the study. The channels were grouped into five categories: broadcast network (ABC, NBC, CBS, and Fox), independent broadcast (Los Angeles–based KCAL, KCOP, and KTTV), public broadcasting (PBS), basic cable (A&E, AMC, Cartoon Network, Disney, Family Channel, Lifetime, Nickelodeon, TNT, USA, VH-1, and MTV), and premium cable (Cinemax, HBO, and Showtime).

In total, the 2,700 hours of television sampled each year resulted in more than 9,500 programs observed across the three-year period. As stipulated in the research contract with the study's funder (NCTA), all types of programs were analyzed for violence except for religious programs, game shows, infomercials, instructional shows, and breaking news. These five categories represented less than 15 percent of the programming each year.

Measuring Violence across Incidents, Scenes, and Programs

NTVS measured violence across three distinct levels or units of analysis. The "violent incident," the smallest unit, was defined as a violent interaction between a perpetrator and a victim. The "violent scene" was defined as a series of related violent incidents that occur without a significant break in the flow violence, such as a bar fight. The largest level of analysis was the entire "violent program." Some contextual features of violence were judged at the level of each violent incident, such as whether the perpetrator was attractive. Other features were evaluated by taking the entire violent scene into account, such as how graphic was the violence. Still other features required a consideration of the entire program as a unit, such as whether there was an overall theme of antiviolence in the show. By analyzing violence at all three levels, the researchers were able to provide comprehensive information about the meaning of violence on television.

Coding and Training

An elaborate codebook was developed to provide detailed and precise definitions of terms such as "credible threat," "rewarded violence," and "long-term consequences." The codebook also provided extensive rules of judgment for coding. Each year, more than fifty undergraduate students at the University of California, Santa Barbara, were trained to become highly skilled at applying the definitions and rules laid out in the codebook. These coders received approximately forty hours of classroom instruction and twenty hours of laboratory practice to help them learn the complex coding scheme. Once trained, the coders worked individually in quiet laboratories as they assessed programs for violent content.

It took approximately twenty weeks each year to complete all the coding. Every week during this time, half of the coders independently evaluated the same program to assess consistency across individuals. Agreement or reliability was at least 80 percent on nearly all the measures coded each year.

Major Findings

The NTVS researchers found a remarkable degree of consistency in how violence was portrayed across the three years of the study. They also found that the way that most television violence is portrayed does in fact pose risks to viewers. What are some of the portrayals that can be harmful?

First, much of television violence is "glamorized," or cast in a positive light. Across three years of the study, nearly 40 percent of the violent incidents on television were initiated by "good" characters who can serve as attractive role models (see Figure 1). The risk here is that viewers of all ages, but especially children, are likely to emulate characters who are perceived as attractive.

Another aspect of glamorization is that physical aggression is often condoned on television. For example, more than one-third of violent programs featured bad characters who are never punished anywhere in the plot. Violence that goes unpunished poses risk because it can encourage the learning of aggression among viewers. In addition, fully 71 percent of violent scenes contained no

FIGURE 1. *Patterns of glamorized violence on television.*

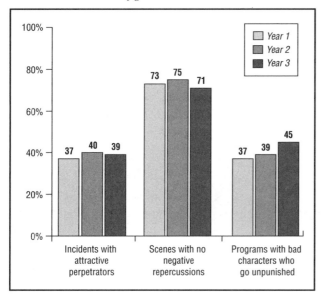

FIGURE 2. *Patterns of sanitized violence on television.*

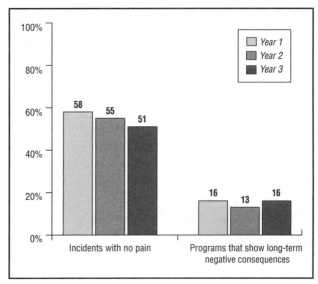

remorse, criticism, or penalty for violence at the time that it occurs. This is especially problematic for viewers under the age of seven years who focus mostly on immediate repercussions and lack the cognitive ability to consider punishments for aggression that may occur later in a program.

Second, most television violence is "sanitized," or shown with minimized negative consequences. In fact, roughly half of the violent incidents on television showed no physical harm or pain to the victim (see Figure 2). Not only are short-term outcomes often missing, so are long-term consequences. Over the three-year period, only 15 percent of the violent programs showed any prolonged negative effects of violence on the family, friends, or community of the victim. As discussed above, the portrayal of negative outcomes such as pain and suffering can decrease the chances that viewers will learn aggression from media violence.

Third, much of the serious violence on television is "trivialized," or shown as less serious than it is. Across the three-year study, more than half of the violent incidents featured physical aggression that would be deadly or incapacitating if it were to occur in real life (see Figure 3). Yet much of this serious violence is undercut by humor. In fact, about 40 percent of the violent scenes on television are shown in a humorous context. Exposure to serious violence that is made to seem trivial can contribute to both desensitization and imitation among viewers.

FIGURE 3. *Patterns of trivialized violence on television.*

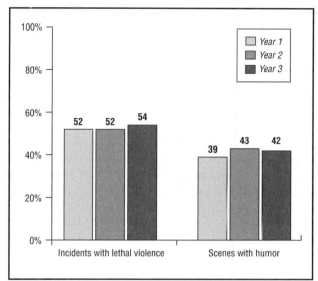

FIGURE 4. *Programs with violence by channel type.*

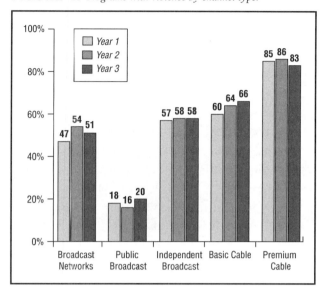

Fourth, very few programs emphasize an antiviolence theme. A program can include violence in a way that is actually educational rather than promotional of violence. For example, violence can be shown to have strong negative consequences or alternatives to violence can be promoted. Less than 5 percent of violent programs featured an antiviolence message across the three years of the study.

Thus, what is the prevailing message? Violence on American television is typically presented as an acceptable and often beneficial way to solve problems, and it rarely results in any serious or lasting damage.

The NTVS researchers also looked at the sheer prevalence of violence, independent of how it is portrayed. Over the three years of the study, a steady 60 percent of programs across the television landscape contained some violence. However, the prevalence of violence varied quite a bit across the different channel types, with premium cable the most likely to feature violent programs (more than 80% of the programs on these channels contained violence) and public broadcasting the least likely (fewer than 20% of the programs on this channel contained violence) (see Figure 4).

The researchers also looked at the concentration or amount of violence within a program. They found that the typical violent program featured at least six violent incidents per hour. Each of these incidents involved a different perpetrator and victim, and many of them included multiple acts of physical aggression. In fact, more than 60

percent of the violent incidents contained repeated behavioral acts of aggression on a victim. In other words, it is rare for a television perpetrator to hit, shoot, or stab someone only once.

The last major finding concerns what the NTVS researchers called "high-risk" portrayals. Depictions were labeled "high risk" when several plot elements that encourage the learning of aggression are all featured in one scene. A high-risk portrayal features an attractive perpetrator, engaging in justified violence that goes unpunished, that results in minimal consequences to the victim, and that seems realistic to the viewer.

The researchers found that for children under the age of seven years, high-risk portrayals of violence that teach aggression are found most often in cartoons, the very programs that are targeted to this age group. Of course, cartoons pose little risk for older, more mature viewers who routinely discount animated content as unrealistic. But preschoolers have difficulty distinguishing reality from fantasy on television, and therefore are susceptible to imitating fantasy violence that occurs on television.

Taking into account the typical viewing habits of children in the United States, the researchers concluded that the average American preschooler who watches mostly cartoons is exposed to more than five hundred high-risk portrayals of violence each year. These portrayals contain a potent set of plot features that strongly encourage the learning of aggression in some of the most vulnerable members of the television audience: young children.

Implications

The NTVS received a great deal of public attention. The findings each year made headline news in major newspapers such as *The New York Times, The Washington Post, USA Today,* and the *Los Angeles Times.* In addition, the study was featured on CNN, on the ABC, CBS, and NBC news programs, and on the "Jim Lehrer Online NewsHour."

The study also was recognized by prominent policymakers. Senator Paul Simon (D-IL) described it as "a solid report that should be a strong signal to the television industry and to the public that glorified violence is harmful and that we still need improvement" (Simon, 1996). Representative Joseph P. Kennedy (D-MA) stated that "The National Television Violence Study shows the problem is not going away. The television industry must work together and clean up media violence for the sake of public health—our children's health" (Kennedy, 1997). Even the president of the United States acknowledged the study. The researchers briefed the White House regarding the findings, and President Bill Clinton issued a statement noting that the study "shows that there is still too much violence on the television, and that we must all continue the important work we have begun" (Clinton, 1997).

However, the effect of the study was not limited to political rhetoric alone. In 1996, Representative Edward Markey (D-MA) argued that NTVS was instrumental in helping to pass V-chip legislation, mandating that a blocking device be installed in new television sets. Markey (1996, pp. 5–6) described the study's report as "devastating" for the television industry, noting the following:

> It shredded the industry argument that the V-chip was unnecessary because voluntary action was working. Instead, the authors found that in the programs studied, perpetrators were going unpunished in 73% of all violent scenes, and only 4% of violent programs emphasized anti-violence themes. . . . This may have been the greatest paradox of all—that a study initiated in 1994 to block passage of the V-chip should become one of the most powerful arguments to go forward with the V-chip in 1996.

Beyond policymaking, the study has had an effect on science as well. The American Psycho-

logical Association (1998) called it "the gold standard against which other research on television violence will be measured." George Comstock and Erica Scharrer (1999) described NTVS as "the most powerful content analysis in the history of mass communication research." And Steven Chaffee (1999), a distinguished scholar of media effects, described the content analysis as "an exemplary model for researchers for years to come." Already, researchers in Great Britain and Portugal have used the NTVS methods and coding scheme to analyze television violence in their own countries.

Conclusion

The ultimate measure of the effect of any study is whether it has long-term scientific and practical significance. If NTVS encourages future researchers of television violence to focus not so much on the number of shootings, stabbings, and fistfights, but instead on the meaning of this aggression within the context of the plot, then it will have lasting scientific value. If the study helps parents to navigate the television landscape and make informed choices about their children's viewing habits, then it will have practical significance as well.

See also: ANTIVIOLENCE INTERVENTIONS; AROUSAL PROCESSES AND MEDIA EFFECTS; CHILDREN'S PREFERENCES FOR MEDIA CONTENT; DESENSITIZATION AND MEDIA EFFECTS; FEAR AND THE MEDIA; RATINGS FOR TELEVISION PROGRAMS; SOCIAL COGNITIVE THEORY AND MEDIA EFFECTS; TALK SHOWS ON TELEVISION; V-CHIP; VIOLENCE IN THE MEDIA, ATTRACTION TO; VIOLENCE IN THE MEDIA, HISTORY OF RESEARCH ON.

Bibliography

American Medical Association. (1996). *Physician Guide to Media Violence.* Chicago: American Medical Association.

American Medical Association (1998). "AMA Says New Study 'Definitive Confirmation' That TV Violence Is Harmful." Press release from the American Medical Association, April 16.

American Psychological Association. (1993). *Violence and Youth: Psychology's Response.* Washington, DC: American Psychological Association.

Chaffee, Steven. (1999). "National Television Violence Study 3." *Journal of Communication* 49(3):194–196.

Clinton, William J. (1997). "Statement by President

Clinton on the Release of the second Annual National Television Violence Study." Washington, DC: The White House Office of the Press Secretary, March 28.

Comstock, George, and Scharrer, Erica. (1999). *Television: What's On, Who's Watching, and What it Means.* New York: Academic Press.

Friedrich, Lynette K., and Stein, Aletha H. (1973). "Aggressive and Prosocial Television Programs and the Natural Behavior of Preschool Children." *Monographs of the Society for Research in Child Development* 38(4, Serial No. 151).

Getlin, Josh. (1999). "Grim Show Is Only the Latest for America's Violent Culture." *Los Angeles Times*, April 22, p. A17.

Hoffner, Cynthia. (1998). "Framing of the Television Violence Issue in Newspaper Coverage." In *Television Violence and Public Policy*, ed. James T. Hamilton. Ann Arbor: University of Michigan Press.

Huesmann, L. Rowell. (1986). "Psychological Processes Promoting the Relation between Exposure to Media Violence and Aggressive Behavior by the Viewer." *Journal of Social Issues* 42(3):125–140.

Johnson, Roger N. (1996). "Bad News Revisited: The Portrayal of Violence, Conflict, and Suffering on Television News." *Peace and Conflict: Journal of Peace Psychology* 2(3):201–216.

Kennedy, Joseph P., II. (1997). "The TV Industry Must Work Together and Clean Up Violence." Press release from the Office of Representative Joseph P. Kennedy II (D-MA), March 26.

Markey, Edward J. (1996). "It Takes a V-Chip." <http://www.house.gov/markey/chip.htm>.

National Institute of Mental Health. (1982). *Television and Behavior: Ten Years of Scientific Progress and Implications for the Eighties (Vol. 1). Summary Report.* Washington, DC: U.S. Government Printing Office.

National Television Violence Study, 1. (1997). Thousand Oaks, CA: Sage Publications.

National Television Violence Study, 2. (1998a). Thousand Oaks, CA: Sage Publications.

National Television Violence Study, 3. (1998b). Thousand Oaks, CA: Sage Publications.

Nikken, Peter, and Peeters, Allerd L. (1988). "Children's Perceptions of Television Reality." *Journal of Broadcasting and Electronic Media* 32:441–452.

Paik, Haejung, and Comstock, George. (1994). "The Effects of Television Violence on Antisocial Behavior: A Meta-Analysis." *Communication Research* 21:516–546.

Pew Research Center. (1999). "Teens and Traffic Top Community Concerns." <http://www.people-press.org/may99rpt2.htm>.

Simon, Paul. (1996). "Reaction of Senator Paul Simon to the Cable-Funded Audit of TV Violence." Press release from the Office of Senator Paul Simon (D-IL), February 6.

Wright, John C.; Huston, Aletha C.; Reitz, Alice Leary; and Piemyat, Suwatchara. (1994). "Young Children's Perceptions of Television Reality: Determinants and Developmental Differences." *Developmental Psychology* 30:229–239.

BARBARA J. WILSON

■ NETWORKS AND COMMUNICATION

Network analysis is the study and interpretation of influences on, forms of, and outcomes from, patterns of relations among entities. The overall structure of a network, the relationships among the network members, and the location of a member within the network, are critical factors in understanding social behavior. They influence, among other things, access to resources, the distribution of social and organizational power, the spread of new ideas as well as diseases, career success and mobility, workplace diversity, job satisfaction, and even personal health and longevity.

The network approach has been applied to studying a wide range of topics, such as referrals among community helping agencies, overlaps in company boards of directors as part of antitrust investigations, changes in friendship among elementary school students, rumor diffusion in organizations, interactions among transients and regular patrons at late-night diners, citation patterns among members of scientific disciplines, the role of formal organizational communication networks compared to emerging informal networks, the structure of international telecommunication traffic, and contributions to nonprofit agencies. Georg Simmel's 1908 *The Web of Group Affiliations*, and Jacob Moreno's 1934 *Who Shall Survive?* were some of the first books to describe and apply this approach. Other early studies considered kinship networks in tribal villages, relational patterns among families, interactions among workers in manufacturing or mining sites, and the development of class and group identity through joint attendance at social events.

Network Data, Measures, and Analysis

Network data are fundamentally different from the typical social science approach, which collects information about a variety of variables (such as demographics, attitudes, performance) from a (ideally) random set of individuals (such as students, managers, organizations). This approach assumes that the individuals are independent, so the topic of interest is the association among variables. Typical data are thus a "people by variable" matrix.

For network analysis, the data consists of the relationships among the entities. The entities may be people, organizations, words, events, and so on. The relations may be communication, trade, co-occurrences, hierarchies, or the like (though the rest of this entry will refer to "people"). The strength of such relations among the people might be measured by such things as frequency, attraction, length, and dependency. This is thus a "people by people" dataset. The relations among people might be identified by observation, surveys, archival data, information-system-collected data, transcribed conversations, or analysis of printed material, diaries, legal records, and so on. For example, an organizational study might use a survey that has a section listing all the members of the organizational department, which asks respondents to indicate how frequently they communicate with other members of that department. Note, however, that network data are usually collected along with variable data, and often analyzed together. Further, a "people by variable" matrix can be converted into a "people by people" matrix.

Data about these relationships can be collected at, and analyzed by, several levels of analysis. The most basic levels are the individual and the network level.

Data collected at the individual or "ego" level involves measures of the relations in general of a set of individuals or their relations to specific others, without knowledge of the complete network of relations among all the others. These might include the number of friends a person has at school; the number of times a manager asked for advice from, or gave advice to, coworkers; or the number of suppliers an organization uses. Analyzing such individual-level data would allow researchers to differentiate the people as being more or less popular, seekers or givers of advice, or more or less dependent. The network level of analysis would describe or compare groups of people (say, part-time and full-time employees) on such individual-level measures.

Data collected at the network level involves measuring relations among all the members of a particular network (a group, an organizational department, an academic discipline, an industry). This allows analysis of the interdependencies among the members, including indirect relations and both presence and absence of relations. Such analysis can characterize individuals' network properties, including the in-degrees (the number of links a person receives from others), out-degrees (the number of links a person gives to others), density (percentage of all possible links each person has), centrality (the extent to which the person is close to or is part of all other relations in the network), integrativeness (the extent to which a person's direct relations are also related), power/prestige (the extent to which a person receives relations from others who are also powerful), reciprocity (the proportion of relations that flow both to and from a person), and roles or positions.

Typical organizational communication network roles include being a member of a group (or "clique"), the liaison (who connects groups but is not a member of any group), the bridge (who belongs to one group but provides a direct link to another group; this may include the "gatekeeper"), the isolate (who does not belong to any particular group), the opinion leader (to whom others turn for leadership and legitimization of group norms), and the boundary spanner, environmental scanner, or cosmopolite (who provides a link between the organization and the environment). Other roles include the broker (who passes information or resources along), a follower (who provides links to but not from others), a leader (who receives links from but may not provide links to other), and people who occupy similar positions (who are "equivalent" even though they may not have direct relationships among themselves).

Such analysis can also characterize network properties of dyads (such as reciprocity and similarity in the network) or triads (such as transitiveness, the extent to which a relation between entity A and B and a relation between B and C also involves a relation between C and A). Finally, network-level analysis can characterize properties of the network as a whole, such as overall density, centrality, integrativeness, power/prestige, reciprocity, transitiveness, and other measures of structure. However, network-level analysis can also provide a wide array of network-level portrayals, such as separate and overlapping cliques within the network, positions within the network that include people that are similar to each other with respect to their relations to all other entities, multidimensional visual portrayals of the relations among the entities within the whole or portions of the network, or clusters of people that are grouped together in hierarchical fashion depending on the strength of the relation.

To summarize, then, researchers can collect network data at the individual or network level. They can then analyze individual-level network data at the individual level, or describe and compare that individual-level network data within different groups. Or researchers can collect network data at the network level, and then analyze that data to produce individual-level or network-level measures and results. Finally, they can analyze the combined individual- and network-level measures. Further, researchers can collect any of these kinds of data across time, to compare individuals and networks longitudinally. For example, studies have shown that organizational mergers often fail because the work networks of the two companies do not become more densely connected over time, or the network of the acquiring company remains centralized. Or, the use of electronic mail allows organizational members to overcome physical, temporal, and hierarchical obstacles and thus participate in more decentralized communication networks over time. Researchers can also collect and combine data from several networks, such as within an organization, formal and informal work relations, interdependence among tasks, sources of resources, and power relations, and test their relative influence, interaction, or change over time.

Developments and Debates

Network analysis has typically been used to study relations among individuals or organizations, but, as noted above, the possible applications are endless. One specific application is semantic network analysis, where text is analyzed to determine some measure of the extent to which words are related (such as how frequently words co-occur) within a given meaning unit (such as paragraphs in organizational documents). Then, this word-by-word network of relations is analyzed to produce measures for or clusters of the words. These results can be directly interpreted, used in other analyses, or compared between different groups, such as types of organizations, or a single organization before and after a major change.

A primary enduring theoretical issue involves the relative influence of "structure" (location of the individual in the network, and overall network characteristics) and "agency" (individual attributes and behaviors). An extreme structuralist would argue that almost all individual attitudes and behaviors are heavily constrained by the networks in which one is embedded. Extreme agency argues, in turn, that individuals shape the form and nature of their relationships and the resulting networks. More-integrated approaches attempt to understand the relative influences of individual and network factors on particular social phenomena, and, in turn, their effects on individual and network factors. Networks both constrain and facilitate social action, and, in turn, are constrained and facilitated by social action. Thus, one can study both the effect of preexisting networks and what affects the development and emergence of new network structures. Typically, then, network research would measure both individual and network attributes across time periods, and test one or more theoretical models as to the relative influence and causality of structure and agency.

An application of this debate in an organizational setting is the analysis of the extent to which members use a new communication medium, such as the Internet, because of task/individual factors (such as simplifying the work to be done) or because of social/structural influences (such as a manager expresses the opinion that the medium should be used or a coworker demonstrates extensive use of the medium). Network analysis provides both theory and measures to test the relative role of individual versus social influences. For example, a traditional study would measure each individual's usage of, attitudes toward, and outcomes from, electronic mail, as well as individual attributes such as demographics, type of task, prior experience, personality traits, and so on. A network study would also measure the extent to which all members of a department communicate with each other about work in general, and the new medium in particular, and other structural measures such as location in the organizational hierarchy, from which network measures would be computed. By combining these two kinds of data, analysis could then show how individual and network factors interact to explain each individual's assessment of the new medium. These kinds of studies have shown that such network influence as exists is predominantly from coworkers (though also from managers when that person is a role model or opinion leader), is more likely if the medium is perceived as highly innovative or uncertain, and is stronger early on in the process, giving way to more individual-level influences such as task demands, perceived benefits, access and ease of use.

Another central theoretical and empirical debate centers around the distinction between cohesion and position. Cohesion approaches presume that direct relations among entities best represent network influences. Cohesion measures include in- and out-degrees, reciprocity, and cliques of densely interconnected members. So, for example, diffusion of an innovation would be best explained by patterns of direct and multi-step communication between an early adopter and later adopters. Position approaches presume, instead, that what is more important than direct relations is the extent to which people occupy the same, or even similar, positions in the network. Position measures include the similarity of present and absent relations (as well as similarity of the relationships among the relations of an entity) throughout the network, such as correlations, closeness in multidimensional space, clusters, factor loadings, and various measures of equivalence. So, for example, here diffusion would best be explained by initial adoption by members of one's own position, even if those members do not communicate directly with each other, or by members attempting to emulate the adoption behavior of an influential position (such as "managers," not necessarily one's own manager). There are theoretical arguments supporting each approach, and many studies attempt to test the relative influence of cohesion versus position conceptualizations of networks. As with the structure and agency debate, studies often find that both approaches provide somewhat different contributions to explaining social behavior and attitudes.

Resources

Simple network analysis (such as drawing "sociograms" that show the relations among entities and computing some individual-level measures such as in- or out-degrees) can be done by hand. Somewhat more complex or large-scale networks can be analyzed through standard statistical software. However, it is more typical that proper processing of the data and analyses will require specific network analysis software. Perhaps the most widely used software of this type is UCINET (originally used at the University of California, Irvine).

See also: COMMUNITY NETWORKS; INTERNET AND THE WORLD WIDE WEB; ORGANIZATIONAL COMMUNICATION; RELATIONSHIPS, TYPES OF; RESEARCH METHODS IN INFORMATION STUDIES.

Bibliography

Baker, Wayne. (1994). *Networking Smart: How to Build Relationships for Personal and Organizational Success.* New York: McGraw-Hill.

Borgman, Christine, ed. (1990). *Scholarly Communication and Bibliometrics.* Newbury Park, CA: Sage Publications.

Degenne, Alain, and Forse, Michel. (1999). *Introducing Social Networks.* Thousand Oaks, CA: Sage Publications.

International Society for Social Network Analysis. (2000). "Welcome to the International Network for Social Network Analysis." <http://www.heinz.cmu.edu/project/INSNA/index.html>.

Moreno, Jacob. (1934). *Who Shall Survive?: A New Approach to the Problem of Human Interrelations.* Washington, DC: Nervous and Mental Disease Publishing Company.

Nohria, Nitin, and Eccles, Robert, eds. (1992). *Networks and Organizations: Structure, Form, and Action.* Boston: Harvard Business School Press.

Rice, Ronald E. (1993). "Using Network Concepts to Clarify Sources and Mechanisms of Social Influence." In *Progress in Communication Sciences: Advances in Communication Network Analysis,* eds. William Richards Jr. and George Barnett. Norwood, NJ: Ablex.

Rogers, Everett M., and Kincaid, D. Lawrence. (1981). *Communication Networks: Toward a New Paradigm for Research.* New York: Free Press.

Scott, John. (1993). *Network Analysis: A Handbook.* Newbury Park, CA: Sage Publications.

Simmel, Georg. (1908). *The Web of Group Affiliations.* New York: Free Press.

Valente, Thomas. (1995). *Network Models of the Diffusion of Innovations.* Cresskill, NJ: Hampton Press.

Wasserman, Stanley, and Faust, Kathryn. (1994). *Social Network Analysis: Methods and Applications.* New York: Cambridge University Press.

Wasserman, Stanley, and Galaskiewicz, Joseph, eds. (1994). *Advances in Social Network Analysis.* Thousand Oaks, CA: Sage Publications.

Wellman, Barry, and Berkowitz, Stephen. (1997). *Social Structures: A Network Approach,* updated edition. Greenwich, CT: JAI Press.

RONALD E. RICE

▌■ NEWS EFFECTS

According to Harold Lasswell (1948), communication in society serves three essential functions: (1) the surveillance of the environment, (2) the correlation of adaptive responses to the environment, and (3) the transmission of social inheritance. The institution of the news certainly serves these functions, although it does each to different degrees. Surveying the physical and social environment for threats and opportunities would have to be considered the primary function of news. Citizens are informed of happenings; but as a rule, actions toward these happenings are not suggested. The news may also, however, aim at instigating and coordinating civic action when such action can be considered, with some degree of consensus, to serve the welfare of the citizenry. Finally, the transmission of cultural information is obviously another component of the news.

In the interest of survival, humans have, no doubt, monitored their environments throughout the ages, looking for both perils and opportunities. For thousands of years, individuals had to rely on personal observation and the observations of a limited number of other people. This condition was dramatically changed, of course, with the coming of message distribution by the mass media via print, radio, television, and computer. Countless others now share, through these media, their experiences, observations, and beliefs quasi-instantaneously with massive audiences. Lasswell characterized this development as an extension and an overcoming of the limited capacity of people to survey their environment. The surveyed environment is now truly global. News organizations gather enormous amounts of information from around the world, reduce it to what, according to some agreed-upon criteria, is deemed newsworthy, and present it to the public for further selective sampling. It is this multitude of available information that defines the context for the exploration of news effects.

News Reception and Interpretation

Whatever the format of presentation, news must be perceived and interpreted. Whether the informational displays that convey the news are manifest in printed language, spoken language, or language that is supplemented by drawings and photographs or by motion-picture sequences, recipients must pay attention to these displays in order to obtain information from them. The interpretative extraction of meaning is necessary, in turn, for news to have the effects that news is designed to bring about—first and foremost, to inform the citizenry of pertinent environmental and social developments (in terms of both threats to the well-being of citizens and opportunities for improving their wellness), and, according to writers such as Davis Merritt (1995), to inspire or instigate social action in the interest of communal or societal welfare.

Before these ends can be served, it is obviously necessary for recipients to comprehend the news. The mediation of comprehension is commonly considered in the context of schema theory. Doris Graber (1988), among others, has employed this theory to elucidate the information processing and information elaboration that is entailed in making sense of the news. Schemata are conceived of as discrete yet interconnected active memory structures that consolidate related past experiences and that foster expectations and interpretations that are based on these experiences. According to Graber, schemata control all relevant processes in news reception and interpretation. Specifically, they are thought to determine what recipients notice, process, and store during exposure to the news; to help recipients to evaluate and structure information in accordance with established beliefs; to facilitate the interpretation of information about unfamiliar, novel situations; and to aid in the construction of coping strategies. Essentially, then, the reception and interpretation of news is seen as a result of sequential filtering by the subjectively defined schemata of the recipients.

An experimental investigation conducted by Mary Beth Oliver (1999) of stereotypical interpretation illustrates the suggested filtering. White viewers were exposed to a news broadcast that included a wanted poster of a murder suspect. The race of the suspect was indicated solely by the poster, which featured either a white or a black person. A person identification test was administered immediately after exposure and again three months later. The findings revealed that, especially with the passage of time, white respondents tended to misidentify white suspects as being black. Additionally, negative attitudes toward blacks led over time to fewer misidentifications of white suspects and more frequent misidentifications of black suspects. Such findings could be interpreted as a result of stereotypes manifest in "race filters," stereotypes that appear to have been particularly pronounced in the filters of recipients with negative attitudes toward blacks.

It should be clear from this illustration that schema theory can be profitably applied, *post facto,* to shed light on the subjectification of the news. It should also be apparent, however, that the theory lacks predictive power in that specific interpretations of the news cannot be forecast, as the mediating schemata are typically presumed rather than empirically ascertained.

Information Acquisition and Retention

Much is known about the acquisition of information from the news and about its retention. It has been shown, for example, that when news items are presented in sequence, as is typical for radio and television broadcasts, items that are placed at the beginning or toward the end of a sequence are better recalled than items in the middle of the sequence (Gunter, Furnham, and Gietson, 1984). It is also apparent that attention to, and recall of, news items can be influenced by the contents of preceding and following items. It has been shown, among other things, that emotion-arousing news items foster extended cognitive preoccupation after exposure and that, as a result, attention to subsequently presented items tends to be greatly impaired (Scott and Goff, 1988; Mundorf, Drew, Zillmann, and Weaver, 1990). It is further apparent that the presence of images generally improves the recall of information from news reports (Graber, 1990). Imagery that is consistent with and that highlights the verbally presented focal message of news reports has been found to be particularly effective in enhancing recall (Brosius, Donsbach, and Birk, 1996). Attention to specific content categories has also been examined. It has been observed, for example, that

violence-laden news items, irrespective of their mode of presentation, are better recalled than nonviolent items and that men recall violent news items better than do women (Gunter, Furnham, and Gietson, 1984). Influences of other contents, of style, and of display variables on recall have also been examined. It has been demonstrated, for example, that image-evoking text can facilitate recall almost as much as actual images (David and Kang, 1998) and that actual images tend to facilitate the recall of accounts of concrete, perceivable situations more than that of abstract, difficult to visualize phenomena (David, 1998).

In research, news recall is commonly ascertained shortly after exposure to the news. Such assessment can be seen as tapping information extraction and comprehension. Research that focuses on longer-term retention of the acquired information has essentially shown that most of this information is soon lost (Gunter, 1987). The surprisingly poor retention of the news after days, weeks, or months has been deemed deplorable by some observers. It may also be seen as serving the public well, however, because retention of the specifics of news reports (which is what recall tests usually assess) tends to have little utility. Part of the subjectification of the news by filtering in schema-theoretical terms, as suggested by Graber (1988), allows recipients to select personally salient messages from the flood of news information, focus on them, and commit them to memory, while proficiently discarding the remainder.

It should be recognized that attention to, information acquisition from, and recall of the news does not constitute a meaningful end in itself. The object of the news, put simply, is to apprise the public of developments that affect their welfare. It is to provide a reliable overview of happenings in the immediate communal environment of citizens as well as in extended frames, such as state, nation, and the world at large. The purpose of the news, in other words, is to furnish the material for the construction of perceptions of, beliefs about, and dispositions toward relevant incidents and phenomena. As the mediators of individual and social actions, these perceptions, beliefs, and dispositions constitute the ultimate news effects that are worth examining. Receiving, interpreting, and comprehending the news, then, are necessary intermediate processes for news to serve its designated purpose.

News and Public Discourse

In contrast to the limited capacity of citizens to survey their extended environments by their own actions, news organizations can gather information about countless happenings around the globe and relay this wealth of information quasi-instantaneously to local, national, and worldwide audiences. Information is not gathered in random fashion, however. Editors and news directors give specific assignments to reporters and correspondents, and they further reduce the number of incoming reports by selecting only those that, according to prevailing news criteria, are considered newsworthy. Reports are thus judged, classified, and implicitly or explicitly ranked by importance. Those deemed important are included in the news, and those deemed especially important are featured more prominently than others.

The news, then, predetermines what the public will get to know (by implication, also what it will not get to know) and signals the degree of importance of individual reports. Maxwell McCombs and Donald Shaw (1972) explored this function of the news and labeled it "agenda setting." The influence focus of this approach is on the determination of issue salience. News is seen as bringing significant issues into public consciousness, as inviting reflection, and as providing the means for independent judgment rather than as influencing the public to adopt suggested positions on the issues.

The agenda-setting paradigm has generated much supportive research. It has been tested, essentially, in the correspondence between issues presented in the news and, usually after some passage of time, public awareness of these issues (McCombs, 1994). Additional demonstrations showed a correspondence between presentational prominence of items in the news and the perception of the importance of these items by the public. It has also been observed, however, that the news media are sensitive to public awareness of issues and respond to it with pertinent news reports (Brosius and Kepplinger, 1990). The news may thus set the public agenda while, on occasion, the public also sets the news agenda.

News and Issue Perception

News influence is not limited, however, to signaling the salience of presented issues and then letting the public render judgment. The news, by presenting events in particular ways, can narrow interpretational leeway and thereby guide recipients to adopt specific perceptions of relevant issues. By framing or contextualizing reports, aspects of secondary importance can be highlighted and given disproportional influence on the interpretation and perception of issues and, ultimately, on expectations and dispositions concerning the issues.

The contextualizing exemplification of phenomena of public interest (i.e., the presentation of selected cases to illustrate broader phenomena) has been found to have especially potent influence on the perception and evaluation of issues. Dolf Zillmann and Hans-Bernd Brosius (2000) examined exemplification in this context. They found exemplars to permeate all facets of the news. In the form of people who relate their experiences, exemplars are considered to humanize the news. If employed in impartial fashion, exemplars may be expected to aid recipients in forming appropriate perceptions and judgments. It appears, however, that exemplars are often arbitrarily, sometimes carelessly, and, on occasion, recklessly selected. When this occurs, the resulting selections are biased and likely to foster inappropriate, distorted perceptions and dispositions.

The influence of exemplification has been demonstrated, for example, in an experiment employing a news report on the crime of carjacking (Gibson and Zillmann, 1994). The report, presented as a news-magazine article, related facts about carjacking, including information about the risk of harm to its victims. Specifically, the report indicated, either verbally in "greater than" comparisons or numerically in percentages, the ratios that were associated with fatal outcomes, crippling injuries, minor injuries, and trivial injuries. Fatal outcomes were said to be extremely rare (or less than 1%), crippling injuries to be rather rare as well (or about 4%), minor injuries to be comparably frequent (or about 20%), and trivial injuries to be very frequent and typical (or about 75% of all cases). The report featured two exemplars (i.e., explicit and vivid descriptions of the carjackings, especially with regard to the outcome for the victims). The carjackings either resulted in the brutalization and death of the victims, led to crippling injuries, yielded only minor injuries, or were inconsequential for the health of the victims.

Respondents indicated their perceptions of the danger of carjacking to the public either shortly after reading or one week after reading one of the eight article versions (i.e., they read an article in one of four outcome conditions with the incidence rate of the particular outcome indicated either by rather vague verbal description or in exact percentages).

The findings indicated that concrete and vividly detailed exemplars can profoundly influence the assessment of issues. They also suggest that, in contrast, the provision of abstract, pallid, quantitative information, although usually more reliable, tends to be of little moment. Specifically, on the basis of two exemplars of extremely violent but rare occurrences, the respondents grossly overestimated the incidence rate of fatal and crippling carjackings. At the same time, these respondents grossly underestimated the incidence rate of carjackings that resulted in minimal harm to its victims. This misperception of the danger of carjacking to the public grew markedly over time (i.e., it was more pronounced after a week's time), and it materialized despite the presence of corrective quantitative information (i.e., verbal specifications or percentages). Numerous similar investigations (e.g., Brosius and Bathelt, 1994) have shown the same dominant effect of exemplars over abstract, quantitative information in the perception of social issues. Recipients were found to base their assessments of issues on the distribution of exemplars, even in cases where quantitative information suggested the opposite.

Experiments on the influence of exemplification in the news have also demonstrated that this influence extends to personal dispositions toward issues. Research on the effects of so-called gut-wrenching interviews with people who are suffering various misfortunes, as frequently featured in broadcast news, suggests that recipients not only perceive an increased risk of such misfortunes for the public, but for themselves as well. For example, respondents considered themselves at greater risk of salmonella poisoning from dining in fast-food establishments after seeing highly emotional footage of victims than after seeing nonemotional footage of the victims or no such exemplification at all.

A related investigation on the danger of contracting skin cancer from excessive sunbathing revealed that protective dispositions can also be created (Zillmann and Gan, 1996). An informative health newscast that urged the use of sun-block lotions was manipulated to show melanoma either in sanitized images or in explicit, shocking images. Two weeks after exposure to the program, respondents who had seen the version that contained shocking images considered the melanoma risk to the public and to themselves as being greater than did those who had seen the version with sanitized images. The former group also indicated greater commitment to using sun-block lotion than did the latter group. News influence, then, is not limited to the perception and interpretation of social issues. It is capable of affecting beliefs about dangers and opportunities, and these beliefs are capable, in turn, of affecting related dispositional changes.

The theoretical framework used to explain the indicated influence is that of cognitive heuristics (Higgins, 1996). Built-in automatisms of information processing are thought to yield efficient but often imprecise assessments of phenomena. Regarding news influence, the accessibility heuristic is of particular importance. It projects that memory access to information related to phenomena under consideration is a function of the frequency and recency of activation of this information. Novelty and perceptual vividness of the stored information are also known to facilitate access.

The effect on the assessment of the risk of contracting melanoma that was observed two weeks after exposure to the newscast that featured threatening images, for example, becomes explainable as the result of the vivid memory of these images (in contrast to the sanitized images) that imposes itself at the time when the risk is assessed or reassessed. Essentially, then, aspects of a phenomenon that enjoy superior chronic accessibility come to exert disproportionally strong influence on judgments that are rendered some time after exposure. The paradigm also applies, however, to immediate interpretational influences, such as those that are fostered by framing. It has been shown, for example, that directly quoting sources, as compared to paraphrasing their statements, shifts attention and emphasis, thereby facilitating access to the contents and enhancing influence on judgments that are rendered shortly after message reception (Gibson and Zillmann, 1998).

In order to bring a personal angle to the story of famine in Somalia, a news camerawoman followed a U.S. Marine around as he shook hands with Somali children in the city of Baidoa in 1992. (David & Peter Turnley/Corbis)

News and Emotions

An essential part of the news function is to apprise the public of immediate and impending threats and dangers. This assignment accounts for the preponderance of reports of the victimization of others only in part, however, as most of the reported ill fortunes, tragedies, disasters, and catastrophes are of no direct consequence to the news recipients. The well-documented dominance of so-called bad news appears to reflect a strong interest in reports of danger and mayhem on the part of the news audience, an interest that is commercially exploited.

The bad-news dominance has been amply criticized, mostly on grounds of the suggestion that it fosters bad moods and feelings of depression in the audience. The research evidence tends to support this contention. Tragic revelations, especially displays of the suffering of victims, are consistently found to evoke emotional distress, this distress being particularly intense in highly empathic recipients (Aust and Zillmann, 1996). To the

extent that threats of reported victimizations are also directed at the news recipients, emotional reactivity is adaptively involved in the creation and maintenance of apprehensions and fear. Such fears may be warranted and inspire due caution. If reported dangers do not threaten the news recipients at all, however, the formation of apprehensions and fear can be maladaptive and unduly burden recipients emotionally.

The convention of placing an uplifting or amusing report at the end of television newscasts appears to have been instituted in an effort to counteract adverse emotional reactions to preceding distressing reports. There is an indication that these efforts are effective. In an experimental investigation that was conducted by Zillmann and his colleagues (1994), respondents were exposed to a broadcast of a series of reports that presented threatening, depressing national and international issues. The newscast was varied only in that it either ended with a threatening report or featured an added-on human-interest story. Respondents evaluated the threats upon conclusion of the entire newscast. It was found that the concluding addition of an entertaining and amusing report altered the retrospective assessment of the threats. Specifically, after being amused by the concluding report, respondents deemed the national and international threats that were presented earlier to be less severe and less depressing.

Reports of the misfortunes and suffering of others need not result in depressive emotions, however. They may evoke indignation and outrage or feelings of pity. These reactions, in turn, may instigate social action that is aimed at correcting the deplored conditions. A case in point is the news coverage of the famine in Somalia during the early 1990s. In particular, the barrage of images of starving and deformed Somali children is believed to have greatly upset American viewers and compelled them to action. In fact, the resulting public pressure on the government to intervene in Somalia in order to end starvation is believed to have driven, if not dictated, foreign policy (Sharkey, 1993).

Moreover, conditions exist under which news reports of the setbacks, misfortunes, and suffering of others evoke joyous rather than depressive reactions. It has been demonstrated that negative affective dispositions (i.e., disrespect, contempt, resentment, anger, and the like) toward publicly known people are commonly held and motivate pleasure in response to news revelations of the misfortunes of such people (Zillmann, Taylor, and Lewis, 1998). Some politicians, for example, may be disliked, even despised and hated, and these dispositions may foster euphoric reactions to news about their demise. Analogously, negative dispositions that are manifest in the news recipients' opposition to particular political causes and social objectives can foster reactions of joy upon learning of failure by, and the devastation of, the opposed parties.

The emotions of the public in response to news about the misfortunes and suffering of others thus should not be expected to be uniformly negative. Because emotional reactivity is mediated by affective dispositions toward the parties whose bad fortunes are reported in the news, reactions of either distress or delight may be expected as a result of the status and intensity of prevailing dispositions.

See also: AROUSAL PROCESSES AND MEDIA EFFECTS; MINORITIES AND THE MEDIA; MOOD EFFECTS AND MEDIA EXPOSURE; NEWS PRODUCTION THEORIES; SOCIAL CHANGE AND THE MEDIA; SOCIAL GOALS AND THE MEDIA; SOCIETY AND THE MEDIA.

Bibliography

Aust, Charles F., and Zillmann, Dolf. (1996). "Effects of Victim Exemplification in Television News on Viewer Perception of Social Issues." *Journalism and Mass Communication Quarterly* 73(4):787–803.

Brosius, Hans-Bernd, and Bathelt, Anke. (1994). "The Utility of Exemplars in Persuasive Communications." *Communication Research* 21(1): 48–78.

Brosius, Hans-Bernd; Donsbach, Wolfgang; and Birk, Monika. (1996). "How Do Text–Picture Relations Affect the Informational Effectiveness of Television Newscasts?" *Journal of Broadcasting & Electronic Media* 40:180–195.

Brosius, Hans-Bernd, and Kepplinger, Hans M. (1990). "The Agenda-Setting Function of Television News: Static and Dynamic Views." *Communication Research* 17(2):183–211.

David, Prabu. (1998). "News Concreteness and Visual–Verbal Association: Do News Pictures Narrow the Recall Gap Between Concrete and Abstract News?" *Human Communication Research* 25:180–201.

David, Prabu, and Kang, Jagdeep. (1998). "Pictures, High-Imagery News Language and News Recall." *Newspaper Research Journal* 19(3):21–30.

Gibson, Rhonda, and Zillmann, Dolf. (1994). "Exaggerated Versus Representative Exemplification in News Reports: Perception of Issues and Personal Consequences." *Communication Research* 21(5):603–624.

Gibson, Rhonda, and Zillmann, Dolf. (1998). "Effects of Citation in Exemplifying Testimony on Issue Perception." *Journalism and Mass Communication Quarterly* 75(1):167–176.

Graber, Doris A. (1988). *Processing the News: How People Tame the Information Tide*, 2nd edition. New York: Longman.

Graber, Doris A. (1990). "Seeing Is Remembering: How Visuals Contribute to Learning from Television News." *Journal of Communication* 40(3):134–155.

Gunter, Barrie. (1987). *Poor Reception: Misunderstanding and Forgetting Broadcast News*. Hillsdale, NJ: Lawrence Erlbaum.

Gunter, Barrie; Furnham, Adrian; and Gietson, Gillian. (1984). "Memory for the News as a Function of the Channel of Communication." *Human Learning* 3(4):265–271.

Higgins, E. Tory. (1996). "Knowledge Activation: Accessibility, Applicability, and Salience." In *Social Psychology: Handbook of Basic Principles*, eds. E. Tory Higgins and Arie W. Kruglanski. New York: Guilford.

Lasswell, Harold D. (1948). "The Structure and Function of Communication in Society." In *The Communication of Ideas: A Series of Addresses,* ed. Lyman Bryson. New York: Harper & Brothers.

McCombs, Maxwell. (1994). "News Influence on Our Pictures of the World." In *Media Effects: Advances in Theory and Research,* eds. Jennings Bryant and Dolf Zillmann. Hillsdale, NJ: Lawrence Erlbaum.

McCombs, Maxwell, and Shaw, Donald L. (1972). "The Agenda-Setting Function of Mass Media." *Public Opinion Quarterly* 36:176–187.

Merritt, Davis. (1995). *Public Journalism and Public Life: Why Telling the News Is Not Enough.* Hillsdale, NJ: Lawrence Erlbaum.

Mundorf, Norbert; Drew, Dan; Zillmann, Dolf; and Weaver, James B. (1990). "Effects of Disturbing News on Recall of Subsequently Presented News." *Communication Research* 17(5):601–615.

Oliver, Mary Beth. (1999). "Caucasian Viewers' Memory of Black and White Criminal Suspects in the News." *Journal of Communication* 49(3):46–60.

Scott, Randall K., and Goff, David H. (1988). "How Excitation from Prior Programming Affects Television News Recall." *Journalism Quarterly* 65:615–620.

Sharkey, Jacqueline. (1993). "When Pictures Drive Foreign Policy: Somalia Raises Serious Questions About Media Influence." *American Journalism Review* 15:14–19.

Zillmann, Dolf, and Brosius, Hans-Bernd. (2000). *Exemplification in Communication: The Influence of Case Reports on the Perception of Issues.* Mahwah, NJ: Lawrence Erlbaum.

Zillmann, Dolf, and Gan, Su-lin. (1996). "Effects of Threatening Images in News Programs on the Perception of Risk to Others and Self." *Medienpsychologie* 8(4):288–305, 317–318.

Zillmann, Dolf; Gibson, Rhonda; Ordman, Virginia L.; and Aust, Charles F. (1994). "Effects of Upbeat Stories in Broadcast News." *Journal of Broadcasting & Electronic Media* 38(1):65–78.

Zillmann, Dolf; Taylor, Kay; and Lewis, Kelley. (1998). "News as Nonfiction Theater: How Dispositions Toward the Public Cast of Characters Affect Reactions." *Journal of Broadcasting & Electronic Media* 42(2):153–169.

DOLF ZILLMANN

NEWSPAPER INDUSTRY

At the same time that the debate over the structure and effects of the emerging global media industry is being influenced by the values that are most represented by newspapers, the newspaper industry is in what appears to be an almost certain and inevitable decline. Although there is substantial evidence to refute the charges that the industry is a "dinosaur" and in terminal danger, there is little doubt that the relative importance of the newspaper as an information conveyer, a public policy agenda-setter, and an economic power is declining.

Indications of decline have been around since the nineteenth century. Some people in the 1830s criticized the change that transformed newspapers from expensive business, political, or literary publications (limited to elite audiences) into inexpensive, advertising supported, mass media. Certainly, the pejorative terms "yellow journalism," "tabloids," and "jazz journalism" were part and parcel of the criticism that newspapers had lost their way in the 1890s and 1920s. Of course, these are qualitative judgments that neglect the power of newspapers' importance in cultural development, particularly in the pretelevision era. This power can be seen in the contributions that newspapers have made in the struggle to expand literacy, create a common language and national culture, argue for social and political reform, entertain the masses, encourage and implement technological change, and develop the most important of all journalistic values—the hallmarks of objectivity, fairness, the watchdog function, and civic responsibility.

A Future for Newspapers?

In addition to the qualitative criticisms that have long been made about the newspaper industry, discussions of the decline of the newspaper follows one of the most conventional wisdoms in media analysis. This is that the combination of digital and online communications and the World Wide Web component of the Internet, in particular, will become *the* conduit for virtually all forms of mediated communication that are delivered in homes and based on the specific desires of the user. Although there is not yet enough distance between diffusion, adoption, and use of new technology to be sure of this "wisdom," traditional mass communication vehicles such as the newspaper and broadcast television clearly are making efforts to adapt to changing circumstances. As is common, old media adapt to new media, but they do not disappear.

There will continue to be print newspapers in the future. They will exist along with many other forms of digital media that are brought about by technological diffusion and economic policy decisions. The qualities of ease of use, reasonable cost, and utility will still be relevant for the preservation of newspapers in the digital online era.

However, the ongoing redefinition of media communication cannot be reversed, and it will have enormous effect on all aspects of the newspaper industry. The brand name of many newspapers will be used in virtually every media form. The websites and the cobranding arrangements with local television and radio, which are becoming ubiquitous, will continue and expand. As is increasingly clear, the newspapers that prosper will increasingly generate revenues as electronic conduits or portals for information and entertainment in various forms. An increasing number of people will choose to have their "newspaper" delivered electronically, and many of these people will print out a hard copy. Journalists will see their work presented in various formats and will increasingly be trained to be writers and multimedia producers. A considerable number of "users" (a more accurate term than "readers") will choose to design and edit their newspapers, individually emphasizing only the content that they choose. Advertising will be targeted according to these choices, as well as the demographics and psychographics of the audience.

Traditional versions of newspapers that offer a little something for everyone will become more expensive, as the consumer has to pay for the privilege of being in a niche group that depends on or prefers a carefully edited product with a diversity of information. As is the case with magazines, careful testing of consumer cost and advertising mix will become more important for newspapers as they seek to maximize desirable audiences for sale to advertisers and to eliminate undesirable audiences (i.e., those who have little or no value for advertisers).

As for content, print newspapers are likely to become increasingly local in orientation in a continuation and enhancement of the trends toward suburban metropolitan zone newspapers and such movements as civic journalism. National news is likely to get minimal attention, as it will be so readily available from other media sources. However, analysis and interpretation of all types of news are likely to take up even more space, as will local sports, entertainment, and lifestyle information. Moreover, more and more material is likely to be bylined by highly paid and heavily promoted "stars" who can help the print newspaper stand out as an important "brand" among a glut of competitors for the attention of consumers.

These relatively mild predictions are based on the acceleration of existing trends, many of which came into existence with the advent of television. As is the case with almost all media, as the newspaper has peaked in terms of influence and faced the challenge of new competition, it has had to refocus and, to some degree, specialize. Although this seems economically necessary, too much or the wrong type of specialization has a high cost for newspapers—the loss of identity as a mainstream medium.

What Is the Newspaper Market?

Tables 1 and 2 provide snapshots of the status of the U.S. newspaper industry. In many respects, the industry is financially healthy and culturally influential. Despite the evident decline in the percentage of Americans who read a daily newspaper, more than half continue to read a daily. Although the number of daily newspapers is decreasing, the ones that remain are, in most cases, left in a dominant if not monopoly position within their markets. Because of their ability to offer a blend of classified, local, and national advertising of various types at a reasonable cost, daily newspapers still generate about 25 percent of all U.S. advertising revenues.

Two of the major trends in newspapers since the 1950s have been the lessening of competition and consolidation of ownership. Newspaper chains own about 80 percent of all daily newspapers, with the largest chains, in terms of total circulation (Gannett, Knight-Ridder, Newhouse, Times Mirror, New York Times), also typically having ownership interests in other media, including various forms of television and online ventures. Perhaps instructive of the future of media consolidation is that the largest newspaper group in assets as of the mid-1990s was Capital Cities/ABC (a part of the Walt Disney Company), which generates most of its income from nonnewspaper media and entertainment activities.

Here, as in most accounts of newspapers, the large metropolitan daily newspaper is given the most attention for the obvious reasons of its economic position and social influence. However, there are other forms of print newspapers that

TABLE 1.

Trends for Daily and Sunday Newspapers

Year	Number of Dailies	Number of Sundays	Daily Circulation (in millions)	Sunday Circulation (in millions)
1950	1772	549	53.8	46.6
1960	1763	563	58.9	47.7
1970	1748	586	62.1	49.2
1975	1756	639	60.7	51.1
1980	1745	736	62.2	54.7
1985	1676	798	62.8	58.8
1990	1611	863	62.3	62.6
1995	1533	888	58.2	61.2
1998[1]	1489	898	56.2	60.1

[1] Preliminary data.

SOURCE: Newspaper Association of America (1999c).

TABLE 2.

Daily Newspaper Readership Trends by Percentage

Year	Men	Women	All Adults
1970	77.5	77.8	77.6
1975[1]	73.2	71.4	72.3
1980	69.2	64.8	66.9
1985	67.1	61.6	64.2
1990	64.5	60.5	62.4
1995	63.1	56.0	59.4
1998[2]	62.2	55.2	58.6
1999[2,3]	—	—	56.9
2000[2,3]	—	—	55.1

[1] Combined data for 1974 and 1975.
[2] Top 50 market data only.
[3] Fall quarter only.

SOURCES: Hernandez (2000); Newspaper Association of America (1999a, 1999b).

should be considered in any overview. Robert Picard and Jeffrey Brody (1997, pp. 8–10), for example, define nine "general categories" of newspapers, with an example of each:

1. international and national daily newspapers (*USA Today*),
2. metropolitan and/or regional daily newspapers (*Pittsburgh Post-Gazette*),
3. local daily newspapers (*North Hills News Record*),
4. nondaily general audience newspapers (small towns and alternative city newspapers such as *In Pittsburgh*),
5. minority newspapers (*New Pittsburgh Courier*),
6. newspapers that are published in secondary languages (*El Diario-La Prensa*),
7. religious newspapers (*National Catholic Register*),
8. military newspapers (on most major bases), and
9. other specialty newspapers (*Baseball Weekly*).

Not included here are the free shoppers that increasingly have suburban or neighborhood news in addition to many local advertisements. These categories are helpful in reminding people that a newspaper can be many things and has strengths of convenience and cost that will ensure a future for print. They also remind people, by their continuing success, that specialization works in print as it did in motion pictures, radio, and, increasingly, television. As the "mass" in mass communication continues to be redefined as a mass of people who are making use of various specialized or niche media, this will become more and more important.

The various types of newspapers are also commonly used by media economists, such as Picard and Brody (1997) and Stephen Lacy and Todd Simon (1993), to demonstrate via the "umbrella model" that even with fewer than 2 percent of communities having competing newspapers, there is a competitive market for newspapers because most Americans have easy local access to several different types of newspapers.

The U.S. newspaper industry employs about 500,000 people who work in editorial, advertising, circulation, production, or other types of business operations. Technology and the consolidation of operations, along with a decrease in the number of newspapers, leads to a relatively gloomy U.S. government assessment of employment prospects, particularly in the newspaper reporter workplace. According to the U.S. Bureau of Labor Statistics (1999), employment in this area is expected to continue to decline for print newspapers. However, the bureau concludes that "online newspapers and magazines should continue to grow very fast and create numerous job opportunities."

Eras and Adaptations

The U.S. newspaper industry faces major issues about its place in the American economy and in the hearts and minds of the public. This is not the first time that this has occurred. The first "end of an era" occurred with the corresponding development of broadcast news and the suburbanization of the United States, which eventually relegated the newspaper to a secondary medium for an ever-increasing number of people. Tables 1 and 2 show that the trend is continuing with a shrinking, albeit still substantial, percentage of the population being regular newspaper readers and an overall circulation that is beginning to slip noticeably. Another particularly ominous concern for newspapers is that younger people do not read newspapers regularly, and they show little inclination to become regular readers as they age. In a report prepared for the Newspaper Association of America, Stu Tolley (1999) presents data that suggests that if this trend is not reversed, the audience for daily newspapers will decline to zero in the latter part of the twenty-first century.

Despite their decline as the primary news source since the 1950s, newspapers were able to adapt well to a changing media environment by using such tactics as increasing industry consolidation and group ownership, switching to mainly morning publication cycles, getting the government to legalize joint operating agreements (JOAs), offering more specialized content, increasing the amount of analytic and opinion pieces, and upgrading the graphics and visuals. In addition, the newspaper industry was able to maintain a major, if no longer dominant, position as a national cultural power through its continuing ability to set the agenda for issues by helping to define what was newsworthy and by setting the standards of what constituted proper journalistic practice. These standards have long been the foundation of journalism education in the United States, and they follow students into various media positions. In addition, many radio and television stations continue to rely on major newspapers to set the agenda for what they are going to cover.

A look at the data in Tables 1 and 2 demonstrates that as long as broadcasting was the primary competition for news consumers, the newspaper industry did extremely well economically and in reaching the masses. Despite the many critics who believe the marketing orientation of the newspaper business has compromised its ability to serve the public properly, this type of orientation has been essential in keeping the industry economically strong in the face of considerable adaptation and change.

The newspaper industry, and for that matter the entire media industry, in at the end of another era. The twin "Cs" of economic consolidation and technological convergence are changing the traditional role and nature of media in ways that are difficult to predict. However, one thing that is very clear is that the dividing lines between once disparate media, such as the telephone and the television or the television and the newspaper, are fading in importance to users, media owners, and policymakers. The end result is that the newspaper increasingly is becoming just another platform for a rapidly developing global media oligopoly, losing much of its distinctiveness.

Another obvious result of consolidation and convergence is the increasing number of information and entertainment options that are available to the average person. The number of options dwarfs the competition that newspapers have previously had from electronic media. To stand out and maintain distinctiveness as a major medium in such a crowded landscape is *the* major issue for the newspaper industry.

Beginning in the mid-nineteenth century, newspapers ushered in the era of mass communication and relatively democratic access to news and information. Their low cost, easy availability (at least in urban areas), and mass appeal content, all spurred by the growth of industrial capitalism and the accompanying rise of mass advertising, made the newspaper a powerful instrument for the setting of civic agendas from the municipal to the federal level. Newspapers were often involved in campaigns against perceived social ills and for social improvements. They were powerful enough forces in American life to contribute to the development of local civic identities, the leveling of cultural differences, and the development of a distinctive American culture. They have reflected and sometimes helped to create local values, and, in many cases, they themselves became important business and cultural institutions within their market areas. At the same time, standardization of industry operations and techniques, the development of wire services and syndicates, the corporatization of ownership, and the national expansion of advertising helped to develop a set of national media values that are associated with journalism.

Despite the relatively successful adaptation of newspapers to broadcasting, the pretelevision era is likely to be regarded as the heyday of newspapers. This was the time when the newspaper *was* the news for the vast majority of the population. It was a time of enormous political and economic power for the industry, as politicians and businessmen sought favor and support from major newspapers in a way that has since become more common for television. It was also a time in which the industry codified standards of journalistic practice in professional codes, trade associations, and higher education. The newspaper industry will never again be as prominent in the United States or in the world. There are several interrelated reasons for this assertion.

First, broadcasting and especially television took away the immediacy of the newspaper, one of its fundamental reasons for being. Ever since the 1950s and 1960s, Americans have looked more to television as their primary news source. The Internet and other newer communication technologies expand the competition to an unparalleled degree.

Second, television in its various forms (i.e., local, national, syndicated, broadcast, cable, satellite) has consistently chipped away at the leading position that newspapers hold in the generation of advertising revenue. Although daily newspapers continue to generate more advertising revenue than any other medium, their percentage continues to decline as new forms of television and the Internet are increasingly able to compete for the lucrative local display and classified advertising that has long been the major strength of print newspapers.

Third, the newspaper industry is beginning to see the firewall between editorial and advertising dissipate, as marketing becomes a primary mantra for the industry and newspapers work to service better their primary customer—the advertiser. Although this is also true of other media, the cost is much higher for newspapers because of their position as the originator and keeper of such values as objectivity and the watchdog function. In allowing the erosion of the firewall, the newspaper becomes just another medium, just another platform for the display of commercial messages, just another media commodity.

Fourth, the Internet is a decidedly mixed blessing for the industry. It certainly does provide a critically important new distribution system and potential revenue center. Of course, this would not be all that important if the Internet did not provide the outlet for all sorts of new competition for the newspaper. There are two particularly important effects that the Internet has on newspapers. First, it is rapidly developing the capacity to serve local display and classified advertisers at reasonable cost with increasing market penetration in a visual and interactive fashion that is impossible for print to replicate. Second, while many newspapers have been early adopters of Internet publishing, they are forced to compete in a more direct way with the many other content providers that do not have "roots" in the newspaper business. Although the brand equity of many newspapers is substantial and certainly lends credibility to Internet efforts, the World Wide Web makes other providers functionally equivalent for many readers and consumers. For example, CNN's website looks and reads very much like many newspaper-operated sites. The distinctiveness of the newspaper as a print medium and the cultural cache that it carries (e.g., literate, thorough, for the thinking person) versus television and its traditional cultural baggage (e.g., headline service, shallow, emotional appeals) is being obliterated by the Internet.

Fifth, the newspaper industry faces a continuing dilemma in terms of purpose and function. The trend of specialization in media, which was set in motion with the introduction of commercial television, continues to accelerate as advances in digital technology and the Internet provide a seemingly ever-increasing number of specialized and navigable "channels" for many Americans. Although the newspaper industry has reacted to this with increased internal specialization for zoned editions, the newspaper remains so amorphous (with "a little something for everyone") that it continues to decline in relevance for a public that is increasingly offered more specialized content in virtually all competing media. However, the traditional daily newspaper is constrained in making more radical changes toward unit specialization (i.e., all content on a similar subject or appealing to a specific audience target). To move in this direction would seriously risk both its financial well-being (by alienating traditional advertisers and readers) and its cultural capital (by compromising its position as a relatively objective "voice" of the community). This dilemma has led to much soul searching within the newspaper industry as it struggles to maintain its position. At the same time, there is little doubt that the biggest success stories in the industry are related to those newspapers that serve smaller and, at least geographically, specialized audience segments.

The Newspaper Legacy

The importance of print newspapers is fading, but they will remain influential far into the future. This will be true even as the distribution system evolves into some form of online digital transfer for an increasing number of users. The hope is that this will also be true even as the newspaper becomes more commodified as a constituent part of a complex and increasingly global multimedia entertainment and information industry. Print is too convenient a form to disappear completely, and newspapers have built up such strong brand equity that they will be able to extend their brand in both print and electronic forms. In addition, the vitality of specialized print publications will continue to provide much traditional reading material to the public.

Perhaps more important, the values and traditions of civic responsibility that were developed primarily in and by the U.S. newspaper business are infused to one degree or another in all American mass media (and for that matter, much international media), they form the basis of the educational system for newspaper workers, and they often frame the debates about the proper function and structure of all communication industries. Included here would be the tension between economics and service or, more specifically, between the seeking of ever-higher profits and the role of public forum that newspapers have, at times, provided. Unlike the electronic media, with its public-interest roots in transportation law and policy and the concomitant emphasis on licensing and regulatory oversight, the U.S. newspaper has a direct link to the U.S. Constitution and the philosophers who influenced it. As explained by Lacy and Simon (1993), this is one of the keys to the intellectual market of newspapers. In fact, without the newspaper and its print "brethren" (e.g., one-sheets, pamphlets, books), many of the ideas that influenced the Constitution would not have been disseminated as powerfully and as rapidly as they were. The newspaper in the United States has, with few exceptions, been the commercial media form with the greatest influence in promoting relatively free and democratic speech.

This legacy is more important than ever in a time when complex shifts are occurring in the dynamics and definition of mass communication and media. Major media firms increasingly have holdings in various media forms and in various parts of the world. As television and online communications become one, and as newspaper content becomes available to new audiences through the Internet and other technology, differences between media—in terms of form, mission, and national orientation—have the potential to narrow and be subsumed by purely revenue-generation goals.

Using the values and traditions of U.S. newspapers to frame the argument is perhaps the best and only way for interested citizens and media professionals to work toward the goal that the newspaper first promised and that newer communication technologies have the potential to deliver. These values and traditions include the insistence on fairness in coverage, public participation in the information forum, and limits on government or corporate power over media. The challenges obviously are staggering. Much of media history is riddled with promises that were either unfulfilled or subverted. However, to give up or not even try is more than acquiescence. It is a subversion of the original ideals of the U.S. newspaper industry.

See also: INTERNET AND THE WORLD WIDE WEB; JOURNALISM, HISTORY OF; JOURNALISM, PROFESSIONALIZATION OF; NEWSPAPER INDUSTRY, CAREERS IN; NEWSPAPER INDUSTRY, HISTORY OF; NEWS PRODUCTION THEORIES; TECHNOLOGY, ADOPTION AND DIFFUSION OF.

Bibliography

Dizard, Wilson, Jr. (2000). *Old Media, New Media: Mass Communications in the Information Age,* 3rd edition. New York: Longman.

Heil, Scott, and Peck, Terrance W., eds. (1998). *Encyclopedia of American Industries,* Vol. 1, 2nd edition. Detroit, MI: Gale.

Hernandez, Debra Gersh. (1999). "ABC FAS-FAX Shows Slight Slips in Circulation; Newspaper Industry Moves to Sieze New Opportunities." <http://www.naa.org/about/news/article.cfm?Art_ID=227>.

Hernandez, Debra Gersh. (2000). "Slight Declines in Readership, Circulation Offset by Gains Online and in Overall Reader Satisfaction, According to NAA." <http://www.naa.org/about/news/article.cfm?Art_ID=322>.

Lacy, Stephen, and Simon, Todd F. (1993). *The Economics and Regulation of United States Newspapers.* Norwood, NJ: Ablex.

McChesney, Robert W. (1997). *Corporate Media and the Threat to Democracy.* New York: Seven Stories Press.

Newspaper Association of America. (1999a). "The Competitive Media Index." <http://www.naa.org/about/cmi/top50_99.html>.

Newspaper Association of America. (1999b). "Daily Newspaper Readership Trends." <http://www.naa.org/marketscope/databank/tdnpr.htm>.

Newspaper Association of America. (1999c). "Newspaper Circulation Volume." <http://www.naa.org/marketscope/databank/circvol.htm>.

Picard, Robert G., and Brody, Jeffrey H. (1997). *The Newspaper Publishing Industry.* Boston: Allyn & Bacon.

Squires, James D. (1993). *Read All About It! The Corporate Takeover of America's Newspapers.* New York: Times Books.

Tolley, Stu. (1999). "The Abyss That Is Destroying Daily Newspaper Reading." <http://www.naa.org/marketscope/research/cohort.htm>.

U.S. Bureau of Labor Statistics. (1999). "Occupational Outlook Handbook: News Analysts, Reporters, and Correspondents." <http://stats.bls.gov/oco/ocos088.htm>.

ROBERT V. BELLAMY JR.

NEWSPAPER INDUSTRY, CAREERS IN

Careers in the newspaper industry offer a breadth of opportunities from story composition to publication layout to advertising design. The reporter is the most basic unit of a newspaper staff. Reporters serve as the eyes and ears of the newspaper and its readers. General assignment (GA) reporters cover any type of news from city council meetings to murder trials. Beat reporters are assigned to focus on specific topics, such as the local textile industry or school news. A key difference between the two types of reporter is that beat reporters typically generate their own stories while GA reporters are tipped to breaking news.

In addition to reporters, newspapers employ other types of writers. Investigative journalists spend days or months sorting through facts in an attempt to find and uncover news. Columnists write specifically about topics that are important to them, and they are allowed to mix personal opinions with facts. Finally, editorial writers, similar to

The prominence of computers in the offices of London's Daily Mirror underscores the necessity for newspaper editors and writers to have a strong computer background or at least a high degree of computer literacy. (Adrian Arbib/Corbis)

columnists, express personal stances on social issues that are of interest to readers. Editorial writers are under no obligation to present both sides of an issue, and they commonly promote a stance that is taken by the editorial board of the newspaper.

Newspapers also employ staff other than writers. Photojournalists tell stories through photographs, relaying the relationship between individuals and events to readers by supplying images to go with the copy. Editorial cartoonists offer humorous and often satirical comments on society through combining artistic skill with a critical eye. Overseeing writers, photographers, and design artists are various types of editor. Editors coordinate news activities by assigning stories, scrutinizing copy, and overseeing layout for final publication. Assisting with the editing function are copy editors and proofreaders. Copy editors are usually entry-level employees who read manuscripts for errors in grammar, spelling, punctuation, and style. Additionally, they check facts and occasionally assist in layout. Proofreaders serve much the same function but are more concerned with comparing materials that are ready for printing against the edited manuscripts from which those materials were created. Once materials have been edited, page and layout designers manufacture the newspaper using copy, headlines, photographs, graphics, and advertisements. Ultimately, layout staff serve a unique journalistic function in that they control the means by which information is disseminated.

In addition to these careers that are traditionally associated with the industry, newspapers also employ people in advertising sales and circulation departments. Because advertising is responsible for up to 80 percent of the revenue of a newspaper, the advertising staff is vital. Advertising staff employees oversee local and national advertising sales as well as the classified advertisements department. Also, on many newspaper staffs, the advertising department often designs local advertisements. In the circulation department, employees must coordinate street sales, home delivery, and mail subscriptions. Working in the circulation department also entails developing marketing campaigns and subscription promotions.

Outside of local opportunities that are available for a journalist, some careers in the industry allow the reaching of a wider audience through news organizations, regional publication of national newspapers, and syndication. News organizations establish bureaus in various locales, cover the news as it occurs in the area, and then sell stories and photographs to newspapers that are unable to send correspondents to the location. The Associated Press, for example, is a news organization with 3,500 employees working at 240 worldwide bureaus. More than 1,500 U.S. newspapers subscribe to the service of the Associated Press. Certain national newspapers also establish bureaus to facilitate covering of regional news and attracting of wider audiences. For example, *The New York Times* has twelve national bureaus and twenty-seven foreign news bureaus. In addition, the national edition of *The New York Times* is printed at ten sites throughout the United States, providing additional career opportunities. Finally, columnists on large newspapers often sell their columns to other newspapers via syndication.

Preparing for a career in any of the copy-production positions on a newspaper staff or in a news organization typically involves training in news reporting. Because reporters make up the majority of newspaper staffs, most entry-level employees begin their careers as reporters. These employees are expected to have earned a journalism degree or a degree in English with extensive training in writing for the press. More than four hundred colleges and universities offer journalism degrees consisting of three-fourths liberal arts classes and one-fourth journalism classes such as basic reporting, copy editing, and media law and ethics. A college degree in journalism alone, however, is often not enough to land a job on a newspaper staff. Increasingly, entry-level employees are expected to have experience working for the press. School newspapers and internships afford media students the opportunity to apply classroom knowledge to a real-life press environment. Students should make an effort to garner this experience before entering the job market. While photojournalists and layout specialists may not anticipate a career in producing copy, the entry-level requirements are not dissimilar from those of reporters. Journalism degrees and experience again are prerequisites for these careers.

Individuals who are aspiring to editorial positions normally begin their careers as reporters or copy editors and advance through the ranks of the staff. A typical newspaper has a number of editors, beginning with copy editor and progressing up to department or section editor to managing editor to editor-in-chief. The normal succession to the top editorial post involves stops along the way at the various sublevels. With each increasing level comes more responsibility for managing subordinates. Also, as editors advance through the newspaper hierarchy, a wide breadth of knowledge is imperative. Students hoping to become editors would do well to pursue a double major in college with a focus in political science or economics to complement their journalism training.

Employees who are working in advertising sales offices typically also have a background in journalism and an understanding of how a newspaper works. Again, journalism degrees are common, as are degrees in advertising and marketing. Employees working in upper-level circulation positions also are expected to have journalism training in addition to marketing skills. Just as internships provide practical experience for other staff, those aspiring to a career in newspaper advertising or circulation should acquire a working knowledge of the business before seeking employment.

See also: EDITORS; NEWSPAPER INDUSTRY; WRITERS.

Bibliography

Ferguson, Donald L., and Patten, Jim. (1993). *Opportunities in Journalism Careers*. Lincolnwood, IL: VGM Career Horizons.

Fuller, Jack. (1996). *News Values: Ideas for an Information Age.* Chicago: University of Chicago Press.

Goldberg, Jan. (1999). *Careers in Journalism,* 2nd edition. Lincolnwood, IL: VGM Career Horizons.

Morkes, Andrew, ed. (1998). *What Can I Do Now?: Preparing for a Career in Journalism.* Chicago: Ferguson.

COY CALLISON

NEWSPAPER INDUSTRY, HISTORY OF

The creation of movable type marked the beginning of mass production of the written word and thus was essential to the newspaper industry's development. In general, this accomplishment is credited to Johannes Gutenberg, who was working in Mainz, Germany, in the mid-1400s. Other printing techniques existed prior to that time, including a form of movable type in Egypt and other areas of the Mediterranean. In 1295, Marco Polo brought Europe word of advanced printing techniques that were being used in Chinese. Furthermore, the Aztecs of South America hung colored banners in their main public squares to spread the "news" without the use of Gutenberg's or anyone else's "modern" technology. Still, when Gutenberg produced his movable type, the process of information dissemination underwent a revolution.

What, specifically, was Gutenberg's revolutionary invention? Gutenberg had used woodcuts to print pictures and came up with the idea of carving letters in wood and moving them around to create words that, when coated with ink, could be used to print. A worker whom Gutenberg hired suggested that wood would produce blurry letters and that using metal letters might work better. The rest, to use a cliche, is history. Using this new process, Gutenberg printed the Mazarin Bible, which is believed to be the first full book to be published. Without the ability to mass produce the written word, the process of disseminating the news would not have been able to become an "industry." Centuries later, the basics of the movable type that Gutenberg had created were still in use in England's North American colonies.

Colonial America

Public Occurrences, published by Benjamin Harris in 1690, is recognized as the first newspaper in what later became the United States. Although Harris intended the newspaper to be a monthly, it was published only one time. Harris failed to submit his newspaper for government censorship, so it was shut down. The first newspaper to be published on a regular basis in the colonies was the *Boston Newsletter,* which appeared from 1704 to 1719. It was a weekly and its editor was also the local postmaster, John Campbell.

The survival of a newspaper in the American colonies was contingent upon the government. The editors almost always were printers first—the concept of journalism as it is known today did not develop until much later. Printers had to import their presses from England or Germany because none were made in the colonies. In addition, the patronage system existed where the printers relied not on money from advertising and circulation but rather on money from the government in order to print messages to the citizenry. Because their principal income was provided by the government, printers had little incentive to print dissenting opinions or to take on political issues. The early newspapers also served the needs of commerce. Goods being shipped from England to the colonies were important, so newspapers would print information about what was going to arrive and when. Boston, New York, and Philadelphia were the areas that served as the centers for commerce, politics, and education during this period, so they were also the primary locations in which printers lived and worked. The paid circulation, even of the largest newspapers, during the colonial period was only in the hundreds—with a large number of people reading a single copy that was from one person to another. About 70 percent of the males in the colonies in the early 1700s were literate, but even the illiterate people could benefit from newspapers if they gathered in public places to hear a literate person read the newspaper aloud. Along with schools and churches, newspapers and books were the main educational tools and entertainment in the colonies.

Some history books emphasize the conflicts between the colonists and the English government—and obviously that conflict eventually led to the independence of the colonies—but the majority of printers during the colonial period were very timid. They were afraid of the potential financial ramifications of losing the work that was involved in printing government announcements,

An undated illustration depicts the public burning of issues of John Peter Zenger's Weekly Journal on November 6, 1734. (Bettmann/Corbis)

and they were afraid, in the worst case scenario, of losing their official licenses to publish. James Franklin's *New England Courant* (1720) was one of the first newspapers in the colonies to criticize the government while operating without a license. Franklin challenged the government's program of forcing citizens to get inoculated against smallpox. It was not that Franklin was adamantly against inoculation; it was more about Franklin struggling for authority and freedom in an effort to gain power. He was jailed on contempt charges but resumed his activities upon his release from incarceration. He was forbidden from ever printing the *Courant* again without a license, but when the government pressed its case, a grand jury would not endorse the charges (i.e., indict him). As a result, the law that required printers in the colonies to purchase licenses remained on the books, but it no longer could be enforced. Thus began the principal of no prior restraint by the government.

While the licensing of newspapers became all but ignored, laws that pertained to seditious libel

remained. The most often cited case that led to the concepts of freedom of the press and freedom of speech involved John Peter Zenger, the printer/editor of the *New York Weekly Journal*. Zenger started the *Journal* in 1733, and in 1735, he was charged with seditious libel. Zenger wrote that the colonial governor William Cosby was corrupt, greedy, and tyrannical, among other things. Zenger's attorney, Andrew Hamilton, did not dispute the nature of the charges; instead, he argued for the freedom of the colonies. After only ten minutes of deliberations, the jury found Zenger not guilty. Although the seditious libel law remained on the books, the government shied away from prosecuting such cases.

As the unrest in the colonies increased in the latter part of the 1700s, the colonial press changed. Newspapers emerged as the most important forum for information exchange. There were around thirty-five newspapers in existence prior to the American Revolution, and there were around thirty-five operating after the war—although they were not the same newspapers; some had gone out of business, and others had sprung up to take their place. The debate, between 1765 and 1775, over what direction the colonies should take was carried out in large part through newspapers. Unlike the objectivity ideal that surfaced in the late 1800s and early 1900s, neutrality was not accepted. The so-called Patriots (or Sons of Liberty) tolerated neither neutrality nor pro-English stances by newspapers. With the Tories pledged to continue loyalty to the British Crown and the Whigs upset over British economic sanctions, the Patriots' goal was to win over the Whigs. Therefore, the war had certainly started with words—largely published in newspapers—long before the first shot was fired.

Sam Adams was essentially the Patriots' propaganda minister. Adams published an account of the Boston Massacre, where six colonists were killed in an exchange with the British, in the *Boston Gazette*. His account painted a picture of British thugs and criminals slaughtering innocent citizens. Other publications, which technically cannot be described as newspapers, also helped in creating dissidence in the colonies.

Post-Revolutionary Partisanship and Technological Advancement

Historian James Mott has described the years following the American Revolution, specifically from 1789 to 1814, as the "Dark Ages of American Journalism." Mostly, Mott abhorred the fact that the partisan press was allowed to exist after the revolution. Others see the period as an extremely exciting time for newspapers and the country. The great debate between the Federalists and the anti-Federalists (or Jeffersonians) about what kind of government would be best for the fledgling country eventually led to the passage of the Bill of Rights, but the debate did not end there. Most historians agree that much of what was printed in the way of political debate during this period was mean spirited and that neutrality still was not tolerated. Editors would often walk the streets with canes, and some were known at times to beat on rival editors because they had alleged printed lies.

Meanwhile, until 1832, no political conventions were held; instead, candidates were nominated through the newspapers and spoke through the newspapers. The newspapers wielded an amount of political power that they had never had before and have never had since. From 1789 to 1850, the newspaper was virtually inseparable from the political system. By 1840, some separation was occurring. For example, William Henry Harrison became the first presidential candidate to make a public address. Still, for the most part, candidates made their statements through newspapers.

Meanwhile, technological advances allowed newspapers to be produced cheaper and more easily. In the 1820s, printers made a discovery that wood pulp could be used to create paper. In the 1850s, some of the larger newspapers adopted a new stereotyping process that allowed multiple copies of the same page to be printed at the same time. By 1861, R. Hoe Company designed a rotary press that took advantage of the stereotyping process and made the printing process even faster. In addition, the company's later "web perfecting press" was able to deliver thirty thousand copies of an eight-page newspaper in one hour. The "web" referred to the continuous roll of paper, and "perfecting" referred to printing on both sides of one sheet of paper at the same time.

The distribution of newspapers also benefited from advanced technology. In the beginning, newspapers could only be delivered over short distances. However, in 1875, the Pennsylvania Railroad started operating, which allowed newspapers from New York and Philadelphia to be distributed as far west as Chicago. Further, the telegraph was introduced in 1841, which allowed quick communication between distant cities, and in 1878, the first telephone exchange was created in New Haven, Connecticut. Because the telegraph had instantly become popular with newspapers, the change to using telephones was not considered to be necessary. Therefore, the telephone did not supplant the telegraph for use in newsgathering activities until several years after it had already become popular with the public.

The Penny Press

In 1833, a dramatic shift began in the newspaper industry caused by new technology and the changing world. Benjamin Day's printing business was on the decline, so he decided to put together a newspaper that concentrated on local happenings and news of violence. He decided that the newspaper would be sold on a per-issue basis and financed with advertising. The result was the *New York Sun*, which became the first of the so-called Penny Press newspapers. After the first six months of publication, the *Sun* had a circulation of eight thousand, and by 1837, the circulation had risen to thirty thousand, which was more than the total of all other New York newspapers combined. The Penny Press was quite different from anything that had existed before. Many historians see the Penny Press as the birth of the modern newspaper. They were sold for one penny per issue (giving them their name), directed toward the common person, hawked by street vendors (i.e., newsboys), financed through advertising (many of which made fantastic claims about patent medicines), and written by local reporters who were paid to provide news. Editors were no longer printers who simply published newspapers as a side business; editors were fully dedicated to the newspaper business. In addition, editors became more concerned about delivering the news rather than opinion—a decided shift from earlier years.

While it was not the first Penny Press newspaper, James Gordon Bennett's *New York Herald* (first published in 1835) certainly became the most innovative Penny Press newspaper. Bennett relied on crime stories and sensationalism, and he had no equal in this area. Bennett pushed the envelope more than anyone else did at the time. For example, he arrived at murder scenes and wrote vivid descriptions of the corpses. As a result, he became a kind of social outcast, and in the 1840s, what is described as a "moral war" was waged against him. Bennett did not hesitate to use terms such as "pants," "shirts," "legs"—all of which were socially unacceptable terms to put in print at the time. People boycotted his newspaper and asked hotels to dispose of it, but Bennett won out; people kept buying and reading.

It would be unfair to characterize Bennett strictly as a "tabloid" journalist. He was innovative and created many journalistic practices that continue to be used. He opened a Washington, D.C., bureau for his newspaper in 1841. He created the country's finest financial page for business people. He created a "letters" column, printed comments from readers, carried a review column, and published society news. Bennett eventually offered sports news and religious news in his newspaper. He even hired news correspondents to cover Europe, Mexico, and Canada. As a result of his sensationalist style, Bennett dealt with an increasing number of libel suits, but he was still feared by politicians and businessmen because the newspaper's popularity provided Bennett with a considerable amount of power.

The Penny Press expanded quickly to Philadelphia, Baltimore, and many other cities, but the most significant expansion was to the west. Horace Greeley, who owned the *New York Tribune* (first published in 1841), rejected sensationalism, and, as a result, his newspaper was always behind the *Sun* and the *Herald* in terms of circulation numbers. However, it was his weekly edition of the *Tribune* that essentially became the first national newspaper—circulated to the western frontier. Greeley considered his newspaper to be an intellectual publication for the non-elite, and he was ahead of his time in believing that all people—white and black—could share in the prosperity of the country. He is often credited with the phrase "Go West, young man, go West." As in the old colonial press days, newspapers in the western frontier needed to publish notices and information about new laws that had been passed by the government. Greeley recognized the growing literacy in the population and took seriously these people's need to know what was going on, as well as their need for entertainment. He became known as the "father" of the editorial, promoting various political or partisan points of view, much as had been done in the years previous to the creation of the Penny Press. Further, Greeley practiced the art of boosterism, singing the praises of the city, town, or state in which the newspaper was going to be circulated.

During the peak of the Penny Press era, Henry J. Raymond started *The New York Times* (first published in 1851), which would become arguably the best newspaper in the United States. This newspaper was more expensive to produce than the Penny Press newspapers, and it served a higher calling. Raymond considered the newspaper to be an outlet for social concerns, a watchdog over business and government, and he focused on specialized coverage of society, arts, religion, and international news. *The Times* highlighted decency in reporting and has continued to maintain that theme.

Photography

Technological advancements in the 1800s allowed for some dramatic changes in the way in which newspapers looked and marketed themselves. Linotypes (typesetting machines) and faster presses, striking typography and layout, color printing, cartoons, and photographs all allowed for editors to make a more vivid, eye-catching newspaper. One of the most important developments occurred in the area of photography. In 1837, Louis Daguerre invented positive photographic plates that allowed, for the first time, the creation of readily usable photography. However, the process required twenty to thirty minutes of exposure time, and no copies could be made. William Henry Talbot and Sir John Herschel, between 1837 and 1840, developed the Collotype Process, which allowed for multiple prints under a positive-negative process. In 1851, Frederick Archer created the Collodion Wet Process, which used glass negatives and required a much shorter exposure time of twelve minutes. In 1871, Richard L. Maddox created the Dry Plate Process, which cut exposure times to seconds. This series of developments, among other refinements in photography, made it easier for photographs to be taken and reproduced.

The U.S. Civil War is recognized as the first war to be thoroughly covered with the use of photographs. Mathew Brady is credited with chronicling the war through pictures. Brady had been a portrait photographer in New York, but in July 1861, he received permission from Union commanders to accompany the troops at his own expense. Brady put together traveling darkrooms that consisted of photographic plates, plate holders, negative boxes, tripods, and cameras. As a result, Brady is credited with bringing the "terrible reality" of the war to the country's "dooryard." Although there was no demand for his photographs after the war and Brady died in poverty, the thirty-five hundred photographs that he and his crew produced are now considered to be a national treasure.

Twentieth-century developments in photography made the use of photographs in newspapers easier and more economical. In 1912, faster film was developed for use in the Speed Graphic camera, which was also smaller. The Speed Graphic, which used 4-inch by 5-inch film, became the standard for newspaper photography for nearly fifty years. The 35-mm camera first appeared in the 1920s, but it was initially less reliable and more difficult to use effectively than the Speed Graphic. On the positive side, the 35-mm camera had a faster lens and used more sensitive film, both of which eliminated the need to have subjects pose and allowed for the creation of informal, realistic, nonintrusive photographs.

Yellow Journalism

Toward the end of the nineteenth century, a form of journalism known as "yellow journalism" (or "new journalism") emerged. This new form of journalism was typified by unethical and unprofessional tactics that were used primarily to boost circulation. The newspapers of Joseph Pulitzer and William Randolph Hearst were the most prominent practitioners of this style. Pulitzer left the *St. Louis Post-Dispatch* in 1883 to move to New York and take over the *New York World*. Borrowing from the advances that had been made by Day and Bennett, Pulitzer added the innovations of short news clips, columns, large headlines, and the use of a worldwide news service. Pulitzer managed to reinvent himself before his death (lending his name to the most prestigious journalism award in the country—the Pulitzer Prize), but early on he led the way in sensationalized irresponsible journalism. For example, eleven people were trampled to death on a pedestrian walkway next to the Brooklyn Bridge in May 1883. Keeping in mind the newness of the bridge, the headline on Pulitzer's newspaper read, "Baptized in Blood." In 1895, Hearst took over the *New York Journal* and raided Pulitzer's staff. One of the most sensational quotes to be attributed to Hearst during this

Mathew Brady's photographs of the Civil War allowed newspaper readers to see for the first time the actual events of war, including this occasion where observation balloons were prepared for use in observing enemy maneuvers on June 1, 1862, near Fair Oaks, Virginia. (Medford Historical Society Collection/Corbis)

period had to do with the Spanish-American War. In 1897, Frederic Remington was serving as a correspondent in Cuba, but he wanted to return home because it did not look like there was going to be a war. Hearst reportedly sent a telegram to Remington saying, "You provide the pictures; I'll provide the war." Unlike Pulitzer, Hearst was never able to reinvent his public image in order to distance himself from his early days of sensationalism. The term "yellow journalism" comes from the Yellow Kid, a comic strip character that was created by Richard Felton Outcault. Pulitzer was the first to publish Outcault's character, but the artist was later lured away to work for Hearst. This event only served to escalate the battle between the two publishers.

While Hearst and Pulitzer squared off, *The New York Times* was rescued from bankruptcy and did not give in to the temptations of the day. In 1896, Adolph Ochs bought the newspaper and rebuilt it. His hiring of top-class editors and reporters set the tone for *The Times* and maintained the original intent of its founder.

Changing Formats and Increasing Objectivity

As the twentieth century began, newspapers reached a saturation point. There were more than twenty-two hundred daily newspapers in the country; there were twenty-nine dailies in New York City alone. Newspapers were facing a changing world, and never again would they be as dominant a medium as in the late 1800s. As the 1920s began, there was disillusionment with Democrats because of World War I, radio was on its way to becoming the new dominant medium (until television), and business was king. The silent film industry was thriving, magazines were becoming more sophisticated with quality color printing, and cities were getting larger (i.e., the mostly rural country was becoming a more urban country).

Newspapers, at least many of them, adapted to the environment. The reaction was the creation of the tabloid. Compared to newspapers, tabloids were more visually pleasing, smaller, and more compact (in order to be easier to handle when riding on a streetcar or in a subway). Short punchy stories were more common as magazines and films cornered the market on good storytelling. Further, responding to the radio commentators, political columnists became more prevalent in publications. The *New York Daily News,* first published by Joseph Medill Patterson in 1919, is a good example of the new newspapers of this period. Patterson aimed his newspaper at the lowest literate class of people in New York, and he patterned it after successful New England publications. The *New York Evening Graphic,* which was first published in 1924, used a tabloid format, but it also used "yellow journalism" tactics. This newspaper pioneered the doctoring of photographs (e.g., taking people from two different photographs and creating a composite photograph to make it look as if they appeared together).

It would be irresponsible to avoid addressing the issue of objectivity when talking about the newspaper industry. Some historians trace the journalistic ideal of objectivity—the idea of reporting information fair and accurately without personal bias leaking into the news—as far back as the Penny Press. Compared to the opinion-laden newspapers that were published before, during, and soon after the American Revolution, the newspapers of the Penny Press were certainly more fact driven. Another group of historians believes that objectivity took root about the time that the Associated Press started disseminating news nationwide in the mid-1800s. Because the news was used in all areas of the country, it had to be reported as fairly as possible in order

to guarantee that it did not offend anyone. In addition, the evolution of photography lent itself to the idea of objectivity because photographs were considered to be little pictures of "reality." A final group of historians believes that objectivity as a journalistic ideal did not start until the 1920s and 1930s. The rise in public relations (which was often considered to be "creating" the news) and the failure of big business (with the Great Depression) caused journalists to look for a scientific approach to newsgathering. Things such as identification of news sources, creation of nonpartisan research councils, and the professionalism of journalism all occurred in response to dissatisfaction with the existing system. Several of the most famous journalism schools started during this time, and the Society of Professional Journalists (Sigma Delta Chi) adopted objectivity as part of its code of ethics, declaring, "We honor those who achieve it."

Modern Technological Innovations

In the period between 1945 and 1974, another revolution led by technology hit the newspaper industry. One of the major developments was the Teletypesetter system of the 1950s. Used in conjunction with the old Linotype machines, the Teletypesetter helped to create a trend toward uniformity in the newspaper industry. It was easier for an editor to print a national wire service story than to assign a local reporter to go through the entire process of production. The Teletypesetter had a set type of punctuation, abbreviations and capitalization styles to which the Associated Press, United Press, and International News Service all agreed to adhere. Photocomposition and offset printing were other major technological breakthroughs that occurred in the decades immediately after World War II. The old Gutenberg raised type had been the standard for centuries, but photocomposition produced type by photographic processes. Offset printing, a form of lithography, used a photographic process to produce the plate for printing, which all but eliminated the large and noisy linotype machines by the end of the 1960s. The computer started taking over the newsroom in the 1980s. This new process was aptly called "desktop publishing," and it included the use of laser printers, personal computers, and software that created both text and graphics. By 1987, half of the newspapers in the United States had already converted to desktop publishing.

The number of daily newspapers declined steadily during the twentieth century. Other than the creation of *USA Today* by the Gannett Company in 1982, virtually no new major newspapers have surfaced since the mid-1970s. Instead, many cities have undergone a joining of two newspapers into one or the loss of one or more newspapers. *USA Today,* which is second only to the *Wall Street Journal* in circulation, was the first modern-day national newspaper. Initially, *USA Today* was damned by most of the newspaper establishment, who said that it was television in print. Still, when it became both popular and profitable, local newspapers all over the country suddenly started to copy it.

In the 1990s, newspapers, by and large, joined the new media arena. Most of the daily newspapers in the United States established some kind of Internet presence, even though there was little or no evidence that a website would prove to be profitable. If the estimates that indicate that there are more than eight thousand online newspapers in existence are correct, then the number of online newspapers has already surpassed the number of traditional print newspapers.

See also: BENNETT, JAMES GORDON; BLY, NELLIE; GREELEY, HORACE; GUTENBERG, JOHANNES; HEARST, WILLIAM RANDOLPH; INTERNET AND THE WORLD WIDE WEB; JOURNALISM, HISTORY OF; JOURNALISM, PROFESSIONALIZATION OF; NEWS EFFECTS; NEWSPAPER INDUSTRY; NEWSPAPER INDUSTRY, CAREERS IN; NEWS PRODUCTION THEORIES; PRINTING, HISTORY AND METHODS OF; PULITZER, JOSEPH.

Bibliography

Boyce, George; Curran, James; and Wingate, Pauline. (1978). *Newspaper History from the Seventeenth Century to the Present Day*. Beverly Hills, CA: Sage Publications.

Emery, Edwin; Roberts, Nancy L.; and Emory, Michael C. (1999). *The Press and America: An Interpretive History of the Mass Media*. Englewood Cliffs, NJ: Prentice-Hall.

Folkerts, Jean, and Teeter, Dwight L. (1997). *Voices of a Nation: A History of the Media in the United States*. New York: Macmillan.

Sloan, William David, and Startt, James D. (1996). *The Media in America: A History*. Northport, AL: Vision Press.

LAWRENCE N. STROUT

■ NEWS PRODUCTION THEORIES

News carries with it a powerful mythology, leading people to regard news as a mirror that is held up to society, a window on the world that tells "the way it is." Moving beyond this unproblematic view of journalism opens a wide range of important questions to research, predicated on the idea that news, like other forms of knowledge, is socially constructed.

The many attempts to explain the production of news have often taken a sociology of media view, which considers how media power functions within a larger social context. More narrowly, this approach is equated with the newsroom ethnographies that have been carried out by sociologists such as Herbert Gans and Gaye Tuchman. Taken more broadly, it suggests that the structural context of journalism must be tackled, moving beyond the more narrow attempt to psychologize the news process through the attitudes and values of individual practitioners, or "gatekeepers."

In her interpretive sociological approach to news, Tuchman (1978, p. 12) asserts that "making news is the act of constructing reality itself rather than a picture of reality," a view that leads her to think of news as a "frame." Newswork is viewed as the process of transforming occurrences into news events. Her ethnomethodological analyses of journalists in local news organizations examines how people make sense of the everyday world in its "taken for grantedness." Journalists, for example, find the meaning of objectivity in the specific procedures of quoting, sourcing, and balancing that have become synonymous with good work. Thus, reference to these steps, the "strategic ritual," as she terms it, rather than any philosophical recourse, is invoked when their work is challenged. Following the work of Peter Berger and Thomas Luckmann (1967), Tuchman's work shows how meaning becomes objectified in the institutional "newsnet," rendering "historically given" the journalistic reports that are embedded in the time rhythms and geographical news "beat" arrangements of legitimated, official settings.

Framing the News

As a particularly influential concept in news study, the idea of "frame" is defined by Erving Goffman (1974) as the principles of organization that govern people's interpretation of and subjective involvement with social events. Interest in framing responds to the recommendation by Robert Hackett (1984) that studies of news move beyond a narrow concern with bias—deviation from an objective standard—to a more fruitful view of the ideological character of news, thoroughly structured in its content, practices, and relations with society. The notion of bias suggests that a faithful reflection of events is possible, while framing underscores the constructed quality of news. The surge of interest in framing highlights important issues. Precisely how are issues constructed, discourse structured, and meanings developed?

A number of definitions have been proposed to refine the framing concept. According to Robert Entman (1993, p. 52), a frame is determined in large part by its outcome or effect: "To frame is to select some aspects of a perceived reality and make them more salient in a communicating text, in such a way as to promote a particular problem definition, causal interpretation, moral evaluation, and/or treatment recommendation." William Gamson and Andre Modigliani (1989, p. 3) define frame as a "central organizing idea . . . for making sense of relevant events, suggesting what is at issue," signified by the media "package" of metaphors and other devices.

Todd Gitlin (1980, pp. 7, 21) views frames as "persistent patterns of cognition, interpretation, and presentation, of selection, emphasis, and exclusion, by which symbol-handlers routinely organize discourse." His definition lays the emphasis on the routine organization, which transcends any given story and is "persistent" over time (resistant to change). In dealing with information, frames enable journalists to "recognize it as information, to assign it to cognitive categories." This gives frames a power, actively to bring otherwise amorphous reality into a meaningful structure, making them more than the simple inclusion or exclusion of information. In their analysis of social movement coverage, James Hertog and Douglas McLeod (1995) note that if a protest march is framed as a confrontation between police and marchers, the protesters' critique of society may not be part of the story—not because there was not room for it, but because it was not defined as relevant. Thus, it may be said that frames are organizing principles that are socially shared and persistent over time and that

are working symbolically to provide a meaningful structure for the social world.

Hierarchy of Influences Model

To help summarize the forces that figure into the construction, or framing, of news, a "hierarchy of influences" model that is based on levels of analysis has been proposed by Pamela Shoemaker and Stephen Reese (1996). In brief, these levels range from the most micro to the most macro: individual, routines, organizational, extramedia, and ideological, with each successive level viewed as subsuming the prior one(s). The hierarchical aspect draws attention to the idea that these forces operate simultaneously at different levels of strength in any shaping of news content.

Individual Level

At the individual level, the attitudes, training, and background of the journalist (or media workers more generally) are viewed as being influential. American journalists have encouraged a certain mythic image of their distinctive role in society and resisted viewing this product as a construction, like those produced in any other complex organization. Leo Rosten (1937) was perhaps the first to try to describe journalists in his study of Washington correspondents, but not until the 1970s did sociologists begin to apply the same occupational and organizational insights to this as to any other professional group. J. W. C. Johnstone, E. J. Slawski, and W. W. Bowman (1972) are frequently cited as making the first major empirical effort to describe U.S. journalists as a whole.

In more partisan-based research, the tendency of journalists to tilt liberal is sufficient to explain what conservatives view as a leftward slant in news content. S. Robert Lichter, Stanley Rothman, and Linda Lichter (1986), for example, concluded that American journalists (those working at "elite" urban, primarily Northeast media) were more likely to vote Democrat, to express left-of-center political views, and to be nonreligious than were the American public as a whole. Broader surveys, such as those by David Weaver and G. Cleveland Wilhoit (1991), find that American journalists, across the entire country, are much more like the American public than the Lichter study would suggest. They have provided a valuable counterweight to generalizations about journalists that have been based on a few high-profile but unrepresentative cases.

The study of key news decision makers follows from the "gatekeeper" tradition of analysis that was begun by David Manning White (1950), who attributed great influence to the individual editor's subjective judgment. Later perspectives see the gatekeeper as greatly limited by the routines and organizational constraints within which they work (Becker and Whitney, 1982; Berkowitz, 1990).

Routines Level

The routines level of analysis considers the constraining influences of work practices, which serve to organize how people perceive and function within the social world. Analysis taking this perspective often finds the ethnographic method valuable because it allows the effect of these practices to be observed over time and in their natural setting. It is assumed that journalists are often not aware of how their outlooks are so "routinely" structured and would be unable to self-report honestly about it. And indeed, it is assumed that much of what journalists provide as reasons for their behavior are actually justifications for what they have already been obliged to do by forces that are outside of their control (e.g., Tuchman, 1972, 1978). Field observation suits the concern here with the ongoing and structured rather than the momentary or sporadic. The routines that have attracted the most interest have been those that have involved the frontline reporters, such as in local television news (Altheide, 1976; Berkowitz, 1990) and newspapers (Fishman, 1980; Sigal, 1973). A classic field study of national networks and newsmagazines, which was conducted by Herbert Gans (1979), showed how little journalists often know of their audiences, how influenced they are by other media—especially The New York Times—and their news sources, and how, while reflecting the enduring values and hierarchies of society, journalists must assume a detached attitude toward the consequences of their work.

Organizational Level

At the organizational level, the goals and policies of a larger social structure and how power is exercised within it may be considered. If the routines are the most immediate environment within which a journalist functions, the organizational level considers the imperatives that give rise to those routines and how individuals are obliged to relate to others within that larger formal structure. Charles Bantz, Suzanne McCorkle, and Roberta Baade (1980) exemplify this view in their depiction of local television as a "news factory," leading workers to take an assembly line view of their interchangeable commodity products rather than a more professional, craft-oriented perspective. The major questions addressed at this level are suggested by an organizational chart, which maps the key roles and their occupants, in addition to how those roles are related to each other in formal lines of authority. The chart additionally suggests that the organization must have ways to enforce and legitimize the authority of its hierarchy and calls attention to the organization's main goals (economic in relation to journalistic), how it is structured to pursue them, and how policy is enforced. The pioneering work of Warren Breed (1955) showed how social control is exercised nonovertly in the newsroom, ultimately by publishers, leading to self-censorship by journalists.

Newsroom studies often contain elements of both the routines and the organizational perspective, which are clearly related. This more macro level, however, is a reminder that news is an organizational product, produced by increasingly complex economic entities, which seek ever more far-reaching relationships in their ownership patterns and connections to nonmedia industries. While journalists have long needed to be concerned with business considerations influencing their work, now these concerns may stretch far beyond their immediate organization. As news companies become part of large, global conglomerates, it is often difficult to anticipate the many conflicts of interest that may arise, and journalists find it difficult to avoid reporting that has a relationship to one or more aspects of the interests of the parent company.

The organizational level brings different challenges for analysis than the previous two levels. Organizational power is often not easily observed and functions in ways not directly indicated by the formal lines of authority described in accessible documents. As Breed (1955) emphasized, power is not often overtly expressed over the news product because it would violate the objectivity notion, that news is something "out there" waiting to be discovered. Enforcing policy about what the news is to be would contradict this principle. At this level, there is curiosity about how decisions are made, and how they get enforced. By definition, the concern is with power that is exercised periodically, implicitly, and not overtly, which makes it not as readily available to direct observation. Indeed, a journalist anticipates organizational boundaries, the power of which is manifested in self-censorship by its members. Thus, journalists may accurately state that no one told them to suppress a story. This self-policing is more effective than direct censorship, however, because outsiders are often not even aware that anything has taken place.

Extramedia Level

At the extramedia level, those influences that originate primarily from outside the media organization are considered. This perspective considers that the power to shape content is not the media's alone; it is shared with a variety of institutions in society, including the government, advertisers, public relations, influential news sources, interest groups, and even other media organizations. This latter factor may be seen in the form of competitive market pressures. From a critical perspective, the extramedia level draws attention to the way media are subordinated to elite interests in the larger system. While individual journalists may scrupulously avoid conflicts of interest that may bias their reporting, maintaining a professional distance from their subject, their employers may be intimately linked to larger corporate interests through interlocking boards of directors and other elite connections. At this level, then, it is assumed that the media operate in structured relationships with other institutions, which function to shape media content. It is further assumed that these relationships can be coercive but more often are voluntary and collusive. Normative concerns at this level are for press autonomy, assuming often that it is not desirable for the media to be so dependent on other social institutions. Conceptually, this level encompasses a wide variety of influences on the media, but those systemic, patterned, and ongoing ways in which media are connected with their host society are of particular concern.

Ideological Level

Each of the preceding levels may be thought to subsume the one before, suggesting that the ultimate level should be an ideological perspective. The diverse approaches and schools of thought in media studies that may be deemed "ideological" make them difficult to summarize. Here, the concern at least is with how the symbolic content of media is connected with larger social interests, how meaning is constructed in the service of

power. This necessarily leads to the consideration of how each of the previous levels functions in order to add up to a coherent ideological result. In that respect, a critical view would consider that the recruitment of journalists, their attitudes, the routines they follow, their organizational policy, and the 'positions of those organizations in the larger social structure work to support the status quo, narrow the range of social discourse, and serve to make the media agencies of social control. A critical view is likely to be concerned with how power is exerted by the natural workings of the media system, creating a process of hegemony. Gitlin (1980), in his classic study of media marginalization of the student movement in the 1960s, defined this as the "systematic (but not necessarily or even usually deliberate) engineering of mass consent to the established order." At this level, it must be asked how a system of meanings and commonsense understandings is made to appear natural through the structured relationship of the media to society.

Conclusion

Led by the media sociologists, research into the news production process has grown greatly since the early 1970s. These studies provide great insight into precisely how societal power, organizational processes, and individual characteristics of journalists interact to shape the news. The news produced, or "framed," as this constructed reality in turn frames the ways of thinking about social issues and the participation in public life.

See also: Cultural Studies; Culture Industries, Media as; Democracy and the Media; First Amendment and the Media; Functions of the Media; Globalization of Media Industries; Journalism, History of; Journalism, Professionalization of; Social Change and the Media; Society and the Media.

Bibliography

Altheide, David. (1976). *Creating Reality: How Television News Distorts Events.* Beverly Hills, CA: Sage Publications.

Bantz, Charles; McCorkle, Suzanne; and Baade, Roberta. (1980). "The News Factory." *Communication Research* 7:45–68.

Becker, Lee, and Whitney, D. Charles. (1982). "Keeping the Gates' for Gatekeepers: The Effects of Wire News." *Journalism Quarterly* 59:60–65.

Berger, Peter L., and Luckmann, Thomas. (1967). *The Social Construction of Reality*. Garden City, NY: Doubleday-Anchor.

Berkowitz, Dan. (1990). "Refining the Gatekeeping Metaphor for Local Television News." *Journal of Broadcasting & Electronic Media* 34:55–68.

Berkowitz, Dan. (1997). *Social Meanings of News: A Text-Reader*. Thousand Oaks, CA: Sage Publications.

Breed, Warren. (1955). "Social Control in the Newsroom: A Functional Analysis." *Social Forces* 33:326–335.

Entman, Robert. (1993). "Framing: Toward Clarification of a Fractured Paradigm." *Journal of Communication* 43(4):51–58.

Epstein, Edward. (1974). *News from Nowhere*. New York: Vintage.

Fishman, Mark. (1980). *Manufacturing the News*. Austin: University of Texas Press.

Gamson, William A., and Modigliani, Andre. (1989). "Media Discourse and Public Opinion on Nuclear Power: A Constructionist Approach." *American Journal of Sociology* 95:1–37.

Gans, Herbert. (1979). *Deciding What's News*. New York: Vintage.

Gitlin, Todd. (1980). *The Whole World Is Watching*. Berkeley: University of California Press.

Goffman, Erving. (1974). *Frame Analysis: An Essay on the Organization of Experience*. Boston: Northeastern University Press.

Hackett, Robert. (1984). "Decline of a Paradigm? Bias and Objectivity in News Media Studies." *Critical Studies in Mass Communication* 1(3):229–259.

Hertog, James, and McLeod, Douglas. (1995). "Anarchists Wreak Havoc in Downtown Minneapolis: A Multi-Level Study of Media Coverage of Radical Protest." *Journalism & Mass Communication Monographs*, No. 151. Columbia, SC: Association for Education in Journalism and Mass Communication.

Johnstone, J. W. C.; Slawski, E. J.; and Bowman, W. W. (1972). "The Professional Values of American Newsmen." *Public Opinion Quarterly* 36:522–540.

Lichter, S. Robert; Rothman, Stanley; and Lichter, Linda S. (1986). *The Media Elite*. Bethesda, MD: Adler.

Molotch, Harvey, and Lester, Marilyn. (1974). "News as Purposive Behavior: On the Strategic Use of Routine Events, Accidents and Scandals." *American Sociological Review* 39:101–112.

Rosten, Leo. (1937). *The Washington Correspondents*. New York: Harcourt, Brace.

Shoemaker, Pamela. (1991). *Gatekeeping, Communication Concepts 3*. Newbury Park, CA: Sage Publications.

Shoemaker, Pamela, and Reese, Stephen. (1996). *Mediating the Message: Theories of Influence on Mass Media Content*, 2nd edition. New York: Longman.

Sigal, Leon. (1973). *Reporters and Officials: The Organization and Politics of Newsmaking*. Lexington, MA: DC Heath.

Tuchman, Gaye. (1972). "Objectivity as Strategic Ritual: An Examination of Newsmen's Notions of Objectivity." *American Journal of Sociology* 77:660–679.

Tuchman, Gaye. (1978). *Making News*. New York: Free Press.

Weaver, David, and Wilhoit, G. Cleveland. (1991). *The American Journalist: A Portrait of U.S. News People and Their Work*, 2nd edition. Bloomington: Indiana University Press.

White, David M. (1950). "The Gatekeeper: A Case Study in the Selection of News." *Journalism Quarterly* 27:383–390.

STEPHEN D. REESE

NONVERBAL COMMUNICATION

Nonverbal communication has been referred to as "body language" in popular culture ever since the publication of Julius Fast's book of the same name in 1970. However, researchers Mark Knapp and Judith Hall (1997, p. 5) have defined nonverbal communication as follows: "Nonverbal communication refers to communication effected by means other than words." This definition does not exclude many forms of communication, but it implies that nonverbal communication is more than body language. However, determination of the exact boundaries of the field is a point of contention among scholars.

Nonverbal communication is an area of study that straddles many disciplines—sociology, psychology, anthropology, communication, and even art and criminal justice. Each of these fields tends to focus on a slightly different aspect of nonverbal communication. For example, psychology might focus on the nonverbal expression of emotions; anthropology might focus on the use of interpersonal space in different cultures; and communication might focus on the content of the message. However, there is more overlap among these fields than divergence.

The History

It appears that all cultures have written or oral traditions expressing the importance of nonverbal communication to understanding human beings. Over thousands of years, Chinese culture has developed a set of rules about how to judge the character and personality of an individual by observing the size, shape, and relative positions of the nose, eyes, eyebrows, chin, cheeks, and forehead. Someone with wide-set eyes would be a "broadminded" person, while someone with a high forehead would be a "smart" person. Although there does not seem to be much scientific evidence that facial characteristics predict personality, modern people still believe this to be valid.

Ancient Greek culture has also relied on nonverbal communication to understand people. The playwright Theophrastus created a list of "31 types of men" that he made available to other playwrights to assist them in the creation of characters for their plays. Theophrastus relied on insights gleaned from nonverbal communication to describe these personalities; the penurious man does not wear his sandals until noon, and the sanguine man has slumped shoulders. Humans still rely on nonverbal insights like these to judge the personalities and emotions of other people.

In India, the sacred Hindu texts called the *Veda,* written around 1000 B.C.E., described a liar as someone who, when questioned, rubs his big toe along the ground, looks down, does not make eye contact, and so forth. Late-twentieth-century research based on North Americans shows that people still concur with the *Veda* on this description of a liar.

Research into African history has shown that one of the characteristics of an effective tribal chief was his ability to move his subjects with the power of his speeches, made particularly potent by the heavy use of nonverbal communication. This legacy is apparent in the traditions of the African-American church in America. These same principles of strong body language and voice tone accompanying speeches has now been adopted in various forms by the rest of American society and politics because of its ability to persuade above and beyond well-crafted words.

The Function of Nonverbal Communication

Nonverbal communication serves a number of functions. It can define communication by providing the backdrop for communication—a quiet, dimly lit room suggests to people that the communication that occurs within that environment should also be quiet and hushed (as in a religious venue). Brightly lit rooms, with active colors such as yellow and orange, communicate active, upbeat activities. Nonverbal communication can also be connected to the behavior or dress of others in the room. If others are moving calmly, crying, and wearing formal clothes, that sends a nonverbal message that is quite distinct from a room full of people moving with a bounce in their step, laughing, and wearing Hawaiian-print shirts.

Nonverbal communication can also regulate verbal communication. Much of people's conversations are regulated by nonverbal cues so subtle that the average person does not notice them. People nod and smile at particular moments during a face-to-face conversation. This signals the talker that the listener understands and that the talker should continue talking. When the talker is finished, he or she will drop his or her voice tone and loudness to let the listener know. If the talker wishes to continue talking, he or she will fill the pauses that occur with a louder voice, with many "umms, ahhs," and so on. People have learned these rules so well that they adhere to them almost unconsciously. The use of these subtle clues accounts for why people can have conversations without constantly talking over each other, or having to utter the word "over"—like the astronauts—to let the other person know when one is finished speaking. This rule can be tested by violating it. If a person tries to remain motionless while engaged in a conversation with a friend, that person will find this is not only hard to do, but it will cause the friend great consternation.

Finally, nonverbal communication can be the message itself. A frown indicates unhappiness. A wave of the hand signifies "good-bye." A quiver in the voice signifies distress. Raising the index finger to the lips signifies "shhh," or "be quiet," yet raising the index finger into the air in a thrusting manner may mean "we're number one." No words are needed to send these messages. Note that most of these meanings are culturally determined (which is discussed below in detail).

The Relationship Between Verbal and Nonverbal Communication

Paul Ekman proposed that there are six ways in which verbal and nonverbal communication relate. He suggested that nonverbal communication can substitute for verbal communication, as well as repeat, contradict, complement, accent, and regulate verbal communication.

What Ekman meant by substitution is that nonverbal communication can be substituted for verbal communication. If asked whether another helping of mother's wonderful pasta is wanted, a person can shake his or her head up and down to signify "yes," rather than attempting to utter the word "yes" through a mouthful of spaghetti.

Nonverbal communication can also repeat verbal communication. People can simultaneously speak the word "no" and shake their heads side to side. Repeating and substitution seem like the same idea, but substitute means someone does not speak the word or phrase represented by the nonverbal gesture, whereas repeat means he or she does speak the word or phrase.

Sometimes these simultaneous verbal and nonverbal signals will contradict each other. Someone might utter the phrase "this will be fun" and yet display a facial expression of disgust as they speak those words. This is sarcasm; the words seem positive, yet the facial expression is negative.

Nonverbal communication can also complement verbal communication. Someone might say the phrase "I've had a tough day" with their shoulders slumped and their feet dragging. Note that slumped shoulders and dragging feet can express a number of things (e.g., sadness, fatigue, injury, daydreaming), but in conjunction with the verbal message "I've had a tough day," they enrich and focus the message.

Sometimes nonverbal communication will simply accent a particular part of a spoken verbal communication. Someone might say, "It is important to punctuate your speech with nonverbal gestures," while rhythmically moving one hand up and down on each syllable in the word "punctuate." In this situation, the moving hand gestures for the word "punctuate" will accent that word, thereby letting the listener know that this concept is important.

Finally, Ekman proposes that nonverbal communication can regulate verbal communication. As discussed above, there are various unspoken rules that regulate conversations. Listeners provide backchannel communication (e.g., nodding, smiling subtly, saying "uh huh") at particular points during the conversations to let their partners know that they understand and that the partners can continue to speak.

The Structures and Properties of Nonverbal Communication

Judee Burgoon and other scholars have suggested that nonverbal messages conform to many

Les Grimaces, *an early nineteenth-century lithograph by Louis Leopold Boilly, depicts five basic facial expressions—anger, disgust, happiness, sadness, and surprise. (Corbis)*

of the same properties as verbal communication—properties such as structured rules, intentionality, awareness, covert and overtness, control, and private/publicness—but in slightly different ways.

In order to communication meaning, nonverbal messages must be rule bound, similar to speech. The sentence "Floats otter the on sea the" does not make much sense because it does not conform to certain rules applying to word order. "The otter floats on the sea" does follow those rules, and thus makes sense. Nonverbal communication has similar properties, and when the rules are violated, they change the meanings. In North America, there are rules that guide how close people stand next to each other when talking—usually between eighteen inches and four feet. When one person stands too close to another when talking, the other feels compelled to move away to reestablish what they feel is a comfortable distance. The violation of this rule causes one person to feel that the other person is too pushy or aggressive, and the other person to feel that the other is too unfriendly or standoffish.

People assume that the vast majority of spoken communication is intentional; they choose the words they speak. Likewise, most nonverbal communication is intentional. People deliberately wave to others or give an insulting finger gesture.

However, scholars such as Peter Andersen and Joseph Capella have argued that it appears that a greater proportion of nonverbal communication is unintentional. For example, some people may intend to communicate calmness and maturity about the death of their cat, and yet they often unintentionally communicate sadness through their voice tone and facial expression.

Similarly, people are also less aware of their nonverbal communication compared to their verbal communication. Except for unusual circumstances, people can hear all that they speak. People are usually aware of their nonverbal communication (e.g., the clothes they wear, the gestures they use, and the expressions they show), but not always. For example, when lying, a person may feel afraid and yet feel they were able to hide that fear. As scholar Bella DePaulo has shown, despite their beliefs, liars are often unaware that in fact they are expressing clear signs of fear in their face, posture, or speech.

Verbal communication is more overt, and nonverbal behavior is more covert. People are formally trained in their verbal behavior in the schools. Nonverbal communication is less obvious, as in subtle facial expressions and barely perceptible changes in voice tone, and people are not typically formally trained in their nonverbal communication. Children are not often given lessons on how close to stand to others when talking or how to express anger in a facial expression.

Nonverbal communication is also less controllable than verbal communication. Verbal communication is easy to suppress, or to express, and people choose the words they use. Although much of nonverbal communication follows the same pattern (e.g., people choose to display a hand gesture), nonverbal communication is much more likely to have an unbidden quality to it. This is the smile that creeps onto one's face when one knows he or she should not be laughing.

Finally, verbal communication is more public than nonverbal communication. Speaking typically requires an audible or visible message that is available for others to hear or see, not just the intended target of the communication. Once public, this communication is also fodder for public discussion. In contrast, nonverbal communication tends to be more fodder for private conversation. When political candidates speak, people publicly discuss and debate their policies, and not their shoes or their gestures. This trend is changing, with more focus being placed on how the candidate delivers a message, rather than on the message itself.

The Origins of Nonverbal Communication

Nonverbal communication comes from both culture and biology. Most nonverbal communication is learned the same way as language, one word or gesture at a time. Words have different meanings in different languages or cultures, and likewise, gestures can have different meanings in different cultures. In North America, a raised index and middle finger typically means "peace" or "victory," regardless of whether the palm is turned inward or outward. In Australia or the United Kingdom, this same gesture with the palm turned outward means "victory," but with the palm turned inward, it is an insult ("screw you"). People learn how to cross their legs, fold their arms, how much to gesture with their hands when speaking, how much to express with their faces, how close to stand to others, and so on.

However, what distinguishes nonverbal communication from verbal communication is that some nonverbal communication is not learned; it is innate. Charles Darwin argued that the facial expressions people display for certain emotions, such as anger, disgust, distress (sadness), fear, happiness, and surprise (some scholars argue for contempt, embarrassment, and/or interest as well), are part of human evolutionary heritage. These emotions have helped humans (and other animals) to survive, and thus they get passed from one generation to the next. A person who has a fear emotional response to danger will be more likely to escape that danger and thus will survive and reproduce. A person without that response will not survive and thus will not pass his or her genes on to the next generation.

What Darwin and others, including Carrol Izard and Ekman, have argued is that these emotions cause people or animals to act in some way (e.g., to strike when angry, or to flee when afraid). This behavioral intention must be communicated to others in the group. The facial expression thus becomes a visual signal of this intention, which allows others to avoid this person and his or her anger—which prevents a fight. This communication permits all social animals to maintain harmony and cooperation. Even animals without a spoken language will communicate their emotional intentions (e.g., tail wag, raised fur, attentive ears), but they communicate with their bodies and not so much with their faces. Other animals interpret these signals accurately without receiving any formal training.

Darwin, Ekman, and Izard argue that these facial expressions are as much a part of an emotional response as an increased heart rate or sweating, and they cite five sources of evidence that supports their views. First, scholars such as Irene Eibl-Eibesfeldt have shown that children who are born blind will smile when happy or make a distressed face when sad—similar to children who are born with sight—even though they cannot see how this expression was made. Second, human's biologically closest animal relatives, the chimpanzees, also seem to show facial expressions that are similar to those of humans. Third, when Ekman and his colleagues asked people to pose those facial expressions of emotion described above, and then showed photos of these expressions to people of other cultures, the people in other cultures were not only able to recognize the expressions but agreed strongly which expression was anger, which was disgust, and so on. Likewise, all cultures spontaneously pose these expressions in the same way (i.e., all people show anger with a furrowed eyebrow and tight lips, and happiness with a smile, and so on). Ekman's research included cultures in Papua New Guinea that at the time had no books, no electricity, and almost no contact with Western culture, so they could not have learned the expressions from movies, television, or outsiders. Izard points out that as one travels in Europe, the nonverbal gestures for particular words or concepts change drastically as one goes from village to village—yet the facial expressions for these emotions does not. Fourth, Ekman and his colleagues have shown that by posing and holding these facial expressions of emotion, one will experience the emotion shown in the facial expression. Finally, evidence suggests that there are centers in the human brain that respond specifically to the facial expression of fear, and possibly other facial expressions of emotion, thus arguing for the hard-wired perception of these expressions.

However, Ekman and Izard have argued that these facial expressions are not simple reflexes. People can learn to control these expressions, depending on the rules of a person's particular culture or subculture. Boys in North America learn not to cry when distressed, whereas girls typically do not learn that rule. In Japan, people learn not to show anger or disgust to high-status people or in public situations, whereas North Americans do not learn such a rule. Research has shown that both Japanese and Americans, when alone, will show facial expressions of disgust when viewing a gory film. However, when in the presence of a high-status person, the Japanese will smile during the gory film, whereas Americans still show an expression of disgust. Ekman found with closer inspection that the Japanese were still showing expressions of disgust, but they were trying to mask them with the smile. Ekman has called these cultural rules that dictate how and when people should show these facial expressions of emotion "display rules."

Sources of Nonverbal Communication

Nonverbal communication is part of the behaviors of people, as well as the results of their behavior. One source of messages is the environment. Different houses send different messages about their occupants. This is accomplished through the use of color, lighting, heat, fabric textures, photos, and so on. Restaurants will capitalize on the messages sent by these environmental factors to influence the behaviors and impressions of diners. Fast-food restaurants use active, bright colors such as orange, yellow, and red in a well-lit environment with hard plastic seating. These messages subtly urge diners to eat more food more quickly and not to lounge around afterward. In this way, the fast-food restaurants get a quick turnover in order to maximize profits. In contrast, elegant restaurants use dimmer lighting, softer and darker colors, and more comfortable chairs to communicate a more intimate impression, subtly urging diners to feel comfortable and stay around for dessert and coffee, and so on. This will cause diners to spend more money per visit, as well as ensure increase business through positive word of mouth. Thus, the nonverbal messages sent by the environment can help guide the behaviors that occur within that environment.

Another source of nonverbal messages is one's physical characteristics and appearance. Physical characteristics are the static physical appearance or smell of a person. This includes one's height and weight, skin color, hair, eyebrows, cheeks, chin, proportion of eye, nose, and chin size, as well as odors. William Sheldon believed that different body types were predictive of personality: endomorphs (heavier, obese, rounder, softer looking) were sociable and pleasant, mesomorphs (angular, muscular, harder looking) were leaders and strong-willed, and ectomorphs (thin, frail, brittle looking) were withdrawn, smart, and nervous. The media capitalizes on this association by casting actors and actresses accordingly; notice how the leading man is almost always a dynamic mesomorph, the comedy relief is almost always the sociable endomorph, and the smart person is almost always the nerdy ectomorph. Although these beliefs persist, there is no strong evidence that body types predict personality.

Moreover, people have historically made the same judgments of personality based on facial appearance. The ancient Chinese were not the only ones to do this; in the late 1800s, Europeans led by Caesar Lombroso felt they could characterize criminal personalities based on the heaviness of one's eyebrows and jaw. As with the body research, there has been no evidence that one can accurately identify criminals by their facial appearance. Research by Diane Berry and Leslie MacArthur in the 1980s found that adult humans with more babyish looking faces—defined by a higher forehead, proportionally larger eyes, and smaller nose—are seen as more naïve, honest, and less likely to be picked as a leader. Research by Paul Secord in the 1950s showed that although people have reliably assigned personalities to particular faces, their assignments were not accurate. This perhaps best sums up the findings in this area.

Odors also send messages, both at a conscious and unconscious level. At a conscious level, perfumes and aftershaves and lack of body odor send messages about hygiene in North America, but such messages are not so clear in other cultures. Humans subconsciously send pheromones, substances that, when placed under the nose of a woman, make her judge a man as more attractive. Infants can also recognize the smell of their mothers and will show strong preferences for items that carry that smell. Many adults will also note how they are comforted by the smell of loved ones.

Physical appearance clues also include what are called artifactual clues, such as jewelry, clothes, glasses, and so on. People wearing glasses are seen as being smarter. Jewelry sends messages about one's socioeconomic or marital status.

North Americans signal their married status by wearing a solid gold band on their left-hand "ring" finger, whereas Europeans often wear this signal on the right-hand ring finger. Clothing also sends messages about income, group membership, and even respect for others. People who wear jeans to a formal occasion send a message about what they feel about that occasion, although, as in the previous instances, this message can be inaccurate.

An important source of nonverbal messages involves proxemics, or the study of the use of space during interactions. Edward Hall noted that human beings seem to have a series of four concentric zones that surround them, like a portable territory, in which they allow others to enter depending on the occasion and the degree of familiarity between the people involved. Hall called the zone that ranges from touching the body to 18 inches (45 cm) away the "intimate zone," an area that typically only lovers, children, and other intimates can enter. The next zone outward, ranging from 18 inches (45 cm) to 4 feet (1.22 m), was called the "casual-personal zone," the distance at which most casual conversations take place. The next zone, ranging from 4 feet (1.22 m) to 12 feet (3.67 m), was called the "social-consultative zone," the distance at which most formal conversations, as in business meetings with strangers, take place. The final zone, 12 feet (3.67 m) and beyond, was called the "public zone," where public speeches and other events take place. Note that these distances are typical for North Americans; other cultures may have the same series of concentric territories, but the distances may be different. In some Mediterranean countries, strangers will routinely talk to each other while standing less than 1 foot (30 cm) apart. To a North American, this will violate his or her intimate zone, and the North American will feel extremely uncomfortable and will take steps to reestablish a more comfortable distance by backing away. Of course, the Mediterranean person will feel uncomfortable talking to someone so far away and will move closer. This is another example of how cultural differences in nonverbal communication can cause misunderstanding and discomfort by both individuals. Note that neither distance is "right"; they are just different. Of course, other variables besides culture can affect the distance at which people communicate. These variables include how personal or negative the topic is, the age of the individuals (people stand closer to children and the elderly), and so on.

Humans also use nonverbal signals to mark their territories or possessions. Putting down one's books on a desk in a classroom, or placing one's jacket over a chair, will typically mark that desk or chair as temporarily belonging to that person—that is, part of his or her territory.

People send many types of nonverbal messages with their bodies. Ray Birdwhistell referred to the field of inquiry dedicated to the study of body messages as "kinesics." Kinesics includes body postures, such as angle of lean or tightness, and it also includes gestures, touching behavior, facial expressions, eye behavior, and even paralanguage (e.g., voice tones).

Body postures can certainly communicate many things. A person in a job interview who sits slumped in his or her chair will not look attentive and will be judged as uninterested in the job. Another way posture communicates is through the appearance of immediacy; a person who leans toward another, makes eye contact, and modulates his or her voice (i.e., does not speak in a monotone) is seen as very immediate. Research evidence suggests that people who behave in a more immediate fashion are seen as more credible, and teachers who are more immediate are better liked and children seem to learn more from them.

There are many nonverbal gestures that people exhibit to communicate. In the 1940s, David Efron suggested that one type of gesture—called an emblem—takes the place of a word. The "thumbs up" sign means "okay" or "good" in North America. People can say the word or show the gesture. Holding one's nose means something stinks. There are about one hundred emblems in North America. Efron showed that these emblems are learned. He observed that the emblems used by Jewish and Sicilian immigrants were different, and yet the emblems used by their American-born children were identical.

Desmond Morris proposed that these emblems come about through a variety of ways, and he identified mimic, schematic, symbolic, technical, coded, hybrid, relic, and interactive emblems. For example, Morris suggested some emblems mimic in a schematic fashion the object for which the emblem stands; holding both hands to one's head and extending index fingers to resemble the horns of a cow is the emblem for a cow. Others are sym-

bolic, as in crossing the fingers for good luck; the crossed fingers represent a crucifix or "sign of the cross," which early Christians believed would ward off evil or bad luck. Relic emblems derive from ancient practices, such as the Greek "moutza" emblem. This emblem involves throwing a hand up toward another to signify contempt or disdain; it evolved from the ancient practice of citizens throwing garbage onto criminals as they were marched through the streets. The emblem thus mimics the action of throwing garbage onto someone. Morris believes that some emblems represent universal human social experience, such as the emblem for the word "no," being a side-to-side headshake. He suggests that this derived from the side-to-side head action that an infant exhibits to reject his or her mother's breast when not hungry. All people throughout the world experience this, and that is why virtually all cultures use the horizontal headshake to indicate "no."

A second type of gesture is an illustrator. Illustrators do not take the place of words, but they help facilitate speech by being intimately tied to the content and flow of speech. Thus, when people move their hands as they speak, they are illustrating. Sometimes these illustrators are used to help find a word; sometimes they are used to keep the rhythm of the speech; sometimes they paint pictures of what the speaker is referring to; and sometimes they show motion. Illustrators are not confined to the hands; people can illustrate with their eyebrows by raising them as they emphasize an important point.

A third type of gesture is a manipulator, or adaptor (the words are used interchangeably). Manipulators occur when a person manipulates an object or other part of his or her body. Thus, touching one's nose, rubbing one's chin or ear, twirling one's hair, playing with one's glasses, chewing on a pencil, and biting one's lips are all examples of manipulators. There is some evidence that manipulators increase when people are nervous.

Touching behavior is another form of rule-bound nonverbal message. In North America, heterosexual males tend not to touch other males. If they do touch, it is typically on the upper arm, in a strong fashion. Heterosexual females touch each other more and in other body spots besides the upper arm. However, in the context of a sporting event, male teammates will pat each other on the rear end—a touch that would not be socially sanctioned in any other time or place. Of course, a pinch or a punch is a form of touch that sends a very different message than a gentle caress.

Facial expressions provide some of the more obvious forms of nonverbal communication. In addition to the six to nine universal facial expressions discussed above, humans have learned expressions as well. A wink may mean different things in different cultures. One raised eyebrow may be an illustrator. People can even pose expressions to communicate that they are thinking (eyebrows pulled down, lower lip pushed up), or are exasperated (raising the eyebrows slightly, and puffing cheeks and then blowing out the air), and so on.

People send nonverbal messages though eye behaviors. Eye behaviors typically involve staring or gazing, but they also include pupil dilation (where the pupil increases in size). When heterosexual couples are attracted to each other, they gaze into each other's eyes longer, and their pupils dilate. Researchers note that women with dilated pupils are seen as more attractive. When people are going to fight, they glare at each other. There are also great cultural differences in eye contact—members of some cultures gaze longer at strangers than do members of other cultures. When speaking, members of some cultures show their respect for other people by looking them in the eye; members of other cultures show their respect by not looking other people in the eye.

Finally, nonverbal messages are sent in the paralanguage of others. Paralanguage includes voice tone, pitch, pauses, and so on. This is has led to the adage "it is not what you say, but how you say it." People can say a positive statement and, using their voice tone, make it sound sarcastic, thereby producing two very different meanings from the very same sentence.

Conclusion

Everyday decisions are made based on people's readings of nonverbal communication. Nonverbal communication affects interpersonal encounters ranging from police interviews to first dates, doctor visits, job interviews, and advertising. For the most part, people are good at interpreting these nonverbal communications, although some people are better at it than others, despite the fact that the nonverbal message that is sent often does not equal the message that is received, and vice versa.

In addition to relying on nonverbal communication to clarify communication and make day-to-day interactions flow more smoothly, people also use it as an indicator of the true essence of a person. As Chinese philosopher Confucius stressed thousands of years ago, one can better understand others by looking into their eyes, rather than listening to their words.

See also: ANIMAL COMMUNICATION; INTERCULTURAL COMMUNICATION, ADAPTATION AND; INTERPERSONAL COMMUNICATION; INTERPERSONAL COMMUNICATION, CONVERSATION AND; INTERPERSONAL COMMUNICATION, LISTENING AND; LANGUAGE ACQUISITION; LANGUAGE AND COMMUNICATION; LANGUAGE STRUCTURE; MODELS OF COMMUNICATION; SYMBOLS.

Bibliography

Andersen, Peter. (1999). *Nonverbal Communication: Forms and Functions*. Mountain View, CA: Mayfield.

Argyle, Michael. (1988). *Bodily Communication*. London: Methuen.

Berry, Diane S., and McArthur, Leslie Z. (1986). "Perceiving Character in Faces: The Impact of Age-Related Craniofacial Changes on Social Perception." *Psychological Bulletin* 100:3–18.

Birdwhistell, Raymond L. (1970). *Kinesics and Context*. Philadelphia: University of Pennsylvania Press.

Burgoon, Judee K.; Buller, David B.; and Woodall, W. Gill. (1996). *Nonverbal Communication: The Unspoken Dialogue*. New York: Harper & Row.

Capella, Joseph N. (1991). "The Biological Origins of Automated Patterns of Human Interaction." *Communication Theory* 1:4–35.

Darwin, Charles. (1872). *The Expression of the Emotions in Man and Animals*. London: John Murray.

DePaulo, Bella M., and Friedman, Howard S. (1996). "Nonverbal Communication." In *The Handbook of Social Psychology*, 4th edition, eds. Daniel T. Gilbert, Susan T. Fiske, and Gardner Lindzey. New York: McGraw-Hill.

Efron, David. (1941). *Gesture and Environment*. New York: King's Crown Press.

Eibl-Eibesfeldt, Irene. (1979). "Universals in Human Expressive Behavior." In *Nonverbal Behavior, Applications and Cultural Implications*, ed. Aaron Wolfgang. New York: Academic Press.

Ekman, Paul. (1982). *Emotion in the Human Face*. Cambridge, Eng.: Cambridge University Press.

Ekman, Paul. (1992). *Telling Lies*. New York: W. W. Norton.

Ekman, Paul, and Friesen, Wallace V. (1969). "The Repertoire of Nonverbal Behavior: Categories, Origins, Usage, and Coding." *Semiotica* 1:49–98.

Fast, Julius. (1970). *Body Language.* New York: M. Evans.

Hall, Edward T. (1959). *The Silent Language.* Garden City, NY: Doubleday.

Hall, Edward T. (1966). *The Hidden Dimension.* Garden City, NY: Doubleday.

Izard, Carrol E. (1971). *The Face of Emotion.* New York: Appleton-Century-Crofts.

Knapp, Mark L., and Hall, Judith A. (1997). *Nonverbal Communication in Human Interaction,* 4th edition. New York: Harcourt Brace.

Morris, Desmond. (1977). *Manwatching: A Field Guide to Human Behavior.* New York: Harry N. Adams.

Morris, Desmond. (1985). *Bodywatching.* New York: Crown.

Secord, Paul F.; Dukes, William F.; and Bevan, William. (1954). "Personalities in Faces: I. An Experiment in Social Perceiving." *Genetic Psychology Monographs* 49:231–270.

MARK G. FRANK

▌■ NUTRITION AND MEDIA EFFECTS

An Australian study by the Food Commission (1997) reported that more than one-half of nine- to ten-year-old children believe that Ronald McDonald knows best what is good for children to eat. Is television truly this persuasive, and can it shape the eating habits of the children of an entire nation? The answer appears to be yes. Poor diet is related to a number of problems in both health and quality of life. Obesity (the prevalence of which is on the rise among children) is the most obvious, but it is only one consequence of a national diet in which food is abundant, readily available, inexpensive, and promoted very heavily.

Television viewing appears to be an important factor in keeping both children and adults from being physically active. The influence of television is especially powerful in children. Many spend long hours watching television, a setting that promotes eating because children are inactive and are exposed to thousands of persuasive food advertisements. William Dietz (1990) noted that children spend more time watching television than doing any other activity except sleeping. Considering that children spend more time with television than in school, television has the potential for enormous influence.

Obesity results from an imbalance between the amount of energy (calories) consumed and the amount of energy used (through metabolism and physical activity). Weight gain occurs when a person eats more than the body burns. Television can affect this balance on both sides of the equation, by keeping children away from physical activity and by increasing food consumption. It is clear from research that children consume extra calories while watching television. The great majority of food advertisements aimed at children are for foods that are low in nutritional value.

Research has shown a positive association between television viewing and obesity. Although some studies have found only weak links between television viewing and obesity, many have found significant positive relationships. In 1985, Dietz and Steven L. Gortmaker published a study reporting that the amount of television viewed by children was directly related to measures of their body fat and that the rate of obesity in the children rose 2 percent for every hour of television viewed per day. The results of this research have been supported by numerous other studies that also indicate an increase of obesity associated with television viewing. Even those researchers who report finding weaker associations note that the health risks of obesity are of such magnitude that the topic merits further research. The message appears clear—more television, more obesity.

The content of what children watch is critical. A 1997 report by The Center for Media Education stated that children view one hour of advertising for every five hours of television watched and that the average child sees more than twenty thousand television commercials per year. Most young children do not understand that the purpose of advertising is to sell a product. Therefore, the line between programs and commercials is blurred as advertisers use popular television and movie characters to induce children to buy their products.

The majority of television commercials aimed at children are for food products, most of which are foods high in sugar, fat, and salt. A 1996 report by Consumers International (Dibb, 1996) on television food advertising directed at children indicated that food items represented the majority of products advertised to children in almost all of the thirteen countries studied. Candy, sugared breakfast cereals, and fast-food restaurants accounted for more than one-half of the food advertisements, with salty snacks, prepared foods, soft drinks, desserts, and dairy products also being widely advertised. Many advertising campaigns directly target children through promotional items in children's meals and tie-ins with popular cartoon and movie characters. Advertisers know that children control a large portion of family spending, either directly through purchases or indirectly through purchase requests, so they tailor their campaigns to capitalize on the children's market.

Studies have shown that the food choices of children are closely related to what they see on television. Television viewing in children has been linked to poor eating habits, increased caloric intake, supermarket requests for unhealthy foods, and misunderstanding of nutritional principles. Howard L. Taras and his colleagues (1989) conducted a study of mothers with children between three and eight years of age and found that food requests by children paralleled the frequency with which those foods were advertised on television. Weekly viewing hours correlated significantly with the food requests of children, purchases of advertised foods by parents, and the caloric intake of children.

Gerald Gorn and Marvin Goldberg (1982) showed through an experiment that children who watched candy commercials chose more candy than fruit as snacks, but children who saw either no commercials or public service announcements chose more fruit. Several studies have supported the finding that children who see advertisements for unhealthy foods make less-healthy food choices than children who view healthy-eating announcements. Thus, pronutritional public service announcements may be a largely untapped resource for using television to encourage healthier eating.

The Children's Television Act of 1990 limited the number of advertisements in children's programming on broadcast stations to 10.5 minutes per hour on weekends and 12 minutes per hour on weekdays. In 1996, the Federal Communications Commission (FCC) expanded the Children's Television Act, requiring broadcast stations to air at least three hours of programming designed to educate and inform children between two and sixteen years of age. Although the number of so-called educational and informational programs on broadcast stations appears to have increased, the positive effect of these programs remains to be demonstrated.

Television has a powerful influence on children, and that power can be used responsibly to promote healthy lifestyles. Advocacy groups have called for increased pronutritional public service announcements, which have been shown to have a positive effect on healthy food choices, and for greater restrictions on the quantity and content of advertising directed at children. The U.S. government has shown interest in encouraging children to become more physically active with initiatives such as the inception in the 1990s of an annual National TV Turnoff Week. Research has explored the role that parents can play by discussing the content of programs and advertisements with children and by making careful purchasing decisions.

The prevalence of obesity among adults and children has caused observers to highlight the need for intervention on an environmental level. Television is an appealing target area for this type of intervention because it provides opportunities for change on both sides of the obesity equation.

See also: ADVERTISING EFFECTS; BODY IMAGE, MEDIA EFFECT ON; CHILDREN AND ADVERTISING; PARENTAL MEDIATION OF MEDIA EFFECTS; TELEVISION, EDUCATIONAL.

Bibliography

Borum, Cathryn. (Spring 1999). "The Children's Television Act in its Second Year." In *Info Active Kids*, ed. Cathryn Borum. Washington, DC: The Center for Media Education.

Center for Media Education. (1997). "Commercials." <http://www.cme.org/children/kids_tv/commercial.html>.

Dibb, Sue. (1996). *A Spoonful of Sugar: Television Food Advertising Aimed at Children: An International Comparative Survey.* London: Consumers International.

Dietz, William H. (1990). "You Are What You Eat—What You Eat Is What You Are." *Journal of Adolescent Health Care* 11:76–81.

Dietz, William H. (1993). "Television, Obesity, and Eating Disorders." *Adolescent Medicine* 4(3):543–549.

Dietz, William H., and Gortmaker, Steven L. (1985). "Do We Fatten Our Children at the Television Set? Obesity and Television Viewing in Children and Adolescents." *Pediatrics* 75:807–812.

Food Commission, The. (1997). "Advertising to Children: UK the Worst in Europe." *Food Magazine,* January/March.

Gorn, Gerald, and Goldberg, Marvin. (1982). "Behavioral Evidence of the Effects of Televised Food Messages on Children." *Journal of Consumer Research* 9(2):200–205.

Robinson, Thomas N. (1999). "Reducing Children's Television Viewing to Prevent Obesity." *Journal of the American Medical Association* 282(16):1561–1567.

Taras, Howard L.; Sallis, James F.; Patterson, Thomas L.; Nader, Philip R.; and Nelson, James A. (1989). "Television's Influence on Children's Diet and Physical Activity." *Journal of Developmental and Behavioral Pediatrics* 10(4):176–180.

KATHERINE BATTLE HORGEN
KELLY D. BROWNELL

O

■ OPINION POLLING, CAREERS IN

Public opinion research is one of the fasting growing and most diversified career opportunities available. It provides opportunities for work in government agencies, university settings, in political campaigns, and in the business world. Because the work involves a range of possible skills, the field attracts people who are interested in designing studies, managing polls in the field, conducting statistical analyses of data, or working with clients to implement policy or business decisions based on the data analysis.

Public opinion polling takes a number of forms. People who work for news organizations, for example, are interested in measuring opinion about current events or political figures. The most visible form of this work is the preelection polls conducted in conjunction with political campaigns or the exit poll interviews that are collected on the day of an election that are used to estimate the outcomes of elections. People who work for commercial firms are often interested in the attitudes and behavior of consumers with the intent of helping companies understand how to increase their market share or to improve their products. People who work for the government are interested in tracking important demographic trends or the use of government programs and services. Academic pollsters often study such basic research questions as how attitudes are formed and crystallized, how durable they are, and how opinions affect behavior.

Conducting a poll involves a number of steps, and different skills and training are required for each. Many of the people who rely on polling data for making decisions are not well trained themselves in data collection and analysis, so one of the most important needs is for people who can talk to potential users of public opinion data to determine what their needs are. They can help the potential users think about such questions as what the appropriate population of interest is, what questions should be asked, and what shape the analysis should take in order to provide an answer to the original questions. Most polls involve samples of individuals drawn from the population of interest, and sampling is a special skill that is quite different from the ability to write good questions for a poll. Specialists in writing questionnaires are interested in producing unbiased data that are unaffected by the wording of a particular question or by the order in which the questions are asked. People who analyze polling data have a set of statistical skills that are quite different from samplers or questionnaire designers. Most polling is done by telephone, although the use of the Internet for conducting surveys is increasing.

Learning to manage studies while data collection is underway is another important skill that is in demand. The production of a survey, from the design of the sample to writing a questionnaire to collecting data to analyzing them, involves the coordination of staff and facilities. There have to be enough interviewers available to contact potential respondents on the expected days and nights, for example. Managing data collection and analysis on a timely and cost-effective basis is a very important responsibility.

The appropriate training for a career in public opinion polling can be obtained through a number of college disciplines that result in a B.A. degree. Public opinion research is necessarily a quantitative profession, so a person should have some training in statistical methods and feel comfortable with data. People who are interested in becoming survey methodologists who specialize in sampling or data analysis should consider a concentration in statistics, although this path can usually be pursued in conjunction with a substantive specialty in a field such as political science, psychology, or sociology. Survey research training can increasingly be found in programs in communication studies or in interdepartmental programs in the social sciences. For individuals interested in market research, undergraduate training in business would be good background. Most of this undergraduate training would expose a student to an introduction to methodology but concentrate on data analysis. A well-trained undergraduate should understand the steps in the survey process and how to analyze the resulting data. They would be well trained to be a consumer of polling data and to write research reports, but they might not know how to produce data.

There are a growing number of graduate programs that offer an M.A. degree in survey research or public opinion research, and this advanced training can lead to starting positions that have more responsibility and higher salaries. In a graduate program, students learn more about the methodological skills necessary to produce public opinion polling data. In an M.A. program in survey research, students typically take courses in sampling, questionnaire design, and data analysis, as well as in survey management. Most programs involve some kind of practicum course in which the students go through all of the steps in the process, including interviewing. By the time the students finish this course, they are familiar with all of the steps involved in the process.

People in the polling business often belong to one of a number of professional organizations that provide them with the opportunity to meet other people in the field and to network about job placements. The American Association for Public Opinion Research is an organization that publishes a career brochure and provides a job placement service at their annual conference. There is a Survey Methods Section of the American Statistical Association that produces a series of brochures titled *What Is a Survey?* that describe how surveys are planned and conducted. Also, the Council for Marketing and Opinion Research maintains an Internet website to inform members of the public about the research process, their role in it, and the various types of misuses and abuses of the research process that they may encounter

See also: ADVERTISING EFFECTS; AUDIENCE RESEARCHERS; ELECTION CAMPAIGNS AND MEDIA EFFECTS; MARKETING RESEARCH, CAREERS IN.

Bibliography

American Association for Public Opinion Research. (1999). "AAPOR." <http://www.aapor.org>.

American Statistical Association. (2000). "Survey Research Methods Section." <http:www.stat.ncsu.edu/info/srms/srms.html>.

American Statistical Association. (1999). *What Is a Survey?* Washington, DC: American Statistical Association.

Asher, Herb. (1995). *Polling and the Public: What Every Citizen Should Know.* Washington, DC: CQ Press.

Council for Marketing and Opinion Research. (2000). "Consumer Information." <http://www.cmor.org/consumer.htm>.

Gallup Organization. (2000). "How Polls Are Conducted." <http://www.gallup.com/poll/faq.asp>.

Traugott, Michael W., and Lavrakas, Paul J. (1999). *The Voter's Guide to Election Polls.* Chatham, NJ: Chatham House Press.

World Association for Public Opinion Research. (2000). "WAPOR". <http://www.wapor.org>.

MICHAEL W. TRAUGOTT

ORGANIZATIONAL COMMUNICATION

Organizational communication is a process through which people construct, manage, and interpret behaviors and symbols (whether verbal or nonverbal), both intentionally and unintentionally, through interaction (mediated or direct), within and across particular organizational contexts.

An October 2000 search for publications that included "organiz-"and "communicat-" yielded more than 2,000 books or journals in the online Library of Congress catalog and more than 630 doctoral dissertations in the Dissertations Abstract database. ABI/Inform, the online business and organizations database, included nearly 1,300 articles that were indexed with either "organizational" and "communication" as subject words and nearly 200 articles with the two words in the article title. Furthermore, many surveys show that managers rank communication among the most valuable skills new, and veteran, employees should have.

Organizational communication can occur at a variety of levels, involving interpersonal and dyadic interaction, small groups or teams, large meetings, and within or across organizational departments or units, entire organizations, industrial sectors, and national borders. This communication may emphasize specific content (such as a memo providing some information) or may emphasize the nature of the relationship, what is called "metacommunication" (such as that same memo emphasizing that the person providing the information is clearly the expert and the reader should follow orders). The focus of the communication may be on task or social aspects, on administrative or operational functions, and on disseminating or receiving.

Organizational Theories and the Role of Communication

Different theories about organizations involve different assumptions about communication. Developed during the beginning of the 1900s, "classical management theory"—including scientific management theory, administrative management theory, and formal bureaucracy theory—arose in response to the growth of large organizations performing standardized procedures to produce manufactured materials, a result of the industrial revolution. Classical management theory generally proposed that organizations could be efficient and successful through hierarchical structures, downward flow of task information from managers to workers, recognition of monetary and security motivations of employees while ignoring social relations and personal goals, avoidance of ambiguity or subjectivity of information especially in rules and procedures, optimal design of the work process, authority and legitimacy located in hierarchical position rather than in personal and political influence, hiring and rewarding employees on the basis of technical competence and task performance, division of labor to increase efficiency and specialization,

facilitation of horizontal communication when necessary but only with approval of the relevant superiors, and a continuing focus on organizational goals. In classical management theory, communication is highly structured and hierarchical, impersonal, and focused only on the goals of the organization.

Human relations theory arose not so much as a rejection of classical management theory but as a means to manage relationships within hierarchical organizations. However, the famous Hawthorne Studies in the 1920s and 1930s found that humans value social interaction and attention. Thus, organizational communication should allow development of group cohesion and cooperation, relationships within and among workers and management, job satisfaction, managerial skills, and awareness of the organization's community.

By the end of World War II, human resource theory expanded the consideration of social aspects, by emphasizing the importance of genuine participation and involvement of members. Other strands emerged, such as the authority-communication theory, which argued that organizational authority is developed, maintained, and accepted through honest and open communication.

In the 1960s, systems theory conceptualized systems as being embedded in larger systems and consisting of smaller subsystems, each interdependent, each creating something greater than the sum of the parts, and each engaging in general processes. Organizational environments consist of other organizations providing inputs to, using outputs from, and creating constraints on, the focal organization. No longer could organizations be managed as fixed, efficient machines; rather, they must be considered organic, adaptive, and constantly challenged processes that require constant communication within and across system boundaries.

Related concepts include organizational communication networks and roles, such as gatekeepers (who filter communication to a specific manager or upward through the organization), liaisons (who mediate interaction between two groups), bridges (a group member who mediates interaction with outside individuals), cosmopolite or boundary spanner (one who monitors the environment and brings new information into the organization), cliques (members who communicate more with each other than with other members), and grapevines and rumor networks (where members communicate through informal and social networks about salient, time-sensitive topics).

Communication structures influence outcomes (e.g., centralized or decentralized networks are differentially appropriate for different kinds of tasks), are affected by other factors (e.g., accuracy of upward communication is moderated by the level of trust between superior and subordinate), moderate other relationships (e.g., the ability of organizations to respond well to crises), and are both positive and negative influences on, and are both positively and negatively affected by, organizational changes such as the implementation of new media (Johnson and Rice, 1987). Evaluation and use of new organizational media may be influenced by the behaviors and attitudes of others in one's communication network (Fulk and Steinfield, 1990).

Related somewhat to systems theory, as well as to more recent notions of the interpretative and interactive nature of organizational communication, is the theory of organizational sense-making (Weick, 1979). The purpose of organizing is to reduce equivocality, or the extent to which multiple interpretations of a situation are possible. The nature of the environment is largely constructed by what people are able to, or choose to, "enact." To the extent that what is selected from this enacted environment is equivocal, people must either refer to interpretations and responses retained from past activities, or make sense of the situation through interactions with others. Jointly, through agreed-upon patterns of enactment, interaction, and interpretation, organizational members "make sense" of their world so that they can engage in behaviors. Often, however, people must first take action before they can make sense of the situation, what is known as "retrospective sense-making."

More interpretative and cultural conceptualizations view organizations as constituted and structured not by formal flows of downward or horizontal communication but through and in the form of stories, myths, rituals, artifacts, values, logos, trademarks, taken-for-granted behaviors, dress styles, and office landscapes. That is, these cultural symbols are both results of and influences on meanings and behaviors, both positively and negatively, and emerge organically through the communication of members. A powerful example of an interpretative or cultural perspective is the organizational metaphor. Members may be guided, often implicitly, by the organization's "root" metaphor—such as business as "war." These metaphors shape the values and interpretations of the members and thus their decisions and behaviors as well. Metaphors also communicate the organization's image to its members, publics, researchers, executives, and policymakers—such as machine, organism, brain/computer, culture, political system, prisons, self-producing systems, or instruments of domination (Morgan, 1986). Some theorists, such as Stanley Deetz (1992), Michel Foucault (1995), and Dennis Mumby (1988), argue that all organizational power is embedded in discourse—who controls what is communicable within the organizational context. Thus, communication is not just a tool for exercising power; it is the very form of power.

More recent developments in organizational theory focus on quality management (where communication with current and prospective customers is the crucial source of feedback necessary to guide and improve the organization), chaos theory and learning organizations (where organizations are complex, adaptive, self-organizing systems dependent on rich communication that fosters collaboration, shared knowledge, and constant feedback at various levels), and network organizations (where organizational boundaries are becoming blurred as entities engage in temporary relations for particular products or markets, divest or outsource entire divisions so as to take advantage of marketplace resources, or even create virtual organizations that exist only on the Internet).

Applications of Organizational Communication

Motivation theories argue that people may be influenced to take action by salient needs that are not currently being met (Maslow, 1970), by expectations of the likelihood and value of outcomes (Vroom, 1982), or by general perceptions of expectations, opportunities, fulfillment and performance (Pace and Faules, 1994). Each of these processes is moderated by or manifested in communication; for example, expectations can be changed through communication about abilities and outcomes.

Organizational climate—a macro, organizational-level perception of the environment based on one's experiences with and perceptions of organizational elements (such as work and management practices)—influences a variety of communication outcomes (such as open and accurate downward information, and level of consultation in decision making). Communication satisfaction—a micro, individual-level evaluation—represents the extent to which basic communication processes (such as ability to suggest improvements, media quality, and adequacy of information) are acceptable. Both climate and satisfaction influence the attitudes and behaviors of individuals (Pace and Faules, 1994).

The concept of leadership has changed from a hierarchical role that delivers decisions and monitors workers, to a person who helps construct shared meanings and norms, provides support and motivation, and manages the boundaries of the unit. Various studies of leadership styles emphasize different communication aspects, from the appropriate balance among tasks and personal relations, to the extent to which all members can engage in decision making and self-regulation.

Another shift is from fixed organizational positions and specialized tasks to fluid teams and collaborative projects. Teams are often temporary groups that bring together particular expertise for a specific project, accomplish their task, and then disassemble to form new teams. These teams may even be "virtual," with the team consisting of members from different organizations who may be devoting only a portion of their time to each of several teams, and who may not even meet their team members face-to-face, instead collaborating and communicating through new communication technologies. Group decision support systems and other forms of groupware may be used to improve group communication (e.g., through anonymous brainstorming), allowing participation across time and space constraints, and providing different decision tools such as voting or ranking. Even traditional teams must communicate well to evolve through various group development stages and provide the necessary social support as well as task coordination. The necessary communication skills for dispersed and virtual teams are greater, especially as team members will be increasingly diverse—from different locales, organizations, professions, and cultures—and as members will have to switch between teams and adjust to new teams more frequently.

Conflict management and negotiation are fundamentally communication processes, as they are deeply embedded in the language, information, and interpretations available to, and valued by, each of the participants. There are formal and strategic communication styles that experienced negotiators apply in different contexts, for different goals.

Writing, public and group speaking, thinking critically, using new media, and presenting reports and results are increasing in importance. Working with others, especially in management and leadership roles, requires good listening and nonverbal communication abilities, an understanding of persuasive messages, familiarity with new interactive multimedia, interviewing, preparing and evaluating resumes, reading and assessing research reports, understanding the use and evaluation of online information and databases, and managing mediated interactions, such as through videoconferencing or online discussion groups.

Other areas of organizational communication include public relations, cross-cultural interaction, performance assessment, training, socialization, decision making, innovation, globalization, emotions, clothing design and selection, and office decoration. Nearly all organizational communication has ethical and legal implications concerning things such as harassment, discrimination, equity, cultural diversity, gender roles, racism, hiring and promotion bias, false or misleading advertisement, and even termination and retirement.

See also: DIFFUSION OF INNOVATIONS AND COMMUNICATION; INTERNET AND THE WORLD WIDE WEB; NETWORKS AND COMMUNICATION; ORGANIZATIONAL COMMUNICATION, CAREERS IN; PUBLIC RELATIONS.

Bibliography

Barnard, Chester. (1968). *The Functions of the Executive.* Cambridge, MA: Harvard University Press.

Choo, Chun Wei. (1995). *Information Management for the Intelligent Organization: The Art of Scanning the Environment.* Medford, NJ: Information Today.

Deetz, Stanley. (1992). *Democracy in an Age of Corporate Colonization.* Albany: State University of New York Press.

Eisenberg, Eric, and Goodall, H. Lloyd (1999). *Organizational Communication,* 3rd edition. New York: Bedford/St. Martin's.

Fayol, Henri. (1984). *General and Industrial Management,* revised by Irwin Gray. New York: Institute of Electrical and Electronics Engineers.

Foucault, Michel. (1995). *Discipline and Punish: The Birth of the Prison*, 2nd edition, translated from the French by Alan Sheridan. New York: Vintage Books.

Fulk, Janet, and Steinfield, Charles, eds. (1990). *Organizations and Communication Technology*. Newbury Park, CA: Sage Publications.

Gleick, James. (1987). *Chaos: Making a New Science*. New York: Viking.

Jablin, Fred, and Putnam, Linda, eds. (2000). *Handbook of Organizational Communication*. Thousand Oaks, CA: Sage Publications.

Johnson, Bonnie, and Rice, Ronald E. (1987). *Managing Organizational Innovation: The Evolution from Word Processing to Office Information Systems*. New York: Columbia University Press.

Katz, Daniel, and Kahn, Robert. (1978). *The Social Psychology of Organizations*. New York: Wiley.

Likert, Rensis. (1961). *New Patterns of Management*. New York: McGraw-Hill.

Maslow, Abraham. (1970). *Motivation and Personality*, 2nd edition. New York: Harper & Row.

Mayo, Elton. (1986). *The Human Problems of an Industrial Civilization*. Salem, NH: Ayer.

Mintzberg, Henry. (1973). *The Nature of Managerial Work*. New York: Harper & Row.

Morgan, Gareth. (1986). *Images of Organization*. Newbury Park, CA: Sage Publications.

Mumby, Dennis. (1988). *Communication and Power in Organizations: Discourse, Ideology, and Domination*. Norwood, NJ: Ablex.

Nohria, Nitin, and Eccles, Robert, eds. (1992). *Networks and Organizations: Structure, Form, and Action*. Boston, MA: Harvard Business School Press.

Pace, R. Wayne, and Faules, Don. (1994). *Organizational Communication*, 3rd edition. Englewood Cliffs, NJ: Prentice-Hall.

Richmond, Virginia, and McCroskey, James. (2000). *Organizational Communication for Survival: Making Work, Work*, 2nd edition. Boston, MA: Allyn & Bacon.

Senge, Peter. (1990). *The Fifth Discipline: The Art and Practice of the Learning Organization*. New York: Doubleday.

Spencer, Barbara. (1994). "Models of Organization and Total Quality Management: A Comparison and Critical Evaluation." *Academy of Management Review* 19(3):446–471.

Taylor, James, and Van Every, Elizabeth. (1993). *The Vulnerable Fortress: Bureaucratic Organizations and Management in the Information Age*. Toronto: University of Toronto Press.

von Bertalanffy, Ludwig. (1968). *General Systems Theory: Foundations, Development, Applications*. New York: George Braziller.

Vroom, Victor. (1982). *Work and Motivation*. Malabar, FL: R. E. Kreiger.

Weber, Max. (1947). *The Theory of Social and Economic Organization*, ed. Talcott Parsons. Glencoe, IL: Free Press.

Weick, Karl. (1979). *The Social Psychology of Organizing*, 2nd edition. Reading, MA: Addison-Wesley.

RONALD E. RICE

ORGANIZATIONAL COMMUNICATION, CAREERS IN

By the end of the twentieth century, the United States and other developed countries (especially Japan and most of the countries in Europe) had become information- and service-based economies. Due to the need to manage more complex social and institutional activities, and due to the rise of systematic management, communication media, computing systems, and telecommunications networks, more and more organizational activities have become symbolic—the creation, communication, and interpretation of information. Organizational communication and information professionals—"symbolic analysts" or "knowledge workers"—will play an increasingly crucial role in society and the economy.

The U.S. Department of Labor (2000c) predicts that there will be growth in the number of communication and information jobs between 1998 and 2008. Within the industrial sector, which will grow by 14.4 percent overall, the services sector will have the largest growth (31%). The largest expected growth will be in professional specialties (27%), technical and related support (22%), service (17.1%), executives, administration, and managerial (16.4%), and marketing and sales (14.9%). The top ten industries with the fastest wage and salary employment growth will include computer and data processing services (117%), management and public relations (45%), and research and testing services (40%). The top six fastest growing occupations will be computer engineers (108%), computer support specialists (102%), systems analysts (94%), database administrators (77%), desktop publishing specialists (73%), and paralegals and legal assistants (62%). Overall, the top ten occupations with the largest job growth include systems analysts, general managers and top executives, office clerks, and computer support specialists. The rise of the Internet, of course, has generated entirely new classes of communication/information workers (see U.S. Department of Labor, 2000b).

Communication Careers

Disciplinary and association career guides, such as those noted in the bibliography section of this entry, provide good descriptions of the kinds of jobs, the educational and skill requirements, related disciplines, salary ranges, and associations related to communication and information professions.

Communication jobs can be categorized in a variety of ways:

- Advertising (marketing, copy writer, sales manager, media planner, media sales representative, opinion researcher, agency manager, account manager, creative/art director, publicity and promotion, etc.)
- Communication disorders (speech-language pathology, audiology, teaching, research)
- Communication education (media librarian, language arts coordinator, drama or debate director, university professor, etc.)
- Corporate communications (investor relations, environmental affairs, government relations, issues management, crisis management, public affairs, strategic planning, media relations, employee relations, community relations, marketing, special events, publicity, advertising, fundraising, media production)
- Electronic media (radio/television station personnel, film/tape librarian, engineer, community relations director, traffic/continuity specialist, media buyer, market researcher, actor, announcer, account executive, writer, news reporter or anchor, director, lighting director, multimedia developer, Internet information management, website developer, interactive materials producer, music librarian, video specialist, announcer, etc.)
- Publishers (print or electronic reporter, editor, copy writer, script writer, trade magazine representative, advertising sales, direct mail researcher, art and design, archivist/librarian, news service researcher, photography, technical writer, media critic/reviewer, media interviewer, printing, columnist, book editor, contract manager, literary agent, feature writer, freelance writer, etc.)

Tom Grimmer—the communications director for the Credit Suisse First Boston group—speaks to reporters outside the Credit Suisse's Tokyo branch office in October 1999 after the Japanese police had raided Credit Suisse Financial Products on suspicion that it obstructed an earlier inspection by Japanese financial regulators. (Reuters NewMedia Inc./Corbis)

- Public relations (publicity manager, marketing specialist, press agent, lobbyist, crisis management, press secretary, sales manager, media analyst, conference organizer, media planner, audience analyst, public opinion researcher, fund raiser, development officer, account executive, etc.)
- Theater/performing arts (performer, script writer, events organizer, producer, director, arts educator, lighting/design, theater librarian/historian, makeup/costume, theater critic, professor of theater and film, etc.).

Almost all other careers involve multiple aspects of communication and information. Some of the most relevant include business, education, government/politics, foreign service, educational institutions, high technology industries, health centers, international relations and negotiations, law, and social and human services.

Organizational Communication and Information Professionals

Some theorists such as Chester Barnard and Karl Weick have argued that organizations exist only through the process of communicating, whereby members attempt to make sense of information by communicating with others. The work that is performed by managers primarily involves providing oral communication with external and internal information sources, making decisions from incomplete and contradictory information, developing formal and informal communication networks, scanning the environment and spanning organizational boundaries, and depending on organizational structures to filter and evaluate information. Communication and information are central aspects of all organizational activities, from managing offices, developing satisfying jobs and worker relations, motivation and commitment, up to corporate redesign, information systems implementation, and marketplace strategy.

The book *Managing Information for the Competitive Edge* (1996), which was edited by Ethel Auster and Chun Choo and contains good reviews of these topics, argues that "information management" represents the beginning of convergence of the knowledge and skills of a range of professions—as indicated by the rise in executive titles such as chief information officer and by the growth in research and consulting in the fields of information resource management and knowledge management. A United Kingdom report noted in the book listed the following five positions as the most important areas for information management: information strategy, systems development, management of information, training, and liaison among other managers. New university programs and degrees in communication/information include multidisciplinary domains such as information science, information systems, database managers, user-interface and usability evaluator, communication, psychology and sociology, management, health informatics, information management in a variety of institutional settings, and Internet use and evaluation.

The rise of team/project structures, virtual organizations, and groupware or collaborative technology (such as desktop video, audio, and text conferencing, shared files and documents, and asynchronous task management), and contract and outsourced employment, all require greater knowledge of nonverbal, interpersonal, team, and organizational communication.

Jobs involving information handling, networking, managerial awareness of information technology, and project management will become more frequent and important. Four basic organizational information competencies are monitoring performance, correcting performance, improving systems, and designing new systems.

Many organizational communication textbooks discuss job and career opportunities. Development positions include improving team and organizational effectiveness, training managers, developing and delivering training services, providing sales and customer service training, career development, and offering technical and skills training. Public contact positions include public affairs, community relations, media relations, and employee relations, as well as the more familiar marketing and personal sales. Finally, general management careers pervade for-profit and nonprofit organizations.

A search of an online career placement service, using the search term "organizational communication," found more than two thousand job listings. Examples (with the main category capitalized and the communication-related subcategory in lower case) include Account Management, Administrative Support meetings & marketing, Advertising Management, Art Director of Magazine, Business Process Consultant, Clerical Ad Team coordinator, Consulting senior writer, Creative Services corporate communications, Desktop Publishing online senior editor, Education/Training instructional designer, Entertainment audiovisual, Executive director of communications, General Management media ratings, Graphics, Health Care director of needs assessment, Human Resources personnel management, Internet/Intranet/Extranet editor, Marketing Communications manager, Multimedia information architect, Other catalog marketing strategist, Other collaboration, Other Intra/Inter/Net content specialist, Other conference planner, Other media production team, Other corporate communications, Producer online, Public Relations administrator, Publishing assistant, Secretarial communications coordinator, Technology Development technical writing, Trade Services internship coordinator, and Training manager.

Additional Sources

Most professional and academic associations have websites that describe their placement services, career opportunities, listings of related disciplines, and summaries of undergraduate and graduate programs. Particularly relevant associations are the American Society for Information Science, the International Communication Association, the National Communication Association, the Association for Education in Journalism and Mass Communication, the Association for Communication Administrators, the International Association of Business Communicators, and the American Speech–Language–Hearing Association. Most all career and occupational books provide resources for local, regional, and national employers, by job type. The *Dictionary of Occupational Titles,* produced by the U.S. Department of Labor (2000a), provides a comprehensive list of job descriptions.

See also: INTERNET AND THE WORLD WIDE WEB; ORGANIZATIONAL COMMUNICATION; PUBLIC RELATIONS, CAREERS IN.

Bibliography

Auster, Ethel, and Choo, Chun, eds. (1996). *Managing Information for the Competitive Edge.* New York: Neal-Schuman.

Camenson, Blythe. (1996). *Great Jobs for Communications Majors.* Lincolnwood, IL: VGM Career Horizons.

Marlow, Eugene, and Wilson, Patricia O'Connor. (1997). "Appendix I: The Emerging Employment Landscape." In *The Breakdown of Hierarchy: Communicating in the Evolving Workplace.* Boston: Butterworth-Heinemann.

Morgan, Bradley, ed. (annual). *Magazines Career Directory.* Detroit, MI: Visible Ink.

Morgan, Bradley, ed. (annual). *Newspapers Career Directory.* Detroit, MI: Visible Ink.

Morgan, Bradley, ed. (annual). *Public Relations Career Directory.* Detroit, MI: Visible Ink.

Morgan, Bradley, ed. (annual). *Radio and Television Career Directory.* Detroit, MI: Visible Ink.

National Communication Association. (annual). *Pathways to Careers in Communication.* Annandale, VA: National Communication Association.

Noronham, Shonan. (1993). *Careers in Communications.* Lincolnwood, IL: VGM Career Horizons.

Pace, R. Wayne, and Faules, Don. (1994). *Organizational Communication,* 3rd edition. Englewood Cliffs, NJ: Prentice-Hall.

U.S. Department of Labor. (2000a). "Dictionary of Occupational Titles." <http://stats.bls.gov/oco/ocodot1.htm>.

U.S. Department of Labor. (2000b). "Futurework: Trends and Challenges for Work in the 21st Century." <http://www.dol.gov/dol/asp/public/futurework/report.htm>.

U.S. Department of Labor. (2000c). "Occupational Outlook Handbook." <http://www.bls.gov/ocohome.htm>.

RONALD E. RICE

ORGANIZATIONAL CULTURE

Organizational culture is defined by Brent Ruben and Lea Stewart (1998) as the sum of an organization's symbols, events, traditions, standardized verbal and nonverbal behavior patterns, folk tales, rules, and rituals that give the organization its character or personality. Ruben and Stewart note that organizational cultures are central aspects of organizations and serve important communication functions for the people who create and participate in them. These functions include providing employees with a sense of individual and collective identity, contributing to the establishment of structure and control within the organization, aiding the socialization of employees through learning about the customs and traditions of the organization, and fostering cohesiveness among employees.

In their classic book on organizational culture, *Corporate Cultures: The Rites and Rituals of Corporate Life* (1982), Terrence Deal and Allen Kennedy provide extensive examples of organizations with strong cultures. Four of the common characteristics that they found are the following:

1. a widely shared philosophy (e.g., "people are our greatest resource" or "customer service is our top priority"),

2. a belief in the importance of employees (e.g., through flexible jobs and work hours, absence of reserved parking spaces, or open-door management policies),

3. the presence of heroes (i.e., a person or persons who exemplify the philosophy of the organization), and

4. rituals and ceremonies (e.g., pizza parties every Friday afternoon, company sponsored recreational outings, birthday celebrations for all employees, and so on).

Various aspects of an organization can serve as indicators of its organizational culture. For example, modern technology companies often are characterized by their use of open space in which many people work in a large space that is freely accessible to all corporate employees. These companies may also encourage employees to dress casually and to interact in an informal manner. This reflects an organizational belief that hierarchies inhibit creativity and make it difficult for people to do their best work. Contrast this view of organizational culture with a more conservative company in which employees adhere to a generally understood dress code of formal business attire and work in offices that indicate the status of their occupants by the size of the office and the relative quality of its furnishings. These companies believe that formal networks of supervision lead to more productivity by allowing supervisors to monitor employee behavior and provide guidance and sanctions when necessary to keep employees focused on their jobs.

Language is a very important aspect of organizational culture and one that has been studied extensively by scholars of communication. Language both reflects and influences an organizational culture. For example, an organization that describes itself in terms of the family metaphor may provide flextime for employees who want to balance home and work responsibilities, on-site daycare facilities, wellness programs including health club memberships, or organization-wide social activities such as picnics and trips to amusement parks. An organization that uses military-oriented language, such as "we are fighting this battle together" or "success means climbing to the top," may focus more on maintaining a rigid organizational hierarchy and a clear separation between people at different levels in the company.

Stories are an important means to maintaining an organizational culture. Most people in organizations can tell several stories that are indicative of the organizational culture, such as stories about how past employees either succeeded or failed at their jobs or memorable moments in the history of the organization. These stories may be communicated within the company or may be included in messages the organization communicates to the public. Within a company, an employee may tell a story of how the last person to ask for a new office carpet was moved to a smaller office, clearly communicating the message that the company does not encourage employees to focus on office décor. Communicating to the public, a television commercial for a beer company describes a situation in which a town was coping with the aftermath of a severe flood, and the company stopped bottling beer and bottled water instead to distribute to the flood victims. This type of advertisement is designed to communicate to the general public the caring nature of the organizational culture of the company.

Healthy organizational cultures can adapt to changing business needs and technological developments. For example, as technology enables employees to telecommute (either work at home or on the road and still remain in contact with their offices), many organizations have adapted themselves to this phenomenon. Some organizations have set up large areas in which telecommuters can come to the office and make telephone calls and meet customers or other employees as necessary without having individual offices. Other organizations have invested considerable resources in making sure that employees who work from their homes have ergonomically designed equipment that will enhance their productivity. Many organizations are struggling to balance the benefits offered by telecommuting (such as allowing employees to have flexible work schedules and the ability to respond to customer needs immediately) with the difficulties that arise when employees are separated from their supervisors and the day-to-day informal communication that is often beneficial to a healthy work environment.

Katherine Miller (1999) moves beyond the prescriptive approach to organizational culture by noting that some researchers view organizational culture not as a thing but as a process that includes emerging and possibly fragmented values, practices, narratives, and artifacts. Miller argues that the approach to organizational culture scholarship taken by contemporary researchers views culture as complicated, emergent, and not unitary. These researchers are more likely to use qualitative data collection methods, such as participant observation, extensive interviews, and ethnography, to develop a rich understanding of the culture of a particular organizational culture. The goal of this research is to gain an understanding of organizational culture that is grounded in what Miller refers to as "local observations." This research may be reported in a formal, scholarly way, but it can also include stories that are impressionistic and that attempt to capture the essence of an organizational culture that is compelling to the reader.

See also: CULTURE AND COMMUNICATION; ORGANIZATIONAL COMMUNICATION; ORGANIZATIONAL COMMUNICATION, CAREERS IN; ORGANIZATIONAL QUALITY AND PERFORMANCE EXCELLENCE.

Bibliography

Cameron, Kim S., and Quinn, Robert E. (1998). *Diagnosing and Changing Organizational Culture: Based on the Competing Values Framework.* Reading, MA: Addison-Wesley.

Deal, Terrence E., and Kennedy, Allan A. (1982). *Corporate Cultures: The Rites and Rituals of Corporate Life.* Reading, MA: Addison-Wesley.

Deal, Terrence E., and Kennedy, Allan A. (1999). *The New Corporate Cultures: Revitalizing the Workplace after Downsizing, Mergers, and Reengineering.* Reading, MA: Perseus Books.

Frost, Peter J.; Moore, Larry F.; Louis, Meryl Reis; and Lundberg, Craig C., eds. (1991). *Reframing Organizational Culture.* Newbury Park, CA: Sage Publications.

Itzin, Catherine, and Newman, Janet, eds. (1995). *Gender, Culture and Organizational Change: Putting Theory into Practice.* London: Routledge.

Miller, Katherine. (1999). *Organizational Communication: Approaches and Processes.* Belmont, CA: Wadsworth.

Ruben, Brent D., and Stewart, Lea P. (1998). *Communication and Human Behavior,* 4th edition. Boston: Allyn & Bacon.

Schein, Edgar H. (1997). *Organizational Culture and Leadership,* 2nd edition. San Francisco: Jossey-Bass.

LEA P. STEWART

ORGANIZATIONAL QUALITY AND PERFORMANCE EXCELLENCE

Many organizations face common challenges when it comes to achieving quality and high levels of performance. Organizations of all kinds— business, governmental, health care, and educational—create products or services to meet particular sets of consumer needs. To the extent that an organization achieves success and stability, the structures, systems, policies, work practices, and leadership styles that are associated with those accomplishments become accepted and standardized over time. In the short run, these patterns are often a prescription for continued success and vitality. However, in the longer term, these same patterns can lead to rigidity, insulation, lack of innovation, and gradual distancing from the needs of the marketplace and the expectations of consumers.

Over time, changes may also occur in the needs, expectations, or confidence of key consumers or sponsors. Competition, technology, economics, regulatory factors, and other marketplace conditions also evolve, sometimes in dramatic ways, and organizations or industries that are unable to anticipate, accommodate, or shape these changes are at risk as they become increasingly closed systems. Unless new ways of thinking and working and new structures and cultures to support these changes are developed, performance and quality may well deteriorate. The dynamics are quite similar whether one considers the rise and fall of an educational institution, a local video store, a community group, U.S. electronics manufacturers, or the Swiss watch industry.

Six Core Concepts

Originally called "TQM" (total quality management), "the quality/performance excellence approach" has achieved remarkable acceptance as a philosophy and method for addressing quality and performance challenges and dynamics and for identifying and reducing the gaps that confront many contemporary organizations.

Though the terminology varies somewhat from setting to setting, author to author, and program to program, there are six key values that transcend the various approaches to organizational quality and performance excellence: (1) service orientation, (2) leadership, (3) information use, (4) collaboration, (5) communication, and (6) continuous improvement.

Service Orientation

A service orientation directs attention to the needs, expectations, and satisfaction levels of the groups that are served by a private- or public-sector organization. Within the quality framework, these groups are variously referred to as "customers," "constituencies," "stakeholders," "consumers," "publics," "clients," "audiences," "beneficiaries," or "users." The focus on service to consumers is based on a recognition that it is ultimately their judgments of the quality of a product, service, or institution—translated into marketplace behaviors—that are necessary for the continuing viability of the product or service organization.

The quality/performance excellence perspective suggests that practically speaking—as well as theoretically speaking—the definition of quality and value is dictated by the behaviors of consumers in a competitive marketplace for goods and services. No matter how organizational "insiders" assess the value of a particular product or service, those judgments are made in a vacuum (which makes them limited and inevitably incomplete) if the insiders do not take account of the needs, perceptions, and expectations of the consumers for whom the products and/or services are intended.

The concept of service orientation also applies to services provided by support and operational units within an organization for other groups that are internal to the organization. Most basically, the concept of service orientation suggests that it is essential to (1) identify external constituencies for which the organization provides products or services, (2) determine and anticipate their needs and expectations, and (3) satisfy—ideally exceed—those needs and expectations.

Leadership

A fundamental tenet of the quality approach is that leaders are most effective when they are personally involved in creating, communicating, explaining, reinforcing, and exemplifying the organization's mission, vision, values, and service orientation. These directions must be clear, visible, and well integrated into management systems. Leaders should serve as role models through their active involvement and leadership in public and professional activities.

Ideally, the involvement of senior leaders will include a visible commitment to the growth, development, and satisfaction of the employees, and it should encourage productivity, participation, collaboration, and creativity among all personnel. Through ongoing personal involvement in activities such as planning, communication, reviews of performance, and recognition of individual and unit achievements, senior leaders serve as role models, reinforcing the organization's mission, vision, values, and goals and encouraging improved leadership at all levels.

Information Use

The basic concept underlying the value of information use is that organizational well-being and an external focus are possible only with effective systems for information acquisition, analysis, and application. This includes identifying, studying, and comparing an organization's own activities to those of "benchmark" organizations—organizations that represent a standard of excellence and are therefore a focal point for performance comparison and improvement. Specific kinds of information to be collected and used would include the answers to the following questions:

- How do key external consumer groups evaluate products and/or services?
- What criteria do consumers use in assessing products/services?
- What is the relative importance of these criteria?
- Who are the key competitors?
- How do products, services, management approaches, and operational performance compare to those of competitors?
- How do employees evaluate the organization, its performance, management, quality of life, products/services, and processes?
- How do suppliers and gatekeepers evaluate the organization and its products/services?

Depending on what information is needed in order to answer any given question, the data may need to be gathered from external sources (e.g., key constituent groups, other organizations, and suppliers), or it may need to be gathered from internal sources (e.g., from employees and through organizational self-study).

Collaboration

Organizations are considered to be complex systems with numerous internal and external constituencies that interact with and depend on one another. These interactions may take the form of exchanges of goods, services, capital, or information. The viability of organizations as systems and their ability to meet expectations of external constituencies depend largely on whether and how these internal interactions take place.

Traditionally, organizations have been structured based on basic functions that need to be carried out. Thus, a typical manufacturing company has divisions or departments of production, sales, operations, marketing, finance, research and development, and so on. Each division is organized hierarchically, with the staff in that area reporting to supervisors, who report to managers, who report to directors, who report to vice-presidents, who ultimately report to a president and/or a chief executive officer. This results in elaborate vertical structures and reporting relationships within each functional area of the organization.

Vertical structures, sometimes termed "silos," facilitate interaction within functional divisions. At the same time, they set up obstacles to interaction and coordination between units. Individuals and departments often become detached from the overall mission of the organization. Work process fragmentation, compartmentalization, and an "it's not my job" mentality tend to evolve. Thus, for example, the research and development division may design a product without the benefit of full collaboration with manufacturing, operations, and marketing, which can potentially lead to any of a number of unfortunate outcomes, such as a wonderful design for a product that the company cannot easily manufacture and for which there is no longer a viable market.

Simpler, better integrated, "flat" organizations, which facilitate cross-functional and cross-divisional collaboration, coordination, and teamwork, are considered to be a means for addressing consumer expectations, aligning individuals and functional units with the organization's mission, and improving the overall organizational quality.

Communication

Communication is the means through which information is gathered and disseminated to and from stakeholders or consumers, and it is the mechanism through which work process collaboration occurs. It is also the process through which relationships are formed and developed—relationships that are essential to the creation of a culture and spirit of teamwork that is necessary to support and maintain an external focus, collaboration, and a good overall organizational quality.

Continuous Improvement

Quality and high levels of performance do not occur naturally. Rather, they require a substantial commitment of time and resources to a process of continuous improvement and ongoing change—what many people writing in the quality area have called a "journey."

Continuous improvement implies a commitment by everyone within the organization to a recursive process, consisting of planning and testing improvements, evaluating outcomes, learning from failures, implementing and sustaining successes, planning and testing improvements, and so on.

Quality Strategies and Processes

What is the process by which the core quality and performance excellence values are implemented within an organization? Broadly speaking, the process has two phases: assessment and improvement.

Assessment

Fundamentally, assessment is a strategy for evaluating the current level of performance of an organization in relationship to the expectations of its constituencies and the organization's mission and vision. It allows for the identification of service quality gaps, which become priorities for improvement.

One of the most widely used assessment tools is the Malcolm Baldrige National Quality Award. The Baldrige Award, signed into federal law on August 2, 1987, was initiated with the intent of improving quality and workmanship in the United States. The National Institute of Standards and Technology (NIST) directs the award program. Organizations that are interested in being considered for the award must complete a comprehensive self-study and application process. Awards are given in five categories: manufacturing, service, small business, education, and health care.

Quality Improvement

The process of quality improvement usually involves two steps: (1) identifying, planning, and implementing improvement and (2) integrating improvements. Basic to the improvement process are groups, or teams. A team simply is a group composed of individuals who represent various facets and levels of a unit or process earmarked for study and improvement. The team includes individuals who have a broad base of knowledge and experience with the processes that are being addressed.

The team members work together to develop an approach for ongoing monitoring, evaluation, and improvement. Team activities typically consist of the following:

- attending meetings,
- planning improvements,
- understanding the process to be improved,
- understanding the problem,
- collecting information,
- using tools and techniques to analyze and interpret the information, identifying solutions, and
- implementing and managing changes.

Other improvement tools besides teams include strategic planning, advisory groups, work process design or redesign groups, quality and service skills training, partnerships with corporations that are experienced with quality programs, and external consultation.

Conclusion

The quality/performance excellence approach is an interdisciplinary approach to organizational behavior and leadership. The approach addresses significant and enduring issues, and it integrates theories, concepts, and methods from various disciplines and traditions of organizational thought.

See also: CULTURE AND COMMUNICATION; GROUP COMMUNICATION; KNOWLEDGE MANAGEMENT; MANAGEMENT INFORMATION SYSTEMS; ORGANIZATIONAL COMMUNICATION; ORGANIZATIONAL CULTURE.

Bibliography

Al-Assaf, A. F., and Schmele, June A. (1993). *The Textbook of Total Quality in Healthcare.* Delray Beach, FL: St. Lucie Press.

AT&T Quality Technology Center. (1990). *Quality Improvement Team Helper.* Holmdel, NJ: AT&T Quality Technology Center.

Cortada, James, and Woods, John. (1995). *Encyclopedia of Quality Terms and Concepts.* New York: McGraw-Hill.

Hammer, Michael, and Champy, James. (1993). *Reengineering the Corporation.* New York: HarperCollins.

Hiam, Alexander. (1993). *Does Quality Work? A Review of Relevant Studies.* New York: The Conference Board.

Lewis, Ralph G., and Smith, Douglas H. (1994). *Total Quality in Higher Education.* Delray Beach, FL: St. Lucie Press.

National Institute of Standards and Technology. (1987–2001). *Malcolm Baldrige National Quality Award Criteria.* Washington, DC: U.S. Department of Commerce.

Ruben, Brent D. (1995). *Quality in Higher Education.* New Brunswick, NJ: Transaction.

Ruben, Brent D. (2000). *Excellence in Higher Education: A Guidebook for Organizational Assessment, Planning, and Improvement.* Washington, DC: National Association of College and University Business Officers.

Scholtes, Peter R. (1988). *The Team Handbook.* Madison, WI: Joiner Associates.

BRENT D. RUBEN

P-Q

PALEY, WILLIAM S. (1901–1990)

William S. "Bill" Paley was the son of Samuel and Goldie Paley, Jewish immigrants from the Ukraine who founded a cigar manufacturing company in 1896 in Chicago; the company was later incorporated as the Congress Cigar Company and relocated to Philadelphia, where it became a thriving business. At the age of twelve, Paley impulsively added the middle initial "S" to his name. (Some people thought the "S" stood for Samuel.) Paley graduated from the Wharton School of Finance at the University of Pennsylvania in 1922. He had worked for his father's company while in college and joined the company upon graduation. Paley biographer Sally Bedell Smith writes in *In All His Glory* (1990) that while young Paley was vacationing, his father and uncle agreed to sponsor a radio program to advertise their La Palina cigars. This eventually led the company to become a radio sponsor on a regular basis. Smith writes that Paley only reluctantly agreed to his involvement with radio, although Paley, in his later years, suggested that he had been the radio visionary who recognized the power of radio to promote the family's cigars. In any case, Paley's version had become the official network story by the 1940s.

Radio advertising boosted the sale of the cigars and opened young Paley's eyes to the possibilities of radio. La Palina cigars became one of the first sponsors on the newly founded Columbia Phonograph Broadcasting System, later the Columbia Broadcasting System (CBS). In 1928, with Paley buying 41 percent of the stock, and other family members owning the remainder, Paley purchased CBS. Two days before his twenty-seventh birthday, Paley was elected president of the network. One of his early successes came when the network was negotiating program carriage with the local stations (i.e., affiliates). First, Paley doubled the number of network programming hours to twenty hours per week—time that consisted of a combination of programming with sponsors (i.e., sponsored programming) and without (i.e. sustaining programming). Second, he got the affiliates to agree to run all twenty hours and to guarantee that they would not preempt network programming. Third, he got the affiliates to agree to accept money from the network only for the portion of the twenty hours that consisted of sponsored programming. Finally, he got the affiliates to waive this monetary compensation for the first five hours of sponsored programming. Because the network typically included only five hours of sponsored programming in the twenty hours of full programming each week, the affiliates had to run all of the programming for free. More important in the long run, the twenty hours of programming provided affiliates with higher quality national broadcasts that furthered the development of the network and improved the public's perception of radio.

Paley's network competitor and nemesis was David Sarnoff, president of the National Broadcasting Company (NBC). Sarnoff's NBC Red and Blue networks led Paley in the number of affiliates, the number of popular programs, and the length of operation. One of Paley's early accomplishments for CBS was to sign additional affiliates

Frank Stanton presents William S. Paley with a silver gavel on behalf of "The men and women of CBS in grateful appreciation for his resolute and inspiring leadership" to commemorate the company's fortieth anniversary year. (Bettmann/Corbis)

that had previously been with the NBC networks. The affiliate raids ended a "gentleman's agreement" between CBS and NBC not to poach each other's affiliates, and it signaled to Paley's detractors that he was prepared to compete head-to-head in the competitive radio business. Paley was noted for his ability to identify star performers and recruit them for CBS broadcasts. Part of Paley's effectiveness came from his ability to charm the stars through his personality. Paley conducted a series of talent raids to lure stars away from NBC, a tactic he used successfully several times during his career. The talent raids were a success partly because Paley offered the stars more money but also because Paley personally enjoyed lavishing attention on his stars. Following the talent raids, CBS carried the most popular programs, and NBC had to start over and prepare a new programming schedule. Popular CBS performers included George Burns and Gracie Allen, Jack Benny, Will Rogers, Bing Crosby, Kate Smith, and the Mills Brothers.

During World War II, Paley served in the U.S. Army in the Psychological War Branch of the Office of War Information. Paley's assignments included supervising broadcasts to Germany and Occupied Europe and preparing radio messages to accompany the D-Day invasion. Paley described radio broadcasting as a tool of warfare, just as were guns and bullets.

Under Paley's leadership, CBS introduced a color television system in 1945. Because the system was incompatible with existing black-and-white television sets, NBC's Sarnoff successfully lobbied the government not to approve the CBS system. Eventually, CBS withdrew its color television system. CBS was slow to develop television programming, but with help from Frank Stanton, CBS was soon airing *The Jackie Gleason Show* (1952–1970), *I Love Lucy* (1951–1961), *Gunsmoke* (1955–1975), *Arthur Godfrey's Talent Scouts* (1948–1958) and *The Ed Sullivan Show* (1948–1971).

For Paley, CBS was his very life. He waived the company's mandatory retirement rule in 1966 and continued to serve as company president. He selected an outsider, Tom Wyman from Pillsbury, to run the company in 1983 with disastrous results. Paley resumed the chairman's job in 1986 when Laurence Tisch of Loews Corporation was acquiring stock and eventual control of the company. Tisch, at the time of Paley's death in 1990, had succeeded in wresting control of CBS away from Paley and was putting the company through a series of cost-cutting measures and selling divisions of the company.

Paley and his second wife, Barbara "Babe" Paley, were avid art collectors. Their collection included works by Henri de Toulouse-Lautrec, André Derain, Pablo Picasso, Paul Cezanne, and Jackson Pollock. Paley was a longtime president and trustee of the New York City Museum of Modern Art and founded the Museum of Broadcasting, which was later renamed the Museum of Television and Radio.

See also: RADIO BROADCASTING, HISTORY OF; RADIO BROADCASTING, STATION PROGRAMMING AND; SARNOFF, DAVID; TELEVISION BROADCASTING, HISTORY OF.

Bibliography

Barnouw, Erik. (1966). *A Tower of Babel: A History of Broadcasting in the United States.* New York: Oxford University Press.

Barnouw, Erik. (1968). *The Golden Web.* New York: Oxford University Press.

Douglas, George. (1987). *The Early Days of Radio Broadcasting.* Jefferson, NC: McFarland.

Lewis, Tom. (1991). *Empire of the Air: The Men Who Made Radio*. New York: HarperCollins.

Paley, William S. (1979). *As It Happened: A Memoir*. Garden City, NY: Doubleday.

Paper, Lewis J. (1987). *Empire: William S. Paley and the Making of CBS*. New York: St. Martin's Press.

Smith, Sally B. (1990). *In All His Glory: The Life of William S. Paley*. New York: Simon & Schuster.

Sterling, Christopher, and Kittross, John M. (1990). *Stay Tuned: A Concise History of American Broadcasting*. Belmont, CA: Wadsworth.

GREG PITTS

PARADIGM AND COMMUNICATION

Philosopher Thomas Kuhn (1970) is generally credited with having introduced the term "paradigm" to refer to a broad framework that guides the thinking and research of scholars over a long period of time as they conduct research and develop specific theories. Perhaps the most classic illustration of a paradigm was the long-standing view that Earth was the center of the universe, around which center the Sun, moon, and planets revolved. This way of thinking, attributed to Alexandrian geographer and astronomer named Ptolemy (130 C.E.), was widely accepted and used until astronomers encountered discrepancies that were not easily explained by Ptolemy's geocentric paradigm. Inconsistencies of this kind, which Kuhn calls "anomalies," can lead to a scientific revolution and the emergence of a new paradigm. In this case, the new framework, advanced by Nicolaus Copernicus in the fifteenth century, was able to address the anomalies by advancing a new way of thinking, which proposed that Earth rotates on its axis and that the planets (including Earth) revolve in orbits around the Sun. This paradigm replaced the Ptolemaic view and has continued to provide the overarching framework for scholarship and research in the centuries since then.

In communication study, as in astronomy and other fields, the concept of paradigm is quite useful for understanding the evolution of thought. From the earliest formal study of communication by Aristotle and his contemporaries in Ancient Greece, communication was generally viewed as a process through which a speaker conveys messages to influence or persuade one or more receivers. This paradigm emphasizes the importance of a source and his or her intended message. Receivers are typically viewed as being passive recipients of messages, and thus as the endpoint in what is viewed as a straightforward and predictable cause-and-effect process.

This Aristotelian framework remained pervasive in communication study until the middle of the twentieth century. As noted above, paradigms change as a result of anomalies. In the case of communication study, it was observed by a number of scholars that messages sent by a speaker often are not received and/or acted on by receivers in the manner in which the sender or message advocated. These observations were at odds with the traditional paradigm. Gradually, the anomalies led to the erosion of the traditional paradigm and the growing acceptance of a communication paradigm that emphasizes the active and powerful influence of receivers on the process.

Contemporary models of communication assert that receivers play a much more active and discriminating role in the process. They emphasize the variety of ways in which receivers attend to, interpret, and respond to messages. The factors that affect these processes are related to the sender and the message, as well as the channel, the situation, the relationship between sender and receiver, and so on.

Paradigms are important in communication study, as in other fields, because they guide scholarship, research, and sometimes policy and professional practice. For example, based on the earlier communication paradigm, it made sense to think that smoking could be greatly reduced or eliminated if warnings pointing out the health hazards were printed on cigarette packages. Research and observation, however, indicated that the intended message was often ignored or distorted by receivers; it certainly was not reacted to as advocated by the source or message. Anomalies such as these led to a view that suggests the importance of focusing on the intended receiver of messages rather than just on a sender and the intended message.

Paradigms evolve slowly and are sometimes rejected with reluctance even when many anomalies exist. Thus, even though important changes began to take place in the communication paradigm in the middle of the twentieth century, it is still not uncommon to hear the process described in terms that reflect the older view, such as when someone says, "I don't know why he didn't get my message. It was a simple point, and I repeated it two times!" This kind of utterance implies that communication outcomes are primarily influenced by the sender and his or her message; it does not acknowledge the very active role that receivers play and the variety of factors that influence the outcomes of the communication process.

See also: COMMUNICATION STUDY; EVOLUTION OF COMMUNICATION; HUMAN INFORMATION PROCESSING; MODELS OF COMMUNICATION.

Bibliography

Harper, Nancy L. (1979). *Human Communication Theory: History of a Paradigm.* Rochelle Park, NJ: Hayden Books.

Kuhn, Thomas S. (1970). *The Structure of Scientific Revolutions,* 2nd edition. Chicago: University of Chicago Press.

Ruben, Brent D., and Stewart, Lea P. (1998). *Communication and Human Behavior,* 4th edition. Needham Heights, MA: Allyn & Bacon.

BRENT D. RUBEN

■ PARANORMAL EVENTS AND THE MEDIA

The term "paranormal" refers to a wide range of alleged phenomena that appear to defy explanation using scientific understandings of natural law. The term is commonly used to refer to such diverse things as extrasensory perception (ESP), haunted houses, ghosts, devils, angels, spirits, reincarnation, telekinesis, unidentified flying objects (UFOs), space alien abductions, astrology, palm reading, astral projection, the Loch Ness monster, and communicating with the dead.

Public opinion polls and studies by academic researchers indicate that belief in paranormal phenomena is common. In a 1991 national survey of more than one thousand adults, George Gallup and Frank Newport reported that paranormal beliefs were "widespread," with nearly 50 percent of the respondents reporting belief in ESP and almost 30 percent reporting belief in haunted houses. Of some surprise to scholars, studies reveal that paranormal beliefs are not significantly lower among college students, even at institutions that are noted for science and engineering. For example, in a 1994 study of students from Purdue University, Glenn Sparks, Trish Hansen, and Rani Shah found that a variety of different paranormal beliefs were endorsed by many of the respondents. These beliefs included the existence of ghosts (70%), accurate predictions of the future by reading palms (40%) or by relying on psychics (37%), personal ability to use ESP on occasion (44%), and astral projection (30%). The traditional line of research on paranormal beliefs extends back to the late 1960s and focuses on (1) the extent to which various populations express belief in some paranormal phenomenon, (2) the extent to which belief in one paranormal phenomenon corresponds with belief in other paranormal phenomena (i.e., the structure of paranormal beliefs), and (3) the extent to which belief in the paranormal varies according to individual differences in personality or according to membership in some demographic category.

In the 1970s, a group of scholars (including some who conducted basic research on paranormal beliefs) became increasingly concerned about what appeared to them to be a rising tide of paranormal claims that were, for the most part, not challenged by any systematic line of study. Their concern resulted in the formation of the Committee for the Scientific Investigation of Claims of the Paranormal (CSICOP), an organization that is devoted to rational, scientific inquiry into various paranormal claims. CSICOP began to publish a journal, *The Skeptical Inquirer,* in the mid-1970s.

One issue that has been regularly featured in *The Skeptical Inquirer* since its inception is the role that mass media play in encouraging people to believe in various paranormal claims. Typical of the rhetoric that is found in the pages of this journal is the following comment made by Paul Kurtz (1985), chairman of CSICOP and a philosophy professor: "We thought it incredible that so many films, TV and radio programs, news stories, and books were presenting these paranormal claims as gospel truth, even maintaining that they had been proven by science, and that there was little or no public awareness of the fact that when these claims were subjected to careful scientific appraisal they were shown to be either unverified or false" (p. 357).

Even though no scientific content analyses exist to document the presence of paranormal themes in the media, Kurtz's observation about the prevalence of paranormal depictions is not controversial among scholars. Such depictions of one form or another have turned up in books, radio programs, movies, and television shows for almost as long as these media have existed. On Halloween night in 1938, Orson Welles triggered a sensational episode of panic among the radio-listening audience with his *War of the Worlds* broadcast. The radio drama, which aired as part of CBS's *Mercury Theatre on the Air,* featured realistic, on-the-spot "news" reports that told of an invasion of space aliens from Mars. Follow-up research conducted by Hadley Cantril at Princeton University in 1940 documented the fact that many listeners did experience feelings of helplessness and panic as a result of the broadcast.

Until the late 1970s, few studies other than Cantril's study examined fright responses to media depictions, and almost no research existed on how depictions of paranormal themes might influence audience beliefs. In 1981, Joanne Cantor launched a series of studies on children's fright reactions to mass media (see Cantor, 1998). As a result of these studies that were funded by the National Institute of Mental Health, a number of researchers began to work systematically with frightening movies and television programs. Much of the content in this genre was paranormal. For example, *The Exorcist,* a 1973 film that triggered several extreme reactions among audience members (including the need for hospitalization), featured the paranormal depiction of demonic possession. Similarly, *Poltergeist,* a 1982 film that reportedly induced long-term sleep disturbances in many children, featured numerous ghosts and spirits who disrupted the daily routine of a suburban family by haunting their house in frightening ways. Although research on children's media-induced fears shows that the tendency to be frightened by fantasy creatures declines with age, in her 1998 book summarizing the available fright research, Cantor concluded that alien and supernatural phenomena were among the most potent fear-inducers for adolescents. The early studies examined these films for their emotional effect on viewers, but it was only a matter of time before the potential effect of paranormal themes on the beliefs of viewers would also come under scrutiny.

Several factors converged in the 1980s to increase the prevalence of paranormal themes in

Brig. General Roger M. Ramey and Col. Thomas J. Dubose, from the U.S. Air Force, identify metallic fragments found by a farmer near Roswell, New Mexico, as pieces of a weather balloon. (Bettmann/Corbis)

the media. With the proliferation of cable channels, new networks searched for programming formulas that would compete for a share of viewers that was large enough to make a profit. Industry programmers discovered that so-called reality television was relatively cheap to produce and could attract reasonable audience sizes. Consequently, stories about haunted houses, UFO sightings, police psychics, demonic possessions, angelic visitations, and the like began to proliferate. The success of some of these programs inspired the networks to explore paranormal themes in their prime-time lineups and led Hollywood to invest in more movies that revolved around paranormal plots.

In the 1990s, Sparks and his associates began studying the effect of media depictions of the paranormal on the beliefs of viewers. In a 1994 study, Sparks, Hansen, and Shah randomly assigned college students to view a television program about astral projection with one of four possible introductions: one that emphasized that the depicted events had been real, one in which the events were labeled fictitious, one with a stronger disclaimer that emphasized that the depicted events were impossible from a scientific standpoint, and one with no introduction. The introductory messages significantly affected the subsequent beliefs of the students. Relative to the beliefs that they had expressed several weeks earlier, students assigned to the fiction or impossible conditions reduced their beliefs in astral projection and related paranormal phenomena. Students who heard no introductory message increased their beliefs in paranormal phenomena. Students in the reality condition failed to increase their beliefs in the paranormal. Sparks and his colleagues speculated that introductory messages that emphasize the reality of the depiction may cause viewers to become more suspicious about the veracity of the events that are being depicted. This study demonstrated that the way in which paranormal phenomena are depicted in the media can trigger changes in what people believe about the existence of those phenomena.

In a 1995 study by Sparks, Cheri Sparks, and Kirsten Gray, college students who possessed either high or low ability to experience vivid mental images were randomly assigned to view one of two versions of a television program that featured documentary-style reporting of UFO sightings. One version of the program contained depictions of UFOs and space aliens that were created by special effects as part of the original network broadcast of the program. The second version of the program was edited to remove all of these UFO depictions that were created by the network. Students with a high ability to experience vivid mental images increased their belief in UFOs after viewing the version that contained no UFO or alien images. In contrast, students with a low ability to experience vivid mental images increased their belief in UFOs when they viewed the unedited version of the broadcast that contained the special effects. Sparks and his colleagues concluded that the decision to include various UFO images in a documentary-style report can definitely have an effect on the subsequent beliefs of viewers, but this effect may depend on viewer characteristics.

In a 1997 experiment by Sparks and Marianne Pellechia, college students were randomly assigned to read one of four versions of a magazine article about alien abductions. Two of the stories affirmed the reality of alien abductions; the remaining two stories tended to disconfirm their reality. For both the affirming and disconfirming stories, one of the versions featured the testimony of a scientist while the other version simply presented the opinions of the magazine writer. After reading the articles, beliefs in UFOs and alien abductions were highest among the students who read the affirming story that featured the testimony of a scientist. Beliefs were lowest among the students who read either the affirming or disconfirming story that presented only the opinions of the magazine writer. Students who read the disconfirming story that featured a scientist did not express the lowest level of belief in UFOs. Sparks and Pellechia speculated that merely mentioning a scientist in the context of a story about UFOs and alien abductions may tend to bring credibility to the phenomenon and make it more believable. Once again, variation in the way paranormal content was depicted produced a difference in post-exposure beliefs.

In a 1998 experiment by Sparks, Pellechia, and Chris Irvine, college students were randomly assigned to watch one of two different segments about UFOs. The segments were originally broadcast as part of a network news documentary. One segment featured video experts who testified that a video recording of an alleged UFO showed more than a conventional jet aircraft. The other segment featured unchallenged testimony from an alleged eyewitness to a UFO crash. Students who viewed the unchallenged testimony increased their belief in UFOs; those who viewed the video experts decreased their belief in UFOs.

In addition to these experiments, Sparks, Leigh Nelson, and Rose Campbell conducted in 1997 a random-sample survey from a midwestern city to investigate the relationship between media exposure and paranormal beliefs. Exposure to programs that regularly depict the paranormal was positively correlated with paranormal beliefs. Sparks and his colleagues discussed the possibility that prior beliefs lead to selective exposure to these programs, but they concluded that overall, the pattern of evidence from the survey and the experiments supports the idea that media depictions of the paranormal exert a causal force on the paranormal beliefs of viewers. Given the frequent depictions of paranormal phenomena in the media, there is every reason to believe that researchers will continue to investigate their effect.

See also: FEAR AND THE MEDIA; WELLES, ORSON.

Bibliography

Cantor, Joanne. (1998). *"Mommy I'm Scared." How TV and Movies Frighten Children and What We Can Do To Protect Them.* San Diego, CA: Harcourt Brace.

Cantril, Hadley. (1940). *The Invasion from Mars: A Study in the Psychology of Panic.* Princeton, NJ: Princeton University Press.

Gallup, George, and Newport, Frank. (1991). "Belief in Paranormal Phenomena among Adult Americans." *The Skeptical Inquirer* 15:137–146.

Kurtz, Paul. (1985). "The Responsibilities of the Media and Paranormal Claims." *The Skeptical Inquirer* 9:357–362.

Sparks, Glenn G.; Hansen, Trish; and Shah, Rani. (1994). "Do Televised Depictions of Paranormal Events Influence Viewers' Paranormal Beliefs?" *The Skeptical Inquirer* 18:386–395.

Sparks, Glenn G.; Nelson, C. Leigh; and Campbell, Rose. (1997). "The Relationship between Exposure to Televised Messages about Paranormal Phenomena and Paranormal Beliefs." *Journal of Broadcasting & Electronic Media* 41:345–359.

Sparks, Glenn G., and Pellechia, Marianne. (1997). "The Effect of News Stories about UFOs on Readers' UFO Beliefs: The Role of Confirming or Disconfirming Testimony from a Scientist." *Communication Reports* 10:165–172.

Sparks, Glenn G.; Pellechia, Marianne; and Irvine, Chris. (1998). "Does Television News about UFOs Affect Viewers' UFO Beliefs?: An Experimental Investigation." *Communication Quarterly* 46(3): 284–294.

Sparks, Glenn G.; Sparks, Cheri; and Gray, Kirsten. (1995). "Media Impact on Fright Reactions and Belief in UFOs: The Potential Role of Mental Imagery." *Communication Research* 22(1):3–23.

GLENN G. SPARKS

■ PARENTAL MEDIATION OF MEDIA EFFECTS

There is much concern over the negative effects of television viewing on children. Children who watch more television are at a greater risk of experiencing a host of negative outcomes compared to children who watch less television. The good news is that parents can modify or even prevent television-related effects by engaging in a variety of practices known as "mediation."

What Is Mediation?

Mediation has not been defined consistently. As a result, many different definitions of this term exist. However, researchers endorsing the various conceptualizations agree that mediation refers to interactions with children about television. Although a number of individuals can provide mediation, such as siblings, peers, and adults, the term is commonly used to signal parent-child interaction. The focus of this entry, therefore, is on parental mediation.

Parental mediation can take several different forms. Amy Nathanson (1999) has distinguished these forms as active mediation, restrictive mediation, and coviewing. Active mediation refers to the conversations that parents can have with their children about television. Sometimes these conversations are generally negative in tone, such as when parents tell their children that what they are seeing on television is not real or that they disapprove of the behaviors of the television characters or the program in general. In this case, the parent-child communication is called "negative active mediation." However, parents can also say positive things about what their children watch on television. For example, parents can communicate their approval of certain programs or depicted behaviors or point out how certain portrayals are realistic. This kind of interaction is called "positive active mediation." Parent-child communication about television that is neither negative nor positive would likely fall into the "neutral active mediation" category. This type of active mediation includes providing the child with additional information or instruction regarding television content. For example, while watching an educational program, parents might extend the lessons that television introduces. Active mediation—whether negative, positive, or neutral—can take place at any time. In other words, parents can discuss television with their children during viewing or after programs have ended and the television is no longer on.

Restrictive mediation includes the rules and regulations that parents institute regarding the television viewing of their children. Parents can create rules about the kinds of programs that their children are allowed to watch, how much they can watch, and when they can watch it. Parents can also vary in how strict they are in enforcing the rules. That is, some parents may have a lot of television-viewing rules, but may not enforce all of them. Others may have just a few rules that they ensure are never violated. The combination of the kinds of rules and how strictly they are adhered to constitutes the level of restrictive mediation.

Coviewing occurs when parents watch television with their children. Although parents may discuss the television content with their children while viewing with them, it is important to note that coviewing occurs regardless of whether active mediation occurs. As a result, coviewing describes a much more passive form of behavior in which the parent simply watches television with the child. The distinction between active mediation and coviewing is an important one to make, as the two concepts reflect unique forms of behavior that are associated with very different kinds of effects.

Who Gives and Receives Mediation?

Unfortunately, Erica Austin reported in her 1993 article that not all parents use mediation. In fact, it may be increasingly difficult for parents to provide mediation given a number of factors, including the limited amount of time that working parents have to mediate and the easy access of children to television (in fact, many children have television sets in their own rooms). Those parents who do mediate appear to fit a particular profile. In other words, there are certain types of parents who use the various forms of mediation with certain types of children. To begin, active mediation is most often used by mothers as opposed to fathers. It is unclear whether users of active mediation are more educated or not—a 1992 survey by Tom van der Voort and his colleagues suggests that this is the case while research conducted by Patti Valkenburg and her colleagues in 1999 indicates that active mediation is used by parents of all educational levels. It is not surprising that parents who generally like and approve of television are more likely to use positive active mediation while parents who dislike television are more inclined to use negative active mediation. Both boys and girls of all ages are equally likely to receive active mediation.

Parents who use restrictive mediation are also usually mothers. These parents are typically well educated and believe that television can have a detrimental effect on their children. Parents are more likely to restrict the viewing of their younger children as opposed to their older children, who are allowed more viewing freedom. For the most part, it appears that parents are equally likely to use restrictive mediation with their sons as with their daughters.

Research suggests that coviewing is used most frequently by mothers and parents with less education (Austin, Bolls, Fujioka, and Engelbertson, 1999; van der Voort, Nikken, and van Lil, 1992). Like positive active mediation, coviewing occurs more frequently among parents who like and approve of television. Although both boys and girls are likely to receive coviewing, there is some disagreement in the literature regarding whether coviewing is mostly used with younger or older children. That is, a 1999 survey by Austin and her colleagues indicates that parents are more likely to coview television programs with their younger children. If parents believe that coviewing will help prevent negative effects from occurring, then it makes sense that they would use it more with younger children who are often perceived to be more susceptible to experiencing negative effects from viewing television. On the other hand, a 1982 survey by Carl Bybee and his colleagues showed that coviewing occurs more frequently with older children. This could be because of the similarities in the viewing preferences of the parents and the viewing preferences of the children that emerge as children mature. Hence, coviewing that occurs between parents and older children may reflect shared interests rather than conscious attempts at mediation.

Overall, then, mothers use all forms of mediation more than fathers. When they use negative active mediation or restrictive mediation, it is likely that they are trying to protect their children (probably their younger children) from perceived harmful effects of television. In the minds of the parents, making negative statements about television or restricting the access of their children to it should reduce the negative effects of television. However, it is possible that the use of positive active mediation and coviewing by parents is simply the outcome of parents enjoying television with their children.

How Successful Is Mediation?

Researchers have tried to determine whether active mediation, restrictive mediation, and coviewing affect children in a positive way. Given that there is so much concern over the effects of television on children, it certainly would be reassuring to know whether parents can prevent or reduce undesirable effects.

Much of the work on the effects of active mediation has explored whether parents who use it have children who are more sophisticated consumers of television. For example, research has shown that children who receive active parental mediation are better able to understand the plots of television programs, are more skeptical of televised news, and are less likely to believe that what they see on television is real (Austin, 1993; Desmond, Singer, Singer, Calam, and Colimore, 1985; Messaris and Kerr, 1984). However, some forms of active mediation can produce the opposite effects. A 2000 survey by Austin and her colleagues showed that children become less critical of television when their parents make positive comments about it. It certainly seems that what parents say to their children about television is very important in shaping the children's perceptions of the content.

Other research indicates that children whose parents employ active mediation are less likely to be negatively affected by television. Although there exists less research exploring this kind of relationship, the results are promising. A 1997 survey by Nathanson found that children whose parents use negative active mediation are less aggressive than other children. In fact, these children are not only less aggressive in general, but they are also less likely to learn aggression from violent programs they see even when their parents are not present. It could be, then, that negative active mediation "inoculates" children from harmful television-related effects that could occur outside of the home.

Research on the effects of restrictive mediation is less abundant. However, there is some indication that children whose access is restricted to television are less likely to be negatively affected by it, even when they do view it. A 1987 survey by Nancy Rothschild and Michael Morgan found that children whose parents restrict viewing are less likely to be unnecessarily fearful of the outside world (one outcome that is often associated with television viewing). In addition, it has been found that children who receive restrictive mediation are less aggressive—both in general and after viewing violent content on television. It should be noted, however, that there is some evidence that very extreme levels of restrictive mediation will backfire. In other words, children whose parents severely limit access to television may actually become more aggressive, perhaps due to the frustration that results from the deprivation of privileges.

When parents coview television with children, it seems that children are more likely to experience positive feelings and learn from what they see on television. It is possible that the mere presence of parents while viewing makes children feel happy and that this positive emotional state enhances children's learning. Although this appears to be a generally positive effect, negative outcomes may result when parents coview harmful television content. In fact, there is evidence that children whose parents coview are more likely to believe that television is realistic, to uphold gender stereotypes, and to learn aggression from television (Messaris and Kerr, 1984; Nathanson, 1999; Rothschild and Morgan, 1987). The effects of coviewing may depend, then, on what kind of television content the parents and children share.

One reason why the various forms of parental mediation are associated with the outcomes reviewed above could be that mediation teaches children to have a certain attitude toward television that will make effects either more or less likely to occur. In the case of negative active mediation, it is possible that children who consistently hear negative messages about television adopt a disapproving attitude toward it. Armed with this kind of attitude, these children may be less likely to take what they see on television very seriously and, therefore, be less likely to learn from it. This kind of reasoning could also apply to restrictive mediation: When their television is consistently restricted, children may learn that television is undesirable. Once they adopt this perspective, they may be less vulnerable to experiencing television-related effects when they do watch television. However, when children receive positive active mediation, they may learn that television is good and should be taken seriously. This kind of attitude may make effects more likely. And, if children interpret parental coviewing to mean that their parents like the content that is shared, they may develop a very accepting attitude toward television that may enhance effects.

In fact, a 1999 survey by Nathanson showed that the explanation provided above is accurate. It seems that children who receive negative active mediation or restrictive mediation of violent television have more negative attitudes toward violent television than other children. It also appears that these negative attitudes that children develop make it less likely that children will learn aggression from television. It is unclear, however, whether coviewing effects are also attributable to changes in attitudes toward television.

Mediation, then, provides parents with some options for dealing with the television viewing of their children. Depending on the kind of mediation provided and the kind of programs that are mediated, parents can influence how their children are affected by television. However, parents need to be educated about what options exist and the relative effectiveness of these options so that the most successful strategies will be implemented with more children.

See also: Antiviolence Interventions; Fear and the Media; Ratings for Movies; Ratings for Television Programs; Ratings for Video Games, Software, and the Internet; Violence in the Media, Attraction to; Violence in the Media, History of Research on.

Bibliography

Austin, Erica W. (1993). "Exploring the Effects of Active Parental Mediation of Television Content." *Journal of Broadcasting and Electronic Media* 37:147–158.

Austin, Erica W.; Bolls, Paul; Fujioka, Yuki; and Engelbertson, Jason. (1999). "How and Why Parents Take on the Tube." *Journal of Broadcasting and Electronic Media* 43:175–192.

Austin, Erica W.; Knaus, Christopher; and Meneguelli, Ana. (1998). "Who Talks How to Their Kids about TV: A Clarification of Demographic Correlates of Parental Mediation Patterns." *Communication Research Reports* 14:418–430.

Austin, Erica W.; Pinkleton, Bruce E.; and Fujioka, Yuki. (2000). "The Role of Interpretation Processes and Parental Discussion in the Media's Effects on Adolescents' Use of Alcohol." *Pediatrics* 105:343–349.

Bybee, Carl; Robinson, Danny; and Turow, Joseph. (1982). "Determinants of Parental Guidance of Children's Television Viewing for a Special Subgroup: Mass Media Scholars." *Journal of Broadcasting* 26:697–710.

Desmond, Roger J.; Singer, Jerome L.; Singer, Dorothy G.; Calam, Rachel; and Colimore, Karen. (1985). "Family Mediation Patterns and Television Viewing: Young Children's Use and Grasp of the Medium." *Human Communication Research* 11:461–480.

Dorr, Aimee; Kovaric, Peter; and Doubleday, Catherine. (1989). "Parent–Child Coviewing of Television." *Journal of Broadcasting and Electronic Media* 33:35–51.

Messaris, Paul, and Kerr, Dennis. (1984). "TV-Related Mother–Child Interaction and Children's Perceptions of TV Characters." *Journalism Quarterly* 61:662–666.

Nathanson, Amy I. (1999). "Identifying and Explaining the Relationship between Parental Mediation and Children's Aggression." *Communication Research* 26:124–143.

Nathanson, Amy I., and Cantor, Joanne. (2000). "Reducing the Aggression-Promoting Effects of Violent Cartoons by Increasing Children's Fictional Involvement with the Victim: A Study of Active Mediation." *Journal of Broadcasting and Electronic Media* 44:125–142.

Rothschild, Nancy, and Morgan, Michael. (1987). "Cohesion and Control: Adolescents' Relationships with Parents as Mediators of Television." *Journal of Early Adolescence* 7:299–314.

Salomon, Gavriel. (1977). "Effects of Encouraging Israeli Mothers to Co-Observe 'Sesame Street' with Their Five-Year-Olds." *Child Development* 48:1146–1151.

Singer, Jerome L.; Singer, Dorothy G.; and Rapaczynski, Wanda S. (1984). "Family Patterns and Television Viewing as Predictors of Children's Beliefs and Aggression." *Journal of Communication* 34(2):73–89

St. Peters, Michelle; Fitch, Marguerite; Huston, Aletha C.; Wright, John C.; and Eakins, Darwin J. (1991). "Television and Families: What Do Young Children Watch with Their parents?" *Child Development* 62:1409–1423.

Valkenburg, Patti M.; Krcmar, Marina; Peeters, Allerd L.; and Marseille, Nies M. (1999). "Developing a Scale to Assess Three Styles of Television Mediation: 'Instructive Mediation,' 'Restrictive Mediation,' and 'Social Coviewing.'" *Journal of Broadcasting and Electronic Media* 43:52–66.

van der Voort, Tom H. A.; Nikken, Peter; and van Lil, Jan E. (1992). "Determinants of Parental Guidance of Children's Television Viewing: A Dutch Replication Study." *Journal of Broadcasting and Electronic Media* 36:61–74.

AMY I. NATHANSON

■ PATIENT-PROVIDER RELATIONSHIP

See: Health Communication; Provider-Patient Relationships

■ PEIRCE, CHARLES SANDERS (1839–1914)

Born in 1839 in Cambridge, Massachusetts, Charles Sanders Peirce was the second and favorite son of Benjamin Peirce, who was a professor of mathematics and astronomy at Harvard University and was superintendent of the U.S. Coast and Geodetic Survey. Along with Abraham Lincoln in 1863, Benjamin Peirce founded the National Academy of Sciences. Charles graduated with high honors in 1854 from Cambridge High School, where one of his favorite pastimes was the debating society, a source of his reputation as an engaging conversationalist and dynamic lecturer. He then graduated from Harvard with a B.A. in 1859 and an M.A. in 1862. In 1863, he graduated summa cum laude with a B.S. in chemistry from the Lawrence Scientific School at Harvard. He had an erratic and confrontational personality, largely preventing him from permanent employment in the academic world. He was a part-time lecturer in logic at Johns Hopkins University from 1879 to 1884. Despite the persistent efforts of William James, he never obtained a position at Harvard. His more periodic employment with the Coast Survey, and later with the U.S. Assay Commission, fared no better. He suffered seven mental breakdowns between 1876 and 1911 due to a condition now known as trigeminal neuralgia, associated with manic depression. With a small inheritance, he purchased a retirement home at Milford, Pennsylvania, and lived in extreme poverty. During the years between 1903 and 1908, he corresponded on logic and semiotics with Victoria Lady Welby in England. Peirce died of cancer on April 19, 1914.

Peirce comes closest to being America's only systematic philosopher, writing widely and in detail. His principal philosophic system draws from medieval learning focused on the semiotic *trivium* of grammar, logic, and rhetoric—the building blocks of modern communication theory and mathematical (information) exchange theory. But, the behaviorist division of semiotics, proposed by Charles Morris, is better known. For Morris, gram-

Charles Sanders Peirce. (Bettmann/Corbis)

mar is syntactics, or the study of sign structures (codes), whether animal, machine, or human. Logic is semantics, or the study of choices in meaning that govern intention in communication. Last, rhetoric is pragmatics, or the use of discourse to inform and convince. These three elements combine to create the world of human reference (named the "semiosphere" by Juri Lotman).

Peirce uses the covering term "semiotic" to include his major divisions of thought and communication process: (1) speculative grammar, or the study of beliefs independent of the structure of language (i.e., unstable beliefs); (2) exact logic, or the study of assertion in relation to reality (i.e., stable beliefs); and (3) speculative rhetoric, or the study of the general conditions under which a problem presents itself for solution (i.e., beliefs dependent on discourse). This division previews Peirce's famous triadic models of analysis. Peirce goes on to make the distinction between communication (a process) and signification (a system). Communication is the study of messages and the process of meaning, whereas signification is the study of codes and the system of referential signs used. Messages may contain codes (e.g., linguistics or computer programs) or codes may contain messages (e.g., cryptography or measurement). Messages constituting codes are Peirce's doctrine of "tychism," or the study of probabilities where absolute chance is real. What is probable can be understood as the distinction among type, token, and tone. A typology is a category Peirce called "firstness," the condition under which something exists. A token is an example illustrating the type and is a case of "secondness." The tone is "thirdness," a unique individual (a paradigm or prototype example) known by the connection between the type and token. In short, firstness and secondness are two categories held together, related, by thirdness. Thus, types are more probable than tokens; tokens are more probable than tones. For example, one's actual ability to drive a car is more probable than one's ability to own a car, but one's owning a car is more probable than one's buying a new Ford. The communication process of tychism for Peirce is the existential experience of learning how to learn in a general communication experience. When one learns, an object presents itself to the person's consciousness as a sign or "representamen" that "stands to somebody for something in some respect or capacity." An equivalent sign or "interpretant" is created in the mind and this new sign stands for the object. How this communication process of representation (phenomenology) works is the study of signification.

Signification or the doctrine of "synechism" is the analysis of possibilities where codes contain messages. This doctrine holds that all problems can be solved because there is an absolute continuity among things that can be generalized as such. This basic doctrine is applied in Peirce's classification of signs. He divides signs into three basic types, although there are sixty-four subtypes. First, an icon is a sign that has a similarity to its object. Second, an index is a sign that physically connects to its object. Third, a symbol is a sign that arbitrarily links to its object. For example, a statue of a person is an icon, a photograph taken of that person is an index, and the naming noun "person" is a symbol of that person. As Umberto Eco suggests, keep in mind that in complex communication systems the types of signs are often "overcoded" in one object; for example, a traffic stop sign is an icon (similar to a raised hand), an index (red color of danger, octagon shape of convergence), and a symbol (contains the word "stop" on the sign face). Film and television images have much the same overcoded effect. Undercoding occurs when one or more of the signs are taken away, such as when a stop sign does not have the word "stop" on it or when one suddenly loses the audio while watching a television set.

Peirce is noted for his philosophic realism, or the belief that probability and possibility are linked to the actual existence of things or that which can become actual. Hence, people inherit the association of "pragmatism" with a test of real-world application that Peirce called the doctrine of "fallibilism." This existential and phenomenological orientation made Peirce a polymath, according to his biographer Joseph Brent. Peirce was conversant with chemistry, geodesy, metrology, and astronomy. He was the first experimental psychologist in America, a mathematical economist, a logician and mathematician, a dramatist, an actor, a writer, and a book reviewer. He created the modern discipline of semiotics to include all the arts and sciences of communication, information (informatics), and exchange.

See also: LANGUAGE STRUCTURE; RHETORIC; SEMIOTICS.

Bibliography

Brent, Joseph. (1998). *Charles Sanders Peirce: A Life,* revised edition. Bloomington: Indiana University Press.

Eco, Umberto. (1976). *A Theory of Semiotics.* Bloomington: Indiana University Press.

Freeman, Eugene, ed. (1983). *The Relevance of Charles Peirce.* La Salle, IL: The Hegeler Institute, Monist Library of Philosophy.

Lanigan, Richard Leo. (1992). *The Human Science of Communicology.* Pittsburgh, PA: Duquesne University Press.

Liszka, James Jakob. (1996). *A General Introduction to the Semiotic of Charles Sanders Peirce.* Bloomington: Indiana University Press.

Lotman, Juri. (1990). *Universe of Mind: A Semiotic Theory of Culture.* Bloomington: Indiana University Press.

Nöth, Winfried. (1990). *Handbook of Semiotics.* Bloomington: Indiana University Press.

Peirce, Charles Sanders. (1931–1935, 1958). *Collected Papers of Charles Sanders Peirce,* Vols. 1–6, eds. Charles Hartshorne and Paul Weiss; Vols. 7–8, ed. Arthur Burks. Cambridge, MA: Harvard University Press.

Peirce, Charles Sanders. (1976). *The New Elements of Mathematics by Charles S. Peirce*, 4 vols., ed. Carolyn Eisele. The Hague: Mouton Publishers.

Peirce, Charles Sanders. (1982–1999). *Writings of Charles Sanders Peirce: A Chronological Edition*, Vols. 1–6 (with 30 projected), ed. Christian J. W. Kloesel. Bloomington: Indiana University Press.

RICHARD L. LANIGAN

PHILOSOPHY

See: Ethics and Information; Technology, Philosophy of

PIRATE MEDIA

Pirate media refers to media outlets that operate without official license. This is different from alternative media—those outlets that provide in their content and operation a challenge to the dominant media and social systems. In the United States, for example, legally authorized and operated radio stations may be alternative in their programming—for example, Pacifica stations KPFA in Berkeley, California, and WBAI in New York City—but they are not pirate. Likewise, because print media are not licensed in the United States, alternative newspapers abound. Thus, "pirate" typically refers to media otherwise requiring official authority to operate (i.e., radio and television) and to the illegality of their operation rather than to the nature of their content. This does not mean that pirate media are not alternative in their content, because many, if not most, are alternative in content. Despite the fact that they do have illegal operation in common, pirate stations in different countries and different media systems do serve different functions for those countries and systems.

The term "pirate" came into use in Great Britain in the 1960s, when it was applied to illegally operated radio stations broadcasting to English audiences from off-shore facilities. Pirate, then, had a dual connotation—these broadcasters were, like pirates, rogues and law-breakers, and again like pirates, they operated on the high seas.

These pirates, however, were well funded and powerful, richly supported by commercial advertisers and record companies, and operated twenty-four hours a day, every day of the year. Among the most notable were Radio Caroline, broadcasting from the *M. V. Frederika* three and a half miles off the coast of the Isle of Man and drawing a million listeners a day; Radio London, broadcasting from a retired U.S. minesweeper; and Radio Veronica, broadcasting from a ship anchored off the coast of The Netherlands. At the time of their greatest popularity, they offered an alternative to the more controlled and sedate fare of the noncommercial stations of the British Broadcasting Corporation (BBC). Advertisers wanted to reach British consumers, but there were no commercials allowed on the BBC, and record companies wanted to introduce their artists to rock-n-roll hungry kids, a growing audience largely ignored by the government-controlled BBC.

It was the popularity and success of the pirates, in fact, that eventually helped persuade the British government to begin the licensing of commercial radio stations and to create its own popular music service, BBC Radio 1. Nonetheless, pirate stations flourish in England and throughout Europe, but now they are more like pirate stations in the United States—they operate on shoestring budgets, broadcast irregularly, are not-for-profit stations, air content that is politically and community oriented, and like the early British pirates, they are constantly under siege by governmental broadcasting authorities.

Pirate Radio

The early pirate stations in Europe operated in defiance of the continent's noncommercial broadcasting systems, trying to sound as much as possible like American commercial stations—employing witty disc jockeys to play snappy slogans and jingles while spinning contemporary rock and pop music discs. The experience of pirate radio in the United States, however, is just the opposite; it began and continues to operate in opposition to the dominant commercial broadcasting system.

Pirate radio in the United States goes by several names: microbroadcasting, free radio, low-power broadcasting, rebel radio, and, of course, pirate radio. Yet many people involved in this unlicensed broadcasting reject the term "pirate," arguing that it is the government, through the Federal Communications Commission (FCC), and giant, moneyed corporations that are the real thieves, having "stolen" the people's airwaves. For example, as recently as the 1980s, the most radio stations one entity could own in the United States was seven nationally and two in any one city (one AM and one FM). The FCC imposed these limits in an effort to ensure a diversity of sound and opinion on the air. However, through deregulation and the Telecommunications Act of 1996, virtually all ownership limits have been removed. A single company, Clear Channel, for example, owned 830 stations in 1999, and it and a score of others own as many as eight in a single city. It is this "corporatization" of the radio dial that has breathed new vigor into pirate radio.

The philosophy of the movement is encapsulated in the manifesto of pirate station Radio4All:

Radio for *whom*? The airwaves nominally belong to the people, but the reality is most of the media outlets worldwide are owned by a steadily smaller number of large corporations who use them to expand their wealth and power. Even so-called "public stations" increasingly take corporate money or emulate corporate paradigms. This means communities and individuals are increasingly shut out of the process of determining what information they receive. A right of "Free Speech" that only the rich can exercise is no right at all!

This belief is embodied in the type of programming found on the low-power pirates. Beginning operation in Springfield, Illinois, in 1986 as Black Liberation Radio, Human Rights Radio broadcasts African-American music and literature, political and social commentary, and addresses by local community residents. WTBS (The Pirate Station) in Milwaukee, Wisconsin, began operation in 1983 as an outlet for music that local commercial and college stations would not play. Free Radio Gainesville in Florida plays an eclectic mix of music emphasizing local artists, community news, and poets and writers reading their works. Radio Clandestino in Los Angeles programs bilingual, leftist Latin American fare. There are pirate stations serving the Hasidic Jewish community in Miami, Florida; family farmers in North Dakota; and small merchants who are unable to afford the cost of advertising in the major media in Cincinnati, Ohio.

Pirates typically transmit at a power of from 1 to 100 watts (as compared to the 50,000 to 100,000 watts of licensed stations) and reach an area from 2 to 15 miles. The necessary audio and transmitting hardware is inexpensive (often less than a few hundred dollars), can fit comfortably in a backpack, and can be legally purchased from scores of outlets. Websites such as Pirate Radio Central and Radio4All provide instructions on how to get started, operate, avoid detection, and deal with the authorities if caught.

There are more than 1,000 unlicensed low-power radio stations operating in the United States at any given time, despite the efforts of government officials to stifle their growth and operation. In 1998, for example, the FCC shut down 270 pirates nationwide, 19 in a single December day in Miami, Florida. These closures are frequently accomplished with the aid of armed SWAT teams, but just as the early British pirates forced change in the BBC's radio landscape, the pirates in the United States have been successful in moving the FCC to consider altering that of the United States. Citing "the most dramatic increase in consolidation in the broadcast industry in our history" and the hundreds of microbroadcasters willing to face fines and even jail to meet the needs of their listeners, FCC chairman William Kennard announced in 1999 that the commission intended to create a new type of radio: legal microbroadcasting. The aim, according to Kennard as reported by Bill McConnell (1999, p. 100), is to "maximize the use of the spectrum for the American public" and to "give voice to the voiceless," goals so close to the hearts of the pirates that the FCC received 13,000 inquiries for low-power licenses in the first few months after Kennard's announcement.

Still, some pirates either will not wait for (or simply reject) legal microbroadcasting, arguing that because U.S. law requires that all new frequencies be auctioned off to the highest bidder, the same corporate commercial giants who dominate high-power radio will inevitably dominate low-power radio. There have been several challenges, therefore, mounted against the FCC's rules that limit unlicensed microbroadcasting. These efforts have two similar themes: (1) the FCC ban on licensing stations of under 100 watts is a violation of the First Amendment's protection of free speech and press, and (2) the federal government should have no say in the regulation of low-power radio stations whose signals do not cross state lines.

Abie Nathan operated a pirate radio station from The Peace Ship, which sailed in the international waters of the Mediterranean Sea from 1972 until 1993. (Moshe Shai/Corbis)

Clandestine Broadcasting

There is another type of pirate broadcaster, the ones whose primary intention is the overthrow of an entrenched political power; these are clandestine broadcasters. According to Lawrence C. Soley and John S. Nichols (1987, p. vii), "Clandestine stations generally emerge from the darkest shadows of political conflict. They frequently are operated by revolutionary groups or intelligence agencies." There have been antigovernment or antiregime clandestine broadcasters as long as there has been officially authorized broadcasting. In the 1930s, radio pirates aired the grievances of communist sympathizers in Czechoslovakia, Germany, and Hungary, while the Irish Republican Army broadcast in Belfast and anti-Nazi dissidents broadcast in Germany and Austria. During World War II, clandestine stations encouraged German submarine sailors to sabotage their U-boats in harbor to avoid near-certain death at sea at the hands of the Allies. False reports were intentionally broadcast for a variety of reasons. For example,

Atlantic Station and Soldiers' Radio Calais, posing as two of the many official stations run by the German military for the enjoyment of its personnel, broadcast false reports of the invasion of Normandy. In addition, by making false reports of such verifiable facts as the death of Field Marshall Erwin Rommel, the clandestine broadcasters forced the official German media to counter with accurate reports, thereby providing the Allies with just the information they wished to know.

It was during the Cold War, however, that clandestine broadcasting truly flowered. In the years between the end of World War II and the fall of European Communism in 1989, thousands of radio, and sometimes television, pirates took up the cause of either revolutionary (pro-Communist) or counterrevolutionary (anti-Communist) movements. In addition, other movements tangentially related to this global struggle—especially the anti-Colonial movements in South America, Central America, and Africa—made use of clandestine broadcasting.

The Cold War pirates typically operated outside the nations or regions to which they broadcast, because to have operated within those borders guaranteed discovery, capture, and imprisonment or death. Those relatively few pirates who operate inside the areas to which they transmit are indigenous stations, and those pirates who broadcast from outside the areas to which they transmit are exogenous stations. Indigenous Radio Solidarity, the underground voice of the successful Polish anti-Communist, antigovernment movement, began operating a network of transmitters inside the borders of Poland in 1982, four months after embattled pro-Soviet dictator General Wojciech Jaruzelski declared martial law. Leipzig-based Kanal X transmitted pirate television from inside East Germany, in opposition to that regime's adherence to Soviet-style Communism until the Berlin Wall—and the Communist regime—fell. Exogenous Voice of Free Africa, the pirate station of the Mozambique National Resistance Movement, broadcast its antigovernment message into Mozambique from South Africa during the late 1970s and early 1980s.

These illegal operations can be further classified as "black stations" (i.e., those that disguise both their purpose and source of support) and "gray stations" (i.e., those that are open in their aim to subvert the existing government while disguising the source of their support). During the war in Vietnam, for example, the U.S. military operated a black station, Liberation Radio, which was a duplicate of a North Vietnamese gray station by the same name. This black station broadcast false reports of South Vietnamese military victories in an effort to demoralize North Vietnamese soldiers and to boost morale among the South Vietnamese army. The gray Liberation Radio, broadcasting into South Vietnam from and with the support of the government of North Vietnam, had just the opposite goals. Implicit in this example is another characteristic of the large majority of clandestine stations that operated during the Cold War—they drew their support from foreign powers who were also hostile to the targeted nation.

Regardless of their specific nature—black or gray, indigenous or exogenous—there is not a major Cold War or anti-Colonial conflict that has not seen the involvement, if not the success, of broadcast pirates. Unauthorized, illegal broadcasts have been enlisted to further the cause of all sides of the conflict in Northern Ireland, both sides in the push for and against Apartheid in South Africa, both the pro- and anti-Castro Cuban partisans, and the leaders of the ill-fated Hungarian Revolution against Communist rule in 1956.

Modern Pirates

Modern pirate broadcasters, rather than being truly politically motivated clandestine stations, are more likely to be free-broadcasting advocates; that is, they object to either excessive corporate or government control of radio and television. Political clandestine stations do exist, however. Inside Israel, for example, ultra-Orthodox Jewish pirate stations broadcast from Jerusalem in opposition to what their operators believe is the secular drift of the elected government. Exogenous, black Radio Caiman, transmitting from Guatemala and rumored to be funded by the U.S. Central Intelligence Agency, has been broadcasting rock-n-roll, Latin music, and anti-Castro matter into Cuba since 1994. Indigenous Radio Patria Libra, urging the overthrow of the Colombian government, transmits from that country's Medellin region. In the United States, neo-Nazi Voice of Tomorrow illegally broadcasts from Virginia its racist propaganda designed to "raise the consciousness" of supposedly "threatened White Americans."

Still, the large majority of pirates operating in the United States and around the world has the somewhat less overtly political goal of subverting or at least challenging what it sees as officially sanctioned information monopolies. In the United States, as discussed above, this activity exists in the form of low-power radio pirates broadcasting to local audiences the music and commentary that is otherwise ignored by the commercial media. In Europe, also discussed above, these low-power stations exist to challenge the noncommercial as well as commercial media. Another difference between the U.S. and European pirates is that the European pirates are more likely than U.S. pirates to employ television. Radio is the medium of choice for most pirates, regardless of location, because of its low cost, the portability of the necessary equipment, and the ease with which pirates can avoid detection and seizure. The technology for pirate television, while not as cheap and not as small as that for radio, is becoming increasingly so. Still, in the United States, there has been no significant pirate television movement, in large part because local commercial television, licensed low-power independent stations, and the public access channels of cable television provide numerous outlets for independent video producers and activists.

This has not been the case in Europe. Beginning with the 1977 free-broadcasting movement in France, illegal television stations went on the air with the stated intent of breaking the government broadcasting monopoly. They did so by flagrantly and openly defying the law, going so far as to announce the date, time, and place of broadcast, and televising live the inevitable police raids. Television pirates have forced the French and Italian governments to open their television systems to large numbers of independent stations, resulting in greater diversity and citizen involvement. As the number of these stations has grown, pirate television has become as rare in these countries as it is in the United States. This is the reason that most discussions of pirate broadcasting have come to deal almost exclusively with pirate radio.

See also: BROADCASTING, GOVERNMENT REGULATION OF; CABLE TELEVISION, REGULATION OF; FEDERAL COMMUNICATIONS COMMISSION; FIRST AMENDMENT AND THE MEDIA; RADIO BROADCASTING; TELECOMMUNICATIONS ACT OF 1996; TELEVISION BROADCASTING.

Bibliography

Hind, John. (1985). *Rebel Radio: The Full Story of British Pirate Radio.* London: Pluto Press.
McConnell, Bill. (1999). "FCC Tunes Microradio." *Broadcasting & Cable,* January 25, p. 100.
Messinger, Evelyn. (1990). "Pirate TV in Eastern Europe." *Whole Earth Review,* Fall, pp. 119–124.
Pirate Radio Central. (2000). "Pirate Radio Central." <http://www.blackcatsystems.com/radio/pirate.html>.
Radio4All. (2000). "Welcome to Radio4All." <http://www.radio4all.org>.
Schechter, Danny. (1999). "(Low) Power to the People." *The Nation,* May 24, p. 10.
Smith, Jeremy, and Rosenfeld, Howard. (1999). "Radio for People, Not Profit." *Dollars & Sense,* May–June, pp. 8–10.
Soley, Lawrence C., and Nichols, John S. (1987). *Clandestine Radio Broadcasting: A Study of Revolutionary and Counterrevolutionary Electronic Communication.* New York: Praeger.

STANLEY J. BARAN

◼ POLITICAL ECONOMY

In the field of communication and information studies, "political economy" is a term generally used to describe scholarship concerned with the relationships among economic, political, and communications systems within the structure of global capitalism. The tradition is rooted in the classical political economy of Adam Smith, David Ricardo, and John Stuart Mill, among others, and the radical political economy of Karl Marx. Their works, spanning the late eighteenth to late nineteenth centuries, sought to understand the nature of the emerging industrial phase of capitalism. Though the original political economists had relatively little to say about communications systems, they established a holistic and normative approach upon which contemporary political economists of communication and information have built.

Beginning in the late nineteenth century, classical political economy gave way to neoclassical approaches that displaced political and moral considerations from the study of economics for the purposes of establishing a discipline in the tradition of normal science. This pattern was replicated in almost every branch of the social sciences, including communications studies. By the late 1950s, the quest to make communications studies a science had relegated critical analysis of media institutions and organizations to the margins. Increasingly, however, communications scholars raised questions about the control of communication and information systems, as social and political changes in the late 1950s and 1960s brought them to the fore. In the 1970s, the search for answers led to a renewed interest in the work of the Frankfurt School on the culture industries and inspired the emergence of critical political economy of communications as a distinct approach within mass communications theory.

Communication and Class Struggle (1979, 1983), a two-volume collection of original and republished essays edited by Armand Mattelart and Seth Sieglaub, and *The Political Economy of the Media* (1997), a two-volume compilation of reprinted articles and book chapters edited by Peter Golding and Graham Murdock, document the origins and continuing evolution of this perspective. In *The Political Economy of Communication* (1996), Vincent Mosco categorizes the various approaches within critical political economy by the regional contexts in which the work was produced. Dallas Smythe, Herbert Schiller, and Thomas Guback pioneered a North American approach. Nicholas Garnham, Golding, Murdock, and Mattelart developed a distinct European approach. These scholars influenced, and were influenced by, political economists working in third-world countries. By the late 1990s, a fifth generation of critical political economists began entering teaching and research positions in the academy.

Most political economists take Marx's critique of capitalism as their starting point. Marx showed how the logic of capital shapes the reproduction of human existence in particular ways. Political economy studies have extended this analysis to the communications system, examining the ways in which the logic of capital affects the structure and output of the information and culture industries. For example, Marx argued that capitalism has an inherent tendency toward concentration as capitalists logically seek to control their markets through horizontal and vertical integration in hopes of maximizing their profits. The political economic history of the media and telecommunications industries, as well as the accelerated concentration occurring in these sectors of the economy in the late 1990s, reflect this tendency.

For political economists, concentrated and centralized control of the communications system has ramifications that extend beyond the high prices, artificial scarcity, and poor quality usually associated with monopolistic control of basic goods. In addition to the ability to influence markets and reap excess profits, those who have ultimate control of the culture and information industries can use their power and wealth to influence public opinion and policy. Schiller's groundbreaking *The Mind Managers* (1973) serves as a touchstone for understanding how the capitalist class extends its power through both the media and the state. Ben Bagdikian's influential text *Media Monopoly* (1983) falls outside the neo-Marxist tradition, yet it provides ample evidence of ways in which institutional networks link the capitalist class, the government, and the culture industries. Such networks operate to affect media content, from the censorship of news deemed harmful to specific and general corporate interests to the promotion of causes that are regarded as beneficial. In *Manufacturing Consent* (1988), Edward Herman and Noam Chomsky develop a propaganda model to study systematically how these institutional networks shape media coverage of U.S. foreign policy in similar ways.

Political economists who study the media as culture industries also focus on how the pursuit of profits affects the form and substance of the output of mass media. The culture industries, following common oligopolistic practices, seek to manipulate consumer demand through heavy investments in marketing and promotion. However, the demand for informational and cultural products is inherently harder to influence than in markets for basic consumer goods. Accordingly, in order to minimize economic risks, culture industries tend to rely on imitation, formula, sequels, series, spin-offs, stars, and other sorts of strategies to attract already existing audiences. Additionally, culture industries dependent on advertising revenues must produce content to attract audiences within the demographic range desired by advertisers (i.e., those with the ability to consume). The result is increasingly homogeneous informational and cultural output distributed globally.

The primary challenge to the critical political economy tradition has come from cultural studies. Cultural studies theorists have criticized the tradition for reducing the analysis of communications systems to economic determinants at the site of production and distribution while ignoring the polysemic nature of texts and the interpretive capacities of audiences. Another challenge comes from information policy studies that emphasize the dynamic processes at work in information and communications markets largely generated by continuing development and deployment of new technologies.

Political economists have responded to these challenges by returning to their roots, such as the retrieval of Raymond William's concept of determination, defined in *Marxism and Literature* (1977, p. 87), as a process involving the "setting of limits" and the "exertion of pressures" rather than a strict one-to-one causal relationship. The response also involves the recovery of Marx's dialectic relationship between social structures and human agency. To paraphrase Marx, while human beings are born into specific social conditions they have the capacity to change them, which leaves plenty of theoretical space for polysemic texts and readings. Similar to information policy studies, political economists recognize the central role of communications in processes of social change. However, political economists reject the notion that technology alone can bring it about.

See also: CULTURAL STUDIES; CULTURE AND COMMUNICATION; CULTURE INDUSTRIES, MEDIA AS; WILLIAMS, RAYMOND.

Bibliography

Bagdikian, Ben H. (1983). *The Media Monopoly*. Boston: Beacon.

Golding, Peter, and Murdock, Graham, eds. (1997). *The Political Economy of the Media*, 2 vols. Cheltenham, Eng.: Elgar Reference Collection.

Herman, Edward S., and Chomsky, Noam. (1988). Manufacturing Consent: The Political Economy of the Mass Media. New York: Pantheon Books.

Mattelart, Armand, and Sieglaub, Seth, eds. (1979, 1983). *Communication and Class Struggle*, 2 vols. New York: International General.

Mosco, Vincent. (1996). *The Political Economy of Communication*. London, Eng.: Sage Publications.

Schiller, Herbert I. (1973). *The Mind Managers*. Boston: Beacon Press.

Williams, Raymond. (1977). *Marxism and Literature*. Oxford, Eng.: Oxford University Press.

RONALD V. BETTIG